FOUNDATIONS OF REHABILITATION COUNSELING
WITH PERSONS WHO ARE BLIND OR VISUALLY IMPAIRED

J. Elton Moore,
William H. Graves, and
Jeanne Boland Patterson
Editors

PRESS
NEW YORK

Printed in the United States of America

Library of Congress Cataloging-in-Publication Data

Foundations of rehabilitation counseling with persons who are blind or visually impaired / J. Elton Moore, William H. Graves, Jeanne Boland Patterson, editors.
p. cm.
Includes bibliographical references and index.
ISBN 0-89128-945-3 (alk. paper)
1. Blind—Rehabilitation—United States. 2. Visually handicapped—Rehabilitation—United States. 3. Rehabilitation counseling—United States. I. Moore, J. Elton. II. Graves, William H. (William Hughes), 1942–. III. Patterson, Jeanne Boland.
HV1795.F68 1997
362.4′186—DC21 97-4409
CIP

The development of this publication was funded in part through Cooperative Agreement No. G0086C3502 from the National Institute on Disability and Rehabilitation Research (NIDRR) (PR Award No. 133BH60014) awarded to Mississippi State University. The opinions or policies expressed herein do not necessarily reflect those of the granting agency, and no official endorsement should be inferred.

The mission of the American Foundation for the Blind (AFB) is to enable persons who are blind or visually impaired to achieve equality of access and opportunity that will ensure freedom of choice in their lives.

It is the policy of the American Foundation for the Blind to use in the first printing of its books acid-free paper that meets the ANSI Z39.48 Standard. The infinity symbol that appears above indicates that the paper in this printing meets that standard.

CONTENTS

PART THREE Rehabilitation Services and Resources

FOREWORD

Like everyone else, individuals who are blind or visually impaired have needs that are as diverse as are their strengths. Effective service delivery to people with visual impairments needs to be based on an awareness of the importance of these individual differences. Rehabilitation counselors are often the key coordinators who orchestrate the services delivered to blind and visually impaired persons, and it is therefore essential that counselors' recognition of this diversity be particularly keen.

In the past, rehabilitation counselors have not had at their disposal comprehensive information in one volume to help them understand the abilities and requirements of the blind and visually impaired clients with whom they worked. With the publication of *Foundations of Rehabilitation Counseling with Persons Who Are Blind or Visually Impaired,* the American Foundation for the Blind (AFB) has taken steps to remedy that situation. It is hoped that this new text, the first in almost thirty years to provide information on the subject of rehabilitation counseling with persons with visual impairments, will have far-reaching influence on the effectiveness of counseling services.

The appearance of a comprehensive text in any discipline is of notable importance. However, in consolidating the knowledge base relating to the field of counseling individuals who are visually impaired, we at AFB believe that the contributors to this volume have given service providers important tools with which to help people develop or resume the independent pursuit of satisfying lives. Whether as part of university training efforts or in the daily practice of counseling, *Foundations of Rehabilitation Counseling with Persons Who Are Blind or Visually Impaired* will be an invaluable resource for the blindness and rehabilitation fields.

Carl R. Augusto
President
American Foundation for the Blind

PREFACE

In an age of powerful and global market forces and enormous advances in a number of areas of technology, the profession of rehabilitation counseling has been confronted with more challenges and has been offered more opportunities than ever before. This is the world that students of rehabilitation counseling have entered and the place where their knowledge and skills will be constantly tested; however, the rewards that await them (and their successful clients) are surely worth the preparation and work they have undertaken to become facilitators of human achievement and growth.

In the pages of this book, rehabilitation counselors and students learning to become rehabilitation counselors will find knowledge that has been shared by experts who serve the blindness community. They will learn facts that can become the tools to build productive relationships with consumers. They will explore resources that may become the bridges that their clients can cross to reach the goals of greater independence and contribution to society. And they will gain insights that will help them develop partnerships with their clients, which in turn can become the foundation for new opportunities, both for themselves and for their clients.

It is hoped that rehabilitation counselors will make the most of this book and will consult it often throughout their careers. Some of the information may change over time, such as that relating to legislative and funding trends reflected in service delivery in this country, and various approaches to the art and science of counseling may evolve beyond current conventions. However, in addition to the knowledge that counselors will learn from these writings, they may also absorb a deeper understanding upon which they can build careers. *Foundations of Rehabilitation Counseling with Persons Who Are Blind or Visually Impaired* can enable counselors to become trusted partners to blind or visually impaired people who will continue to make important choices in their lives, take on responsibility for their futures, and give back to society as full participants in the American dream.

Charles H. Crawford
Commissioner,
The Massachusetts Commission for the Blind and
President,
The National Council of State Agencies for the Blind

ACKNOWLEDGMENTS

Although we are very grateful to all the authors who have devoted so much time and effort to this project, we are particularly appreciative of the suggestions of a number of other individuals who extended themselves behind the scenes to make this text as complete as possible. These include Dr. John J. Benshoff of Southern Illinois University, Dr. Michael Bina of the Indiana School for the Blind, Gary Everhart of the Texas Commission for the Blind, and Dr. Michael Gandy of the Mississippi Office of Vocational Rehabilitation for the Blind, who also provided material for the glossary.

Special thanks are likewise extended to those individuals who reviewed and critiqued selected chapters, including Kitch Barnicle, Jay Leventhal, and Mark Uslan of the American Foundation for the Blind (AFB), Pat Brown and Dr. Jimmy Cotton of the Addie McBryde Rehabilitation Center for the Blind, Carolyn Mezger of the Texas Commission for the Blind, and Amy Pais of Lions World Services for the Blind. We especially appreciate the contribution of Dr. Samuel B. Johnson, Chairman of the Department of Ophthalmology at the University of Mississippi Medical Center, who was helpful in reviewing clinical material that has appeared throughout this text. The late Dr. Arthur H. Keeney, a Distinguished Professor of Ophthalmology at the University of Louisville, was also especially helpful in reviewing material of a medical and clinical nature. Additional thanks are also extended to Dr. Alfred Rosenbloom of the Chicago Lighthouse for People Who Are Blind or Visually Impaired for his review and comments on various eye reports and low vision charts, to Lisa Ashmore for her significant contributions in corresponding with authors and updating manuscripts, and to Olean Outlaw, who has provided ongoing clerical support. In addition, we would like to thank the Jewish Guild for the Blind and the Pinellas Center for the Visually Impaired for their cooperation and graciousness in helping to provide some of the photographs appearing in these pages.

This book would never have been produced without the initial endorsement and support of William F. Gallagher, former Executive Director of the American Foundation for the Blind, who agreed to support this project through AFB Press [then AFB's Publications and Information Services Department] and in collaboration with the National Institute on Disability and Rehabilitation Research. Special thanks are also extended to Dr. Charles Talor, who served as an initial reviewer of manuscripts while employed as a research scientist at the Rehabilitation Research and Training Center on Blindness and Low Vision at Mississippi State University.

Last, a significant debt of gratitude is owed to Natalie Hilzen and Kathy Campbell of AFB Press for their ongoing support, guidance, and patience in finalizing the manuscript for publication. Without this support and guidance, the publication would never have gone to press.

INTRODUCTION

Foundations of Rehabilitation Counseling with Persons Who Are Blind or Visually Impaired is written mainly for preservice professionals who will soon begin providing rehabilitation counseling services to individuals who are blind or visually impaired. Although it is intended primarily as a graduate-level text for the education of rehabilitation counselors, it is also designed as a resource and desk reference for practicing counselors and other human resource development specialists who work with people who have visual impairments. Not since the publication of Thomas A. Routh's *Rehabilitation Counseling of the Blind* (1970) has a rehabilitation counseling textbook specifically geared to professionals working with persons who have visual impairments been available. Rehabilitation professionals have long recognized the fact that the needs of people who are blind or severely visually impaired are unique and require a special knowledge and expertise in the provision and coordination of rehabilitation services. The overriding purpose of vocational rehabilitation in the blindness field is to meet the employment and independent living needs of people with visual impairments. This objective permeates the entire rehabilitation process and is the foundation of all service delivery.

With the passage of the Rehabilitation Act of 1973 and the Rehabilitation Act Amendments of 1992, the U.S. Congress has acknowledged not only the necessity for education and training of professionals to provide rehabilitation services more effectively to persons who are blind or visually impaired, but also the urgency of increasing the supply of personnel available for employment in public and private nonprofit rehabilitation agencies involved in the vocational rehabilitation, the independent living rehabilitation, and the supported employment of individuals with severe visual impairments. Given the ongoing need to train new rehabilitation counselors and to maintain and upgrade the basic skills of staff members already employed as providers of rehabilitation services to individuals who are blind or visually impaired, the editors hope that this text will serve as a resource for those who are charged with the instruction of counselors. The rehabilitation counseling process (that is, case finding and referral processing, evaluation and assessment, plan development, service delivery and coordination, and job placement and follow-up) for professionals who work with people who have visual impairments is very similar to the process followed by practicing professionals who work with people who have other disabilities. However, the types of services offered to visually impaired individuals and the emphasis applied to various process components tend to differ significantly from those involved in work with members of other groups because of the singular needs of persons who are visually impaired. In addition to mastering their basic coursework in rehabilitation counseling, it is essential that counselors possess the knowledge and skills that enable them to work with visually impaired individuals and that they comprehend the medical aspects of vision and issues related to assessment, functionality, and adaptation vis-à-vis vision loss. Understanding the roles of the other members of a rehabilitation team, such as a rehabilitation teacher and an orientation and mobility specialist, and being knowledgeable about the community resources that can contribute to the rehabilitation of visually impaired persons enable the rehabilitation counselor to forge and carry out a successful rehabilitation plan.

FORMAT OF THE CHAPTERS

The editors of this text have attempted to provide a broad overview of a multitude of issues faced by rehabilitation counselors who work with persons who are blind or visually impaired. How can a counselor obtain accurate information about a client with a visual impairment to develop an appropriate and effective rehabilitation plan? Which assessment tools can counselors use to help them identify a client's needs and strengths so that the client's vocational goal is consistent with his or her functional ability? How can a rehabilitation counselor determine career development interventions and suitable job modifications for a client with a visual impairment? These are just a few of the questions examined in *Foundations of Rehabilitation Counseling.*

The book is divided into three parts. Part One provides an overview of blindness and visual impairment, including a survey of the anatomy and function of the visual system, a consideration of the impact of the age of the individual at the time of onset of blindness, and an introduction to low vision and low vision devices. Part Two discusses the medical, vocational, and psychological assessments of people who have visual impairments and the importance of assessment in the rehabilitation process. Demographic and cultural issues are also addressed in Part Two, along with issues relevant to counseling people who have multiple disabilities. Part Three deals with rehabilitation services and counseling, and explains the roles of the rehabilitation team members, the purpose and use of assistive technology, and the major activities in the rehabilitation process, such as those relating to career development, job readiness, job placement, supported employment, job retention, and job accommodation. Each chapter contains a Learning Activities section that can be used in class assignments or during in-service training. All bibliographic references are listed in alphabetical order at the end of the book. The appendixes provide sample forms, which will be helpful to rehabilitation counselors in their work with clients. The Professional Code of Ethics for Rehabilitation Counselors, another appendix, has been printed in its entirety. There is also an extensive glossary for easy access to clear definitions of terms, as well as a resources section listing sources of information and assistance to professionals in the field.

REHABILITATION COUNSELING

Rehabilitation counseling in the field of blindness is a challenging profession with a rich history and a promising future. Rehabilitation counselors recognize the dignity and worth of people who have visual impairments, the importance of choice, the value of independence and work, and the responsibilities they have in regard to promoting consumer empowerment. In the face of legislative and funding shifts that have a dramatic impact on service availability, counselors need to be knowledgeable facilitators. *Foundations of Rehabilitation Counseling* offers a wealth of resources for strengthening the delivery of rehabilitation services in the field of blindness, and it is for this reason that it will serve as a touchstone in teaching rehabilitation counseling to professionals who work with individuals who are visually impaired.

THE CONTRIBUTORS

J. Elton Moore, Ed.D., is Professor of Counselor Education at Mississippi State University, Mississippi State, Mississippi, where he also serves as Director of the Rehabilitation Research and Training Center on Blindness and Low Vision. A former Switzer Fellow and a recipient of the 1996 Mississippi MAER (Mississippi Association for Education and Rehabilitation of the Blind and Visually Impaired) Outstanding Service Award, he is the author of numerous articles, book chapters, and monographs and a frequent speaker at national and international conferences. Dr. Moore is a Certified Rehabilitation Counselor (CRC) and a licensed professional counselor. He is also a former director of Mississippi Vocational Rehabilitation for the Blind, a past president of the National Council of State Agencies for the Blind, and a former president of Prevent Blindness—Mississippi, as well as past chair of the Association for Education and Rehabilitation of the Blind and Visually Impaired's Council of Division Chairs.

William H. Graves, Ed.D., is Dean and Professor of Counselor Education in the College of Education at Mississippi State University at Mississippi State. He is a former editor of *RE:view* and the author of numerous articles and book chapters on such topics as vocational rehabilitation, rehabilitation research, and policy decisions in rehabilitation research. Dr. Graves is the former director of the National Institute on Disability and Rehabilitation Research in the Office of Special Education and Rehabilitative Services at the U.S. Department of Education, a past chair of the Interagency Committee on Disability Research at the U.S. Department of Education, and a former director of the Rehabilitation Research and Training Center on Blindness and Low Vision at Mississippi State University.

Jeanne Boland Patterson, Ed.D., is Director of the Council on Rehabilitation Education. Previously she was a professor and coordinator of the Rehabilitation Program at the University of Georgia in Athens, as well as a program coordinator and faculty member at Utah State University and Florida State University. A former Switzer Fellow, Dr. Patterson has written and co-written numerous training manuals, book chapters, and articles in the areas of rehabilitation education, ethics, consumer satisfaction, and job development and placement of individuals with disabiliities, and has presented papers on these topics at conferences throughout the world. She is past president of the National Council on Rehabilitation Education, past president of the American Rehabilitation Counseling Association, and past chair of both the Commission on Rehabilitation Counselor Certification and its Commission on Standards and Accreditation.

Chapter Authors

Stephen S. Barrett, M.Ed., is Executive Director of the Pinellas Center for the Visually Impaired in Largo, Florida.

Anna Bradfield, Ph.D., is Professor and Chair of the Department of Counseling and Special Educational Programs at Stephen F. Austin State University in Nacogdoches, Texas.

Larry R. Dickerson, Ph.D., is Director of the Center for Research on Teaching and Learning at the University of Arkansas in Little Rock.

Randal R. Elston, Ed.D., is Professor and Coordinator of the Graduate Rehabilitation Counselor Training Program of the Department of Human Resources at East Central University in Ada, Oklahoma.

Kathleen E. Fraser, O.D., is Director of the Santa Rosa Low Vision Clinic in San Antonio, Texas.

Don Harkins, M.S., is Director of Vocational Services at the Rehabilitation Institute in Kansas City, Missouri.

Kathleen Mary Huebner, Ph.D., is Assistant Dean and Associate Professor in the Department of Graduate Studies in Vision Impairment, and Director of the Community Rehabilitation Services Program at the Institute for the Visually Impaired at the Pennsylvania College of Optometry in Philadelphia.

Samuel B. Johnson, M.D., is Professor and Chairman of the Department of Ophthalmology and Assistant Professor in the Department of Pathology at the University of Mississippi Medical Center in Jackson.

Lynne Luxton, Ed.D., is Director of Rehabilitation at Helen Keller Services for the Blind in Brooklyn, New York.

B. J. Maxson, M.Ed., is Executive Director of CARE Ministries, Inc., in Starkville, Mississippi, and Project Director of the Information and Resource Referral Project at the Rehabilitation Research and Training Center on Blindness and Low Vision at Mississippi State University in Missisipi State.

John H. Maxson, M.S., is Training Director at the Rehabilitation Research and Training Center on Blindness and Low Vision at Mississippi State University in Mississippi State.

Lynn W. McBroom, Ph.D., is Senior Research Scientist at the Rehabilitation Research and Training Center on Blindness and Low Vision at Mississippi State University in Mississippi State.

Connie S. McCaa, M.D. and Ph.D., is Professor of Ophthalmology and Director of Corneal Services at the University of Mississippi School of Medicine in Jackson.

Gerald Miller, M.S., is Executive Director of the Employment Program for Recovered Alcoholics and former director of National Services in Rehabilitation and Employment at the American Foundation for the Blind in New York City.

Jeffrey J. Moyer, M.R.A., is a consultant on access, an adjunct faculty member at Kent State University, and a motivational speaker, songwriter, and disability advocate in Highland Heights, Ohio. At the time of writing, he was Director of Rehabilitation and Education Services, Storer Sight Center, at the Cleveland Society for the Blind.

Michael D. Orlansky, Ph.D., is Foreign Service Officer, specializing in educational and cultural affairs, at the American Embassy in Guatemala. He was, at the time of writing, Professor of Special Education at Ohio State University in Columbus.

Priscilla A. Rogers, M.A., is a consultant at the American Foundation for the Blind in New York City, and was, at the time of writing, Program Director of the Division of Blind Services in Tallahasse, Florida.

Sharon Zell Sacks, Ph.D., is Professor in the Division of Special Education and Rehabilitative Services at San Jose State University in San Jose, California.

Sue A. Schmitt, Ed.D., is Dean of the School of Education at Seattle University in Seattle, Washington.

Geraldine T. Scholl, Ph.D., is Professor Emerita of Education at the University of Michigan in Ann Arbor.

Steve Shindell, Ph.D., is Clinical Associate Professor at Emory School of Medicine and Georgia State University, Atlanta, and a consulting psychologist. He has a private practice in Atlanta, Georgia.

Pat Bussen Smith, Ed.D., is Chairperson of the Department of Rehabilitation and Coordinator of the Rehabilitation Teaching of the Blind graduate programs at the University of Arkansas in Little Rock.

B. C. Starkson, M.S., is Supervisor of Computer Training at the U.S. Department of Veterans Affairs in Birmingham, Alabama.

Dean W. Tuttle, Ph.D., is Professor Emeritus in the Division of Special Education at the University of Northern Colorado in Greeley.

Marjorie E. Ward, Ph.D., is Associate Professor in the College of Education, School of Teaching and Learning, at Ohio State University in Columbus.

Richard L. Welsh, Ph.D., is Vice President of Pittsburgh Vision Services in Pittsburgh, Pennsylvania.

Karen E. Wolffe, Ph.D., is a career and rehabilitation counselor, and a private consultant in Austin, Texas.

PART ONE

Vision and Visual Impairment: An Overview

A knowledge of disabilities and their impact on the individual is the feature that differentiates rehabilitation counselors from other types of counselors. In the field of blindness and low vision, rehabilitation counselors are further distinguished by their knowledge of blindness and visual impairment and the system of services and resources available to minimize or accommodate effects of a visual impairment. To understand the system of services and resources available in this area, rehabilitation counselors need a foundation on which to build successful rehabilitation programs. Such essential information includes an awareness of the prevalence and incidence of visual impairments, an understanding of the terminology that is used in the field of vision, a familiarity with the anatomy, physiology, and functioning of the eye, a comprehension of the etiology and effects of common visual impairments, and a sensitivity to the individual and societal response to visual impairments. The rehabilitation counselor requires this basic knowledge to facilitate communication with individuals who have visual impairments and with other service providers.

Numerous myths and stereotypes surround blindness—for example, the belief that people who are blind have extraordinary compensatory powers, such as clairvoyance. Understanding this and other myths and stereotypes related to blindness can help rehabilitation counselors appreciate the psychosocial and employment issues that may be faced by individuals with visual impairments. Because the beliefs of counselors reflect those of the general public, it is equally important for counselors to examine their own views and values and confront any stereotypes they may have.

Rehabilitation counselors also need to understand the physical makeup of the eye, how it functions, and the different impairments associated with the eye. When a client says, "I have macular degeneration," the rehabilitation counselor should have some knowledge of the condition, the typical course of treatment, common functional limitations, and a sense of the questions the client might raise about his or her impairment. Although each client's condition is unique, a basic understanding of the structure of the eye and a knowledge of common visual impairments can help the counselor identify appropriate questions to ask in relation to a particular client. Because rehabilitation counselors work most frequently with individuals who are not totally blind, they also need to know about low vision and about severe visual impairment and low vision devices.

Individuals who are congenitally blind or visually impaired frequently have different life experiences from those of individuals who acquire visual impairments later in life. Part One of this book provides an overview of blindness and visual impairment, a brief presentation of the visual system, important background information on the implications that the time of onset of vision loss may have for vocational counseling, and an introduction to low vision and low vision devices.

CHAPTER 1

An Overview of Blindness and Visual Impairment

Larry R. Dickerson, Pat Bussen Smith, and J. Elton Moore

Human beings probably depend on vision more than all the other senses combined, and it has even been estimated that approximately 80 percent of the information we derive comes through our eyes (Morris, 1985). At any given moment, some 1.5 million simultaneous messages are being received by the 137 million cells of the retina. When we smell, feel, or hear something, we rely on our eyes to confirm it. The importance that modern civilization places on vision is evident in the often-used phrase "seeing is believing" (Vickers, 1987).

Visual impairments and blindness may affect anyone, regardless of age, gender, wealth, physique, or personality. A person may be born with impaired vision (i.e., a congenital visual impairment) or may experience an impairment that develops later in life (i.e., an adventitious visual impairment). The actual onset of a visual impairment or loss may be sudden or gradual. There is great diversity of both visual characteristics and rehabilitation needs within the population of individuals with impaired vision. The loss of visual acuity can range from slight to profound. The visual field loss may be predominately peripheral or central, with severity ranging from slight to profound. Other vision problems may also exist, such as night blindness, color blindness, decreased contrast sensitivity, sensitivity to glare, or prolonged recovery from the effects of glare. The extent of the impairment created by a vision loss depends not only on the nature and extent of the loss and when it occurs but also on the needs, aspirations, attitudes, and physical abilities of the individual involved. Some of the more significant functional problems resulting from impaired vision typically include diminished ability to read, recognize faces and facial expressions, perform visually guided motor tasks, be aware of the important features of the immediate environment, and move freely within the environment. All of these factors influence the rehabilitation process. The objectives of this chapter are to (1) explore commonly used definitions and terms relating to blindness, (2) describe the incidence and etiology of visual impairments in the United States, and (3) identify some of the psychosocial and employment issues associated with blindness and visual impairment.

DEFINITIONS

There is no universal definition of blindness. The World Health Organization (WHO) (1973) has identified multiple international definitions, and various definitions of blindness are used by numerous agencies in the United States. Although the term *blindness* is often used to denote a total absence of light, most individuals with vision loss have some usable vision, and it is estimated that in the United States over 75 percent of individuals who are legally blind have some remaining vision (Sardegna & Paul, 1991). The term *legal blindness* refers to a specified loss of vision that makes individuals eligible for benefits and services of government programs or rehabilitation agencies (Bailey & Hall, 1990).

WHO (1980) defined blindness as corrected visual acuity less than 20/400 (or 6/120, its metric equivalent) in the better eye (that is, the person can see at 20 feet what a sighted person can see at 400 feet). This is the internationally accepted definition of blindness and indicates the inability of an individual to count fingers held up by an examiner at a distance of 20 feet or to walk around unguided. In the United States, a frequently used definition of blindness is the clinical measure for legal blindness established by the American Medical Association (AMA) House of Delegates in 1934. The AMA definition stated that "a person shall be considered blind whose central visual acuity does not exceed 20/200 in the better eye with correcting lenses or whose visual acuity, if better than 20/200, has a limit to the central field of vision to such a degree that its widest diameter subtends an angle of no greater than 20 degrees" (Koestler, 1976, p. 45). A more generic definition is given in the *American Medical Association Encyclopedia of Medicine* (Clayman, 1989), which defines blindness as a total or partial inability to see, even with ordinary eyeglasses. Hoover and Bledsoe (1981) defined blindness as anatomic and functional disturbances of the sense of vision of sufficient magnitude to cause total loss of light perception.

The need for delineating the range of vision between unimpaired or "normal" vision and total blindness has resulted in a variety of terms, including *low vision* and *severe visual impairment.* Although *blindness, visual impairment,* and *visual disability* are frequently used as synonyms, these terms are also sometimes assigned different meanings. The term *visual impairment* is generally used in the field of blindness to refer to any deviations in vision. However, the term *visual disability* is also used in the field of rehabilitation counseling to refer to a visual impairment of sufficient magnitude that an individual requires the specialized services of a counselor or agency serving individuals with vision loss.

The International Classification of Diseases (Colenbrander, 1976) identified three levels of vision loss as moderate, severe, or profound, with further distinctions and definitions given at each level. These levels and definitions were adopted by WHO for international reporting, effective January 1, 1979. In these classifications, severe low vision was determined to be visual acuity in the better eye equal to or less than 20/200 or a visual field of 20 degrees or less; moderate low vision was described as visual acuity of 20/70 or less, or a visual field of 60 degrees or less. At a 1992 meeting of WHO, a person with low vision was defined as (Best & Corn, 1993):

> . . . one who has impairment of visual function, even after treatment and/or standard refractive correction, and has a visual acuity of less than 6/18 to light perception or a visual field of less than 10 degrees from the point of fixation, but who uses, or is potentially able to use, vision for the planning and/or execution of a task. (p. 309)

In frequent discourse, however, the term *low vision* is usually used to refer to "a vision loss that is severe enough to interfere with the ability to perform everyday tasks or activities and that cannot be corrected to normal by conventional eyeglasses or contact lenses" (Jose, 1992, p. 209).

The use of various terms, therefore, has been discussed and examined frequently (for a full discussion, see Corn & Koenig, 1996). In the field of rehabilitation, however, the term *blind* is typically reserved for individuals with no usable sight whatsoever, and the designations *visual impairment* and *low vision* are used to describe those who have some usable vision, regardless of the amount of loss. In this book, the term *visual im-*

pairment encompasses any deviation from low vision to total blindness.

Measurement of Legal Blindness

One reason for the great disparity frequently encountered in the estimates of the number of people who are visually impaired in the United States is the lack of agreement about the definitions of legal blindness within various service delivery systems. For example, discrepancies in meanings have been reported between the medical establishment and the rehabilitation community (Silverstone, 1988). The medical establishment definitions, which generally measure the need for medical services, and which include acuity and extent of visual field and etiology, are used to specify medical procedures to restore vision and to maintain and enhance residual vision functions. In contrast, the definitions used by the rehabilitation community determine deficits or limitations in performing the activities of daily living used for identifying training and support services that are needed to assist individuals in performing work and daily living activities. These functional measures, such as the ability to perform specific tasks, are useful in determining the need for nonmedical rehabilitation services. Consequently, definitions of blindness and visual impairment depend on the intent and purpose of the designation and the agency providing that definition.

In addition to the designation of blindness given by the medical and rehabilitation communities, most states have also created their own statutory definitions of "blindness." One reason for these statutory definitions is that approximately 27 of the 50 states in the United States maintain registers of individuals who are "legally blind." In these states, ophthalmologists and optometrists are required to register legally blind persons with the state agency responsible for serving those people who are blind or severely visually impaired. The purposes of maintaining legal blindness registers are as follows: (1) to attempt to know how many residents have visual impairments, which is necessary in allocating resources for state-provided services, and (2) to furnish a means for social service agencies to identify those individuals who may benefit from their services. Although several states also register people who are visually impaired, Table 1.1 contains a list of states that register individuals who are legally blind. Because state registers are based on state law, the number of states who require registration can change at any time. The variety of definitions of "legal blindness" also demonstrates that legal blindness does not always mean a total loss of light perception. Moreover, in some systems the definition of blind-

Table 1.1. States Maintaining Legal Blindness Registers

Alabama	New Jersey
Connecticut	New Mexico
Delaware	New York
Florida	North Carlina
Hawaii	Oklahoma
Indiana	Oregon
Iowa	Rhode Island
Kansas	South Carolina
Louisiana	South Dakota
Maine	Tennessee
Maryland	Utah
Massachusetts	Vermont
Minnesota	Virginia
New Hampshire	

Source: V. DeSantis and J. D. Schein, "Blindness Statistics (Part 2): Blindness Registers in the United States." *Journal of Visual Impairment & Blindness,* 80 (1986), p. 570.

ness may be precisely defined, but based on prognosis or functional need, and may be interpreted either narrowly or broadly.

As might be assumed, defining legal blindness based on the diverse state-made assessments of visual acuity and extent of the visual fields (e.g., scanning ability, depth perception, and contrast sensitivity; see Chapters 2 and 4) has produced variability in the estimates of the number of individuals with visual impairments. Many of the widely used, chart-type instruments for measuring visual acuity, such as the Snellen Eye Chart, are not as precise when used near the level of acuity that defines legal blindness. Specifically, some chart-type assessments have progressively larger steps beginning at high levels of acuity, compared to steps on the chart that denote lower levels. For example, a chart might have steps from 20/20 to 20/30 acuity, which are smaller than steps from 20/100 to 20/200 acuity. The smaller step at the high level of acuity increases the precision of measurement at that level compared to levels with larger steps. When the definition of legal blindness is a measured level of acuity of 20/200 and the assessment instrument is an acuity chart with less precision in the area of legal blindness, it is possible that people with significant visual impairments are not determined to be legally blind.

The application of the definitions of legal blindness also frequently reflects different interpretations of the term *best correction.* Some people may interpret best correction to mean regular prescription eyeglasses or contact lenses, while others may interpret this to encompass the use of special low vision devices (see Chapter 4). In addition to this disparity, this definition does not consider the etiology and prognosis of the vision loss, the individual's age at the time of onset, the type of onset, and the length of time that has elapsed since the onset. For example, Dale (1992) discussed how the etiology may influence the psychosocial adjustment to blindness, specifically the difference between traumatic onset and blindness caused by a more insidious disease process. All of these factors influence the formation of concepts, the adjustment to blindness, and, hence, the services required, which are all important considerations in the rehabilitation process.

Functional Definitions

Although the definition of legal blindness with the emphasis on the measurement of distance visual acuity and visual fields may provide guidance in determining eligibility for various services and programs, rehabilitation and educational professionals have found that the visual acuity assigned to a person does not reflect how well the individual utilizes that vision. Two individuals with the same visual acuity may possess different abilities to use their vision, and may in fact see differently, just as two people of the same height and weight may have different physical abilities. Consequently, the need arose for a functional definition of blindness, to better address the effects of the reduced visual acuity on the functions and activities in a person's daily life. Because the definition is often based on one specific task, such as the ability to read small print, recognize an individual across the street, or obtain a driver's license, functional vision (similar to legal blindness) may also be defined in various ways by the different sectors working with people with impaired vision.

An example of a functional definition is that used by the National Center for Health Statistics (NCHS, 1975), which defines a person with severe visual impairment as someone who is unable to read ordinary newspaper print even with the aid of corrective lenses, or, if under six years of age, a person who is blind in both eyes or has no useful vision in either eye. Another type of functional definition has been set forth by the National Federation of the Blind (Jernigan, 1974): "An individual may properly be said to be blind . . . when [he or she] has to devise so many alternative techniques . . . to function efficiently . . . that his [her] pattern of daily living is substantially altered" (p. 2).

Eligibility for Services

Eligibility for vocational rehabilitation services in the United States for individuals with impaired vision is determined primarily by meeting the definitions of legal blindness, which, as discussed in the previous section, are based on the medical definitions of blindness and visual impairment. For example, the Rehabilitation Services Administration codes visual impairments according to etiology (i.e., cataract; glaucoma; all other diseases; congenital condition, accident, poisoning, exposure, or injury, ill-defined and unspecified causes) using the following categories: (1) blindness, both eyes, no light perception, (2) blindness, both eyes (with correction not more than 20/200 in better eye or limitation in field within 20 degrees, but not [1]), (3) blindness, one eye, other eye defective (better eye with correction less than 20/60, but better than 20/200, or corresponding loss in visual field), (4) blindness, one eye, other eye good, and (5) other visual impairments. The provision of client services, however, is determined by the rehabilitation community definitions of the functional limitations in performing activities that are imposed by the client's personal visual ability. Although eligibility for services is a medically ascertained issue, the provision of specific services is a determination of functional visual ability. Accordingly, rehabilitation counselors working with people with visual impairments need to be familiar with definitions used by both the medical and rehabilitation communities.

Eligibility for such social service programs as Social Security Disability Insurance (SSDI) is also based on specific criteria. This program uses a definition similar to that used by the Randolph–Sheppard Vending Facility Program for the Blind (34 CFR 395.1) (see Chapter 10), which defines a person as blind if the person is determined to have (1) not more than 20/200 central visual acuity in the better eye with correcting lenses, or (2) an equally disabling loss of the visual field as evidenced by a limitation to the field of vision in the better eye to such a degree that its widest diameter subtends an angle of no greater than 20 degrees.

PREVALENCE AND INCIDENCE ESTIMATES

As already suggested, the lack of agreement on a standard definition of blindness and visual impairment and the various purposes of those definitions have made it difficult to estimate the number of people who are "legally blind" or "totally blind." Estimates from WHO indicate that, worldwide, there are 28 million people who are blind, a figure that rises to about 42 million if the estimates include those who have visual acuities of 20/200 (6/60) or worse (Vaughan, Asbury, & Riordan-Eva, 1995). WHO (Best & Corn, 1993) also estimates that 1.5 to 2 million children in the world have low vision or are blind. In the United States, an estimated 4,293,360 noninstitutionalized civilian individuals have severe visual impairment (Nelson & Dimitrova, 1993), with severe visual impairment defined as: "self- or proxy-reported inability to see to read ordinary newspaper print even when wearing glasses or contact lenses; for children under age 6 it is the caregiver's

Table 1.2. Distribution of Visual Impairments, by Age

Age	Percentage
0–17	2
18–44	8
45–54	8
55–64	14
65–74	25
75–84	28
85 and over	15

Source: K. Nelson and G. Dimitrova, "Statistical Brief #36: Severe Visual Impairment in the United States and in Each State, 1990." *Journal of Visual Impairment & Blindness,* 87 (1993), pp. 80–85.

(usually the mother's) report that the child lacks useful vision" (p. 80).

When visual impairment is viewed in relation to age group (See Table 1.2), estimates suggest that 82 pecent of visually impaired individuals are age 55 or older (Nelson & Dimitrova, 1993). The 1984 NCHS survey obtained data about older individuals who were living in a community setting. That survey, which defined visual impairment as blindness in one or both eyes and any other trouble seeing, estimated that the number of people with impaired vision between the ages of 65 and 74 was 26,290,000; between the ages of 75 and 84 was 8,073,000; and 85 and over was 1,990,000 (Havlik, 1986).

COMMON ATTITUDES AND STEREOTYPES

Regardless of the definition of blindness that is employed, many people hold a number of stereotypes about both blindness and people who are blind. Jernigan (1992) suggested that these misconceptions or stereotypes, rather than the actual physical loss of sight, constitute the real problem of blindness, and noted the need for changing public attitudes. Prevailing misunderstanding and stereotypes often have a significant negative effect on self-esteem, availability of services, and employment opportunities for individuals who are visually impaired. In 1976, when Frances Koestler wrote about the myths, taboos, and stereotypes, many people believed blindness to be one of the most universally dreaded of all disabilities. Although some people may argue that fear surrounding the topics of cancer or acquired immunodeficiency syndrome (AIDS) is currently more pronounced than the dread related to being blind, there is no doubt that many people fear blindness and loss of vision.

Impact of Stereotypes

A stereotype is an image of a person that incorporates widely held beliefs about the characteristics of the group to which that person belongs (Vickers, 1987). The effect is to deny the differences that undoubtedly exist among members of the group and thus concentrate on similarities, usually to an extent that goes beyond the facts. Many commonly held fears of blindness result from this wide range of divergent and stereotyped characteristics that has been attributed to individuals who are blind. Some of these characteristics are negative, such as a belief that people who are blind are being punished for sins. Other characteristics are idealized, for example, the presumption that individuals with visual impairments have miraculous compensatory powers, such as "second sight" or clairvoyance is widespread (Wagner-Lampl & Oliver, 1994). Occasionally blindness is equated with loss of intelligence or diminution of one or more of the other senses, particularly hearing. Also, the fear of the dark inherent in many young children can leave a lasting impression; in the minds of many individuals, blindness is synonymous with blackness or the complete absence of light. Wagner-Lampl and Oliver (1994) also described the "folklore" of blindness, including the various myths that perpetuate many negative stereotypes and misconceptions. These superstitions range from not touching an individual who is blind (because blindness is contagious) to keeping a room dark when a person has measles (to avoid becoming blind). Parents can also perpetuate myths about blindness through such statements as "crying too much causes blindness," or "reading in poor light causes blindness."

Other sources also confirm the perpetuation of the stereotypes about people who are blind. Wainapel (1989) indicated that the general public tends to view individuals with visual impairments as (1) either totally blind or fully sighted without recognizing the types and levels of visual impairment, (2) having other disabilities such as mental retardation or deafness, (3) helpless objects of pity who are unable to live independent lives, or (4) unable to work except in certain types of jobs, such as operating vending programs or working as court stenographers.

Patterson and Witten (1987) identified a

number of myths related to disability in general, which have also been applied to individuals with impaired vision. These include the following: (1) disability is a constantly frustrating tragedy, (2) the more severe the disability, the greater the psychological impact, (3) persons with disabilities do not recognize their limitations or abilities, (4) persons with disabilities worry about more "important" things than their sexuality, (5) employment problems for such people are almost always caused by disabilities, and (6) people with disabilities have special personalities or special abilities. Although these myths certainly do not reflect accurate views of people who are blind, they encapsulate a stereotypical perspective that is widespread in our society.

Stereotypes and Counseling

When we reject a stereotype, we tend to concentrate on the person as an individual; we differentiate that person from other members of the same group. We can also be aware of similarities to members of other groups or, more important, the similarity to ourselves. It is essential for the rehabilitation professional to remember that some stereotypes may be positive and may concentrate on favorable characteristics of the group, either real or imagined. Negative stereotypes, on the other hand, are often held about groups whom we fear. If the combination is used as a basis for action, it amounts to prejudice. The perpetuation of a stereotype is often encouraged by ignorance or misinformation and a strong element of denial, so that evidence against the validity of the stereotype is ignored. Many agencies, organizations and information services on vision and eye health, such as Prevent Blindness America, have tried to distinguish between fact and fiction regarding eyesight and eye care by publishing and distributing material explaining the facts. For a list of common eye-related myths, see Sidebar 1.1.

The general beliefs that society has about people who are blind (e.g., that they are helpless, docile, dependent, melancholic, and so forth) create a stigma about blindness that makes it difficult for sighted people to accept a person who is blind as an equal human being (Scott, 1969). The social stigma associated with disabilities in general, and vision loss in particular, is difficult to overcome. Rehabilitation professionals who work with people who are either blind or severely visually impaired can help eliminate social stigma and negative stereotypes by advocating on behalf of individuals with impairments, and providing counseling and appropriate support services.

Attitudinal Barriers

Attitudinal barriers can be even more defeating to individuals with visual impairments than an inaccessible environment (Bishop, 1987). Attitudinal barriers have been defined as "a way of thinking or feeling, resulting in behavior that limits the potential of . . . [people with disabilities] to be independent individuals" (Regional Rehabilitation Research Institute, 1981, p. 4). It is important that rehabilitation counselors understand attitudinal barriers, particularly as they affect employment opportunities for persons who are blind. Because employers hold the same or similar views as the general public, when making employment decisions, they bring their own unique versions of the prejudices, attitudes, and generalizations that have become part of our culture—attitudes that are held about blindness and persons who are blind, as well as those that are held about other impairments. Thus, the attitudes of employers, which exist in varying degrees in all people, can have the effect of either barring or restricting access to employment and career opportunities that should be available to all individuals, including those with visual impairments (Dixon, 1983). (For more about counselors, stereotypes, and job placement, see Chapters 6 and 11.)

Although legislation, technology, and the consumer movement have helped bring people with disabilities from the margins of society into the main current of community life, stereotyped attitudes still persist (Resnick, 1983). Even with

SIDEBAR 1.1

Common Myths About Eyesight

Myth: Reading in dim light can damage your eyes.
Fact: Reading in dim light can cause eye fatigue, but it will not hurt the eyes.
Myth: Watching television too closely or for too long will damage your eyes.
Fact: There is no evidence to suggest that watching television sitting too closely or for too long will damage the eyes. Young children often sit close to the television screen because they have a greater ability to focus on close-by objects than adults do. Consequently, children hold their reading material close as well. However, as they grow older, these habits usually change. If not, the youngsters may have myopia (nearsightedness). To detect signs of possible eye problems, children should have regular eye examinations.
Myth: Eating carrots will improve your vision.
Fact: Although it is true that carrots, as well as many other vegetables, are high in vitamin A, which is an essential vitamin for sight, only a small amount is necessary for good vision. A well-balanced diet with or without carrots, provides all the nutrients that are needed. In fact, taken to the extreme, too much vitamin A, D, or E may actually be harmful.
Myth: Too much reading of fine print will wear out or damage your eyes.
Fact: This is one of the more widely held myths about vision. Many older people in particular feel they should not read too much because it will wear out their eyes. Although extensive or prolonged reading of fine print can cause eye fatigue, there is no evidence to suggest that it will damage or wear out the eyes.
Myth: Failure to use proper eyeglasses will hurt your eyes.
Fact: This statement does have some truth in it for a small number of persons. Some children have eye problems that can be corrected, and it is important that they wear their eyeglasses. But vision problems caused by heredity or physical injury remain whether or not we use eyeglasses. Although corrective lenses or contacts are needed to improve eyesight, using one's eyes, with or without eyeglasses, will not damage them further.
Myth: An eye examination is necessary only if an individual is experiencing problems with his or her eyesight.
Fact: Everyone should follow a proper eye health program that includes a regular eye exam, whether or not they're having any noticeable signs of problems. Children should be tested at six months old, before entering school (age 4 or so), and then periodically throughout their school years. For adults, the frequency depends on the doctor's advice and may be every other year or more often.

Source: Adapted, by permission of the publisher, from "Common Eye Myths" flyer (Schaumburg, IL: Prevent Blindness America, 1993).

the Americans with Disabilities Act, many reports exist of discrimination in housing, recreation, insurance, jury duty, parenting, and employment. Moreover, employment rights do not guarantee comfortable interpersonal relationships with coworkers, and educational rights do not guarantee that sitting next to a sighted student in school will ensure welcomed participation in social life. Integration in the sense of mutual acceptance frequently has not occurred

With an appropriate rehabilitation program, people who have a visual impairment can be trained to use assistive devices to accomplish the same work-related tasks that sighted individuals perform.

(Resnick, 1983) between people with and without disabilities.

Attitudes of Counselors

Misunderstandings about the nature of blindness often originate because of a lack of knowledge concerning the point at which declining vision comes to be recognized as such in medical parlance, legislative provision, or eligibility for supportive services. Such misunderstandings present major attitudinal barriers to individuals with visual impairments. Rehabilitation counselors live in the same culture as the general population and are no more immune to disability myths than others (DeLoach & Greer, 1981). Because these attitudinal barriers and myths operate primarily on a subconscious level, they are less easily detected in day-to-day rehabilitation program operations (Holmes & Karst, 1990). Moreover, because much of what culture teaches is on a subconscious level, people may perceive their own behavior as normal and peculiar behavior in others as either irresponsible or psychopathic (Hall, 1976). These concepts are significant for the rehabilitation service-delivery system, because rehabilitation counselors work in settings in which the welfare of clients must often be weighed against agency policies and financial limitations. Subconscious attitudes can hamper the professional behavior of counselors and the ability of rehabilitation programs to achieve their missions.

Accordingly, counselors are advised to carefully examine the extent to which they believe the

SIDEBAR 1.2

Attitudes of Persons Who Have Visual Impairments

The importance of attitudes of persons who have visual impairments was demonstrated in a focus group on employment that was held to determine the outlook of those individuals who had been highly successful in their fields. The commonalities that were found among the focus group participants included the following:

- "We don't blame everybody else." Participants took responsibility for their lives (i.e., they did not blame agencies or society for their problems), they had high expectations of themselves, and they believed in the value of work.
- "You want to be passionate about your work." In order to be passionate about work, the participants believed it had to have personal relevance, be viewed as worthwhile, and have challenges to advancement.
- "They are not going to rearrange the world for you." The focus group members took responsibility for educating employers, anticipating employers' concerns, and recognizing that they lived in a sighted world to which they needed to adapt.
- "Blindness is a characteristic of you, not you." The importance of blindness as a secondary characteristic rather than as a primary characteristic was stressed, along with the importance of developing common interests with coworkers, often through leisure activities.
- "You have to develop alternative skills to function." Mastery of skills, such as a knowledge of braille and travel skills, contributes to the self-esteem of individuals with visual impairments. In turn, the heightened self-esteem and self-reliance allowed individuals to feel that they could compete with sighted individuals.
- "Most of us get jobs because someone else believes in us." The importance of role models and mentors with and without visual impairments was stressed by focus group participants.

Source: Adapted from C. E. Young, "A Focus Group on Employment." *Journal of Visual Impairment & Blindness News Service,* 89 (1) (1995), pp. 14–17.

general myths about disabilities or specific myths related to blindness, and they should ensure that (1) clients are not taught such myths, (2) such beliefs are not reinforced in clients, when clients believe in myths or stereotypes, and (3) such myths are dispelled. Rehabilitation professionals are also reminded that a review of the literature (Wallace, 1972) showed that poor adjustment to disability, including blindness, more frequently results from the attitudes of society rather than from the disability itself (see Sidebar 1.2).

Rehabilitation counselors are challenged to facilitate these feelings of self-worth and self-esteem in individuals who are experiencing negative societal attitudes. Rehabilitation professionals can improve the rehabilitation service-delivery system by recognizing disability myths for what they are, refusing to stereotype clients, and advocating on behalf of individuals with visual impairments. Part of advocacy is working to change negative attitudes; however, attitudes are complex phenomena. Recognizing that there are both emotional and cognitive aspects of attitudes, Verplanken, Meijnders, and van de Wege (1994) found that both level of experience and contact correlated positively with the emotional component and knowledge, but did not have a direct relationship to the cognitive component. The statements concerning the results of their study further describe the complexity of attitudes:

> On the one hand experience and contact may enhance positive feelings toward . . . persons [with visual impairments], whereas on the other hand, experience may increase knowledge: for example, through experience, a person may gain more insight into the problems and needs of . . . people [with visual impairments]. In other words, our data suggest that the degree of experience leads to more *differentiated* attitudes toward . . . persons [with visual impairments]. That is, more experience and contact does not result in more favorable or less favorable attitudes in general, but in more favorable feelings, on the one hand, and more realistic perceptions, on the other hand. (p. 508)

Various approaches have been used to change attitudes, including the provision of information, simulation activities, contact with individuals with impairments, and a combination of these (Shaver, Curtis, Jesunathades, & Strong, 1987). Research suggests that neither contact nor information alone is effective in changing attitudes, but that both are required (e.g., Anthony, 1984; Sampson, 1991). Further research (e.g., Wetstein-Kroft & Vargo, 1984) also suggests that more positive changes occur when individuals with and without disabilities are of the same status, have perceived similarities, and have structured direct contact. Because all of the research is based on expressed beliefs, as opposed to behaviors, however, there is no research to support that changes in behavior actually occur. This is an important consideration, because in addition to knowledge and feelings, there is a third component of attitudes—behavior. And, as Van Hoose and Kottler (1985) pointed out, there is no perfect correlation between what people believe, what they say they believe, and how people actually act on the basis of their beliefs.

Counselors must be knowledgeable about the problems that vision loss causes, the capabilities of individuals with visual impairments, and the range of help that is available for those with either congenital or adventitious blindness. Only then can the rehabilitation system and the rehabilitation professional provide the best possible services to persons who are severely visually impaired (see Sidebar 1.3).

Attitude Formation and Psychosocial Issues

Lukoff and Whiteman (1970) suggested that there is no generalized attitude of society about individuals who are blind and blindness itself. Attitudes are changed or modified based on other characteristics of the person who is blind, such as age, education, and level of perceived independence. This means that in addition to the myths and stereotypes that exist, those individuals with impairments can perpetuate or refute existing stereotypes. Perceived independence and perceived coping are two means of refuting negative stereotypes. For example, McGowan and Porter (1967) indicated that the individual's status is primarily determined by a perception of either independence or dependence by society. The more dependent an individual is viewed, the more the person will lose in personal dignity, prestige, and self-esteem, not only within the immediate family unit, but also in society in general. The ability to cope is viewed in a manner similar to independence. Wright (1990) stated that individuals with disabilities are viewed more favorably when they are perceived as coping with their problems and making the most of their abilities. Consequently, an important role of rehabilitation is to help individuals with visual impairments learn independent living skills not only for functional purposes but also for promoting more positive attitudes by the individuals themselves and the public in general. (For a more complete, in-depth coverage of attitudes and psychosocial issues, see Chapter 3.)

Public attitudes tend to be formed through generalizations obtained from limited contact with individuals who are visually impaired and

SIDEBAR 1.3

The Counselor–Client Relationship

The following letter to a rehabilitation counselor addresses a number of attitudinal issues and behaviors of counselors that influence the counselor–client relationship. It also highlights the importance of sensitivity toward the person with whom the rehabilitation counselor is working.

Dear Rehabilitation Counselor,
I realize that ATTITUDE plays a crucial part in our relationship. I am willing to comply [with] the following terms to maximize our productivity. I submit them for your consideration.

A: ACCEPT the fact that the party on the other side of the desk is only human. You, as a counselor, are not perfect in your opinions and actions, just as I, as a client, am not perfect in my opinions or follow-through.

T: TOLERANCE. A certain amount of tolerance goes a long way. I will allow you to have a bad day but you need to extend me the same courtesy.

T: TOUGH. What we are going through is tough. Losing my eyesight is tough no doubt. Cutting through the paperwork jungle when you were trained to give service, not fill out forms, is tough.

I: INITIATE. We need to learn to initiate. I, as a client, should not rely solely on you, the counselor, to guide the way to my future. I need to initiate potential solutions. You should be willing to initiate new and innovative ideas for rehabilitation.

T: TOGETHER. We are in this thing together. Not only do I, the client, gain a job or an education or whatever I decide to gain from the agency, but you, the counselor, gain a closure for your record and the satisfaction of assisting someone to reenter society.

U: UNDERSTAND. I, as a client, understand that you, as a counselor, have to conform to standards set by the agency. You may make some innovations but you will always be limited in some way, usually financially. You need to understand that I am limited in ways as well. I do not know what I can achieve. Along with the frustration of the physical reality of blindness, I also have to cope with the frustration of acceptance by society, the bureaucracy of service agencies, and my own lack of self-confidence at times.

D: DEVELOP. We will develop. You, as a counselor, will develop a sense of what my talents are, what types of areas I might be inclined toward, and you will also develop a sense of me as a human being rather than a case file to be completed by the numbers. I will develop a sense for the endless paper trail you must leave when I request something. I will develop my own skills so that I will not expect you to come to my rescue or to do all the work for me. I will develop a sense of you as a human being, not just the great power which governs my life by the approval or denial of service.

E: EXCELLENCE. We will strive for excellence. The work we each have to do is hard. I must look at myself as the sighted world sees me and keep that image in mind. You must try not to become disenchanted with those people who do not meet your expectations or are held back by some force you cannot break. We should both try to be the best we can at what we do, and not worry about how well or how badly anyone else does what they do.

Source: Adapted from J. McKeown, "Letter to a Rehabilitation Counselor." *The Braille Forum,* 30 (4) (1992), pp. 20–22.

People with visual impairments can make the most of their abilities and become self-reliant through learning independent living skills, like reading braille.

unrealistic portrayals in the media. Negative attitudes can be held by people who are visually impaired, the general public, and professionals working in the field of blindness. Often people may not be conscious of the fact that they have negative attitudes.

Luck and Cull (1980) described two theories of attitude formation based on visually impaired people who have negative beliefs that are internalized. First, attitudes may be formed by a process of self-inclusion; prior to the onset of blindness, some people who hold negative attitudes about people who are blind maintain these negative attitudes after onset and then apply these attitudes to themselves. In the second theory, attitudes can be formed by a process of generalization, in which negative attitudes toward oneself are generalized to all people who are blind. Luck and Cull believed that self-inclusion and generalized inclusion processes can occur together and result in preventing a positive adjustment to blindness, or contributing to a negative adjustment or adaptation to blindness.

The attitudes of people with congenital blindness, like the attitudes of everyone else, are initially formed by the attitudes and expectations of important people in their lives, such as parents, siblings, teachers, and peers. Children who are blind often do not realize their visual impairment until early childhood when they question how other people "know" something that is not apparent to them. Erin and Corn (1994) explore the manner in which children first understand their visual impairments, and the subsequent questions parents need to address. They have found that the three major questions related to (1) "when"—will I be able to see when I am older?, (2) "why"—why did God make me blind?, and (3) "how"—how do you know the door is open? Awareness of vision loss occurs as early as age two, with most children being aware by age four. How children are informed about their visual impairment will also have an effect on their acceptance and attitude toward their own blindness and the blindness of other individuals. Erin and Corn (1994) stated: ". . . some children with visual impairments have come to understand that discussing their visual impairment is a taboo. Perhaps, even at an early age, they do not wish to upset their parents further or to talk about a part of them that has been deemed ugly or unspeakable" (p. 138).

The attitudes of parents of children who are visually impaired are influenced by prior experiences and their belief systems, as well as the manner in which they are informed of a child's loss of vision. Too frequently, parents are informed in medical settings, where negative attitudes and misinformation (or lack of information), especially in relation to educational concerns, may be conveyed by medical doctors, who usually do not have contact with educational and rehabilitation programs. The poignant comments of one parent help explain commonly encountered parental actions and feelings:

> My daughter Julie was diagnosed with retinitis pigmentosa (RP) when she was two years old, in 1969. Although I was born into a large family of eight brothers and sisters, all of whom had children, I was the only one with a child who had RP. This was a new world for me. I had no background; I did not know where to go for information. I did not know how to help my daughter or what resources were available for her. . . . The doctors felt Julie should not be told about her RP. Even though my "motherly instincts" made me feel she should know as soon as she was old enough to understand, I followed the doctor's counsel and did not tell her. I relied on doctors because I felt that they had the training and knowledge to advise and guide me. As I consulted with more and more of them (in the first year Julie saw 200 doctors), I realized that all my hours at the medical library had made me more informed and knowledgeable about RP than most of the doctors I consulted. I've had many negative, heartbreaking experiences with the medical profession. One well-respected pediatrician told me Julie would not live to see her eighth birthday. She is now 20 years old. I don't want to be completely negative; many doctors were caring and helpful and were not afraid to admit they did not have all the answers. (Goar, 1988, pp. 73–74)

Many parents may feel guilty, become overprotective, or exhibit other characteristics, both positive and negative, which can influence the child's concept of self.

Low vision can also create other problems for individuals that may influence their own attitudes as well as the attitudes of others. The visual functioning of individuals with low vision often fluctuates depending on such factors as etiology, time of day, physical health, weather, and environmental conditions, for example, lighting and color contrast. This lack of control over knowing how one will be able to function visually from one situation to the next can be very frustrating for the individual with a visual impairment. Individuals with low vision may also "bluff" or attempt to conceal their impairments in situations that require more vision than they have at that particular time. Moreover, many people with low vision feel they neither "belong" in the sighted population nor in the blind population. Variations in visual functional ability can also confuse families, as well as the general public, in terms of what a "blind person" can do. Some family members may even feel that the person with partial sight is "faking it" in order to gain more assistance and attention than is necessary.

INDIVIDUAL RESPONSE TO VISUAL IMPAIRMENT

Lukoff (1970) stated that "perhaps the most common complaint in the literature by . . . people (who are blind) is that their blindness appears to overwhelm all other attributes they possess, and dominates the responses they receive from sighted persons they may encounter. The fact of blindness penetrates into every aspect of the relationships in which they engage" (p. 1). Although written nearly 30 years ago, in many instances this statement is still true today.

The response to visual impairment frequently differs between individuals with congenital and adventitious blindness, in large part because those with congenital blindness have never had the experience of vision. Individuals with adventitious loss are more likely to experience the wide range of emotions (e.g., shock, denial, fear, anger, and depression) that are similar to the feelings of any individual who acquires any severe disability. (For more on the differences between congenital and adventitious loss of vision, see Chapter 3.) Dale (1992) indicated that the response to an impairment brought on by traumatic onset differs from the response to blindness caused by a more insidious disease process. He stated that for a person with a traumatic onset of blindness, "(1) the denial period may be longer, (2) the person usually attributes the causes of blindness to a specific person or object,

(3) the wish for revenge may preoccupy the person, (4) the motivation to improve oneself may be offset by the need to depict oneself as badly injured in the hopes of a larger monetary compensation, and (5) posttraumatic stress disorder may be present" (p. 142). Furthermore, an older individual's response to vision loss is shaped by a lifetime's experience of responses to other difficult or stressful situations. As a general rule, those individuals who have coped well with other situations can be expected to face vision loss in much the same manner. Similarly, the severity of the impairment and whether it occurred gradually or suddenly, may also affect the individual's response to the vision loss. There is also significant variation among peoples' ability to make the best use of whatever visual capacity they have.

When individuals become blind or visually impaired later in life, they often fear that they will lose their jobs and their ability to support themselves. Many fear that they will be unable to take care of themselves or that they will become objects of pity. Because vision loss frequently threatens an individual's independence, there is often concomitant diminishment of self-esteem, which sometimes can cause a person to be reluctant to accept assistance offered by others, including rehabilitation services.

The psychological effect of adventitious vision loss may be profound and may frequently result in severe loss of self-confidence. Depending on the nature and severity of the vision loss, many vocational and daily living skills are affected and will have to be relearned. New methods of moving safely from place to place will have to be mastered, as will skills for reading, writing, and general communication. A person with vision loss often needs time to adjust psychologically before being able to begin the rehabilitation process (Resources for Rehabilitation, 1990). The amount of time needed by individuals before they adapt to their vision loss and are able to benefit from rehabilitation services is a personal matter and may be days, months, or even years. In most cases, people who are visually impaired and who are slow to adjust to their changed circumstances will benefit from discussing their situation with a professional counselor or with others who have gone through similar experiences. The role of the professional rehabilitation counselor may be crucial in determining an individual's response to blindness or severe visual impairment (Resources for Rehabilitation, 1990). "All too often insufficient attention has been given to the level of self-confidence or self-esteem that the student or rehabilitation client has . . ." (Johnson, 1997, p. vii).

One of the more important elements of a rehabilitation program is the recognition that people with impaired vision are individuals with different capabilities, hopes, and dreams—the same as everyone else. Every adult has the right to choose the level of independence and potential to be achieved in a lifetime. With the assistance of the vocational rehabilitation system and teamwork with the professionals, that potential can become a reality. Professional service providers, such as rehabilitation counselors, need to assist those with visual impairments in assessing their functional abilities and potential, and then help them to achieve as much independence as they desire and to gain as much self-sufficiency as they are capable of acquiring.

GENETIC ISSUES

One area that is especially challenging to rehabilitation counselors is addressing the additional psychosocial and rehabilitation issues associated with inherited blindness and visual impairments. Rehabilitation professionals, medical practitioners, and even the general public tend to be more aware of the visual impairments and disorders that result from accidents and diseases and so are familiar with names, symptoms, and consequences of glaucoma, cataracts, and diabetic retinopathy. A significant number of visual disorders, however, result from genetic makeup and have the potential to be inherited by offspring (Vaughan, Asbury, & Riordan-Eva, 1995). Although medical professionals are knowledgeable regarding the best practices for medically limiting the progression of genetic visual disorders and rehabilitation practitioners are effective in limiting the functional disabilities caused by the vision loss, relatively few people in either group know what to do about accompanying psychosocial difficulties.

When individuals or family members (primarily parents) first learn that they have or their child has a hereditary visual disorder, the initial questioning reactions often include: "How did this happen?," "Where or from whom was it inherited?," "Is this life threatening?," and "How will it affect our lives?" As children with inherited visual impairments grow older, they may wonder: "How much vision will I lose?," "Will this disorder cause more physical pain and suffering in years to come?," "Will I die at a younger age than most people?," " Will my children inherit the same impairment?," and, ultimately, "Should I marry and have children?"

Most physicians and ophthalmologists view their role in assisting a patient with visual disorders as limited to curing the disease or containing the vision loss and improving the person's vision. The personal adjustment issues created by the visual impairment are often left to others, even though from a technical standpoint, the physician ostensibly has the background in genetics to address many of these expressed concerns. Practical experience suggests, however, that physicians, special educators, rehabilitation professionals, and other human service providers usually do not raise these personal adjustment issues with individuals. In some instances, inaccurate or misleading information may even be provided. People with inherited visual impairments frequently report being told that they should not have children because the children will inherit the same visual impairment. Accordingly, rehabilitation professionals are cautioned against providing quick solutions to complex issues that are based on personal opinion or limited information, because such behavior is unprofessional, unethical, and, in many cases, misinformed.

Hereditary visual and related disorders may follow a particular specific hereditary pattern. For example, ocular albinism is inherited in a sex-linked recessive pattern. Various forms of RP may be inherited in autosomal dominant, autosomal recessive, or sex-linked recessive patterns. [An autosome is "any non-sex-determining chromosome of which there are 22 pairs in a man" (Bolander & Bolander, 1992, p. 20). Sex-linked means the trait for hereditary purposes is located on the one pair of sex-determining chromosomes.] Other such disorders as diabetes mellitus and open-angle glaucoma (see Chapter 2) have a hereditary base but follow an as yet undetermined pattern. Therefore, a rehabilitation professional should have a very complete medical and family history of a client with a genetic visual impairment or loss to be of maximum assistance in providing counseling and education. Although many rehabilitation professionals will not have the expertise to provide genetic counseling, some guidelines and rules that can provide assistance are as follows:

1. Know which disorders have a genetic base, know the implications of the hereditary and medical information, and give this information to the client as accurately as possible. This information can be found in the library and in medical texts. Rehabilitation professionals can also gain much of this information by talking to the agency's medical consultant or a local ophthalmologist.
2. Help the client to understand the information without telling the client what to do. A rehabilitation professional should not provide an opinion about what the client should do with this information.
3. Assist the client in finding a reliable genetic counselor. Most genetic counselors are located in large metropolitan areas and are affiliated with major medical treatment facilities. Because hereditary visual disorders are uncommon in relationship to other genetically based

health problems, most genetic counselors have limited experience with individuals who are blind or visually impaired. Therefore, rehabilitation counselors in rural areas and many working in cities may have some difficulty in locating appropriately qualified genetic counselors.

4. Assist clients in determining the hereditary patterns for their disorders. If a genetic counselor is not available, the rehabilitation professional may be able to assist the client in developing a genetic pedigree or family tree for such purposes. The information provided by a genetic pedigree helps determine the probability that the client's children will have the disorder. When discussing probabilities, it is important to remember that each child has the *same* probability of inheriting the disorder as the previous child. If the hereditary pattern suggests that 25 percent of the children will have the disorder and one child already has it, the chances of a second child with the same parents having the disorder are still 25 percent. Also, the best indication of how severe the client's symptoms or vision loss will be from a hereditary disorder is based on the experience of other family members who also have had the disorder.
5. Provide supportive counseling to the client to deal with the information gained as it affects the client's life.

It is important for rehabilitation professionals to attend to the genetic counseling needs of individuals who are blind or have low vision. Rehabilitation professionals working with individuals who are visually impaired are urged to raise and respond to genetic counseling issues; this type of action would help to fill a major gap in the current client service programming. Furthermore, the psychological stress surrounding the uncertainty of genetically based visual disorders could be dramatically reduced.

UNEMPLOYMENT AND VISUAL IMPAIRMENT

Kirchner and Peterson (1988a) estimated a chronic unemployment rate of between 65 and 70 percent among working age people with severe visual impairments. Kirchner (1988) later speculated that the reasons for lack of employment among this population were the result of employment discrimination, discouragement in seeking employment, and disincentives to work. The first two reasons result, in part, from the attitudes, stereotypes, and misconceptions about people with visual impairments that are held by employers, family members and friends, and the clients. Regardless of the reason, the effect of not holding an appropriate job and earning a living is significant to the unemployed individual in terms of self-concept and personal satisfaction. Many citations in the literature suggest that "Not working is perhaps the truest definition of what it means to be disabled" (Bowe, 1990, p.2). It is also expensive to society in terms of lost wages, reduced taxes, and increased benefit payments.

How serious is the unemployment of people with visual impairments? In reviewing the U.S. Bureau of the Census's March 1988 Current Population Survey (CPS) for *all* individuals with disabilities, Bowe (1990) found:

- Only 32 percent of working-age adults with disabilities work or actively seek employment (two-thirds of adults with disabilities are not working). Seventy-nine percent of nondisabled adults in the same age range are in the labor force.
- Only 27 percent of women with disabilities are participating in the work force, while 69 percent of nondisabled women are working or seeking employment.

- Twenty-two percent of the blacks with disabilities participate compared with 79 percent of nondisabled blacks.
- Hispanics with disabilities are participating at a 23 percent rate versus a 74 percent participation rate for nondisabled Hispanics.

Significant to this analysis is the fact that labor market participation among individuals with disabilities is decreasing. In 1970, the proportion of individuals with disabilities participating in the labor force was as high as 41 percent. Bowe accounts for this decrease by citing recessionary influences on the U.S. economy in 1974, 1979, and 1982, with individuals with disabilities being the "last hired and first fired." Present economic conditions support continued difficulty in maintaining employment of workers with disabilities. Other factors influencing this decrease in labor force participation of workers with disabilities include the 1974 nationwide introduction of Supplemental Security Income (SSI) and the frequently lower educational levels of those with disabilities that often allow them to qualify for only entry-level, minimum wage employment.

In Bowe's analysis of the 1988 CPS data, he found several other relevant characteristics of individuals with disabilities attempting to participate in the labor force. These include:

1. Adults with disabilities, from ages 16 to 64, were four times more likely than nondisabled individuals of the same age group to have never completed the eighth grade. Twenty-three percent of individuals without disabilities have college degrees, while only 9 percent of individuals with disabilities have this level of educational achievement.
2. Approximately 14.2 percent of both men and women with disabilities in the 1988 labor force were unemployed. This compares with 6.2 percent and 5.2 percent for nondisabled men and women during the same period of time. The unemployment rates for workers with disabilities are double to triple that of the individuals without disabilities.
3. Approximately 28 percent of working-age adults with disabilities have incomes from all sources (including governmental support programs) that place them below the poverty line. The median income of all working-age adults with a work disability was $6,323 in 1987; the mean was $9,364. Among people with severe disabilities, a group where most people with visual disabilities might be found, the figures were $5,246 and $6,618, respectively.
4. Of the 4,974,000 working-age adults with disabilities who had jobs at any time during 1987, the mean earnings for individuals with disabilities were $12,253. That was 35 percent less than the $18,951 mean for workers without disabilities in the same age range. This suggests underemployment and underpayment of workers with disabilities. Possibly the most significant finding of this study was the fact that 10 percent of the 1,362,000 individuals with disabilities in the 16 to 64 age range reported no income at all in 1987.

Similar data have been reported by Louis Harris and Associates (1986a, 1986b, 1994) polls. The 1994 Harris survey, conducted for the National Organization on Disability, found that having a disability: (1) limited mobility, (2) curtailed the person's social life, (3) resulted in less education, and (4) decreased individual income. In 1994, Harris also found that:

- Seventy-five percent of individuals with disabilities have at least a high school education and the percentage of individuals with disabilities who have completed college is similar to the population of individuals who do not have disabilities.
- The educational statistics have not contributed to higher earnings of individuals with disabilities. Twenty-two percent of

adults with disabilities live in households with earnings of $25,000 or less.

- Although 79 percent of working-age adults (i.e., individuals between the ages of 16 and 64) would like to be working, two-thirds are not working.
- Thirty percent of adults with disabilities who are working or who would like to be working have experienced job discrimination. Almost half of the adults with disabilities who are working do not believe their work requires their "full talents and abilities" (p. 7).
- Twenty-five percent of adults with disabilities who are working or who would like to work need special equipment or technology to work in the jobs they prefer, with the most frequently mentioned technology being computer equipment.
- Although a majority of adults with disabilities believe that public attitudes and access to public facilities and transportation have improved, two-thirds reported that their disability limits their access to activities of daily living outside the home and to social activities.
- A majority of individuals with disabilities who are not working and who are not looking for work, base their behavior on fear of losing benefits (e.g., income or healthcare). "Almost half of adults with disabilities get at least some portion of their personal income from benefits and insurance payments" (p. 8).
- Fifty percent of individuals with disabilities who are of working age are not familiar with the Americans with Disabilities Act.

Kirchner and Peterson's analysis (1988a) of the 1976 U.S. Bureau of the Census and 1977 NCHS data on individuals with visual impairments reveals similar trends. They have found that less than one-third of working-age individuals with visual impairments were in the labor force, compared to almost three-fourths of the U.S. population. Only 20 percent of the women with visual impairments were in the labor force compared to 43 percent of visually impaired men. Thus, it appears that women with visual impairments are significantly more disadvantaged than men with visual impairments in securing satisfactory employment. In terms of individuals between the ages of 16 and 21 who are out of school and working, the employment picture is equally bleak. Sixty-two percent of people without impairments are working, compared to only 24.3 percent of individuals with visual impairments and the unemployment rate for persons with congenital vision loss is 80 percent (Kirchner & Peterson, 1988a).

The unemployment statistics for individuals with visual impairments are reflected in their reported rates of poverty. The poverty rate of people with severe visual impairment (23 percent) is twice that of individuals who do not have disabilities (12 percent). The poverty rates for those with visual impairments vary by age; the highest rate (33 percent) is that of people in the 15 to 64 age group and the lowest is for individuals over age 65 (18 percent). Nonetheless, the poverty rate for older individuals is still three times that of those in the same age group who do not have disabilities (6 percent) (Demographics Update, 1995a).

Students with visual impairments represent only about 1 percent of the students with disabilities who are served by special education programs (Kirchner, 1988). They also participate in postsecondary activities at a higher rate than individuals with other disabilities (Fairweather & Shaver, 1991). Head, Maddock, Healey, and Griffing (1993) reported that a majority of students who attend residential schools for individuals with visual impairments graduate and 81 percent are involved in education or training programs or are employed full-time.

Although the national trend of decreased labor-force participation by adults with disabilities may suggest similar employment problems for the individuals with visual impairments, it is important to note that the increased use of computers with voice output and other assistive devices has dramatically changed their employability in terms of opportunity and variety of jobs. Also the long-range consequences of legislative initiatives in recent years, including the Americans with Disabilities Act, should have a positive effect on the labor-force participation of individuals with visual impairments.

SUMMARY

Multiple definitions of blindness and visual impairment are used throughout the world. The most widely accepted definition of legal blindness in the United States is the following: central visual acuity not exceeding 20/200 in the better eye with the best corrective eyeglasses or contact lenses, or visual acuity, if better than 20/200, with a limit to the central field of vision to such a degree that the size of the field of vision is reduced to an angle of no greater than 20 degrees. Over 75 percent of those individuals who are determined to be legally blind, however, have some residual vision. In the field of rehabilitation, the term *blind* is generally used for those individuals with no usable sight, whereas the terms *visual impairment* and *low vision* are used to describe persons who have some usable vision. Because the visual acuity of a person does not reflect how well the individual utilizes that vision, functional definitions are typically applied to determine the services needed by people who are blind or visually impaired. Functional definitions describe what an individual is able to do under specific conditions (e.g., read a newspaper, drive, and so forth). The lack of agreement on standard definitions of blindness or visual impairment and the various purposes of the definitions have made it difficult to estimate the number of individuals who are affected by vision loss. It is presently estimated that nearly 11.5 million people in the United States have some degree of visual impairment, including the inability to read newsprint.

The attitudes and stereotypes that are commonly held about individuals with visual impairments, and the resultant barriers (e.g., to employment, social interactions, and so on) created by inaccurate generalizations are still prevalent in our society. Inaccurate perceptions of visually impaired individuals are not limited to the general public, but are also held by professionals, including rehabilitation professionals and even some individuals with vision loss, which contributes to some of their psychosocial adjustment issues. Other factors include previous coping styles, the severity of the impairment, the type and time of onset, and the ability to use their remaining vision. Vision loss may also enhance fears, which in turn has an effect on a person's self-esteem and self-confidence.

The statistics on the participation of people with disabilities in the labor market is also highly significant. The fact that two-thirds of adults with disabilities are not working and 60 percent of adults with disabilities live in households with earnings of $25,000 or less are disturbing statistics. Equally unsettling is the fact that one study showed that only 60 percent of the individuals with disabilities surveyed were familiar with rehabilitation services and only 13 percent had used rehabilitation services.

These statistics, along with the issues related to the definitions, incidence, attitudes, and psychosocial factors explored in this chapter have a number of implications for rehabilitation professionals. Although the rehabilitation professional may use a legal definition, with information provided by the medical professional, to determine eligibility for various rehabilitation services or programs, that same professional will typically use a functional definition in determining the types of services that will be most beneficial to the individual with a visual impairment. This use of two differing perspectives can create confusion for both the professional and the client, as well as the general public. Rehabilitation professionals have a major role to play in educating the public about visual impairments in dispelling myths, promoting employment opportunities, and informing potential recipients of rehabilitation services of the availability of such services. Rehabilitation counselors provide an important service—counseling—to individuals to help them adjust to a loss of vision, to parents to help them understand the needs and services that are available to children with visual impairments, and to some individuals to help them know how to deal with the genetic implications of vision loss. In addition, their concrete efforts in the direction of helping individuals learn adaptive techniques, find and retain employment, and secure services can immeasurably enhance the quality of life of individuals with visual impairments.

LEARNING ACTIVITIES

1. Interview an individual with a visual impairment to learn more about the individual and to answer the following questions:

    a. Is the impairment or loss congenital or adventitious?

    b. Has the individual used services from a rehabilitation agency? If so, what services were provided and how does this person evaluate the quality of services offered?

    c. What attitudinal or employment barriers has the individual experienced?

    d. What recommendations does the person have for rehabilitation professionals who work with individuals with visual impairments?

2. Use a blindfold for four hours while doing your daily activities. Based on your experience, list the pros and cons of such an experience. Also identify the skills that you would need to learn to function more effectively with diminished vision.

3. Interview a rehabilitation counselor who works with people with visual impairments. Based on your interview, answer the following questions:

    a. What does the counselor believe to be the most important skills in working with individuals with visual impairments?

    b. What education or training has the counselor received relating to visual impairments?

    c. Does the counselor perceive differences in working with individuals with congenital versus adventitious visual impairments? If so, what are these differences?

4. Watch a video on blindness or visual impairments (e.g., *What Do You Do When You See a Blind Person?* available from the American Foundation for the Blind [see Resources]). What myths or stereotypes are presented in the video? What commonly held myths or stereotypes are refuted in the video?

CHAPTER 2

The Visual System: Anatomy, Physiology, and Visual Impairment

Marjorie E. Ward with Samuel B. Johnson

Our five senses enable us to receive information from our surroundings. But there is much more to learning about the people who are with us and what surrounds us than passively receiving stimuli from our auditory, visual, tactile, olfactory, and gustatory receptors. The receptors and their neural pathways transmit data to the various brain centers for information processing, storage, and retrieval. This transmission process involves electromagnetic, hydraulic, chemical, and electrical energy, which relies heavily upon the precise and complex interactions of the muscular, metabolic, and vascular systems. These systems are, of course, part of a larger intricate organism, the human being, and a human being is much more than the sum of his or her parts. Although we will focus our attention on one system in this discussion of the process of seeing, we need to keep in mind the human being—the person—of which that system is a part.

For most people, the sense of sight serves as the primary mediator of information picked up by the other senses and helps us organize and negotiate our environment to bring order and understanding out of the maze of objects, aromas, sounds, flavors, tactile impressions, and people we encounter. But for a significant number of children and adults who are visually impaired, the sense of sight is limited or not available for the tasks of work and daily living. Therefore, it is recommended that rehabilitation counselors working with individuals who are blind or visually impaired understand the visual system, its disorders, and how to interpret reports from eyecare specialists. This information should enhance the skills of rehabilitation counselors in their efforts to assist their clients to meet the challenges of home, travel, employment, and leisure activities.

The objectives of this chapter are to (1) present information about the anatomy of the eye and how it functions, (2) give an overview of the visual system and what can happen if any of the components of the system malfunction, and (3) illustrate how clinical information from eye specialists can be used by rehabilitation personnel and related professionals.

ANATOMY AND PHYSIOLOGY

Knowledge of the basic anatomy of the visual system introduces us to just how complex and intricately designed, yet powerful and efficient this

The author gratefully acknowledges the review of this chapter by Gary L. Rogers, M.D. and Rae Fellows, M.A. from Columbus Children's Hospital, and Larry Lytle, M.D., in private practice in Columbus, Ohio.

system can be when all components function at peak capacity. The component most obvious in the visual system is the eyeball with its protective padding and housing. The following discussion of the eye and how it functions will begin with consideration of the orbit where the eyeball is situated.

Orbit and Eyelids

The bony orbit is the pear-shaped cavity in the skull that houses the eyeball, the optic nerve (second cranial nerve, or CN II) that exits from the posterior portion of the eyeball, and the six muscles that attach to the eyeball. These muscles are anchored to the walls of the orbit and are innervated by CN III (oculomotor), CN IV (trochlear) and CN VI (abducens). The muscles of both eyes are yoked in function and enable the two eyes to move together to see visual targets at both near and distant points. Figure 2.1 illustrates how the muscles attach to the eyeball.

In addition to the eyeball and muscles, the orbital cavity also contains blood vessels, nerves, the lacrimal gland, and the fat and connective tissue that surrounds the eyeball to provide protection and cushioning. The lacrimal gland, located in the upper outer quadrant of the orbit, secretes tears that flow down over the front surface of the globe into the cul-de-sac below the margin of the lower eyelid and finally drain out through the nasolacrimal system that empties into the nose and nasopharynx.

For additional protection against bumps, blows, dirt, perspiration, and even bright lights, the eyelids close off the anterior opening of the orbit where the eyeball is exposed. In the eyelids are specialized glands that secrete oils and other elements that help lubricate the cornea (the front portion of the eyeball) and prevent the evaporation of tears (Vaughan, Asbury, & Riordan-Eva, 1995). Blinking the lids aids the flow of the tears across the front parts of the eye, the sclera and cornea, and the tissue that lines the lids, the conjunctiva.

The conjunctiva, in addition to lining the posterior surface of each eyelid, covers the white part of the eyeball, the sclera, to the point where

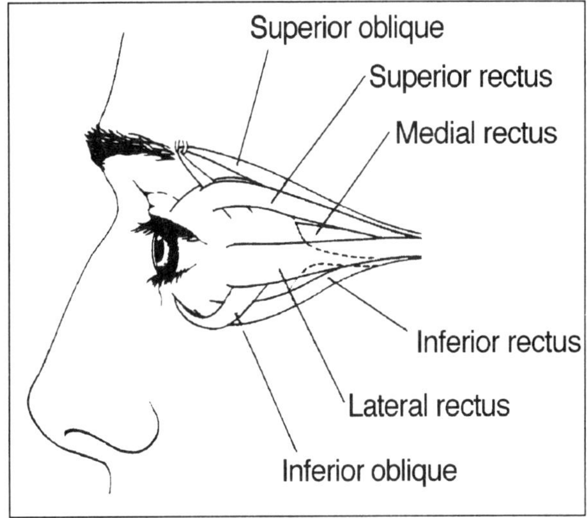

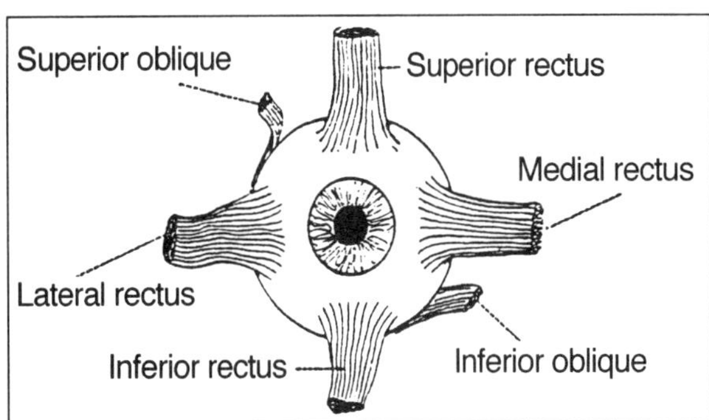

Figure 2.1. The six muscles of the eye that control eye movement. *(Top)* A side view of the left eye.

Source: Reprinted, by permission of the publisher, from K. W. Heller et al., *Understanding Physical, Sensory, and Health Impairments* (Pacific Grove, CA: Brooks/Cole, 1996), p. 218.

***(Bottom)* A frontal view of the right eye.**

Source: Reprinted, by permission of the publisher, from H. M. Katzin & G. Wilson, *Rehabilitation of a Child's Eyes* (St. Louis, MO: Mosby, 1961), p. 96.

the sclera and cornea meet. When this thin, transparent mucous membrane becomes irritated or inflamed, the eye appears pink or red; this condition called conjunctivitis is the most common eye disease worldwide (Vaughan et al., 1995).

Eyeball

The eyeball measures approximately one inch on the horizontal axis in the normal adult eye. It has three structural layers, which are (1) the protec-

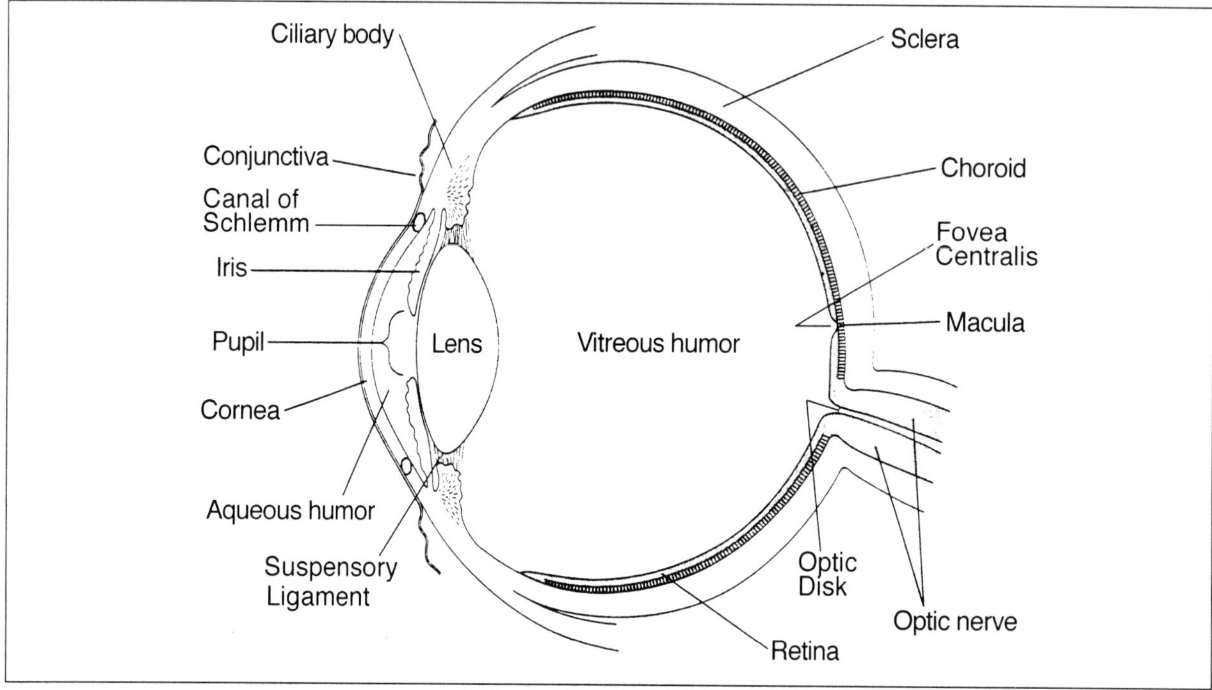

Figure 2.2. A schematic section of the external and internal structures of the human eye.
Source: Adapted, by permission of the publisher, from Heller et al., *Understanding Physical, Sensory, and Health Impairments* (Pacific Grove, CA: Brooks/Cole, 1996), p. 219.

tive outer layer, (2) the vascular middle layer, and (3) the nerve or retinal inner layer where light rays entering the eye should come to a point of focus. Light causes chemical changes in the cells of each retina that result in the transmission of information in the form of electrical impulses along the optic nerve to the occipital lobes at the back of the brain. There, these impulses from each retina are given meaning in the process of interpretation, storage, retrieval, and use. (See Figure 2.2.)

The outer protective layer is made up of the fibrous, white sclera and the transparent, avascular (i.e., without blood vessels) cornea through which light first enters the eyeball. The sclera continues around the entire eye and merges with the dural sheath that covers the optic nerve at the posterior of the eyeball where the optic nerve exits. The cornea has five distinct layers, although it is only about .65 mm at the periphery where the sclera and cornea meet and thins to about .54 mm at the center. To remain transparent so that light can enter and pass through to the cells of the retina, these five layers of the cornea must maintain a balanced state of relative dehydration (deturgescence). Corneal abrasions or infections can allow germs to enter these layers, upsetting this balance and leading to risks for serious infection (keratitis) and scarring.

The choroid, the ciliary body, and the iris make up the middle layer of the eyeball. This layer is also called the uveal tract. The choroid lies between the sclera and the inner retinal layer and provides the blood supply for the retina.

The ciliary body consists of the ciliary muscle and the ciliary process. The ciliary muscle portion helps to adjust the thickness of the transparent lens by regulating the tension of the suspensory ligaments, which are the fibers that connect to the lens capsule and to the ciliary muscle to hold the lens in place. The lens sits just behind the pupil, the opening created as the iris muscles contract or relax. Changes in the tension of these suspensory fibers (also called the zonule of Zinn), alter the thickness of the lens, which affects the ability of the lens to bend light rays. The ciliary process portion of the ciliary body produces the aqueous humor, a watery fluid that flows from the posterior chamber through the pupil into the anterior chamber where it leaves through the trabecular meshwork and the Canal of Schlemm.

Although the lens is technically not a part of the uveal tract, the function of the lens, as mentioned in the foregoing, is controlled largely by action of the ciliary muscle on the suspensory ligaments that hold the lens in place behind the pupil. The function of the lens is to refract the light rays so they will come to a clear focus on the retina. The cornea refracts light rays as they first enter the eye, but the cornea cannot alter its curvature, as the lens can, to do the fine-tuning necessary for the light rays to land precisely on the retina and produce sharp, clear images whether using near or distant vision. The natural aging process results in a gradual loss of the elasticity in the lens, a condition called presbyopia, which leads to the decrease in accommodative power. At approximately age 45, most individuals begin to notice that seeing details at close range, such as telephone numbers, becomes difficult. Reading glasses or bifocal lenses added to prescription lenses usually compensate for these changes related to aging.

Another change not uncommon with aging is a decrease in the transparency of one or both lenses, leading to cataracts. A cataract is not a growth, but rather is a clouding or opacity of all or part of the natural lens that eventually may become dense enough to prevent light rays from passing through to the retina of the eye. At present there is no "cure" for a cataract lens that returns it to a transparent state. The opaque lens can, however, be removed surgically by various techniques described later in this chapter. Without the natural lens, the optical system of the eye is underpowered because it has no way to fine-tune light rays to focus them on the retina. To compensate, an individual may wear strong eyeglasses or contact lenses. The eyeglass lens may produce excess magnification in relation to the unoperated eye, or may limit peripheral vision and depth perception (Padial, 1986). Today, the most frequent management after cataract removal in selected adults is the use of an intraocular lens implant (IOL). Usually, the IOL is inserted in the posterior chamber approximately where the natural lens had been. The IOL has a precalculated refractive power to converge light rays that can now pass through to the retina; however, it has no accommodative capacity as the natural lens had to adjust its curvature. As a result, eyeglasses are frequently necessary for close work and are also worn with the contacts.

The retina, the inner nerve layer of the eyeball, lies next to the choroid and is composed of 9 distinct cell layers. The thinnest portion of the retina, called the macula, lies about 3.5 mm lateral to the optic disk (blind spot) and is the area of clearest vision (Vaughan et al., 1995). In the center of the macula is the fovea centralis, about the size of the head of a pin. Cone cells that are sensitive to bright lights and give the clearest, sharpest sense of color and resolution are packed into the fovea and macula. The cones give way to the rod cells that increase in number and dominate the peripheries of the retina. Rods are activated by even low levels of light and enable us to see at dusk and after dark.

Some premature infants who have low birth weight must receive oxygen over a period of time to sustain life. The retinas in the eyes of these babies may not develop normally, a situation that is related primarily to low birth weight and length of gestation. The retinas are not developed sufficiently to handle even the carefully monitored levels of oxygen necessary to sustain life; their response is abnormal vascularization. These changes that occur in the retinas and the capillaries that nourish them are termed retinopathy of prematurity (ROP).

As with the lens, the macula and the retina are also vulnerable to the effects of aging. Such degenerative diseases as macular degeneration, which compromises cone cells, can decrease or even destroy central vision and color vision. Other conditions, for example, retinitis pigmentosa (RP), can disrupt the normal function of the rod cells and result in decreased night vision or loss of all peripheral vision. Retinal function is also impaired if the blood supply to the retina is reduced or cut off. Diabetes of long standing increases the risk of retinal problems associated with retinal hemorrhages and neovascularization. Judicious laser therapy in the early stages of this disease may prolong useful vision 10 to 15 years. Certainly any retinal detachment can lead to loss of retinal function.

The rods and cones of the retina, after being activated by light, send their messages to other layers of the retina where ganglion cell axons finally pass the information on in the form of electrical impulses to the some million fibers that make up the optic nerve (CN II). The fibers of the optic nerve extend through the scleral foramen and out the back of the globe, leaving the orbit of the eyeball through the optic canal, and continue into the middle cranial cavity. There they come together as the optic chiasm in which certain fibers from each optic nerve decussate (cross over) to the opposite side (Vaughan et al., 1995), as illustrated in Figure 2.3. Some information from each eye is transmitted to each side of the occipital lobe of the brain. Injury to a portion or portions of the optic pathways can, in some cases, be pinpointed by checking an individual's field of vision to locate blind spots or field restrictions. For example, if an injury occurred posterior to the optic chiasm, portions of the visual field of each eye could be affected. Conversely, damage to one of the optic nerves anterior to the optic chiasm would affect only one eye.

In addition to the structures of the eye, there are three chambers through which light rays must pass as they travel to the retina. Behind the cornea and anterior to the surface of the iris lies the anterior chamber. Behind the iris and anterior to the lens and its supporting fibers lies the posterior chamber. The aqueous humor, the watery fluid secreted by the ciliary process, flows from the posterior chamber through the pupil into the anterior chamber and, in a healthy eye, drains out through the trabecular meshwork and Canal of Schlemm in the peripheral anterior chamber. A leading cause of blindness among the adult population over 40, especially among African-Americans and individuals with diabetes, is glaucoma (Prevent Blindness America, 1994), a condition in which drainage of the aqueous humor is blocked either partially or completely. Hence, intraocular pressure rises and, without treatment, can lead to insidious or immediate blindness.

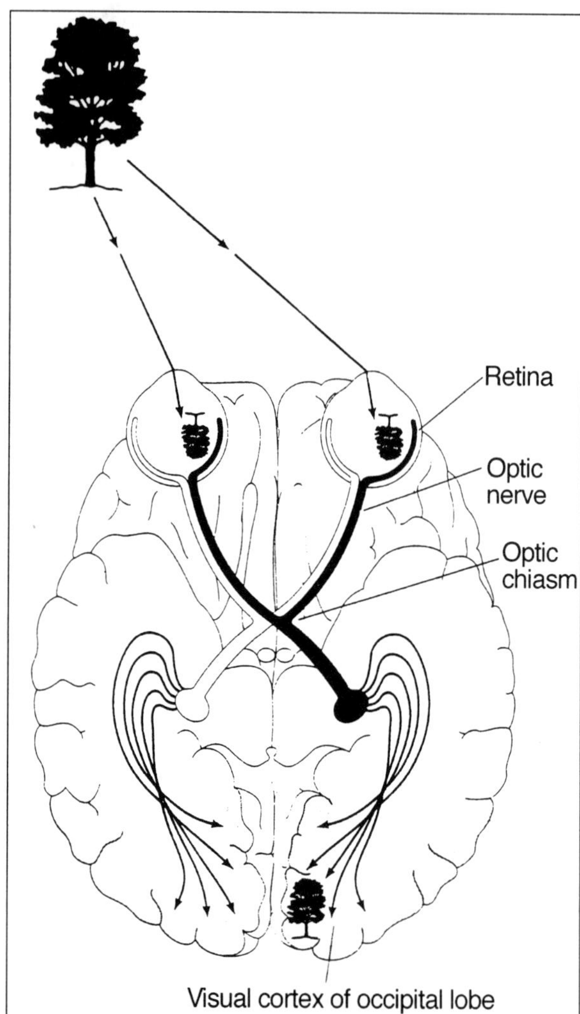

Figure 2.3. The optic pathways as seen from above the brain.

Source: Adapted, by permission of the publisher, from Heller et al., *Understanding Physical, Sensory, and Health Impairments* (Pacific Grove, CA: Brooks/Cole, 1996), p. 221.

Behind the lens lies the third chamber of the eye, the large vitreous cavity, that is filled with a transparent physiological gel that is 99 percent water. This vitreous gel and its surrounding cavity accounts for 75 percent of the weight and about 66 percent of the volume of the globe. Any injury or insult that allows the vitreous gel to escape can result in the collapse of the eyeball. If the vitreous is stained by blood, for example, because of the hemorrhages that can occur as a result of diabetic retinopathy, both color vision and clarity of vision can be affected. Blood-generated impairments can lead to cicatricial or scar bands and should be carefully evaluated for surgical excision by an ophthalmologist.

Structural Defects Affecting Function

Light rays must pass through the cornea, the anterior chamber, the pupil, the lens, and the vitreous before coming to a point of focus on the retina. Many people, however, have refractive errors, which means that light rays do not come to a point of focus on the retina. In myopia (nearsightedness; that is, only objects at near range are focused properly on the retina), light rays converge at a point slightly in front of the retina, usually because the eyeball is longer than normal on the horizontal axis. In hyperopia (farsightedness; that is, only objects at far range are focused properly on the retina), the rays converge at a hypothetical point behind the retina, and in astigmatism they meet at different points in relation to the retina, generally because the surface of the cornea is oblong rather than spherical. These refractive errors lead to blurred vision. (See Figure 2.4.)

To correct many refractive errors, eye specialists prescribe eyeglasses, contact lenses, or both. In some cases, such surgical procedures as radial keratotomy or eximer laser sculpturing are options to correct myopia or astigmatism, but not all people with these conditions are candidates for these procedures and some of the newer techniques are still undergoing trials and refinement.

In eyeglasses and prescriptive lenses, concave spherical (divergent or minus) lenses are used to compensate for myopia and convex spherical (convergent or plus) lenses are used to compensate for hyperopia. Cylindrical lenses are prescribed to correct astigmatism, as they can be shaped with different refractive powers along specific meridians to compensate for the convergent or divergent power a specific eye lacks to bring light rays to focus on the retina.

The term *binocular vision* refers to the ability of the two eyes to focus on one object while the brain fuses these slightly differing images from each eye into one single image. In cases of muscle imbalance, the paired muscles of the eyes do not work in a coordinated fashion to produce conjugate eye movements in the six cardinal directions of gaze. If these muscles are not innervated equally (Hering's Law), if muscle strength is unequal, or if there is any muscle paralysis, then the eyes may not appear straight and may not achieve good, clear, binocular vision. The term strabismus refers to the condition in which an eye deviates from parallel with its yoke muscle. An eye may turn toward the nose (eso-), toward the temple (exo-), or up (hyper-) or down (hypo-) in relation to the horizontal axis. This turn may be constant (-tropia) or an occasional tendency (-phoria). For example, a person whose left eye is always turned in has a left esotropia; whereas a person whose left eye turned in only after long hours of close work would have a left esophoria. Strabismus is a broad term used to refer to any of these instances of deviation from parallel.

Strabismus can also cause diplopia (or double vision) because the images in both eyes do not focus on corresponding places on each retina. Double vision may be the result of strabismus, or an injury, or it may be caused by an object that is exerting pressure (e.g., a tumor), which moves the eyeball out of alignment.

Treatment of strabismus can take a variety of courses, which include (1) correction of any refractive errors, (2) medical treatment for any pathologic condition, (3) patching or occlusion of the good eye for prescribed periods of time each day to stimulate use of the weaker eye and equalize the visual acuities, (4) orthoptic exercises in selected cases, (5) medication to force use of the weaker eye, and (6) surgery. The goals of any treatment are good (normal) acuity in each eye, cosmetically straight eyes, and binocular vision (fusion). In cases of long-standing strabismus however, an individual may not achieve binocular vision (Vaughan et al., 1995).

Refractive errors and muscle imbalance in many individuals can be treated or managed to the degree that few children or adults experience serious visual impairment from strabismus. In situations in which one eye is so affected that functional vision is decreased, even after treat-

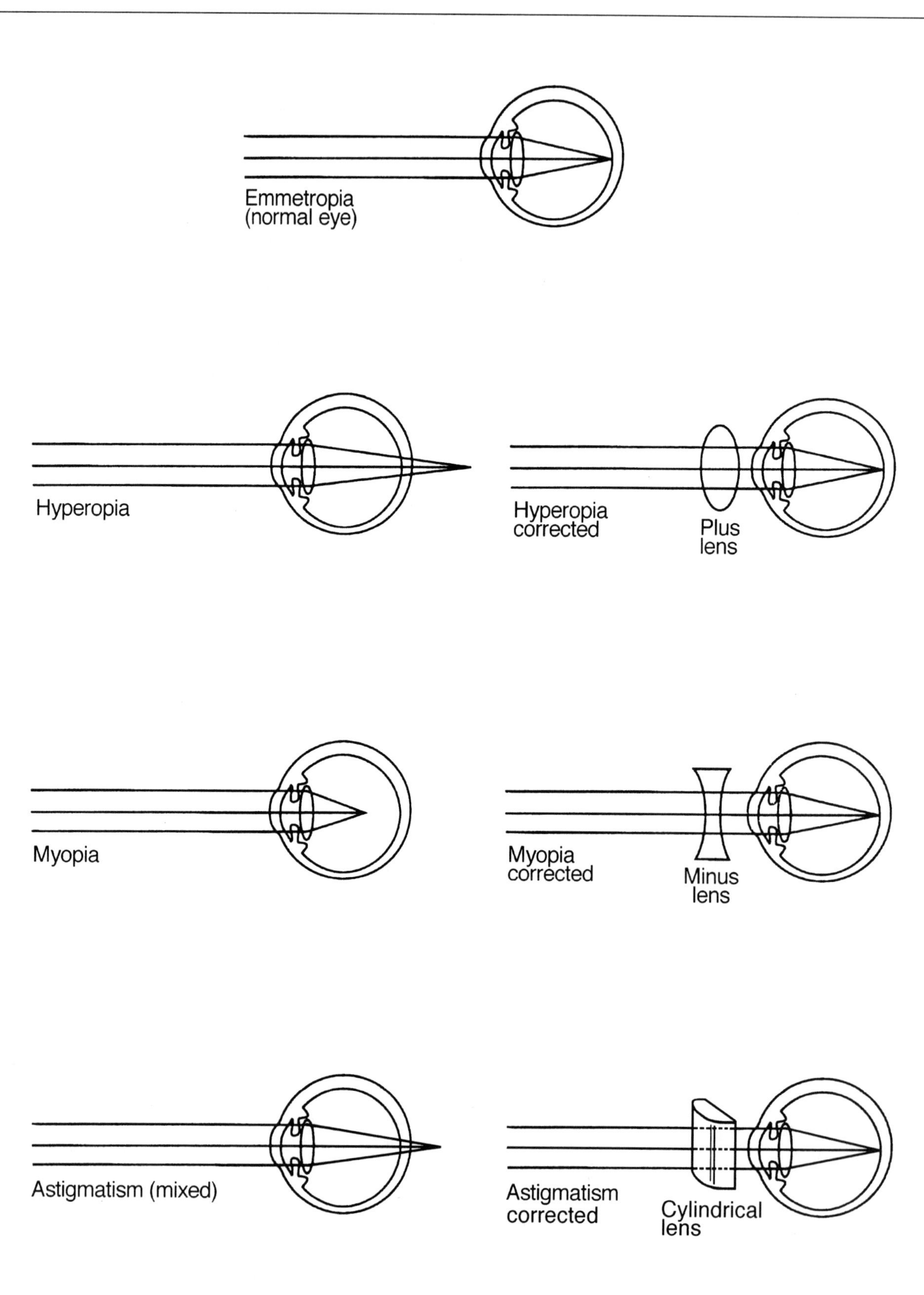

Figure 2.4. Refractive errors and the lenses used for correction.

ment, the other eye often retains good visual function.

THE EYE AND THE AGING PROCESS

Just as other parts of the human body experience changes related to the aging process, so does the eye (Weinstock, 1987). At birth, the eyeballs appear large because the actual size of the newborn's eyes and head as compared to the less-developed limbs and torso is quite large. The eyeball reaches adult size in 7 to 8 years, but the cornea reaches its full size usually by the end of the second year. It typically becomes flatter over the years, especially on the vertical axis. The crystalline lens, although totally without blood vessels, continues to grow as a tree trunk by adding fiber layers at the periphery; however, its growth is slower in later years. The lens material in youth is softer, which facilitates accommodation, but in later years typically becomes harder, leading to presbyopia or a loss of the ability to focus at close range. As the years go by, there may be deposits or particles in the vitreous that appear as thin strings or floaters that flutter through the visual field. If these occur suddenly or in large numbers, however, they may be indicative of retinal detachment or hemorrhage into the vitreous. They may be central or in the periphery and are often intermittent. Nevertheless, in most cases floaters are clinically insignificant, albeit bothersome (Chalkley, 1982; Vaughan et al., 1995).

Changes associated with aging also occur in the arterioles of the eye, much as they cause arteriolosclerosis of other parts of the body. With hypertension, changes in the retinal arterioles may suggest either recent, reversible pathology or fixed, longstanding alterations. Other typical age-related changes are reduction in contrast sensitivity, decreased pupil size, which necessitates more illumination for tasks, and reduced near visual acuity as a result of the loss of the ability to accommodate. These changes can be exacerbated in elderly individuals who have other physical problems or who are on medication that may have side effects on vision (Morse, Silberman, & Trief, 1987). The signs of potential eye problems in adults and elderly persons are summarized in Sidebar 2.1 to alert professionals to signs that should be noted and discussed further with clients.

ETIOLOGY OF BLINDNESS AND VISUAL IMPAIRMENT

Conditions that can lead to blindness or visual impairment may originate during the prenatal period as a result of genetic propensity, genetic transmission, maternal injury or disease, or sometimes for unknown reasons. In some individuals, a problem may occur during the birth process, during the developmental years, or as the person matures and enters the late adult years. Conditions that manifest themselves at birth are called congenital; those that are acquired later or are caused by accidents are called adventitious. Some inherited conditions may not be manifest until months or even years after birth. The point to remember is that not all hereditary conditions are considered congenital and not all congenital conditions are considered hereditary. For example, difficulties with night vision and other symptoms of retinitis pigmentosa (RP), which is inherited, may not appear until the adolescent years or later.

Major Causes of Blindness and Visual Impairment

In the United States, the leading causes of blindness are glaucoma, cataracts, diabetic retinopathy, and macular degeneration (Newell, 1996). In the over-40 age group the leading causes are the same, but macular degeneration moves to the top of the list (Prevent Blindness America, 1994). Knowing about the major causes of blindness helps prepare the rehabilitation counselor to respond to questions from clients and their families

SIDEBAR 2.1

Signs of Eye Trouble

APPEARANCE
- Swollen eyelids
- Protrusion of the eye
- Crusty rims or a discharge
- Crossing of one eye
- Red eyes
- Twitching eyes
- Difference in the size of the eyes

BEHAVIOR
- Eyes do not move smoothly in all directions of gaze
- Covering one eye, tilting the head, or shutting one eye
- Sense of limited field of vision or loss of side vision
- Rubbing the eyes excessively
- Fluctuating blurriness in central vision
- Shielding the eyes from light

COMPLAINTS
- Eyes itch, burn, or feel scratchy
- Dry eyes
- Light sensitivity
- Loss, distortion, or dimness of vision overall
- Pain in or around the eye
- Double vision
- Flashing lights, halos around lights, floaters, spots in visual field
- Severe headaches
- Loss of ability to tell shades and hues of colors

and to anticipate changes in vision status over time, which could influence the short- as well as the long-term planning process. The following discussion focuses on these conditions and several others that occur frequently among individuals who have been referred to social service agencies serving individuals with visual impairments.

Macular Degeneration

Age-related macular degeneration (AMD) is the overall leading cause of legal blindness in the United States and in people over the age of 60 (Newell, 1996). In AMD, cells of the macular area break down. The result is a decrease in central vision and the ability to see fine detail and color; side or peripheral vision is not affected. In approximately 80 percent of AMD cases, nonexudative, or "dry," AMD occurs, which manifests as yellowish spots of waste materials (called drusen) and sometimes clumps of pigment scattered throughout and around the macular area. In exudative, or "wet," AMD, blood or serous fluid leaks through the thin tissue separating the choroid and macular area of the retina. New and very fragile blood vessels may grow and rupture (American Academy of Ophthalmology, 1984; Vaughan et al., 1995). (See Figure 2.5.)

There is no treatment for "dry" AMD. However, the degenerative progress is typically slow and may even stop. For "wet" AMD, laser photocoagulation to seal off leaking blood vessels may be helpful in stopping the progression of the disease; however, the surgery must be done very early in the development of the disease—sometimes even a day can make a difference.

Ophthalmologists can make a diagnosis of AMD by examination with an ophthalmoscope to view the back of the eye and the macular area. In addition to this device, an Amsler grid test for visual fields and a color vision test can reveal areas of visual impairment and problems with color discrimination that suggest poor macular function. Fundus fluorescein angiography (FFA), discussed later in the section on diagnostic procedures, can show where abnormal vessels are growing and where leaks have occurred.

Although macular degeneration usually

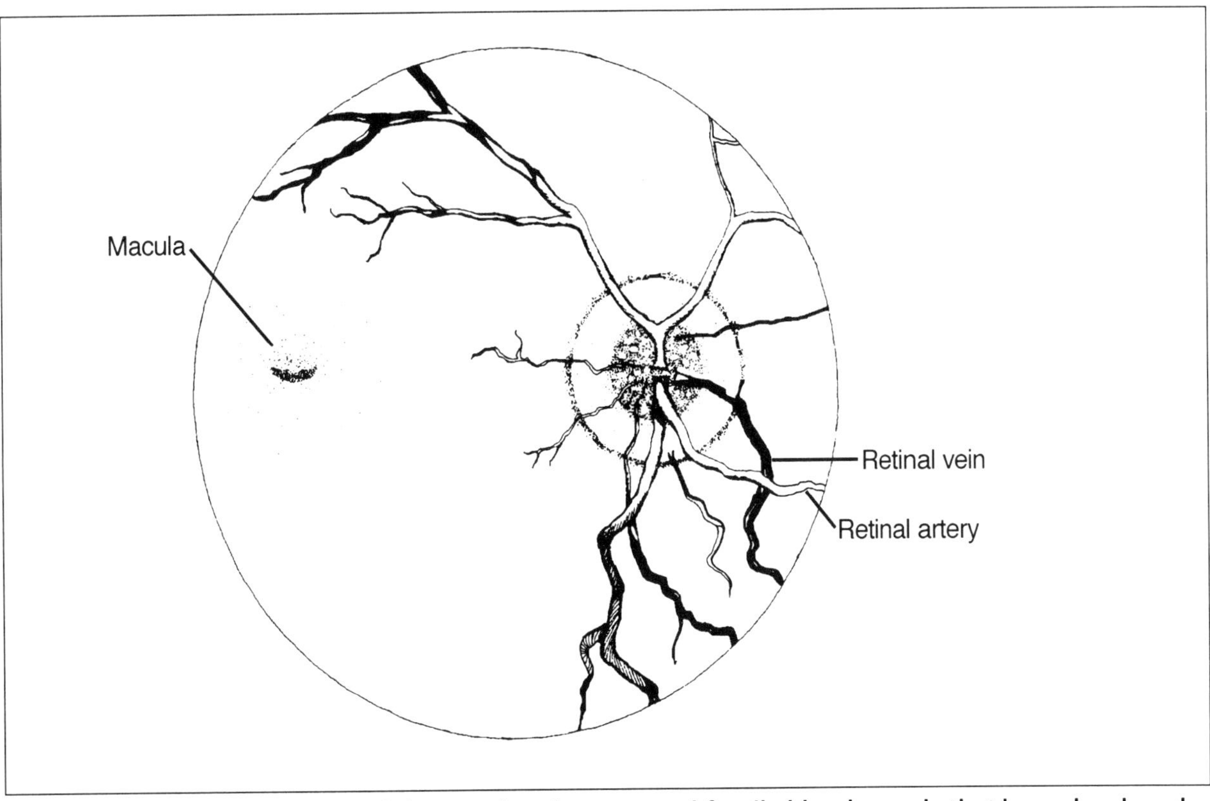

Figure 2.5. A view of the back of the eye showing new and fragile blood vessels that have developed in macular degeneration.

occurs in the older population, non-age-related macular degeneration can occur in children and young adults or can appear secondary to other eye conditions. It can also develop as a complication after surgery.

Glaucoma

Glaucoma is not only the leading cause of blindness in the United States, but the rate of glaucoma in African Americans is four to eight times that of Caucasians (Prevent Blindness America, 1994). With glaucoma, pressure inside the eyeball increases beyond the tolerable level because the aqueous humor does not drain properly out of the anterior chamber. This drainage can be impeded by a number of problems. In chronic, primary, open-angle glaucoma (POAG)—the most common type of glaucoma—the aqueous humor does not filter through the trabecular meshwork and out of the Canal of Schlemm as a result of some degenerative changes in the meshwork. Typically, the course of POAG is slowly progressive, insidious, bilateral, and asymptomatic until loss of visual field is noticed, either by the individual or upon testing of visual fields. In addition to elevated intraocular pressure (IOP), there can be optic nerve damage and visual field defects if the pressure is not reduced. The optic nerve damage may be the result of tension or stress and strain, not just as a direct result from hydrostatic pressure against nerve cells (Vaughan et al., 1995).

In primary, acute, closed-angle glaucoma, the flow of aqueous humor is obstructed by the narrowing or blockage of the angle where the iris and cornea meet. IOP rises, and the individual typically experiences sudden, blurred vision, feels excruciating pain in the eye, and sees halos around lights (Kweskin, 1985; Vaughan et al.,

1995). Some individuals, however, have chronic, angle-closure glaucoma that manifests itself as a gradual blockage of the angle instead of a sudden and painful block; others may have a mixed mechanism of impaired drainage channels and angle closure.

In addition to primary, open-angle and closed-angle glaucoma, elevated IOP may also develop secondary to an injury, hemorrhage, inflammation, neovascularization, the growth of fragile, new blood vessels, or the use of certain drugs. There is also a low-tension glaucoma in which the IOP is within the normal clinical range but examination reveals optic nerve damage and visual field loss typical of glaucoma. Also, some babies are born with glaucoma apparently because of defective development of the angles of the anterior chamber; others develop glaucoma in the early months of life.

At present, there is no specific prevention for any form of glaucoma, but there are several options for treatment to stabilize the IOP within a tolerable range. The goal of treatment is reduction of IOP either with drugs to increase drainage of aqueous humor or to inhibit production of aqueous humor, or with surgery to open up the trabecular meshwork or to create an additional escape route for the aqueous humor (Eye Research Institute of Retina Foundation, 1988a). If left untreated, all types of glaucoma will lead to loss of vision. Compliance with drug therapy is absolutely critical to control IOP and to prevent blindness.

Cataracts

A cataract is any opacity or clouding of part or all of the lens of the eye. In turn, this opacity or cloudiness blocks the passage of light rays through the pupil to the retina. Age-related cataracts (sometimes still called senile cataract) are very frequent in advanced age. The development of lens opacity is generally slow and many years may pass before removal of the lens is necessary. Congenital cataracts, however, can occur in infants and may require surgery within the first few months of life. Eyeglasses or contact lenses are then prescribed to encourage normal visual development. Some individuals develop a cataract secondary to other eye disease, such as chronic uveitis (inflammation of all or part of the uveal tract), glaucoma, RP, or as a result of having taken certain medications. A fourth type is traumatic cataract, which occurs as a result of injury such as a hard blow or a puncture cut of the lens. Cataracts may also be caused by overexposure to intense heat or radioactive materials.

There is no known way at present to clear the lens or stop the progression from transparency to opacity. The only existing treatment for a cataract is removal of the lens, which can be accomplished with a variety of surgical techniques. The most frequently used method is to extract all of the lens except the posterior capsule or back membrane by means of phacoemulsification. Using this method, the surgeon maneuvers an ultrasonic probe that breaks down and removes lens tissue by means of a combination of ultrasonic vibration, an irrigation system, and suction. In some patients, an IOL can then be implanted in the position where the original lens was located to compensate for the removal of the natural lens.

Although research and clinical trials are underway with bifocal and multifocal lens implants, most IOLs provide correction for only one focal distance. IOLs cannot change refractive power to accommodate for changes in distance from objects the way a young natural lens can. Therefore, an individual who has an IOL will usually need eyeglasses as well. A person who is not a candidate for an IOL will compensate for the loss of his or her natural lens as a result of cataract surgery by wearing eyeglasses, contact lenses, or a combination of both (Vaughan et al., 1995). Visual rehabilitation after cataract surgery has become much simpler and more quickly achieved by virtue of the IOL.

Diabetic Retinopathy

Diabetes is a systemic metabolic disorder in which the islets of Langerhans within the pancreas either do not produce enough insulin for the body to use to metabolize starches and sugars

Loss of peripheral vision, such as the simulation shown here, and eventual blindness, can frequently result if glaucoma is left untreated.

into glucose needed for energy (insulin-dependent, type I) or the body does not properly use the insulin produced (non-insulin-dependent, type II). Insulin-dependent diabetes, type I, usually develops before the age of 30 and requires insulin therapy and a carefully controlled diet for a lifetime. Non-insulin-dependent diabetes or type II is the more common form. type II typically appears after the age of 40, and often can be controlled with diet, weight loss, and exercise. In some cases, oral medication or insulin may also be necessary. Both forms of diabetes can have serious effects on the blood vessels of the nerves, kidneys, and eyes (U.S. Department of Health and Human Services, 1982).

Diabetic retinopathy is a disease of retinal blood vessels. Although it usually occurs in people who have had diabetes for 15 to 20 years, it can also occur shortly after onset and is sometimes one of the first signs of diabetes. Even individuals whose diabetes has been well-controlled can develop diabetic retinopathy (Vaughan et al., 1995); however, effective control generally postpones the advent of this complication.

Retinal changes associated with diabetes include blood vessels that leak fluid, blood, or fatty substances and reduced perfusion or flow of blood through retinal vessels that have become clogged. The growth of fragile new blood vessels (neovascularization) may lead to breaks and may hemorrhage into the retina or vitreous (National Society to Prevent Blindness, 1980). (See Figure 2.6 for an illustration of these changes.) The advent of both laser photocoagulation in the 1960s and the surgical removal of bloody vitreous in the 1970s has improved the prognosis for maintaining useful vision by an additional 10 to 15 years.

Diabetic retinopathy can be classified into two major types, which are background diabetic retinopathy with aneurysms and leaking, and proliferative diabetic retinopathy with neovascularization. Background diabetic retinopathy is the milder of the two, but with poor control can progress to the proliferative diabetic retinopathy

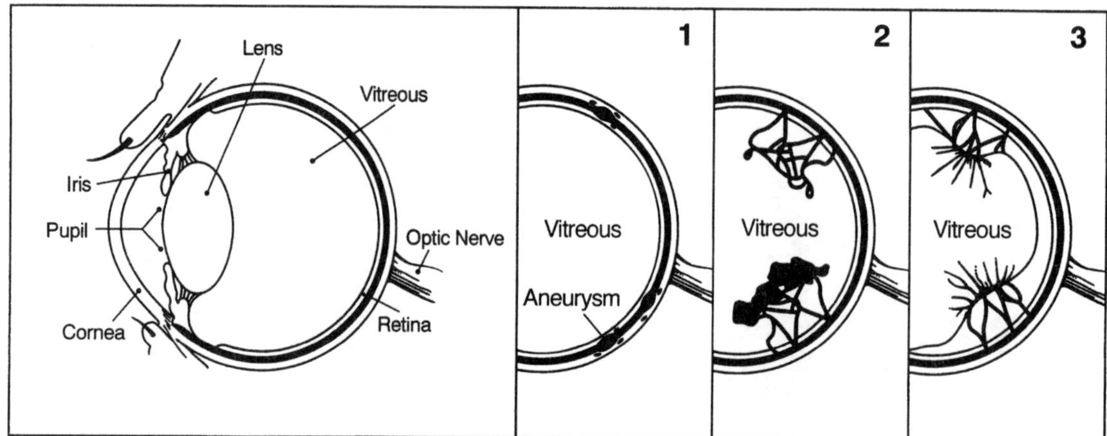

Figure 2.6. In diabetic retinopathy, retinal blood vessels may expand (1), and burst and leak fluid (2), and the resulting scar tissue mass contract the vitreous and pull the retina, tearing or detaching it from the choroid (3).

Source: Adapted graphic courtesy of Prevent Blindness America®.

with hemorrhages, formation of scar tissue, retraction of the vitreous away from the retina, and retinal tears or detachments from the choroid layer. Fundus fluorescein angiography (FFA) can demonstrate the status of the retinal vessels and indicate where deposits, hemorrhages, and tears or detachments have occurred. Sterile fluorescein dye is injected into the bloodstream for this examination. As it circulates through the blood vessels in the eye, photos are taken to reveal the perfusion of blood through the retinal arterioles and veins. The fluorescence of the dye gives detailed pictures that are very helpful in planning treatment (Vaughan et al., 1995). The closer proximity to the macular area that problems develop, however, the greater the threat to useful central vision.

Treatment of diabetic retinopathy centers on the control of blood sugar levels, and the frequent monitoring of these levels. In some cases of early proliferative retinopathy, photocoagulation with an argon laser seals off leaking vessels and destroys the tiny, new, abnormal vessels and thus slows progression (Vaughan et al., 1995). A surgical procedure called vitrectomy, in which some or all of the vitreous gel is removed to eliminate blood as a result of hemorrhage along with any extraneous fibrous tissue, can improve useful vision for some patients.

It is highly recommended that rehabilitation professionals understand the importance of careful monitoring and follow-up for all clients with diabetes, even if retinopathy is not presently apparent. Diabetes is more common in the over-40 age groups, when other age-related eye problems also begin to increase. The presence of diabetes, however, increases the need for regular eye exams every 6 to 12 months to detect signs of changes in visual function.

Optic Atrophy

The optic nerve is part of the central nervous system. Damage to the optic nerve can result from occlusion of the central retinal artery, degeneration of the retina, direct injury to the optic nerve, or pressure against the nerve from a tumor or aneurysm. In the latter case, if the pressure can be relieved, vision may improve; in other cases, often little can be done. Loss of vision may occur slowly and may be the only symptom of the problem (Vaughan et al., 1995).

Retinitis Pigmentosa (RP)

A hereditary disease that can be transmitted as autosomal recessive, autosomal dominant, or X-linked, with many genetic variations, RP typically manifests itself in the early teenage years.

The first sign of RP is usually poor night vision. Rod cells of the peripheral retina slowly degenerate and the field of vision constricts gradually and concentrically. The rate of progression is unpredictable, however, and the macular area may or may not be involved in the later years. Such electrophysiological tests as electroretinopathy can detect subclinical signs of RP before a person is even aware of any field loss or night blindness. Such testing is very important for those individuals who have an unexplained congenital hearing loss and who may have Usher's syndrome (congenital deafness and RP apparent during adolescence) (see also Chapter 8). Rehabilitation professionals working with clients who have both visual impairment and hearing loss as a result of Usher's syndrome or other causes will need to concentrate on ensuring that appropriate modes of communication are well-established and that concerns about maintaining skills for independent living and mobility are addressed.

Retinal Detachment

Retinal detachments are most common in nearsighted individuals over the age of 60, but they can occur at any age and with any refractive status. Retinal detachments often result from some problem with the vitreous that causes shrinkage of the gel, which fills up the center of the eye and helps to hold the retina in place next to the choroid. If the vitreous shrinks and pulls away from the retina, retinal tears can be produced. Other causes are eye injuries (particularly bruising or contusion), inflammations, hemorrhages and retinal vascular abnormalities related to diabetes, degenerative myopia, complications from eye surgery such as after cataract surgery, hereditary predisposition to detachment, or retinal weakness related to other systemic conditions (Eye Research Institute of Retina Foundation, 1988b).

If the retina breaks away from the choroid, vitreous fluid can slip behind the retina and lead to further separation and tearing. If untreated, the cells of the detached retina will lose nutrition and cease to function. Various procedures that permit an eye surgeon to repair a detachment or at least decrease the risk of further detachment are as follows: (1) photocoagulation using a laser for "spot welding," (2) cryo surgery using extreme cold to seal off tears, (3) scleral indenting or buckling to reduce the circumference of the globe and push the scleral wall against the retina, (4) and other surgical techniques, including vitrectomy, depending on the size and position of the detached area.

Retinopathy of Prematurity (ROP)

The administration of high concentrations of oxygen for extended periods of time to newborn infants of low birth weight led to many cases in the late 1940s and 1950s of what was then called retrolental fibroplasia (RLF). Oxygen, which is necessary in many instances to preserve the life of the infant, triggers changes in the retinal blood vessels and in some cases proliferation of vessels into the vitreous with predisposition to retinal detachment. For many babies, the net result is blindness, and for others, it is low vision. When the relationship between low birth weight, prematurity, and the administration of high concentrations of oxygen over extended periods of time was discovered in the early 1950s, monitoring procedures were introduced, and the incidence of RLF decreased dramatically.

There are still cases of what is now called ROP in premature infants whose birth weights are very low, and whose retinas are not as developed as they would be at full term. ROP may occur even though the amount of oxygen and the length of time it is administered are carefully controlled and monitored (Newell, 1996). Infants at greatest risk are those under 1500 grams (or 3.5 pounds) at birth (Newell, 1996; Palmer & Phelps, 1986). Cryotherapy, a technique for the surgical treatment of ROP using a freezing probe, holds some hope for babies whose ROP progresses to advanced stages in which the probability of limited functional vision is high. Many of these infants also have other physical problems stemming from extreme prematurity and the efforts necessary to sustain life. Some may also show developmental delays, which means that some of these youngsters may become clients of rehabilitation agencies in the years to come.

Nystagmus

Nystagmus is a condition that frequently is found in children and adults whose vision has been impaired since birth or shortly thereafter. Nystagmus is an involuntary, rhythmical oscillating movement of one or both eyes from side to side, up and down, in a rotary pattern, or in some combination of these. The movement can be pendular and regular or jerky with a comparatively slow move in one direction and a rapid return. Nystagmus may accompany other eye conditions—usually those that have existed for an extended period of time. It can be congenital or can originate during the first two or three years of life as happens with albinism. Treatment is directed at the primary condition if the nystagmus accompanies another condition. Nystagmus alone is usually asymptomatic (Faye, 1984) or may be associated with decreased acuity, but some children and adults may turn or tilt the head in an effort to decrease the speed, amplitude, or duration of the eye movements. Some may also locate a "null point," in which direction there is the least amount of nystagmus and the best possible vision.

The mechanism for nystagmus is not fully understood (Vaughan et al., 1995). Under certain circumstances, nystagmus can be elicited in individuals with normal vision by having them look as far to one side as possible for a period of time, by watching a rotating drum marked with alternating dark and light bands, or by looking at railroad cars moving along the tracks. This elicited optokinetic nystagmus, however, is a normal response in such situations and should not be equated with any pathological nystagmus (Vaughan et al., 1995). Other individuals may have latent nystagmus in which occlusion of either eye causes the other eye to go into nystagmus with reduction in its acuity.

The previous discussion has focused on only major causes of visual impairments. Many more contribute to the numbers of people who are blind or visually impaired. Tumors, corneal injuries and scarring, trachoma (inflammation of the cornea and conjunctiva, which is a leading cause of blindness in developing countries), vitamin deficiencies, such systemic diseases as multiple sclerosis, infectious diseases, for example, maternal rubella, therapeutic drug side effects, which lead in many cases to temporary visual impairment, venereal diseases, and eye injuries are additional causes of impaired vision. Of great concern are the large numbers of individuals for whom the cause of visual impairment is not reported, or for whom the cause is simply not known or "unknown to science." The various types of glaucoma—except for those secondary to disease or trauma—fall into this category because, in most cases, the reason for the increase in pressure within the eye is not evident.

DIAGNOSIS OF VISUAL IMPAIRMENTS

Parents and teachers may be the first to suspect that something is wrong with a child's eyes. But who looks out for adults whose vision may change in slow, subtle, and often "expected" ways as a result of the aging process? What happens to those whose eye conditions exist but do not produce noticeable changes in functional vision? What about those individuals who do notice changes but fear what they might mean and decide, consciously or unconsciously, to ignore them? What happens to elderly people who live alone and who experience sudden pain or blurriness or loss of vision, and simply do not know what to do? Unless they receive professional help or have family or friends to help them solicit care, eye disorders will continue to develop and will possibly lead to visual impairment and blindness, even though treatment may be available.

Treatment for visual impairments is provided by ophthalmologists, optometrists, orthoptists, and opticians. An *ophthalmologist* is a medical eye specialist, a physician, who concentrates on the diagnosis and treatment of defects and diseases of the eye by prescribing lenses and drugs, performing surgery, and carrying out other forms of medical treatment. An *optometrist* is a trained and licensed specialist who provides a variety of services, including diagnosis of visual conditions, prescription of optical corrections, and other noninvasive procedures. Some optometrists and ophthalmologists specialize in the evaluation of patients for possible use of low vision devices. In some low vision clinics, both of these eye specialists are on the staff. Working in conjunction with some eye specialists is the *orthoptist*, who is trained in various aspects of ocular analysis and can recommend eye exercises in cases of muscle imbalance and suppression of foveal stimulation. An *optician* is a technician trained to grind prescription lenses, fit contact lenses and eyeglasses, and adjust eyeglass frames to the wearer (Bailey & Hall, 1990). For a more detailed discussion of the role of eyecare specialists, see Chapter 10.

Eye specialists use a wide variety of diagnostic procedures and tests in their assessment of the integrity, health, and function of the eye and the optic pathways that lead to the occipital lobe of the brain. The eye specialist will typically decide which of the following common procedures are required in any given situation:

1. Notation of symptoms reported by patients, such as pain, double vision, tearing, dryness, blind spots, halos around lights, floaters, photophobia (light sensitivity), poor night vision, blurriness, and difficulty in reading. In combination with a carefully compiled family and previous medical history of the patient, this information will help determine the type and extent of further testing.
2. Notation of the appearance of eyes with attention to such items as size, shape, position, swelling, color, presence of discharge, and inflammation.
3. Measurement of central visual acuity at distance is usually checked with the Snellen letter chart or the E chart (see Chapter 4 for a reproduction of the Snellen and E charts). The Snellen Chart presents lines of letters (or, in the case of the E Chart, lines of Es) in gradational sizes to represent distances. The E Chart is preferred for individuals who, for whatever reason, cannot accurately identify letters. For many preschool children and youngsters with visual impairments, the "HOTV" test is suggested because all that a child is required to do is match letter shapes (Simons, 1983). These four letters (H, O, T, and V) cannot easily be confused with other letters and do not have mirror images that indicate other letters in the alphabet. Visual acuity in the near or reading range is also checked for each eye with a standardized chart such as the Revised Jaeger Standard. This is less precise, however, than are measurements at 20 feet.
4. Determination of the field of vision. The normal field of vision covers approximately 150 degrees on the nasal to temporal axis and approximately 110 degrees on the superior to inferior axis (Jose, 1983) as measured with a standard Goldmann III 4e stimulus. (See Figure 2.7.) A number of different confrontation techniques or grids and screens can be used to determine defects in the central or peripheral field of vision in each eye (Vaughan et al., 1995). The eye specialist will select the most appropriate to the specific situation. At times, it is helpful to do a binocular field examination with both eyes open. (For more information regarding the Goldmann perimetry, see Chapter 4.)
5. Examination of lids and anterior portion of the eyeballs with a slit lamp for magnification (biomicroscopy). Use of a slit lamp with high-power magnification and illumination provides the eye specialist with a more detailed view of the eyelids and eyeballs.
6. Measurement of IOP (tonometry). Some types of tonometry require the

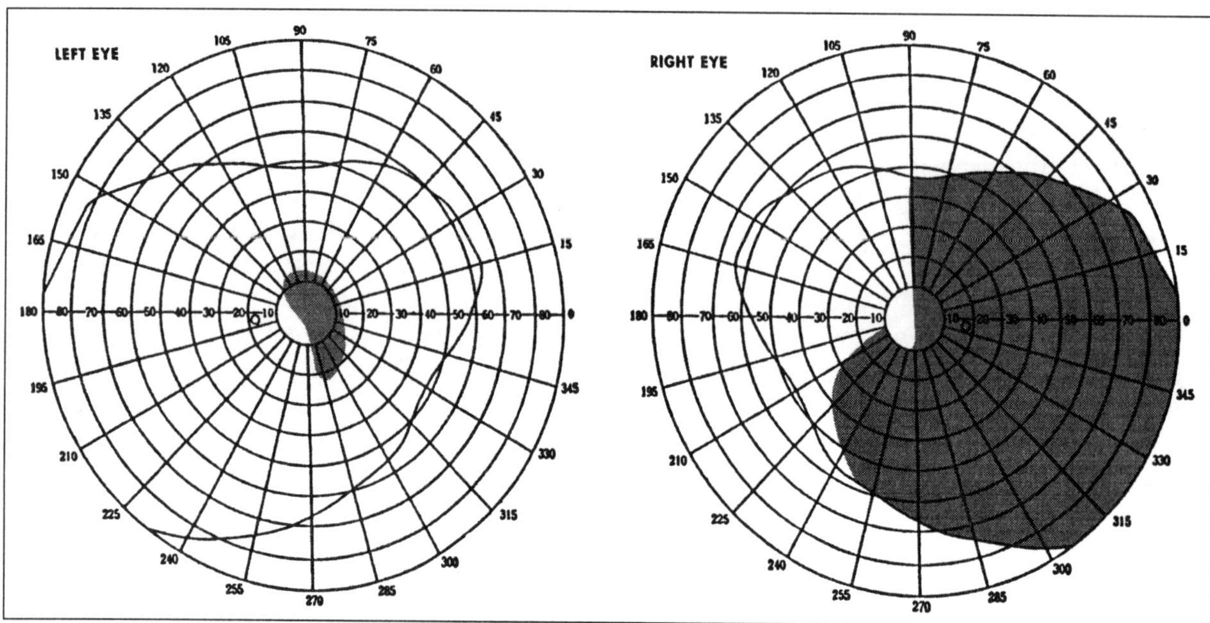

Figure 2.7. The Goldmann perimetry, a record of which appears here, can be used to determine defects in the central or peripheral field of vision.

Source: Visual field portion of eye examination report adapted with the permission of the New Jersey Commission for the Blind and Visually Impaired, Newark.

use of a topical anesthetic solution on the eye to permit an instrument to touch the cornea without discomfort. In some cases, the tonometer measures pressure inside the eye by indicating the amount of force necessary to flatten a small area of the cornea (applanation or Goldmann tonometry). Another technique used since the discovery of the human immunodeficiency virus in tears is a hand-held electronic tonometer. This type of tonometer has a throwaway latex rubber cover that is replaced with each use, thus avoiding any possibility of cross-contamination. Older tonometers measure pressure by indicating the amount of force necessary to indent the cornea (indentation tonometry). Glaucoma screening programs may use yet another technique, noncontact tonometry, that involves touching the eye only with a puff of air. This type of procedure is quite satisfactory for initial screening purposes, but applanation and indentation tonometry are more precise for clinical purposes.

7. Ophthalmoscopic examination. Examination with the direct and the indirect ophthalmoscope provides a good view of the retina and the internal structures of the eye. An ophthalmologist (and now in many states, an optometrist) instills a mydriatic, a drug that dilates the pupil but does not affect accommodation, so as to obtain visual access to the peripheral retina, as well as the posterior pole of the eye (fundus) (Vaughan et al., 1995).

8. Examination of anterior angle of anterior chamber with a gonioscope (gonioscopy). Particularly in suspected cases of glaucoma, gonioscopy is performed as a special type of contact-lens technique to examine the anterior chamber angle by either direct or indirect visualization. Topical anesthetic, special lighting, a special microscope, and a goniolens are required for the examination.

9. Corneal staining. To reveal corneal abrasions and irregularities, or to help

locate foreign bodies in the eye, a dye may be instilled on the eye. Sterile fluorescein dye is frequently selected for this purpose, and the eye is then examined under special lighting.

10. Testing for color perception. Tests for color perception require that the individual identify patterns—often numbers—composed of colored dots on a background of dots of a different color, but identical saturation and brightness. The colors are selected so that patterns are not discernible to people with color perception defects. Red-green confusion is the most common problem in both males (8 percent) and females (0.4 percent), and blue-yellow confusion is extremely rare in both sexes (Vaughan et al., 1995). Problems with color vision that are not associated with eye disease are almost always sex-linked and are usually transmitted through the mother to the male offspring.

11. Detection of blind spots in the area of central vision using an Amsler Grid (see Chapter 4 for a reproduction of an Amsler Grid). To detect blind spots or scotomas in the central or near central visual field, a person may be asked to focus on a dot in the center of a grid chart and then indicate any area of distortion or absence of the grid pattern. Blind spots in the field can indicate where on the retina or in other structures there may be damage.

Sometimes for a variety of reasons, both children and adults will try to fake poor vision. Using prisms and special lenses and mirrors, eye specialists can identify attempts to feign poor vision or blindness.

The previous list of assessment procedures and techniques contains those most frequently encountered during an eye examination; however, there are many other more sophisticated noninvasive procedures as well. Some of these specialized diagnostic procedures are described in Table 2.1.

Depending on the type of condition, the site, the severity, the natural history, or anticipated progression of the condition if left untreated, more invasive procedures may be warranted than those listed in Table 2.1. Some of these procedures are described in the next section.

SURGICAL PROCEDURES

Many surgical procedures involving the eye can be performed on an outpatient basis and may be done under either a local or a general anesthesia. If the latter is used, the patient will require some period of time to recover after surgery and to become alert enough to return home. Any surgical procedure carries with it a degree of risk; therefore, it is obvious that the surgeon and individual will need to discuss the associated risks and the expected outcomes as a result of having or not having a particular procedure performed.

Operations on the Eyelids (Blepharoplasty)

Operations performed on the eyelids most often are to move the lids to better functional or cosmetic positions. Some eyelid operations are for "entropion," in which the lid turns in, for "ectropion," in which the lid turns out, or for "ptosis," in which the lid droops over the eyeball. If the lid is lax and does not fit smoothly against the eye, or does not provide proper moisture to the cornea, or does not constantly wash the front of the eye with tears by blinking, the cornea can become dehydrated. If the lid is too tight, the lashes will sometimes turn in and painfully scratch the covering epithelium of the cornea. If the lid droops over the front of the eye, or if there is too much redundant skin hanging down over the line of vision, either the upper lid is elevated by shortening the muscle(s) that holds it up or the redundant skin is excised.

Table 2.1. Specialized Diagnostic Procedures

Visually Evoked Potential (VEP) This is an objective measure mainly of macular function as measured with scalp electrodes placed over the occipital cortex. The VEP can be used to detect lesions in the optic nerve and pathways to the brain (Sherman & Bass, 1984).

Electroretinopathy This is considered the "best single objective test of overall retinal function" (Faye, 1984, p. 223). The electroretinogram (ERG) measures electrical responses from the retina when a checkerboard pattern or flashing lights are presented to both the light- and dark-adapted eye. The pattern, amplitude, and latency of the wave form that results from the stimulation of the retina by the flashing lights or the reversing pattern are displayed on the ERG (Vaughan et al., 1995). A depressed ERG is particularly useful in the diagnosis of retinopathy of prematurity, even before the presence of symptoms or visible fundus lesions or without patient reporting.

Electro-oculography (EOG) A test of the function of retinal pigment epithelium, the EOG requires that the patient be able to cooperate during the testing time by changing fixation from one visual target to another. Skin electrodes pick up shifts in corneal-retinal electrical potential as the gaze switches, and changes in potential are considered indicative of problems in the retinal pigment epithelium, one of the nine layers of the retina. Sherman & Bass (1984) report that the ERG is a better test of overall retinal function than the EOG, which is not widely used in clinical practice.

Ultrasonography This test provides a measure of the structural integrity of the eye by using the reflection of extremely high-frequency waves to determine shape, size, thickness, position, and density of soft tissue in the orbit and the eyeball. Ultrasonography (also called echography) is helpful in locating tumors and foreign bodies, and in detecting detached retinas.

Contrast Sensitivity (CS) This test is a subjective measure of an individual's ability to detect and discriminate objects and fine detail under conditions of reduced or low contrast (Sherman & Bass, 1984). CS curves indicate how a person can see large targets (low-spatial frequency) of poor contrast, in addition to such small targets (high-spatial frequency) as letters or road signs of poor contrast. Sherman & Bass (1984) noted that CS curves may help explain why functional vision for the visual tasks during the course of a normal day may present problems, even when Snellen acuities are within the normal range. CS tests can provide additional data in evaluation of people with cataracts, multiple sclerosis, early glaucoma, and amblyopia (Sherman & Bass, 1984).

Fundus Fluorescein Angiography (FFA) This procedure shows capillaries, arteries, and veins of the choroid and retina. A sterile dye, fluorescein, is injected into the arm and a fundus camera with special filters takes pictures at half-second intervals to start and then at longer intervals to record the passage of the fluorescein through the choroid and retinal blood vessels. FFA is especially helpful in the diagnosis of and the determining of appropriate treatment of diabetic retinopathy, retinal vein occlusion, and macular degeneration. Vascular leaks, edema, neovascularization, and hemorrhages can be detected by observation with an ophthalmoscope during the procedure and by examination of the fundus photographs later (Jose, 1983; Vaughan et al., 1995).

Scanning Laser Ophthalmoscopy (SLO) This procedure involves a movie camera that permits viewing the surface of the retina and its deeper structures as they function. The SLO requires lower levels of light than FFA. The television display of what the SLO is recording is immediately available for analysis. The laser beam can be projected as an image onto the retina at specific points and the individual can report if an image is visible. This enables researchers to determine areas of the retina that do or do not function. Used in conjunction with FFA, the eye researcher can track the flow of the fluorescein through the choroidal and retinal blood vessels and study the dynamics of the flow.

Source: Adapted from Marjorie E. Ward, "The Visual System." In G. Scholl (Ed.), *Foundations of Education for Blind and Visually Handicapped Children and Youth* (New York: American Foundation for the Blind, 1986), p. 49.

Operations on the Orbit

Operations on the orbit are usually performed for the removal of a tumor or mass behind the eye, or for the drainage of the cerebrospinal fluid that surrounds the optic nerve. Collectively these procedures are called "orbitotomy." Often the direction of the surgical approach will be indicated, as lateral, medial, transnasal, or transantral. For this type of operation, most individuals are admitted to the hospital and are given a general anesthesia.

Sometimes a cosmetically acceptable blind eye can have the pain stopped or eased sufficiently to be able to tolerate the injection of 95 percent ethyl alcohol into the space behind the globe in the orbit. The alcohol kills the nerves that carry the pain; the eye is essentially denervated. This procedure usually works, at least to some extent, but often has to be repeated in a few months. Sometimes it also kills one or more of the nerves that supplies the muscles that move the eye, or the muscle that holds up the upper lid. As a result, some deviation in the position of the eye or the upper lid may occur. Usually, but not always, this clears within a few months because the nerves often regenerate. The client should be willing to accept the possibility that normal eye movement may not be regained after surgery.

Operations on the Extraocular Muscles

Operations on the extraocular muscles are performed for eyes that are turned in (esotropia), turned out (exotropia), turned up (hypertropia), or turned down (hypotropia). The surgical procedure either tightens or loosens one or more extraocular muscle. A resection tightens and a recession loosens a muscle. "Resection, left lateral rectus" is usually written or spoken as "resection, LLR." Similarly, "recession, right medial rectus" is usually indicated as "recession, RMR." These procedures have a major impact on binocularity and binocular coordination.

Operations on the Lacrimal Drainage System

Operations on the lacrimal drainage system reestablish the drainage ducts that normally carry tears from the eye into the nose. "Dilatation of the punctum" refers to the expansion with small metal dilators or probes of the opening at the beginning of the drainage system on the lid margin of each of the four lids. In almost all cases, this is an office procedure. "Probing the ducts" involves running small metal probes of progressively increasing diameter through the opening, sac, and nasolacrimal duct into the nose. Sometimes plastic tubing will be put through the entire length of the tear drainage system and left in place for several months. If the system is extensively scarred, a new drainage passage system may be surgically established (dacryocystorhinostomy). Often tubing is put in to keep the newly constructed drainage system open during the healing process. Occasionally, the lacrimal sac will be so infected as to require removal (dacryocystectomy). Although these lacrimal-removal operations can be done under a local anesthesia, bleeding may be on a moderate level; therefore, most patients and surgeons prefer general anesthesia. These procedures rarely require hospital admission.

Operations on the Cornea

The most common major operation performed on the cornea is cornea transplantation (keratoplasty), of which there are two kinds. The first, described as lamellar, is when the cornea is split much as layers of plywood can be split. The second, called penetrating, is a procedure in which the full thickness of the cornea is removed. Transplants are also noted as "total" if the whole circumference of the cornea is replaced, or "partial" if only the central portion is replaced. In any of these cases, the removed corneal tissue is replaced by donor tissue obtained from an eye bank. Most corneal transplants are performed while the client is under general anesthesia. During these procedures, the diseased area of cornea is simply cut out with a "cookie cutter"-type instrument and a graft is sutured in place. The client must be careful during the postoperative period because healing takes many weeks and minor bumps or contusions to the eye can rupture the sutures. The client is usually hospitalized for a few days, although surgery is sometimes done on an outpatient basis. As with all transplanted material, however, the graft may be immunologically rejected and turn white. The result of this rejection is a secondary corneal opacity, which requires a secondary, full thickness graft. With repeated operations, a clear transplanted cornea is usually obtained.

Pterygia are fleshy nodules that can develop close to and on the top of the cornea. They are common in near-tropical and dusty, windy parts of the world among people who are outside much of the time. A pterygium impairs vision by warping the cornea, even if it has not yet grown across the central visual axis. Removal of these nodules usually takes place in an office or in an outpatient surgical suite, and involves removing the pterygium and dissecting off a thin layer of underlying normal cornea. Individuals often postpone this operation for too long, although the best results require removal before the growth has extended into the pars optica or before it has encroached on the visual axis. Pterygia are commonly bilateral and are prone to recurrence.

Operations on the Iris

The two most frequent operations performed on the iris are (1) iridectomy, which refers to the surgical removal of a piece of the iris, and (2) iridotomy, in which a hole is cut in the iris. Both procedures are used to make an opening to facilitate the flow of aqueous humor from the posterior chamber behind the iris into the anterior chamber and anterior chamber angle in front of the iris. The surgery is indicated when the anterior chamber angle becomes too narrow for the aqueous humor to flow out through the trabecular meshwork. The client generally develops the acute, painful form of glaucoma known as closed-angle glaucoma. This may or may not occur in individuals who have already been diagnosed with glaucoma. Usually corrective surgery can be done under local anesthesia with a laser, either the type that "burns" (e.g., argon, dye, or krypton) or the kind that "cuts" [e.g., neodymium: yttrium-aluminum-garnet (Nd: YAG)]. If a laser is used, often the procedure can be done in an ophthalmologist's office or in a hospital outpatient department.

Trabeculoplasty is another glaucoma laser procedure (usually Argon) involving the trabeculum, which is the area where the fluid flows from the eye. The trabeculum is located in the far periphery of the anterior chamber. During this operation, it is burned with a laser, which increases the outflow of aqueous humor. Trabeculoplasty is also often an outpatient office procedure.

Retinal Operations on the Vitreous

Surgical removal of the vitreous is called vitrectomy. The vitreous gel can contain strands running through it that can sometimes be quite strong. Often, the surgeon must use a machine with a cutting head approximately the size of a ball point pen refill. The cutter cuts the vitreous, small bits at a time, and an irrigation fluid and suction system carries the bits of old blood or scar tissue out of the eye.

Operations on the Retina

Generally, operations on the retina (those that do not simultaneously involve a vitrectomy) are performed for any condition in which a discrete scar to hold the retina to the choroid must be made, or when a lesion must be destroyed. Making a discrete scar usually means that retinal tears without detachment have been found during a routine examination, or when the client has noted blood or new floating material in the visual field. Laser (light), cryopexy (cold), or diathermy (heat) may be used to seal the retina to the choroid. Because no incision is made into the eye, such operations may be done in the office and there are only modest postoperative restrictions. Laser, cryopexy, and diathermy can also be used to destroy pathologic lesions in the eye, commonly as part of the treatment of diabetic retinopathy. For example, lasers can destroy the new budding capillaries and vessels in the retina that indicate neovascular proliferation. They may also be used when a vascular membrane is invading a critical area, as in subretinal or epiretinal neovascular membrane, which is one of the many types of macular degeneration. The use of the laser in all these conditions is a tradeoff, in which it is accepted that a limited destruction of retina will take place during the attempt to prevent a much greater loss if the eye is left untreated. Often, retreatment once or twice yearly is necessary, as these conditions are characteristically progressive with new vascular changes occuring as time passes.

Retinal detachment and retinal separation repairs usually include vitrectomy, because the vitreous, if contracted, literally pulls the retina off the choroid layer of the eye. Laser energy may be applied directly onto the retina to seal the retina back to the choroid after the retina has been replaced in its original position, or it may be sealed with either cryopexy or diathermy. If the retina cannot be put back in place by cutting free that which pulled it off, for example, when vitreous traction bands are present, then air or any of several gases that are absorbed more slowly may be injected into the eye. This is usually called "gas fluid exchange." Or, a silicone oil or a heavy liquid may be injected into the vitreous cavity to help push the retina back in place. Sometimes small incisions must be made through the sclera and choroid to tap the subretinal fluid that could not otherwise be drained. Whatever the procedure, the purpose is to cut free or remove that which is holding the retina away from the choroid, and, after the retina is back in place, seal it in place with one of these methods. If the retina will not go back as far as is required, the entire eye may be made smaller by putting a band around the outside of the eye at the equator. This is usually referred to as a "buckle" or a silicone "band."

Retinal detachment operations are usually done in a hospital with the client under general anesthesia. The hospital stay is typically a few days; however, individuals are generally restricted from strenuous activities for some weeks after surgery. Because the retina gets its nourishment from the choroid and if separated from the choroid can become "starved" for nutrients, the clarity of vision after successful retinal reattachment surgery is sometimes less than the preoperative condition. For individuals who have concomitant retinal disease, such as diabetic retinopathy, these problems are compounded. If the vitreous has been injured from the passage of a foreign body, industrial accidents (e.g., grinding wheel or metal saw), gunshot wounds, or laceration or rupture of the globe, the contracting vitreous and resultant retinal detachment are just parts of the larger problem.

Removal of the Eye

If the eye must be removed in evisceration or enucleation, or if the entire orbital content must be removed in exenteration, the individual must clearly understand that the process is to save life, not sight. Evisceration involves taking out all the contents of the eye and sometimes the cornea, leaving only the scleral shell. A smaller, plastic globe is implanted within the scleral shell, and the muscles that move the eye are left intact. Evisceration usually allows the fitting of a prosthesis, an artificial eye, that moves well and has good cosmetic results. Enucleation, the most commonly performed of these three procedures, involves the removal of the entire eyeball. Each of the six muscles attached to the sclera along with the optic nerve, all the blood vessels, and small nerves that serve the eye must be severed. Usually an acrylic implant (or one of a similar material) approximately the same size as the removed eye is secured within Tenon's capsule from which the eyeball was removed (Newell, 1992). There are many types of implants that allow the muscles to be attached to the implant in an effort to retain movement. The implant must be inserted at the time of surgery and is completely covered with tissue. It cannot be seen postoperatively.

In exenteration, which is the least commonly performed of these three procedures, the entire contents of the orbit is removed. This procedure is almost always done because of malignancy. A thick, split graft of non-hair-bearing skin is applied to the orbital bones to facilitate healing of the cavity.

When an eye is completely removed, an ocularist can make a prosthesis to precisely fit the individual. Usually the fitting of a prosthesis is done about six weeks after postoperative healing. In cases of evisceration or enucleation, a shell painted to resemble an eye is placed so that it fits between the lids and in front of the now healed conjunctive tissues that cover the implant in the case of enucleation, or that cover the downsized scleral shell in the case of evisceration. Artificial eyes are of many types and may be "stock" or custom designed and painted.

Provided that surgery preserves the stump and allows either the implanted material or a modified scleral shell to move, a custom-made prosthesis will usually be difficult to detect as being artificial. Because a custom eye is made by hand to fit the socket, built up on the front to make the lids assume a normal position, and a handpainted color match of the other eye, it is by far the better choice than a stock eye for nearly all people who need this type of prosthesis. A custom eye from an ocularist will cost several times more than the stock eye costs, but is very much worth the cost difference.

In the case of an exenteration of the orbit, the artificial eye is only part of a much larger prosthesis or dam that fills the larger orbital cavity. This type of prosthesis may have artificial lids and sometimes part of the nose. Because fewer of these are made, the person will need the services of an ocularist who is experienced in creating this type of prosthesis.

INTERPRETATION OF EYE REPORTS

Most state and private agencies providing services for individuals with visual impairments require that an eye report be completed by an eye specialist, either an ophthalmologist or an optometrist. Although no single report form has been uniformly adopted by agencies or eye specialists, the information contained in most reports generally pertains to patient/client identification, the history of the eye condition and other medical history of particular significance to the eye condition, clinical measurements of acuity and visual field, present eyeglasses prescription, the cause of the condition if such can be determined, a prognosis, and recommendations. The eye report may be used to determine eligibility for services from the agency, and to determine eligibility for such special benefits as income tax deductions, supplemental social security benefits, or reader services.

The eye report usually becomes an intrinsic part of the client's permanent record. Much of the information is clinical in nature and provides the underpinnings for objectives related to rehabilitation, orientation and mobility (O&M) instruction, or strategies for fostering independent living skills. The delineation of impairments is valuable to the rehabilitation counselor, teacher, or any other professional who requires a basic understanding of client needs.

Identifying Information

A record of the client name, age, date of birth, address, occupation, and referring agency, if any, identifies the individual for whom the eye report is requested. The social security number is also helpful as several individuals may have the same name. Usually, the client gives the eye report form along with a cover letter explaining why the report is needed to the eye specialist at the time of the examination.

History

Most healthcare professionals view obtaining a complete and accurate history of previous health problems, treatments, and habits as the most critical component of any type of general or special evaluation or report. Many elements of both the prior health and present illness history are important for the rehabilitation counselor to know also, not only for what they directly contribute to the understanding of the immediate condition of the client, but also for what they suggest regarding past eyecare, compliance, possible risks for other or future family members, and prognosis.

Individuals who have had little or no functional vision since birth bring to the rehabilitation setting very different experiences than those persons who have had good, useful vision most of their lives. An important piece of information is, therefore, the age at onset of the eye condition. The counselor should look also for prior eye problems that have required medical treatment and the age of the client when those problems occurred, the medication(s) taken and any that are presently prescribed, any hearing impairment, and any systemic diseases that could affect the eyes, such as diabetes or hypertension. A medical history of others in the same family with similar or identical problems is important, especially if these are congenital disorders that can be inherited. Such information carries implications for both short-term and long-range planning.

Clinical Measures of Vision

Clinical measurements of vision include distance and near visual acuities with and without correction, a report of the type of correction that has been prescribed for eyeglasses or contact lenses, any additional correction added for reading (e.g., bifocals), a record of the field of vision for each eye, and information about any problems with color vision. All of these measures can suggest to the counselor those functional visual capabilities that the client may possess for independent living, work, and leisure activities.

Distance visual acuity and the extent of field loss are typically used to determine eligibility for services. A distance visual acuity at 20/200 or less in the better eye after correction will usually qualify an individual for service. Distance visual acuity often is reported with and without correction. If the individual has no eyeglasses, or has forgotten or lost them, then no acuity with correction can be reported. If the client does not need to wear eyeglasses at the present time, it is recommended that the counselor check to see if lenses or eyeglasses had been prescribed in the past and how long they were used.

For educational and vocational purposes, near visual acuity is very important. As with distance visual acuity, near visual acuity is usually reported with and without correction, although it is subject to more variation than measurements at 20 feet. If a person has been fitted with a low vision device, either a binocular or monocular device for distance viewing or some type of magnifying device for close work, visual acuity may be reported when using the device. In addition to devices, some clients depend heavily on extra lighting or natural daylight for enhancing visual acuity.

Acuity measures taken in a clinical setting often can be anxiety producing and unsettling. They may give a fair picture of visual function in that setting but will not reveal how efficiently a person uses vision at home, in a work setting, or for travel. The counselor and rehabilitation teacher will need to supplement that clinical information with careful observations and additional information about use of vision in other settings, the lighting conditions or environmental modifications that might improve use of vision, and the length of time that a person can work on a visual task and still perform proficiently and efficiently.

It is important to consider the distance from the visual target at which visual acuities are taken. For distance vision, the usual distance is 20 feet or the simulation of 20 feet. Sometimes a person with a visual impairment will be able to see the largest visual target on the test chart only at some distance closer than 20 feet. The examiner may then report an acuity such as 10/400, which means that the individual recognized at a distance of 10 feet that which a person with normal vision—or 20/20—could recognize at a distance of 400 feet. Such information may be helpful for some purposes (e.g., eligibility for services), but again may not reveal much insight in regard to visual efficiency and performance in the nonclinical setting. Table 2.2 contains the abbreviations that are frequently used on reports of visual acuities.

Table 2.2. Abbreviations Frequently Encountered in Eye Reports

OD	ocular dexter (right eye)
OS	ocular sinister (left eye)
OU	oculi unitas (both eyes)
△	prism diopter
+	plus or convex lens
–	minus or concave lens
x	at (used in recording correction for astigmatism to indicate location of added cylindrical power)
X	number of times of magnification, as a 10X magnifier that enlarges 10 times
CF	count fingers
HM	hand movements
LP	light perception
NLP	no light perception

Lenses

Knowing how to read a prescription provides information about the strength or power of the lenses a person is to wear and can suggest factors that both counselors and teachers are advised to keep in mind when discussing ways to improve visual function. A detailed explanation of prescription lenses is beyond the scope of this chapter; that which follows is basic information to aid in understanding the data that often appear on an eye report. (For a more comprehensive discussion of prescription lenses, see Chapter 6).

Prescriptions for corrective lenses are reported in terms of the refracting or light bending power of the lenses. The power of a lens is measured in diopters (D). The stronger the lens, the shorter the focal distance or the distance necessary to bring light rays to a point of focus. A convex (plus) lens that converges light rays is used to correct for hyperopia; a concave (minus) lens that spreads or diverges light rays corrects myopia. A convex lens with a power of 10 D is stronger than that of 5 D, just as a −10 D concave lens is stronger than a −2 D lens. (See Figure 2.8.)

Corrective lenses can be spherical or cylindrical. A spherical lens has the same refractive power on all axes (or meridians); a cylindrical lens has more power along one axis than along any other. Spherical lenses are prescribed for simple refractive errors and cylindrical lenses are used to correct astigmatism. Many times, an individual will need additional correction in the form of a bifocal, or in some cases a trifocal, to make reading and other close work more comfortable. The additional power is reported as an ADD, for example, OU ADD +3 D, which indicates that refractive power has been added to both eyes in the amount of 3 D.

Knowledge of the ways in which lenses can be used is helpful for rehabilitation professionals. Such information can usually be gleaned from a careful reading of the client's eye report form and record of lens prescriptions.

Power of the Lens

The power reported for the lenses coupled with near and distance acuities can give the counselor some idea regarding a client's functional vision without correction. Typically, the stronger the correction, the poorer the vision without correction. This information can support the importance of wearing corrective lenses either at all times or when particular visual demands are present. An exception to this is the nearsighted individual who may have good near vision without any correction and who may remove glasses for near vision tasks. Also, because of increasing minification brought on by increasing minus dioptric lens power, some nearsighted individuals may prefer not to wear their eyeglasses at all times.

Presence of Astigmatism

With astigmatism, it becomes even more important for individuals to wear eyeglasses and to keep them properly adjusted on their faces so the power of the corrective lenses matches up accu-

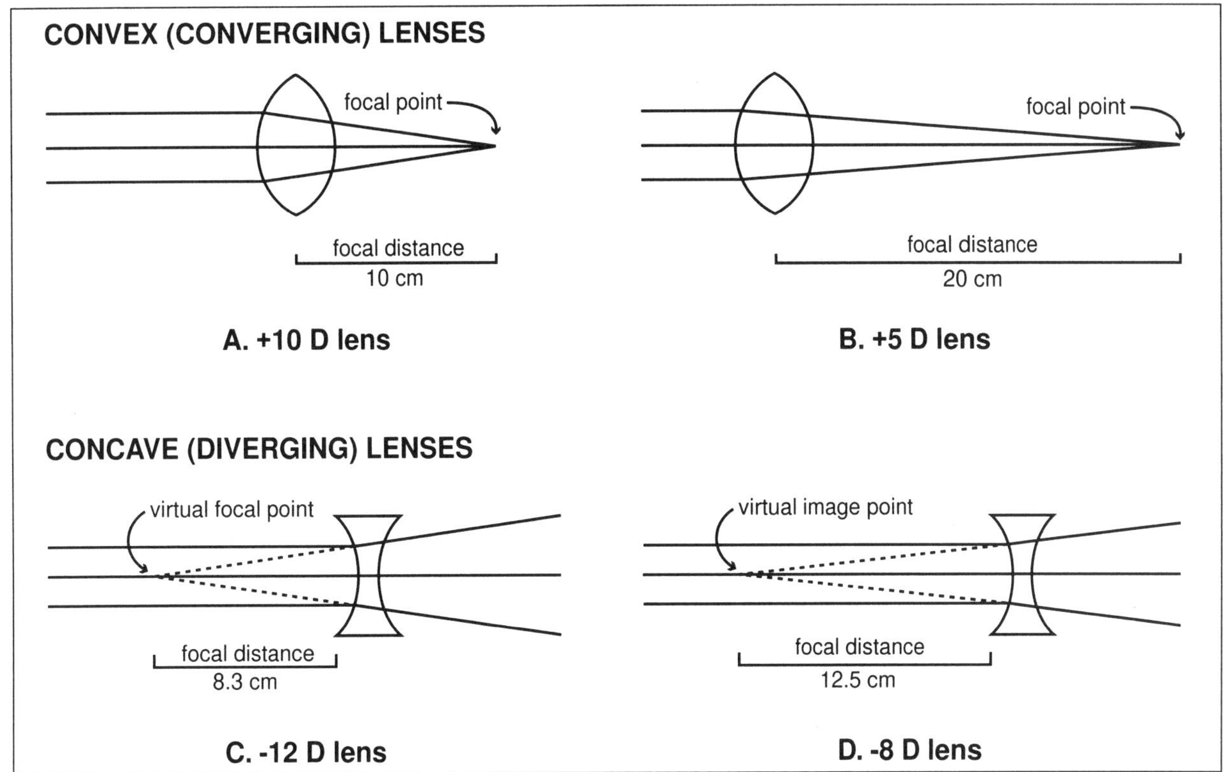

Figure 2.8. Lenses of different powers are commonly used to converge or diverge light rays passing through them. The stronger the lens, the shorter the distance required to bring light rays to a point of focus.

rately with the power of the person's eyes on the various meridians. Most individuals with astigmatism prefer to wear their corrective eyeglasses during all waking hours.

Power of a Lens Greater than +12 D

The power of a lens greater than +12 D could suggest that the person's natural lens has been removed. That suspicion can be confirmed or rejected by checking other parts of the report to see if the person is aphakic, that is, has had surgery to remove the lens. It could also mean that the person is extremely hyperopic (farsighted). Sometimes in extreme cases of hyperopia, distance vision after correction may not be very clear.

Power of Minus Lens

A very strong minus lens, −6 D to −8 D or more, suggests that the client is very myopic (nearsighted) and may achieve better vision (that is, less minification) with contact lenses than with eyeglasses.

Disparity Between the Strength of Correction

When the difference between the powers of the two lenses is large, as in the case of a person who is extremely farsighted in one eye and very nearsighted in the other (anisometropia), the person may tend to favor one eye for such tasks as reading or watching television. A converging lens, used for the hyperopic eye, tends to increase the size of the image on the retina. To decrease or eliminate any confusion, the person may simply use only one eye for any particular activity.

Safety Lenses

Safety lenses in eyeglasses should be standard issue today to prevent injuries. Each year, Prevent

Blindness America (see Resources) receives reports of many preventable visual impairments caused by shattering lenses, cut eyelids, or penetrating wounds in the cornea or deeper into the globe, which could have been prevented by the use of safety lenses.

Low Vision Devices

If a device has been prescribed or a recommendation has been made that a person be evaluated at a low vision clinic to determine whether a device might be helpful, then it is recommended that the counselor be certain that the person actually has the device and knows how and when to use it. It is also highly advisable that the counselor find out whether the appointment has been made or kept for the low vision evaluation. (See Chapter 4 for a discussion of low vision and low vision devices.)

Field of Vision

Field of vision refers to the entire area that can be seen with the eye staring straight ahead or in some other fixed position. A field of vision loss may occur in one or both eyes and may be in different locations in each field. Some individuals have scattered patches or islands of useful vision that may necessitate redirecting their gaze in order to allow light rays to activate these portions of the retinas that still function and respond to light. Some people may have good central acuity where cone cells dominate but may have losses in peripheral vision because of problems with rod cells.

Usually the eye report for a person having a field of vision loss will show an illustration to depict where the fields are restricted, or to what degree in terms of a specified stimulus size and brightness. Field of vision losses can be detected and plotted several different ways with methods ranging from the relatively quick tangent screen with lights or light-colored objects against a dark screen, to the more sophisticated Goldmann perimeters (Vaughan et al., 1995). (See Figure 2.7 for an example.) Inferences can be drawn from the patterns that emerge about those portions of the retina that still receive and respond to light. An individual whose visual field is restricted, whose macula is compromised, or who has patches of useful vision can learn to turn the head so the visual target reflects light rays onto those portions of the retinas that still function. There are also auditory and other cues that can be useful in making sense of the environment. Such information is helpful to the client, as well as the rehabilitation counselor or teacher to confirm where the areas of functional field of vision remain and to suggest different directions of gaze that might collect more stimuli than a direct gaze could, especially if the client's central vision is not clear or sharp. These off-center directions of gaze are sometimes referred to as eccentric gaze.

Color Perception

Problems with color discrimination are much more common in males than in females (Vaughan et al., 1995). Complete absence of color vision (achromatopsia) is quite rare—0.3 per 100,000 in males and even lower in females (Jose, 1983). Most people who have difficulty interpreting color have normal visual acuity, however (Vaughan et al., 1995). Children and adults may confuse colors because their retinal cone receptors lack the necessary pigment or because their cones are less sensitive in general to light waves and levels of light intensity and do not detect red-orange, yellow-green, or blue light wavelengths.

Generally, there are no serious learning problems or other problems brought on as a result of a lack of color perception, as long as the client whose color vision is deficient and any rehabilitation professionals are aware of the difficulty the person has distinguishing colors and hues. One particular area of concern for the client with a visual impairment, in some occupations, however, could be tasks with color-coded objects or instructions. Color deficiency can be a frustrating problem when trying to follow color-coded diagrams, maps, or instructions, or maintaining employment in occupations that require the best possible perception of all colors. Another area of concern is the recognition of color in traffic lights when the person must cross light-controlled intersections alone. Rehabilitation professionals are advised to note in referral letters or on the eye report if problems with color vision are present.

Vision in One Eye

Some individuals who have only one eye or who have normal vision in only one eye but limited vision in the other may need assistance in developing compensatory skills, but may not require even minor modifications for most tasks after those skills are mastered. For example, individuals with temporal field of vision losses may need to be alert for sound cues that people or objects are approaching from that particular side and then remember to turn their heads in that direction to detect visual cues with the other eye. Persons with poor central vision in one eye should experiment to determine where to hold reading materials to ensure comfort and efficiency for using the good eye.

A person with useful vision in only one eye will probably also want to develop strategies to use monocular clues in the absence of depth perception. Such monocular clues include looking for shadows and intervening objects (overlapping contours) and using knowledge of distance perspective to help determine the space between objects or the space between the viewer and other stationary or moving objects. Size, aerial haze, and convergence of lines at distance all help. Knowing situations in which judgment of distance is particularly difficult is also important. These situations include running on a playground, participating in sports during which balls or sticks of any size are used, reaching for objects on a desk or shelf or items in a cafeteria line, or driving behind a pickup truck from which boards or poles are extending. An individual with good vision in only one eye must pay particular attention to the selection of sports and recreation activities. Activities with low risk of eye injury include track and field events, swimming, rowing, and walking. High-risk sports include hockey of any kind, racquet sports of any kind, lacrosse, baseball, volleyball, football, and all other types of handball. Extremely high-risk sports include boxing, full contact karate, and any other combat sports. Sports with high risk for eye injuries are not wise choices for any athlete with functional vision in only one eye (Vinger, Knuttgen, Easterbrook, Pashley, & Schnell, 1988). Risk of injury and damage to the good eye can be greatly reduced by wearing such adequate protective eyewear as molded polycarbonate frames and lenses, face masks, or helmets with face protection.

Causes of Blindness and Visual Impairment

On many eye reports the counselor will find some notation of the probable past and present causes of the individual's eye condition. In such degenerative disorders as degenerative myopia, or conditions that require regular monitoring, as with glaucoma, the clinical measures cannot reflect the whole picture; for example, some causes of blindness call for restricted physical activity because bumps or falls could increase the risk of a detached retina. The rehabilitation professional needs to be cognizant of the implications of eye conditions and is advised to examine carefully all information on the etiology of the disorder.

Usually, the eye specialist will indicate if the condition can be inherited. If the genetic patterns of transmission (i.e., autosomal dominant, autosomal recessive, or sex-linked) are known, the eye specialist usually notes what they are. The counselor should investigate how clearly the client understands the pattern(s) of transmission. The client can use this information in discussing with other family members the importance of examinations for those family members who may be at risk either because they manifest clinical signs of the condition or because they may be unaffected carriers.

With adolescents and young adults, questions may come up about their eye conditions and whether or not these can be passed on to their children. Teachers and counselors may be those who field these questions. Most rehabilitation counselors or teachers, however, are not experts in genetics, patterns of transmission, frequency of occurrence within a generation (penetration), severity within a particular individual (expression), or how to lay out a record of occurrences (pedigree) within a family. But it is highly recommended that the counselor at least be able to recognize the importance of these questions and be able to locate or refer clients to appropriate genetic counseling clinics or other resources.

Prognosis and Recommendations

If at all possible, the eye specialist notes any information regarding the stability of the eye condition. If the condition may deteriorate, both the client and the counselor are encouraged to be aware of those signs that might be a warning of some significant change. For example, light flashes or dark spots in the visual field may be signs of retinal detachment or hemorrhage, or eye pain and discomfort may be a sign of increased IOP brought on by glaucoma. The presence of a significant sign calls for prompt action on the part of the client or the client's family to arrange for examination by an eye specialist, even when there is doubt about how serious the situation might be.

The eye specialist will usually report what treatment is recommended and when the patient's next examination should be scheduled. The rehabilitation professional may want to discuss with the client the importance of follow-up and compliance with instructions, especially if noncompliance is perceived to be a problem.

In the elderly population noncompliance may be the result of many factors, not just "stubbornness" or refusal. For example, not keeping appointments may be a result of transportation problems, forgotten dates, illness related to other physical conditions that are quite separate from the eye condition, or bad weather. And failure to take medication may be caused by misunderstanding the directions, forgetting to fill the prescription, lacking money to pay for the prescription even though reimbursement is forthcoming, forgetting, difficulty in measuring liquid dosage or instilling drops, wanting or needing further instructions or assistance when none is available, or feeling discomforting side effects. All of these problems can usually be handled in some way by the counselor, but first they must be recognized.

A special note about drug interactions and side effects: adults and elderly people who have such systemic conditions as diabetes, chronic infections, cardiovascular disease, allergies, pulmonary disease, or asthma, need to report to the eye specialist exactly what medications, if any, they are presently taking. Certain systemic conditions warrant careful consideration and selection of medication for the eye condition to avoid unwanted drug interactions or adverse reactions. For example, Timolol (TM), a beta-blocker, is very commonly prescribed for the treatment of glaucoma, but there can be uncomfortable and even severe side effects for individuals with bronchial allergies, or cardiopulmonary or cardiovascular disease (Vaughan et al., 1995). Also, not everyone realizes that just about any drug may have negative side effects in addition to the positive effect the drug is supposed to have and the reason for which it is prescribed. For example, allergy medicines may make you sleepy, cold remedies may make you feel tired, and pain medicines may leave you feeling pain-free but limp. To achieve the desired effect, the undesired effects may have to be endured. Or, if unsafe or intolerable, the medicine may have to be changed or the dosage reduced. Therefore, to criticize a client for noncompliance is not productive; what is really needed is a discussion about the factors that may be contributing to noncompliance with medications or follow-up appointments and what to do about it. For more information about clients with prescribed medications, see Sidebar 2.2.

SIDEBAR 2.2

Rehabilitation Counselors and Clients with Prescribed Medications

Many individuals in rehabilitation programs have to take long-term medications, as prescribed by their eyecare specialists. It is important that the client's relationship with his or her eyecare specialist be maintained, particularly with reference to prescribed drugs whose continuance is essential to the client's welfare or life. It is recommended that a counselor (1) be aware of what medications the individual's doctor had prescribed, (2) reinforce the necessity of medications with the individual, and (3) encourage the individual to schedule eye examinations routinely. Many people do not maintain regularly scheduled examinations because they have been told by an eyecare specialist that nothing more can be done for their eye diseases. In such cases, it is important that counselors emphasize to these individuals the fact that eye conditions can develop. Counselors should encourage clients to maintain their periodic visits to eyecare specialists even though they might regard them as a low priority.

When a counselor makes the first appointment with a different eyecare specialist for a client, the counselor should make certain that the doctor is given all of the medical information that he or she has about the client. Time delays, increased medical costs, and most important, delayed medical treatment often occur when eyecare specialists are not supplied with essential data. It is recommended that the client carry all medications he or she has used and is currently using to the appointment. This might mean that the clients will have to take empty bottles and the bottles of medications that are no longer being prescribed for them. The person's rehabilitation will be enhanced if the eyecare specialist has been given a full medical history, including a list of which medications helped in treating the person's condition, and which did not.

Counselors also need to be aware of potential side effects from medications and that these can take almost any form at some point during a particular individual's treatment. If a client is put on a new medication and then he or she develops new symptoms or side effects, these should be reported to the eyecare specialist. The common side effects of specific medications that do not warrant alarm usually will be communicated by the doctor at the time the prescription is given. In general, the following symptoms or signs should be reported:

1. For medications applied locally (e.g., eye drops, ointment for the eye or lids), if there is an increase in swelling, redness, itching, increased tearing, scaling of the skin, or wet, moist fluid containing blebs, it should be reported. It is recommended that a counselor report anything that tends to get worse after the medicine is started and that is not part of the original disease process.
2. For medications that change the pupillary size, if enough medication runs through the lacrimal drainage system into the nose and is absorbed into the blood stream, it might cause the same effect on the smooth muscles within the body. Therefore, a drug that dilates the pupil by stimulating the dilator muscles, if absorbed, will perhaps cause constriction of the blood vessel muscles and increase blood pressure. Or a pupillary drug that relaxes the pupillary constrictor muscles, if absorbed may cause a

(continued on next page)

Rehabilitation Counselors and Clients with Prescribed Medications (continued)

red rash and a fast pulse. These are not sensitivities or "allergies," they are simply the systemic or full body effects of a medication given for its consequences on the eye only.

Many medications given for other diseases can affect the eyes. Similarly, every drug has the capacity to cause unwanted side effects or sensitivities (Fraunfelder, 1966). As previously noted, the rehabilitation professional should be sensitive to any new symptom or complaint from the individual that begins after a new therapeutic agent has been prescribed.

Some eye conditions (e.g., degenerative myopia) may call for a restriction of physical activities, primarily those that have a high probability of hard physical contact with other players or with equipment. Such limitations are usually noted on the eye report and it is advised that rehabilitation professionals help the client explore other physical activities and athletic events.

Additional Information on Eye Reports

Some eye specialists may add information about visual function under specific circumstances or at a certain distance, or they may provide qualitative information about light awareness or projection. Some may report the type size that the individual was able to read in the clinical setting. While sometimes useful, what will probably prove to be more useful in the future will be computer screen size and variables related to computer usage.

A chart showing the normal field of vision for each eye is often provided for the examiner to shade in the portion of the field that is constricted and the areas of the central field where scotomas exist or macular degeneration has caused reduced visual acuity. The target or stimulus size and brightness must also be recorded. The completed chart can show the extent of where the patient may find "islands" of vision useful for certain tasks or specific situations. These field drawings also help explain why particular individuals turn their heads slightly when attempting to see an object or person directly in front of them. Information about field defects is very important to review with the client, the family, and any significant others involved with the client.

The counselor who brings to the examination of a clinical eye report a good, working knowledge of anatomy and physiology of the eye, the process of seeing, and eye disorders and their implications for vocational rehabilitation and education will contribute significantly to the quality of the services ultimately deemed appropriate for the client. Clinical eye reports are not always completed to the satisfaction of the rehabilitation professional, however. The rehabilitation counselor is urged to be persistent in securing required, essential information if any spaces are left blank on the eye report. Missing or incomplete information will require ongoing communication with the eye specialist or medical consultant.

CASE STUDY

An eye report (see Figure 2.9) for 59-year-old Mrs. Marguerite McNally, a widow, was completed by an ophthalmologist. Mrs. McNally has slight sensorineural hearing loss in her right ear and a significant weight problem. She also has high blood pressure and is trying to reduce her salt intake

Eye Examination Report

Patient's Name Marguerite McNally Date of Birth 2-14-38 Social Security No. 123-45-6789

Address 168 West 12th Street City Old Pine State10 OH Zip 43000

Ocular History (e.g., previous eye diseases, injuries, or operations)

Age at onset 58 History Macular degeneration, with drusen; open-angle glaucoma

Visual Acuity

If the acuity can be measured, complete this box using Snellen acuities or Snellen equivalents or NLP, LP, HM, CF.

Without Glasses		With Best Correction	
Near	Distance	Near	Distance
R 14/70	R 20/200	R J8 14/42	R 20/60
L 14/70	L 20/200	L J10 14/56	L 20/100

Acuity with glare testing, if applicable: R ________ L ________

If the acuity cannot be measured, check the most appropriate esimation.

☐ Legally Blind
☐ Not Legally Blind

Extra Ocular Muscle Function ☐ Normal ☐ Abnormal Describe ________

VISUAL FIELD (Goldmann preferred)

LEFT EYE (O.S.)
Remaning field:
________ DEGREES
Circle applicable code(s)
H Hemianopsia-like
S Central Scotoma
O Other handicapping field loss
N Normal field
I 40° or less
B 20° or less

RIGHT EYE (O.D.)
Remaining field:
________ DEGREES
Circle applicable code(s)
H Hemianopsia-like
S Central Scotoma
O Other handicapping field loss
N Normal field
I 40° or less
B 20° or less

TANGENT SCREEN
INSTRUMENT
TARGET SIZE
COLOR
INTENSITY

INTRAOCULAR PRESSURE CHECK ONE: ☐ POSITIVE ☐ NEGATIVE ☐ BORDERLINE	RIGHT EYE (O.D.) Tension in mm: 36	LEFT EYE (O.S.) Tension in mm: 28
	Instrument Used: Computer automated perimeter	Instrument Used:

(continued on next page)

Figure 2.9. The eye examination report for Mrs. McNally.

Source: Adapted with the permission of the Texas Commission for the Blind, Austin, and the New Jersey Commission for the Blind and Visually Impaired, Newark.

Eye Examination Report (*continued*)

Color Vision ☐ Normal ☐ Abnormal
Colors involved:

Photophobia ☐ Yes ☐ No

Diagnosis (Primary cause of vision loss)

Age-related macular degeneration with drusen, slight optic cupping; open-angle glaucoma

Prognosis ☐ Permanent ☐ Recurrent ☐ Improving ☑ Uncertain ☐ Progressive ☐ Communicable ☐ Can Be Improved

Treatment Recommended

☐ Glasses Refraction Record:

	Sph	Cyl	Axis	ADD	Prism
R	+4.75			+3.00	
L	+4.00			+3.00	

☐ Patches (Schedule):

R ____________________

L ____________________

☐ Medication ____________________

☐ Refer for other medical treatment/exam:

____

☐ Surgery

☐ Hospitalization will be needed for approximately ________ days.

Name of hospital ____________________

Name of anesthesiologist or group:

☐ Low Vision Evaluation

☑ Other Return in 2 weeks for refraction. See family doctor (high b.p., wt.)

Precautions or Suggestions (e.g., lighting conditions, activities to be avoided, etc.)

Scheduling When should patient be re-examined? in two weeks

Date of Next Appointment 12/9 Time

Clifford R. Bates, M.D.
Print or Type Name of Licensed Ophthalmologist or Optometrist

Signature of Licensed Ophthalmologist or Optometrist

861 East Fir Street
Address

10/6/97
Date of Examination

Old Pine | OH | 43000
City | State | Zip

(614) 123-4567
Telephone Number

RETURN COMPLETED FORM TO:

Name

Address

Olag Corp., Dept. of Human Services
Agency

City State Zip

and lose weight to bring her blood pressure under control. She does not drive and takes the bus to work. She lives alone in a large old house where she and her husband raised their three children, who are now all married and living out of state. Mrs. McNally's recent noticeable decrease in vision, which she mentioned to her close friend at church, has her quite worried. She is hesitant to say anything at work (where she is a quality control checker) because recent job cutbacks and the installation of robotic machines have led to the elimination of some jobs similar to hers on the production line. Although quality control checkers are still needed on the line, her decrease in visual acuity has made her work more tiring and she finds it more difficult to keep up the pace on the line. She often comes home with headaches and even had to leave the production line early on three occasions during the last month.

After much urging on the part of her friend at church and her youngest daughter in Alaska, Mrs. McNally went to the company's health clinic and asked if someone might help her get new glasses, "So I can read my mail, see the labels on the boxes at work better, and not get so many headaches." The nurse at the clinic checked Mrs. McNally's distant visual acuity and then referred her to Dr. Bates, one of the company's ophthalmologists, whose office is closest to Mrs. McNally's bus stop.

After the eye examination had been completed, Mrs. McNally's report was reviewed by the nurse at the company clinic. The nurse then sent a copy of the report to a counselor in the company's department of human services. The counselor looked at the report and, not fully understanding the significance of all the information, decided to forward it to the rehabilitation agency to which employees with physical and sensory impairments are referred.

The following thoughts and questions were considered by the rehabilitation counselor while reviewing Mrs. McNally's eye report:

History

1. Not much clinical history is reported. Let's look under etiology as well. I wonder if Mrs. McNally has known about the macular degeneration and glaucoma. The referral letter that came with the report states she has worked for some years on the packing line at the plant and has recently been complaining of localized headaches and trouble seeing shipping labels and packing lists.
2. When did Mrs. McNally acquire her present eyeglasses? She could not remember the name of the eye specialist who had prescribed her present lenses.
3. Do others in Mrs. McNally's family have glaucoma or know to be checked? She did not mention glaucoma to the clinic nurse. We will need to talk about that.

Measurements

1. According to the present prescription, what must Mrs. McNally's refractive error be? She has a bifocal ADD, which makes sense given her age. There's no correction for astigmatism. How strong is her bifocal? Does she wear her eyeglasses all of the time? I see that Dr. Bates wants her to return for refraction in two weeks, after she has seen her regular physician.
2. Does her performance in the ophthalmologist's office resemble her performance in her work settings?
3. Are Mrs. McNally's lenses safety lenses? Are they plastic? Are they properly adjusted? Do they stay positioned at the right spot on her nose?
4. Do Mrs. McNally's eyeglasses really give her improvement for reading? Jaeger 8 is equivalent to adult textbooks and Jaeger 10 to the size of young children's books. I should ask her to bring some labels and packing slips with her when she comes in so I can see the type size. We will have to wait until after Mrs. McNally's next appointment with Dr. Bates to see how much her near visual acuity can be improved; perhaps we may need to think

about some type of low vision device for her to wear at work, or for a higher ADD bifocal, which would give some near range magnification.

5. Does Mrs. McNally have any field of vision loss? Yes. Any scotomas? What will she need to learn to help compensate for her restricted peripheral vision, especially in her left eye? What problems might she have with scanning print? Going up or down steps? Getting on and off the bus? Searching for landmarks? Finding objects dropped on floors—with or without carpet? Will she be able to keep up with the work pace on the production line?
6. Mrs. McNally's IOP is above the average normal range. What might that mean in terms of medication? Could the field of vision loss be related? What about her headaches? Did she get a prescription for any medication?

Causes of Impaired Vision

1. What are the probable causes of Mrs. McNally's eye problems? What treatment has been prescribed? How long has she worn eyeglasses? What type of refractive error does she have? How much does she want/need to read beyond her job? Because she lives alone, she must be able to handle her own bills and bank records.
2. What are drusen? I think they are deposits within the layers of the retina, typically associated with macular degeneration, but may also appear within the optic nerve head. Where can I look for more information? What is the best way to be certain that Mrs. McNally understands AMD?
3. Does Mrs. McNally understand what glaucoma is and, most important of all, does she understand why she must use her drops every day? We need to talk about checking when her prescription must be refilled and how to make certain her drops actually get into her eyes.
4. Is there any relationship between AMD and glaucoma other than high incidence among those age 55 and over? I will see if many other clients with AMD also have glaucoma. This is also the age when cataracts become more frequent.

Prognosis and Recommendations

1. Because of the instability of her condition, what signs or problems should Mrs. McNally watch for and report to her ophthalmologist immediately?
2. Dr. Bates mentions Mrs. McNally's high blood pressure, diet, salt intake, and an appointment next week with her own physician. Mrs. McNally should be certain to report what medicine she is using for her glaucoma in case she has to start taking medicine for her high blood pressure, or for anything else. How can I best assist Mrs. McNally without encouraging compliant, passive behavior or diminishing her independence? I also sense that Mrs. McNally is reluctant, even fearful, of talking openly with me because she feels her job is in jeopardy.
3. When is Mrs. McNally to return for her next eye examination? Has the appointment been made? Can she or will she make her own arrangements?
4. Are any physical limitations mentioned?
5. Has the report been signed and dated?
6. Has a copy been placed in Mrs. McNally's confidential record?

Other questions will probably emerge after Mrs. McNally's next appointment. It may be that Mrs. McNally will not need any ongoing help from the rehabilitation agency to which the company nurse and department of human services have referred her. She may not even be eligible for service after all the information has been gathered and reviewed. She still must return for a refraction after she has been using her medicine for two weeks.

The rehabilitation counselor who can respond to the situation and the questions outlined above is well on the way to an understanding of visual impairments and their implications for individuals of any age who must learn to go on with their lives in new ways. The counselor needs to be in a good position to assist clients who are blind or visually impaired to focus their energies and analyze and deal with whatever situations they may face. Client and counselor together can create ways to strengthen the client's skills to meet the challenges of daily living, travel, employment, and community life.

SUMMARY

This chapter first presented a brief discussion of the structures of the eye and how they function to enable us to gather visual information from the environment. Because the normal aging process, disease, and injury can all affect the efficiency and integrity of the visual process, the discussion moved on to major causes of blindness and visual impairment. Following were sections on the various diagnostic and surgical procedures the rehabilitation counselor might encounter in reviewing clients' eye reports and medical records. Even though eye specialists may report information to counselors in many different formats, most reports contain the same basic information. For that reason, the types of information generally included in any eye report were reviewed along with some discussion to help the counselor interpret that information to clients who might have questions about their diagnosis, treatment, and prognosis. Finally, to illustrate how knowledge of anatomy, physiology, etiology of visual impairment, function of corrective lenses, and diagnostic procedures are used in the counselor's work with clients, the reader was introduced to the case of Mrs. Marguerite McNally. Information from this chapter should contribute to a better understanding of some of the concerns and uncertainties a client might bring to the counseling situation and should enhance the counselor's skills in assisting the client to explore the future with confidence.

LEARNING ACTIVITIES

1. Describe the path of light rays from the environment through the eye to the retina. Draw a picture of the pathway. What medium does most of the refracting? What structure can alter its curvature and thus its refractive power? Why is this desirable?
2. What protection does the eyeball have against mechanical injury? Against excessive light?
3. What are three major layers of the globe? What is the primary function of each?
4. Describe three major types of refractive errors and explain their correction.
5. What are the major causes of blindness among the general population in the United States over 40 years of age? Which of these are age-related? Which of these are secondary to other systemic conditions?
6. On the diagram drawn for Activity 1, place a check on the parts of the eye affected by the four leading causes of visual impairment in the age groups 20 years of age and older.
7. Define the following terms:

ophthalmologist	optometrist	accommodation
perfusion	suppression	presbyopia
visual acuity	field of vision	lens opacity
fovea centralis	power of a lens	IOP

8. Describe the types of information usually included in an eye specialist's report of an examination. What are important contributions each type of information can make to a rehabilitation professional's understanding of how a person might function visually?

CHAPTER 3

Congenital and Adventitious Blindness

Richard L. Welsh and Dean W. Tuttle

Each person who is blind or visually impaired is unique; however, the individual's age at onset of a visual impairment can strongly influence the types of rehabilitation services that he or she may need. Also, individuals who are congenitally blind have some different experiences, and therefore different needs, from those who are adventitiously blind. The three-fold purpose of this chapter is to review the various experiences and specific needs of individuals with either congenital or adventitious blindness, describe the implications of these differences and needs, and identify the various services that may be needed. An appreciation for the consequences of variations in age at onset, the accompanying differences in life experiences, and other related factors will better equip the rehabilitation counselor to develop meaningful rehabilitation programs that can enhance the independence and vocational success of their clients. People with visual impairments have many individual abilities and strengths and rehabilitation counselors are encouraged to target those strengths and assets, rather than try to remediate what might be thought of as deficits that, in some cases, might be circumvented rather than remediated. Because people who are blind are much the same as sighted persons, the psychological principles that have been developed to understand the behavior of all people are adequate and sufficient to understand the behavior of individuals with visual impairments.

CONGENITAL VISUAL IMPAIRMENTS

The term *congenital visual impairment* refers to a condition of blindness or severe visual impairment that is present at birth or occurs at an age when the absence of vision probably will alter a person's conceptual development. An individual whose blindness occurs prior to ages 3 or 4 will in all probability not retain any visual imagery or visual memory, which provides important building blocks for the development of many basic and important concepts (Lowenfeld, 1981a).

There are no statistics available to indicate or to permit an estimation of the number of people—both children and adults—at any one time whose blindness can be considered a congenital visual impairment. However, a national survey was conducted of 500 direct labor workers with visual impairments who were employed by agencies associated with the National Industries for the Blind. From this survey Moore, Crudden, and Giesen (1994), were able to report about half (52 percent) of the workers had been blind since birth, with the remaining 48 percent being adventitiously blind.

Effect of Personal Characteristics on the Need for Services

A review of the research literature and practice reports confirms the impression that no two adults who are congenitally blind are exactly alike. This is true of all people—visually impaired or not. Each person with a congenital visual impairment needs first to be viewed by the rehabilitation professional as unique, and then a thorough assessment needs to be conducted to determine that person's individual strengths and rehabilitation needs. Some documented developmental delays in children who have visual impairments, such as in the areas of social skills and concept development (Warren, 1994), are frequently able to be remedied prior to adulthood and none of these characteristics has been identified as appearing in every child. Similarly, research has not identified any particular traits, abilities, or impairments that are characteristic of all or even a majority of adults who are congenitally visually impaired or blind. The deductions drawn from the research reported regarding the characteristics of children with congenital visual impairments that may have relevance to the needs and types of rehabilitation services to be provided are discussed in the next section.

Sensory Abilities

A common misconception about persons who are congenitally blind is that they have been given or have developed superior abilities in using their other sensory systems. There is no research evidence of the truth of this belief, and what abilities do exist seem to be related to improvements that come from practice with or dependence on these other sensory systems. For example, Hare, Hammill, and Crandell (1970) found no difference in the auditory discrimination between children with and without sight from 6 to 10 years of age. Witkin, Oltman, Chase, and Friedman (1971), however, did find differences in the auditory skills of teenagers with congenital blindness and matched sighted subjects. They explained these results by suggesting that the teenagers with visual impairments had learned over the years to attend better to auditory stimuli. Warren (1994) summarized research on tactile discrimination and indicated that, on a variety of measures, there are no striking differences in children with or without sight. When differences do appear, they tend to favor children who are blind, although not strongly. Therefore, it is suggested that rehabilitation counselors not assume superior sensory skills and instead consider appropriate client assessments to determine abilities, particularly if employment that requires special tactile discrimination skills is being contemplated.

It should also be noted that significant progress has been made to help children with congenital visual impairments learn how to use whatever visual capacity they may have to its best advantage. More than three decades ago, Barraga (1964) demonstrated the effectiveness of a vision training program that she had developed, and training in visual efficiency is often received by students. It should not be assumed, however, that all individuals have received and benefited from such training. Therefore, the rehabilitation counselor needs to take steps to assess independently the visual efficiency of the person with a visual impairment, unless clear documentation of a recent low vision evaluation exists (see Chapter 4).

Similarly, the counselor cannot assume that the client with a congenital visual impairment has been evaluated for, has received, and is making the most effective use of low vision services. For example, many adolescents are reluctant to consider low vision devices because they feel socially awkward using them or believe that they are cosmetically unattractive. When young adults who are visually impaired start a rehabilitation program, however, they may display a greater interest in using low vision devices than they did during their school years.

Cognitive Abilities

There is strong agreement among theorists and researchers that congenital blindness that results in no visual input has a definite effect on cognitive functions. Lowenfeld (1950) identified the following three areas as those particularly limited or affected by a lack of vision: (1) the range and variety of experiences the individual has had, (2) the ability to get around, and (3) the interaction of the individual with the environment. Each of these areas affects the cognitive development of the person with congenital blindness. Vision is the sense that usually provides the information from which most of a person's concepts are formed. This is especially true for concepts that reflect distance, color, and size. Hearing and touch also provide a portion of the information that is used for conceptual development. Dependence on the verbal descriptions of others limits the accuracy and richness of the concepts developed by a person who has congenital blindness. Tuttle and Tuttle (1996) described it as follows:

> While unimpaired vision enables a person to perceive the whole and then subsequently its parts and the relationship of the parts to each other and to the whole, the tactile-auditory process requires that a person, after examining the parts, integrates the parts into a mental whole. The latter conceptualization process is much less efficient and much more susceptible to deficient or incomplete concepts. (p. 47)

As a consequence of growing up without vision, many adults may not fully develop certain abstract concepts, which in turn can sometimes result in functional difficulties in such areas as mobility, leisure activities, or work. For example, because of an incomplete sense of the concept of directionality, a person after finding his or her way to the driveway while traveling with a cane, may not be able to find a way off the driveway. Similarly, the person may be unable to understand the pattern required by a particular craft activity, or a skill required on an assembly line job may be unachievable. It is recommended that the rehabilitation counselor be alert to the possibility of such gaps when attempting to understand a performance problem that the client is experiencing in a testing, training, or work situation. Frequently, such a gap is indicated when the client can describe a task or a skill verbally but cannot perform the actual skill. When this is the case, special instruction or hands-on experience may need to be provided to address the gap in conceptual development.

Verbal descriptions can produce oral feedback but it is recommended that these descriptions not be used in place of a demonstration of a performance skill. A demonstration of a physical skill by an instructor, followed by an opportunity for practice by the client, coupled with verbal and perhaps tactile descriptions, will help clients develop more accurate concepts of a physical space or a motor skill.

Motor Abilities

Lowenfeld (1950) pointed out that an inherent limitation in the ability to move about the environment accurately and safely accompanies blindness. In addition, Fraiberg (1977) demonstrated how the absence of the "distant lure" provided by visual stimuli interfered with the natural and timely emergence of the ability to crawl and walk in children with congenital blindness. Fraiberg also demonstrated how the child who was showing readiness could be encouraged to crawl or walk by the use of sound stimuli. The frustration of a child's physical development needs encountered at the crawling stage of motor development has also been used to explain the progression of certain stereotypic behaviors, sometimes called "blindisms," which are observable actions or mannerisms that involve an undifferentiated form of energy discharge. For example, a frequently observed "blindism" among persons with congenital blindness is rocking back and forth when standing or sitting.

Independent travel can be facilitated and taught to counter any mobility-related limitations. However, it is suggested that the rehabilitation counselor not assume that all clients have had formal instruction in orientation and mobility (O&M) while in school. O&M is a body of specialized techniques that enable people to move about and travel independently, and these techniques are taught by O&M instructors specially trained to work with individuals who are visually impaired (see Chapter 9). Although many educational programs provide such instruction, not all do. Nor do all students take advantage of the training when it is offered or even benefit from it at the time it is provided. In addition, the home environment, including the attitudes of parents or the neighborhood setting, has an impact on the child's use of any mobility skills that may have been learned. A thorough mobility assessment is recommended, as well as the provision of training to address any gaps in the person's skills in this area—which can be so critical for an individual's personal and vocational success.

Among infants who were blind, Fraiberg (1977) also identified a delay in the development of the skill of reaching for and grasping an object. Characteristically, the children studied maintained their hands at shoulder height and did not use their fingers effectively for exploring objects. Not only did they not reach and grasp at the appropriate time, but, when toys were put into their hands, they showed no interest in exploring them. Fraiberg demonstrated how the proper developmental sequence could be facilitated, but in addition to these perceptions, she observed that many school-age children who were blind may not have accomplished this developmental milestone in a timely manner. Because the hands of many children do not habitually make sensitive discriminations and the individuals do not seek and explore objects, they may not possess some of the special skills needed for reading braille and performing other tactile tasks. For reasons such as these, children who are blind or visually impaired often receive training in sensory awareness and tactile discrimination.

In light of these considerations, the rehabilitation counselor should arrange a thorough assessment of the individual's motor skills, for example, the ability to read braille or successfully manipulate objects or perform other tactile discrimination tasks. An assessment of these skills is important to ensure appropriate vocational training for persons with congenital blindness who have deficits in these areas.

Psychosocial Abilities

Research provides no clear evidence of patterns of behavior, personality, or emotional development that is characteristic of either children or adults who are congenitally blind. When psychosocial problems do arise, Fraiberg (1977) suggested that they result from a lack of bonding between an infant and parent. Because bonding is the basis for the development of other human relationships, Fraiberg demonstrated a method for helping parents understand the basic communication needs of a child who is blind, so that the bonding can occur. More recently, additional attention has been paid to how to enhance infant–parent communication and interaction with children who are visually impaired (see, for example, Ferrell, 1985; Chen & Dote-Kwan, 1995).

Two frequently quoted studies in psychosocial development (i.e., Cowen, Underberg, Verrillo & Benham, 1961; Sommers, 1944) show no significant differences in adjustment between adolescents with and without sight. Focusing on a healthy self-concept as one of the key indicators

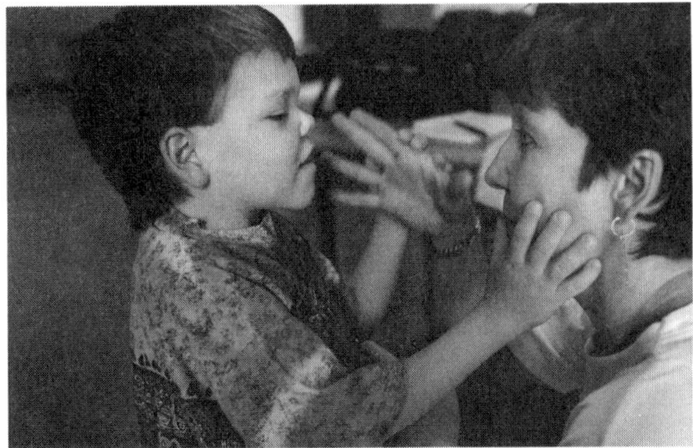

Like every child, a child who is congenitally blind benefits from interaction with his or her parents because bonding is the basis for the development of other human relationships.

of a good personal adjustment, Tuttle and Tuttle (1996) identified several studies, however, that found conflicting results when the self-concepts of adolescents who are blind were compared with those of sighted adolescents. Accordingly, it is advised that rehabilitation counselors not assume that a client reflects any particular set of psychosocial characteristics.

The counselor can benefit from understanding the behavior of clients in the context of the social environment in which they have grown. Children with congenital blindness grow and develop in environments that may frequently reflect the stereotypical and sometimes negative attitudes of people toward blindness in general and toward people who are visually impaired. These factors can have a negative effect on the self-esteem of such children. Also, because blindness is a low incidence impairment, many children who are congenitally blind grow up without adequate role models who are blind. They do not always receive feedback about the inappropriateness of certain behaviors, and both they and their parents often have difficulty sorting out what is an acceptable accommodation to their blindness.

In general, when working with adventitious onset, counselors will spend a large amount of time with clients working through the effects of the traumatic loss of vision and the need to recover a sense of equilibrium. This type of emotional reaction is generally not associated with congenital onset. However, Tuttle and Tuttle (1996) expressed the view that people who are congenitally blind can have certain life experiences that force them to realize in a new way that they are different from their peers. This new realization can have the same type of traumatic effect on a person who is congenitally blind that the sudden loss of vision can have on a person who becomes adventitiously blind.

Travel Skills

It is highly recommended that O&M services begin for the child who is congenitally blind at a very early age. During preschool years, a mobility specialist can serve as a consultant to parents and teachers in relation to basic concept development that will be important later for independent travel. The mobility specialist can explain how to encourage the child to explore the environment and how to employ basic protective techniques when doing so (Ferrell, 1979; see also Chapter 9). More recently, mobility specialists have been experimenting with teaching preschool children how to use the long cane, an important mobility aid (Pogrund, Fazzi, & Schreier, 1993; Pogrund & Rosen, 1989) in addition to other alternative mobility devices (Bobash, 1988).

In general, it is advised that the child who is blind, whenever possible, be given sufficient O&M training to keep up with other children in terms of getting around the home or backyard, the neighborhood, the school, the local business areas, and eventually into larger business areas using public transportation. The recommended pattern is that in which formal instruction is given until the child is appropriately self-sufficient. The use of these skills will help the child to become more confident as the mobility specialist works to provide the next level of skill instruction.

The rehabilitation counselor is encouraged to attempt to understand what the pattern of instruction has been, the client's current level of skill and self-confidence, and the amount of use the client makes of the skills learned. In addition, consultation with the O&M instructor who worked with the client can provide more information than may be conveyed in the formal reports. For example, an adolescent may have received training in how to travel independently, but may not have used those skills for a variety of reasons, such as fear, lack of interest or need, or, perhaps, because of parental overprotectiveness. In such situations, refresher training may be needed as part of the rehabilitation program.

Independent Living and Vocational Skills

Patterns in areas of self-care and other living skills are similar to those observed with travel skills. That is, most students will receive some

The early intervention of training in mobility and protective techniques is important in helping a child who is blind become more confident and self-sufficient.

training in the basic skills required for functioning as an independent person. Critical factors that determine the skill level the client brings to a rehabilitation program will be the amount of use that has been made of the training received and the appropriateness, quality, and thoroughness of the training provided.

In the areas of career education, work experience, and vocational training, a person's lack of the incidental knowledge that is learned through vision is often evident. Hatlen and Curry (1987) pointed out that "sighted children learn much of what they know about the world of work through their observations of others, either in real life or through the media" (p. 11). This process begins in preschool years and continues throughout life. It is recommended that the rehabilitation counselor inquire of all clients with congenital blindness, and of their teachers and parents (when available and appropriate), about the types of learning experiences (i.e., career education, work experience, and vocational training) that were provided while these clients were in school. For an individual who has received little in the way of formal experiences related to career education, it is expected that the counselor will be providing a large amount of much-needed education and information before the client is able to participate fully in making career choices. As with any client with limited exposure to careers, the counselor may want to validate a relatively inexperienced client's verbalized description of vocations and work opportunities, if the description appears unrelated to a functional concept. In a comparison of legally blind adults with congenital and adventitious vision loss, Crudden (1997) found no significant differences between the two groups. Persons with early onset of vision loss work a comparable number of hours, earn just as much money, are as satisfied, and retain their jobs as long as persons with later onset of vision loss.

Other Rehabilitation Considerations

Clients with congenital blindness most frequently enter a rehabilitation program through a direct referral from the school system prior to or immediately following graduation. Others, who may have tried to establish themselves in an adult placement or activity without intervention from the rehabilitation system, may turn to rehabilitation services as a result of experiencing functional, adjustment, or other difficulties. Still others may have had a successful adult experience without rehabilitation assistance and then may experience a further deterioration of vision or another disabling condition that requires rehabilitation assistance.

When a rehabilitation client with congenital blindness has been away from school for a period of time prior to contacting the rehabilitation system, it is suggested that the counselor who is aware of the present operation of the school program not assume that the operation was the same when the client was a student. School programs have undergone important changes in recent years, and, once again, the counselor is encouraged to conduct a thorough interview and assessment to fully understand what previous experiences the client has had and what skill level should be anticipated.

Conversely, rehabilitation counselors may find that clients who have recently graduated from school sometimes lack a sufficient level of maturity to follow through on plans that are mutually established by the client and the counselor. If this is the case, the counselor may have to continue to work with the client to develop skills needed for adult life through a planned program of increasing the clients' self-responsibility in the context of the rehabilitation planning.

Rehabilitation counselors serving persons with congenital visual impairments are also encouraged to learn how to work effectively with parents and other family members. Parents who are concerned about how their children will function on their own after graduation may have a significant effect on a client's feelings and behavior. As much as possible, the counselor is advised to focus the interactions and decision-making on the client, in addition to being sensitive to the most effective use of family involvement.

It is essential that a rehabilitation counselor make early contact with the student who is blind and is about to enter the adult world of careers to determine what vocational services will be needed by him or her in making a career choice.

Because the educational experiences of people with congenital or adventitious visual impairments vary, it is strongly suggested that the rehabilitation counselor make early contact, preferably while a student is still in school. This timely contact will assure the best access to the school's record of services received by the student and, consequently the outcomes of those services. It also promotes direct contact between the counselor and the student's teachers, who can elaborate on the formal reports and provide a more complete picture of the student's experiences.

In addition to early direct contact with students and teachers, it is helpful for the rehabilitation counselor to participate in the Individualized Educational Program (IEP) planning process for anticipated clients while they are still in school. Many teachers and school staff do not have an adequate concept of those skills a student will need after graduation and the opportunities that have to be considered. If the rehabilitation counselor becomes a participant in planning during the student's final school year or some period of time before then, there may be an increased chance to influence the direction of the school program toward skills or experiences that will have the greatest relevance for adult life (Sisson & Babeo, 1992).

Some people who have an adventitious visual impairment can learn to perform visual tasks by using low vision devices, such as hand-held magnifiers.

ADVENTITIOUS VISUAL IMPAIRMENTS

Individuals who at one time were sighted but who have subsequently lost some, if not all, of their vision are described as having an adventitious visual impairment. To individualize programming, it is recommended that the rehabilitation counselor understand the heterogenous, widely varied nature of the group of individuals with adventitious blindness. Some causes of adventitious blindness affect just the visual system, such as retinitis pigmentosa (RP), while others, such as diabetic retinopathy, have a systemic origin, potentially affecting other parts of the body. In certain instances, vision loss is sudden and traumatic, though not necessarily total. For others, the loss is gradual over months, years, or even a lifetime. Some individuals may have good central acuity, but have little or no peripheral vision, while others may have just the reverse. For some people, the loss of vision is stable or is medically stabilized, whereas others have vision that fluctuates daily or in different settings. Certain visual impairments require higher levels of illumination for optimum visibility, while others need lower levels. As Zimmerman (1992) pointed out, "there is no correlation between high levels of illumination and increased visual functioning. Lighting preferences among people with visual impairments are highly individualized. A person with cataracts or glaucoma may require lower light than one with retinitis pigmentosa" (p. 71). Some individuals with visual impairment can be helped to perform visual tasks by using magnifiers, electronic enlargers, or other devices, whereas others are unable to do so. The extreme variability in the nature and extent of vision loss is not always understood by either professionals or the general public, and may become a basis for misunderstanding and confusion.

Factors Relating to Adventitious Blindness

In large measure, a person's beliefs about visual impairment will determine his or her style of adaptation to vision loss. Many false notions about blindness frequently held by society in general are also believed by some people who acquire visual impairments. Rehabilitation counselors are strongly urged to confront and try to dispel these mythical and irrational beliefs. At the same time, there are some significant consequences of vision loss that must be acknowledged. The significance of these consequences varies with the lifestyles of the individuals prior to their visual impairments. Some of the real-life consequences (e.g., difficulties with pouring coffee or reading a book) are only temporary until adaptive or alternative skills are mastered; other consequences (e.g., the inability to drive a car or play tennis) are of a more permanent nature. Even in regard to the more permanent consequences, however, there are substitute strategies and activities that can be learned and that may be able to facilitate the satisfaction of basic needs and desires.

Those individuals who have lost part or all of their vision as young adults or as adults have in general already learned basic life skills as sighted persons. The process of "unlearning" techniques that require more sight than that which remains and then learning new approaches and unfamiliar coping strategies to accomplish formerly routine tasks may be both time consuming and frustrating. The areas that usually need to be addressed include personal and home management, communication, travel, recreation, and vocational skills (Tuttle & Tuttle, 1996). It is advised that an individual who acquires a visual impairment learn to build upon previous visual experiences without allowing them to interfere with learning to rely on the other senses.

Even without continued visual input, the organizational function of the visual experience continues to be effective after the onset of blindness. The differences in performance of the more complex spatial tasks between people who are congenitally blind and those who are adventitiously blind point to the enduring efficiency of the visual frame of reference even after the loss of vision (Warren, Asooshian, & Bollinger, 1973). Researchers have found that because individuals with adventitious blindness have been able to maintain and utilize a visual frame of reference, their concepts of their spatial environment are more accurate than those of persons with congenital blindness (Dodds, Howarth, & Carter, 1982; Lockman, Rieser, & Pick, 1981; Marmor, 1977; Rieser, Guth, & Hill, 1982).

However, rehabilitation counselors are encouraged to be aware that the visual imagery within that frame of reference becomes dated over time. This reality relates to two additional areas in which vision plays a dominant role for sighted individuals. First, it is through vision that many incidental bits of information are learned. This information is not sought but is accidentally observed (e.g., the name and location of a new fast-food establishment, a tree in the park that has recently been cut down, or the presence of a moving van in the neighborhood). Second, it is also through vision that nonverbal information is communicated in interactions between people. The frown, the shrug, or the stiffening of the body all send messages that are visually observed. Consequently, access to incidental information and to nonverbal communication will be limited in direct proportion to the amount of vision that has been lost. Learning to ask the right questions and being sensitive to such nonverbal clues as tone of voice or silence can compensate for some of these difficulties. For optimal adjustment to take place, the ability to develop personal life skills and adaptive behaviors needs to be accompanied by the internalization and assimilation of the newly acquired visual impairment into the individual's ego structure and self-concept.

Reactions to Loss of Vision

Various individuals (e.g., Carroll, 1961; Cholden, 1958; Tuttle & Tuttle, 1996) have described the process of adapting to a visual impairment. One of the classic scholars in this area was Cholden (1958), a psychiatrist. His beliefs are not generally accepted today, because he proposed that individuals who had lost their vision were essentially and fundamentally different from other people. Cholden also believed that rehabilitation was "a total reconstitution of the being to someone different from the previous being, in preparation for a different life" (p. 110). He adhered to the stage theory in describing the experiences of individuals who recently lost their sight, outlining a number of phases through which the person typically passed. Cholden indicated that individuals who lost their sight experienced shock, and frequently, depression before recovery was possible. The shock period, which might last from a few days to a few weeks, was viewed "as a period of protective emotional anesthesia which is available to the human organism under such stress" (pp. 73–74). A short period of mourning that Cholden termed "grieving for their 'dead' eyes," followed shock. Cholden believed that the successful accomplishment of some quickly attainable short-term goals and tasks facilitated the movement out of depression.

Father Carroll (1961), a chaplain for the Blinded Veterans Association for many years and another classic figure in the field of blindness, viewed loss of vision as a serious and complete disruption to the entire organism. "The blows which blindness deals to a person, the losses suffered, do not come on one by one to be dealt with one by one, but all together—whether blindness itself overtakes one slowly or suddenly" (p. 9). Carroll's religious orientation can be seen in his view of acquired blindness as a death and rebirth experience. "Loss of sight is a dying. . . . It is death to a way of life that had become part of the man. It is the end of acquired methods of doing things, the loss of built-up relationships with people, of ingrained relationships with an environment" (p. 11). In order to come to terms with oneself, Carroll believed that the sighted person must die and the new individual, the person who is blind, must emerge to once more become a whole person, but only if the individual is willing to go through the pain of death to sight.

Long before the concept became popular, Carroll (1961) identified the importance of grieving the loss of vision to the rehabilitation process. "Thus, in dealing with the . . . person [who is newly blinded], our first job is not to counsel that it is not bad, certainly not to say that it is not blindness. Rather it is to communicate the recognition that . . . person is lovable and loved, and that in their grief they do not grieve alone. Then, gradually, we can let the . . . person [who is newly blinded] see that it is possible that 'life is changed, not taken away.'" (p. 12). Carroll enumerated 20 losses that he felt were imposed upon the individual who loses vision. Each one is severe enough individually, but "together they make up the multiple handicap which is blindness. Each loss involves a painful farewell, (a 'death')" (p. 13). These losses can be summarized as follows:

- ◆ Basic losses to psychological security (involving physical integrity, confidence in the remaining senses, reality contact with environment, visual background, and light security);
- ◆ Losses in basic skills (involving mobility and techniques of daily living);
- ◆ Losses in communication (involving ease of written communication, ease of spoken communication, and informational progress);
- ◆ Losses in appreciation (involving visual perception of the pleasurable and visual perception of the beautiful);
- ◆ Losses concerning occupation and financial status (involving recreation, career, vocational goal, job opportunity, and financial security);
- ◆ Losses to the whole personality (involving personal independence, social adequacy, obscurity, self-esteem, and total personality organization).

Other models of adjustment to blindness have refuted the "loss" model, as described by Carroll and Cholden. For example, Tuttle and Tuttle (1996), rather than seeing adjustment problems as unique to individuals who are blind, viewed the adjusting process as a normal, healthy process used by all persons in responding to a severe trauma or crisis in their lives. Although Cholden (1958) and Carroll (1961) described the adjusting process in terms of a total reorganization of the self with the emergence of a new person, Tuttle and Tuttle argued that the person before and after blindness is essentially the same with the same personality and behavior traits, the same interests and abilities—except for vision—and the same likes and dislikes. Tuttle and Tuttle (1996) stated that the self-concept must be revised, which involves the examination of one's own attributes and values in light of the new trait of a visual impairment and the replacement of some previously perceived personal attributes and values with new ones; some are modified only partially, and, in the final analysis, most of these values and attributes can be left untouched. Dodds et al. (1994) developed an alternative, "structural" model of adjustment. Instead of viewing adjustment as focusing on grief work and addressing unconscious processes, Dodds's group looked at possible relationships between learned helplessness (Seligman, 1975, 1981), stigma and social stereotypes (Goffman, 1963), locus of control (Rotter, 1966), self-efficacy (Bandura, 1977), attributional style (Abramson, Seligman, & Teasdale, 1978), and hopelessness–depression (Abramson, Metalsky, & Alloy, 1989). Based on the results of their research, Dodds and colleagues suggested that (1) variables that counselors generally relate to motivation should be viewed as adjustment issues, instead of motivational issues, (2) counseling, in and of itself, may not enhance self-worth, but it can change the motivational factors that produce improvements in self-worth, and (3) cognitive counseling is the best approach, when counseling is indicated, because individuals view the success of rehabilitation as resulting from their own efforts, rather than the efforts of the rehabilitation professional.

Of particular importance for rehabilitation counselors, substantiated by the work of Dodds and his colleagues is that the requirement of mourning or a required period of mourning (Wright, 1990) should be eliminated from the counselor's repertoire of expectations. They offer the following example:

> Traditionally, clients receive skill training, combined with some form of counseling, or simply emotional support during rehabilitation. However with regard to the psychological needs of clients, it must be recognized that counseling, in whatever form it takes, and the acquisition of independent living skills are not mutually exclusive approaches. Clients who are obviously severely distressed require additional emotional support, whereas those who appear to be well-motivated and "together enough" to go straight into independent skill training should not have to undergo a "cure" for a condition from which they do not suffer. (p. 494)

Adjustment and Adventitious Blindness

It is a universal truth that everyone needs self-esteem, a sense of personal worth and personal adequacy, including self-respect and self-approval. In general, there are two primary sources for a person's self-esteem. Younger, less mature, more dependent people may rely almost exclusively on reflections from others, such as "what others say about me." Older, mature, independent people tend to develop an internal self-evaluation process for their sense of competence. Judgments about the degree of competence in their life's activities involve personal goals, standards, and values. The onset of an impairment, however, can diminish these feelings of personal competence.

Adjusting (or adapting) is the process of responding to the ever-changing demands in life and, as a result, is a lifelong endeavor. Tuttle and Tuttle (1996) do not believe that there is an ultimate static state of adjustment, for no sooner is a state of equilibrium reached than some new event or condition requires attention and disequilibrium is once again experienced. People with vision loss do not "adjust" to their impairments. Instead, adjusting can be described as the process of responding to life's demands, with the added stress of a visual impairment. This impairment is simply one of many personal attributes, some representing strengths and others representing limitations, with which an individual faces life's challenges.

Psychological Trauma

Trauma is the event or series of events that produces a sense of disequilibrium, incongruity, or vulnerability, creating stress and making a person anxious or upset. There are several possible occurrences that may precipitate a psychological trauma: experiencing the initial onset of a vision loss or subsequent losses, meeting new psychological situations or old unresolved problems that resulted from the loss of vision, and, encountering the devaluing stigma of blindness frequently expressed by society. When an individual has been prepared mentally and emotionally for any or all of these psychological traumas, the adjusting process will usually be less disruptive.

For the person who is adventitiously blind or visually impaired, a trauma may begin in the ophthalmologist's office or hospital when the doctor informs the patient of the loss of sight. On occasion, the rehabilitation counselor or spouse may also be involved in the awkward and difficult process of communicating this information. In any case, it is advised that the disconcerting news be shared with kind and gentle understanding, with direct and simple frankness, and without pity or condescension. At this very vulnerable time, the rehabilitation counselor is encouraged simply to provide physical and emotional support rather than yielding to the temptation to provide immediate direct intervention.

The nature and extent of the response varies considerably from one individual to the next. One 35-year-old man, after a car accident, suddenly became aware of his total blindness when bandages were removed from his eyes, while he was still recovering in the hospital. A middle-aged housewife, who had her prior suspicions confirmed when the ophthalmologist diagnosed her illness as macular degeneration, found the onset of trauma to be much more gradual. A veteran who lost his sight was not so much traumatized by the loss of vision as by the negative reactions of close family members.

Shock and Denial

Shock is a psychic anesthesia that numbs the mind, preventing disintegration. Denial is one method to escape coping with the requirements and implications of the disequilibrium caused by the onset of an impairment. Shock and denial are natural—and even healthy—responses if they are experienced only temporarily. If the denial persists, techniques can be employed that help individuals confront the reality of their situations. For example, a teacher with bilateral detached retinas was convinced that laser surgery would restore her vision. She stated how she had deliberately buried in the back recesses of her mind the unwanted thoughts of impaired vision. When a series of surgeries failed, some of her friends encouraged her in the belief that God was going to perform a miracle in her life. No miracle came. Through the use of these denials, she was able to maintain some semblance of normal daily routine. She felt no trauma at the time because she ignored all of the indicators.

Mourning and Withdrawal

As the shock begins to wear off, a person may become aware of a general state of incongruity or a global sense of loss. This phase is characterized by mourning and self-pity, which are frequently accompanied by withdrawal and isolation. It is recommended that individuals be allowed to mourn their loss of vision because giving expression to their sadness may be therapeutic (Riffenburgh, 1967). However, individuals who are engaged in self-pity tend to cut themselves off from their own support network, which can perpetuate feelings of isolation and loneliness. Hostility and anger may also begin to emerge and may be directed toward anyone who happens to be available.

During this phase, the person may experience a general loss of confidence, adequacy, or self-esteem due to either the recent vision loss or the negative, devaluing reflections from others. In either case, a troublesome sense of being more different from rather than being the same as others may be experienced. It is advised that the rehabilitation counselor continue to be an attentive, discerning listener while beginning to counteract the individual's feelings of inadequacy and incompetence by providing some easily mastered, practical solutions to personal and social management problems. New information or skills can serve as convincing evidence that all is not lost, that life is indeed manageable as a person with impaired vision (Tuttle & Tuttle, 1996). At this time, it is also highly recommended that the attitudes and behaviors of the family members be analyzed and addressed, if necessary, because adapting is more difficult when living with significant others who are exhibiting predominantly negative attitudes (Emerson, 1981).

Succumbing and Depression

As the shock continues to wear off, the individual may begin to ponder the many implications of decreased or lost vision. This phase is often characterized by the phrase "I can't." However, people's perceptions of what they can and cannot do are frequently distorted and unrealistic. As a result of pessimistic and negative perceptions of themselves and their abilities, individuals may have degrees of depression, which are common and usually temporary. For example, the father of a 6-year-old boy was gradually losing his vision to RP. He had enjoyed the outdoors, particularly contact sports. The son's innocent question asking to play ball triggered a chain reaction of thoughts: "I will never be able to play football with my son or take him hunting or teach him to drive or. . . ." This event ushered in a period of extreme depression in his life.

Through conversations with persons with visual impairments and family members, the rehabilitation counselor can obtain a fairly accurate picture of their feelings toward themselves and toward blindness. If they have any illogical, dysfunctional, or distorted beliefs about themselves or their visual impairments, the rehabilitation counselor is urged to reflect these attitudes and beliefs back and, if necessary, gently but firmly challenge them. It is also recommended that misconceptions about the consequences of visual impairment be corrected. The use of role models or biographies are sometimes helpful to individuals in developing more positive, realistic self-statements. When this happens, they are usually ready to begin identifying their assets and strengths, permitting a shift from "I can't" to "I can." Taking responsibility for their own behavior is encouraged and making excuses for irresponsible behavior is not acceptable. Finally, it is advisable that the rehabilitation counselor, through the use of role models with visual impairments and other techniques, provide convincing evidence that life is worthwhile, that life as a person with a visual impairment can be rich, full, and satisfying (Tuttle & Tuttle, 1996).

Reassessment and Reaffirmation

During the phase of reassessment and reaffirmation, individuals reevaluate their personal attributes, goals, and values. This may lead to a search for a personal identity and for the meaning of life. The individual becomes aware that some challenges can be avoided, some can be prevented by restructuring prior circumstances, and still others can be conquered through the development of adaptive and coping skills.

At this very delicate time, it is highly recommended that the rehabilitation counselor exhibit acceptance, respect, and understanding—now more than ever. The existential questions regarding meaning and purpose of life, free choice, and responsible action need to be explored after such a trauma as loss of sight. The rehabilitation counselor can help facilitate the redefining of individuals' perceptions of their assets and strengths. Based on these perceptions, individuals can then clarify their goals and values in life, pursuing some without any need for modifications, altering others, and substituting still others with those that are more appropriate. It is important that people who have acquired vision loss be able to reaffirm themselves and reaffirm the possibilities of life.

The process of reassessment and reaffirmation is experienced in various ways. One woman, after breaking glass cookware containing creamed corn, came to the realization that there was nothing to do but clean up the mess, because to give way to self-pity would only prolong continued defeat. Another person began to recognize that, although the visual impairment was certainly an inconvenience because it interfered in many ways, it was not the worst thing that could ever happen. Someone else described life as a card game with a hand that held no trumps; instead of throwing the cards on the table, the person decided to stick it out. In each case, the realization that came from within became the turning point.

Coping and Mobilization

In the coping and mobilization phase, the individual focuses on the development of suitable coping skills and adaptive behaviors. To accomplish this, a person must mobilize both internal and external resources. The goal is to enable individuals who have acquired visual impairments to manage more effectively the daily demands in their physical and social environments. Through improved coping skills, individuals can gain both self-assurance and self-confidence.

As a starting point, the rehabilitation counselor can begin focusing on planning a program that enables the individual to develop adequate coping skills and adaptive behaviors by involving him or her in formulating behavioral goals and objectives. A variety of techniques may be employed, such as precision teaching for social skills, behavior modeling, role playing, cognitive behavior modification, and behavior rehearsals (Corey, 1991). The individual may also need a restatement of or additional information about the condition or disability (e.g., cause, extent of impairment, or prognosis). The counselor is encouraged to take every opportunity to facilitate the individual's development of healthy attitudes toward self and the visual impairment.

An individual's efforts to acquire coping skills and adaptive behaviors are reminiscent of an adolescent's struggle toward independence. An older graduate student who had recently become blind discovered that she enjoyed being creative and finding new and different ways to accomplish formerly routine tasks. She found the use of technological aids and devices particularly challenging and rewarding. Some inner drive compelled her to prove to the world, and to herself, that she indeed was still competent and capable of functioning independently with a surprising degree of self-sufficiency.

Self-Acceptance and Self-Esteem

Too many rehabilitation counselors stop at the coping and mobilization phase because of their conviction that all psychological issues have been addressed. Rehabilitation counselors are encouraged to address self-acceptance and self-esteem needs. However, it is apparent that people can learn to live with their impairments without ever accepting themselves, much less developing any sense of self-worth. During this next phase, individuals learn not only to accept the visual impairment, but also to accept themselves as human, as people with many attributes, only one of which is the visual impairment. They discover that self-acceptance includes feelings of being comfortable with themselves, being at peace with themselves, and liking themselves, feelings that can be encouraged and nurtured. Self-acceptance frees noqindividuals to accept others which, in turn, allows them to be accepted and valued by others. This exchange is the basis of self-esteem. Vash (1981) refers to this level of the disability experience as "transcending the disability."

The rehabilitation counselor will also want to focus on helping the individual develop strong interpersonal relationship skills. Small group activities, providing Big Brother or Big Sister support to an individual who is coping with the recent onset of an impairment, and volunteer work assignments in the community are examples of opportunities that can foster the development of positive relationships. It is advised that the rehabilitation counselor allow individuals time and space to exercise independently their newly acquired coping skills. Soon after returning home from the hospital, a Vietnam veteran was approached by his 10-year-old daughter to go horseback riding as had been their custom. The father sadly explained that he was now blind and would be unable to ride. Not understanding or accepting this verdict, the daughter walked with him to the familiar setting of the barn. He discovered that saddling the horses was quite manageable and, with his daughter in the lead to warn him of low overhanging branches, they rode the 5-mile trail together. This little excursion did more than anything else to restore the veteran's self-confidence and his appreciation of life.

There are some common ways in which many individuals will react to the onset of an impairment. Similarities in response can be considered in terms of adjusting, adapting, and coping phases. Not all individuals will experience all of these phases. For that matter, they may not experience any of them. They are not hierarchical, that is, a person need not fully complete one phase before moving on to another. Instead, they are dynamic and fluid, with a significant amount of overlap between one phase and another. The manner in which the individual has previously responded to important life changes will usually suggest how that person will respond to the onset of an impairment.

The services of rehabilitation counselors and other members of the rehabilitation team can help individuals who acquire visual impairments work through whatever phases of the adjusting process they may experience (see Chapter 9). The acquisition of alternative skills and adaptive behaviors, along with appropriate attitudes concerning visual impairments, the self, and others, empowers individuals, increases their independence, and fosters self-esteem. The needs of individuals, however, not only vary from one phase to another, but there are considerable differences with respect to the intensity and duration of the cognitive, behavioral, and emotional reactions during each phase. The issues presented in the next sections represent only a few of the possible factors that influence the adjusting process.

Factors Influencing Reactions to Vision Loss

Vash (1981) identified the following three categories of factors that influence responses to a disability: (1) the nature of the disability, (2) the person, and (3) the environment. These categories are similar to those identified by Hudson (1994) (i.e., social factors, personal factors, and a combination) in a review of the literature on causes of reactions to adventitious blindness. The factors in each of these categories have implications for counselors. Because many of these factors are described in detail in other chapters of this textbook, only selected factors are discussed here.

The Nature of the Impairment

The category relating to the nature of the disability includes such factors as time of onset, type of onset, functions impaired, severity of the impairment, visibility of the impairment, stability of the impairment, and pain.

Degree of Remaining Vision. Individuals with mild vision loss in general require fewer and less extensive adaptive behaviors and skills, whereas individuals with no remaining vision require many more. Individuals at either end of the continuum of vision loss may sometimes have an easier time with the adjustment process than do those in the middle. Many people who are visually impaired may experience the sensation of being in limbo—that is, they are not blind, nor do they have unimpaired vision. On the one hand, some may tend to reject or are unable to profit fully from the adaptive behaviors and skills that symbolize or are associated with "blindness." On the other hand, some may be unable to function fully independently without some basic accommodations. This ambiguous state of affairs can result in a poorly defined self-concept and socially awkward situations (see Corn & Koenig, 1996).

Low vision can afford some individuals the opportunity to hide or conceal their disabilities, acting as if they could see (Wright, 1990), if they choose to do so. As Safilios-Rothschild (1970) pointed out, "the more an individual has a chance to hide a disability, or the more the resulting limitations are diffused and maldefined, the more one tends to avoid integrating the necessary changes into one's body image and self-concept" (p. 96). Similarly, Wright (1990) noted the problems of marginality, of not really belonging to either the blind or sighted group, and the stigma of an impairment, which can prompt an individual to attempt to conceal a condition, even though "concealing the disability does not eradicate it; it still remains in the eye of the person as the barrier to . . . acceptance by the sought-for-group" (p. 138).

Stability of Vision. The stability or constancy of vision, regardless of the degree of vision loss, is another factor influencing how individuals respond to visual impairment. Some conditions are stable or constant for most of a person's life; some losses degenerate slowly over a period of months and even years, and still others fluctuate from one day to another and from one situation to another. Personal uncertainty about one's vision is frequently accompanied by anxiety and fear, and can keep a person's feelings in a state of flux (Schulz, 1980). Referring to the instability of vision among some of their patients, Oehler-Giarrantana and Fitzgerald (1980) commented that "for most of the patients, loss of vision would have been a relief after months and years of fluctuating vision" (p. 464).

A person with gradually deteriorating vision may not experience shock and depression or other phases of the adjustment process until the loss is severe enough to interfere with daily functioning. Subsequent cycles back through the process of adjusting may occur with each succeeding degree of significant sight loss that requires new adaptive behaviors and skills. As Stogner (1980) noted, persons with gradually deteriorating vision may experience psychological adjustment problems, in varying degrees of intensity, with each new degree of vision loss.

Additional Impairments. Another factor influencing adjustment is the extent to which people with visual impairments may also be contending with additional conditions or disabilities that precipitate issues in their lives. This double jeopardy results when two conditions occur simultaneously, each making the person vulnerable to additional medical complications, to discriminatory action, or to being stigmatized. A person with a visual impairment, in addition to a facial disfigurement, or quadriplegia, or deafness, faces increasingly complex issues of adjusting and adapting become more complex.

Some evidence for the additional difficulties experienced by persons with multiple impairments was provided in a study by Barron (1973), who compared individuals with visual impairments resulting from diabetes with those whose vision loss was caused by RP. In general, Barron found that the individuals whose loss of vision was caused by RP were better adjusted and had better coping skills than did the individuals who had impaired vision resulting from diabetes and the multiple health problems associated with it.

Smithdas (1975), who is both deaf and blind, described the group identity issues that accompany deaf-blindness. "Socially the deaf-blind belong to the deaf group, as they use the same communication methods as the deaf; but technically they belong to the blind group, because they use the tools, devices and aids, and many of the methods used by blind persons" (p. 3). The dual impairments of deafness and blindness also produce communication barriers that can impede social development and social interactions. Moreover, in the case of two sensory disabilities, the interaction of deafness with blindness is much more than the sum of two independent impairments.

The Person

Personal characteristics that affect adjustment to vision loss include factors relating to gender; interests, values, goals; activities, remaining resources, and other personality variables.

Personality Characteristics. The individual's personality, including ego strengths and self-concept, established prior to the onset of a disability is a highly significant predictor of the outcome of the adjusting process (Emerson, 1981; Rusalem, 1972; Vander Kolk, 1981). After testing 114 adults who recently became blind, along with a significant other person for each subject, Greenough, Keegan, and Ash (1978) found that those experiencing less depression had been viewed as "assertive, independent, stubborn, venturesome, uninhibited, experimenting, free-thinking, aggressive, and socially bold" (p. 87) prior to their loss of vision, whereas those experiencing more severe depression had been viewed as "humble, mild, obedient, conforming, shy, restrained, conservative" (p. 87).

Vander Kolk (1981), in discussing the personality determinants of adjustment among individuals with recent vision loss, stated that:

> A somewhat dependent person will likely become more dependent. A very independent person may at first feel a greater shock, and perhaps depression, then assert his or her independence to the maximum extent possible. Those who overreacted to the stresses of everyday life are more likely to suffer a great deal emotionally when they lose their vision. The socially introverted person may become a recluse. (p. 142)

Prior Coping Experiences. Along with the basic personality characteristics, previous experiences with traumas or crises help to establish a person's style of coping and pattern of problem solving (Emerson, 1981). "The way the individual has learned to cope with major life problems and emergencies antedating the blindness will largely determine his or her ego-recovery capacity as far as blindness is concerned, assuming, of course that the external obstacles are not too great" (Cholden, 1958, p. 73). It is notable that the pattern of problem solving and the style of decision-making are themselves subject to cultural and ethnic variations.

Prior Attitudes Toward Blindness. An individual's attitudes toward blindness, prior to the onset of blindness, also influence a person's adjustment. For many people with a recent vision loss, these attitudes may be more detached and abstract because they are usually developed long before the actual onset of vision loss. Conversely, the pre-onset attitudes of many who have been visually impaired for a while may be much more personalized because they are referring to a personal attribute. In either case, such pre-onset attitudes tend to be predominantly negative, derogatory, and devaluing, thus potentially placing the person in an inferior status position. These attitudes toward blindness are usually learned unconsciously and incidentally from the portrayals of blindness in the media and literature, from the talk among significant others in a person's social environment, or from an individual's own fantasy or imagination. Regardless of the source, devaluing pre-onset attitudes can have a negative effect on a person's adjusting process.

Age at Onset. The individual's age at onset influences the areas of concern prompted by the vision loss, which may tend to exacerbate previously identified issues. For example, during their adolescent years, many people are struggling with peer pressures and with issues related

An older individual who develops a visual impairment later in life and who may already have to contend with additional health problems may need to learn new approaches and strategies to perform formerly routine tasks on the job and in daily life.

to social acceptance, with their search for identity and independence, and with preparations for their careers. "The older the child when the loss of sight occurs, the greater will be the emotional and physical impact, the longer [s]he will take to adjust to living with impaired vision, and the more support [s]he will need from his[her] family" (Scott, Jan, & Freeman, 1977, p. 13). According to Lowenfeld (1971), the concerns and needs of adolescents are compounded by blindness, especially in the areas of "sex curiosity, dating, the lure of the car, and concern for the future" (p. 184). When onset occurs during adolescence, additional difficulties that arise need to be understood in light of age-typical concerns.

In contrast to adolescents, adults during the working years have usually already (1) established their own identity, (2) achieved an independent status, (3) developed adequate competence and confidence in their own abilities, and (4) established themselves in jobs. Loss of vision during this period may undermine a person's self-confidence, sense of competence, and adequacy. Frequently, it is assumed that a person can no longer continue in his or her vocation, which can precipitate anxiety about future employment and financial independence.

Some people, during their retirement years, may have less flexible patterns of behavior and may have already experienced such other stressors as feelings of diminished value to the community, loss of sensory and mental abilities, additional health problems, decreasing stamina, and diminished monetary resources (Rosenbloom, 1984). Children have left home, and there is an increasing probability of losing friends to death. In light of such circumstances, learning new adjustment behaviors and coping skills can frequently be discouraging and depressing, especially if an individual's pattern of behavior has become somewhat rigid and inflexible. Attempting to cope with a vision loss can be a fearful and unnerving experience for many older people, particularly if they are already coping with other traumas of lowered self-worth and adequacy, undermined confidence, social isolation, and threats to remaining independent. Although some researchers have found a relationship between depression and blindness in older individuals (Branch, Horowitz, & Carr, 1989), it has not been universally demonstrated. Some researchers (e.g., Teitelbaum, Davidson, Gravetter, Taub, & Teitelbaum, 1994) found that depression in older veterans was not predicted by extent of vision loss, age, or the number of systemic diseases, but rather by the self-reports of the participants' general overall health. The researchers hypothesized that the findings may have resulted from envionmental factors such as spousal support and access to the array of services for veterans, for example, psychological therapy, low vision training, monetary benefits, and training in activities of daily living.

The Environment

Environmental factors include the immediate environment (i.e., family acceptance and support, income, available community resources), and the broader cultural environment (i.e., technological support, agencies and services). Spouses, parents, siblings, and friends are all members of an individual's personal support network. When someone experiences a vision loss, his or her significant others also have to contend with their previously held stereotypes and with other issues related to adjustment (Gardner, 1982; Neu, 1975; Schulz, 1980; Scott et al., 1977). As Winkler (1975) stated, "blindness in a single individual inevitably becomes a family affair. All members of that person's family are forced to share it . . . in some way" (p. 19). Similarly, Moos and Tsu (1977) stated that "family members and friends, as well as patients, are affected by the crisis, encounter many of the same or closely related adaptive tasks, and use the same coping skills" (p. 8). As previously noted, understanding, acceptance, and respect, whether from parents, a spouse, siblings, or close friends, contribute greatly to a person's healthy adjustment and positive self-esteem.

Rehabilitation counselors can help family and friends understand the importance of encouragement, praise, and acknowledgment of new accomplishments. They can also help members of the support network to realize the value of emotional support, and some of the problems with providing too much support. By offering too much assistance, the network can inadvertently reinforce the person's "I can't" beliefs, rather than the "I can" beliefs. Similarly, giving too much assistance can contribute to succumbing (i.e., giving in to the disability) and hinder the development of coping skills (Wright, 1990).

SUMMARY

Individuals with congenital blindness frequently have different needs and experiences than do individuals with adventitious blindness. The effect of congenital blindness is often observable in such areas as sensory abilities, cognitive abilities, motor abilities, psychosocial abilities, travel skills, and independent living and vocational skills. However, the research suggests no clear evidence of a pattern of behaviors, personality, or emotional development that is characteristic of children or adults who have congenital visual impairments. Although blindness has a major effect on mobility, travel skills, and selected cognitive abilities, most of these effects of congenital visual impairment can be ameliorated through appropriate educational programs, and some disappear in the course of growth and development. There are no known consequences of congenital blindness or visual impairment that can be seen consistently in all adults with congenital visual impairments.

As with individuals with congenital blindness, there is no unique psychology or personality attributable to a group of individuals solely on the basis of a visual impairment. Individuals with adventitious blindness or visual impairment do, however, usually have to contend with more psychosocial issues associated with the loss of vision. Individuals who lose their vision often have to "unlearn" techniques that require more sight than that which remains, but they can build on their previous visual experiences. The psychosocial issues associated with loss of vision parallel those associated with other acquired disabilities: for example, threats to self-esteem, feelings of competence, and self-worth. Many individuals experience certain response patterns (e.g., mourning, depression, anger, coping) and can benefit from rehabilitation counseling services. There are tremendous variations in response to vision loss that are a function of the impairment itself, the individual, and other environmental factors. Knowledge of these response patterns and appropriate interventions by rehabilitation counselors can assist individuals who have lost their vision, in making the necessary adaptations and learning new skills that can restore a sense of equilibrium to their lives.

LEARNING ACTIVITIES

1. Read an autobiography of a person with a congenital or adventitious visual impairment and analyze the forces and experiences that

seem to have had the greatest effect, both positive and negative, on that person's self-concept.

2. Interview a rehabilitation counselor who works with people with visual impairments. Ask the counselor to identify those elements that are different in working with people with congenital impairments versus individuals with adventitious impairments.

3. Interview an adult whose visual impairment is congenital and identify the age at which the individual first traveled independently in business areas, the age at which the individual had his or her first work experiences, and the age at which the individual first lived independently. Compare that individual's experiences to common experiences of young adults without visual impairments.

4. Interview an individual with an adventitious visual impairment who has retired from a successful employment career and who lost his or her vision at least 15 years prior to retirement. What challenges did the individual experience in maintaining his or her employment or securing new employment?

CHAPTER 4

Low Vision and Low Vision Devices

Kathleen E. Fraser

As already discussed in prior chapters, the majority of individuals who are designated legally blind or severely visually impaired have some usable vision, usually referred to as low vision. Low vision services, which are designed to maximize the individual's efficient use of the visual system, can therefore be a critical component of the rehabilitation plan. Low vision services typically consist of (1) an examination of the individual's visual system and visual functioning, (2) instruction to maximize the use of the client's vision, (3) the prescription of eyeglasses (when appropriate), (4) the prescription of various optical, electro-optical, and nonoptical devices (also when appropriate) designed to enhance visual functioning, and (5) instruction in the effective use of these devices. It is highly recommended that rehabilitation counselors play a role in the provision of low vision services. Often it is the rehabilitation counselor who imparts information to the client about specialized low vision services, facilitates the appointments, and provides support throughout the rehabilitation process. The rehabilitation counselor is strongly urged to understand the processes involved in low vision rehabilitation, as well as the benefits and limitations of the various options available to improve the client's overall functioning. The objectives of this chapter are to (1) review some of the common causes of visual impairment, (2) discuss the functional implications of different types of visual impairments, (3) discuss the clinical measurement of visual functioning, (4) examine the management of different types of vision loss, (5) review the basic functional optics relating to low vision optical devices, and (6) consider the use and range of the various types of optical systems.

In general, the term *low vision* refers to any visual limitation that is not correctable by conventional eyeglasses or medical or surgical treatment that interferes with a person's ability to perform such everyday activities as reading newsprint. (For a discussion of related terms, see Chapter 1.) Vision loss can be quantified as a loss of visual acuity, visual field, or contrast sensitivity. These concepts will be explained later in this chapter.

The Lighthouse National Survey on Vision Loss (1995) has indicated that there are 13.5 million adults (or approximately one in six Americans) over the age of 45 who are visually impaired. The incidence of visual impairment increases with age; over the age of 75, approximately one adult in four reports a visual impairment that interferes with the ability to read regular newsprint with eyeglasses, or to see a face across a room. In addition to these types of age-related impairments, there are also a number of congenital, hereditary, and acquired ocular and systemic condi-

The editors wish to acknowledge the contributions of Dr. Samuel B. Johnson to an earlier version of this chapter.

tions that cause visual impairment in children and young adults. Also, advances in medical care increase the survival of individuals with systemic health conditions, severe physical impairments, and head trauma, many of whom have visual impairments and need low vision care.

Many people with low vision are considered legally blind. Legal blindness is defined by the Social Security Administration (SSA) as "vision in the better eye after best correction of 20/200 or less" or "contraction of the peripheral visual fields in the better eye (1) to 10 degrees or less from the point of fixation; or (2) so the widest diameter subtends an angle no greater than 20 degrees." As indicated in Chapter 1, this definition does not account for the great number of individuals with reduced visual functioning (but who are not blind) that significantly interferes with their ability to do everyday activities. Therefore, for those charged with rehabilitation needs, a more functional approach to specifying visual impairment is appropriate (Corn & Koenig, 1996, Chapter 1). It is useful for rehabilitation professionals to think about vision loss in terms of the area of visual field affected (because loss of visual field can have a significant impact on the person's functional abilities). Faye (1984b) specifies vision loss as one of the following three types:

1. No specific visual field defect, but an overall blur, glare, or haze, impaired central vision without a scotoma [(blind spot)], and normal peripheral vision. This can be because of an abnormality of the refractive media (cornea, lens, or vitreous), or a macular or retinal defect. Examples of this are cataracts, aniridia, and albinism.
2. Central visual field impairment with a scotoma or distortion at or near the macula. Examples of this are macular degeneration, toxoplasmosis, and retinopathy of prematurity (ROP).
3. Peripheral visual field impairment with loss of specific parts of the peripheral vision (hemianopia) or constriction of the field. Examples of this are caused by stroke, glaucoma, and retinitis pigmentosa (RP).

CAUSES OF VISUAL IMPAIRMENT

Any condition that affects not only the eyeball but also the visual pathways, visual cortex, or oculomotor system can interfere with normal visual functioning. There are numerous causes of visual impairment; the more frequently encountered causes are briefly defined in the following subsections, along with the functional implications of each. Table 4.1 lists in a quick reference format additional causes of visual impairment most commonly encountered by rehabilitation counselors.

Readers should note that many of the terms used in this chapter are defined more fully in Chapter 2. They may therefore wish to read these chapters in conjunction with one another (for more comprehensive information, see Corn & Koenig, 1996; Jose, 1983; Newell, 1992; Pavan-Langston, 1985; Vaughan, Asbury, & Riordan-Eva, 1992).

Age-related Macular Degeneration

Age-related macular degeneration (AMD) is also called age-related maculopathy (ARM) and is a degeneration of the central portion of the retina, or the macula, which is responsible for detail vision. The cause is not completely understood, although most affected individuals are over the age of 65. Heredity may also be a factor. Age-related macular degeneration can be classified as either dry or wet. Dry macular degeneration is a gradual process for which there is no effective treatment, although studies suggest vitamin therapy may slow down the progression in some individuals. With wet macular degeneration, there is hemorrhage or fluid leakage in the macular area, which can cause sudden changes in vision, and which may be arrested with laser treatment. However, the end result of both forms of macular degeneration is the same: eventual loss of acuity to be-

Table 4.1. Causes of Visual Impairment

Condition	Structure Affected/ Physical Manifestation	Onset	Cause	Acuity	Visual Field	Other Factors
Achromatopsia	Partial or complete absence of cone cells in retina	Birth	Inherited	20/200	Normal	Color vision loss, nystagmus, photophobia
Albinism, ocular	Lack of pigment cells in eye	Birth	Inherited	20/70 to 20/200	Normal	Nystagmus, strabismus, photophobia
Albinism, oculocutaneous	Lack of pigment cells in skin, hair, eyes	Birth	Inherited	20/200 to 20/400	Normal	Nystagmus, strabismus, photophobia
Aniridia	Failure of iris tissue to grow	Birth	Inherited or sporadic	20/200	Normal	Nystagmus, photophobia, can worsen if secondary or corneal scarring occurs
Best's disease	Cysts in macula rupture and scar	Usually mid-teens	Inherited	May be good early, 20/200 after cyst ruptures	Central scotoma	After cyst ruptures, vision usually stabilizes
Choroideremia	Degeneration of the choroid	Usually mid-teens	Inherited	May be good until middle age	Progressive peripheral loss	Poor night vision can lead to blindness
Coloboma	Variable involvement of iris, ciliary body, choroid, retina, optic nerve	Birth	Inherited or sporadic	Depending on degree of involvement of macula and optic nerve	Superior visual field loss	Nystagmus if acuity is poor, strabismus and photophobia possible
Cone rod degeneration or dystrophy	Cone cells, then rod cells in retina	By age 20	Inherited	20/200 to 20/400	Progressive central and peripheral loss	Nystagmus if congenital, loss of color vision, photophobia
Cortical visual Impairment	Visual pathways or visual cortex	Any age, depending on when injury or insult occurs	Anoxia, trauma, tumor, stroke	Variable, depending on degree of injury	Variable, depending on degree of injury	Poor visual perceptual skills
Histoplasmosis	Inflammation of retina and choroid	Any age, when infection occurs	Systemic fungal infection	Depending on degree of retinal inflammation	If macula involved, central scotomas and distortion	Can recur with further vision loss
Keratoconus	Central corneal thinning and scarring	Usually teens to twenties	Unknown	Depending on degree of corneal distortion, eventually glasses do not correct but contact lenses may	None	Photophobia, may eventually require corneal transplant

Table 4.1. *Continued*

Condition	Structure Affected/ Physical Manifestation	Onset	Cause	Acuity	Visual Field	Other Factors
Leber's congenital amaurosis	Generalized retinal degeneration	Birth or shortly after	Appears to be inherited	20/200 or worse	Central and peripheral vision losses	
Leber's optic atrophy	Optic neuritis leads to optic atrophy	Teens to twenties	Inherited	20/200 or worse	Central and paracentral scotomas	Visual acuity can improve or decline after onset
Macular hole	Retinal hole in macular area	Usually adults	Can be associated with trauma but usually idiopathic	20/200 or better	Central scotoma and distortion	
Malignant myopia	Retinal thinning	Childhood	Severe myopia may be familial	Acuity is dependent on degree of retinal thinning	Can have central or paracentral scotoma	Can be progressive
Micropthalmos	Unilateral or bilateral small, malformed eye	Birth	Growth defect	Acuity is dependent on extent of tissue involvement	Dependent on extent of tissue involvement	If bilateral, nystagmus
Optic nerve hypoplasia	Unilateral or bilateral underdeveloped optic nerve	Birth	Isolated or associated with neurological malformation	Acuity is dependent on extent of tissue involvement	Dependent on extent of tissue involvement	If acuity is reduced, nystagmus
Retinoblastoma	Retinal tumor	Birth	Inherited or sporadic	Acuity is dependent on extent of tissue involvement	Dependent on extent of tissue involvement	Strabismus, if both eyes are involved, may have nystagmus
Retinoschisis	Splitting of retinal layers	Within first decade	Inherited	Near normal or reduced, can progress to 20/200	Can have central scotoma	May have strabismus
Rubella (congenital)	Microphthalmos, cataract, nonprogressive retinitis	Birth	Maternal rubella infection during first trimester of pregnancy	Acuity is dependent on extent of tissue involvement	Dependent on extent of tissue involvement	If acuity is reduced, nystagmus and strabismus
Stargardt's macular degeneration	Retina and retinal pigment epithelium	Usually by twenties	Inherited	20/200 to 20/400	Central scotoma	
Toxoplasmosis	Retinal scarring	Birth	Protozoan infection of mother transferred to fetus	Acuity is dependent on extent of macular scarring	Central or paracentral scotoma	If acuity is reduced, nystagmus and strabismus

tween 20/200 to 20/400, in addition to the development of a central blurred, distorted, or blind spot that is located where the 20/20 acuity formerly was located. The peripheral vision remains good and, in general, individuals with macular degeneration do not become completely blind.

Amblyopia

Amblyopia is unilateral or bilateral reduced vision that is not fully attributable to organic causes, and is usually associated with strabismus or a high uncorrected refractive error. Vision can be improved if aggressive therapy (use of eyeglasses, patching, or other measures) is initiated early in life. Surgery may also be indicated to straighten a strabismic eye.

Cataract

A cataract is the opacification of the crystalline lens of the eye. Congenital cataracts are present at birth or appear within the first three months; these may be unilateral or bilateral, inherited, or associated with other conditions (e.g., microphthalmia, Down syndrome, rubella). Cataracts may be stationary or progressive, and may be so small that they do not interfere with a person's vision. If vision is impaired, however, surgery should be performed as soon as possible. They are also associated with such systemic conditions as diabetes, the use of certain medications, trauma, or the aging process. In adults, cataract extraction is usually followed by intraocular lens (IOL) implantation (unless contraindicated). Implants may also be appropriate for some infants and children. When an implant is not placed after cataract extraction, the focusing power of the crystalline lens must be replaced with eyeglasses or contact lens correction (the optically preferred correction). In some cases, cataract extraction is contraindicated (because of the potential for complications, lack of vision in the other eye, or systemic health concerns that do not permit the surgery). Cataracts can cause reduced acuity, blurriness throughout the entire visual field, poor contrast sensitivity, or photophobia.

Cerebrovascular Accident or Stroke

Vision loss can be caused by a cerebrovascular accident or a stroke resulting from hemorrhage and anoxia in any part of the brain. Depending on the part of the brain that has been affected, there may be little to no visual impairment, or any combination of poor visual acuity, visual field loss, diplopia (double vision), distortion, glare sensitivity, or such visual perceptual difficulties as visual agnosia (objects are seen but not recognized).

Cortical Visual Impairment

Any limitation in visual functioning caused by such problems in the visual cortex as microcephaly, or brain injury from anoxia, trauma, tumors, or stroke is referred to as cortical visual impairment. Although the eyes may be normal, visual input to the brain is not interpreted properly, which results in poor visual functioning.

Diabetic Retinopathy

Diabetic retinopathy is caused by vascular abnormalities of the retina resulting from diabetes. This can cause hemorrhaging, edema (swelling), neovascularization (new blood vessel growth), scar tissue formation, and retinal detachment. Complications also include cataracts and glaucoma. Treatment may involve laser photocoagulation of the retina, or when indicated, vitrectomy, retinal detachment repair, or cataract or glaucoma surgery. Regardless of treatment, there may be reduced visual acuity, central or multiple paracentral blind spots, reduced contrast sensitivity, peripheral visual field loss, poor vision in dim lighting, and glare sensitivity. Refractive error and visual functioning may be affected by blood glucose levels.

Glaucoma

Glaucoma affects the optic nerve, and is usually associated with increased intraocular pressure caused by inadequate drainage of the aqueous humor through the anterior chamber angle. Congenital glaucoma can be inherited, is most often bilateral, and can be associated with other ocular abnormalities (e.g., aniridia, coloboma, Marfan's syndrome). Glaucoma can also be the result of trauma, can be associated with either diabetic retinopathy or aging (the most common cause). Low tension glaucoma is a form of glaucoma in which the nerve is damaged but intraocular pressure is within normal limits. The goal of treatment is to maintain intraocular pressure at a level at which no further damage occurs. Treatment includes topical and/or oral medications, laser surgery, or filtering surgery. Glaucomatous optic atrophy results in reduced visual acuity, peripheral and central visual field disturbances, poor contrast sensitivity, poor color perception, and glare sensitivity.

Nystagmus

An involuntary, rhythmic oscillation of the eyes, nystagmus is most often associated with any condition that causes reduced visual acuity within the first few months of life. Congenital nystagmus refers to this condition but without any other ocular abnormality (i.e., the eyes are normal but they move continuously). The eye movement usually decreases on convergence. Often a gaze angle (or null point) exists at which the nystagmus slows. Sometimes individuals adopt a head turn to maximize this null point. Surgery may be helpful in slowing down the nystagmus or reducing the head turn, but it will not completely eliminate the movement. Nystagmus can also be acquired as a result of multiple sclerosis or brain trauma. If the nystagmus is acquired, oscillopsia will occur. Oscillopsia is the sensation that the world is moving, and is caused by the eye movements. When nystagmus is present at birth or shortly after, oscillopsia is not experienced.

Optic Atrophy

Optic atrophy refers to any loss of function of the optic nerve that results from any condition that damages the nerve. It can be (1) congenital (because of intrauterine insult, anoxia, or brain damage), (2) hereditary, (3) the result of optic neuritis (Leber's optic neuritis, anterior ischemic optic neuropathy), (4) glaucoma, (5) trauma, (6) anoxia, (7) poor nutrition or the toxic effects of alcohol or tobacco, or (8) can be associated with such systemic conditions as multiple sclerosis or diabetes. The amount of vision loss depends on the extent of optic nerve damage; visual acuity, visual fields, contrast sensitivity, and color perception also can be affected to varying degrees.

Retinal Detachment

Retinal detachment is a separation of the retina from the underlying choroid (which provides nutritional support to the retina), resulting in loss of retinal function. Surgery must be done in a timely manner to regain retinal function. Vision loss depends on the extent and location of the retinal detachment. Conditions such as high myopia and retinopathy of prematurity (ROP) are associated with increased risk of retinal detachment.

Retinitis Pigmentosa

Retinitis pigmentosa (RP) is a retinal degeneration that primarily affects the rod cells but eventually also affects the cones. It can be either spontaneous or inherited in one of several ways, and can also be associated with other systemic conditions (i.e., Usher's syndrome, Lawrence–Moon–Biedl syndrome). Initially, the midperipheral and peripheral retina are affected, often showing pigmentary disruption, and eventually optic atrophy and degenerative macular changes also occur. The initial symptom is poor night vision. Eventually, there is difficulty adjusting to various lighting conditions accompanied by significant peripheral visual field losses. Central vision can remain quite good for indefinite periods, however. Cataract formation is also common and can create difficulty seeing clearly in bright light. RP can lead to total blindness.

Retinopathy of Prematurity

Retinopathy of prematurity (ROP) is caused by abnormal retinal growth resulting in scar tissue formation; this condition is the result of oxygen therapy given to premature infants. The premature infant's retinal vasculature stops growing in response to oxygen therapy, but after the infant is removed from the oxygen, the vessels begin to grow again in a faulty manner. This faulty growth can result in scar tissue formation and hemorrhage. The degree of visual impairment is related to the degree of tissue damage.

Traumatic Brain Injury

Traumatic brain injury can cause visual impairment and can be the result of head injury, stroke, or intracranial tumors. It can also be caused by the treatment for a tumor, or anoxia. A traumatic brain injury can result in visual acuity loss, visual field loss, poor binocularity, visual perceptual difficulties, photophobia, or refractive changes.

LOW VISION EXAMINATION

The goal of low vision rehabilitation is to improve visual functioning, and thereby maintain or increase a client's independence. This is achieved through a clinical evaluation of visual functioning and ocular health, followed by the development of a rehabilitation strategy based on the clinical findings and the client's needs. The low vision eyecare practitioner will evaluate and prescribe optical, electronic, and nonoptical devices to improve both visual and overall functioning. Therapy that includes instruction in the use of the vision that a client still retains, as well as use of prescribed lens systems and devices is often necessary. Referral for services outside the expertise of the clinician may also be appropriate.

Evaluation and management of a client with low vision involves a somewhat different examination strategy from that generally used. A thorough history that includes ocular and visual history, general health history, social, vocational, and educational concerns, and discussion of specific visual needs is performed. It is important for the clinician to understand both the individual's visual limitations and specific needs in order to determine the most appropriate rehabilitation plan. The history is followed by a clinical assessment that is modified for the patient's visual, physical, and cognitive abilities. Adaptations include specialized low vision charts, modified refraction techniques, visual field assessments, and assessments of such visual capabilities as contrast sensitivity, glare sensitivity, ocular motility, and color vision. These examination strategies are outlined in the following sections.

History

A comprehensive clinical assessment of the visually impaired person includes a complete visual and ocular history, including the diagnosis and time of onset of the visual disorder, surgical history, stability of the eye condition, and its effect on the individual's visual functioning. For persons with a recent onset of irreversible vision loss, there may be reluctance to accept that the problem cannot be "fixed," an attitude that can interfere with the rehabilitation process. Individuals who have had the visual impairment for a time, however, generally may have more acceptance of their own limitations, and the limitations of low vision devices, and some may already have experience with lens systems. When the disorder or visual functioning is not stable, it may be wise to plan interim strategies or postpone any final decisions in regard to prescriptive devices until there is some stability. The clinician also gathers information on the person's general health history, including medication use. Individuals who self-administer medications must be able to identify medications, measure the correct amounts (as with diabetics), and tell when it is time to take the medication. Some systemic conditions (such as diabetes, arthritis, or stroke), however, can influence the individual's ability to participate in the rehabilitation process, because of physical, cognitive or emotional difficulties.

Social aspects of a client's history will explore support systems, educational, vocational, and avocational needs, transportation issues, and activities in the community. An individual who lives alone in a community with no public transporta-

SIDEBAR 4.1

Visual and Ocular History Questions

When undertaking a clinical assessment of a person who is visually impaired, the following questions will help the counselor elicit the information necessary to create a rehabilitation strategy.

OCULAR AND VISUAL HISTORY

- What is the name of your eye condition?
- How long has your vision been this way?
- Have you had any surgery or treatments to your eyes? Are any (more) planned?
- Do you use any medications for your eyes?
- Do eyeglasses (or contact lenses) help you to see better?
- Does your vision fluctuate? How so (i.e., day-to-day or throughout the day)?
- Are you able to read newspaper print? Large print? Headlines?
- At what distance do you watch television? Is it clear at this distance?
- Can you walk unassisted in an unfamiliar environment?
- Are your eyes sensitive to light indoors? Outdoors?
- Do you use anything to help you see better?
- Can you see at a distance?

GENERAL HEALTH AND MEDICAL CONCERNS

- How is your general health?
- Do you have any specific health problems such as diabetes, heart problems, and so forth?
- Are you taking any medications?
- How is your hearing?
- Are you depressed (about your eye problem)?
- How do you feel most of the time? How do you feel today?

SOCIAL CONCERNS

- Do you live alone?
- Who assists you when you need help?
- Do you work? (Explore work related needs.)
- Are you a student? (Explore educational needs.)
- What do you like to do for fun?
- How do you spend your day?
- What type of transportation do you use?

tion will have a different set of needs from a person who lives with a supportive significant other, or who can still travel independently. People who are either working or seeking employment may have job specific needs, and may require an on-site evaluation to assess the workplace environment and job requirements. Students will have unique needs (i.e., seeing a chalkboard, viewing overhead projections, and perhaps heavier reading demands) that must be addressed so they can function adequately in the educational system.

As a final step, goals will be identified so that the evaluation is problem-oriented, that is, so the clinician can direct the rehabilitation management of the visual impairment as it affects specific activities. It is important to be as specific as possible with goals, describing the tasks, reading materials, working distance needed, and so forth.

Therefore, it is quite helpful to bring samples of unusual work or reading materials. Some of the questions that might be asked during the history are listed in Sidebar 4.1. After a complete history is taken and the person's baseline needs and goals are established, the clinical examination is performed.

Measurement of Visual Function

Visual Acuity

Visual acuity is the specification of the resolving ability of the visual system, or the ability to see detail (see also Chapter 2). Measurement is usually achieved by the identification of letters, numbers, or pictures of varying standard sizes. The target size is specified by the distance (in feet) at which the target subtends a critical angle; a 200-foot target (which is about 3 1/2 inches tall) subtends the same angle at 200 feet that a 20-foot target (which is about 3/8 inches) subtends at 20 feet (see Figure 4.1). Visual acuity is recorded as a fraction (called the Snellen fraction), in which the numerator (first number) is the actual testing distance, and the denominator (second number) is the size of the target identified. (The Snellen chart is a traditional chart whose top line consists of the letter *E* and which is used in most eye examinations.) "Normal" visual acuity is considered to be 20/20, which specifies that a 20-foot target is discriminated at 20 feet. A measurement of 20/40 acuity specifies that the smallest target read at 20 feet is a 40-foot target; a 40-foot target is twice the size of a 20-foot target. Stated another way, 20/40 acuity means that the smallest target seen at 20 feet is that size target that the "average, normally sighted" individual could see at 40 feet. A 20/200 acuity means that the smallest target identified from a 20 foot testing distance could be seen by the "average, normally sighted" person at 200 feet; the 200-foot target is ten times the size of a 20-foot target.

Standard distance visual acuity charts have only a few figures in the lower acuity ranges (20/100 to 20/400), but specially designed low vision charts allow more accurate specification of reduced visual acuity, with a number of targets in

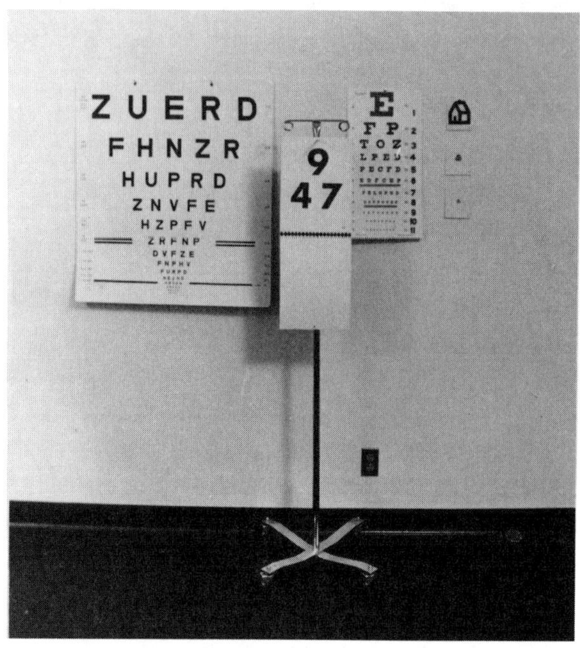

Distance acuity charts, such as those shown here, can be used for assessing a low vision patient's acuity of distance vision, or the ability of the eye to see detail at a specified distance.

the 20/120 to 20/800 range. Typically these charts are used at 10 feet or closer, so that acuity is recorded with the numerator of 10 (or whatever the actual testing distance was) and the denominator is the size of the target read. Conversion to a 20-foot equivalent is done by simple ratio (i.e., 10/100 becomes 20/200). On the standard Snellen projected chart, there are no targets between the measurements of 20/200 and 20/100; however, on many low vision charts, there are targets in this midrange. Although 10/60 can be converted to 20/120 by simple ratio, a person who reads with an acuity of 10/60 on a low vision chart may not be able to see better than 20/200 on the standard Snellen projected chart, as he or she may not be able to see as well as 20/100, which is the next smaller line. For this reason, it is important to specify the actual testing distance, and be aware of the possible discrepancies when different charts or testing distances are used, especially for determining legal blindness. Snellen acuities at 20 feet are used for determining legal blindness. In many cases, a person with an acuity of 10/60 or even 10/40 may not be able to see better than

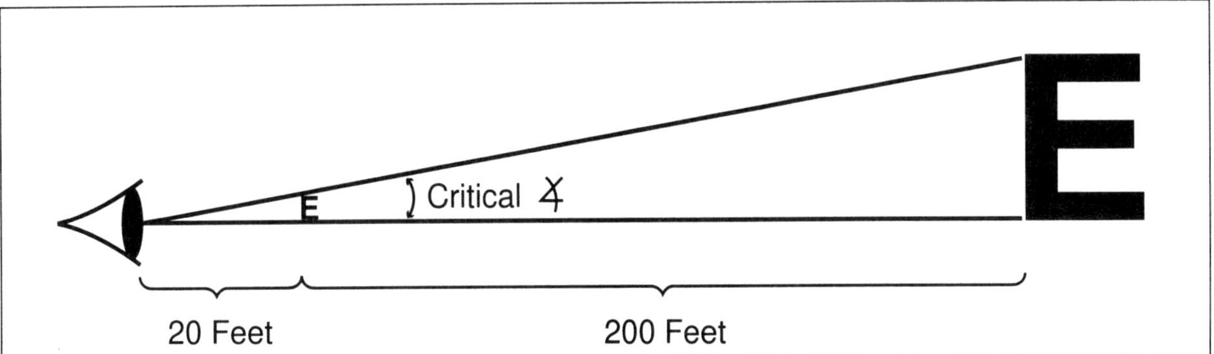

Figure 4.1. In measuring distance visual acuity, the target size is specified by the distance in feet at which the target subtends a critical angle. A 200-foot target subtends the same angle at 200 feet that a 20-foot target subtends at 20 feet.

20/200 on the standard Snellen chart, and therefore would be considered legally blind.

When distance visual acuity cannot be measured with specialized charts, use of objects will allow the clinician to calculate a rough detection acuity, based on the size of the object and the distance at which it was seen (which allows a critical angle to be calculated; see Figure 4.1). This approach is useful for children or nonverbal persons. Detection of hand motion, light projection (i.e., the ability to discern from which direction a light is coming), or light perception (i.e., the ability to tell whether a bright light shining in the eye at close range is off or on) should also be evaluated. The specification of no light perception is an unequivocal measurement, indicating total blindness.

Near visual acuity is often measured during the low vision exam, because it is the basis for determining near magnification requirements. The acuity can be specified as a Snellen fraction, with the numerator representing the testing distance and the denominator, the size of the target read. This allows for easy comparison to the distance acuity. However, the metric (M) system is preferred, recording the distance (in meters) over the M-size target read. M units express the distance in meters at which lower-case letters subtend 5 degress of arc. If the 4M line is read at 40 cm, this is recorded as .40/4M, which is (by simple ratio) equivalent to 20/200 acuity. Other measures of near visual acuity that rehabilitation counselors most frequently encounter include reduced Snellen, Jaeger, and the point system, but these systems can vary from individual card to indivdiual card and can be confusing. A person's single-letter acuity while reading a chart may be better than the ability to read continuous text, and this should also be explored.

Visual Field

The visual field is the total projected area of vision with the eye looking straight ahead. The normal visual field of one eye extends superiorly (up) 50 degrees, nasally (toward the nose) 60 degrees, inferiorly (down) 70 degrees, and temporally (toward the temple) 90 degrees from the straight-ahead gaze. The central visual field is the central 20-degree diameter, whereas the peripheral visual field is that area beyond the central 20 degrees. Visual field testing can be performed with several different instruments.

Measurement of the Central Visual Field. The tangent screen is a simple tool that is used to measure the central 50 degrees, primarily the central visual field. The individual being tested fixates on a central target on a black screen while another small target is moved throughout the central visual field to determine dim or nonseeing areas. The examiner moves a wand with a small target at the tip from a point where the patient cannot see the target to a point where he or she can just see the target. The examiner then marks that point on the tangent screen with a pin

An eye examiner uses a tangent screen to determine a low vision patient's central visual field.

and continues the technique until the examiner determines the patient's central visual field. The presence of central visual field disturbances will interfere with seeing detail, especially with reading.

Another test to qualitatively assess the central visual field is the Amsler grid. When viewing this square grid pattern, distortion in the vision will be seen as waves or bends in the straight lines, and blind areas or scotomas may be seen as blurred, dim, or dark areas. The presence of any distortion may necessitate the modification of prescribed magnification.

Measurement of the Peripheral Visual Field. Goldmann bowl perimetry (or an equivalent test) uses a moving target presented in a bowl-like apparatus to measure the entire visual field, and is called kinetic perimetry because the target is moving. While the patient looks straight ahead, a target is brought in from the far periphery, where it cannot be seen. A buzzer is then pressed to indicate when this target is first seen, and as the target continues to move toward the center, the individual indicates if it disappears at all. Goldmann perimetry yields a visual field map, called an isopter, which is a line connecting the points where the target was seen or was not seen.

Automated static perimetry, (for example, Humphrey or Octopus instruments) uses flashing targets of varying brightness presented randomly throughout the visual field. These measure more precisely the retinal sensitivity at any given point. While looking straight ahead, when the patient being tested sees a light flash anywhere, a response button is pressed. If a target is not seen, the instrument will present a brighter target in the same place at a later time, increasing the brightness until the target is seen (or maximum brightness is achieved). Automated perimeters keep track of false positives (i.e., the patient responds when no target is presented, or in an area which had already been determined to be blind) and false negatives (i.e, the patient does not respond when the target is actually seen). Automated instruments yield a visual field map called a gray scale that indicates how bright the target had to be before it was detected. As of this writing, however, the SSA specifies that Goldmann perimetry done with a III4e target (which specifies the size and brightness of the target) is necessary for determining legal blindness that results from visual field loss, and that automated static perimetry is not acceptable, because it can be more difficult to interpret.

Confrontation testing is a gross measure of peripheral visual field awareness, and is often used as a screening tool. The examiner asks the patient to count fingers or detect a target or movement in the periphery while looking straight ahead. A person with severe peripheral field losses on perimetry may have some residual object or motion detection in the periphery, which may be helpful for mobility purposes.

Contrast Sensitivity

Contrast sensitivity refers to the ability to detect differences in brightness between a target and the background. This is measured clinically with charts that have either stripes or letters of progressively less contrast. The person being tested indicates the lowest contrast target that can be detected. Poor contrast sensitivity is an indication that there may be difficulty seeing low contrast targets in the environment, such as unmarked curbs, or low contrast printed materials, such as newsprint. It may call for the use of extra light, specially designed lens systems to maximize light transmission through the lens, or use of electro-optical devices, such as a closed-circuit television (CCTV), despite relatively good visual acuity. The use of colored filters, such as yellow, orange, or amber, may also enhance contrast sensitivity, especially outdoors.

Assessment of Extraocular Muscle Function

Binocularity is the single, simultaneous perception of an object by both eyes. Under normal circumstances, the two eyes work together as a team affording stereopsis or fine depth perception. The

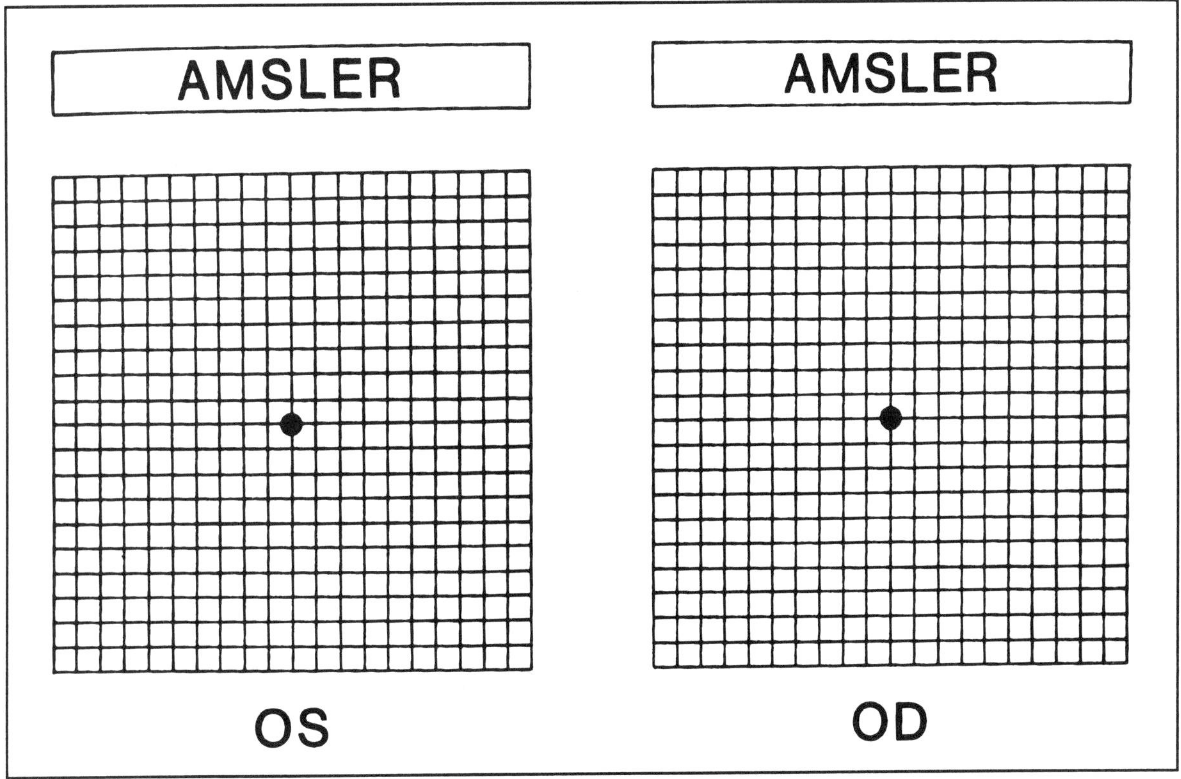

An Amsler grid is used to test the central visual field by assessing the presence of distortion in a patient's vision while viewing the center spot on the grid pattern.

alignment of the eyes is evaluated, as is the ability of the eyes to converge and to move smoothly in all positions of gaze. When there is an eye turn or when a significant difference in visual acuity between the two eyes exists, binocularity is disrupted. If poor binocularity exists, diplopia (double vision) may be present, especially if the poor binocularity has been acquired. Prisms, lenses, or occlusion (covering one eye), may minimize or even eliminate diplopia. (See later discussion of low vision devices.)

Nystagmus is also evaluated, and the type and severity as well as the presence of a null point (position of gaze where the nystagmus slows) is noted. Nystagmus is not a contraindication for the use of optical devices, but compensatory head turns developed by the client to maximize his or her ability to view objects (to achieve a null point) may require special attention to positioning of lenses.

Refraction

Refraction is the clinical measurement of refractive or focusing errors (myopia, hyperopia, astigmatism, and presbyopia). This measurement is the basis for prescribing conventional eyeglasses and contact lenses. An accurate refraction is a critical component of low vision management, and is the basis for any optical, nonoptical, or electro-optical prescriptions. An objective refraction is done by the clinician using a retinoscope and lenses, or an autorefractor (a computerized instrument that measures refractive errors) and requires minimal effort or cooperation by the patient. (An objective refraction is used to determine the prescription of eyeglasses for infants, children, and noncommunicative patients.) A subjective refraction further refines the objective measure by asking the patient being tested to identify the clearest of several lenses. The patient is encouraged to adopt the head or eye position that gives the best vision, to compensate for blind spots in the vision. This information is used to determine the final prescription, based on a number of factors, including the patient's old prescription, the quality of the responses, and whether the patient sees better with lenses. Some conditions can cause fluctuations in the refractive error so that it may be necessary to recheck the refraction at a different time of day or over several weeks before prescribing lenses.

Basic Optics

Optics of Light

Light is a form of energy that travels through space. The sources of light are either a primary source, such as a light bulb, or a secondary source—any object that reflects light. The two ways to think about light are either as waves or as rays. For the purposes of this text, light will be thought of as rays, which travel in straight lines. A source of light emits rays in every direction, but the only rays to be concerned about in this discussion are those that reach the eye. When a light source or object is at optical infinity (20 feet or farther), the bundle of light rays that reach the eye are essentially parallel. If the light source or object is closer to the eye than 20 feet, then the rays will diverge from each other as they travel through space. Light rays that move closer together as they travel through space are converging. Light rays are considered to have zero vergence if they are parallel, negative or minus vergence if they diverge, and positive or plus vergence if they converge (see Figure 4.2). Vergence is the measurement or degree of either convergence or divergence, and is given in diopters. The unit of vergence is the diopter:

$$\text{Diopter} = \frac{100}{\text{object or image distance in cm}}$$

For example, if an object is 20 cm away from the eye, the light rays that reach the eye will be divergent, and will have 100/20 cm = 5 diopters of divergence or −5 diopters of vergence. If the

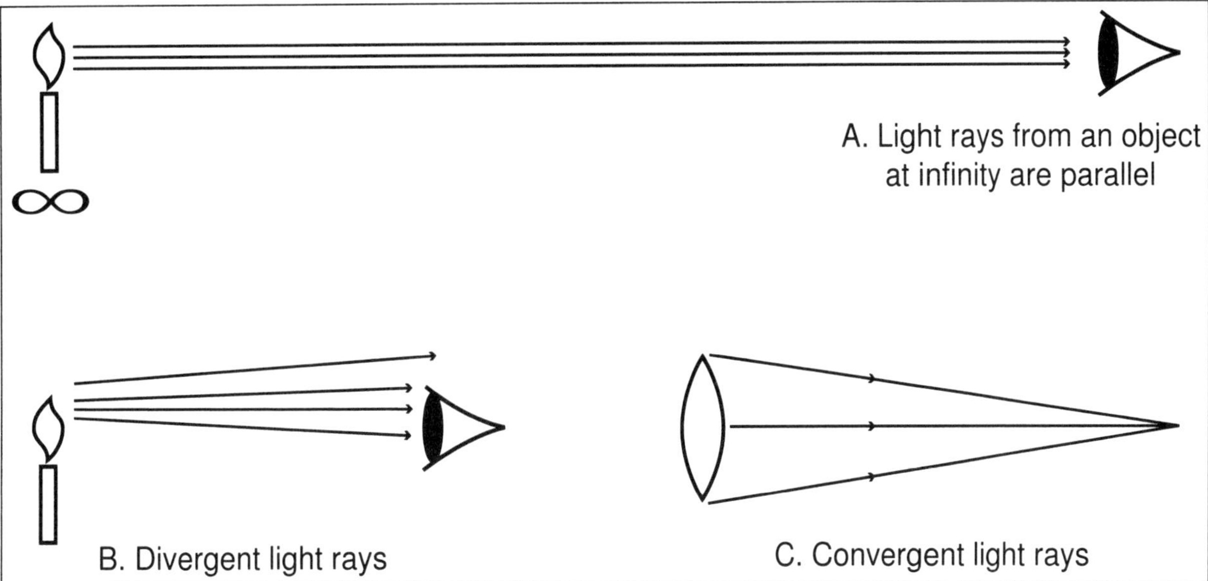

Figure 4.2. (A) When light rays emanate from an object 20 feet or farther from the eye, they are considered to be traveling essentially as a parallel bundle of rays (that is, they do not bend) and to have zero vergence, a circumstance known as optical infinity. (B) Light rays are considered to have negative, or minus, vergence if they diverge, and (C) positive, or plus, vergence if they converge.

same object is viewed at 100 cm, however, the light rays that reach the eye will have 100/100 of negative vergence, or −1 diopter of vergence. The closer the object is to the eye or lens, the more divergent the light rays that reach the eye.

For an image to be formed, the light rays must converge to a single point. If light rays are parallel or divergent, an image will not be formed unless something changes the direction—or vergence—of the rays. Lenses will change the direction of light rays so that they form an image.

Optics of Lenses

Lenses can change the direction of light rays either by reflection or refraction. Light rays may be reflected off the surface of a lens rather than passing through it. Objects reflect light that reaches them, and it is this reflected light that reaches the eye, and allows objects to be perceived visually. Refraction occurs when light rays pass through a lens, and the direction of the emergent light is altered by the curvature of the lens and the lens material (see Figure 4.3). When light passes through a lens it may pass through with the direction unchanged (i.e., zero vergence change), or the light may be either converged or diverged, depending on the curvature of the lens. A convex (or plus) lens will converge light whereas a concave (or minus) lens will diverge light. The lens power is also specified in diopters, which tells the refracting or bending power of the lens. A diopter is the unit of strength needed to bend or refract parallel light to focus at one meter. The focal distance of a lens is the distance at which it focuses parallel light (i.e., light with zero vergence), and is inversely proportional to the power of the lens. The same formula for measuring the unit of vergence is used to measure the lens power:

$$\text{Diopter} = \frac{100}{\text{distance in cm}}$$

The stronger the lens power (which is determined by the curvature of the lens), the more it refracts or changes light direction. A + 1.00 diopter lens will focus parallel light at 1 meter from the lens, a

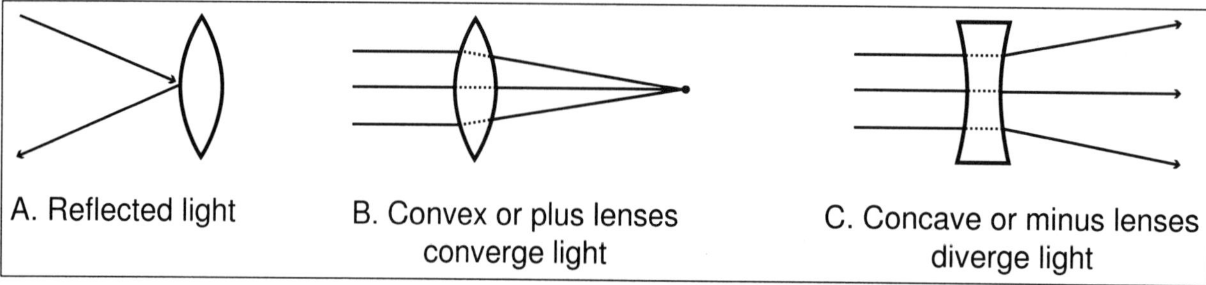

Figure 4.3. Lenses can be used to change the direction of light rays so that they form an image. Light rays can be reflected by the surface of a lens (A); they can be refracted by the curvature of the lens, as by a convex, or plus, lens (B), which will converge light, or by a concave, or minus, lens (C), which will diverge light.

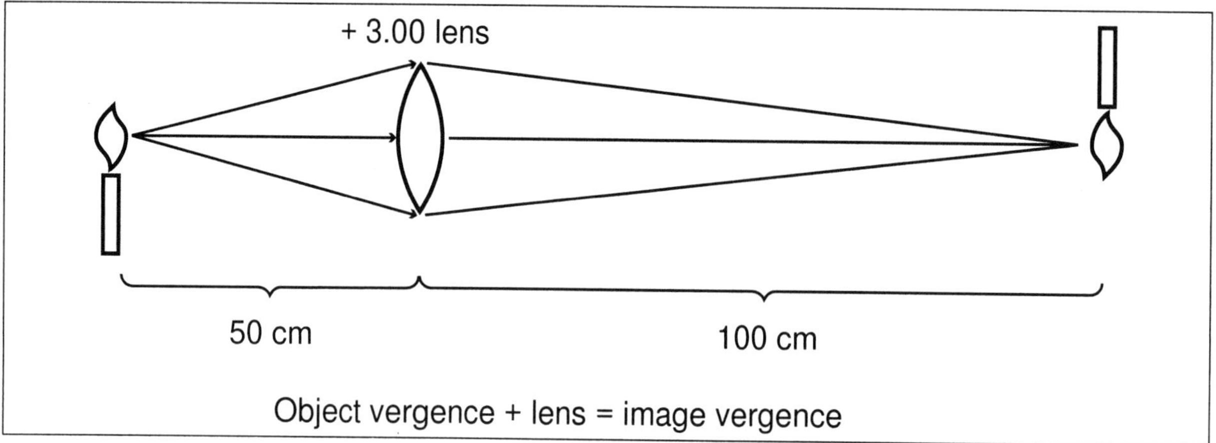

Figure 4.4. Light rays from an object 50 cm in front of a +3.00 lens will emerge from the lens more convergent by 3 diopters and will form an image 100 cm behind the lens.

+2.00 diopter lens will bend the light twice as much, focusing it at .5 meters or 50 cm, and a +4.00 diopter lens has a focal distance of 25 cm. The focal distance of the lens (in centimeters) is determined by the dioptric power of the lens divided into 100. When light is refracted by a lens, an image of the object is formed somewhere in space. The position of the image formed by the light after it passes through the lens depends on the vergence of the light as it hits the lens surface plus the refracting power of the lens. For example, light rays emitted from an object 50 cm in front of a +3.00 lens will emerge from the lens more convergent by 3 diopters and will form an image 100 cm on the other side of the lens (see Figure 4.4). Had the light rays not passed through the lens, they would have continued to travel through space diverging as they went, and would never form an image.

Optics of the Eye

The optical components of the eye refract light, which causes it to focus on the retina. The major refracting surface of the eye is the cornea, providing approximately 66 percent of the refracting power of the eye. The crystalline lens makes up the remainder of the refracting power. If there is a perfect match between the total refracting power of the eye and the length of the eyeball, so that the light is focused perfectly on the retina (as with emmetropia or no refractive error), a clearly focused retinal image will be formed. If there is a mismatch between the refracting power and the length of the eye, the retinal image will be out of focus.

With myopia (nearsightedness), the refracting surface of the eye is either too strong for the length of the eye or the eyeball is too long for the refracting power. In either case, the image is formed in front of the retina so that the retinal image is blurred (see Figure 2.4). Concave (minus) lenses will reduce the total vergence so that the image is moved back to focus on the retina. This is how eyeglasses with minus lenses compensate for myopic refractive errors.

With hyperopia (farsightedness), the refracting surface of the eye is too weak for the length of the eye, or the eyeball is too short so that the image is formed (theoretically) behind the retina (see Figure 2.4). In this situation, the retinal image is also blurred, but convex (plus) lenses can increase the total light vergence so that the image is moved forward to focus clearly on the retina. Therefore, convex lenses are used to compensate for hyperopia.

If the cornea or lens has an irregular curvature, there may be two powers of lens required to focus the light properly on the retina. This common refractive error is called astigmatism, and astigmatic lenses (with cylinder correction) are prescribed to compensate for this.

In addition to supplying part of the refractive power, the crystalline lens of the eye also serves to focus for near-viewing distances. When looking at a distance target, the eye focuses for that distance, and when viewing at a close range (within approximately 3 feet), it refocuses for the closer distance, much like an autofocus lens in a camera. This automatic adjustment to maintain a clear focus is called accommodation. With age, the ability to accommodate or focus at near distances gradually declines, so that at the age of 40 to 45 (approximately) most people cannot focus comfortably at an average 16-inch reading distance through their distance correction. This is called presbyopia, and bifocals or reading glasses are prescribed to compensate for it. Bifocals may also be prescribed for younger patients who have close focusing problems, or to provide magnification for near tasks (see discussion on magnification for near needs).

Contact lenses may be prescribed to compensate for refractive errors or when corneal irregularities exist, as with keratoconus. When the lens is worn on the cornea, rather than in the spectacle plane, there may be better visual functioning as a result of reduced lens distortion and increased peripheral vision awareness. The comfort and cosmetic benefit of eliminating very thick eyeglasses should not be discounted, especially for children and young adults who may be coping with issues of self-esteem. Prosthetic contact lenses should also be considered to improve the appearance of a malformed or disfigured eye.

If the visual system has no defects except a refractive error, when eyeglasses or contact lenses are used to focus the light properly on the retina, a clear image will be seen. However, if there is any additional problem with any component of the visual system, even if the light is focused properly on the retina, the image will not be clear. In the case of macular degeneration or any other condition that causes reduced macular function, eyeglasses will focus the light on the retina but the image may not be seen clearly because the area on the retina where the light is focused is not working properly. The result is low vision despite the best correction with eyeglasses. Nevertheless, the refractive correction must be determined to afford the best corrected visual acuity, and possibly minimizing the amount of magnification required. The refractive correction must also be incorporated into the low vision prescription, to provide the clearest image. In these situations, magnification is beneficial because the image is not only focused on the retina, but also is enlarged (see Figure 4.5).

OCULAR HEALTH ASSESSMENT

Many visually impaired patients are comanaged by several eyecare practitioners, including a primary care doctor, retinologist, glaucoma specialist, and/or low vision specialist. Each clinician must make an assessment of the state of the ocular health as it relates to the specific condition being managed. For the low vision practitioner, it is important to evaluate the eye condition from a functional standpoint. For example, a patient may have a cataract that is not felt to be a significant factor in the visual impairment by the retinologist because macular degeneration is also present. The low vision specialist, however, may recommend the cataract be removed so that the individual can see better with low vision devices, to better remediate the effects of macular degeneration. (For more on medical assessment, see Chapter 5.)

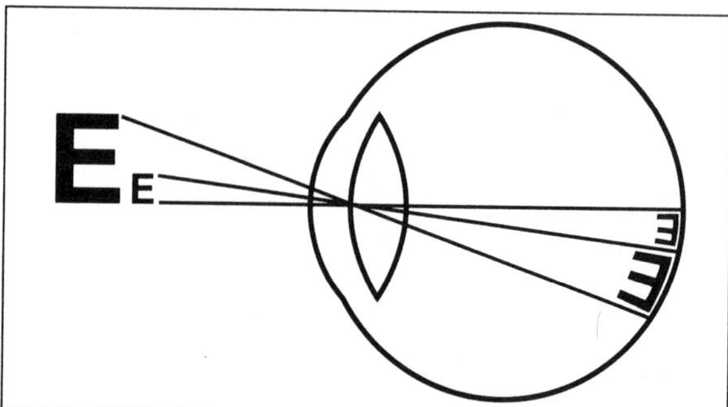

Figure 4.5. In relative-size magnification, the size of the retinal image is increased by enlarging the size of the object. For example, if the size of the object is doubled, the image is doubled in size. Twice the number of cells are stimulated to send an impulse up the optic nerve to the brain, and the object detail is perceived.

Management of Low Vision

Magnification and Reduced Visual Acuity

The goal of most low vision rehabilitation is to improve visual acuity for distance, intermediate, or near activities—or for all three. Magnification improves visual acuity by providing an enlarged retinal image (see Figure 4.5). With 2X magnification, the retinal image is two times larger and thus is more easily seen. Magnification can be achieved by several methods that are described as follows:

1. Relative-distance magnification is achieved by simply moving closer to the target. If the object is moved to half of the original viewing distance, the retinal image will be twice the size, hence a 2X magnification. Moving closer to the television is an example of relative-distance magnification.
2. Relative-size magnification is achieved by making the target itself larger. If print is enlarged by 100 percent on a photocopy machine, the retinal image will be twice the original size. Large print and bold-lined paper are examples of relative-size magnification (see Figure 4.5).
3. Angular magnification is achieved by the use of lens systems that optically increase the apparent size of the object and thus enlarge the retinal image. Telescopes and magnifiers make objects appear larger, increasing the retinal image size by angular magnification.
4. Electronic magnification is accomplished through electro-optical devices that make use of both relative-size and relative-distance magnification. Camera systems and adaptive computer software can enlarge the object (relative-size magnification), and the user can move closer to the screen to benefit from relative-distance magnification.

For convex lenses, magnification units are calculated by the dioptric power of the lens divided by 4 diopters. This formula compares the angular size of the enlarged image to the angular size of the object placed at an arbitrary 25 cm viewing distance (100/25 cm = 4 diopters for one unit of magnification). This simple calculation is useful for eyeglasses and contact lenses, but the optics of magnifiers that are hand-held or mounted in stands complicate the formula so that the true effective magnification is not so easily determined. It is recommended that this be kept in mind when patients self-prescribe or talk about their "10 power" magnifier, which may be a +10 diopter lens, a 10X lens, or neither.

Magnification for Near Needs

Based on the patient's specific needs and best corrected visual acuities, the clinician can determine a starting magnification level or lens prescription. Because reading is the most common goal, the near magnification is evaluated not only with single letters, but also with continuous text charts and, finally, with actual reading materials. It may also be necessary to modify magnification if there is reduced contrast sensitivity or distortion in the central visual field. After the optimum level of magnification for any given task is determined, the lens form can be explored, taking into account the visual field, the working distance (distance from the eye to the task), and the lighting requirements for the task. Magnification for near-vision needs can be provided in several forms, which are described as follows:

1. Bifocals and trifocals are multifocal lenses with different strengths in the upper and lower parts of the lens to focus for different viewing distances. They can be prescribed in standard strengths for presbyopia, low magnification needs, or to facilitate the use of certain optical devices (e.g., stand magnifiers). Specially designed bifocals can be fabricated in higher powers but require closer-than-average working distances.
2. Reading lenses mounted into spectacles are called microscopes. Because they are spectacle-mounted, they afford hands-free magnification, with the largest field of view of any equivalent lens system. The principle of relative-distance magnification involves holding the material at the focal distance of the lens, providing a focused, enlarged retinal image. The focal distance or working distance of a near spectacle lens for near tasks is inversely proportional to the power of the lens; that is, the stronger the lens, the closer the working distance. The focal distance of the lens (in centimeters) is

Spectacle-mounted binocular microscopes can be used for near-vision tasks.

determined by the dioptric power of the lens divided into 100. For example, a +20 diopter lens has a focal distance of 100/20 = 5 cm, or approximately 2 inches. For a person with no significant refractive error, the reading material must be held at 5 cm to be seen clearly through this lens. If there is significant refractive error, this will affect the focal distance. A nearsighted individual will have to hold the material closer, and a farsighted individual will hold it farther away.

Binocular prescriptions can be fabricated up to a certain lens power, beyond which it is impossible to achieve binocularity. Half-eye reading glasses with prisms to help maintain binocularity are available in low magnification (see the section on prisms later in this chapter for more information). For stronger microscope prescriptions in which binocularity is not possible, the eye that is not being used may be frosted or occluded to eliminate confusion or diplopia. Stronger microscope prescriptions can also be provided as full-field lenses, half-lenses, or specially designed bifocals, to minimize distance blur when looking up from the reading material.

As the lens power increases, the field

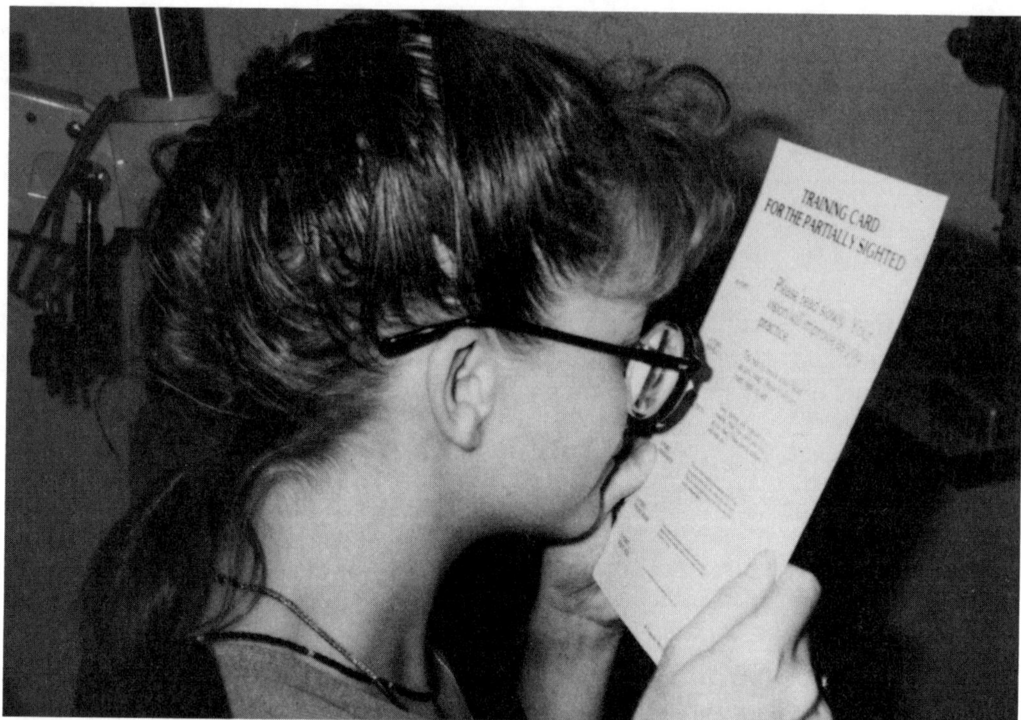

Microscope reading lenses offer hands-free magnification but require the user to be a close working distance from the surface being viewed.

of view through the lens decreases so that fewer printed characters are seen at one time. This may slow reading speed. Even so, as soon as the patient has learned how to properly use reading eyeglasses, the reading speed with this device is often faster than with equivalent-powered magnifiers or telescopes. As might be expected, the greatest difficulty with using a microscope is adapting to and maintaining the close focal distance, which is often less than three inches. Training in the proper use of the lens, along with practice, is required for proficiency. Most patients will see improvements in the ability to use this type of device in three to four weeks of practice.

3. Telemicroscopes are telescopes that are adapted to focus at a near or intermediate distance by the use of a cap or a variable focusing mechanism. Telemicroscopes that are spectacle-mounted also allow hands-free magnification at a greater focal distance than equivalent-powered microscope reading eyeglasses, but at the expense of field of view. The field of view is the width of usable vision when looking through the lens. Because the field of view is reduced, fewer printed letters are seen at the same time. This may slow down reading speed, create difficulty in keeping one's place when reading across a line of print, or in finding the next line. With proper instruction and practice, however, the use of a telemicroscope for reading can be mastered. Binocular telemicroscopes can be prescribed up to a certain magnification level, if the individual is capable of functioning binocularly for near-vision tasks. Telemicroscopes or near telescopes are indicated when it is desirable to maximize the working distance, such as reading a computer screen, typing, or reading music.

4. Hand-held magnifiers provide magnifica-

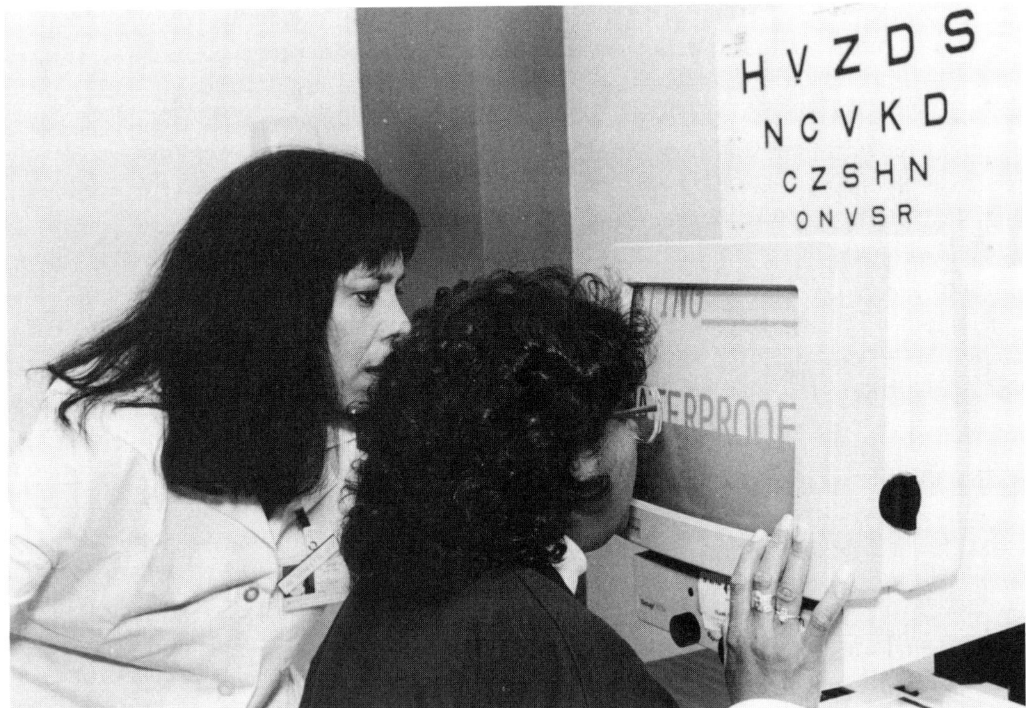

A closed-circuit television (CCTV) provides electronic magnification by using a video camera that, when pointed at an object, projects the image onto a television monitor. The CCTV is generally used as a near-vision device and allows the individual to control the size, contrast, and clarity of the images projected.

tion at variable working distances. The focal distance of the lens (the distance the lens is held from the page or surface to be viewed) is determined by the power of the magnifier. However, the working distance (that is, the distance between the eye and the page or surface to be viewed) depends on how close the lens is held to the eye. The closer the lens is held to the eye, the larger the field of view through the lens. However, the stronger the lens power, the smaller the usable lens because of optical distortions in the lens periphery that increase with increasing lens power. Hand-held magnifiers require some training to teach proper focusing for maximum magnification, and to instruct the bifocal wearer on which part of the eyeglasses to use for maximum benefit (the effective magnification will vary depending on whether the bifocal is used, and at what distance the lens is held from the eyeglasses). Hand-held magnifiers are preferred by many for such short-term reading tasks as reading prices, labels, and bus schedules.

5. Stand magnifiers also allow a greater working distance than equivalent-powered spectacle-mounted microscopes, but they do not allow the hands to be free. The focal distance of the stand magnifier is fixed, so that it is easier to maintain, but the fixed distance usually requires accommodation (close focusing of the crystalline lens inside the eye) or use of a bifocal for the image to be seen clearly. Also, many stand magnifiers are labeled in such a way that the magnification specification is ambiguous. The clinician must determine the most appropriate stand magnifier; this

determination is based on the magnification required and an analysis of the stand magnifier when used in combination with the patient's accommodation or bifocal. As with hand-held magnifiers, the lens area decreases as the lens power increases, and the field of view through any given lens will increase the closer it is held to the eye. There are a variety of illuminated stand magnifiers available, making this a good option for those who need a lot of light or for when illumination cannot be controlled.

6. Electro-optical devices or video magnification devices such as CCTVs are available with black-and-white or color displays. They can be stationary cameras (the material is moved under the camera), hand-held, or head-mounted camera systems. Electro-optical devices not only afford maximum magnification for patients with very poor visual acuity, but also allow for the manipulation of contrast, which is more important for some types of visual impairments, such as glaucoma. Reading duration can also be improved with this type of device. Because the working distance is generally greater than with eyeglasses, postural fatigue may also not be as much of a problem. The use of a CCTV may be indicated if extended reading is a goal. Training will often improve reading speeds with these devices, because the different eye-to-hand coordinations take some practice. But because most of these devices are less portable, almost all people who use them can also benefit from more portable optical devices, such as reading eyeglasses or magnifiers.

Magnification for Distance Needs

The best corrected distance visual acuity and the required acuity for the task will determine the distance magnification needed by the individual. When physically possible, relative distance magnification can increase the visibility of the target viewed. Moving closer to the television or chalkboard is the simplest way to provide magnification for these activities. When moving closer is not adequate or is physically impossible, telescopes can be used to make the target look larger (angular magnification). A telescope is a device with two or more lenses separated by a precise distance. This optical arrangement provides magnification for distance that cannot be duplicated by a single lens system. Telescopes can be monocular or binocular, hand-held, head-mounted, or mounted on eyeglasses. Hand-held telescopes are useful for short-term spotting activities and are preferred for mobility applications. Telescopes mounted in eyeglasses allow hands-free magnification and are optimum for such extended distance viewing activities as classroom activities, theater presentations, or sporting events. The telescope can be mounted in the center of the lens of the eyeglasses so it coincides with the visual axis, or in a bioptic position, mounted off the visual axis, generally above or below, to allow the individual to look around the telescope and use it only for certain viewing needs. Spectacle-mounted telescopes are unusual looking and therefore patients may initially be reluctant to use them. However, if there is a clear indication for this type of device, the benefits are quickly appreciated. Telescopes require practice to develop the ability to find targets quickly (spotting), to survey the environment in an organized manner (scanning), to follow moving targets (tracking) and to adjust the focus for different distances (focusing). Instruction in the proper use of the telescope will help to ensure proficiency.

Some head-mounted video displays are also available for both distance and near application, and provide contrast enhancement as well as magnification. Zoom focus capabilities make these devices extremely versatile, but to attain maximum proficiency, training and practice are required to learn both head control and the manipulation of the instrument panel.

Management of Visual Field Loss

Management of Central Visual Field Defects

Central blurred areas, blind spots, or distortion will significantly interfere with an individual's ability to see in detail, especially with reading. People with central field losses may continue to try to use the blurred or distorted area (because viewing with the macula is a reflex), and may need to be taught how to use the adjacent peripheral vision. Eccentric viewing, or viewing with an off-center part of the retina, will develop in some individuals without training, but most will benefit from instruction and practice to improve this skill. Therapy can be done with or without the use of magnification devices, and because most patients with central visual field loss are interested in reading, print materials are usually used in training. The training materials can be enlarged to a point at which they can be seen without magnification, but most often training is done in conjunction with use of appropriately powered lens systems. The patient is first taught to position the eye properly for best vision around the blind spot. After this has been mastered, he or she is then taught to recognize letters and words with the off-center point, progressing to reading text. This type of training can require several months of in-office and home activities before the individual is able to maintain a consistent eccentric viewing point when reading. Because a blind spot is present in the visual field, fluent reading may not always be possible, but often reading speeds and duration will improve with practice.

Management of Peripheral Visual Field Defects

Peripheral visual field losses interfere primarily with the ability to travel independently. Rehabilitation strategies include teaching peripheral awareness with or without optical systems. The client is taught scanning techniques to maximize the use of his or her remaining vision—techniques that are helpful for all aspects of visual functioning. Lenses that can improve peripheral visual field awareness include prisms, mirrors, reverse telescopes, and minus lenses, and are described in the following paragraphs:

1. Prism lenses shift an image in space so that the object appears to be in a different position than it actually is. The power, placement, and orientation of the prism will depend on the type of visual field loss that is present, as well as the visual acuity; people with visual field loss and reduced acuity may not be candidates for prism lenses. Partial prisms can be placed laterally on the eyeglasses, off of the visual axis, so that they are not seen when looking straight ahead, but by glancing into the prism, objects appear to be shifted more toward the midline so they are detected with a reduced amount of eye movement. Prisms can be helpful for any type of peripheral visual field defect and can be especially useful for hemianoptic defects. (Hemianopia is blindness in one-half of the visual field.) Extensive training is generally needed to teach appropriate and efficient use of the prism.
2. Mirrors can be attached to eyeglasses at an angle and used like rear view mirrors to see into the blind area. Because the image is reversed (left to right and vice versa), mirrors may be more difficult to adapt to perceptually, especially for the head-injured patient. Again, extensive training is usually indicated for patients using mirrors as field awareness devices.
3. Reverse telescopes and minus lenses can be useful for patients with constricted visual fields but who retain good acuity. These lens systems minify objects that are viewed so that more information fits into the restricted visual field, but if acuity is poor, the minification will make the infor-

mation difficult to interpret. As with other so-called field expanders, there is perceptual distortion which requires extensive training to adapt to this type of device.

Low Vision Instruction and Training

Throughout this chapter, references have been made to training the visually impaired client. Instruction in the efficient use of impaired vision, in addition to instruction in the optimal use of low vision devices to maximize use of vision, is an integral part of the low vision service. Instruction in the use of vision may include therapies to improve (1) eye movement skills, (2) accommodative functioning, (3) eccentric viewing skills, (4) peripheral awareness, (5) blur interpretation, (6) visual closure, (7) visual memory, and (8) letter and word recognition. Instruction in the proper use of low vision devices may also include proper care and cleaning of the devices, maintaining the proper focal distance, use of appropriate lighting and other nonoptical devices, learning to move the material rather than one's head, and addressing safety issues. For the use of telescopes, spotting, scanning, tracking, and focusing must be taught. In-office instructional training sessions, supplemented by a training program in the home may be ongoing until the client has mastered the skills necessary to effectively utilize the impaired vision, with or without low vision devices. The rehabilitation professional is advised to remember that motivation and expectations are key components to success.

Management of Reduced Contrast Sensitivity and Glare Sensitivity

The ability to detect targets or objects of low contrast is important not only with respect to reading, but also for independent travel. Poor contrast sensitivity may necessitate modified magnification and illumination for reading print, and for general purposes. Specific task lighting may be required and, therefore, it is recommended that incandescent, fluorescent, and halogen lights or combinations of lighting be evaluated for optimum functioning. Contrast sensitivity issues will also influence the prescription of optical devices; some lens forms provide brighter images and may be indicated for individuals with poor contrast sensitivity. For example, achromatic doublet lenses (reading lenses fabricated from two lenses cemented together) will provide better image contrast than simple single-lens microscopes. Illuminated stand magnifiers afford brighter images than nonilluminated types. For those with relatively good acuity but severely reduced contrast sensitivity, electronic magnification (such as a CCTV) may be necessary, as this is the only approach which allows manipulation of the contrast viewed. This is especially true for patients with glaucoma or inoperable cataracts. Contrast in the environment can sometimes be better detected with the use of special colored filters—yellow, orange, and amber are some of the more commonly prescribed colors.

Glare sensitivity, both indoors and out, can interfere with the ability to use residual vision effectively. Lighting modifications in the home, school, or the work environment can be made—such as sitting with one's back to the window, reducing ambient illumination by removing one or two tubes from a bank of overhead fluorescent lights, or using a flex-arm lamp at the work space, instead of using overhead light. Tinted lenses or filters can be used to reduce photophobia, as well as light to dark adaptation time. Ultraviolet protection should be included in all eyeglasses to reduce any bothersome glare. Frames with side-shields can also be helpful, especially for individuals with severe photophobia.

NONOPTICAL DEVICES

There are numerous nonoptical devices that improve functioning by relative-size magnification, contrast enhancement, or the use of nonvisual approaches. Use of large print, bold-lined paper, felt-tipped pens, big-eye needles, and large-button phone dials or timers are all applications of relative-size magnification. Lighting, filters,

The use of nonoptical devices, such as large-button telephones, handwriting guides, large-print timers and watches, bold-lined paper, and illumination, can help a person with low vision improve his or her performance of common tasks.

and the use of a typoscope (slotted black card to minimize reflected glare off of the page while one is writing) or a signature guide can benefit the client by improving contrast. Contrast can also be manipulated in the environment to improve visibility of targets. For example, putting a dark electrical outlet plate on a white wall, or placing light-colored food on a dark plate will make the target more visible. Reading, music, or flexible-arm typing stands can be used to position reading materials for very close working distances. Tactile markers and such auditory devices as talking watches, clocks, calculators, and bathroom scales, along with taped materials, allow the individual who is visually impaired to do some activities nonvisually. Some visually impaired individuals use both print and braille, as well as taped materials. It is advisable to remember that when the visual system is impaired, nonvisual approaches to some activities may be safer and more efficient.

When indicated for the client's needs, adaptive computer technology can be explored. Sometimes simply moving closer to the computer screen (relative-distance magnification) and using an appropriate near-vision prescription for that distance will be adequate. Stands with adjustable arms can position the monitor at the optimum distance. Using a larger monitor or font size also provides relative-size magnification. The low vision clinician can specify the size of the characters that can be seen comfortably at a given distance, and prescribe the correct reading lenses for that distance to ensure appropriate modifications are made without overcompensating. Enlarging beyond a certain point will actually slow the patient down and may be contraindicated with certain types of visual field loss. Therefore, it is best for the patient to have a low vision evaluation prior to exploring adaptive technology.

THE REHABILITATION COUNSELOR'S ROLE

The rehabilitation counselor plays an important role in the provision of low vision services. First, the counselor should help the client identify those specific goals that can be addressed through rehabilitation. Prior to the evaluation, the client can be helped to formulate reasonable expectations about what will occur. Some individuals may not understand how the low vision examination will differ from their other ophthalmic care. They may be skeptical or have been unsuccessful with over-the-counter magnification devices and may need to be educated about the low vision rehabilitation process. It is recommended that patients be encouraged to bring all eyeglasses, magnifiers, or lenses they are using, as well as samples of reading materials or activities that are important to them but are difficult to see or perform.

The counselor can also assess needs in the home, particularly lighting, as part of the intake process. Assessment of work-related needs can be done as part of an on-site visit, and should be as specific as possible about the client's work environment, job requirements, and safety issues. Communicating this information to the low vision practitioner, typically an ophthalmologist or optometrist (see Chapter 2), will assist in formulating the rehabilitation goals and needs. After the initial visit, the counselor provides support, encouraging the client to follow through with prescribed therapies, to keep follow-up visits, and to use the prescribed low vision devices as intended. Many clients may be overwhelmed with what is involved in the low vision rehabilitation process or may lack internal motivation. It is for these clients that external support is particularly critical. The rehabilitation counselor, while being supportive of the process, can provide the client with a meaningful outlet for expressing any frustrations, discouragement, or negative feelings about such issues as the cosmetic appearance of certain devices, the social awkwardness of using devices in public, and the difficulties involved in mastering adaptive techniques for tasks. Recognizing when counseling or additional therapies are indicated and making appropriate and timely referrals can also help ensure the success of the rehabilitation process.

SUMMARY

Visual impairment can be the result of a number of causes but the end result is a sensory loss that can interfere with the ability to do many activities of daily living. Many individuals who are visually impaired use a variety of approaches to carry out daily living, educational, work-related, and recreational activities and tasks. All people with visual impairments should have the opportunity to evaluate the potential benefits of any appropriate lens system, adaptive equipment, or environmental modifications. This can only be achieved by a comprehensive low vision evaluation and cooperative efforts between the client, the eyecare specialist, and rehabilitation professionals. Low vision rehabilitation is an ongoing process, as vision, a client's needs, and compensatory abilities are not always static. By maximizing the individual's use of remaining vision and enhancing the ability to complete a variety of activities and tasks, low vision services can lay the cornerstone for effective rehabilitation efforts.

LEARNING ACTIVITIES

1. Mrs. Jones has diabetic retinopathy and complains of fluctuating vision. You have received a report that states her visual acuities are OD 10/40–, OS 10/200. Is she "legally blind?" Does she qualify as being visually impaired through your state agency? What other information would you need to have to make these determinations?
2. Explain relative-distance magnification and give examples of how patients can benefit from this principle for simple activities of daily living.
3. Explain the term *refraction* as it applies to lenses. What is meant when an examination for refraction is performed as part of the low vision evaluation? Why is this an important component of low vision care?
4. What are the advantages of reading with a microscope? What are the drawbacks? How can these disadvantages be overcome?
5. Describe the patient's options for seeing a television screen more clearly.

PART TWO

Assessment

The development of a rehabilitation plan involves the assessment of a need for services, the identification of daily living and vocational goals, and the setting of objectives to meet these goals. The plan is based on self-information provided by the client during the initial interview and on medical, vocational, and psychological assessments obtained from other professionals. Rehabilitation counselors must be able to identify the type of information they need, understand the reports they receive, and have the skills to communicate assessment results effectively so that a meaningful rehabilitation plan can be devised.

Part Two of this book outlines the various types of assessments, beginning with the medical assessment. The medical assessment assists rehabilitation counselors in understanding the course of visual impairment, treatment options, and methods of ameliorating or minimizing the effects of impairment in considering vocational goals consistent with an individual's functional capabilities. Psychological and vocational assessments can help the counselor identify an individual's strengths, which when properly established, can contribute to the viability of a rehabilitation plan. They can also help determine deficiencies that may need to be addressed within the framework of the plan. Assessments related to intelligence, aptitude, achievement, and interests may also provide direction. For example, they may validate an individual's expressed interests and capacity to complete a proposed educational program or suggest the need for additional services or adaptive devices. The chapters in Part Two also include demographic information, such as age, gender, culture, and multiple disability issues. These factors influence the selection of assessment instruments, counseling approaches, and the range of services that may be required.

CHAPTER 5

Medical Assessment

William H. Graves and Connie S. McCaa

The provision of appropriate rehabilitation services is contingent upon a comprehensive assessment of the individual with a visual impairment who is seeking those services. Because of its impact on the services that an individual receives later, medical assessment is one of the primary areas of appraisal of the client. The objectives of this chapter are to (1) describe the purpose of a comprehensive medical assessment, (2) identify when comprehensive medical assessments are utilized, and (3) explain the various relationships among nonvisual disabilities, visual impairments, and rehabilitation planning and outcomes.

COMPREHENSIVE MEDICAL ASSESSMENT

One of the fundamental services provided by a rehabilitation counselor is the identification of a client's visual, physical, mental, and emotional functional abilities and limitations. The comprehensive medical assessment, which consists of a complete, general medical examination, a visual examination by either an ophthalmologist or an optometrist, examinations by specialists in medical or related fields, a hearing examination, and clinical laboratory tests and procedures, serves many purposes and can be extremely helpful to the rehabilitation counselor in planning present and future rehabilitation services for a client.

Medical assessment services are an essential part of the total rehabilitation assessment process. These services are tools that rehabilitation counselors use to assist clients with visual impairments to achieve their rehabilitation objectives. In their classic work, McGowan and Porter (1967) stated:

> All individuals involved in the medical study of a rehabilitation client should be aware of the goal of rehabilitation; i.e., the best obtainable vocational adjustment for a client. Their reports and work should reflect this awareness, and the medical evaluation of a client should not become so involved with the diagnosis and treatment of a specific pathology that the goal of rehabilitation becomes overshadowed or secondary. (p. 58)

It is the responsibility of the rehabilitation counselor to coordinate the services provided for a client in the comprehensive medical assessment process. Each of the services increases the counselor's and client's understanding of the client's present health status, the client's needs for visual or other medical services, and the effects of the eye or other disorders on the client's capacity for employment.

Purpose and Function of the Comprehensive Medical Assessment

The inability to work because of a visual impairment is the most common reason individuals apply for services from a rehabilitation agency that serves individuals who are blind or visually impaired. The vision loss is perceived by applicants as the central obstacle to employment. The presence of another disability affecting the employability of the applicant, however, may or may not be known to these individuals. In addition, the relationship of the nonvisual impairment to the visual impairment and its effect on either the visual system or other bodily systems may also be unknown to the applicant.

The potential client may also assume that because the rehabilitation agency serves people with visual impairments, the agency is not concerned about other disabilities and therefore does not provide other types of rehabilitation services. Neither of these assumptions is accurate. Both rehabilitation legislation and policy recognize the importance of meeting all of the needs of the people with visual impairments including those caused by nonvisual disorders or disabilities. These policies and legislation encourage the rehabilitation counselor to provide comprehensive medical assessment services, including hearing evaluations, so that the presence of any other disabilities may be identified. There is general agreement (Hylbert & Hylbert, 1979; Nagi, 1969; Roessler & Rubin, 1992; Wright, 1980) about the purposes of medical assessment, as set forth by McGowan and Porter (1967), and they are as follows:

> (1) to establish through medical diagnostic studies that a physical or mental impairment is present that materially limits the activities that the individual can perform,
>
> (2) to appraise the current general health status of the individual, including the discovery of other impairments not previously recognized,
>
> (3) to determine the extent and means by which the disabling conditions can be corrected, removed, or minimized,
>
> (4) to provide a realistic basis for the selection of an employment objective commensurate with the . . . individual's capacities and limitations. (p. 56)

It is evident that a comprehensive medical assessment is used to (1) identify the presence of one or more disabilities, (2) secure recommendations to remove, correct, or minimize the functional effects of the disability (Wright, 1980), and (3) identify ways to help improve or stabilize the physical, emotional, and mental functioning of the client. There is yet an additional purpose for the medical assessment of individuals with visual impairments: to help and guide the rehabilitation counselor and the applicant in identifying and understanding the relationships among nonvisual disabilities, visual impairments, and the applicant's rehabilitation needs. For example, the systemic nonvisual disorder diabetes mellitus is often associated with the following visual impairments: retinopathies, cataracts, rubeosis iridis, diplopia due to extraocular muscle palsy, iridocyclitis, and optic neuropathy (Vaughan, Asbury, & Riordan-Eva, 1996). Diabetes and each of these related eye disorders will affect the type of rehabilitation program developed by the applicant and the rehabilitation counselor. Failure by the rehabilitation counselor to consider the effects of nonvisual disabilities caused by diseases such as diabetes mellitus, sickle cell anemia, and multiple sclerosis can create other physical and vocational problems that may prevent the client from achieving both vocational and other rehabilitation goals (Giesen & Ford, 1986b). Nonvisual disabilities can also affect the course of the visual impairment. For example, in untreated hyperthyroidism, sight loss due to optic nerve involvement may occur (Vaughan et al., 1995). The appendix to this chapter lists various nonvisual disorders, their characteristics, the associated visual impairments, and recommended actions for both the client and the counselor.

MEDICAL CONSULTATION

When the initial assessment reports are returned from the applicant's medical and eye examinations, the rehabilitation counselor may need assistance interpreting the information in the reports and identifying additional medical or eye-related services required by the client. This assistance can be furthered by a medical consultation. Most rehabilitation agencies employ physicians to provide medical consultation to rehabilitation counselors and other agency personnel. Medical consultation is a regularly scheduled, face-to-face meeting between the agency medical consultant and the rehabilitation counselor during which the client's various medical conditions and their relationship to the rehabilitation plan and vocational goal of the client are discussed and evaluated (McGowan & Porter, 1967).

In many cases, successful rehabilitation depends on the proper use of the medical consultation by the rehabilitation counselor. A medical consultation can be employed to secure an interpretation of medical terms and information, obtain an explanation of information in physicians' reports, relate the visual impairments and nonvisual disabilities to the applicant's functional capacity, identify the need for such additional medical studies as specialty examinations, determine the adequacy of medical information, evaluate the medical prognosis, and determine the functional limitations caused by the impairment.

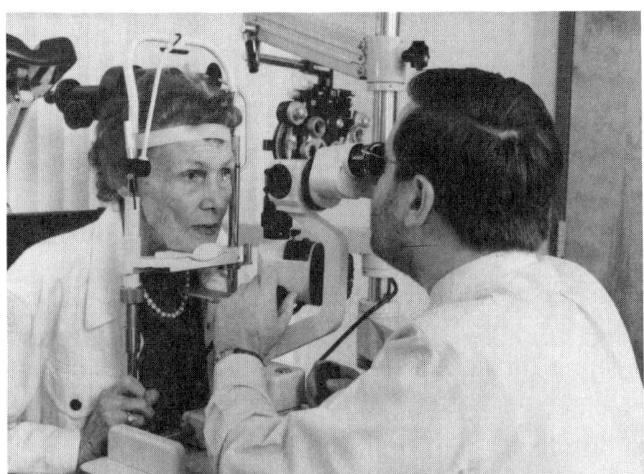
To provide appropriate rehabilitation services, a counselor needs to have access to a complete medical assessment of an individual with a visual impairment. The information received by the counselor includes medical and eye examination reports, and the result of examinations, such as the one shown here.

The information that the rehabilitation counselor obtains from the medical consultation has a direct effect on the planning of rehabilitation services by the counselor and the client. Because the rehabilitation counselor is the primary recipient of medical consultation services, it is the counselor's responsibility to use the medical consultation effectively. The counselor is urged to understand the following:

> (1) the medical terminology, physical findings, diagnoses, and recommendations contained in medical reports;
>
> (2) the amount of impairment attributed by the client to the disorder and how the impairment relates to the client's employability;
>
> (3) how physical restoration services may improve the client's employability;
>
> (4) the areas of expertise of the specialists in the diagnostic study and treatment programs;
>
> (5) the effects of a disorder, the physical stability of the client, and the progress of a client under treatment; and
>
> (6) how the policies of the agency regarding eligibility for services, training, and employment are related to and affected by the comprehensive medical assessment process (McGowan & Porter, 1967, p. 57).

Frequently, the medical consultant working with the rehabilitation counselor serving individuals who are visually impaired is an ophthalmologist.

The ophthalmologist views the visual system as one among all of the bodily systems and by training is aware of the effects of nonvisual disorders on the visual system. This expertise assists the rehabilitation counselor to identify the most appropriate medical care. The medical consultant will also help the rehabilitation counselor develop an assistance plan for the client to achieve medical stability—both visual and nonvisual—before beginning extensive independent living and vocational rehabilitation programs. In those cases in which medical stability cannot be achieved prior to the initiation of the rehabilitation programs, the medical consultant will also aid the rehabilitation counselor in establishing ways to accommodate the medical stability needs of the client during the rehabilitation program.

The following illustrative case study demonstrates the use of medical consultation when there is a possibility of a nonvisual disorder affecting the rehabilitation outcome:

> A 54-year-old man who had been employed as a taxi driver for 25 years was referred by an ophthalmologist for assistance in securing bilateral cataract surgery. The medical examination revealed that the client had arteriosclerotic heart disease, which placed many limitations on his activities. The rehabilitation counselor was unable to determine from the information in the general medical examination whether the heart condition would preclude the client from continuing to work after the removal of the cataracts. The medical consultant assigned to the case recommended an evaluation by a cardiologist. The cardiologist's report indicated that the heart disease was not so severe as to prevent a return to work and recommended trial medications, an exercise program, and dietary planning. The medical consultant then reviewed the recommendations with the rehabilitation counselor. A physical restoration program was recommended by the medical consultant, which included bilateral cataract surgery, follow-up treatment by the cardiologist for six months, and an exercise and diet program under the supervision of a local hospital's cardiac wellness program.

In addition to illustrating the use of the medical consultant, this example also highlights the importance of the general medical examination to identify additional disabilities that may be present.

THE MEDICAL ASSESSMENT AND THE REHABILITATION PROCESS

The medical assessment process is fundamental to the development of any rehabilitation program. Some individuals, who believe they were referred to a rehabilitation agency solely because of their vision impairments, however, do not appreciate the need for a comprehensive medical assessment. Some rehabilitation counselors have also taken the position that a comprehensive medical assessment is either too time-consuming or not relevant. Nevertheless, research (Chase, 1988) shows that a comprehensive medical assessment does not delay the rehabilitation process, but rather provides an opportunity for the client and the rehabilitation counselor to identify the functional effects of all the present and potential disability possibilities. At this time, the effects of multiple disabilities can also be considered by the client and counselor when planning a realistic vocational goal.

A study (Giesen et al., 1985) of 619 clients who were legally blind and whose cases were closed as either employed or unemployed by four state rehabilitation agencies indicated that 66 percent of the clients served by the agencies had at least one secondary disability and 84 percent of the individuals closed as unemployed had a tertiary disability. Of those individuals securing employment in a competitive situation after receiving rehabilitation services, only 22 percent had another disability at referral. This 62 percent difference underscores the significant impact that additional disabilities can have on the outcome of the rehabilitation process for persons with visual impairments. Giesen and Ford (1986b) also reported that the number and severity of additional nonvisual disabilities is associated with unsuccessful outcomes; they found that with each additional nonvisual disability, the probability that the individual would locate competitive employment was decreased. To increase the possibility that clients with multiple disabilities would reach their vocational goals, Giesen and Ford (1986b) suggest that information from comprehensive medical assessments be used in both identifying appropriate vocational goals and planning for the provision of suitable medical and related services.

The foregoing studies document the importance of the comprehensive medical assessment; most clients with visual impairments have an additional disability, and a second disability appears significantly related to unsuccessful rehabilitation outcomes. Therefore, a comprehensive medical assessment is highly recommended to ensure that any nonvisual disability affecting the functioning of an individual with a visual impairment be identified, assessed, corrected, and, whenever possible, minimized. Rehabilitation counselors are encouraged to use the information obtained from the comprehensive medical assessment in the development of the Individualized Written Rehabilitation Program (IWRP) (see Chapter 10) in order to minimize the effects of both the visual impairments and nonvisual disabilities. A sample copy of an IWRP is printed in Appendix A of this book.

Initial Interview

During the initial interview, the rehabilitation counselor is urged to begin planning for the comprehensive medical assessment. To initiate this process with the client, the rehabilitation counselor collects information on (1) when the client's visual impairment was first perceived, (2) what the client believes caused the impairment, (3) the client's symptoms and how they may have changed since the eye problem began, and (4) how the symptoms of the visual impairment interfere with the client's usual work performance. This information reinforces the purpose of rehabilitation service provision and the relationship to the applicant's vocational or independent living goal.

As Wright (1980) stressed, it is important to obtain adequate information about any eyecare the applicant is presently receiving, including the use of eyeglasses or any other optical devices. If the applicant is under the care of an eye specialist, the rehabilitation counselor is encouraged to elicit the nature of the treatment being received, how often the applicant sees the eyecare specialist, and the character of the relationship between the client and the eyecare specialist. Information from the eyecare specialist and other physicians is vital in planning the delivery of rehabilitation services in that it will assist the rehabilitation counselor to understand the relationship of the applicant's specific visual impairment to the rehabilitation process. (Because of the confidential nature of this information, the rehabilitation counselor will need the applicant's permission to contact the eyecare specialist and other physicians and to obtain copies of the applicant's visual and other medical history.)

Based on the information received from the client, the rehabilitation counselor can then contact the applicant's eyecare specialist and physicians to request copies of medical information. In most cases, subsequent to the interview, a general medical examination will be performed by a physician of the applicant's choosing. However, when the applicant has described such multiple physical problems as diabetes, sickle cell anemia, hypertension, heart disease, or respiratory problems, it is highly recommended that the rehabilitation counselor arrange for a comprehensive medical examination to be performed by a physician specializing in internal medicine. A hearing examination is also recommended, because hearing loss frequently accompanies visual impairment and aging. These dual impairments can pose significant constraints on rehabilitation. It is also suggested that the rehabilitation counselor arrange for an eye examination performed either by an ophthalmologist or an optometrist so that the rehabilitation plan will be based on up-to-date information. Usually, the eye examination will follow the general medical examination or can be conducted at approximately the same time.

After all the medical examinations have been performed, the rehabilitation counselor is encouraged to review again the information collected with the medical consultant to determine if the recommendations made by the examining medical and eye specialists are apt to improve the functioning of the client. This medical consultation process may also indicate the need for additional specialty examinations.

Client Considerations

The rehabilitation counselor is responsible for preparing the client for the comprehensive medical assessment process. The preparation process should address any agency policy and procedures that relate to the needs of the client, as well as any emotional issues (e.g., fear or anxiety) raised by the examination process and the presence of a visual impairment. The minimal policy and procedure information needs of the client include (1) why he or she is being referred for a general medical examination, as well as eye and other specialty examinations, (2) the length of time the examinations may require, (3) what the client can expect to learn from the examinations, and (4) how the information from the reports will be used by the rehabilitation counselor (McGowan & Porter, 1967). The counselor should explain that, in most cases, the client will not receive treatment for the impairment during the assessment phase of the rehabilitation process. The time required for the rehabilitation counselor to study the medical reports, review the reports with the medical consultant and applicant, and develop the Individualized Written Rehabilitation Program with the applicant should also be explained. When this information is shared with the applicant, appointments can be made with appropriate specialists. (For more on the responsibilities of a rehabilitation counselor, see Sidebar 5.1.)

Following the medical assessment, rehabilitation counselors may find contradictions between the reports they receive from physicians and the interpretation of the information by an individual client. Such contradictions are not uncommon in light of the fear and anxiety that frequently accompany the diagnosis of an eye disorder, such as macular degeneration, diabetic retinopathy, or cataracts (Zavon & Slater, 1988). In addition to fear and anxiety, contradictions or misconceptions may also result from (1) the point in time at which the information was delivered, (2) the amount of information provided, (3) the provision of incomplete information, and (4) the inability of the client to recall all of the information. Instructional plans, such as those described by Zavon and Slater (1988), can reduce fear and anxiety and enhance communication. Instructional plans provide standardized information in multiple formats. For example, an instructional plan on diabetic retinopathy might include an audiotape or videotape on diabetic retinopathy; information on a support group for individuals with diabetic retinopathy or a support group for individuals with visual impairments; the Internet addresses from which additional information may be obtained; and printed, taped, or braille information about common medical treatments and expected outcomes. Demonstration of assistive devices and appliances may also be beneficial in helping the client cope with feelings of helplessness and despair.

THE IMPACT OF NONVISUAL DISORDERS ON REHABILITATION

People with visual impairments can have one or more of dozens of various nonvisual disorders that affect eye diseases, overall functioning, and, hence, rehabilitation. Rehabilitation counselors have access to medical consultation to assist them in understanding the relationships among

SIDEBAR 5.1

Responsibilities of a Rehabilitation Counselor in the Medical Assessment Process

(1) To identify both visual impairments and nonvisual disabilities,

(2) To determine the extent and nature of the medical case study,

(3) To understand the meaning of the medical and eyecare findings,

(4) To ascertain the possibility of reducing or removing the disorder,

(5) To determine the potential for rehabilitation,

(6) To explain the residual limitations (of the impairment) to the client and those relating to the client's vocational or independent living goals, and

(7) To interpret the effects of the residual impairment on the client achieving her or his vocational goal.

the disorders and the effects of each of them, either singularly or in combination, on the employability of the client. It is important, therefore, that the counselor has a working knowledge about the effects of such frequent nonvisual disorders as diabetes, acquired immunodeficiency syndrome (AIDS), arthritis, multiple sclerosis, and sickle cell anemia. The following subsections briefly describe the rehabilitation implications of diabetes mellitus and AIDS, two conditions commonly encountered by counselors.

Diabetes Mellitus

Diabetes mellitus is one of the leading causes of blindness. Of most concern to rehabilitation counselors serving persons who are diabetic and who also have severe visual impairment is diabetic retinopathy. As mentioned in Chapter 2, there are two major types of diabetic retinopathy: nonproliferative retinopathy, which is also known as background or simple retinopathy, and proliferative retinopathy. Vision is generally not affected until macular edema and proliferative retinopathy develops. Proliferative retinopathy is the most advanced form, and it is almost always associated with severe vision loss. Intensive control prior to development of retinopathy reduces the risk of later vision loss by about 80 percent.

Another serious complication of diabetes is kidney impairment (Needham, Eldridge, Harabedian, & Crawford, 1993; Ponchillia, 1993). Almost all individuals having type I diabetes (juvenile-onset diabetes) have renal damage, although only 35 percent develop signs of nephropathy (Berkow & Fletcher, 1987). After obliterative lesions in glomerular capillaries, renal failure accounts for nearly 50 percent of deaths in people with diabetes with onset before age 20 (Berkow & Fletcher, 1992). Individuals with type I diabetes are often considered as "brittle diabetics," which means the diabetes is very difficult to control. Therefore, it is suggested that rehabilitation counselors encourage regular medical consultation for any clients who have type I diabetes mellitus. In addition to the matters discussed earlier in this chapter, vital issues to be addressed in medical consultation include (1) referral to an endocrinologist, (2) referral to a urologist, and (3) referral to a retinal specialist.

Hypertension (high blood pressure) is also associated with diabetes mellitus (Ponchillia, 1993). It relates to both renal involvement and atherosclerosis. Characteristically, hypertension is accompanied by decreased circulation, increased sensitivity to cold, and prolonged healing time for even mild injuries to the legs and feet. If the lower extremities and toenails are not properly cared for, severe infections can occur that could result in gangrene and eventual amputation of the affected region. Control of hypertension and improved circulation are two of the essential goals of the treating physician.

In addition, impaired nerve conduction or neuropathies frequently accompany diabetes. Symptoms often include persistent tingling and loss of feeling in fingers and toes. For the person with diabetes who is newly blinded, this reduction or loss of sensation in the fingers could prevent either learning braille or becoming proficient in its use. It may also interfere with keyboarding and recording skills and can have a negative effect on activities of daily living (e.g., setting the dials on an oven or measuring insulin). Loss of feeling in the lower limbs frequently means that an injury has gone unnoticed and can also mask other such disabilities as osteoarthritis, infected toenails, or plantar warts.

Strict control of the basic diabetes is necessary to support a healthy visual system. Rehabilitation counselors working with clients whose visual impairments are secondary to diabetes have several tasks. First is to be aware of the fact that insulin therapy is inadequate without diabetic education for the client (Berkow & Fletcher, 1992). The client must monitor the diabetes on a day-to-day basis with blood glucose reagent strips. It is highly recommended that counselors also have some familiarity with the range of devices that are available to clients who use insulin, such as (1) syringes with large display screens, (2) monitors with voice added, (3) magnifiers that snap onto the insulin syringe, (4) syringes that allow for a pre-set dosage, and (5) syringes with plungers that provide an audible "click" (Cleary & Hamilton, 1993; Petzinger, 1993). The surgically implanted insulin pump should also be made familiar to the client with diabetes. As Rosenthal (1993) noted, for diabetic clients who are also visually impaired, the lack of positive feedback from visually seeing a reduction in their blood sugar can make it difficult for some of these individuals to remain self-motivated about following the prescribed diet, the insulin program, or any other vital medication follow-up.

Rehabilitation counselors are also encouraged to stress the importance of caution when taking medications; individuals who have difficulty reading labels increase the probability of taking the wrong medication, particularly when on multiple medications, as illustrated in the following paragraph:

> Many tablets look virtually identical, unless one can discern the print stamped on them by pharmaceutical companies. Although ophthalmic medications are coded by class into different bottle-top colors, many . . . individuals [with visual impairments] cannot tell these colors apart. In some cases, ophthalmic dropper bottles can be mixed with other solutions that come in similar bottles. (One . . . individual [who was nearly blind] . . . accidentally instilled several drops of "crazy glue" into his eye, thinking it was his eye medication, which looked similar.) Sometimes, the errors can result in serious under- or over dosages or in placing the medication in the wrong eye. (One patient devised the handy system of wrapping the medication bottles for use in the right eye with rubber bands and leaving those for the left as is.) (Rosenthal, 1993, p. 332)

In addition to helping clients understand the importance of insulin monitoring, the IWRP for a client with diabetes should, with rare exceptions, include a diabetic education program (Baker, 1993; Williams, 1993). With good education about diabetes, the client should be able to analyze the relationship that the activity level and diet has on blood glucose level and appropriately change the insulin dosage, food intake, or exercise. It is important that the counselor be supportive of efforts by the client and the family to conform strictly to the recommended diet, which may be complicated and usually excludes fast and frozen foods (Rosenthal, 1993). The maintenance of normal or low normal weight is a major objective of diet plans for people with diabetes.

The rehabilitation counselor's second task is to understand the client's work environment and to help the client make informed choices about his or her job. Routine or standard procedures in

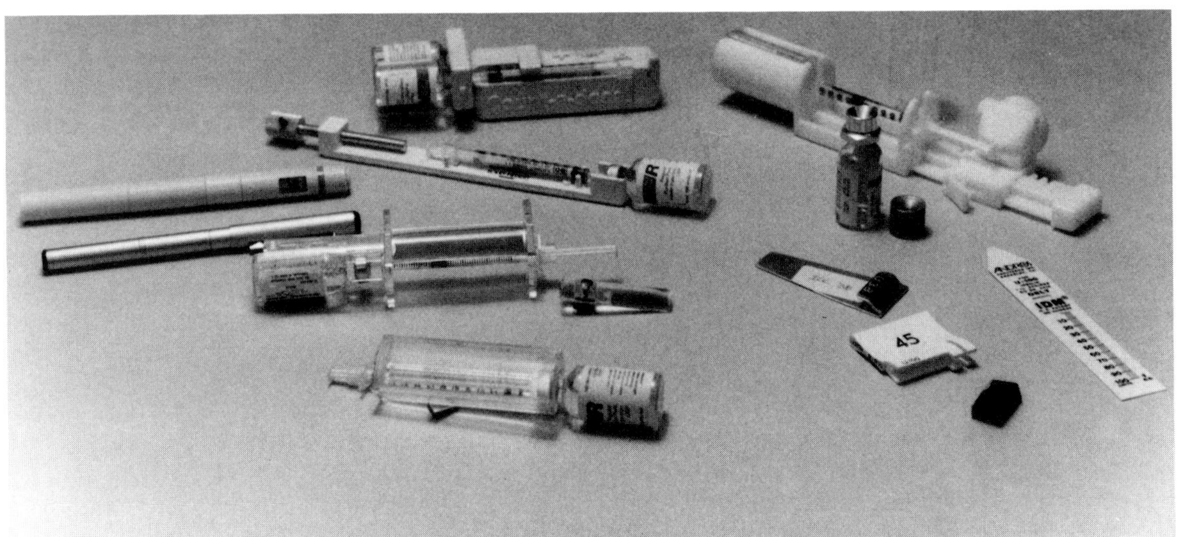

It is important that counselors have some familiarity with the various adaptive insulin measurement devices for diabetic clients who are blind or visually impaired. Clockwise from the left are pen injectors, tactile insulin measurement devices and needleguides, and syringe magnifiers.

the workplace are highly desirable because it is important for the client with diabetes to work at the same pace on a daily basis. Although overexertion is to be avoided, jobs requiring extensive physical activity are acceptable if the physical activities are consistent from day to day. It is recommended that placement in a job with rotating shifts or varying work hours be avoided because these jobs lack the necessary routine. Furthermore, the counselor may consider emphasizing that breaks and meals during the work day be scheduled so that the client's blood glucose level will remain constant.

Employers who do not understand the effects of diabetes need information from both the client and counselor; this information includes (1) what diabetes is, (2) the need for regularly scheduled shifts, lunch times, breaks, and energy expenditures in the workplace, (3) the necessity for regular working hours, and (4) the manifestations of hyperglycemia and hypoglycemia. Without this information, employers may misinterpret the behavior of an employee with diabetes whose blood sugar level is fluctuating. For example, it is possible that an employer would interpret a hypoglycemic reaction as the influence of alcohol rather than recognizing the employee's behavior as a manifestation of low blood sugar. Because these misunderstandings can and do happen, it is important that the employee who is diabetic explain to the employer the symptoms and signs of hypoglycemia or hyperglycemia and explain the appropriate emergency treatment for an insulin reaction or any other problems caused by the diabetes. Rehabilitation counselors can assist clients in this process by (1) providing brochures or pamphlets that clients can give to their employers, (2) role-playing interviews with the client during which the effects of diabetes are explained to the employer, and (3) encouraging the client to become involved in a diabetic support group (Bryant & Vaughn, 1993; Merrill, 1993).

Because of reduced sensitivity in the extremities (peripheral neuropathy), it is important for counselors to help clients understand the problems and the benefits in learning alternatives to sight skills, such as reading braille, using computers with speech recognition, or perhaps learning to utilize a Kurzweil reader or voice pad. The counselor and client may also decide to plan for the client to learn various alternative skills. Along with specific alternatives for reading, the rehabilitation teacher can assist clients in learning to use kitchen appliances and other assistive devices that will enable them not only to prepare food, but also to perform household chores.

For the client with diabetes, basic orientation and mobility lessons may have to be shorter in duration because of the interaction of exercise with low blood sugar levels. It is highly recommended that the orientation and mobility specialist and client monitor blood sugar levels in relationship to the length and type of lessons. Such monitoring will assist both client and counselor in determining the level of physical activity that the client can safely perform. If, for example, mild physical exertion adversely reduces the blood glucose level, the counselor is encouraged to restrict any job searches to sedentary and light exertional work settings, or to confer with the physician concerning reduced insulin dosage.

The third and final task for the rehabilitation counselor is to assess how well the client with diabetes copes with stress. For clients who do not cope well, it is critical to teach stress-management techniques (Needham et al., 1993). Because stress can cause blood sugar levels to vary widely, it is essential that this cause of variability in the blood sugar level be determined and minimized. Many clients have reported that they feel they have no control over their lives since they developed diabetes. It is important for the counselor to help address these feelings so that they may gain respect for the efforts being made to control their diabetes and its complications.

An additional, troubling area for many clients is sex, because sexual performance is often adversely affected by diabetes mellitus. Many men with diabetes report impotence, and both men and women often report a loss of genital sensation. These conditions result from the neuropathies associated with diabetes. Reactions to the conditions vary among clients; some experience depression, whereas others experience fear, anxiety, or anger. When the counselor becomes aware of this issue during the counseling process, it is highly recommended that the client be referred to an endocrinologist and urologist for a specialty examination and treatment recommendations, which may include sex therapy, family counseling, or in some cases penile implants. For a more detailed discussion of these and other issues, see Bryant and Cobb (1997).

Acquired Immunodeficiency Syndrome (AIDS)

AIDS is a disease which, because the immune system fails, paves the way for many potentially fatal opportunistic infections. Cytomegalovirus (CMV) retinitis is the most frequent opportunistic intraocular infection among individuals with AIDS; its prevalence rate is 15 to 40 percent (Henderly, Freeman, Causey, & Rao, 1987). Kiester (1990) stated that 90 percent of the population infected with the human immunodeficiency virus (HIV) carries the CMV virus, which is prone to attack the retina. It can also attack the gastrointestinal system, the adrenal glands, in addition to the brain, resulting in dementia. Studies at the National Eye Institute show that persons with AIDS and CMV retinitis usually have more severe immune deficiency than those without ocular complications (Jabs, Enger, & Bartlett, 1989). The speed with which vision loss occurs varies from months to years (Kiester, 1990).

The first indication of CMV retinitis is blurring or dimness of vision, usually three to six months after the diagnosis of AIDS, followed by retinal bleeding and destruction of retinal tissue (Kiester, 1990). CMV retinitis is frequently bilateral and, if untreated, is almost always progressive, often leading to blindness (Henderly et al., 1987). The drugs ganciclovir and foscarnet generally retard the progression of the disease, but do not cure it.

Infections of the central nervous system are the second most common cause of visual complications of AIDS. The symptoms associated with these infections include double vision, blurred vision, and eye movement difficulties. An important statistic for the rehabilitation counselor to understand is that neurological causes of visual impairments among AIDS patients are more common among intravenous (IV) drug users than other populations infected with HIV (Kiester, 1990).

It is essential that rehabilitation counselors working with people with AIDS address employer attitudes, and their concerns about transmission and absenteeism. The counselor is also encouraged to discuss with the client the rate of progression of the disease, the psychosocial reactions to visual impairment, in addition to issues related to the AIDS diagnosis and client fears (e.g., the social stigma, concerns about a painful death, alienation from friends and family).

SUMMARY

The rehabilitation counselor has two major reasons for obtaining a comprehensive medical assessment. The first is to determine if the applicant for rehabilitation services has a visual impairment and any additional disabilities. The second is to help the person with the visual impairment identify a vocational goal that is congruent with the limitations imposed by the impairment(s).

LEARNING ACTIVITIES

1. Marcie Smith, 39 years old, has been referred to your office for vocational placement. Ms. Smith has been employed as a waitress for the past 20 years. She was recently diagnosed as having systemic lupus erythematosus, as well as retinal damage associated with the lupus. Her present visual acuity is 20/200 with a restricted visual field of 10 degrees. What additional information do you need for vocational planning purposes?
2. You have been asked to prepare a presentation for the local chapter of the NAACP on vision disorders and rehabilitation in the minority community. You decided to focus on medically related issues. Identify the systemic disorders that have visual complications with a higher prevalence rate in minority communities.
3. Ms. Eva Rotenone has been referred to your office. Ms. Rotenone is diagnosed as having CMV retinitis. Although she has a history of IV drug usage, she has been under treatment and is doing well. She is interested in entering postsecondary training as a hairdresser. What are the medical considerations of CMV retinitis and what issues will you have to address in working with Ms. Rotenone?
4. Mr. Louis Chappell has been referred to your office. Underlined in red on the referral form are the words, "Mr. Chappell is a brittle diabetic. Good luck!" Identify the issues that the rehabilitation counselor must address in planning rehabilitation services for Mr. Chappell.

Systemic Disorders and Associated Visual Disorders

Diagnosis	Characteristics	Associated Visual Disorders	Recommended Actions
Acne rosacea	Chronic inflammatory disorder with onset during fourth decade of life or later; characteristics usually occurring in central area of face; vascular lesions, erythema (redness), pimples and pustules, red swollen nose, and increase in volume of flow to face	Rosacea keratitis (uncommon)	Review of medical information with medical consultant
AIDS	A secondary immunodeficiency syndrome, transmitted by body fluids (e.g., blood, plasma, semen), characterized by severe immune deficiency resulting in secondary infections of opportunistic type malignancies, and neurologic lesions	Retinal infections, including CMV	Medical consultations; referral to AIDS specialists; systemic antibiotics; support group; AIDS education; independent living skills
Albinism	A congenital hereditary condition; absence of pigment in skin, hair, and eyes; associated with several hereditary impairments, e.g., esotropia, color vision; may be complete or incomplete	Photophobia; underdeveloped macula; searching nystagmus; lack of pigment in the iris and retina; high refractive errors, especially myopia.	Review of medical information with medical consultant; referral to internist for a comprehensive medical evaluation; dark glasses; avoid sunlight
Alcoholism, ethyl	Physiologic dependence on alcohol with impaired social and/or occupational functioning; peripheral neuropathies; gastrointestinal disorders; autonomic hyperactivity; anxiety and/or depression; avitaminosis	Bilateral loss of central vision; centrocecal scotoma in each eye	Review of medical information with medical consultant; referral to psychiatrist or psychologist specializing in chemical dependency for evaluation and treatment recommendations; referral to internist for comprehensive medical evaluation; consideration of AA; multiple vitamin therapy

(*continued on next page*)

Appendix. Systemic Disorders and Associated Visual Disorders

Systemic Disorders and Associated Visual Disorders (*continued*)			
Diagnosis	**Characteristics**	**Associated Visual Disorders**	**Recommended Actions**
Ankylosing sypondylitis	Chronic, progressive disease of the small joints of the spine, similar to rheumatoid arthritis; 90% affected are young males; gradual onset with mild back pain; immobility of spine; diminished chest expansion; flattening of lumbar curve	Uveitis; scleritis	Review of medical information with medical consultant; referral to internist, rheumatologist, or neurosurgeon or orthopedic surgeon for comprehensive and specialty medical evaluations and treatment recommendations usually including steriods
Arteriosclerotic disease	Syndromes associated with cardiovascular diseases including hypertension, kidney disease, stroke or CVA, atherosclerosis	Retinal emboli; central retinal vein occlusion; atherosclerotic and increased light reflex on retinal arterioles; optic disk infarction	Medical consultation; referral to internist and ophthalmologist for evaluation and treatment recommendation
Avitaminosis A	Chronic deficiency of vitamin A; growth retardation in children; increased susceptibility to infections including upper respiratory and genito-urinary tract infections; hyperkeratosis of the skin	Rod dysfunctions "night blindness;" xerophthalmia; keratomalacia (wasting of cornea); bilateral corneal scarring; blindness	Review of medical information with medical consultant; refer to internist for comprehensive medical evaluation and treatment recommendation; referral to public health service for nutritional planning
Behçet's disease	Aphthae; genital ulcerations; joint pains; possible involvement of central nervous system, heart, and intestinal tract; males slightly more frequently affected than females; age of onset 10 years to 30 years	Recurrent iritis; severe uveitis; retinal periphlebitis; papillitis; conjunctivitis; episcleritis; keratitis; retinal thrombophlebitis; bilateral involvement; optic nerve atrophy	Review of medical information with medical consultant; referral to internist for comprehensive medical evaluation
Brucellosis	Infectious disease caused by ingestion of the bacteria genus *Brucella melitensis* in raw milk of infected cattle, goats, and sheep; relapses of fever; anorexia, weight loss, depression, weakness; emotional instability; sometimes enlarged lymph nodes and spleen; most prevalent in rural areas; occupational disease of meat packers, veterinarians, farmers, and livestock producers	Uveitis with hypopyon; marginal keratitis; granulomatous uveitis; choroiditis; scleritis; retinal perivasculitis	Review of medical information with medical consultant; refer to internist for comprehensive medical evaluation and treatment recommendation

(*continued on next page*)

Systemic Disorders and Associated Visual Disorders (*continued*)			
Diagnosis	**Characteristics**	**Associated Visual Disorders**	**Recommended Actions**
Crohn's disease	Chronic granulomatous inflammatory disease, involving the gastrointestinal tract from the mouth to the anus; characterized by abdominal cramps, bloody stools, mild fevers, anorexia, and weight loss; small intestine and colon may have deep linear ulcerations, obstruction, abscess, or fistula	Recurrent iritis; scleral, episcleral and uveal tract disorders	Review of medical information with medical consultant; referral to internist, gastroenterologist for medical and speciality evaluations
Dermatomyositis	Inflammatory and degenerative changes; fevers; exhaustion; erythematous rash affected muscles; painful swollen muscles; joint pain; brownish skin pigmentation; flat-topped, violaceous papules over the knuckles are diagnostic	Retinopathy; lid edema; periorbital swelling	Medical consultation for case in the skin and voluntary muscles; high management information; referral to internist for comprehensive medical evaluation and identification of treatment alternatives
Diabetes mellitus (type I)	Carbohydrate metabolism disorder characterized by elevated blood sugar and sugar in the urine; absolute or near absolute insulin deficiency; onset usually prior to the age of 25; abrupt onset; symptoms—polyuria, polydipsia, polyphagia, weight loss, and ketoacidosis; controlled with insulin and diet; vascular and neurological changes develop; stability of condition fluctuates and is difficult to control	Retinopathy; cataract; extraocular muscle palsy; optic neuropathy; sudden changes in refractive error; rubeosis iridis; iridocyclitis; neovascular growth above or beneath retina may indicate laser therapy	Review of medical information covering client and family with medical consultant; referral to diabetes clinic for evaluation by diabetologist; consider role of laser therapy; plan for follow-up services by diabetes educators; when stress is psychogenic in origin, consult with diabetes clinical staff and medical consultant for case management issues

(*continued on next page*)

Systemic Disorders and Associated Visual Disorders (*continued*)			
Diagnosis	**Characteristics**	**Associated Visual Disorders**	**Recommended Actions**
Diabetes mellitus (type II)	Occurs predominantly among adults (usually over 40); sufficient insulin to prevent ketoacidosis or hyperinsulinema; Type II non-obese patients may control disorder with diet and hypoglycemic medication; gradual onset; symptoms—polyuria, polydipsia, pruritus, peripheral neuropathy; vascular and neural changes develop later in life; condition fairly stable and usually easy to control; weight control or indicated reduction is important	Retinopathy; cataract; optic neuropathy	Review of medical information covering client and family with medical consultant; referral to internist for comprehensive evaluation and treatment recommendations; referral to diabetologist; plan for follow-up services by diabetes educators; when stress is psychogenic in origin, consult with diabetes clinical staff and medical consultant for case-management issues
Histoplasmosis	Mild to severe respiratory; infection caused by a fungus (*Histoplasma capsulatum*); disease present in damp, humid, rural areas; fever; anemia; enlarged spleen and liver; leukopenia; ulcers of the gastrointestinal tract	Choroiditis; macular lesions	Review of family and client medical information with medical consultant; referral to internist for serologic testing and comprehensive medical evaluation
Hypertension	Persistent blood pressure greater than 150/95 mm; headaches, ringing in ears; dizziness; nervousness; fatigue; or may have no symptoms; possible complications include atherosclerotic heart disease, congestive heart failure, edema, and kidney failure	Retinal hemorrhages; hypertensive retinopathy; narrowing of arterioles; edema in macular area	Medical consultation and therapy; supportive counseling to encourage compliance with antihypertensive medications and dietary guidelines
Hyperthyroidism (Graves' disease)	Enlarged thyroid gland due to toxicity of goiter; occurs most frequently in young women; weight loss, nervousness, disturbances of sleep, excessive heat tolerance and sweating, fine tremors, rapid pulse rate, raised metabolic rate; may follow emotional or physical stress	Exophthalmos; ophthalmoplegia; optic neuropathy; superior limbic keratoconjunctivitis; corneal ulceration; infiltrative ophthalmology is specific for hyperthyroidism; may be euthyroid but still have major infiltration of the extraocular muscles	Medical consultation; possible referral for surgical removal of thyroid gland or ablation of the thyroid with radioactive iodine followed by daily dosage of thyroxin tablets; potential candidate for surgical removal of excess tissue around eyes or orbital decompression

(*continued on next page*)

Systemic Disorders and Associated Visual Disorders (*continued*)

Diagnosis	Characteristics	Associated Visual Disorders	Recommended Actions
Lawrence-Moon-Biedl syndrome	Genetically determined, autosomal, recessive pattern; mental retardation; obesity; polydactyly; underdeveloped genitals	Retinitis pigmentosa	Review of family and client medical information with medical consultant; genetic counseling; referral for psychological evaluation; referral to internist for comprehensive medical evaluation
Leukemia	Chronic or acute disease characterized by unrestrained increase of white blood cells; anemia; infections, internal hemorrhages, and fatigue; pale appearance with multiple purpura; central nervous system involvement; bone and joint pain	Retinal hemorrhage; macula hemorrhage	Review of medical information with medical consultant; refer to internist or to hematologists for examinations and treatment recommendations
Lupus erythematosus (systemic)	Rare inflammatory disease or autoimmune disorder with episodic feverishness and vague constitutional ulcerations on face, upper trunk, and extremities; kidney infections; intermittent joint pains; sensitivity; affects nearly all organ systems, whereas discoid lupus is a skin disease; more common among females between 10 and 40 years of age	Scleritis; conjunctivitis; keratoconjunctivitis; sicca; hypertensive retinopathy; retinal capillary occlusion; proliferative retinopathy	Referral to internist or rheumatologist for current medical evaluation and treatment; if depression seems present, referral for psychiatric or psychological evaluation
Marfan's syndrome	Hereditary condition of connective tissues, muscles, ligaments, and skeletal structures; irregular, unsteady gait; tall, lean body; long extremities including fingers and toes; excessive joint flexibility; flat feet; stooped shoulders; congenital heart disease; possible development of aneurysms; shortened life span	Dislocated lenses; severe refractive errors; megalocornea; cataract, uveal coloboma; and secondary glaucoma	Review of medical information with medical consultant; referral to internist for comprehensive medical evaluation; plan regarding surgical removal of dislocated lenses and possible anterior chamber implant (pseudophakia); careful cardiac monitoring

(*continued on next page*)

Systemic Disorders and Associated Visual Disorders (*continued*)			
Diagnosis	**Characteristics**	**Associated Visual Disorders**	**Recommended Actions**
Multiple sclerosis	Chronic demyelinating disorder of the central nervous system; onset in young adulthood; muscle weakness and ataxia; urinary disturbances; paresthesis; dysarthria due to loss of muscle control; when attempting to coordinate voluntary muscle actions	Blurring of vision; optic neuritis; diplopia; nystagmus, central scotoma; optic atrophy; temporary paravenous sheathing of retinal veinules	Review of medical information with medical consultant; referral to internist, neurologist, and other medical specialists such as a ophthalmologist and urologist
Myasthenia gravis	Weakness of voluntary muscles without atrophy; chronic progressive fatigability; muscle weakness in face and neck; difficult breathing and swallowing; symptoms worsen in evening; associated with hypothyroidism, collagen disease, and diffuse metastatic carcinoma; more common in females	Marked bilateral extraocular muscle weakness (ptosis, diplopia); progressive ophthalmoplyia	Review of medical information with medical consultant; referral to internist for comprehensive medical evaluation and trial of Prostigmin therapy; possible thymectomy
Polyarteritis nodosa	Connective tissue inflammation and ischemia of small and medium-size arteries with resulting functional impairment of tissues supplied by arteries; disease manifested with fever, severe pain in the abdomen or lower limbs, arthritis, muscle pains, cardiac failure, hypertension due to renal impairment, bronchial asthma, purpura or purple skin hemorrhages, urticaria, edema, and erythema	Episcleritis; scleritis; retinal hemorrhage; optic disk edema; fluctuating course, may mimic orbital pseudotumor, or lead to death from terminal nephritis	Medical consultation for patient management and therapy; referral to internist for comprehensive medical evaluation; may respond to steroid therapy
Reiter's syndrome	Triad of symptoms including urethritis, arthritis, and conjunctivitis occurring primarily among sexually active younger men; persistent diarrhea; acute or subacute arthritis in feet, ankles, knees, and sacroiliac joints; recurrences are common; fatalities are rare	Bilateral conjunctivitis; scleritis; keratitis; uveitis	Review of medical information with medical consultant; referral to internist or rheumatologist for comprehensive medical and speciality examination and treatment

(*continued on next page*)

Systemic Disorders and Associated Visual Disorders (*continued*)			
Diagnosis	**Characteristics**	**Associated Visual Disorders**	**Recommended Actions**
Rheumatoid arthritis (adult form)	Chronic, progressive systemic polyarthritis characterized by inflammation in joints; subcutaneous nodules over pressure points; swelling and pain at joints; involvement usually symmetrical; persistent inflammation leads to local neurosis; fatigue; muscle atrophy; active phases associated with stress; symptoms most severe after periods of inactivity	Bilateral scleritis; episclerities; keratoconjunctivitis; marginal degeneration of cornea	Review of current medical information with medical consultant; possible speciality evaluations by rheumatologist, internist, pain center, or psychiatrist or psychologist; trial of anti-inflammatory drugs
Rheumatoid arthritis (juvenile form)	Similar in most respects to adult form; tends to affect larger joints; alteration of growth and development; bird-like facial appearance result of impaired growth of lower jawbone; spleen enlargement; tendency for diseases of the lymph nodes; more favorable prognosis than adult form	Chronic insidious uveitis with high incidence of anterior segment complications; band shaped opacities of cornea; secondary cataracts	Review of medical information with medical consultant; referral to internist or rheumatologist for comprehensive and speciality medical evaluations; possible trial of steroids and anti-inflammatory drugs; recommendations for physical and occupational therapy.
Rubella (German measles)	A contagious disease that has mild constitutional symptoms that may result in abortion, stillbirth, or congenital defects from mothers who were infected during the early months of pregnancy; about 2/3 of infants with congenital rubella will be free of any abnormality at birth; classic syndrome by the combination of cataracts, cardiac, and hearing defects, although infection and defects can occur in every system; mental retardation often accompanies the syndrome	Bilateral retinopathies of pigmentary type; cataracts; microphthalmos and strabismus may occur	Review of medical and obstetrical information with medical consultant; referral to pediatrician for comprehensive medical evaluation

(*continued on next page*)

Systemic Disorders and Associated Visual Disorders (*continued*)			
Diagnosis	**Characteristics**	**Associated Visual Disorders**	**Recommended Actions**
Sickle cell anemia, sickle cell trait, and sickle cell disease	An inherited hemoglobinopathy causing chronic hemolytic anemia occurring almost exclusively in blacks; characterized by sickle-shaped red blood cells; chronic punched outulcers around ankles; abdominal pain and disorders; back and joint pain; neurological disturbances resulting from blockage of intracranial vessels; pneumonia and other infections common; progressive decreases in pulmonary and renal function among older individuals; life expectation beyond fourth decade	Retinal arterial tortuosity and occlusions; vitreous hemorrhages; in the more serious cases there are marked tortuosities and proliferative retinopathies; angioid streaks	Medical consultation; referral to internist or hematologist for evaluation and treatment; contact with sickle cell anemia support groups; supportive counseling for client and family; educational program; genetic counseling
Syphilis (congenital and acquired)	Infectious, chronic, venereal disease due to *Treponema pallidum*); characterized by lesions involving any organ or tissue; develops in three stages; cardiovascular and central nervous system involvement occurs during the tertiary stage	Affects all components of the eye; interstitial keratitis; chorioretinitis; iritis; iridocyclitis; uveitis; vitritis; retinal vasculitis; ischemia; ocular motor nerve palsy; internal ophthalmoplegia; optic neuritis; visual field with marked and irregular peripheral construction; nodules and gummas in tertiary stage	Review of patient's medical information and contacts with medical consultant; refer to internist for comprehensive medical evaluation and treatment plans; consult agency policy regarding reports to state public health agency; responds to high dosage penicillin

(*continued on next page*)

Systemic Disorders and Associated Visual Disorders (*continued*)

Diagnosis	Characteristics	Associated Visual Disorders	Recommended Actions
Toxoplasmosis	A generalized or central nervous system granulomatous disease caused by the *Toxoplasma gondii;* asymptomatic infections are common; blood studies show that from 7 to 94 percent of various populations are infected; two types—congenital and acquired; there are three types of acquired toxoplasmosis: mild lymphatic form; fulminating, disseminated infection; and chronic form; chronic form is characterized by severe retinochoroiditis, muscular weakness, weight loss, headaches, possible diarrhea; derived from domestic and wild rodents and birds; congenital type may be fatal	Retinochoroiditis	Pregnant women with febrile episodes need immediate attention from a physician; (posterior uveitis) persons with the acquired types do not require specific treatment unless a vital organ is involved or the symptoms are persistent and severe; consultation with physician is required for recommendations for additional speciality examinations
Tuberculosis	Infectious disorder caused by various *Mycobacterium* bacteria; organism usually injested or inhaled; primary site of infection is lungs, but any organ or tissue may be involved; weight loss; cough; chest pain; spitting up of blood, difficulty breathing; fatigue; lack of stamina; responds to appropriate medication; increasingly rare	Tuberculous uveitis; tuberculous chorioretinitis	Medical consultation; contact state health department; refer to internist or pulmonary physician; treatment usually consists of up to four drugs; bed rest; hospitalization; corticosteroid therapy in severe cases
Ulcerative colitis	Chronic lower gastrointestinal tract disorder of young adults; symptoms include chronic diarrhea characterized by bloody mucus or pus, offensive smelling watery stools; intermittent fever; fatigue; abdominal pain and tenderness	Scleral, episcleral, and uveal tract	Review of medical information with medical consultant; referral to internist, gastroenterologist, psychiatrist, or psychologist for comprehensive medical and speciality evaluations

(*continued on next page*)

Systemic Disorders and Associated Visual Disorders (*continued*)			
Diagnosis	**Characteristics**	**Associated Visual Disorders**	**Recommended Actions**
Usher's syndrome	Progressive congenital sensorineural hearing loss combined with pigmentary retinal dystrophy	Progressive retinitis pigmentosa (critical losses occur in second decade); frequent mental retardation and myoclonic epilepsy	Medical consultation; contact Helen Keller National Center for Deaf-Blind Youths and Adults for assistance; genetic counseling; hearing evaluation
Wegener's granulomatosis	Autoimmune syndrome characterized by inflammation of arteries and the glomeruli of the kidneys; lower respiratory tract infections; uremia; often fatal, particularly affects young or middle-aged adults	Conjunctivitis, episcleritis; scleritis; uveitis; retinal vasculitis; orbits usually involved by continuity of lesions	Medical consultation for granulomatosis management information; referral to internist and urologist for comprehensive and speciality medical evaluations

CHAPTER 6

Vocational and Psychological Assessments

Lynn W. McBroom, Steve Shindell, and Randal R. Elston

In American society, vocational choice is important for all people. Individuals with visual impairments, however, have often been limited in their career opportunities. They face restricted choices because others often underestimate their capabilities, or because people with visual impairments often restrict themselves to the jobs they believe they can perform (see Sidebar 6.1). The vocational assessment process assists the counselor and client in identifying needed services and making informed career and work choices. In certain circumstances, vocational assessment information can educate clients and potential employers about the client's capability by identifying both strengths and limitations and, at the same time, by providing information about how the client with a visual impairment will perform the job. Each individual is a complicated puzzle of strengths and weaknesses, likes and dislikes, learned skills, and hidden talents. Assessment begins at first contact with the individual who is seeking rehabilitation services. The type and nature of assessment testing vary by setting and purpose. For example, such questions as "What are the individual's vocational strengths?" and "What knowledge does the individual possess regarding the world of work?" relate to vocational assessment. In contrast, such questions as "Does the individual possess the emotional stamina to handle the stress associated with this particular job?" or "Does the individual possess the capacity to learn this particular skill?" or "How do we maximize this person's capacity to learn to participate in a vocational training program?" are more related to psychological assessment. The eight major objectives of this chapter are to (1) assist rehabilitation counselors to develop an understanding of the significance of assessment in rehabilitation service delivery, (2) define the difference between the kinds of testing done in schools and standardized assessment, (3) determine the applicability of certain assessment instruments (tests) for people with visual impairments, (4) explain the basic strengths and weaknesses of assessment as it applies to visually impaired people, (5) define the role of the rehabilitation counselor in requesting assessments and in determining the parameters of testing, (6) assist rehabilitation counselors to understand and use the assessment information (7) assist clients to understand their educational and vocational potential, and (8) identify potential ethical issues related to the assessment of individuals with visual impairments.

VOCATIONAL ASSESSMENT

The goal of vocational assessment is to determine vocational strengths, weaknesses, and interests of individuals with visual impairments to enhance their opportunities for education, training, and

Vocational Opportunities: Why Are the Choices So Limited?

SIDEBAR 6.1

According to researchers and rehabilitation counselors, the reasons for high rates of unemployment and underemployment for people with visual impairments include the following:

1. lack of transportation
2. negative attitudes of employers
3. work disincentives such as SSDI
4. lack of housing
5. lack of access to employment information
6. lack of motivation
7. need for additional training and educational opportunities including activities of daily living, job seeking skills, job retention skills, and job readiness skills
8. need for assistive technology or job restructuring
9. health problems
10. difficulty in finding appropriate employment

employment. Vocational assessment is not performed to limit choices, but rather to assist clients in selecting and choosing appropriate careers. The vocational assessment is different from work evaluation. Vocational assessment is the comprehensive process of using standardized tests, observations and interview techniques to gather data about an individual. A work evaluation uses real or simulated work to evaluate the individual's skills (Peterson, Capps, & Moore, 1984). Both standardized vocational assessments and work evaluations are two means of gathering vocational data.

A thorough vocational assessment takes into consideration:

- medical, social, educational, and vocational information;
- vocational and psychological test scores;
- skills, abilities, and aptitudes;
- interests and leisure activities;
- personality and temperament;
- values, attitudes, and motivations;
- physical ability and work tolerance;
- ability to learn from training or education;
- employment potential;
- social skills;
- work habits;
- and work adjustment (Bauman, 1975; Power, 1991; Pruitt, 1977).

In addition to vocational assessment and work evaluation, individuals with low vision might need to receive a low vision evaluation and an adaptive technology evaluation (see Chapter 4). Many individuals with visual impairments may need to be evaluated in some or all of these areas. However, not every individual participating in the rehabilitation process requires a complete work evaluation as part of the vocational assessment process.

The vocational assessment strategy must be tailored to the special needs of the client (Nadolsky, 1977), including the effects of visual impairment upon the client's functioning. For example, a client who wants to attend college may only need an assessment of academic and cognitive ability. Conversely, for an individual who has never had a job before and does not know about available and appropriate vocational choices, a complete work evaluation may be required.

STANDARDIZED TESTS

Standardized tests used in assessment can include tests of achievement, personality, intelligence, aptitude, interests, and motor skills (Botterbusch, 1978b). Standardized tests compare an individual's performance with the performance of a representative sample group. When such tests are used appropriately, they can provide significant information about the individual being tested (Hursh, undated). However, if standardized tests are used inappropriately, (usually for some reason other than for what they were developed), test results may actually screen out individuals desiring training programs or seeking job possibilities (Elston, 1997; Peterson, 1986). Therefore, it is essential that standardized tests be administered by someone who has formal training in standardized testing and is licensed to administer such standardized tests. It is equally important that the evaluator understand the specialized issues relative to visual impairment.

WORK EVALUATION

Work evaluation (also called vocational evaluation) consists of using real or simulated work, to informally assess an individual's work skills, capabilities, and interests (Pruitt, 1986). When requesting a work evaluation, the rehabilitation counselor should provide the evaluator with specific objectives or questions that outline the purpose of the work evaluation (Power, 1991; Roessler & Rubin, 1991). The counselor should also provide all necessary data about the individual being referred for a work evaluation (McGowan & Porter, 1967). The data provided by the counselor along with information obtained from the individual during the initial interview allows the evaluator to determine the extent and need for work evaluation and to develop the individual vocational evaluation plan (Pruitt, 1986).

Only by including the client's goals and aspirations can a thorough and accurate analysis be obtained. Otherwise, at the conclusion of the evaluation, the work evaluator may make recommendations that have no relevance for the client. Significant family members and others may also be able to provide additional information about the individual being evaluated both at the beginning of the process and at the end. Because family members can be a rich source of information about the client's history and development, strengths and weaknesses, and abilities and interests, Murphy and Hagner (1988) suggested that, *with the permission of the individual being evaluated,* important family members and significant others be involved in the decision-making meeting during which final recommendations are made. Family involvement in the evaluation process will probably lead to a continuation of support throughout the rehabilitation process and into job placement (Elston & Housley, 1988; Wehman, 1981; Westin & Reiss, 1979).

The availability of work evaluation services for people with visual impairments must also be considered in the total vocational assessment process. Because the availability of services varies greatly among local communities, services may not be available at all, leaving the rehabilitation counselor responsible to perform any required vocational assessment procedures (Roessler & Rubin, 1991).

The cost factor must also be considered when developing a work evaluation plan. The length of a vocational evaluation varies according to the purpose, but generally takes no more than one week. The concept of supported employment has changed the focus of some evaluations by placing more emphasis on situational or functional assessment approaches and on-the-job training. Although cost must be considered, short-term evaluations may not be appropriate for all people, especially those with multiple impairments or little or no work experience. Longer-term evaluations may allow these individuals to develop work skills and increase self-esteem. For an ex-

Case Study

SIDEBAR 6.2

The following case study illustrates one type of vocational evaluation, the manner in which the results were utilized, and issues that sometimes surround the identification of a vocational objective in the rehabilitation process.

Andy, a 19-year-old high school student with a severe visual impairment was referred to a vocational rehabilitation counselor by his school counselor. Andy indicated that although his parents wanted him to attend college, he was not interested in any type of education and wanted to begin working. He stated that he had never worked before and was not sure what he wanted to do. After the rehabilitation counselor explained the vocational evaluation process, Andy indicated that he wanted to go through such an evaluation. A time for the evaluation was set and agreed upon by Andy, his parents, and school personnel.

The evaluator found Andy to be fairly outgoing, friendly, and cooperative. His counselor reported, however, that he occasionally annoyed female coworkers and staff. His dress was appropriate for the evaluation setting and he demonstrated other job-readiness skills. Andy indicated to the evaluator that he would like a job working with his hands, but could not name a specific type of work. He was willing to attempt all evaluation tasks.

Because Andy indicated that he was interested in manual work, the vocational evaluator chose to administer only the following psychometric tests: Wide Range Achievement Test (WRAT3) (Wilkinson, 1993) and the Minnesota Importance Questionnaire (MIQ). According to the WRAT3, Andy's reading ability was at the 8.5 grade level and his math ability, at the 5.5 grade level. When given time beyond the standardized allotted time of the math portion of the WRAT3, Andy was able to increase his math level to grade 7.5. Verbal administration of the MIQ and information from Andy indicated that he could be satisfied working in an industrial setting.

Andy was also tested using the Purdue Pegboard and the Pennsylvania Bi-Manual Work Sample in order to determine his degree of bimanual dexterity. According to standardized results of both tests, there was the possibility that Andy could be successful in work requiring manual and finger dexterity. His ratings improved after additional practice on both tests, indicating that his dexterity became sharper with practice. When given the bench assembly unit of the Singer Vocational Evaluation System, Andy scored a below average rating on time, but an above average rating on work quality. When allowed to repeat the work sample tasks, his time rating improved while the quality of his work remained the same. This also indicated that Andy's dexterity improved with practice.

Because Andy was interested in jobs that involve working with his hands and the evaluation results indicated he had good manual skills and finger dexterity, the evaluator decided to evaluate Andy's ability and willingness to assemble a fishing reel. The simulated job sample was developed by the evaluator after doing a job analysis of the tasks required of an assembly line worker at a local industry making different types of fishing reels. The simulated job sample included the use of the same tools, materials, and tasks as that of the actual job. Andy showed enthusiasm and gladly attempted the tasks. As before, his time rating was slow, but the quality of work was

Case Study (continued)

good. Andy followed directions well. He repeated the job sample and improved his time rating. He indicated interest in this type of work and stated he thought he would like to work at the local factory. No additional work samples were administered because the evaluator felt the rehabilitation counselor's questions about Andy's manual dexterity, ability to follow directions, willingness to attempt and stay with work tasks, and interests had been answered.

Based on the results of Andy's vocational evaluation and his interests, it was recommended to the rehabilitation counselor that Andy be considered for a job tryout at the fishing reel job site, with the goal being job placement at that industry. This company was known for hiring people with various disabilities and the work evaluator believed that Andy would be able to make production goals within three weeks with the assistance of a job coach. Counseling was also recommended for Andy's behavior around females. In addition, family counseling was recommended to help Andy's parents accept that Andy wanted to work rather than attend college.

Andy was placed in a two-week job tryout at the local fishing reel factory by the rehabilitation counselor. According to his job coach and work supervisor, Andy made much improvement in both time and work quality during the two-week tryout. He was hired and no longer needed the job coach. He was able to achieve production quotas and was now enjoying the job. His parents finally accepted that Andy was not going to college and were able to offer him encouragement.

ample of a complete vocational assessment, see Sidebar 6.2.

There are various types of work evaluations available, but those most often referred to in the literature include work samples and situational assessment (Botterbusch, 1983). The next two sections examine these kinds of work evaluations.

Work Samples

Some rehabilitation professionals believe that the most valid way to determine an individual's work skills, capabilities, and interests is to have the individual perform the actual work [Albright, 1980; Halpern, Lehman, Irvin, & Heiry, 1981; Nadolsky, 1985; Thornton & Byham, 1982; Vocational Evaluation and Work Adjustment Association (VEWAA), 1975]. A number of standardized commercial work samples have been developed, which compare more to standardized tests than to any other type of work evaluation.

Commercial work samples have been categorized as being either trait-oriented or task-oriented. Trait-oriented work samples assess measures of perceptual, sensory, and cognitive characteristics that are necessary for a client to perform a job. Significant traits to consider when assessing a person with a visual impairment include kinesthetic memory, spatial relations, imaging ability, auditory discrimination, sound localization, tactile discrimination, physical orientation, and equilibrium (Bauman, 1976).

By contrast, task-oriented work samples measure the ability of an individual to perform a specific job task, for example, an individual's ability to measure yards of material or to type 50 words per minute. There are two kinds of task-oriented work samples: job samples and occupational cluster-work samples. To replicate real jobs that exist in the community, job samples utilize the same tools, materials, procedures, and work standards as those for specific jobs. Occupational cluster-work samples are derived from the more common work tasks associated with a cluster (or group) of related jobs (Peterson et al., 1984). In other words, although job samples mimic specific jobs in their entirety, occupational cluster-work samples emphasize select tasks common to several different jobs. Task-oriented work samples are criterion-referenced tests that compare an individual's performance with an expected level of mastery. In some instances, there are advantages in using commercial work samples rather than standardized tests. Many work samples are the same as work because the testing is done with the actual tools and materials used on real job tasks. This use of real tools and materials can help to increase motivation in some individuals because they may not feel as insecure or anxious when attempting work-sample tasks as compared to taking standardized tests. In addition, employers may be more familiar with work-sample reports than standardized test scores (Sakata & Sinick, 1965), because work-sample reports are presented in work-task or work-behavior oriented language. However, work-sample reports may not provide a complete picture of an individual's overall ability level as does a work evaluation that uses standardized tests.

Situational Assessment

One of the more widely used approaches in work evaluation is the situational assessment. Situational assessment is the systematic observation of a person's work behavior in work situations (Peterson, 1986; Pruitt, 1983). The four types of situational assessment are (1) simulated job situation, (2) community rehabilitation program setting, (3) job tryout or job-site evaluation, and (4) vocational classroom tryout. In some instances, these types of assessment may be the most effective way to evaluate clients because of their approximations to real work. However, two weaknesses in situational assessment that may make situational assessment a less accurate measure of an individual's ability are inter-scorer reliability and the lack of a standardized measurement.

Simulated job situations or homemade work samples are similar to traditional work samples, but they are not standardized. For example, a work evaluation center may not have an appropriate assessment instrument to evaluate individuals for a specific job. Therefore, to develop a simulation of that particular job, the evaluator visits the job site, performs a job analysis to determine the tasks and skills required for that job, and develops a simulated work sample. That resultant work sample allows the evaluator to assess specific performance, work, and learning skills, as well as general work skills and behaviors (Pruitt, 1986). (Also see the following section on job analysis and work sample development.)

The community rehabilitation program setting is one of the most widely used settings for situational assessment. The appropriateness of utilizing such facilities varies greatly because some community rehabilitation programs have a large variety of job choices while others have only limited choices. Also, not all community rehabilitation programs have qualified staff to perform assessments (Pruitt, 1983).

Job tryouts, sometimes referred to as job-site evaluations (Botterbusch, 1978a), are situational assessments in which individuals perform actual work tasks on real jobs either in the community or in community rehabilitation programs. This type of assessment is closer to actual employment than any other situational assessment technique. In this procedure, individuals are actually "trying out" jobs as their performance, work, and learning skills are assessed. Some of the different types of job tryouts include (1) full-time or part-time jobs in competitive placement, (2) group placement in competitive employment, (3) institutional work stations, (4) competitive jobs within rehabilitation facilities, and (5) facility-owned businesses. The situational assessment process at sheltered industry production settings usually lasts for several days with individuals being paid for any work produced (Pruitt, 1983). However, job tryouts are generally not utilized until more formal assessments have occurred.

Finally, vocational classroom tryouts are appropriate for individuals who are interested in attending vocational training programs. During the classroom tryout, individuals observe the class and interact with the teacher, perform work samples or informal performance samples, pair with students in ongoing classroom tasks, and try tasks similar to those occurring at the beginning of class (Peterson, 1986). Vocational classroom tryouts are also helpful in career exploration and to determine vocational interests. Teachers use vocational classroom tryouts to make recommendations about the potential of individuals for attending and completing vocational training programs. Again, more formal assessment is often required prior to vocational classroom tryouts.

JOB ANALYSIS AND WORK SAMPLE DEVELOPMENT

According to Pruitt (1983, p. 185), ". . . job analysis is a systematic procedure for determining what a worker does on a job." The results of the job analysis determine the amount of vision or accommodation needed to perform a specific job. Job analysis is critical both in job placement and the development of work samples. During the job analysis, tasks required to perform a job are identified and incorporated into the work sample. As a result, the work sample utilizes the same equipment and materials and includes the same work tasks as the job located in the community. (See Appendix B for a sample of a completed Job Analysis Worksheet.)

Two of the more widely used methods of conducting job analysis for work-sample development are job-site analysis and the use of the *Dictionary of Occupational Titles* (DOT) (U.S. Department of Labor, 1991). Job placement may be facilitated by using job-site analysis because performance and work tasks required in the work samples are very similar to actual job requirements. Although work samples based on job-site analysis are very similar to the actual performance of the real job, high performance ratings on work samples do not always guarantee job success in the community. It is very difficult, if not impossible, to create the actual job climate in the work evaluation setting because of other components required for successful job performance (Pruitt, 1986). Examples of these components include the effects of fatigue, interactions with coworkers, lighting, and noise (McBroom, Seaman, & Graves, 1987).

Although the utilization of the DOT is beneficial in job analysis for work-sample development, not all the information provided will be applicable for the local community because the DOT is based on national guidelines (Peterson, 1986). Also, local jobs may use the same job titles as listed in the DOT, but the actual work tasks may vary significantly. Work tasks provided by the DOT are generalizations based on the analysis of a small number of jobs with the same title. Therefore, the DOT and local job analyses should be used together to ensure that the vocational evaluation process considers the local job market (Peterson, Capps & Moore, 1984).

ASSESSMENT ISSUES

Norms are the standards that provide an indication of the average performance of a specified group (Gilbertson, 1973). These standards allow one person's performance to be compared with the performance of others. Norms are based on groups of people with such common characteristics as education, disability, or job setting. The client's performance score is interpreted within the context of a comparison group or groups. A test without developed norms or with a norm group that differs from the client may give the evaluator an idea of what a person can do, but allows no standardized basis for comparison (Hall, Scholl, & Swallow, 1986).

Parker and Schaller (1996) noted that in situations in which multiple norms are available, the determination of whether to use general or special norms is left to the rehabilitation professionals. They recommend selection based on the purpose of the assessment (e.g., description or prediction). For example, prediction industrial-worker norms, which are based on the performance of experienced industrial workers, would be an applicable basis of comparison for clients who have previous industrial work experiences who are seeking competitive employment within an industrial setting. However, if this is first-time employment, a better group for comparison might be industrial applicants or beginning industrial workers who do not have previous industrial work experience. When norms are used for descriptive purposes, both general and specific norms may be used (Parker & Schaller, 1996).

One difficulty often faced when using industrial norms is that individuals with visual impairments may be screened out of vocational training programs and jobs (Elston, 1997). For example, many times, evaluators report that an individual with a visual impairment—who scored at the ninth percentile level of a standardized work sample using industrial norms—would not be ready for vocational training or employment in that vocational area. The ninth percentile ranking actually indicates that the individual scored as high as or higher than nine people out of 100 *who are actually working on the job.* Elston argued that the individual should be further assessed using situational assessment including on-the-job tryouts.

By contrast, vocational assessment devices based on criterion-referenced or competency-based assessment procedures use industry standards to indicate whether or not the person exhibits mastery of specific tasks. Performance is not compared with the average performance of a comparison group as in norm-referenced assessment, but with an absolute level of ability needed to complete the task (McCray, 1979; McDaniel & Couch, 1980; Peterson et al., 1984). A designated cut-off point indicates whether or not the person can perform the task.

The norm group is important, however, because it is used to establish two statistical measures: validity and reliability. Validity measures the degree to which an assessment device accurately reflects the concept or task it was designed to measure (Anastasi, 1988; Pruitt, 1977). This is an important concern for vocational evaluators and psychologists, because it ensures that they are actually testing the skill or ability they intended to measure. Reliability measures the extent to which data demonstrates consistency on repeated trials across time or from one part of a test to another (Anastasi, 1988; Pruitt, 1977). An assessment device is reliable if clients consistently score near the same level regardless of the number of times they take the test (Babbie, 1975).

Norms are also important in psychological assessment. When choosing tests for people with visual impairments, it is important for the psychologist to understand not only the appropriateness of individual items on the test, but also to have the ability to generalize from the normative group scores when assessing the individual client. Crucial knowledge in regard to the visual functioning of the normative group includes the length of time since the onset of the visual impairment, and whether this impairment was acquired at birth, within their formative years, or later in life. This information will aid the clinician in evaluating the usefulness of the test. (For more on the individual members of the rehabilitation team, see Chapters 9 and 10.) For example, a client who became blind early in life has a general fund of knowledge and experiences that would vary significantly from someone who developed partial sight loss in his or her later years. In comparison, individuals with congenital blindness probably have more experience utilizing their tactile sense for learning such tasks as braille, but may have less understanding of the gross motor skills necessary to ride a bicycle. Differences such as these can cause misinterpretation of testing results, if clients are compared to an incorrect normative group. It is recommended that great care be exercised in matching clients and the peer group to which they will be compared.

TESTING INDIVIDUALS WITH VISUAL IMPAIRMENTS

The use of standardized tests and standardized work samples often creates difficulties in the assessment of people with visual impairments. It is vital that these individuals not be given tests that require sight without making the appropriate modifications and accommodations. Although modifications to standardized procedures do affect the validity of the assessment results, if there are no modifications made, the result may be that individuals will be restricted from either vocational training programs or jobs (Elston, 1997). Table 6.1 contains a list of a few of the many possible adaptations that can be used either with people with low vision or with people who are totally blind. Some of these adaptations, such as "verbal instructions," can be applied to both groups; other adaptations, such as braille, can only apply to one particular group. Certain tests, however, will not be adaptable no matter what modifications are made. For example, with present technology, there is no practical way for a person who is totally blind to sort items by color.

Factors to consider when using norm-referenced tests and standardized work samples include time limit, test length, test content, type of administration, and access devices (Power, 1991). Many standardized assessment instruments are timed so that people with visual impairments are not able to complete the assessment instrument in the amount of time allotted. For example, while many braille readers can read about 80 words per minute, large-print readers often read slower due to use of a closed-circuit television (CCTV) or other adaptive devices. Eye fatigue is also often a factor. Individuals with visual impairments who read regular-size print sometimes have visual field losses that may cause them to have a slower than average reading

Table 6.1. Adaptations for Vocational Assessment Instruments

Adaptations for Low Vision	Adaptations for Blindness	Adaptations for Both Low Vision and Blindness
Large print	Braille	Thorough orientation
Closed-circuit television	Optical Chacter Recognition Systems	Verbal instructions
Adequate illumination	Computers and calculators with voice technology	Cassette tapes
Bold lines and heavy markers	Abacus	Tactile items and markers
Color contrast	Slate and stylus	Sample models
Large-print rulers	Jigs	Needle threader
Hand-held magnifiers	Braille rulers	Adaptive tools and devices
	Light sensing devices	Protective barriers
	Clicking torque wrenches	
	Thermometer with voice technology	
	Audible tools and devices	
	Audible tools and devices	

speed. The results may be more a reflection of reading speed than of job knowledge. When reading is part of the job, speed of task completion should be included in the final results. Elston (1997) suggests that the evaluator mark the amount of work completed at the end of the allotted time and again when the task was finally completed. By doing this, data can be gathered both on how individuals compare to the norm group, as well as how they perform overall on the assessment tasks.

The length of assessment instruments should also be considered when evaluating persons with visual impairments. Many of these assessment instruments are lengthy and it is probably in the best interest of individuals to break them into parts, administering them separately in order to obtain optimal results (Power, 1991). Power also suggests administering instruments in the morning when the client is rested. People who experience eye strain and subsequent impaired performance can better demonstrate their optimum performance ability when allowed to take breaks and perform when rested.

It is recommended that the content of assessment instruments be checked to determine if the items contained in the test discriminate against people with visual impairments. For example, tests based on some traits identified in the DOT may not be appropriate because of faulty assumptions about vision requirements for a job (McBroom & Seaman, 1987). Some computerized job-matching systems incorporating the DOT analysis of the vision requirements of jobs also rule out careers such as law and teaching when, in fact, there are many individuals with visual impairments who are successfully employed in these occupations (McBroom, Seaman, & Graves, 1987).

In addition, individual or group assessment may affect the performance of a person with a visual impairment. Individual assessment may enhance the probability of acquiring valid data in determining the person's capabilities and skills, whereas group assessment may inhibit effort and induce additional stress during the testing situation (Power, 1991). Some people might not have experienced group work and might not know how to assert themselves in the group setting. However, when assessments occur in group settings, people can be assessed on whether or not they are able to work well in a group.

When using adaptive technology to make tests or work samples accessible to people with visual impairments, it is highly recommended that rehabilitation counselors help clients to become totally familiar with the adaptive devices being used. Counselors are encouraged not to put clients in the position of testing poorly because they did not know how to use adaptive devices.

The age of the individual at onset of the visual impairment can affect performance in the assessment process. According to Botterbusch (1976), people with adventitious visual impairments have such established concepts as colors, shapes, and visual aspects of the environment because they previously functioned as sighted persons. By contrast, individuals with congenital visual impairments may not understand or may have difficulty establishing concepts because they have never functioned with sight and would be at a disadvantage when being tested using materials having visual concepts. Individuals with recently acquired visual impairments may still be coping emotionally and physically with the vision loss and may not be able to perform as well as they could at a later time. Therefore, it is suggested that the rehabilitation counselor consider age and recency of onset when interpreting assessment results.

Life experiences—or lack of them—can also affect test results because some life experiences of people with visual impairments can be quite different from those of sighted individuals (Botterbusch, 1976). For example, many items in an interest inventory may be unfamiliar to the visually impaired person, and consequently not chosen. According to Bauman (1973), overprotection by family, friends, school personnel, and others, the exclusion of these individuals from activities in school systems, and lack of accessible learning materials all restrict life experiences of people with visual impairments.

Another factor that can affect the testing re-

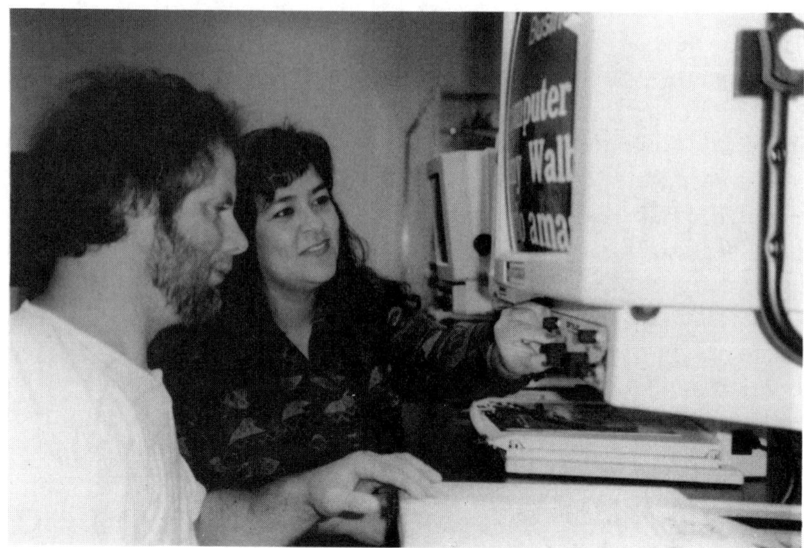

Rehabilitation counselors can help clients with visual impairments to become familiar with adaptive devices before the adaptive technology is used in a situational test or work sample.

sults of people with visual impairments is the psychological effects of the impairment. For example, some people adjust to visual impairment more easily than others. Those who have not made positive adjustments may lack self-confidence. A lack of self-confidence may keep such people from putting forth their best efforts when attempting vocational evaluation tasks. Vocational evaluators are encouraged to recognize adjustment difficulties in order to report more valid assessment data and make more appropriate recommendations (Elston & Housley, 1988).

In addition to the foregoing difficulties, the use of norm-referenced tests and standardized work samples can also discriminate against minorities, especially African Americans, Native Americans, and Hispanics. Research also indicates that individuals from low socioeconomic or disadvantaged homes do not score as well on standardized tests as those from middle- and upper-class homes (Sax, 1974). This additional discrimination may compound the already-difficult problem of assessing persons with visual impairments, because some minority groups are more susceptible to diseases that result in blindness. For example, more than other groups, African Americans have a tendency to develop high blood pressure and diabetes both of which can lead to blindness; as a group, they are also more susceptible to sickle cell anemia, which may result in sickle cell retinopathy (Goldman, Dunham, & Dunham, 1978; Stolov & Clowers, 1981).

These factors are only a few of the possibilities that may affect the evaluation results of people with visual impairments. It is recommended that rehabilitation counselors, psychologists, and vocational evaluators remain aware of these types of conditions as well as others that may affect evaluation results throughout the assessment process. Rehabilitation counselors are encouraged to request the inclusion of such information and observations along with evaluation testing data in the final work or psychological evaluation report.

PROVIDING TEST RESULTS TO CLIENTS

At the completion of the vocational evaluation process, it is suggested that the rehabilitation counselor arrange a meeting with the client during which evaluation results are explained and recommendations are discussed in order to develop a vocational rehabilitation plan. The rehabilitation counselor is urged to be fully prepared to interpret the vocational evaluation results to the client. When reporting the evaluation data, the counselor can make the evaluation results more meaningful by relating them to the behavior of the client (McGowan & Porter, 1967). Throughout the interpretation session, the rehabilitation counselor can encourage the client to express feelings about the results.

Negative data must be carefully explained and data describing the vocational strengths emphasized. Power (1991) suggested interpreting intelligence tests in ranges, such as "average," rather than as specific, numbered intelligence quotient (IQ) scores. The purpose and meaning of personality tests can be explained using functional terms instead of psychological terms (McGowan & Porter, 1967). In addition, personality strengths and limitations can be identified and related to work requirements and vocational goals. As a result of the strengths and limitations that have been discussed, various services, including therapy or work adjustment, may be recommended (Power, 1991).

At the end of the meeting, it is recommended that the counselor ask the client to summarize the vocational evaluation results (McGowan & Porter, 1967). This summation allows for any client misunderstandings or misinterpretations to be clarified. All pertinent vocational information should be emphasized as the client and the counselor prepare for the rehabilitation planning process.

More work has been done with the psychological assessment of people with visual impairments than with vocational assessment. Vocational assessment instruments are available for a wide range of occupations; however, instruments written or adapted specifically for visually impaired people are typically in the area of production assembly work with the exception of a few standardized vocational assessment batteries. Because people with visual impairments are successfully employed across all occupational levels (Kirchner & Peterson, 1988a), the emphasis on production and assembly is inappropriate and unnecessarily restrictive. Of the vocational assessment instruments summarized in the *Work Assessment Database* (McBroom, Seaman, & Freeman, 1987), only 48 were found that were either developed or adapted for people with visual impairments. Only 13 of the 48 tests contain statistical data about norms, reliability, or validity. The majority of the 48 were developed by National Industries for the Blind and are dexterity tests. Because dexterity is only one small measure of work ability, tests that were developed for clients other than those with visual impairments

Because people with visual impairments can be successfully employed across all occupational areas (for example, this employee works with a check encoder), vocational evaluation tests need to be used to appropriately assess individuals who are visually impaired.

may need to be used for assessment. Evaluators giving these tests may be making adaptations to procedures and methodology which eliminate any comparisons to reliability and validity scores established by the test authors.

PSYCHOLOGICAL ASSESSMENT

The purpose of psychological assessment as it relates to the vocational rehabilitation process is the identification of vocational potential. Vocational potential can be thought of in various ways: cognitive, academic, behavioral, social, linguistic, or physical. The psychological assessment is designed to identify the individual's strengths and limitations, which need to be either remediated or accommodated within the rehabilitation process.

As with the work evaluation, rehabilitation professionals are urged to clearly specify what questions they are seeking to answer from the psychological assessment. Referrals that are written in a vague manner without a clear idea of what information is being requested, will yield a general, and potentially useless, psychological report. By specifying what information is needed, the rehabilitation counselor and psychologist can work as an effective, cooperative team. For example, the following is an excellent, answerable question: Can this client work productively and happily for a number of years in an unstructured, low physical demand, low socially reinforcing setting such as telephone sales? In contrast, a question such as: "What about giving the Minnesota Vocational Interest Inventory?" shows an inappropriate focus on scores and no emphasis on the person. The following is an example of a referral request for a psychosocial assessment in the fictitious case of "Jane Rhymer":

> *Referral Question:* What is this person's readiness to return to her previous employment?
> *Background Information:* Ms. Rhymer is a 55-year-old woman with legal blindness of six months duration secondary to age-related maculopathy. Her acuities are 20/200 with a large central field loss in both eyes. She has no other medical difficulties and reports to be in good health. She recently took disability retirement from her job as head nurse on a busy hospital ward where her job responsibilities involved staff recruitment and supervision, administrative duties, writing and reading handwritten and typed reports in a timely manner, and utilizing the hospital computer system for access to patient records. She was not responsible for direct patient care in this position, but attended staff conferences and ward rounds. She has a 30-year history of satisfactory performance in this and similar capacities. She is motivated to return to employment, both for financial reasons and for her self-worth.

This referral does several things:

1. It immediately addresses the issue by asking the question: What is this person's readiness to return to her previous position?
2. It describes the criteria for success, by delineating the specific tasks this person needs to do to adequately reach her goal.
3. It describes pertinent medical information, including the person's medical limitations, length of time with the disability, and other factors that might influence either the assessment or her performance on the job.

The psychologist is left with these assessment questions: (1) Does this person have the motivation to return to her previous employment and if not, do other employment options interest her? (2) Does this person have sufficient skills to enter new learning environments, for example, rehabilitation, education, or new vocational pursuits? (3) Is there a need for orientation and mobility training, braille instruction, or other aspects of rehabilitation? (4) Are there any psychological interventions necessary to either aid in adjust-

SIDEBAR 6.3

Referral Questions

The following are examples of referral questions that will facilitate the provision of vocational evaluation services utilizing the Comprehensive Vocational Evaluation System (CVES):

1. At what general level of vocational competency is the person functioning (e.g., professional/technical, skilled, semi-skilled, transitional, etc.)?
2. What are the individual's vocational interests?
3. What type of training is most appropriate for the person in terms of his or her goals, ability profile, and disability-related functional limitations (e.g., university, community college, technical/trade school, short-term vocational training, on the job training)?
4. What are short-term and long-term training/placement options?
5. Are the person's goals realistic?
6. Would the client benefit from job coaching services? If so, are long-term (supported employment) services necessary or is fade-out possible?
7. If job coach services are needed, are they required for task analysis/mastery or behavioral modification?
8. Does the person demonstrate any inappropriate behaviors?
9. What are the person's vocational strengths and limitations?
10. Is the person's presentation consistent with referral information?
11. What accommodations, if any, would facilitate training/placement for a person with disability-related functional limitations?
12. What are the person's transferable skills?
13. Based upon the vocational evaluator's observations, are further referrals to other professionals needed or appropriate to best serve the consumer (e.g., psychological evaluation, neuropsychological evaluation, pharmacological evaluation, etc.)?
14. Does the person appear motivated to work?

Jack G. Dial, Ph.D.
Dallas, Texas

ment or to improve the success potential of the first three questions? and (5) What type of additional rehabilitation interventions might be considered? See Sidebar 6.3 for a list of referral questions.

The psychologist begins the assessment process with an interview in order to determine the need for further devices to aid the assessment. For example, if Ms. Rhymer came in the office demonstrating good coping mechanisms, a positive adaptation to her sight loss, and concrete realistic ideas on how to do her job-related tasks, a more formal assessment may not be necessary. She has told the psychologist in behavioral terms how she will function in the vocational setting. In contrast, if she came in appearing passive, aided by family members, and unsure if she could or would continue in nursing even if her sight were restored, the assessment in terms of adaptation to sight loss, vocational interest, and general abilities would become much more reliant on standardized tests.

PSYCHOLOGICAL ISSUES

Rehabilitation is a biopsychosocial process in which the psychological makeups and coping styles, social environments, and the various visual impairments of individuals combine to determine the potential for adaptation and success. Such differences as congenital or adventitious blindness, partial or total sight loss, and special school placement or mainstreaming can affect both the person being assessed and the choice of assessment devices. Both the psychologist and the rehabilitation counselor are encouraged to be aware of the potential effect of these differences, as well as the many stereotypes that exist regarding people with visual impairments.

The stereotype of people with visual impairments as having a "blind personality" is totally unfounded. Usually, this stereotype is described by the uninformed as one of frequent depression, passivity, dependence, chronic anger, immaturity, substance abuse, and divorce as a result of chronic adjustment issues relating to the visual impairment. No study in the literature supports this stereotype (Vander Kolk, 1987). The research literature supports the notion that adaptation to sight loss normally occurs without professional intervention. Few long-term differences have been found between groups of sighted individuals and groups of visually impaired individuals on measures of life satisfaction (Shindell, Muray, & Needham, 1987). It is important to note that although the average person with a visual impairment does not show a need for psychological intervention, individual clients may need psychological services, and evaluation is recommended to determine whether psychological services are necessary especially for purposes of assisting with adjustment to the impairment. There is a tremendous variability in individuals, sighted or not, in respect to their abilities to understand and cope with stressful events within their lives.

Also, a number of studies in the rehabilitation literature have noted that adaptation to disability is not negatively correlated with the amount of disability (Vander Kolk, 1987). People with partial sight do not "have it easier" than people who are totally blind. The process of rehabilitation brings forth numerous unique feelings and situations for both people with partial sight and those who are totally blind. The person with partial sight may respond to issues related to possessing a hidden impairment that may fluctuate or progress over time. Others may feel that this person does not have a "real impairment" or that this person should feel lucky for not being totally blind. The person with low vision may feel devalued and less in control, and may not feel comfortable utilizing any rehabilitation services. This "marginal" status can cause a great deal of stress and concern. Indeed, the person with low vision may greet more vision loss with ambivalent feelings (Mehr & Mehr, 1969; Shindell, 1988).

Many studies in the rehabilitation literature (e.g., Brown, 1987) suggest that severe depression is a relatively infrequent phenomenon in rehabilitation settings. However, it is one problem that is greatly overidentified by staff members. It is possible that people overidentify depression in populations of individuals with disabilities as a response to their own anxiety toward interacting with people with disabilities (Wright, 1990).

Learning how clients view the disability, and what coping mechanisms they have used for stressors in the past are important variables that are best understood through a psychological assessment. One of the strongest contributions of the field of behavioral psychology is the notion that past behavior is the best predictor of future behavior (Goldfried & Davidson, 1976). How someone has reacted to challenges in the past (e.g., anxiety, depression, resourcefulness) will be the best predictor of their behavior in such future situations as employment following disability.

Given these various psychological issues, it is essential for the psychologist to have both exposure and training in regard to people with visual impairments to most accurately interpret a client's behavior. Knowledge of visual impairments is also an important consideration in the selection of various psychological tests.

TYPES OF PSYCHOLOGICAL TESTS

Intelligence Tests

Intelligence tests for people with visual impairments fall into two categories. The first category contains those tests that were originally developed for the general population, but that have been adapted. The second category comprises those tests specifically made for use with people who have visual impairments. Each category has inherent strengths and weaknesses dependent on such factors as the size and nature of the normative group, and the ability of the test to generalize to "real world" criteria. The psychologist is urged to decide on a case-by-case basis which type of test will be most functional in achieving the desired results of better understanding the client and answering the referral questions.

It is important to remember that intelligence tests measure one type of intelligence—the type reinforced in the American academic system. Test scores on these measures are very good at predicting academic success, but are not designed to measure mechanical, artistic, or social intelligence. They depend on how well the person has been integrated into the predominant culture of the society. Thus, a Hispanic Spanish-speaking mechanic with a fifth grade education will probably score poorly on the intelligence test. Without significant interventions and support, it could be predicted that this individual's chances of academic success are poor. The low score does not provide information on whether the mechanic is good at his present job as a mechanic, whether he is a good father, or whether he has strong potential for advancing to foreman or supervisor. Again, tests are tools, and, to quote Maslow, "If the only tool you have is a hammer, it is tempting to treat everything as if it were a nail" (Maslow, 1969, p. 15–16).

Intelligence tests are, by and large, excellent tests of that which they were designed to test. However, for some individuals, the idea of producing a numbered intelligence quotient, "IQ," may imply attributes that far exceed what the score really means. The rehabilitation counselor and psychologist need to be aware of what each test measures before predicting performance from a client's scores. The psychologist should report upon subtest variations, as well as intellectual potential.

The use of all the performance subtests with the general population of people with visual impairments is inappropriate because of the heavy emphasis on visual tasks that characterizes the subtests. However, individual performance of any of the tasks may prove to be useful in addressing questions regarding the person's efficiency in using any remaining sight. Scores derived from these subtests are, of course, measurements of a completely different phenomenon and cannot be directly compared to scores of the normative samples provided in the test booklet. For example, having a person with partial sight perform such a task as the block design subtest, which requires manual manipulation of objects, spatial orientation, problem-solving ability, frustration tolerance, and concentration will give an experienced examiner an indication of how the individual will solve problems with similar tasks in his or her own environment. It will reveal to the examiner information regarding the client's style of responding. The main determinant in the normative scores, however, is the speed with which these results are given. The speed with which the answers are given is too dependent on visual acuity to allow comparison between samples of individuals with either full or partial vision. The results should be taken as a behavioral sample and the psychologist is urged to be careful to ensure that he or she possesses sufficient background and experience to correctly evaluate the results.

Wechsler Adult Intelligence Scale-Revised

The Wechsler Adult Intelligence Scale-Revised (WAIS-R) is a well-known multitask intelligence test with normative groups comprised of fully sighted individuals ages 16 to 74. The WAIS-R is commonly thought of as a general "IQ" test. It is useful in predicting future academic success, and subtest variability can give evidence of sought-after potentials and weaknesses (Lezak, 1983). No significant differences have been found in WAIS-R verbal scores between persons who have adventitious blindness or those who have congenital blindness (Vander Kolk, 1982); similarly, no significant variation has been proved between those with partial sight, and those people who are totally blind (Jordan & Felty, 1968).

Other Intelligence Tests

Other intelligence tests include the Haptic Intelligence Scale for the Adult Blind (Haptic) and the Stanford-Ohwaki-Kohs Block Design Intelligence Test. Although it is no longer widely used, the Haptic is a tactile performance test designed to replace the performance subtests of the WAIS and WAIS-R for use with people who have no usable vision. The Stanford-Ohwaki-Kohs Block Design Intelligence Test was originally developed in 1923 as a nonverbal measure of problem solving. This latter test is familiar to most psychologists because one subtest or section of it is given in both the WAIS-R, as well as the Wechsler Intelligence Scale for Children-Third Edition (WISC-III). Norms for both of these tests (i.e., Haptic and Stanford-Ohwaki-Kohs) were created by using individuals with partial sight who were blindfolded for the purpose of taking the test. Therefore, the resultant scores have little predictive value and frequently are in conflict with verbal WAIS-R scores (Vander Kolk, 1982). Consequently, extreme caution should be exercised when reporting scores derived from either the Haptic or the Stanford-Ohwaki-Kohs; however, observing the cognitive styles used with these tests can be of some value to the psychologist when determining how clients approach and resolve problems.

The Cognitive Test for the Blind (CTB) was designed as a standardized and quantitative method of assessing cognitive, intellectual, and information-processing skills. It differs from traditional intelligence tests, such as the WAIS-R, by focusing on actual problem solving, learning, and memory, in addition to acquired knowledge and experience. There are five verbal subtests. They include Auditory Analysis, Immediate Digit Recall, Language Comprehension and Memory, Letter Number Learning, and Vocabulary. There are five nonvisual performance subtests: Haptic Category Learning, Haptic Category Memory, Haptic Memory Recognition, Pattern Recall, and Spatial Analysis. The CTB is an integral component of the Comprehensive Vocational Evaluation System (CVES) used as the primary measure of verbal-spatial-cognitive functions. (Dial et al., 1992).

Although differences on measures of intelligence have not been found between adults with congenital and adventitious blindness, it is important to realize that experiencing the environment can differ drastically for these two groups. One of the purposes of giving an intelligence test is to determine an individual's available fund of knowledge and information. Therefore, variances may not show up in a standardized intelligence test, but the environmental experiences can cause difficulty in other aspects of a person's life. It is very possible that these difficulties may be viewed as indications of pathology by psychologists who are inadequately trained in assessing people with visual impairments. For instance, a congenitally blind woman with advanced educational degrees, who had never flown in a plane before, made the assumption that airplanes flap their wings as birds do to become airborne because airplane flight was explained to her as being analogous to "flying like a bird" (Smith, 1987). Similarly, Foulke and Uhde (1974) reported on a male with congenital blindness who, after having a sex education class, accurately described intercourse, but thought that the vagina was located somewhere near the armpit. Consequently, clinicians are strongly urged to explore an individual's gaps in learning to determine the effect of previous experience and learning on that individual's test performance.

Personality Tests

Personality tests are administered to determine basic characteristics of individuals that can be used to predict their reaction to various situations. These tests are designed to give an indication of a person's psychological strengths and weaknesses, coping styles, and the ability to handle various forms of stress. For example, an assessment may examine a client's ability to receive and integrate negative feedback within a supervisory situation at work.

In many cases, the measurement of personality characteristics in clients with visual impairments is done by reading the test to the examinee or using audio tape, large-print, or braille versions of existing tests. The advantages and disadvantages of each of these techniques are most dependent on a client's skill in using these media, the client's remaining vision, and the type of information that is being presented. For example, large amounts of information that do not require scanning or graph presentation are probably best presented in audio tape format. Braille or large print are preferable if information has to be retrieved from embedded text, or choices need to be made from a number of options, such as in a multiple choice examination. The examiner should be aware of the fact that each of these methods will greatly extend the time needed to take the test and may compromise the results.

It is recommended that tests be carefully selected so as not to confuse or fatigue the client. Clients with visual impairments cannot efficiently scan material, nor can they deal effectively with multiple choice questions that require extensive mental comparisons and manipulations. They cannot scan their answers to determine patterns in a way that often influences fully sighted individuals. Finally, there is always the concern that examinees may vary in their performance when an examiner is present and is recording their answers. Because a staff examiner who is recording responses can possibly influence those responses, the utilization of clerical volunteers who are unfamiliar to the examinees may be helpful in protecting impartiality. Also, use of cards with raised markings can enable examinees to respond without feeling pressure from examiners. Examinees can insert cards into appropriate choice slots in a response box.

Personality test measures that have been specifically designed for people with visual impairments can be organized into two groups: measures of general personality and measures of adaptation to visual impairment. Most measures of personality designed for people with visual impairments follow the pattern of intellectual tests in that they are attempts to take existing tests used with people with full vision in order to develop analogous forms useful in the field of visual impairment. Numerous similar tests, including the Auditory Projective Test, the Bas-Relief Projective Test, the Draw-a-Person Test, the Smith-Madan Projective Test, the Sound Test, and the Twitchell–Allen Three Dimensional Apperception Test have fallen into disuse, because it is extremely difficult to simply "translate" a test into another sensory modality and expect it to assess the same phenomena. One projective measure that is fairly easy to adapt to an auditory presentation is an "incomplete sentences blank" test. There are a variety of incomplete sentences blank tests in use. Many are geared toward a variety of populations and issues and many have been found to work well with individuals who are blind or visually impaired.

Vocational Tests

There are two categories of vocational tests: vocational interest inventories and occupational/industrial tests of abilities. Interest tests, such as the Strong–Campbell Interest Inventory, the Kuder Occupational Interest Survey, and the Minnesota Vocational Interest Inventory, measure individuals' interests in various tasks and jobs and compare them to people who are successful and content in those occupations (Anastasi, 1988). This process can be very useful for individuals with visual impairments who may be either unaware of occupations available to them or who are considering alternative fields of employment that have qualities similar to those they enjoy, such as outdoor or indoor work, regular hours, and human contact (Barker, White, Reardon, & Johnson, 1980; Scholl & Schnur, 1976). Because these tests are based on likes and dislikes, there has not been a need for normative groups of people with visual impairments.

Tests of occupational abilities, for example the General Aptitude Test Battery (GATB), are useful in determining a person's skill in various job-related situations. Because these tests usually measure a person's ability to perform a task in a real-world situation, adaptations can be made during the testing that are similar to the types of accommodations that could be made on an actual job. In this situation, a reference group composed of people with visual impairments is meaningless, because these tests, by definition, are approximations of real-world situations.

Adaptation to Disability

Tests that assess the ability of a person with a visual impairment to adapt and adjust are available in myriad forms. Many are adaptations of similar scales (e.g., the Teare Sentence Completion Test, the Rhode Hildreth Sentence Completion Test); others are tests specifically designed for use with people with visual impairments, such as the Belief About Blindness Scale (BABS) (Ehmer & Needham, 1979). Scores on the BABS have been shown to correspond to staff ratings of improvement in patients involved in rehabilitation (Needham & Ehmer, 1980). The BABS is easily administered within 10 minutes and yields information specific to a person's attitude toward his or her visual impairment. When used by various healthcare and rehabilitation professionals, significant differences have been found (Ehmer, Needham, Del'Aune, & Carr, 1982; Shindell, Muray & Needham, 1987), which suggests that professionals without exposure to people with visual impairments tend to have more dysfunctional attitudes toward them. This reinforces the need for the rehabilitation counselor to assess the background and training of the psychologist performing assessment and providing treatment for visually impaired clients.

Other personality tests specifically designed for people with visual impairments include The Anxiety Scale for the Blind (Hardy, 1966) and The Emotional Factors Inventory (Bauman, 1968), which measure attitudes, sensitivity, somatic symptoms, attitudes of mistrust, and depression of people with visual impairments. However, The Emotional Factors Inventory has been found to be confusing to clients because it contains several double negative questions, thereby limiting its accuracy and reliability.

Neuropsychological Tests

The ability to administer neuropsychological tests to people with visual impairments is critically important because long-standing skill deficits may become evident only after sight loss. For example, a person who has always had a very poor auditory memory may have compensated for this deficit with an outstanding visual memory and imagery. After the onset of visual impairment, this individual would be left with no outlet for these positive skills and, hence, must rely on an undeveloped auditory memory. This person may appear to have suddenly decreased skills in both behavioral and standardized measures, when, in fact, the person's cognitive abilities have not significantly changed.

Three common neuropsychological tests are the Halstead–Reitan Battery (Reitan & Davidson, 1974), the Luria–Nebraska Battery (Golden, 1991), and the McCarron–Dial System (McCarron & Dial, 1976). The revised Halstead–Reitan Battery includes measures of concept formation, sensorimotor functions, spatial organization and kinesthesis, a measure of sustained attention and nonverbal auditory discrimination, and a measure of finger tapping speed. Taking between four and six hours to complete, this battery, which results in an index of possible brain damage, is often supplemented with other tests, such as the WAIS-R, the Wide-Range Achievement Test-3 (Wilkinson, 1993), and the Minnesota Multiphasic Personality Inventory (Hathaway & McKinley, 1970).

The Luria–Nebraska Battery takes about half as much time to complete as the Halstead-Reitan. It is used to assess motor functions, rhythm, tactile and visual functions, receptive and expressive speech, reading and writing skills, arithmetic skills, memory, and intellectual processes.

Although both the Halstead–Reitan and Luria–Nebraska are useful in diagnosis, they do not contribute as much to vocational planning efforts as does the McCarron–Dial System. The McCarron–Dial System was developed as a vocational evaluation battery using a neuropsychological conceptual model. Although this test system has been revised and extended for individuals with various types of disabilities, at different ages and functional levels, many of its basic measures are not applicable to individuals with visual impairments. Even when modifications are made for the limited norms, a lack of technical manuals to assist with interpretation remains problematic.

The CVES, however, was developed to assess vocational functioning of individuals for whom the Halstead–Reitan, Luria–Nebraska, and McCarron–Dial were inappropriate due to their vision requirements. The CVES, developed on the McCarron and Dial model of evaluation, is useful in both describing and predicting vocational potential and provides important information that can be used in the development of rehabilitation or education plans. It is also an appropriate neuropsychological assessment for individuals whose visual functioning level affects their performance on traditional test measures (Dial et al., 1992, p. 14). (A sample of a complete CVES report that is based on the McCarron–Dial model appears in Appendix C of this book.)

ISSUES IN PSYCHOLOGICAL ASSESSMENT

In any assessment situation, the psychologist relies on three main sets of information: (1) the behavioral observations of the client in the testing situation, (2) the clinical interview, and (3) the formal test scores that are developed from standardized tests. Many of the issues in psychological assessment are similar to those in vocational assessment. For example, the psychologist uses both formal and informal means to assess each individual's behavior and attitudes, compared to those of a reference group. Psychologists need to decide which tests to use in each situation and must also determine which existing reference groups are the most appropriate for comparison purposes. As in the work evaluation, choosing an inappropriate reference group can lead to conclusions that are not relevant to the person's abilities, and can ultimately be counterproductive to the client's successful rehabilitation.

Many behaviors that are unique to people with visual impairments can confuse the psychologist in assessing the frequency or "normalness" of such behavior in terms of the person's reference group. For example, a person with a visual impairment may arrive several hours early to the assessment interview, or have very rigid requirements concerning scheduling and length of time in testing. Often this behavior is based on the difficulty of coordinating available transportation and should not be interpreted as a sign of resistance. The rehabilitation counselor is encouraged to aid the psychologist by describing any unusual life situations that may impinge on the interview process and may lead to a false appraisal of the client by the psychologist.

If the psychologist is determining suitability for various occupations that require speed, visual scanning, and similar skills, preparing the testing materials to be presented only verbally is useless. A more appropriate approach might utilize such dexterity tests as the Purdue Pegboard or the

Minnesota Rate of Manipulation Test. Similarly, if the presentation of materials in other forms is unwieldy, cumbersome, and creates fatigue in the client with a visual impairment, the validity of using norms based on sighted subjects is questionable, regardless of how closely the individual items match on the alternative presentation.

Moreover, many individual test items make no sense when translated into verbal form. One example includes tasks in which the purpose is to determine differences between items that are normally viewed visually. Another example is the Picture Completion subtest of the WAIS-R, in which pictures of various items are presented to the subject and the task is to determine what important piece is missing from the picture (e.g., how is this picture different from the "ideal"). Describing the task verbally, including all of the missing parts or differences, would be too much help to the client and would not produce an accurate assessment of the faculties that this test was designed to measure.

The process of assessing someone with a visual impairment goes beyond giving a test "translated" for his or her use. In selecting tests, it is recommended that the psychologist examine the process that was used in developing each test, the types of items used to test each skill domain, the evidence that the items validly meet their intended purpose, and the populations on which norms have been based. Because the data on people with visual impairments are limited for psychological tests, although slightly less limited for vocational tests, the psychologist is urged to use existing data from various sources as a metaphorical series of template overlays that define and illuminate the boundaries in which each individual could be expected to perform, rather than using just one set of results with a matched normative group. It is recommended that psychologists not limit themselves to a specific group of tests for people with visual impairments, but rather assess each situation individually to determine the means that will provide useful information to the referral questions. This requires a concerted effort between the psychologist and rehabilitation counselor in defining and answering the questions that are most important in each client's situation.

ETHICAL ISSUES IN ASSESSMENT

Each of the professionals involved in the assessment of individuals with visual impairments is guided by a different set of ethical standards. Just as rehabilitation counselors are guided by the Code of Professional Ethics for Rehabilitation Counselors (see Appendix D at the end of this book), vocational evaluators are urged to adhere to the Vocational Evaluation and Work Adjustment (VEWAA) Code of Ethics to ensure appropriate standards of conduct in the vocational evaluation of people with visual impairments. Psychologists are guided by the American Psychological Association (APA) Ethical Principles of Psychologists and Code of Conduct, as well as government guidelines (Sherman & Robinson, 1982) that outline the dilemmas facing psychologists who test people with disabilities in a variety of settings. For example, it is strongly urged that the psychologist provide enough information and unambiguous stimuli to clients to ensure that what is being measured is, in fact, that which is being tested.

Rehabilitation counselors, seeking to refer people for vocational evaluations and psychological assessments, are encouraged to assess not only the general qualifications of psychologists and work evaluators, but also their experiences in working with people with visual impairments. Although the various codes of ethics all address competence issues, evaluators or psychologists may not view themselves as incompetent (even though they may be very inexperienced). Therefore, the importance of using professionals with training and experience in assessing clients with visual impairments cannot be overemphasized.

It is also important for the rehabilitation counselor to be aware of biases in evaluations or descriptions of behavior that may misrepresent a client's current status due to stereotypes held by either the evaluator or the psychologist. If there is any question about the validity of a particular test or the manner in which a score is interpreted, the rehabilitation counselor is strongly urged to seek clarification before attempting to use or interpret the results to a client.

SUMMARY

Vocational and psychological evaluations can provide information that is useful to the rehabilitation counselor and client to identify career opportunities and vocational objectives. Both vocational and psychological evaluations should be conducted by qualified professionals who also have expertise in assessment of individuals with visual impairments. It is also important that care be taken in the selection of various tests to ensure the applicability of any norm group comparisons, as well as their reliability and validity for a particular client. It is recommended that the rehabilitation counselor also ensure that tests do not discriminate against individuals with visual impairments, and that the individuals conducting the assessment do not hold inappropriate client stereotypes based on disability.

Assessment is an identification of strengths and potential, rather than only a compilation of scores on individual tasks. Psychologists and evaluators are urged to rely on their abilities in observing behavior, as well as the formal test scores that are developed within the context of any assessment. An effective team composed of a rehabilitation counselor specifying clear referral questions and psychologists and evaluators with experience concerning assessment issues for people with visual impairments can lead to significant client benefits. The assessment of people with visual impairments is a complex responsibility and also an integral part of the rehabilitation process that can assist in identifying client strengths, needed services, and required accommodations, all of which promote integration, self-sufficiency, and self-esteem.

LEARNING ACTIVITIES

1. List five potential referral questions that could best be answered by a psychological assessment.
2. Summarize the special accommodations that should and should not be made when assessing an individual with a visual impairment.
3. Contact and interview a psychologist or vocational evaluator in your area. The interview should include the following topics:
   a. How many people do you evaluate each year? How many people have visual impairments? Please describe some of the visual impairments that you have encountered.
   b. What types of tests and assessment instruments do you use during your evaluation? What modifications do you use when testing a person with a visual impairment? Specify modifications that are appropriate for different levels of visual functioning.
   c. Please identify any additional issues you have found to be important in the assessment and evaluation of people with visual impairments. For example, few tests are normed on people with visual impairments. How does the lack of norms affect test selection and interpretation?
4. Attempt to complete an assembly task from a vocational evaluation kit while wearing either low vision simulation goggles or a blindfold. (Do not look at the assembly task without low vision goggles or a blindfold.) Measure the amount of time needed for assembly and successfulness of the assembly. Alternatively, perform a manual dexterity task while wearing either low vision simulation goggles or a blindfold. Discuss the effects or noneffects of wearing low vision simulation goggles or a blindfold on the task.

CHAPTER 7

Demographic and Cultural Considerations in Rehabilitation

Priscilla A. Rogers, Sue A. Schmitt, and Geraldine T. Scholl

Within the population of individuals who are visually impaired, there is great diversity. This chapter addresses aspects of that diversity by focusing on the rehabilitation issues and needs of individuals with visual impairments, based on three demographic variables: age, gender, and cultural diversity. Research suggests that rehabilitation counselors need to know the manner in which these variables influence access to rehabilitation services, as well as the types of rehabilitation services provided, because older individuals, women, and non-Caucasian individuals have been underserved by many rehabilitation systems (Taheri-Araghi & Hendron, 1994). These groups also have a high prevalence of additional disabilities. For example, the incidence rate of severe visual impairment increases steadily with age, and 68 percent of individuals with severe visual impairments are over age 65 (Nelson & Dimitrova, 1993). The groups are also not mutually exclusive; a majority of older individuals are women and a substantial number of individuals from culturally diverse groups have visual impairments.

OLDER INDIVIDUALS WITH VISUAL IMPAIRMENTS

In the United States, people over age 65 represent a majority of the population who are visually impaired. It is anticipated that the number of older individuals with visual impairments will increase from 3.5 million in 1990 to 7 million by 2030 (AFB Fact Sheet, 1997). Crews and Frey (1993) stated:

> The impact of aging and blindness is intensely personal and private, and its implications are profound. It affects an older person's ability to perform tasks and establish relationships that are second nature to us all. And it may compromise the traditional roles that provide identity, self-esteem, and quality of life. (p. 10)

Despite the profound implications of aging and blindness, until recently older people have traditionally been underserved by state agencies charged with the rehabilitation of individuals who are blind. Because funds to serve this population have been limited, agencies have been unable to provide comprehensive services. Moreover, Kirchner (1988) estimated that 66 percent of persons who are older and visually impaired have other disabilities, including such sensory losses as hearing, loss of taste discrimination, decline in sense of smell, and diminution of touch sensitivity. In reviewing the impact of these sensory losses in elderly persons, Saxon and Etten (1987) stated,

> Sensory changes with age are some of the most crucial and possibly most underrated changes

Services for Older Individuals

SIDEBAR 7.1

A wide range of services is available to older individuals who are visually impaired. The rehabilitation counselor should consider all of the following in developing a rehabilitation program for such individuals:

1. Vision care services, including low vision evaluation.
2. Rehabilitation services, such as training in mobility, daily living skills, communications, use of talking books, and use of low vision devices.
3. Recreational and leisure services.
4. Public transportation and escort services.
5. Counseling in regard to depression or coping with vision loss.
6. Information about visual impairments and other disabilities.
7. Information on, demonstration of, and provision of consumer aids and appliances, such as large button telephones and watches with large-print numerals (Mann et al., 1993).
8. Assistance in employment or volunteer participation.
9. Access to peer groups or other older people who are coping with similar vision problems (Hiatt, 1986).
10. Intervention with family members or significant others.
11. Availability of a variety of such support services as reader services, meals on wheels, and homemaker services.

> associated with the entire aging process. . . . Changes in each of these systems interferes with the ability to gather pertinent information about the environment essential to high quality life and even to the maintenance of life itself. (pp. 19–20)

Other physical problems in the older population have also been documented. For example, in individuals 85 years of age and older, 53 percent reported difficulty walking, 24 percent reported difficulty getting in and out of a chair or bed, 45 percent had cardiovascular disease; 54 percent had hypertension, and 48 percent reported a hearing loss (Havlick, 1986). In addition to these problems, changes in metabolic function may bring about diminished body control over blood pressure, body temperature, and blood sugar. The inability of the older person's body to control these functions means that death can result from even mild cases of the flu or exposure to extremes in temperature (Jernigan, 1981).

Cognitive changes may also occur that slow decision-making processes or alter the way in which individuals learn. Research has indicated that fluid intelligence (i.e., the ability to perform on learning tasks that are fast-paced, perceive complex relations, and form concepts) depends greatly on physiological factors including vision (Bennett & Eklund, 1983a; 1983b). Fluid intelligence is modifiable by behavioral intervention, willingness to use intellectual capacities fully, and learning to compensate for vision loss (Bennett & Eklund, 1983a; 1983b). Furthermore, crystallized intelligence (i.e., the ability to reason and perceive relationships based on previous knowledge) may actually increase as the individual is exposed to more education and experiences (Franz, 1983).

Other research indicates that older adults do not have problems learning or performing if such key factors are considered as (1) pacing the materials to be learned, (2) instructing learners to organize material as it is presented, (3) rehearsing material after it has been learned, and (4) providing techniques for remembering. Motivation and learning are generally greater when the task has meaning for the older adult (Edinberg, 1985).

Many of the impairments described above significantly affect an individual who is 85 years or older, but may be lesser problems for individuals in the age range from 65 to 70. It is the rehabilitation counselor's responsibility to assess the implications of multiple impairments (Hiatt, 1981) on individuals and to help older people adjust and adapt their lifestyles.

Rehabilitation Needs

Although older individuals constitute approximately 66 percent of the total number of persons who are blind, in 1995, only 2 percent of the population served by the state-federal vocational rehabilitation program were 65 years of age or older (RSA, 1995). The failure to serve this population results from (1) a lack of knowledge on the part of rehabilitation professionals, (2) a lack of funding, (3) negative attitudes on the part of professionals (Ebener, 1992), and (4) the discrepancy between the service-delivery needs of older people who are blind compared to the traditional age groups (i.e., ages 16 to 55) served by the state-federal vocational rehabilitation program (Benedict & Ganikos, 1981). This latter problem is compounded by the large numbers of individuals rehabilitation counselors have on their caseloads who require attention, in addition to the tendency of counselors to work with individuals whom they understand and for whom they are expected to help attain employment.

The advent of funding for independent living for older and visually impaired persons has resulted in an additional 22,103 older individuals receiving services in 48 states, as of 1995 (Stephens, 1996). These numbers should increase with the availability of funding to every state. (Sidebar 7.1 includes a list of some of the available services.)

Rehabilitation counselors and other health-care professionals have a responsibility to ensure that older individuals receive services or are referred elsewhere for appropriate services. Consider Margaret Crofton (1985), a retired physician, who lost her vision in 1983 and was placed in a nursing home. She said:

> My doctor didn't know what else to do with me. . . . My doctor never made mention of the program available to rehabilitate the visually impaired or any of the aids and devices currently on the market which enable the blind to carry out daily living skills. If he had, I could have been spared the five months of frustration, anger, and depersonalization I experienced while in the nursing home. . . . (p. 2)

Eventually, through the help of a friend, Dr. Crofton contacted a rehabilitation center, where she learned vital adaptive skills. She stated,

> The Lighthouse has given me back my freedom and my independence. I am once again a responsible adult making my own decisions and living my own life. Losing one's sight is not the end of one's existence. You simply need to relearn how to do basic tasks with a few adaptations. . . . I am grateful to be in my own home again. Yet, I wonder how many other elderly people with a vision loss are trapped within the walls of a nursing home when they too could be in their own home living a full and independent life. (p. 2)

The rehabilitation counselor can play a major role in helping people who are both older and blind maximize their capacities for independent living. Often older individuals with visual impairments are generally unaware of the services that are available or of their potential to live more independently. They need to learn about these possibilities in addition to receiving help to overcome any stereotypic views they may hold on either blindness or aging. Some older individuals may reject assistance because of fear, loss of self-esteem, or feelings of loneliness, uselessness, an-

Rehabilitation counselors need to help older individuals with visual impairments obtain training in adaptive independent living skills and arrange for appropriate referrals.

ger, depression, or denial. By recognizing these feelings, the rehabilitation counselor can assist the person who is older and blind with the adjustment process (Jolicoeur, 1970).

Ed is an example of the positive results that can come from working with an individual who is older and blind. Ed, a 68-year-old man who was totally blind, contacted his state's Division of Blind Services. He talked to the rehabilitation instructor, who made the following report:

> [Ed] wanted to know what services we offered, which I explained in limited detail and suggested that I visit him later for a conference and additional information. At the time of this visit, he very pointedly emphasized that all he wanted was some information, that he was not requesting services, and he did not wish to go through the application procedures. No application for services was taken at this time. He did ask me if I would return to visit with him again. From various things during our initial visit, I could detect the fact that there were numerous services which would greatly benefit this gentleman. I felt strongly that he should be a client and should be able to make use of the available services. Consequently, I informed him that I would return to see him in a couple of weeks. He did agree to let me apply for library services for him. I felt that a man of his interests, education, and background would utilize the library services extensively if he could be persuaded to accept them initially. Both a cassette player and a record player were ordered to take advantage of the wide selection of reading material offered in both media. As expected, he is now going through six to eight books and magazines per week. Following each home visit during the last couple of months, Ed seemed more and more interested in having me return for additional information. His case has now been opened and registered. (Griggs, 1986)

Subsequent to this dictation, the instructor continued with home visits. The instructor stated:

> He finally acquiesced to letting me show the Braille system to him. After a couple of visits he got quite interested and began to work on it with enthusiasm. In a short time he had completely mastered Grade I Braille. He once again went back to his life-long hobby of writing political and social satire in poetry form. He has given me a number of these and not only is his braille good, but I am sure the organized thought and mental stimulation required to achieve this is also very good for him.
>
> Ed was finally led to the conclusion that he could not remain confined to his single room. For the sake of sanity, he came to realize he must return to an active life even though it may not be on the same level as in previous years. The real beginning arrived when I was able to bring him into town and spend the majority of the morning on the streets learning basic mobility and cane techniques. He was quite surprised at the ease and efficiency with which he could travel in this manner. He at once became an enthusiastic learner.
>
> Ed is well known in his small community and everyone is very supportive and very glad to have him active in the community again. Two weeks ago he was appointed as Chairman of the Crime Watch Committee and has had two successful meetings of that group. For many years Ed had been active in the Boy Scouts. Recently he was convinced of his usefulness to the organization and [was] persuaded to accept the position of District Commissioner of Boy Scouts. (Griggs, 1986)

This report not only shows the importance of continuing to work with a client but also illustrates the importance of involving older individuals who are blind in identifying service needs and developing service plans. Effective counseling involves balancing a helping role while facilitating the client's control over his or her own rehabilitation.

In working with individuals who are older, counselors are advised to try to understand the client's expectations of the rehabilitation counselor as a helper. Research on helping (*Rehab Brief*, 1983, pp. 3–4) indicates that help can have the effect of (1) overwhelming and reducing control over recipients' lives, (2) hindering the acquisition and maintenance of useful skills, and (3) creating confusion about who gets credit or blame for the outcomes. For these reasons, the researchers suggest that "helpers may help most by assisting and sorting what recipients can control from what they cannot control."

Therefore, people who are older and blind may require counselor assistance in assessing their own needs and discovering solutions, and yet, may also need to be able to make their own decisions about what course their rehabilitation will take without being patronized. "The Independent Living philosophy stresses that clients who have the ability or potential should be in charge of their own case management. If clients lack this ability, then one goal is to help them get to the point where they have it" (Weil & Karls, 1985, p. 279).

Employment Considerations

In assessing the older person's capacity to work, the counselor is urged to be aware that "... age, in and of itself, does not prevent qualified individuals from performing satisfactorily ..." (Dickey, 1975, p. 220). Health, client motivation, and employer, family, and counselor attitudes are the important factors relating to employability and performance. In addition to these factors, a study conducted by the Rehabilitation Research and Training Center on Blindness and Low Vision at Mississippi State University identified rehabilitation process variables as significant discriminators for predicting employment outcomes among persons who are older and blind. Included in these variables were expenditures for personal and vocational adjustment and rehabilitation facility training; expenditures for restoration services including diagnostic services and hospital convalescent services; expenditures for trade school training; and skill level of the occupational goals contained in the Individualized Written Rehabilitation Program (IWRP). This study found that although 18 percent of those sampled did find competitive employment, they experienced much lower wages than others in the sample. Furthermore, older women were more apt to be closed as homemakers, which was the largest category of closures studied (Giesen & Ford, 1986a). This situation is still true. The Rehabilitation Services Administration Case Service Report for 1995 indicates that 84.3 percent of women over the age of 65 were closed as homemakers (RSA Case Service Report 911, 1995, unpublished).

Health problems can be mitigated by helping individuals who are older and visually impaired find jobs that require less physical capacity or that allow them to pace themselves or to use "other strengths" (Walters, 1980). The Research and Training Center Study also urges the counselor to review carefully the older person's occupational background when identifying realistic job possibilities for the IWRP (see Chapter 10). It is also suggested that secondary and tertiary disabilities be documented and restorative services and technological resources be employed to maximize the older individual's potential for employment (Giesen & Ford, 1986).

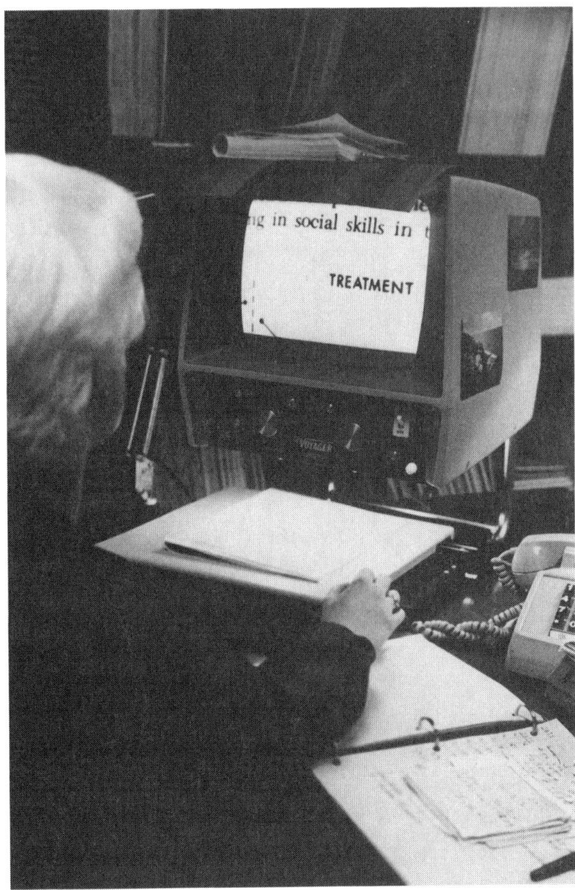

To help an older individual with a visual impairment retain or find new employment, a counselor can consider ways to modify a work station. Accommodations might include the use of low vision devices, such as a closed-circuit television, and methods to improve lighting, reduce glare, or provide appropriate contrast sensitivity.

Older individuals who are visually impaired often do not feel that they can continue to work and thus are not motivated to seek employment. Counseling, participation in rehabilitation training, and support from family members can help older individuals decide to continue to work or reenter the work force (Thomas, 1981). Early intervention (i.e., before individuals lose their jobs or when they can be restored to previously held jobs) is also more apt to result in vocational success for individuals who are older and blind (Dunn, 1981). In these situations, the counselor is encouraged to focus on the employer-employee relationship and try to capitalize on the assets of the older person.

In placing older workers in new jobs, the counselor should be ready to anticipate employer objections to hiring a person who is both older and blind by preparing effective, factual answers to the commonly stated concerns of employers. Some of these concerns can be countered by assuring employers that older people overall (1) are less apt to change jobs than are younger workers, (2) have fewer work accidents than younger workers, (3) are generally as productive as younger persons given their health constraints, (4) have good attendance and punctuality, and (5) have a commitment to quality, loyalty, and practical knowledge (Dickey, 1975; Morrison, 1991; Walters, 1980).

It is also suggested that counselors look for modifications that can be made to the work environment in terms of lighting and working distance, with particular attention to such factors that affect the older worker as glare, contrast sensitivity, and speed of visual processing. Low vision devices can also be considered, depending on the older worker's vision and job requirements. The employer will also need to know that a systematic retraining program may be required, if the older worker is expected to take on new tasks or if work expectations are changed. However, the ability to draw on past experiences can give the older worker the edge in learning or adapting to new tasks (Work, Aging, and Vision, 1987).

It is also suggested that full-time versus part-time work be considered by the counselor and client, depending on the older worker's ability or desire to work full-time. Sometimes, part-time employment is more feasible because of physical capacities or when loss of social security benefits is a concern. When considering sources of work, senior citizens' employment agencies may provide useful job leads.

Mobility Issues

When working with individuals who are older and blind, it is important that the counselor be aware that older individuals are often socially and physically isolated, because of actual or perceived inability to interact or move freely in the environment. Age and activity levels are related. People over 65 years of age have been found to be significantly less active in information gathering, using transportation, and accessing public activities than individuals in the younger age groups (Genesky, Berry, Bikson, & Bikson, 1979). Fear, embarrassment, motivation, physical capability, unfamiliarity with geography, lack of training (Welsh, 1981), and self-reported decline in vision may all contribute to this lack of mobility (Long, Boyette, & Griffin-Shirley, 1996). For these reasons, orientation and mobility (O&M) training for those who are older and blind is essential. Such training may restore hope to the older individual who has virtually given up, who feels helpless and incapable, and whose feelings are often reinforced by family and friends (Hill & Harley, 1984). O&M instructors have a major role to play in helping older people become less isolated and more involved in the community by providing individualized instruction in the immediate environment (Welsh, 1981).

Another factor that affects mobility is fear of trauma—for example, being robbed or victimized (Mann, Hurren, Karuza, & Bentley, 1993; Pava, 1994). To alleviate the fears and feelings of physical vulnerability experienced by older individuals, counselors might suggest taking a course in self-protective techniques and acquiring information on making their homes more secure. Another fear is that osteoporosis and balance problems may lead to falls and possible fractures. The counselor is therefore encouraged to suggest ways to avoid accidents in the home, such as

> adding non-slip treads or carpet to stairs, painting the top and the bottom steps a light color, installing staircase handrails and extending them beyond the last step, installing non-slip rubber mats and horizontal grab bars in bathtubs, eliminating scatter rugs or utilizing non-slip backing on the rugs, tacking down edges of rugs, providing adequate lighting in stairways and storage areas, and designing shelving low enough so that climbing is minimized. (Price, 1978, p. 40)

The use of low vision devices can enhance mobility skills and help the older individual who is visually impaired to function more adequately in performing tasks of everyday living. Older individuals may not be aware of the variety of low vision, assistive devices that are available, however, and some assistive devices may need to be modified to meet their needs. For example, Mann, Hurren, Karuza, and Bentley (1993) have found that older individuals wanted mobility canes that also provided support. Older persons may not always respond to the use of assistive devices and low vision devices and may need help in (1) learning how to use them appropriately, (2) dealing with the frustration of using the

Large-print books, heavily lined writing paper, and handwriting guides like the one pictured here are just a few examples of nonoptical devices that can be useful to older individuals who are visually impaired.

devices and having to hold material closer, and (3) overcoming embarrassment about needing to use such devices. A period of adjustment may be required for a person to feel comfortable in using assistive, low vision devices, because such use does call attention to the individual using them (Genesky & Zarit, 1986; Mann et al., 1993). It is suggested that the older individual who lives with family members be encouraged to use devices to participate in such everyday family activities as watching television, playing cards, and sewing. For individuals who live alone, attention can be centered on performing tasks such as reading mail, medicine bottle labels, and canned goods. Nonoptical devices such as large-print books, heavily lined writing paper, and watches with large-print numerals can also be of great value to older individuals who are visually impaired (Rosenbloom, 1982).

Low vision devices can also assist the older individual who is visually impaired by restoring privacy. Carroll (1961) documented the problem of deprivation of privacy, saying "... the greatest loss (in communication) ... is the ability to read one's own mail, to keep up one's personal correspondence without the intrusion of another party" (p. 46). Many older people who are blind also live alone and may depend on someone outside the family to read their mail and do other personal tasks. In addition to the personal indignity often felt in this situation, this dependency can pose a threat to older individuals, who may fall prey to con artists.

Reimbursement for low vision devices and low vision exams can also be problematic; Medicare and Medicaid generally do not cover these services. Older individuals who are blind generally do not have extra funds available to underwrite the cost of either the devices or the exams. This point is of particular concern to older women, who are a majority of the older, blind population, and because so many of them are impoverished (Bader, 1986; Kirchner, 1988). For a complete discussion of low vision devices, see Chapter 4.

Role of Support Networks

Families of older persons with visual impairments provide 80 to 90 percent of the care of the older individual (Crews & Frey, 1993). These families can play a very crucial role in the rehabilitation of older family members by supporting the family member in his or her efforts and by avoiding overprotective behaviors (Moore, 1984). Older individuals with visual impairments may need assistance in performing some tasks regardless of their capabilities—which may complicate family relationships (Goodman, 1985).

Counselors are encouraged to be aware of the importance of family members and to bring them into the rehabilitation process so that families can understand both the process and their role in it. Rehabilitation professionals have not always done an adequate job of including family members, nor have they fully explored appropriate intervention strategies for family members (Hiatt, 1981). Utilizing the family support network can not only benefit the individual who is older and blind but can also help fill gaps in the formal service delivery or funding system (Yeadon, 1984).

When investigating the concerns of family members who had an older family member with a visual impairment living in the home, Crews and Frey (1993) found that the stress levels of families were greater than anticipated. Major concerns of spouses and adult children who were living with the parent at the time the older family member entered the rehabilitation program included (1) safety, (2) transportation, (3) demands on their time, and (4) knowledge of how, when, and how much to help. Crews and Frey found that rehabilitation efforts primarily targeted to the older individual resulted in substantially reduced stress levels for family members. They stated, ". . . these gains were serendipitous in many respects. If more intense services could be directed toward family members, one would suspect that greater gains could be achieved" (p. 10).

Peers may be another source of support for older individuals with visual impairments. Helping the older person who is blind to develop a peer support network is extremely important both to the rehabilitation process and to socialization efforts. There are a number of challenges that may need to be addressed, however, to the development of peer support networks. For example:

1. Fear of dependency has been cited as the greatest fear of elderly persons (Saxon & Etten, 1987). To develop positive, mutually satisfying relationships, the person who is blind may need a great deal of help in suppressing this fear. Sighted peers may also have concerns about dependency. They may be concerned that their friend who is blind may become dependent on them for social and psychological support, and help in shopping and other everyday tasks. These fears of dependency may become a major barrier in continuing relationships after the onset of visual impairment.
2. Friends may feel uncomfortable with a person who is newly blinded and individuals who are still adjusting to visual impairment are not always able to alleviate the uncomfortable feelings or fears of sighted friends. Some authors (e.g., Ainlay, 1981, Carroll, 1961) have equated becoming blind with the death of the formerly sighted person. Misunderstandings about the implications of visual impairment may also contribute to negative feelings. Sighted peers may be coping with personal feelings about blindness, including fear and denial that such an "affliction" could happen to them. Moreover, many older individuals who are blind have adopted the same negative myths and stereotypes about aging and being blind as the rest of society.
3. Friends who could constitute the peer support network may withdraw because they lack knowledge of how to interact appropriately with an individual who has impaired vision. Explaining partial vision and its functional implications is difficult. For example, the peer may not be able to understand why the friend with a visual impairment can walk around without problems, but is unable to recognize facial features. Inability to use eye contact as a form of communication also tends to limit many relationships.

Peer support networks, composed of other individuals with visual impairments can be an excellent adjunct to the support of sighted peers and family members and may be essential in those situations in which sighted peers are unable to provide support and encouragement. Many benefits are associated with peer groups, including reducing the fears and anxieties that accompany O&M training (Seybold, 1993). Other perceived benefits of peer groups by older individuals with visual impairments include:

> (a) socialization and friendship, including reducing isolation and loneliness; (b) understanding, support, and sharing concerns and experiences, including support from those with the same problem; (c) independence, confidence, self-esteem . . . ; (d) information about resources, events, and devices; (e) coping with specific issues, such as depression and anxiety; and (f) the opportunity to help others. (Kalafat & Dehmer, 1993, p. 113)

Ainlay (1981) documented that a person's ability to cope effectively with the loss of vision is related to peer support from other individuals who have recently lost their vision. Byers-Lang (1984) found that clients engaged in a rehabilitation program using peer counselors made more rapid progress with rehabilitation goals, were better able to handle frustration, and more apt to function independently than were individuals without peer support. Also, Van Zandt, Van Zandt, and Wang (1994) found that peer support groups composed of people with visual impairments provided individuals with levels of support that they were unable to obtain from other types of support groups. Other research (e.g., Evans, Werkhoven, & Fox, 1982) showed that a simple telephone group conference with a client brought about a decrease in loneliness on the part of an individual who is visually impaired and increased that person's activities related to doing household chores.

Family and peer support are also important for socialization needs. The importance of recreational and leisure outlets for older individuals with visual impairments should never be underestimated. It is recommended that the counselor explore these needs and introduce clients to activities in which they can still engage. The older person who is visually impaired might not be aware of specially adapted games or low vision playing cards, for example, which can be used in settings with sighted individuals. The counselor is also urged to learn about community programs for older individuals, the means of accessing such programs, and how to help integrate the person into them.

WOMEN WITH VISUAL IMPAIRMENTS

As previously indicated, because women have a longer life expectancy, the majority of individuals with visual impairments over the age of 65 are women. The National Society to Prevent Blindness (1978) (now called Prevent Blindness America) also found that 52 percent of all individuals who are legally blind are women, and of individuals who are newly blinded, women outnumber men in the over age 65 group by 21 percent. Among individuals in the working-age group, women with visual impairments tend to be older (i.e., 45 percent of women, compared to 35 percent of men who are in the upper working-age range of 55 to 64); they are also less educated, and have less work experience. With incomes often at the poverty level, these women generally live alone or with relatives, and a larger number tend to be divorced, separated, or widowed.

Gender Stereotypes

As with older individuals, myths and stereotypes have contributed to educational, social, and occupational restrictions on women with visual impairments. Because of the high percentage of visual impairments among poor, African-American, and older women, the effects of the impairment are multiplied when the stereotypes associated with socioeconomic status, race, and age are considered. Rehabilitation counselors are not immune to societal myths and stereotypes. The decisions they make about eligibility and rehabilitation services are affected by their values and beliefs, including myths and stereotypes. Beliefs, often subtle but powerful, in regard to the importance of education and the range of occupations appropriate to women influence the evaluation and placement outcomes for women who are visually impaired, as much as rehabilitation technology or reconstructive surgery options do. The counselor's views on sexuality or gender also determine whether this counseling need is addressed or ignored. Because of interrelationships among sexuality, self-esteem, and risk-taking behavior, ignoring this aspect of the person can directly affect independent living and employment.

The effect of vocational stereotypes was demonstrated in a study by Packer (1983), who found that both male and female rehabilitation counselors, when given hypothetical case studies of male and female clients who were blind, chose sex-stereotyped vocational outcomes, with homemaker status listed more often for female than male closures. Occupations highly dominated by females were indicated for 12 percent of the jobs suggested for men, whereas only 8 percent of jobs suggested for women were in highly male-dominated occupations. The occupation of typist/transcriptionist/braillist was suggested twice as often for women, and secretary was suggested 15 times as often for women. Computer programmer/specialist was chosen 57 times for men and only 24 times for women. Men were placed in computer-operator jobs and women were placed in word processor positions. Computer sales, selected for men, was not an occupation indicated for women.

Despite national interest in women's issues, general information is lacking related to women with disabilities and their need for rehabilitation counseling services (Carrick & Bibb, 1982; Degouvea, 1977), particularly women with visual impairments. This is a critical omission, because Schmitt (1984) found that the issues faced by women with visual impairments are more gender- than disability-related, particularly in terms of employment (Corn, Muscella, Cannon & Shepler, 1985).

Gender Issues

There are a number of gender issues that are specific to or have implications for women. These include perceptions of disability, self-esteem, sexuality, and physical vulnerability, in addition to rehabilitation services, health-related issues, race, socioeconomic status, education and training, and earnings. The next sections explore the implications of these issues on women with visual impairments.

Perceptions of Disability

Peterson, Lowman, and Kirchner (1978) found that although a majority of individuals who considered themselves disabled or impaired were women over 65 years of age, the majority of people who were blind and considered themselves as "handicapped" were males under 65 years of age. The authors attributed this to male role expectations of performing work outside the home, in which case mobility and transportation become problems, and to society's expectations of student and housekeeping roles for females.

In reviewing autobiographies of individuals with visual impairments, Asch and Sachs (1983) found that males sought typical male roles and aspired to and achieved professional and business occupations. Sighted partners were sought, and males married more often than females. When males reached their goals, they tended to take credit for their accomplishment. Females, on the other hand, tended to seek employment with individuals who were blind, referred to relationships less often and married less frequently, saw themselves as asexual, were more religious, and sought nurturing occupations. When goals were achieved, the women were less apt to take credit.

In a study of the self-perceptions of 41 working-age women with visual impairments, Corn et al. (1985) found that women who were visually impaired perceived themselves as having substantially more barriers to employment than sighted women. The authors of that study felt that "the research community needs to discover the sources of these fears before agency interventionists can develop appropriate strategies to facilitate the full employment" of women with visual impairments (p. 461).

Self-Esteem and Sexuality Issues

Fears about one's appearance, the inability to apply makeup, uncertainties about the ability to buy attractive clothing, lack of sexual knowledge, and uncertainty about socially acceptable behavior may lead to an unwillingness by women who are visually impaired to pursue training or employment goals. Positive role models, with and without visual impairments, were cited by high-achieving visually impaired women as important sources of influence. Women who are visually impaired used role models to help understand relationships with men and how to be attractive and appealing (Pfanstiehl, 1983). Role models are needed to expand the visions of all the possibilities for women who are visually impaired and to help them explore the various advantages and disadvantages of different options.

Negative perceptions of society and professionals also have an effect on sexuality. These perceptions include images of women with visual impairments as (1) asexual or oversexed (Knappett & Wagner, 1976; Selvin, 1979), (2) perpetual children or disabled in all areas (Who Cares, 1979), or (3) devoid of sexual thoughts and feelings (Dodge, 1979). Society's denial of the ability of people with visual impairments to develop realistic, positive identities as sexual beings and to have opportunities for sexual relationships and expression results in restricted development. When individuals who are visually impaired are denied the opportunity to develop social skills, their ability to socialize comfortably and appropriately with the opposite sex may be negatively affected (Dodge, 1979). If denied this aspect of their humanity, they will not be able to fully develop the positive self-image that is important for success.

Development of a positive self-image is a particular concern to women who become visually impaired prior to or during adolescence. Adolescent girls who are blind are concerned about whether they "fit in" in terms of the right fashions, makeup, and actions (Kent, 1983). Many adolescent girls with visual impairments have delayed emotional and social maturity, which Mangold and Mangold (1983) attributed to lack of appropriate role models and guidance from support systems.

Physical Vulnerability

Pava (1994) investigated the vulnerability of men and women with visual impairments to physical assault. Although vulnerability was a concern of both men and women, women perceived themselves to be more vulnerable to either physical or sexual assault. Men and women reported a similar number of attempted or actual assaults, but women appeared to be more significantly affected by these experiences than men. Because women's training in self-defense was closely related to the failure of attempted assaults, and to increased self-confidence among trainees, rehabilitation professionals are urged to recognize the vulnerability of women and continue to encourage them to participate in self-defense training.

Rehabilitation Services and Outcomes

The statistics on services and rehabilitation outcomes for women demonstrate the existence of serious gender problems. For example, Hill (1989) found that of the 18,394 clients with visual impairments who were rehabilitated by the state-federal vocational rehabilitation program in 1982, 8,032 were men and 10,362 were women. However, of those 18 thousand-plus people, 65.3 percent of the men compared to 35.7 percent of the women were placed in competitive employment. Moreover, three times more women than men were closed as "homemakers." In looking at the demographic variables, Hill found that

> Rehabilitated women were on average 9 years older than rehabilitated men. Women were less likely to be white and were more likely to have a major secondary disabling condition. On average, women had one-half year less schooling than men. In terms of services provided, men were more likely to have received college training, vocational training, on-the-job training, and maintenance than were women. On aver-

> age men received a broader array of services than did women. (pp. 224–225)

Several other issues provide evidence of discrepancies based on gender, and other research studies are consistent with Hill's findings. These issues are examined in the next sections.

Health-related Issues

Declining health has been linked to unemployment (Berkowitz, 1980; Kirchner & Peterson, 1979; Schecter, 1979). Among individuals with visual impairments, approximately 66 percent gave health and physical disability as the reason for not working (Kirchner & Peterson, 1979). Schmitt (1984) found that few women who were blind (14.4 percent) reported only one impairment, while a larger percentage (31.3 percent) reported at least three impairments. In examining the closure status of women, those who were older and received more medication and treatment were more often closed as either homemakers or nonrehabilitated.

Race

Despite the higher incidence of visual impairment in non-Caucasian women, these women have also been inadequately represented in the rehabilitation system. Caucasian representation is greater than nonwhite representation in rehabilitation studies of women with disabilities (e.g., Johnson, 1983) and women with visual impairments (Schmitt, 1984). Race is also reflected in closure status (Schmitt, 1984).

Socioeconomic Status

People with lower incomes have a higher incidence of visual impairments, and more visually impaired women than men live in poverty. Women who are black and those who are elderly are among the poorest (Myers, 1980). In a group studied by Kirchner and Peterson (1981), 33 percent of the women compared to 19 percent of men with visual impairments were in poverty.

The lack of a work history affects the level of benefits for which women are eligible (Kirchner & Peterson, 1981). Supplemental Security Income (SSI), often at poverty rates, is received most frequently by women (Holcomb, 1983; Kutza, 1981) and although more women than men received aged, blind, and disability payments, women's rates of pay were lower than men's. Non-Caucasian women were also found to have the lowest representation in all three benefit groups (U.S. Department of Health and Human Services, 1983).

In terms of rehabilitation outcomes, those persons who were closed in competitive employment status are recipients of benefits less often than those who were closed in homemaker, sheltered, and nonrehabilitated status (Kirchner & Peterson, 1982; Schmitt, 1984). Among women who are blind, the largest percentage receiving Social Security Disability Insurance (SSDI) at closure are closed in homemaker status, while the largest percent of SSI recipients are closed in competitive status (Schmitt, 1984).

Education and Training

Although women with more education participate more often in the labor force (Blaxall & Reagan, 1976), education has typically been less accessible to women than to men (U.S. Department of Labor, 1980). Access to education is important, however, because rehabilitation has a greater effect on women with more education (Greenblum, 1979) and better educated women are more apt to return to work after acquiring a disability (Schecter, 1979). A higher level of education also often predicts salary level (Gandy, 1988; Johnson, 1983) for both men and women.

Educational level also differentiates individuals closed in sheltered or homemaker status. Johnson (1983) showed a higher educational level for women with disabilities who were rehabilitated compared with women who were not rehabilitated. Women with visual impairments who were closed in competitive status have a higher educational level at referral than women who were closed as nonrehabilitated (Schmitt, 1984).

Despite the importance of education, women with disabilities, particularly African Americans, Hispanics (Bowe, 1983), and older persons (Fergeson, 1979), have lower educational levels. These findings are significant in view of the high number of women with visual impairments who are non-Caucasian and elderly. The percentage of women with visual impairments who reported merely a high school education was actually lower than that which was reported overall for women in the labor force (Blaxall & Reagan, 1976).

Schmitt (1984) found that only 15 percent of individuals who were closed received any institutional training and 60 percent received no training at all. The frequencies of training were as follows: (1) on-the-job—12 percent, (2) college—8 percent, (3) vocational school—4 percent, (4) other academic—4 percent, and (5) business—1 percent. When funds spent on training were evaluated, Schmitt found that 86 percent of the women received no expenditure for institutional training and 89 percent received no expenditure for such noninstitutional training as on-the-job training. Elder (1983) also found that fewer women than men with visual impairments received training, and fewer women were referred to the Arkansas Enterprises for the Blind (now known as Lions World Services for the Blind).

Labor Force Participation, Occupations, and Earnings

Since the 1940s, the labor force participation rate of women has increased. Women with visual impairments, however, participate in the labor market at lower rates than women without impairments (Kirchner & Peterson, 1979). Women are faced with the added disincentives of child-care costs and social sanctions for remaining at home. Beliefs that they would not be hired, that accommodations would not be made, and that travel problems would be unmanageable contribute to this low labor force participation (Kirchner & Peterson, 1979).

As was true for women with disabilities in general (Holcomb, 1983; Rehabilitation Services Administration, 1982), more women than men with visual impairments are closed as homemakers and this closure status appears more acceptable to women than men (Packer, 1983). Fewer women (44 percent) are closed in wage-earning status than in homemaker status (76 percent) (Kirchner & Peterson, 1982). Goal changes to homemaker are also more frequent in adults under the age of 30.

Despite the presence of more women in the labor force, their wages and work status have not improved (Carrick & Bibb, 1982). In fact, more women than men with disabilities are closed in limited occupations, low-paying jobs, and unpaid positions (Fine & Asch, 1981; O'Toole & Weeks, 1978; Vash, 1982). In various studies of vocational rehabilitation closures of women with visual impairments, there was a high incidence of closure in clerical occupations (Johnson, 1983; Johnson & Hafer, 1985; Schmitt, 1984), although some women with visual impairments are also closed in professional, technical, service and managerial positions (Corn et al., 1985; Johnson, 1983; Schmitt, 1984). When compared to women with other disabilities, however, more women who were blind were closed in professional and service areas, while women with other disabilities were closed more frequently in clerical or managerial positions. In interviewing 30 women with various disabilities, Johnson (1983) found that the blind women in this larger sample, when closed in managerial positions, were all employed by non-profit blind agencies. These findings substantiate those of Vash (1982) who found many women in "mini ghettos" helping their "own kind."

The foregoing results are not surprising as women in general are placed in lower-paying service industries rather than higher-paying, goods-producing industries (U.S. Dept. of Labor, 1983; Van Dusen & Sheldon, 1978; Vash, 1982). Despite increased educational and employment opportunities created by legislation, women with disabilities continue to occupy low-paying and low-status jobs (Atkins, 1982; Barker, 1982; Vash, 1982).

When compared with salaries of orthopedically impaired women and female households, women with visual impairments have lower salaries. Salary ranges for women with orthopedic disabilities ($40 to $461 per week) were greater than those for women with visual impairments ($16 to $396 per week) in Illinois. The Statistical Abstracts for the U.S. (1982–83) reported that median salary for visually impaired women was $7,200 per year although the national average for all households was $17,710 and that of female households was $10,830 (Johnson & Hafer, 1985). Of 30 successfully rehabilitated women, none of the women with visual impairments made more than $30,000 per year (Johnson, 1983).

Schmitt (1984), in a study of 363 women with visual impairments, found that despite a pay range of zero to $513 per week at closure, 67 percent of the women who were blind had no income, 30 percent earned from $1 to $200 per week, and only 2 percent of all closures earned over $201 per week. When closures in competitive status were considered, 50 percent earned between $101 and $200 per week and only 8 percent earned over $201 per week. Despite these meager salary ranges, of the original 90 percent who reported no referral income, 31 percent had improved their financial status at closure.

Implications for Rehabilitation Counselors

The statistics from these studies highlight the need for counselors to examine their beliefs, values, and potential gender biases that perpetuate both the unemployment and underemployment of women. There are a number of other implications for rehabilitation counselors, which are listed as follows:

1. Counselors are urged to be sensitive to the self-perceptions of women with visual impairments. For example, as a result of limited or no work experience, limited educational and social opportunities, and lowered expectations, women who are visually impaired may not perceive themselves as capable of seeking diverse, nontraditional, higher paying jobs.
2. It is highly recommended that counselors be careful when changing the employment goals of women to "homemaker" to ensure not only that this status change is based on needed services but that "homemaker/unpaid family worker" closures are not used for those women who are able and willing to meet competitive or sheltered goals. Thoughtful evaluation of past work history and educational preparation will help the rehabilitation counselor to determine whether placement or home employment might be more appropriate than homemaker status for women. Homemaker status, however, may be a positive outcome if appropriate services are provided; counselors can help legitimatize this closure status by carefully documenting the services.
3. Because increased mobility and the ability to use whatever visual capacity they continue to have are important for both independent living and work, and because the provision of these services has been low (i.e., 44 percent receive O&M training and 22 percent receive low vision devices), the counselor is urged to ensure that these options are considered in rehabilitation planning and are presented to the client regardless of age or rehabilitation goal. In some cases, the provision of these services might provide an incentive for women with visual impairments to pursue more challenging goals (see Sidebar 7.2).
4. The importance of role models for women with visual impairments is an essential concern of rehabilitation counselors. Using role models can be a strategy in which counselors can assist visually impaired women to deal with

Raising the Aspirations of Women Who Are Visually Impaired

SIDEBAR 7.2

It is recommended that the counseling and other services provided to help women with visual impairments address the lack of societal and personal expectations. Otherwise, the effects may be:

1. Lowered aspirations.
2. Limited job experience.
3. Lack of risk-taking skills.
4. Fear of failure and success.
5. Overprotection.
6. Lack of self-knowledge.
7. Lack of basic social skills.
8. Being seen as less feminine or aggressive or maladjusted when attempting to increase competence and independence.

Assistance is also encouraged to help develop coping mechanisms, self-defense, and independent style. Such services as assertiveness training and training in independent living skills, in addition to opportunities for role-playing, job try-outs or volunteer activities in which new skills can be developed and attempted, and networking are recommended. The opportunity to take risks and to learn that failure is a normal part of risk-taking is a vital part of the rehabilitation process for women who are visually impaired.

problems of dependency, limited expectations, and fear of failure (Koestler, 1983). Women with and without disabilities can also be valuable role models for adolescent girls with visual impairments. These adolescents can also benefit from counseling to help them understand that all adolescents feel "different" and that they are more similar to their sighted peers than they are different from them (Mangold & Mangold, 1983).

5. It is highly recommended that rehabilitation counselors be comfortable with their own sexuality and acknowledge the importance of sexuality as part of the rehabilitation process. Counselors are urged to be sensitive to, and not ignore, the effect that a visual impairment may have on a person's sexuality.
6. Because of the impact of health on employment status for women with visual impairments, rehabilitation counselors are encouraged to recognize the importance of obtaining a complete evaluation of physical status and its implications prior to developing a rehabilitation plan. A clear understanding of what the client thinks and feels the implications of the visual impairment may be, as well as any other physical conditions, is essential. The need for and the ability to obtain insurance, the cost of medications, the identification of situations that may exacerbate the physical conditions, and special transportation needs are all important issues to be considered.
7. Because of the high prevalence of blindness in persons who are nonwhite and poor, counselors are urged to utilize outreach techniques to reach these women. Careful evaluation of the needs and types of services offered is also recommended to ensure that nonwhite individuals and individuals from lower socioeconomic groups are not screened

out of the rehabilitation process. Among the poorest groups are women who are elderly, disabled, and African American—which compounds the racial issue. Because the labor force participation by African-American and Hispanic women is generally lower than that of Caucasian women, counselors are encouraged to consider additional needs that may exist for these women in terms of career exploration, work experience, training, and job-seeking skills.

8. It is suggested that counselors be sensitive to the needs of women with visual impairments who are poor and consider how their sources of income and economic status affects their ability and willingness to participate in the rehabilitation process. Counselors are also advised to examine whether insensitivity to the possible range of services needed is affecting discrepancies between SSDI and SSI recipients and their closure status (i.e., homemaker versus competitive employment). Because recipients of benefits are closed less often in competitive employment, the rehabilitation counselor is urged to examine whether there are added disincentives—for example, loss of medical coverage, loss of transportation benefits, the age of the recipients, and the average wage and potential fringe benefits associated with the occupations being suggested. Higher-paying jobs may be needed to offset disability benefits and may, therefore, affect the willingness of women who are visually impaired to participate in the rehabilitation process. This is particularly true for women who have dependents and must be concerned about childcare costs and lost benefits. It is also important to determine whether there are remedial services that might be needed because of missed opportunities resulting from lack of income.

   The higher prevalence of poverty also means that these women have fewer dollars with which to make such major changes in their lives as relocation for employment or for training opportunities, or to cover costs of transportation, clothing, and job-related equipment. When support is not available to cover these costs, the counselor is encouraged to provide assistance through direct financial support from the vocational rehabilitation agency or to assist the client in identifying other resources, such as college grants, loans, and scholarships; and employer contributions toward the purchase of equipment. The identification of the person's concerns regarding the costs associated with training and initial employment, in addition to fears related to loss of benefits, are all important considerations. It is recommended that counselors be sensitive to the relationship between the selection of an occupational goal and potential earnings. If the earnings are not at an appropriate level, then the rehabilitation counselor will be a partner (albeit unwillingly) in rehabilitating women with visual impairments into poverty.

9. Because educational level affects participation in the labor force and access to higher-paying jobs, education or some form of training becomes particularly important for those individuals who are receiving benefits. Counselors are encouraged to be aware of the need to increase the educational levels of women to expand their job opportunities and to increase their chances of escaping the poverty cycle. Counselors are strongly urged to attempt to provide options through which educational levels can be increased. This may mean involvement in and support of more diagnostic and remedial activities than are usually sup-

> ported by rehabilitation agencies. Given that educational level predicts salary and that women with visual impairments tend to live in poverty and be the recipients of benefits, it is important that they be given every chance to increase their opportunities by furthering their education.

In considering access to and outcomes of rehabilitation, it is suggested that counselors carefully consider the different variables that are identified with various closure statuses. The following variables have been associated with those individuals successfully rehabilitated: (1) disabled at a younger age, (2) fewer non-eye disabilities, (3) younger, (4) not having received SSDI during service, (5) higher weekly earnings at referral, (6) a higher level of vocational choice on the first rehabilitation plan, (7) receiving vocational school services, and (8) more expenditures for prostheses (Schmitt, 1984). These findings imply that people who acquire disabilities later in life, who have multiple disabilities, who are older, who are receiving disability benefits, and who have fewer financial resources may be a higher risk for nonrehabilitation closures and will therefore need additional attention during the evaluation and planning phase of the rehabilitation process. The information on higher levels of vocational choice may indicate that those who have not had past work experience or who have limited vocational information may need more career exploration before a plan is developed. It may also mean that people who have been disabled at a later age have had less time to experience living with a visual impairment and may need counseling related to the number of options available to persons with visual impairments. The data that link training and prostheses to competitive employment reemphasizes the importance of providing additional education and prosthetic devices when appropriate. Counselors are urged to be aware that women face multiple forms of discrimination and stereotypes associated with gender, ethnicity, age, and disability. This cycle will be broken only by recognizing the importance of (and by providing) services that can improve the self-image of women, expand their concept of their potential, and increase their opportunity to take risks in a supportive environment.

ISSUES OF CULTURAL DIVERSITY

Every individual is unique, but when rehabilitation counselors find themselves working with clients from cultural or ethnic groups different from their own, this uniqueness is occasionally lost. The United States is usually considered to be a nation with a majority of its residents classified as "white," and a minority, as "nonwhite." This dichotomy of "white/nonwhite," however, is not very meaningful. Nonwhite includes such extremely heterogeneous groups as Native Americans, African Americans, Hispanics, and Asian Americans. For example, there are distinct language and cultural differences among Asian Americans depending on their country of origin. Similarly, Hispanics from Cuba, Mexico, or Puerto Rico differ greatly in their cultural backgrounds. Among Caucasians, there is also great diversity—factors such as speaking English as a second language, national origin with strong cultural and religious identifications, and long-term geographical isolations have resulted in the development of totally different cultures (e.g., Cajuns and Creoles in Louisiana, Amish in Pennsylvania, and Shakers in New York).

The 1990 U.S. Census used self-identified responses: White, Black or African American, Indian (American), Eskimo, Aleut, Chinese, Filipino, Hawaiian, Korean, Vietnamese, Japanese, Asian (Indian), Samoan, Guamanian, and Other. This system mixes ethnic, racial, and cultural differences and has little meaning because lines between these differences are often blurred. Thus, there is at the present time no classification system to satisfactorily describe individuals who have differing backgrounds. Difficulties arise because the differences themselves raise questions.

For example, is Judaism an ethnic or religious difference? Do Hispanics have racial, or ethnic, or linguistic differences? Yee (1983), in reviewing the many difficulties inherent in racial classifications, has made a strong case for using the terms "ethnic group" and "ethnicity." These terms refer to any group that has a distinct difference derived from ancestry and culture and that share common identifications in such aspects as language and food.

In considering ethnicity, it should be noted that the term "majority" is relative, and the majority in one community can be a minority in another. For example, African Americans constitute the majority of the population in Washington, D.C., but are a minority in Albuquerque, New Mexico. Second, differences within any one ethnic group may be greater than the differences between that ethnic group and the majority or any other ethnic group. Third, counselors should refrain from concluding that a client is from a particular ethnic group based on surnames, appearances, or language spoken in the home. As an example, a school social worker described the home of a kindergarten child referred for a school problem as being "a very American home for an immigrant family." She was basing her conclusion on the German surname and that the child spoke German to both his parents and to a German-speaking teacher. In reality, the child's parents were born in this country, as were the mother's parents and grandparents. Finally, there are distinct intergenerational differences among cultural groups (i.e., first, second, and third generation immigrants). It cannot be concluded that recent immigrants have much in common with third generation immigrants. Over the years, cultural evolution may have changed both in the mother country and in the adopted land, leading to distinctly different cultures.

As our society becomes increasingly diverse, cultural homogeneity is rare even in very small communities. It is, therefore, highly recommended that rehabilitation counselors acquire knowledge about the various ethnic differences in the particular community in which they work and the potential effect these cultural differences may have on the delivery of rehabilitation services to a particular client.

Extent of Cultural Differences

The number of people who are considered a "minority" has been increasing in recent years, partly because of increased immigration. By the year 2000, it is estimated that the number of ethnic minorities will constitute approximately one-third of the total population in the United States (Bouvier & Davis, 1982; Johnston & Packer, 1987). Statistics on the proportion of various ethnic groups, however, are difficult to obtain. The lack of agreement on terminology, the absence of a common classification system, and the general homogenization that has occurred over the years, all contribute to the problem of data collection.

Data on the number of individuals with visual impairments and who come from different cultural backgrounds is also limited. It is usually assumed that visual impairments are distributed among all groups on an equal basis. However, prevalence rates for visual impairments appear to be greater among nonwhites (Kahn & Moorhead, 1973; Kirchner & Peterson, 1988b). [For example, one study found that African Americans had about twice the prevalence rate for being visually impaired as whites in a particular urban area (Tielsch, Sommer, Witt, Katz & Royall, 1990); another found that glaucoma may be as much as four to five times more common among African Americans than whites (Prevent Blindness America, 1994).] Diabetes has been noted in epidemic proportions in some Native American tribes (Orr, 1993) and thus, the incidence of diabetic retinopathy is greater for Native Americans than for the general population. In fact, according to Ponchillia (1993),

> There [is little] data to indicate exactly how many Native Americans lose their vision because of diabetic eye disease, but health and rehabilitation professionals anticipate record numbers in the future because cultural beliefs, poverty, isolation, the lack of education, or the lack of access to basic health care interfere with

the early diagnosis and treatment of diabetic eye complications. (p. 333)

Because nonwhites are overrepresented in the lower socioeconomic groups, they also tend to have a higher prevalence of visual impairments, as well as other disabilities. Because of these dual conditions (i.e., cultural difference and low socioeconomic status), the rehabilitation counselor can expect to work with a number of individuals from various cultures who are also from the lower socioeconomic groups.

The rates of unemployment and underemployment among people with visual impairments is high (Kirchner & Peterson, 1988a, 1988b). Available data for some ethnic groups reflect the same situation. The national unemployment rate for individuals age 20 and over for a recent quarter (U.S. Department of Labor, Bureau of Labor Statistics, 1997) was 5.5 percent, but the rates by ethnicity were as follows: White (4.5 percent), African American (10.9 percent), and Hispanic (8.3 percent). When visual impairments occur in combination with cultural variations, the rehabilitation counselor will be challenged to provide rehabilitation services to those clients who have two significant differences (Chinn, 1979; Walker, Akpati, Roberts, Palmer & Newsome, 1986). The question of which of the two differences is more critical in the rehabilitation planning process may depend on community attitudes and acceptance of cultural variations. In a community where there is a high level of acceptance of cultural differences, the visual impairment will undoubtedly have priority. For example, in a predominately Hispanic community with active and respected Hispanic leaders, the client's Hispanic background will probably not be a significant factor in job placement. On the other hand, if cultural differences are not accepted in the community, if there is a high rate of unemployment and a history of discrimination, then cultural variation may require the major emphasis in the rehabilitation process. It is highly recommended that the client's individual needs in regard to both the visual impairment and the cultural difference be assessed against the background of the community in the total rehabilitation planning process.

Implications of Cultural Differences

Cultural differences have an impact on the attitudes, values, and behavior the client brings to the rehabilitation counseling setting, which in turn affect the services that are provided by the rehabilitation counselor. An appreciation for these differences can help the rehabilitation counselor avoid misinterpreting and possibly shortchanging the client through misunderstanding or ignorance. For example, the apparent nonresponsiveness of a Native-American client could be interpreted by the rehabilitation counselor as lack of interest in the vocational options being described. In reality, the client may have no experience with the job titles and descriptions being presented and thus may not understand what the counselor is attempting to communicate.

Because intragroup differences may be larger than intergroup differences, the rehabilitation counselor must take exceptional care to avoid stereotyping particular ethnic groups and to be very cautious in generalizing about "typical" behaviors or characteristics of any subculture. Nonetheless, some examples of cultural beliefs and their implications for rehabilitation counselors may provide some practical assistance. For example, Table 7.1, developed by Ponchillia (1993), provides examples of cultural beliefs and potential implications for service providers who are working with Native Americans. Table 7.2 provides a comparison between Eurocentric attitudes and values that also may be relevant in the rehabilitation process, and cultural variations. Attitudes and values are included together in this table because of their close relationship to each other. For further clarity, attitudes are likes and dislikes toward people, groups, issues, or objects based on feelings or dispositions or reactions, whereas values are the usefulness or importance or merit of something to the possessor. Attitudes

Table 7.1. Examples of Native American Cultural Beliefs and Potential Implications for Service Providers

Cultural Values/Practices	Implications
Respect elders, experts, and those with spiritual powers.	Always recognize, greet verbally, or shake hands with people, especially elders.
The circle of life, group life, is primary.	Work with the individual and his or her supporters as a team.
Silence is valued; unnecessary talking may be considered foolish.	Listen. Be patient when waiting for answers. Do not interrupt or jump to conclusions too quickly.
Introverted, concern for privacy in regard to personal matters.	Do not just start asking questions; tell why you need to know something.
Hospitality is valued.	Food or drinks are often offered to guests; it is traditional to offer a drink of water or coffee when you are a "host."
Pragmatic. Accept "what is." Health and vision problems may be the result of past behavior.	Preventive health care may not be part of the culture; hence, testing glucose and administering eye drops may seem unnecessary.
Extreme modesty, reluctance to show pain or discomfort.	A heightened awareness of the comfort level of a client is indicated.
Illness sometimes thought to be supernatural.	Showing an anatomic model of the body or the eye may help explain the problem more concretely.
Negative thoughts, actions, or words may cause something bad to occur.	Occluding a client or family member may be viewed as a way to cause future blindness. Cautionary statements should be stated in a positive manner.
The concept of time is viewed differently; hours and minutes are not important. Lifestyle, environmental factors, and weather all have an effect on a person's "schedule."	Family events and other special events take precedence over appointments with teachers and caseworkers. Appointment times may need to be flexible.
The concept of the traditional healer-medicine person reinforces the "cure" of the problem.	Blindness professionals may be expected to cure the problem, rather than teaching coping strategies.
Healers traditionally give tangible objects.	Leave something at the end of an interview or lesson (a cane or a pocket magnifier, for example).

Source: S. Ponchillia, "The Effect of Cultural Beliefs on the Treatment of Native Peoples with Diabetes and Visual Impairments," *Journal of Visual Impairment & Blindness, 87* (1993), p. 335.

and values cannot be observed but rather must be inferred. Table 7.3 presents some cultural differences in behavior in everyday situations that can often be exhibited during the rehabilitation interview. Again the Eurocentric values may, at times, overlap with variations noted in other cultures. Communication is probably the most critical factor among those included in Table 7.3 in terms of its effect on the client–counselor relationship.

Table 7.2. Selected Attitudes and Values

Attitude/Value	Eurocentric Perspective	Cultural Variations
Disabilities	Goal is independence Work toward acceptance	Sent by God or some higher being Person chosen to have disability prenatally Liability to welfare of group Hidden away Punishment for past deeds
Women	Equal rights	Inferior status Matriarch of the group
Time	Punctuality expected	Casual about appointments
Work	Work essential part of life Strive for successreach the top Competitive	Casual about work Noncompetitive
Education	Formal education necessary for success	Education is vehicle for economic and political advancement Strong beliefs in value of education Education not meaningful, has low value Does not lead to a job
Independence	Competition encouraged Dependence not valued	Dependence encouraged especially in females Cooperation emphasized Individuality and independence training begun in early childhood
Family	Nuclear/one parent families	Extended family Entire extended family involved in decisions with implications for family Elders respected Male/female roles clearly defined Strong social unit Male dominates Matriarch dominates
Religion	Frequently a social outlet High rate of church attendance	Religious holidays important aspect even when not church attender Strong religious beliefs Nonchurch attender

Effective communication is essential to achieve the goals of the rehabilitation process. Among the many subtleties that can influence communication is the manner in which an individual is addressed. As a general rule, counselors are encouraged to always use the more formal forms of address, such as "Mr." or "Mrs." instead of addressing a client by his or her first name. The use of the first name may be considered patronizing in some cultures (e.g., Hispanic or Asian).

Table 7.3. Selected Behaviors

Behavior	Eurocentric Perspective	Cultural Variations
Greetings	Firm handshake, often with a nod or smile	Ranges from gentle to vigorous handshake Hug or other form of physical contact Handshake with both hands Hand slapping Bow for formal greeting; nod for informal greeting Kiss on one or both cheeks (not on initial meeting)
Eye Contact	Eye contact important Blind person faces speaker	Little or no eye contact Eye contact avoided with an older person, or a female, or one of higher status or position of authority Females do not make eye contact
Communication	**Eurocentric Perspective**	**Cultural Variations**
Non-English Speaking		Facial expression may indicate lack of understanding Another person (family, friend, advocate) accompanies to interpret Pretends to understand
Verbal	Talkative Silence is uncomfortable Reasonable physical distance from speaker's face	Reluctance to ask questions Sparse conversation Dislikes probing questions Silence valued Close contact with face of speaker Overlapping speech (talk at same time) Speech may be greatly accelerated
Nonverbal	Restrained body movements Facial expression of interest but not high emotion	Ranges from absence to effusive body movements Intense facial reactions Active gesturing Expressive hand and body movements
Touching	Low touch culture	Ranges from absence to much touching Strict rules regarding who touches whom Men may hold hands walking together but not appropriate for a man and a woman

It is suggested that the rehabilitation counselor be sensitive to and prepared to informally assess the client's abilities in both receptive and expressive language. Because some individuals may behaviorally indicate that they understand something that, in fact, is not understood, it is necessary to determine whether the person cannot hear well, or does not understand the content of the counselor's communication, does not understand English, or if other reasons exist (e.g., if the client has inhibitions regarding authority figures). If a hearing problem is suspected, the counselor can vary the volume of speech and observe the client's reactions. If the client does not seem to understand the content, it is recommended that the counselor rephrase the sentence in simpler language and then observe whether the client gives evidence of understanding. Sensitivity to nonverbal cues is essential to determine whether the person cannot hear well or does not understand. The counselor may also ask the client to state his or her understanding of the conversation to assess the degree to which actual understanding is occurring.

Other modifications may also be necessary if English is not the first language. Frequently, another person, sometimes a child, is brought along to interpret. This situation requires that the counselor be sensitive to the dynamics related to having a third person present. Should the counselor address the interpreter or the client? The latter is customary when working through an interpreter for people who are deaf and is probably the more appropriate alternative. How can the rehabilitation counselor obtain sensitive information from the client through another person? This will require tact and sensitivity particularly if a child or other relative is brought to interpret. Perhaps the best plan is to wait until rapport and a trusting relationship have been established before attempting to obtain such information. Some agencies have recruited paraprofessionals from the particular ethnic group (Rogler, Malgady, Costantino, & Blumenthal, 1987) or hired translators (Hendel, 1987) to function as interpreters and cultural consultants. These alternatives may have some disadvantages, such as eliciting personal information necessary for the intake from a stranger, but they may have the advantage of providing access to services for non-English-speaking clients.

When home visits are necessary, it is suggested that the rehabilitation counselor remember that entering the home of a client may be considered to be an intrusion on that person's private space. Permission from the client is essential before making a home visit. In some ethnic groups, certain members of the family may not be included in the discussion. For example, in some Native American groups, women may excuse themselves when the rehabilitation counselor comes to the home. This should not be attributed to a lack of interest but rather to a cultural pattern that women do not participate in some types of activities and discussions.

Because it is impossible to generalize concerning these aspects, it is necessary for rehabilitation counselors to (1) be observant of any behavior that does not seem to be consistent with the typical behavior in that particular community, (2) attempt to seek an explanation for the differences from individuals knowledgeable about the particular culture, and (3) be sensitive to the implications that behavior may have when working with the client.

Implications for the Rehabilitation Process

The cultural differences noted in Tables 7.1 through 7.3 can affect various elements of the rehabilitation process, including referral, initial interview, assessment, training, and placement. Despite the high prevalence of visual impairments in African Americans, as a group they are poorly represented in the rehabilitation system (Asbury, Walker, Belgrave, Maholmes, & Green, 1994). Caucasian representation was greater than nonwhite representation in rehabilitation studies of women who were disabled (Johnson, 1983; Kirchner & Peterson, 1982) and women who were visually impaired (Schmitt, 1984). The large number of Caucasians in these studies may lend support to the findings of Grigg, Holtmann, and Martin (1970) that race is related to program acceptance and the findings of Hollingsworth and Pease (1980) that race affects labor force participation.

Conscious or unconscious racial prejudice appears to affect not only acceptance rate (Dziekan & Okocha, 1993) but also the type of services recommended and the range of options presented. For example, Schmitt (1984) found that a high percentage of Caucasian women who were blind were closed in competitive work status compared with the high percentage of African-American women who were blind and closed in sheltered employment status. These findings support those of Kirchner and Peterson (1982).

Referrals

For a variety of reasons, people from different cultures with visual impairments frequently do not receive necessary rehabilitation services. Kirchner and Peterson (1988c) found that sources of referrals to the state-federal vocational rehabilitation program differed for whites, Hispanics, and African Americans. Whites were more apt to be self-referrals or referred by family or friends. Hispanics and African Americans were more likely to be referred by medical resources. Therefore, an agency in a community with a large Hispanic or African-American population but few clients from those groups might target its outreach efforts to the private physicians and medical service agencies in the community in order to reach the unserved population.

Initial Interview

The rehabilitation counselor's observational skills during the initial interview will often reveal cultural differences. For example, did the client arrive on time for the appointment? If not, was there an explanation? In some cultures, time is less valued and being punctual may not be important or critical (Correa, 1987). In such cases, it is suggested that the counselor review the concept of punctuality with the client before job placement in order to help the client understand why prospective employers view punctuality as an important factor in the workplace.

At the first meeting, the rehabilitation counselor should permit the client to take the lead in the type of greeting, such as a handshake. The counselor can then follow that lead with a similar greeting. Eye contact should also be noted. Does the visual impairment permit the use of vision to provide eye contact? If so, what kind of eye contact? Does the client face the counselor? If not, is this behavior due to limited social skills that were never taught or does it reflect a cultural pattern? Allowing the client to take the lead in the initial interview may also help the rehabilitation counselor assess the client's verbal skills. When accompanied by another person, is the client obviously dependent on that person? In what way(s)? Is it for assistance in mobility or does the other person enter actively into the discussion, "speaking for" the client? It is possible that the counselor will be able to assess the client's degree of dependence and whether it is appropriate to conduct future interviews with the client alone.

Assessment

The area of assessment is critical for clients with cultural differences because results can often determine the direction of the client's future. The use of instruments that have been standardized based on individuals without visual impairments are frequently not appropriate for persons with visual impairments and a cultural difference may distress the client even more. Often the application of informal or nonstandardized procedures may be more appropriate. Some vocational aptitude and interest instruments may not be appropriate for use because of the limited experience the client has had with the materials. Observation, informal conversations, and trial work placements may prove to be more meaningful in assessing interests and abilities.

Cultural differences can also have a significant impact on the client's performance, particularly on standardized tests of intelligence. For example, one young Native American woman scored in the dull normal range on the verbal series of the Wechsler Adult Intelligence Scale (WAIS). The examiner, noting her reluctance to speak and her long periods of silence, sensed that her abilities were greater than the verbal score indicated. In spite of her limited vision, the client scored above average on the performance scales and was highly motivated by the subtests. If vocational planning had been based solely on the verbal test scores, she might have been guided into a routine job. However, her considerably better performance scores indicated a higher level of intelligence and she was counseled into post-secondary education.

Many people from different cultural backgrounds have a low self-esteem usually arising from life experiences in a majority culture in which their own customs, values, and beliefs are devalued (Sue & Sue, 1990). Often such individuals are isolated from the majority culture because of their differences. The counselor is encouraged to be sensitive to the experiences that clients from various cultures and ethnicities bring to the rehabilitation process. The motivation for employment may be low and it may initially appear that some clients are not capable of vocational success. However, these clients may be aware of the high unemployment or underemployment ratio or may have adopted attitudes of learned helplessness. Pointing out successful role models, and helping them accept themselves as valuable individuals who can make a contribution to society can build confidence and self-esteem.

Some recent immigrants (e.g., emigrants from Vietnam, Cambodia, and El Salvador) often present a special challenge. Many left well-paying, prestigious jobs in their countries. Their skills need to be assessed carefully to determine the factors that might impede their ability to obtain comparable jobs in the United States—limited English-speaking ability, for example. In such cases, appropriate remedial programs may then be planned to prepare them for job placement after their English-speaking skills have improved. In the interim, they may need supportive counseling to assist them in overcoming feelings of frustration over not immediately finding jobs of equal status in the United States.

Training

Previous experiences with a variety of occupational possibilities may be limited for some individuals. It is suggested that exploratory experiential opportunities be provided to help clients select an appropriate vocational objective that meets their interests and needs. Meeting and talking with successfully employed persons from both their own and other ethnic groups in the community may expand the clients' knowledge of the range of vocational possibilities. Such an activity may also help them realize that success can be theirs—with both interest and work on their part. It is highly recommended that the rehabilitation process also include attention to other aspects of the client's life, particularly leisure activities, independent living, and social skills. In some cultures, there may be resistance to learning skills of independent living. Upper-class children in some countries may be accustomed to having servants, and their parents may see no need for their children to learn to bathe or dress themselves if there is a servant present in the home to perform this function. In an extended family situation, a mother or sister may always be available. This attitude may also carry over into adulthood, particularly for males. It is possible that the rehabilitation counselor will have to overcome cultural resistance before introducing the client to a program of independent living skills.

Rehabilitation directed only toward employment may be successful, but without attention to adjustment in the community to which the client will return, the rehabilitation process may not result in a successfully rehabilitated person (Orlansky & Trap, 1987). The visual impairment, in addition to any cultural differences, may lead to isolation from peers and family. Training in social skills and in techniques of effective communication may be necessary to help the person become an accepted member of a social group. Encouraging clients to join a church or community social group may spur their interest in and participation with others. Community adult education courses may also be helpful in broadening their horizons.

Because a person's day is not exclusively spent on the job, attention to the development of leisure and recreational activities is also necessary. Assessing the client's interest in, and preference for appropriate activities available in the community setting and encouraging participation in such activities will enable the client to spend time after work productively. A survey of available leisure and recreational resources in the community will help the counselor to determine those activities that might be most appropriate to recommend for the client.

Frequently, housing presents a greater challenge than employment to integration into the community (Coche, 1992; Colbert, Kalish & Chang, 1973). The counselor might explore the various choices with the client and assist in selecting the option that best suits that individual's interests, abilities, and needs. A group home placement may be necessary for the less adept client, prior to moving into an independent living situation.

Placement

Careful selection of the placement objectives based on the assessment information and the environmental demands the person will meet when the program is completed is highly recommended. For example, for a Native American who will return to a rural reservation to work, such O&M skills as learning to cross a busy street may be viewed as a waste of time and the counselor's motivational efforts will meet with failure. The approach to teaching job skills may also need to be modified. If language skills are limited, demonstrations of the specific job skills may be useful. Simulation can be a helpful technique to prepare for either a job interview or the first day on the job, or perhaps in dealing with negative reactions of fellow workers. Video taping such sessions can be an effective teaching tool for a group discussion. It is recommended that the goals of rehabilitation be selected based on the clients' interests, beliefs, and the setting to which they will return. Successful placement will be enhanced if the rehabilitation counselor has assessed the interests and abilities of the client and if the counselor has attempted to find the niche that most nearly provides a "fit" between the client's ethnic characteristics, his or her visual impairment, and the requirements of the job.

Counselor Sensitivity

The rehabilitation counselor is highly encouraged to be sensitive to differences and look at the services being offered from the client's perspective. Effective counselors are "genuinely and demonstrably sincere in their relationship with those being helped; . . . accept the person with whom they work as a separate, different, and worthwhile individual; and . . . are empathic—able to see the person's private world of feelings and attitudes . . ." (Bernard, 1972, pp. 14–15).

To work effectively with people from different cultural backgrounds, it is suggested that rehabilitation counselors acquire information about the cultural backgrounds and local norms of behavior in the communities where these individuals work (Correa, 1987). Locust (1995) provides an example of what can happen when the counselor lacks cultural sensitivity. She described a young Native American man who was told by his rehabilitation counselor to cut his hair. Because his long, braided hair was indicative of his respect for his elders and tribal history, the young man did not return to the rehabilitation counselor. Leaders in the community and advocacy groups are often excellent resources for culturally specific information. If none of these resources is available, the public library may have reference materials about the community and its diverse residents. Counselors with limited knowledge about the cultural characteristics of their communities may need to discuss frankly their lack of knowledge with clients and request the help of clients and families in interpreting needs from their own perspective.

Counselor attitudes are critical in developing successful rehabilitation programs. Counselors are encouraged to assess their attitudes, particularly as they relate to individuals whom they perceive as different, because of the tendency to withdraw from or avoid the extra time and attention it takes to learn about and to deal effectively with this new or different situation. The result may leave the client among those who fall between the cracks (Baker, 1987). Each client from a different cultural background is an individual. It is vital that the client be treated as an individual rather than being viewed in stereotypic terms (Orlansky & Trap, 1987). These clients do present a greater challenge but successful placements will often be more gratifying because of the challenges their cultural differences present.

Many people from different cultures have had experiences with the "system" that cause them to be suspicious and lacking in trust (Rogler et al., 1987; Sue & Sue, 1990). Many have had unsatisfactory dealings with welfare, health, and education agencies, as well as with such community resources as recreational facilities. The rehabilitation counselor is encouraged to be aware of potential resistance and to develop a rapport with the individual before attempting to work out any rehabilitation program.

Successful rehabilitation work with clients from different cultural backgrounds comes when counselors develop a respect for differences. Many individuals in the helping professions bring to their positions a middle-class perspective. The literature discusses the need for people from different backgrounds in the helping professions to assist in giving their teachers and peers another perspective (Ayers, 1971; Baker, 1987; Correa & Kief, 1986; Orlansky & Trap, 1987; Sue & Sue, 1990; Townsend, 1970). Finally, if and when rehabilitation counselors suspect there are more clients from the cultures represented in their community than are being served by their agency or facility, it is highly recommended that the counselors become active advocates and work in cooperation with other community resources to develop outreach programs to serve all people with visual impairments who are in need of rehabilitation services.

SUMMARY

This chapter provided an overview of rehabilitation considerations in working with older individuals who have visual impairments, women with visual impairments, and culturally diverse individuals with visual impairments. Research suggests that these groups have not had equal access to rehabilitation services, although both individually and collectively they comprise a large percentage of the population of individuals with visual impairments. Furthermore, when they are accepted for services, they tend to receive fewer services and to be placed in lower-paying occupations or nonremunerative positions.

Older people who are visually impaired need support and consideration from family members, friends, and other professionals to achieve maximum independence and life satisfaction. Rehabilitation counselors can have a significant effect on quality of life issues for individuals who are older and blind, by (1) ensuring that they receive appropriate information on services and have the maximum participation in the development of rehabilitation programs, (2) addressing vocational issues, and (3) facilitating family or peer support networks. Rehabilitation counselors are encouraged to be sensitive to the needs of women and adolescent girls in terms of their self-perceptions and experiences. Counselors are also urged to avoid occupational stereotyping for both women and adolescent girls. It is the rehabilitation counselor's objective to ensure that women's interests and aptitudes (rather than their gender) are dictating vocational goals.

It is also suggested that rehabilitation counselors increase their sensitivity to cultural diversity issues, by recognizing that each client is an individual with unique needs. In addition to showing respect for elements of a client's background that may differ from the counselor's, counselors are urged to find common bonds of communication, both verbal and nonverbal, when interacting with individuals of culturally diverse heritages. It is recommended that counselors assist in outreach efforts that can promote the delivery of rehabilitation services to individuals from various ethnic groups and allow each client's interests, goals, and living situation to determine the direction of the rehabilitation plan.

LEARNING ACTIVITIES

1. Analyze the community resources in your community that might be of assistance in working with an older individual with a visual impairment. What gaps do you see in the services that you have identified?
2. Interview an older individual who is blind. Has the person required additional devices or accommodations as a result of aging? What are the individual's recreational or leisure activities? What support is provided by family or friends in terms of socialization activities? What advice does the individual have for a rehabilitation counselor working with an older person who is blind or visually impaired?
3. Make a list of ten occupations that are traditionally male dominated. Review the list of stereotypes associated with being blind or visually impaired. What might be the effect of these stereotypes on women with visual impairment entering these ten occupations?
4. Read *Reaching the Hidden Majority: A Leader's Guide to Career Preparation for Disabled Women and Girls* by Hopkins-Best, Murphy, and Yurcison (Cranston, R.I.: The Carroll Press, 1988). Compare the findings with your own experiences.
5. Obtain the statistics on representation of various ethnic groups in your state. Compare these statistics with those of the state vocational rehabilitation agency serving individuals with visual impairments. What groups are underrepresented?
6. Interview an individual with a visual impairment from an ethnic group that is different from your own. Determine (1) if the person's rehabilitation counselor was from a similar or different ethnic group than the individual with an impairment, (2) if the individual felt that ethnic differences hindered the rehabilitation process, and (3) what advice the individual can provide about working with individuals from different ethnic groups.

CHAPTER 8

People with Multiple Disabilities

Sharon Zell Sacks, Stephen S. Barrett, and Michael D. Orlansky

This chapter addresses individuals who have multiple disabilities, that is, physical, mental, or emotional disabilities in addition to their visual impairment(s). Individuals with multiple disabilities, including people who are deaf and blind, have some special rehabilitation needs that must be considered by rehabilitation professionals. With this diverse group, we are considering both high-incidence and low-incidence disabilities. For example, there is general agreement that a sizable percentage of children, teenagers, and adults with visual impairments also have additional disabilities that result in significant challenges in their education and rehabilitation programs. However, in the United States, the incidence of people who are both deaf and blind is small; estimates range from 30,000 to 40,000 (Helen Keller National Center, 1991) to 735,000 (*Rehab Brief,* 1990), depending on the definition used. Therefore, the objectives for this chapter are to consider some of the characteristics and rehabilitation needs of individuals with a visual impairment and one or more other disabilities, as well as individuals who have the dual sensory disability of deaf-blindness.

MULTIPLE DISABILITIES

Individuals with multiple disabilities exhibit two or more disabilities which, in combination, cause difficulties that generally cannot be effectively remediated through educational or rehabilitation programs designed solely for people with only one disability (Schloss, 1987). Sometimes one disability is considered to be primary and the other secondary, as might be the case with a person who is congenitally blind and who also has mild motor impairment from cerebral palsy. Often the combination of problems is so severe, however, that it is difficult or impossible to identify one disability as "more disabling" than the other (Hart, 1988).

It is important to note that with multiple disabilities, one plus one may not always equal two. That is, the cumulative effects of multiple disabilities on an individual may well be greater than the effects of either disability alone. A child who has severe mental retardation in addition to a visual impairment, for example, will be at a greater disadvantage in learning appropriate language and in gaining an understanding of basic concepts. An adult who is blind from birth and who also has frequent outbursts of self-injurious behavior will need specialized and perhaps prolonged intervention, as well as follow-up services to be placed and retained in an employment setting.

Most programs that were originally set up to provide special services to people with visual impairments, such as state vocational rehabilitation systems and centers for older persons with impaired vision, today include at least some individuals with multiple disabilities among their client populations. Similarly, a generation ago educational programs for students who were blind or visually impaired usually were reluctant to admit individuals with severe multiple disabilities, but today most have shifted away from an exclusively academic emphasis and have adapted their programs to serve individuals with multiple disabilities. The present enrollment at the 52 residential schools for students with visual impairments in the United States consists largely of students with such additional disabilities as mental retardation, behavior disorders, and orthopedic impairments (Heward & Orlansky, 1992). Local education agencies, too, now serve many children and adolescents with multiple disabilities; one survey found that 36 percent of the students placed in public school programs for students with visual impairments were classified as having multiple disabilities (Harley, Garcia, & Williams, 1989).

Ever-increasing numbers of people with multiple disabilities are also included in employment programs for those who are visually impaired. A national survey of all rehabilitation clients with visual impairments who were successfully rehabilitated revealed that 15.2 percent were reported as having a "major secondary disabling condition" (Hill, 1989). Thus, rehabilitation counselors, as with other professionals who provide services to people who are visually impaired, can expect to encounter a substantial percentage of clients with additional disabilities.

Disabilities That Frequently Occur with Visual Impairments

Visual impairments can occur with any other type of disability (e.g., mental, physical, auditory, or emotional). Although being blind is considered to be a severe disability by most people, a visual impairment in conjunction with another disability may or may not have been adequately identified and addressed.

Mental Disabilities

A visual impairment may occur in conjunction with mental retardation, which is generally defined as "significantly subaverage general intellectual functioning existing concurrently with deficits in adaptive behavior, and manifested during the developmental period" (Grossman, 1983, p. 11). The word "significantly" refers to a score of two or more standard deviations below the mean on a standardized test of intelligence, equating to an intelligence quotient (IQ) of 70 or below. If IQ scores were used as the sole criterion for defining mental retardation, then about 3 percent of the population would fall into this category. "General" implies that the deficit is present throughout most or all areas of intellectual functioning. Individuals who scored significantly below average in tests relating to reading and expressive language use, but otherwise were in the normal range for their age groups, would not be classified as mentally retarded, because the deficit is specific rather than general. Such terms as "general" or "pervasive" developmental disabilities are sometimes used as synonyms for mental retardation, to differentiate it from specific learning disabilities.

The phrase "concurrently with deficits in adaptive behavior" indicates that performance on an intelligence test cannot be the sole criterion for a diagnosis of mental retardation. A person must also exhibit problems in adaptive behavior, "the effectiveness or degree with which the individual meets the standards or personal independence and social responsibility expected of his or her age and social group" (Grossman, 1983, p.11). Many aspects of adaptive behavior are critical determinants of a person's ability to succeed in an employment setting—for example, the ability to eat independently, use the toilet, travel, attend to personal hygiene, and refrain from odd or injurious behaviors.

"The developmental period" is most often considered to be the first 18 years of life, with the person's intellectual and behavioral deficits occurring during this period. A person who incurred such deficits after age 18 (e.g., a young adult with a severe head injury or an elderly person with Alzheimer's disease) would not be considered mentally retarded, even though some of that person's needs might be similar to the needs of those with mental retardation.

Mental retardation, like all disabilities, occurs with varying degrees of severity. Mild and moderate disabilities are far more prevalent than severe and profound mental retardation. Halpern (1981) also pointed out that a sizable body of research evidence, dating back 50 years or more, documents that most adults with mild mental retardation are capable of achieving independent or semi-independent community adjustment, including successful competitive employment. As the emphasis in rehabilitation has shifted toward the provision of services to people with more severe disabilities, more individuals with the combined disabilities of visual impairments and mental retardation have received rehabilitation services and many have benefited from supported employment services.

Emotional Disabilities

Individuals with visual impairments may also have emotional disabilities. Many efforts have been made to define and describe emotional disabilities, and no single definition is universally accepted or entirely satisfactory. There is no clear agreement as to what constitutes "good emotional health," and it is difficult to measure emotional function with any degree of precision. It is probably safe to say that (1) all people display disordered or inappropriate behavior at certain times, (2) behavior is strongly influenced by an individual's ethnic and cultural background, and (3) the label of "emotionally disturbed" itself can have a negative effect on a person's behavior and on the way in which other people interact with the individual so labeled. It is generally agreed, however, that to be classified as having an emotional or behavioral disability that requires treatment, a person's behavior must deviate markedly and chronically from established societal and cultural norms. The extent to which an individual can function in major life roles is an important rehabilitation consideration, with severe mental illness (or chronic mental illness) defined by diagnosis, duration, and attendant disability. Role impairment occurs in several of the following five areas: (1) self-care and direction, (2) interpersonal relationships, (3) learning and leisure activities, (4) independent living, and (5) economic self-sufficiency.

Caution should always be used in applying the designation of "emotionally disturbed" to anyone. Some individuals with visual impairments have been viewed as exhibiting behavior patterns that are "deviant" or "abnormal" primarily because of others' limited understanding of blindness and their lack of ability to assess the emotional states of clients who are visually impaired. As is sometimes the case with members of any minority group, many so-called disturbances reflect the social expectations of persons outside the group more than the actual behavior of the person. A counselor, particularly one who does not have firsthand experience in the blindness field, is advised to be wary of concluding that a client who is visually impaired is attempting to "pass" as fully sighted, or that a client who is recently blinded and reluctant to use a long cane is demonstrating a symptom of emotional disturbance.

The above considerations notwithstanding, there are some people with visual impairments and other individuals who have behavioral or emotional problems that present serious demands to their vocational potential, social adjustment, or personal fulfillment. Blindness, particularly when its onset is sudden or unexpected, can represent a loss of such magnitude that skilled intervention by a counselor, psychiatrist, or other mental health professional may be both necessary and advisable. The assistance of a specialist with specific training and extensive experiences in addressing the emotional difficulties of individuals may be indicated, and some successful, innovative group counseling techniques have been described (Freeman, 1987; Oehler-Giarratana & Fitzgerald, 1980).

Autism, a relatively rare disability, is usually classified as primarily emotional and behavioral in nature, is sometimes considered to be a concern among certain populations of people who are visually impaired. Several characteristics of autism that have been enumerated include the following:

- Pervasive lack of responsiveness to other people;
- Gross deficits in language development;
- Peculiar speech patterns, if speech is present, such as echolalia; and
- Bizarre responses to the environment, such as resistance to change and peculiar interest in or attachment to animate and inanimate objects (American Psychiatric Association, 1994; Sullivan, 1994).

Behavior that is similar to autism has been thought to occur with greater than expected frequency in children and young adults whose impaired vision is a result of retinopathy of prematurity (formerly termed retrolental fibroplasia) and maternal rubella (Chess, 1987; Lowenfeld, 1980). The reasons for such attributions are not entirely clear. Without discounting the possibility of physiological causes of autism in certain populations, it should be noted that some individuals with multiple disabilities engage in very limited social and physical interaction with people around them, and thus may be seeking self-stimulation by uttering repetitive words and phrases, by engaging in such repetitive actions as finger-flicking or body-rocking, or by becoming unusually attached to objects. Behaviors such as these may diminish when people respond to the communicative efforts of the individuals who are demonstrating behavior thought to be autistic and thereby reduce their isolation by making a range of activities and choices available.

Substance Abuse

Drug and alcohol problems are often unidentified secondary disabilities and may even be the major contributing factor to an individual's primary disability (Heinemann, 1993). An individual who is adventitiously blinded as a result of an automobile accident caused by intoxication could serve as an example. In her examination of alcoholism, drugs, and individuals with disabilities, Glow (1989) described the lack of information on the treatment of people who are blind or visually impaired with codisabilities of alcoholism or substance abuse. Specific demographic data related to the number of individuals with these codisabilities who are served by vocational rehabilitation counselors today are noticeably absent, although statistics indicate that a significant percentage of individuals with disabilities are also substance abusers (Beck, Marr, & Taricone, 1991; Nelipovich & Buss, 1991).

Cherry (1993) indicated that 10 percent of any population will have "serious" drinking problems and another 10 percent will have drug problems (i.e., with prescription, over-the-counter, or illicit drugs). Therefore, it can be estimated that at least 20 percent of the individuals with visual impairments also have a drug or alcohol problem. One visual disorder that is unique to individuals who have a history of a chronic, severe drinking problem is that of alcohol amblyopia, which involves loss of vision, including scotomas (blind spots) and decreased visual acuity within the central portion of the visual field. This condition is closely related to that of tobacco amblyopia, which involves the painless, bilateral loss of vision that gradually worsens because of constricted blood vessels and swelling of the optic nerve. Alcohol amblyopia is also sometimes referred to as tobacco-alcohol amblyopia because of its clinical association with heavy smoking. This relatively rare disorder involves retrobulbar neuritis with optic nerve atrophy, color blindness, and loss of acuity, most often found in malnourished individuals with alcoholism (Knight & Longmore, 1994).

Screening questions that can help rehabilitation counselors identify individuals who have substance abuse problems are listed in Sidebar 8.1. When individuals who are visually impaired also have a substance abuse disability, rehabilita-

Screening for Alcohol Abuse

SIDEBAR 8.1

Individuals with multiple disabilities may have an alcohol problem. In fact, alcohol abuse may be the cause of the visual impairment. To help determine if an individual is an alcohol abuser, the counselor can ask the following questions:

- How often do you drink?
- How many drinks do you have on a typical day?
- How often do you have six or more drinks on one occasion?
- Have you ever found yourself unable to stop drinking after you started drinking?
- Have you ever found that you needed a drink in the morning to begin your day's activities?
- Have you ever been unable to remember what happened after you started drinking?
- Are your family, friends, or doctor concerned about your drinking?
- Have you ever missed work because of your drinking?
- Has anyone ever been injured as a result of your drinking?

tion counselors may be challenged to identify treatment programs that are knowledgeable about working with individuals with sensory impairments. Many service agencies that focus on substance abuse also report an absence of braille or audio tape materials for individuals with visual impairments.

Brain Injuries

Brain injury is a leading cause of death and disability among people under 24 years of age (Zitnay, 1995). Visual impairments can also be a permanent physical consequence of brain injury (sometimes referred to as traumatic brain injury, acquired brain injury, or head injury). Zasler (1990) pointed out that vision problems are common after traumatic brain injury, but provided no specific demographic data related to the numbers of clients served by vocational rehabilitation counselors. Zasler also noted that visual acuity can be compromised by injury to the second cranial nerve (the optic nerve) and usually occurs within the first post-injury week. Other visual deficiencies that may result from traumatic brain injury include blindness, color vision problems, photophobia, scotomas, and various eye movement disorders.

In their discussion of driving after brain injury, Handler and Patterson (1995) noted that a visual assessment is part of most driving evaluations; however, various studies examined different aspects of vision and visual processing. Visual processing is defined as "the entire process by which we receive visual information, integrate it, perform an action and adjust behavior accordingly" (Cohen & Rein, 1992, p. 531). Research concerning driving and vision suggests that many individuals with brain injuries are unaware of their neurologically based partial losses of vision and many visual field problems may not be detected in standard optometric examinations or conventional visual acuity tests (Gianutos, Ramsey, & Perlin, 1988; Johnson & Keltner, 1983). Warren (1992) suggested that such higher level visual skills as visual memory and visual cognition are dependent on midlevel skills including visual attention, scanning, and pattern recognition. Both higher and midlevel skills are dependent on such basic visual skills as oculomotor control, acuity, and visual field. Therefore, it is generally agreed that specialized rehabilitation optometric examinations are necessary for all individuals who have sustained brain injuries.

Physical and Motor Disabilities

Physical, motor, and neurological disabilities may also accompany vision loss. Some conditions, including premature birth, Rh factor incompatibility, and perinatal anoxia (i.e., lack of oxygen around the time of birth) are known to cause impairments in both visual and motor functioning. Of course, people who have visual impairments may acquire physical disabilities at any time in life as a result of metabolic disorders (e.g., diabetes), progressive diseases (e.g., muscular dystrophy), or accidents involving spinal cord injury, head trauma, or amputations. Gradual loss or diminution of certain fine motor and gross motor functions is also often associated with the aging process.

Visual impairments and physical disabilities, in combination, can present severe obstacles to the development of a person's independence and vocationally related competencies. It is universally agreed that effective orientation and mobility (O&M) skills are desirable, if not essential, but individuals who do not have control of their motor functions will generally find it difficult to develop such skills. Although there are few O&M training programs that are especially geared toward people who have severe physical or motor disabilities, resourceful O&M professionals may be able to adapt certain techniques to meet the needs of individuals who have both visual impairments and physical disabilities, including those who use wheelchairs, crutches, or other adaptive devices (Bailey & Head, 1993). Physical and motor disabilities may also affect speech production, head control, braille or print reading, use of computers, and the ability to sit for prolonged periods of time.

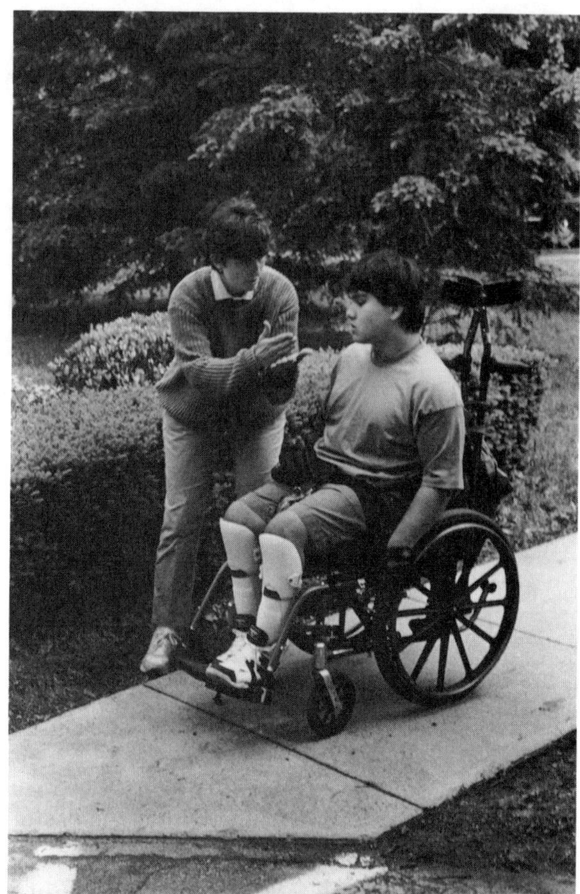

Multiple disabilities in addition to a visual impairment can present numerous challenges to the development of a person's independence. Through the use of certain communication techniques, such as the close-range signing depicted here, an individual's needs can be met.

Cerebral palsy is a general term applied to disorders of posture and voluntary motor function that result from brain injury during the period of early brain growth (i.e., from before birth up to about six years of age) (Alexander & Bauer, 1988). Cerebral palsy is one of the most prevalent physical disabilities found in people with visual impairments. Careful positioning, regular physical or occupational therapy, and, in some cases, medication, surgery, and the use of adaptive equipment and technical devices, can help individuals who have both visual impairments and cerebral palsy move, work, and communicate more effectively.

Individuals who are visually impaired may also exhibit some form of neurological dysfunction. Causes of neurological disorders vary and can be due to maternal infection, injury during the birth process (e.g., anoxia), injury or trauma after birth (e.g., brain tumor, blows to the head), or strokes. For example, clients may have some form of seizure disorder or epilepsy, which occurs when the stimulation of neurons in the brain is interrupted along the neural pathways by chemical inhibitors. It is important for the rehabilitation counselor to recognize the possible side effects of anticonvulsant drugs on a client's physical and behavioral performance. Side effects can range from lethargy to impulsive, combative behavior. Close communication with the medical profession is critical to help these clients maintain a level of control in their daily routines.

Other insults to the brain due to trauma or strokes may result in a form of cortical blindness. Cortical blindness occurs when there is damage to any part of the visual pathways in the brain. Sometimes the optic chiasma (the point at which images are transmitted to the right or left brain) may be injured and unable to transmit the visual impulses. Individuals who are cortically blind may exhibit a reduced visual field or a hemianopia (blindness in half of the visual field).

When working with individuals who have a visual impairment in conjunction with another physical, mental, or emotional disability, rehabilitation counselors are advised to be aware of the client's level of visual functioning in order to develop appropriate job modifications to ensure successful employment and living outcomes. They are also urged to be familiar with community resources, because many service providers (e.g., community mental health centers) may have had little experience working with individuals with multiple disabilities. Supported employment (see Chapter 12) has been successfully used to enhance employment opportunities for many individuals with multiple disabilities, including those individuals who are deaf and blind.

DEAF-BLINDNESS

Deaf-blindness can be an extremely isolating and debilitating condition. Either deafness or blindness can be traumatic and it has been observed that the co-occurrence of two such significant impairments typically produces multiplicative effects, with each magnifying the other. The combined effects of dual sensory impairments severely impede the development of communication, social, and vocational skills, especially when such tertiary impairments as developmental disabilities are also involved, as is presently the case with many students classified as being deaf-blind. When a person's hearing and vision are both impaired, this compounded impairment is far greater than a combination of other disabilities, because each of these sensory impairments continually impinges upon the other. Educational and training methods used with people whose hearing is impaired often call for good vision, whereas strategies employed with people whose vision is impaired often rely heavily on adequate hearing. Thus, unique and individualized techniques are called for, as appropriate to each person's needs (Baldwin, 1991; Heward, 1996; Tedder, Warden, & Sikka, 1993; Trybus, 1984). Although the number of people who are both deaf and blind is relatively small when compared to other individuals with disabilities, this group faces greater challenges in their tasks of daily living and greater risk for exclusion from the work force than other individuals with disabilities.

Most attempts to define "deaf-blindness" have been concerned with eligibility for service, in an attempt to reflect how the condition affects a person's ability to function in different domains (Barrett, 1987). For example, the U.S. Department of Education's Office of Special Education Programs (OSEP) defined children who are deaf and blind as those individuals who have "concomitant hearing and visual impairments, the combination of which causes such severe communication and other developmental and educational problems that they cannot be accommodated in special education programs solely for deaf or blind children" (*Federal Register,* 1977, pp. 42, 479). In contrast, the Rehabilitation Services Administration (RSA) defined a person who is deaf-blind as one who is considered to be legally blind under the laws relating to vocational rehabilitation in his or her state, and "who has a chronic hearing impairment so severe that most speech cannot be understood with optimum amplification and the combination of the two disabilities causes extreme difficulty for the person to obtain independence in activities of daily living, psychosocial adjustment, or in the pursuit of a vocational objective" (Konar & Rice, 1984, p. 14).

Although the population may be relatively small, the individuals comprising this population vary from one another as much as persons in any segment of the population, in terms of the etiology of deaf-blindness, age of onset, degree of severity, limitations imposed, intellectual capacity, and vocational goals and abilities (Maxson, Tedder, Marmion, & Lamb, 1993). The incidence of individuals with both visual and hearing impairments is estimated to be about 735,000 in the United States; however, "the limited information available indicates that 75 to 80 percent of the expected population are unknown to service providers" (*Rehab Brief*, 1990, p. 2).

A widely discussed segment of the population of people who are both deaf and blind are the approximately 5,000 individuals who were born during the rubella epidemic that broke out from 1963 to 1965. Although there is continual concern for these individuals, most of whom are now in their early to mid-thirties, the annual child-count data provided by State Coordinators for Deaf-Blind Children also shows a steady incidence of individuals who are deaf-blind and under the age of 22 (OSEP, 1987). In 1991, OSEP data showed 7,297 children and youth under the age of 22 characterized as being both deaf and blind. This number is constant even though it no longer includes the children from the rubella epidemic. Children born with profound and multiple disabilities, including deaf-blindness, are surviving in greater numbers, because of the advances in medical treatment and technology.

Beyond special education, there is no official government-mandated system for identification and registration of persons who are both deaf and blind. The Helen Keller National Center (HKNC) maintains a nationwide register that is dependent upon voluntary submission of information for determining the characteristics of the population. There are approximately 12,000 persons of all ages listed on the HKNC national register (*Rehab Brief*, 1990).

Causes of Deaf-Blindness

Although many causes of deaf-blindness have been identified, the single leading cause is a condition known as Usher's syndrome (HKNC, 1991). This is a genetic condition with autosomal-recessive characteristics; both parents are unaffected carriers. Statistically, one of four children of parents who are carriers will be born with the condition, although there are numerous cases involving three or more children in the same family.

Individuals with Usher's syndrome are born with profound deafness and experience loss of vision later in life resulting from retinitis pigmentosa (RP). Although the progressive vision loss resulting from RP renders some individuals almost totally blind at an early stage of life, others have been known to retain usable vision well into their sixties or later (Barrett, 1988). Onset and degree of ultimate vision loss vary greatly among individuals and many are unaware of their impending blindness until their late twenties or early thirties (Tedder, 1987).

Other medical conditions have also been associated with deaf-blindness. A seven-year study of the medical characteristics of 141 children who were diagnosed as having deaf-blindness, conducted by the Siegel Institute for Communicative Disorders at Michael Reese Hospital in Chicago, reported a high incidence of neurological disorders, orthopedic problems, language and communication disorders, and other medical problems in addition to vision and hearing impairment (Stein, Palmer & Weinberg, 1980). More recent research has focused on the delayed manifestations of the congenital rubella syndrome, including diabetes, thyroid disease, ocular damage, and other effects (O'Dea & Mayhall, 1988; Sever, South & Shaver, 1985).

Implications for Rehabilitation

Communication

Communication is the primary concern for individuals who are both deaf and blind. Although it is important to avoid generalizing about this diverse group, many adults who are both deaf and blind have one of four combinations of visual and hearing impairments, which greatly affect their style of communication. These combinations include persons who are (1) congenitally deaf and adventitiously blind, (2) congenitally blind and adventitiously deaf, (3) adventitiously deaf-blind, or (4) congenitally deaf-blind. Each combination presents its own implications for communication and rehabilitation. For example, the communication methods and preferences of individuals born, raised, and educated as persons who are deaf, who later lose their vision, will differ greatly from those of individuals who lose their hearing much later in life (Wynne, 1987).

Relatively few people who are both deaf and blind are completely without residual vision or hearing; thus the category of "complete deaf-blindness" is somewhat rare. Rehabilitation professionals should assist individuals who are both deaf and blind in taking full advantage of any residual hearing or vision and provide low vision and audiological services (HKNC, 1991).

Given the heterogeneity of the population, the diversity of etiology, age of onset, educational background, and severity of loss, it is not surprising that many methods of communication have been utilized. Communication must be tailored to the needs and desires of the individual, taking into consideration all of the foregoing factors. A total of 21 methods of communication has been identified. Some include the American One-Hand Manual Alphabet, American Sign Language, braille, Two-hand Tactile Sign Language, and the use of many technological devices such as the Tellebraille (*Rehab Brief*, 1990; Wynne, 1980).

Communication methods may be formal or informal. The use of informal gestures or "home signs" is not infrequent. The individualized assessment of a person's communication methods and preferences is a major component in establishing a rehabilitative program, and is considered to be the single most important factor (Wynne, 1980). If a rehabilitation counselor is unable to communicate in the mode preferred by the client, then a qualified interpreter skilled in the preferred mode must be identified (*Rehab Brief*, 1990).

Planning and Service Delivery

Planning issues involve concerns for program structure, priority, funding, staff training, and related topics. Service-delivery issues are concerned with such topics as case identification, assessment, coordination, consumer input, and the provision of appropriate services. Both planning and service-delivery issues are unique when applied to a population often described as "low incidence/high need." The caseload of any rehabilitation counselor serving people who are either deaf or blind in an urban environment is unlikely to include more than a few people who are deaf and blind. Some counselors may serve only one to three individuals who are both deaf and blind in their caseload during the course of a year.

A national resource to rehabilitation professionals and other service providers, HKNC instituted its Affiliation Program in 1975 in order to help state and private agencies establish specialized service projects for this low incidence/high need population. HKNC's regional offices also have many services available to assist with identification of the population, needs assessment, and service planning.

Early identification is especially important in order to facilitate the delivery of appropriate services. Casefinding is usually done in cooperation with special education programs serving children and adolescents with disabilities, yet it is equally important to identify those elderly individuals who are experiencing problems in their daily living routines because of failing hearing and vision. The two distinct groups of people who are elderly with hearing and vision problems are (1) those who matured with relatively normal vision and hearing who now are experiencing dual sensory problems related to aging, and (2) those who grew up being both deaf and blind and who are now growing older. Each group has its own service priorities and needs, which call for close coordination of services with gerontology and in-

Individuals with multiple disabilities can use a variety of adaptive techniques to perform daily living activities. Here a deaf-blind customer makes a purchase by having a store clerk write letters on the palm of his hand; he places his other hand on hers to help identify the letters as she prints.

dependent living resources. Another target group for casefinding are those individuals who reside in institutions for people with mental illness or mental retardation. In some instances, individuals who are both deaf and blind were placed in such settings many years ago, for lack of a better alternative.

Casefinding, as well as the provision of services, requires interagency coordination and comprehensive services. No one agency can meet all of the needs of persons who are deaf and blind. Also, agencies serving persons who are blind and agencies serving persons who are deaf both have specific qualifications and contributions to serving people who are deaf-blind. Agencies serving individuals with visual impairments tend to have expertise in adaptive skills for independent living, and agencies serving individuals who are deaf typically have expertise in specialized language and communication methods. One of these agencies, however, needs to take the lead role in providing services to those who are both deaf and blind. In some states, there is a clear mandate for one agency or the other to serve as the lead agency, while in other states, there is no clear directive. In this type of case, the needs and communication methods of the consumer should determine the lead agency.

Comprehensive rehabilitation services are needed by a person who is deaf and blind because the condition affects so many diverse yet interrelated areas of the individual's life. People who are blind learn how and when to depend on their hearing, especially for mobility, and conversely, individuals who are deaf depend on their vision, especially for communication. In comparison, being deaf and blind affects not only mobility and communication but also learning, personal and social development, access to information, recreation, leisure, and vocational development. Therefore, no single service agency can meet the range of needs when comprehensive services are required.

In addition to talking to representatives from two or more agencies, it is highly recommended that parents and consumers be involved in planning services. These service groups, each with a different perspective but a common goal, can also share resources for case identification, staff training, and development of new service alternatives. Such consumer groups as the American Association of the Deaf-Blind (AADB) and the National Parent Network (NPN) are vitally important resources.

Other rehabilitation issues that need to be addressed are community resources, which can assist with evaluations, as well as personal adjustment services. Client assessment may be especially problematic, however, because, as Nelipovich and Naegele (1985) noted,

> Few general rehabilitation counselors, psychologists, or evaluators have the knowledge, skill, or experience to appropriately assess . . . [an individual who is deaf-blind]. Misdiagnosis, particularly of mental retardation or mental illness, is highly likely and often occurs when standard measures are administered and interpreted by professionals without sufficient knowledge of and exposure to the implications of the disabilities involved. (p. 106)

Also, the programs providing other services will seldom have expertise in working with individuals who are both deaf and blind. Other community resources, such as vocational and technical centers, can often be accessed through the support provided by sign language interpreters.

In considering services, clients and rehabilitation counselors are also encouraged to obtain medical advice on the feasibility of cochlear implants, which have not received much support from the deafness community. Nonetheless, the decision to use cochlear implants is an individual choice and may be appropriate for some individuals who have profound bilateral sensorineural hearing loss and who cannot benefit from conventional amplification devices. Chute and Nevins (1995) noted that the benefits of cochlear implants are greatest for adults with postlingual deafness and children who have become deaf after they developed speech and language skills. All members of the rehabilitation team, however, are urged to understand the capabilities of individuals, even with cochlear implants. As an example, Miner (1995) described a student who, because of her cochlear implant, was mistakenly treated as a "hearing-blind" student by her O&M instructor during a night mobility lesson, which rendered her totally blind. Miner explained:

> Joanne, who has a cochlear implant and had been hit by a car, was taken out for a night mobility lesson, a situation in which she is rendered totally blind. Her O&M instructor mistakenly thought that the cochlear implant meant that Joanne could not hear and treated her as a hearing-blind student. Joanne described being belittled about her fear of crossing a major intersection, but complied and crossed, despite her terror, relying on her O&M instructor to protect her from danger. The O&M instructor discontinued this practice after the cochlear implant team explained the limitations of the implant. (p. 290)

Individuals who receive the cochlear implant must also have realistic expectations concerning the results of the implant. Miner (1995), describing one teenager who was enraged about her blindness and thought the cochlear implant would allow her to hear, stated that "candidates for cochlear implants need to be psychologically healthy, accept their deafness, and have a clear understanding of what the implants can and cannot do" (p. 291).

There are also case-management issues that need to be addressed by rehabilitation counselors, such as increased amounts of time for meeting with clients and more frequent home visits. Counselors may have to handle more matters in person or use the mail, instead of the telephone, because most individuals who are both deaf and blind do not have a special telecommunication device for the deaf (TTY/TTD) (*Rehab Brief*, 1990).

In terms of employment, counselors are advised to (1) provide employers with information about the various communication methods and resources available to them, (2) help coworkers and peers overcome communication barriers, and (3) arrange alternative transportation services, when public transportation is not an available option. It is recommended that counselors recognize that most employers, and most citizens for that matter, have never met an individual who is both deaf and blind. Supported employment has also been an effective placement method for some individuals who are deaf-blind.

SUMMARY

This chapter focused on individuals who face great challenges because their visual impairments are combined with other physical, mental, or emotional disabilities. In particular, in working with individuals who are both deaf and blind, the most important consideration of counselors is that of communication. Rehabilitation counselors need to become familiar with techniques for accurate assessment of individuals with multiple impairments as well as the development of appropriate rehabilitation programs. Although resources are increasing, much needs to be done to ensure that they receive equal access to rehabilitation services, as well as educational and employment opportunities.

LEARNING ACTIVITIES

1. Plan to observe a case management meeting for a client with multiple disabilities. Observe the following:
   - **a.** Role of each participant (Who attended?);
   - **b.** Sharing of information (Was there a group facilitator or leader?);
   - **c.** Team functioning (Did the group work together or independently?);
   - **d.** Role of the client (Was the client an active participant?);
   - **e.** Role of family members (Did family members play an active role in team decisions?);
   - **f.** Outcomes of the meeting (What decisions were made and what follow-up strategies were agreed upon?).
2. Read Joanne Greenberg's novel, *Of Such Small Differences* about a young man who is deaf and blind (Signet Books, 1988). What information in the book supports or refutes rehabilitation considerations described in this chapter?
3. Discuss the importance of onset and etiology as they relate to methods of communication used by individuals who are deaf-blind.

PART THREE

Rehabilitation Services and Resources

No single professional can effectively meet all the service needs of an individual with a visual impairment. Part Three of this book introduces rehabilitation counselors to other professionals with whom they will work most closely in developing and implementing rehabilitation plans; to the services that are used in the rehabilitation of individuals with visual impairments; and to the various service systems and resources of which they may avail themselves.

The full benefits of a team approach to service delivery can be realized when individual team members have an appreciation for and understanding of each member's role and functions. In addition to the valuable contributions from members of the medical profession, the rehabilitation counselor often relies on the expertise of the rehabilitation teacher and the orientation and mobility (O&M) specialist, because the achievement of a client's vocational goal is often contingent on attaining the skills taught by these professionals. Another important team member, whose professional training may be in one of the previously mentioned disciplines, is the individual who is knowledgeable about assistive technology. The use of assistive technology expands the range of occupations available to individuals with visual impairments and enhances their quality of life.

Team members, including rehabilitation counselors, may work in a variety of settings, such as the state-federal vocational rehabilitation program, the U.S. Department of Veterans Affairs, or one of the many private agencies that provide services to individuals with visual impairments. Knowing the types of agencies and organizations that are available to provide services can help rehabilitation counselors make appropriate referrals (such as to consumer organizations) and aids them in their own continuing education (for example, through membership in professional organizations).

The following chapters explore three critical services (counseling, job development, and placement) offered by rehabilitation counselors. Counseling skills are used throughout the rehabilitation process in the delivery of these services. Consequently, counselors need to recognize the accommodations they will need to make in their counseling styles and in the physical arrangement of their settings to enhance the psychological and physical well-being of their clients. Successful employment, which is frequently the goal of the rehabilitation process, is often dependent on the rehabilitation counselor's ability to develop relationships with employers, to analyze jobs, and to make appropriate job modifications. Counselors also need skills to assist clients in obtaining and retaining jobs. This section highlights the skills that are essential to rehabilitation counselors in effecting successful employment outcomes for clients.

CHAPTER 9

The Rehabilitation Team

Lynne Luxton, Anna Bradfield, B. J. Maxson, and B. C. Starkson

This chapter provides an overview of three professional groups whose members are vital components of the rehabilitation team. Two of the professional disciplines, rehabilitation teaching and orientation and mobility (O&M) instruction, focus on enhancing the independence of individuals with visual impairments by providing instruction in such areas as reading (e.g., using braille), daily living skills, study skills, communication skills, and travel skills. The third group represents a number of different professionals, who are collectively referred to as assistive technology (AT) specialists. Those who specialize in computer technology are called computer access technology specialists and are drawn from a variety of disciplines, including rehabilitation engineering, electrical engineering, rehabilitation teaching, computer science, O&M, and low vision rehabilitation. They are responsible for identifying computer equipment and access devices that assist the client who is visually impaired in overcoming visual barriers to employment and independent living. Because this discipline has developed during the last 15 years, the job titles and professional training requirements vary considerably.

To realize all of the advantages of the team approach, it is important for rehabilitation counselors to make appropriate referrals and to communicate effectively with rehabilitation teachers, O&M instructors, and assistive technology specialists. It is also essential to be able to explain the services these groups offer to individuals with visual impairments. Therefore, the objectives of this chapter include (1) describing the roles and functions of rehabilitation teachers, O&M instructors, and assistive technology specialists, (2) identifying the services and service settings in which rehabilitation teachers and O&M instructors work, (3) describing the educational preparation and certification of rehabilitation teachers and O&M instructors, and (4) identifying various types of assistive technology and computer access devices. When rehabilitation team members understand each others' roles and functions and communicate effectively, the overall rehabilitation process is more effective and the goals of individuals with visual impairments are more readily met.

THE TEAM CONCEPT

The rehabilitation team consists of selected professionals and family members who help provide the information, assessment, and services necessary to assist the client and rehabilitation counselor formulate rehabilitation goals for the client that will lead to successful job placement. Members of the team may include occupational therapists, physical therapists, low vision clinicians, ophthalmologists, optometrists, physicians, psy-

A rehabilitation team can meet the service needs of a person with a visual impairment effectively by working closely in developing and implementing a rehabilitation plan. Team members might include a rehabilitation teacher, an orientation and mobility instructor, a rehabilitation counselor, an assistive technology specialist, a school teacher, and parents or other family members.

chologists, mental health professionals, social workers, family members, counselors, educators, rehabilitation teachers, O&M instructors, and computer access technology specialists. The team may meet formally in an initial or regularly scheduled meeting, as is often done in rehabilitation centers or facilities. In field-based settings, team members more commonly provide services and written assessments to the client and counselor without formal meetings.

The rehabilitation counselor and the client should jointly select and coordinate the professional services necessary for a successful outcome. As much as possible, the client is the ultimate decision-maker. The rehabilitation counselor is responsible for providing information and resources to assist the client in making realistic decisions and to provide guidance and direction as appropriate. Because the counselor will often be instrumental in obtaining the financial support for various services, a cooperative relationship between counselor and client is extremely important to the overall success of the program.

Three potential team members, whose roles are considered in this chapter, are those with expertise and training in rehabilitation, blindness, and visual impairment. Rehabilitation teachers and O&M instructors have for years provided essential instruction in specific areas related to adjustment to blindness.

Rehabilitation teams vary with the age of the client (e.g., school-age, working-age adult, or older adult) and characteristics of the individual or the impairment. For example, the rehabilitation team for individuals with diabetes includes the diabetes educators and other members of the healthcare community, as well as the rehabilitation community (Baker, S., 1993; Hunt, 1993; Williams, 1993). In the case of a student involved in transition from school to work, the team may be composed of the school teacher, rehabilitation counselor, O&M specialist, assistive technology specialist, rehabilitation teacher, and the parents. Whatever the composition of the team for whatever purpose, teamwork enhances both prevention and intervention efforts, increases the possibility of successful rehabilitation, and multiplies the benefits of the services of a single provider.

REHABILITATION TEACHING

Rehabilitation teaching is an essential adaptive service for adults with visual impairments. Employed in residential rehabilitation center programs, in itinerant community agency programs, and as private contractors, rehabilitation teachers provide instruction and guidance in the following independent living skill areas: (1) home management, (2) personal management, (3) communication and education, (4) leisure activity, and (5) home orientation skills (Asenjo, 1975). The process of rehabilitation teaching includes an assessment phase, a planning phase, and a learning and teaching phase (Ponchillia & Ponchillia, 1996).

Rehabilitation teaching is a dynamic process. Grounded in the principles of adult education, rehabilitation teachers facilitate learning experiences and respond to the needs of clients. Changes are made in skills to be taught, teaching methods, development and use of teaching materials, use of adaptive equipment, sequence of instruction within a specific skill area, and the integration of all the skill areas into comprehensive rehabilitation teaching plans.

The discipline of rehabilitation teaching draws elements from adult education (teaching methods), special education (communication skills and adaptive technology), recreation therapy, home economics, counseling or social work, and rehabilitation (theory and case-management practices). In addition to academic preparation, rehabilitation teachers need the personal attributes of good teachers: patience, concern, creativity, and problem-solving skills. The rehabilitation teacher is an invaluable member of the rehabilitation team because people who are unable to label and organize their belongings, obtain and prepare food, maintain their clothing appropriately, or use effective communication skills will be difficult clients to place in competitive employment settings. Furthermore, the inability of individuals who are visually impaired to perform these activities diminishes their self-esteem, self-confidence, and independence (Beach, Robinet, & Hakim-Larson, 1995).

Roles and Responsibilities: Diversity from the Beginning

Rehabilitation teaching ("home teaching") began in the United States in 1882 with the founding of the "Pennsylvania Home Teaching Society and Free Circulating Library for the Blind" in Philadelphia, Pennsylvania. It was modeled after the home teaching societies in England that were started in the 1850s by Dr. William Moon, a minister who was adventitiously blind. The first home teachers were educated women who were blind. These women volunteered to teach tactile reading to homebased adults who were blind; serving as role models, they also helped solve daily living problems.

These first home teachers in the United States taught five types of tactile reading and six crafts, along with case finding, "adjustment to blindness" counseling, and public education. They worked from their own homes, using guides to travel to clients' homes. By 1925, some 26 states had home teaching programs (Koestler, 1976). In addition to the benefits provided to those being assisted, home teaching provided employment for women with visual impairments when other vocational opportunities were scarce.

During the 1920s and 1930s, home teachers emphasized crafts instruction for remunerative home industry products. People with visual impairments were stereotyped as being incapable of competitive employment and were seldom considered as candidates for vocational rehabilitation (Rubin & Roessler, 1987). However, the Social Security Act (1935) and other federal programs requiring eligibility determination prompted state agencies to add social casework to home teachers' duties (Dickinson, 1956). Some teachers with backgrounds in social work added casework and counseling services to the other services they provided; however, other teachers maintained teaching as their primary duty. Presently, rehabilitation teacher job duties continue to include "adjustment to blindness" counseling (Leja, 1989).

Certification standards were initiated in the 1940s, and, based on college education and experience, were refined in the 1950s—regardless of vision. Yet, agencies continued to preferentially hire people who were blind (and female) to be empathetic role models and teachers. The advent of university training programs expanded the personnel and scope of the discipline and rehabilitation teachers have now become a heterogeneous mix of professionals (Hansen, 1980).

Education and Certification of Rehabilitation Teachers

Continuing the legitimization of rehabilitation teaching, the federal Office of Vocational Rehabilitation supported the national study of home teachers by Elizabeth Cosgrove, which resulted in the 1961 monograph, *Home Teachers of the Adult Blind: Who They Are, What They Could Do, What Would Enable Them to Do It.* Among Cosgrove's recommendations were clear job descriptions, equitable salaries, office space, administrative support for teachers, and the establishment of university programs for personnel preparation. In 1963, Dr. Ruth Kaarlela started the first master's degree program in rehabilitation teaching at Western Michigan University (Kaarlela, 1966). Following this important step, in 1966 the Commission on Standards and Accreditation of Services to the Blind (COMSTAC) and the American Association of Workers for the Blind (AAWB) changed the job title of "home teacher" to "rehabilitation teacher" (Uslan, Asenjo, & Peck, 1982). Further, COMSTAC (1966) defined the rehabilitation teacher's role as planning and providing instruction in adaptive techniques and skills, and possessing an understanding of the nature of problems caused by visual impairments.

The Rehabilitation Teaching University Personnel Preparation Guidelines were approved by the Association for Education and Rehabilitation (AER) Board of Directors in 1990. The guidelines were developed over the preceding year and a half through the collaboration of the rehabilitation teaching university faculty, vocational rehabilitation professionals, consumers, and national leaders in rehabilitation teaching (Wiener & Luxton, 1994). The Rehabilitation Teaching University Personnel Preparation Guidelines also specify curricular content, internship requirements, university administrative support, and faculty qualifications for rehabilitation teaching undergraduate and graduate programs. The guidelines also stipulate that rehabilitation teachers who work with children must have courses both in child development and education, and in working with parents and families.

Rehabilitation teachers work closely with occupational therapists, who are trained in physical and psychiatric disabilities, to provide services for persons with multiple disabilities. They also work in association with diabetes educators and other members of the diabetes care team (Cleary, 1994). Rehabilitation teaching is a diverse field requiring competencies in multiple areas of independent living, as well as close working relationships with professionals in allied disciplines. Professional certification, which is discussed in the next section, formalizes the knowledge and skills of rehabilitation teachers.

Rehabilitation teachers are certified through the AER. AER Division 11 (Rehabilitation Teaching and Independent Living Services) grants two types of five-year renewable certifications. The first is Type AA for those with degrees in rehabilitation teaching, and the second is Type A for individuals with degrees in education or related fields. Although the standards are the same for both professional certifications, candidates for Type A certification must document additional continuing education to demonstrate that they possess the knowledge and skills needed to work with adults with visual impairments (e.g., braille, daily living skills, rehabilitation theories, adaptive technology). Certified rehabilitation teachers (CRT) with Type AA certificates are also qualified to teach in college and university programs (Ponchillia & Ponchillia, 1996; Wiener & Luxton, 1994).

Although the profession continually promotes standards and certification of rehabilitation teachers and national efforts are underway to develop state licensing for specialists in services to adults with visual impairments, rehabilitation teacher certification is not a requirement for employment by all state or local rehabilitation agencies (Smith, 1992). Certification may not be required, in part because of the shortage of rehabilitation teachers. The large demand for rehabilitation teachers in nonvocational areas (e.g., older individuals and children) has caused the supply of rehabilitation teachers to become inadequate, particularly in rural areas (Shaw & Nye, 1993).

Rehabilitation teaching includes instructing clients in the use of adaptive technology to maintain personal and home management skills.

Rehabilitation Teachers: Services and Settings

Rehabilitation teachers are employed by federal, state, and community agencies as staff members or as private contractors. The organizational structure of an agency determines the specific rehabilitation teaching job tasks. For example, the rehabilitation teacher and counselor positions may be combined into a "teacher/counselor" position, which results in one person teaching independent living skills, managing casework, and providing counseling services. Another arrangement might call for rehabilitation teachers to be assigned to teach in one such skill area as daily living skills, computer access technology, or braille (Luxton, 1993). In itinerant settings, rehabilitation teachers often carry two or three caseloads simultaneously. Each caseload requires such case-management systems as (1) adult vocational rehabilitation clients, (2) nonvocational rehabilitation clients, for example, older people who are blind in Title VII—Chapter 2 programs, (3) independent living rehabilitation clients, and (4) transition-aged youths. Rehabilitation teachers adjust their instruction and guidance to meet the different needs of programs and individuals (Smith, 1992; Moore & Stephens, 1994). Small gains in rehabilitation skills may enable older people to maintain themselves and their households (Crews & Luxton, 1993). Younger people learn skills to maintain themselves, families, jobs, and new careers for the years to come.

Rehabilitation teaching services are provided in either residential rehabilitation center-based programs, which are appropriate for young adults through senior adults, or they are provided through itinerant services in clients' homes, community settings, and work settings. Center-based services differ in a number of significant ways from itinerant services (see Sidebar 9.1).

There are obvious advantages and disadvantages to both types of programs. One of the concerns raised about center-based programs is whether clients can transfer their newly acquired skills to the home and work environments. Ponchillia and Kaarlela (1986) found that clients successfully transferred their adaptive

SIDEBAR 9.1

Center-Based and Itinerant Rehabilitation Services

Counselors who are familiar with the differences between center-based and community-based programs will find it easier to guide clients in choosing the most appropriate services.

In center-based services:

- The rehabilitation program is a specific length of time (e.g., 12 weeks);
- The curriculum is more detailed and in-depth;
- The lessons are usually in groups of two to four adults;
- There are different rehabilitation teachers in such specific areas as adaptive kitchen skills, budget and household management, housekeeping, personal management (including grooming), print (handwriting, typing) communication skills, listening and auditory skills, braille and tactile communication skills, recreation and leisure skills, shopping and consumer education skills, and low vision training;
- Lesson time is concentrated with lessons scheduled on at least a daily basis. Teaching materials and adaptive equipment are available on-site;
- Vocational training is available with "high tech" electronic equipment and advanced instruction in braille, low vision utilization, listening and other interpersonal social skills;
- Related services that a client needs are available, often on-site. These include nursing care and personal health education, psychological testing and counseling, vocational evaluation and training, low vision and ophthalmological care, and related medical services;
- Peer groups are readily available to the client for support, sharing of experiences and coping hints, and social interaction; and
- Team meetings for case reviews are scheduled regularly.

In itinerant or community-based programs:

- The length of the rehabilitation program is uncertain because of changing client and family situations, health conditions, vocational plans, and rehabilitation goals;
- The rehabilitation teaching curriculum and teaching sequence will vary for each client based on immediate needs and long-term goals. Generally, the overall rehabilitation teaching program is not as detailed as a center-based program although specific areas may be just as detailed;
- Individual lessons are scheduled for one to two hours on a weekly, biweekly, or monthly basis. Some case-management systems allow for more frequent instruction and some, particularly in larger districts, are scheduled only every four to six weeks;
- One rehabilitation teacher provides instruction in all areas. The rehabilitation teacher brings teaching materials and adaptive equipment to the client's setting;
- Utilization of community resources is vital to providing full rehabilitation services;
- The rehabilitation teacher assists clients in becoming involved in community agencies (e.g., recreational facilities) and work settings;
- The rehabilitation teacher observes the client's skills in the actual environments with the actual equipment. Modifications and adaptations are made immediately to foster success;
- The client's family is directly involved in the rehabilitation process;

Center-Based and Itinerant Rehabilitation Services (continued)

- Rehabilitation teachers provide adjustment to blindness and guidance/counseling;
- The rehabilitation teacher has limited rehabilitative and technical assistance support if other rehabilitation teachers are not available or the supervisor is not knowledgeable in rehabilitation teaching;
- Clients with multiple disabilities need additional health-related personnel from community resources; and
- The community-based service team has fewer opportunities to confer than the center-based team has.

skills instruction to their home and work environments.

Guidance and Counseling

A frequent question asked by rehabilitation teachers is "When should I refer a client for social work or counseling services?" Rehabilitation teachers may encounter complex family situations, such as strained interpersonal relationships, financial hardships, and emotional or mental health problems. These situations are not uncommon in caseloads in which counselors provide case-management services but not ongoing client counseling (Ponchillia & Ponchillia, 1996). The rehabilitation teacher is therefore urged to become familiar with the counselor's skills and resources for counseling.

Rehabilitation teachers provide counseling for clients within the course of their instructional programs, but the rehabilitation teacher's roles for further client and family counseling are not clearly defined. It is generally agreed, however, that preexisting family, financial, vocational, or social problems are not in the purview of rehabilitation teachers. Rehabilitation teachers are encouraged to refer individuals with problems in these areas for professional counseling. When clients continually have counseling needs that interfere with achieving instructional objectives, it is also recommended that they be referred for professional counseling. On itinerant caseloads, there will also be emergency situations that rehabilitation teachers must address during lesson time. The rehabilitation teacher is advised to carefully document the presenting situation and response. Rehabilitation teachers generally are neither trained for nor should they be expected to provide professional counseling to clients (McBride, Butler & Nickolson, 1979; Ponchillia, 1984).

Independent Living

The influence of the independent living movement and the increased population of older people in need of rehabilitation services have increased the need for rehabilitation teachers, particularly in community-based systems (Crews, Frey, & Peterson, 1987; Farish & Wen, 1994). Some agencies have also responded to the need for additional staff through the use of rehabilitation teaching assistants and private contractors. Agencies first train assistants and then assign them duties to fit the agency's staffing needs, under the supervision of a rehabilitation teacher. Rehabilitation teachers (as private contractors) are hired by counselors to provide rehabilitation teaching case services. Although reimbursement practices to private contractors vary, payment is usually for teaching contact hours only. Such additional services needed by clients as counseling, agency referrals, or adaptive equipment concerns are handled by the counselor. Of course, the roles of staff rehabilitation teachers and private contractors vary by agency in terms of supervision, support, resources, adaptive equipment, and technical assistance.

Peer groups (Merrill, 1993), which are gaining momentum in every locale, are an extension of independent living programming and are usually started by rehabilitation counselors or rehabilitation teachers with the ultimate goal of "group self-rule." Rehabilitation staff members may serve as liaison from the agency to peer groups. Although the activities of various groups may range from social and leisure events to peer counseling, peer groups do provide an opportunity for clients to learn about available agency services, adaptive equipment, and consumer empowerment (Byers-Lang, 1984).

Rehabilitation teachers and counselors frequently use volunteers who work with clients as personal and audio tape readers, drivers, follow-up instructors, guides to medical appointments, recreational activity assistants, and large-print and braille transcribers. Volunteers also have a long history of working for people with visual impairments as agency board members, certified braille transcribers, and as repair people for talking-book machines. Volunteers are recruited, trained, supervised, and discharged by the agency's written policy guidelines. Recognition events and ongoing support for volunteers are vital to maintaining volunteer programs.

Transition-age Youth

Rehabilitation planning for transition-age students (i.e., those who are leaving high school for work, college, or other vocational rehabilitation services) has prompted the development of programs for high school or precollege students. The emphasis is on the mastery of independent living skills and, if appropriate, college survival skills (see Sidebar 9.2). Simpson (1986) clustered the activities of daily living for transition-age youth into the broad categories of (1) personal adjustment, (2) community adjustment, and (3) vocational adjustment, which are useful categories for program planning and organizing skills.

The regulations that govern teaching students within a school setting differ by state, but generally, personnel must be certified by state education departments. Because rehabilitation teachers' professional certification is not the same as teacher certification by state education departments, careful planning must be used to include rehabilitation teaching services for school students. For example, one way to include rehabilitation teaching is to list it as a "related service" and include it in the student's Individualized Education Plan (IEP). Rehabilitation teachers can also provide valuable consultation to special education and home economics teachers in the school setting for teaching daily living skills to students who are visually impaired.

A popular and successful option for introductory transition programs are weekend programs or short-term training projects. These are usually arranged by rehabilitation agency staff and include both students and their parents. Activities usually focus on vocational exploration, independent living training, and introduction to adult rehabilitation services. They also provide excellent opportunities for networking (Houser, Moses & Kay, 1987; Raver & Drash, 1988).

Client Assessments

Rehabilitation teachers assess each client in the five fundamental skill areas of personal management, home management, communication and education, leisure activities, and home orientation skills. Sensory skills and low vision are also assessed individually, and integrated into the overall assessment process (Flax, Golembiewski, & McCaulley, 1993). Assessments are based on the combination of verbal interviews and skills demonstrations by clients. The rehabilitation teacher and client determine the priority areas, set overall goals, and plan a schedule of lessons with objectives that will meet those goals.

Each client brings a different set of life experiences, skills, knowledge, and attitudes to the rehabilitation process. It is advised that a thorough evaluation include the client's values and own sense of priorities. Initial assessments provide a profile of the client's abilities and capabilities of functioning with the visual impairment. The as-

Goals for Transition-Age Youth

SIDEBAR 9.2

Students who are entering high school or college benefit from the mastery of the following independent living skills:

1. Securing housing
2. Meal planning
3. Shopping
4. Food preparation
5. Clothing selection
6. Housekeeping and laundry
7. Signature writing
8. Personal budgeting
9. Money management
10. Eating etiquette
11. Social graces
12. Sex education
13. Personal healthcare and grooming
14. Recreation and leisure activities

College-bound students should also master the following:

1. Note-taking
2. Study and organizational skills
3. Hiring and firing readers
4. Library skills
5. Community living in a dormitory
6. Typing and computer skills
7. Securing of braille or recorded books, supplies, and adaptive equipment

sessments, which identify areas of need in (1) safety, (2) skill levels, (3) efficiency of task completion, (4) motivation and interest in learning, and (5) strengths and abilities to learn, result in the identification of immediate, intermediate, and long-range goals (Smith, 1992).

Frequently, assessments are based on a deficit-skill approach. The rehabilitation teacher may ask the client, "What tasks are you having problems doing?" With this approach, some clients may be hesitant to identify problems that seem "simple," or those that they think "blind people can't do." Checklists of skills are helpful to rehabilitation teachers in overcoming the hesitancy of some clients, to prompt other clients, and to ensure that all skills are discussed during the assessment.

Checklists for skill demonstrations have narrative- or numerical-rating scales. The client demonstrates skills and receives a rating mark ranging from "inability to do skill" (Level 1) to "does skill independently" (Level 4). There can be other types of levels including "is not interested or skill not applicable to client." Checklists can include comments for notes and recording results of the verbal interview. The commercially available assessment tools for activities of daily living (ADL assessments), however, have not been validated for adults with visual impairments. If the assessment is taking place in a work environment, the rehabilitation teacher and counselor are urged to be aware that both assessments and lessons are more successful when clients know they are not being watched by peers or supervisors.

During verbal interviews, the client describes how tasks and activities are accomplished on a typical day. This gives the rehabilitation teacher insight into the client's lifestyle. For example, in a home setting, if the client always buys and prepares the same foods, the rehabilitation teacher may consider whether this behavior relates to a need for (1) labeling techniques, (2) cooking instruction, (3) eating skills, or (4) recorded food preparation directions (Paskin, & Moloney-Soucy, 1994). In the work setting, if the client waits for a secretary to be free for mail reading, the rehabilitation teacher may consider whether the behavior suggests a need to (1) change the client's job duties, (2) schedule the secretary for reading mail, (3) arrange for regularly scheduled paid or volunteer readers, or (4) investigate other accessible technology.

Clients receive two types of instruction based on assessments. One method is a step-by-step guide for teaching skills that are new to the client—braille, for example. The second method is learning adaptive techniques for existing skills or relearning these skills with limited or without any visual assistance. Examples of adaptive skills are learning tactile techniques for either signature writing or handwriting for the client who already has writing skills. It is highly recommended that clients with adventitious visual impairments develop auditory and tactile methods of learning, because vision may no longer be their primary learning channel (Ponchillia & Ponchillia, 1996).

Assessment results need to be discussed openly with clients. And it is important for clients to agree with their rehabilitation teaching program goals or the result will be frustration and not rehabilitation. Although the vocational rehabilitation client must sign his or her Individualized Written Rehabilitation Program (IWRP), it is also very beneficial for nonvocational rehabilitation clients to sign their plans, because this provides a form of a contract and establishes an agreement for working toward the stated goals in the plan (see Chapter 10). When changes that affect the client's learning develop, they are discussed with the client, recorded in the progress notes, and brought to the counselor's attention.

Evaluations

Evaluations, as with assessments, are ongoing for adult clients and take place as clients work through instructional skills and tasks. Informal evaluations, when previous learning is reviewed, are a regular part of lessons. In itinerant settings, clients make progress on their own by learning adaptive techniques as daily living problems arise. If these techniques work safely and efficiently, rehabilitation teachers will move on to the next lesson. Naturally, the pace of a client's progress will vary by client and that client's skill.

It is highly recommended that the formal evaluation method match the assessment method and be accurately recorded in the case files. Case records show initial assessment ratings and date, middle evaluation dated ratings, and final evaluation dated ratings, with narratives supplementing final evaluations. At a minimum, the evaluations document basic skill level attainment for essential daily living (survival) skills or indicate how clients are meeting these needs. It is advised that narratives indicate that both problem-solving skills and the skills for self-learning are sufficient for clients to learn on their own, without assistance, after rehabilitation services are finished.

Finally, and most important, evaluation is client-based. Although a counselor or rehabilitation teacher may believe that learning or using a skill is necessary for a particular client, the task or activity must be deemed worthwhile by the client for the client to use successfully the skill in daily life. It is helpful for professionals to remember that all people have skills that, at one time or another, they choose not to use for personal reasons. Not using a particular skill does not make the counselor or rehabilitation teacher less "independent," and the same is true for individuals who are visually impaired. See the case study in the appendix to this chapter for an example of rehabilitation services provided for a client who is legally blind from proliferative diabetic retinopathy.

Teamwork: Counselor and Teacher

The counselor and rehabilitation teacher have a number of similar and complementary skills, but for maximum benefit, they need to understand each other (Ponchillia & Ponchillia, 1996). For example, the counselor is encouraged to know the rehabilitation teacher's skills, teaching sequences, and use of community resources. One easy way to initiate communication and begin acquiring this information is for the counselor to ask the rehabilitation teacher how rehabilitation teaching services should be described to potential clients. Counselors may also wish to review the case files of mutual clients and follow lesson progress reports or ask to review the rehabilitation teacher's individual client progress notes. Counselors can learn about other local resources by inquiring about the community resources frequently used by the rehabilitation teacher. Counselors are advised to ask rehabilitation teachers for signs and indications of the need for specific rehabilitation teaching to consider while in the client's setting. For example, rehabilitation counselors (who travel to clients' homes) may observe conditions in a client's household that indicate the need for specific rehabilitation teaching services—such as open containers of food, which suggest a need for labeling and organizational skills, or mismatched or soiled clothing, which indicates a need for laundry and clothing care skills. Counselors may find that such general books as *Whatever Works* (Paskin & Moloney-Soucy, 1994) and *Creative Recreation for Blind and Visually Impaired Adults* (Ludwig, Luxton & Attmore, 1988) can be handy resources with helpful hints for use when interviewing clients and families.

ORIENTATION AND MOBILITY

Orientation and mobility (O&M) consists of a collection of skills and abilities that people use when they traverse through an environment and maintain their awareness of relationship of themselves and of places within that environment. Welsh and Blasch (1980) defined O&M as "the ability to move independently, safely, and purposefully through the environment . . . a skill of primary importance in the development of each individual" (p. 1). Visual impairment often limits this ability. Workers may have the necessary experience to perform a job, but if they are not able to travel to work or move around the job site in a safe and efficient manner, their ability to obtain or maintain employment is severely limited. It is the task of the O&M instructor to provide training to develop or adapt skills for travel. Instruction in O&M consists of the techniques that are used to develop a person's skills in environmental awareness and travel (Hill & Ponder, 1976). The skills and abilities used in O&M consist of a complex set of perceptual and cognitive processes. Both orientation skills and mobility skills are used simultaneously during travel.

For the sighted person, environmental information can be obtained from visual cues, with the path of travel guided by the arrangement of traffic lights, sidewalks, buildings, and street signs. Environmental information is also available through auditory, tactile, and kinesthetic cues. A skilled traveler with a visual impairment can listen at an intersection, interpret traffic patterns, and determine the safest time to cross the street. The touch of the foot or cane on cement or grass line edge gives information about the path of the sidewalk down the block. The slope of a driveway and smell of gas and exhaust gives information about the location of a gas station. A telescope may allow a person who is visually impaired to read a street sign. However, the information provided by these cues must be carefully collected and interpreted. Auditory, tactile, olfactory, and kinesthetic information about the environment is not usually as instantly accessible and comprehensive as visual information.

The pedestrian with a visual impairment must learn to collect sensory information, one piece at a time, compare it with previous experiences, and make decisions regarding the route to travel. The skills involved in collecting the sensory information and extrapolating that information into a usable form are the most important focus of orientation training.

Mobility, "the ability to move within one's environment" (Hill & Ponder, 1976, p. 115), enables the person who is visually impaired the freedom to travel independently without concern for safety. A reasonable fear is caused by the inability of pedestrians to see the upcoming curb or stairs, a tricycle on the sidewalk, or a light pole. Mobility training for people with visual impairments provides a means for locating objects or people in the line of travel before accidents happen. The common mobility tools include the sighted guide, long cane, dog guide, and electronic travel

O&M instructors teach clients who are blind or visually impaired outdoor mobility skills for safe and independent travel.

aids (ETA). The instructor provides training in the use of the appropriate mobility devices so that safety and efficiency of walking are maintained. The extent of instruction is based on the individual safe mobility practices and effective orientation skills. Although changes in the demographics related to visual impairment have necessitated adaptations of old techniques and the development of new instructional procedures, much of what is considered the practice of O&M remains the same as when it was first developed in the mid-twentieth century.

Historical Overview

Although the use of a cane for mobility was chronicled in the 18th century, in the United States, the first formal instruction of O&M was begun at The Seeing Eye, Inc., in 1929. This program also incorporated the use of dog guides for safe mobility. No other mobility device was taught in a structured manner until World War II. Among the casualties of the war were large numbers of veterans who had been blinded and in response to these veterans' need for "foot travel," a group of techniques involving the use of a long cane was developed by Richard Hoover and his colleagues at Valley Forge Army Hospital. These techniques were adopted by veterans' hospitals across the United States, with Hines Veterans' Hospital becoming the recognized leader in training (Bledsoe, 1980).

As the 1950s progressed, educators and rehabilitation specialists outside the Veterans' Administration made requests for access to the mobility techniques. In 1958, the Office of Vocational Rehabilitation established the training of O&M specialists as a high priority in order to provide greater access to training for all people with visual impairments (Wiener & Welsh, 1980). In 1960, the first university degree program in peripatology was begun at Boston College and by 1961, the second program in O&M at Western Michigan University was accepting students. The actual number of programs in the United States has varied over the years with an average of ten university programs in O&M across the country at any time.

As the college level mobility training programs produced graduates and more service providers began to enter the field, professionalization of O&M progressed. To assure "the type of accountability and standardization needed in view of the continuing expansion of the field" (Wiener & Welsh, 1980, p. 638), a certification process was begun by the AAWB in 1968. With some modifications, the certification process is currently administered by AER, Division 9 (O&M). Because certification is not legally required to practice, O&M specialists are now seeking state licensure as a means of ensuring service quality (Hill, Hill, & LeBous, 1994).

Another development in the profession is the supervised training and use of mobility assistants (OMAs) to address the critical shortage of O&M specialists (Jones, 1993; Uslan, Hill, & Peck, 1989;

Wiener & Bussen, 1988; Wiener & Joffee, 1993; Wiener & Uslan, 1990). OMAs are paraprofessionals who have been taught the basic skills of O&M so that they may support and provide practice to clients. Specifically, OMAs can instruct clients in the use of sighted guides, as well as monitoring and supporting skill development in the areas of protective techniques, indoor diagonal cane technique, and basic concepts and sensory skills (Wiener & Hill, 1991). OMAs are instructed by certified O&M specialists who are also trained to be OMA trainer supervisors. The education and certification programs for OMAs are under the auspices of AER, Division 9, O&M and AER's Continuing Education Program.

The practice of O&M has changed over the last 30 years specifically as it relates to specialized groups within the population of people who are visually impaired. The largest segment of people with visual impairments are those individuals over the age of 65. Although no O&M preparation programs are designed to train professionals to specifically work with this group, courses in geriatrics are becoming more common in O&M program curricula. A major issue in the provision of services to older individuals with visual impairments is the lack of accessibility of O&M resulting from the inadequate funding of seniors' programs. Some professional training programs are also oriented toward preparing O&M specialists to address the unique needs of children with visual impairments. In fact, almost 50 percent of all O&M specialists are employed within the special education system (Beliveau-Tobey & De l'Aune, 1990).

When O&M techniques were first developed, they were designed to be used with people who were totally blind. Up-to-date estimates of caseload distribution, however, indicate that about 60 percent of clients have some usable remaining vision (Beliveau-Tobey & De l'Aune, 1990). New teaching procedures are needed for clients who are visually impaired but not totally blind, but only some progress has been made in this area (Dodds & Davis, 1989).

O&M techniques have also been found to be useful for persons with disabilities other than visual impairment (Hirschkatz, 1990; Laus, 1977). Approximately 50 percent of clients being served by O&M instructors have at least one additional impairment (Beliveau-Tobey & De l'Aune, 1990). The type of additional disability (i.e., physical, mental, or emotional) and accompanying functional limitations determines the degree to which the O&M process is influenced by the secondary disability (Courtney & Halton, 1993; Uslan, Russell, & Wiener, 1988). Although these and other issues and trends within the field need to be addressed fully, the development of the profession of O&M within the short span of 30 years has been rather remarkable.

MAJOR MOBILITY SYSTEMS AND CURRICULUM AREAS

To understand the roles and functions of O&M specialists, it is important to be aware of the formal mobility skills for travel and techniques of orientation used by individuals who are visually impaired. The four major mobility systems for people with visual impairments are (1) the sighted or human guide, (2) the long cane, (3) ETAs, and (4) the dog guide. With the exception of the dog guide, the O&M specialist is responsible for instruction in the use of these systems. "These systems are not mutually exclusive, as many blind travelers use more than one system or a combination of them. In some instances, low vision devices may also be considered a system of mobility" (Hill, 1986, p. 316).

Formal mobility skills are taught to clients on a one-to-one basis progressing from simple to complex environments as clients become familiar with new techniques and more confident in their own travel abilities. Orientation skills are taught in conjunction with mobility skills so that the client can travel safely and be aware of his or her position and travel path simultaneously.

Knowledge of body image, laterality, and basic positional and environmental concepts are needed for effective training of formal mobility skills. Clients who have problems discriminating left from right will find it difficult to learn cardinal directions. For example, knowing the location and position of the hand and arm are critical to understanding cane position. Some clients who lack this knowledge can be instructed in these basic areas either before or during mobility instruction. The evaluation of basic concepts usually occurs during the initial phases of training. The O&M instructor provides specific lessons to address the concepts and then incorporates their use into travel activities. The following discussions provide an overview of sighted guide and other formal mobility techniques. [For more in-depth information refer to Hill and Ponder (1976), Tooze (1980), and Jacobson (1993).]

Sighted Guide Technique

Sighted guide procedures are usually taught first because they provide an efficient, safe, and quick means of travel. They also encourage movement and provide a means of safe mobility to clients who have been inactive. Sighted guide techniques have been defined as "a cluster of techniques in which a sighted individual physically guides the individual with a visual impairment through the environment. The basic sighted guide techniques include traveling through doorways and narrow passages, traversing up and down stairs, and seating" (Zimmerman, 1992, p. 67). Although the sighted guide procedures involve a number of techniques, knowledge of the basic sighted guide position is critical to all procedures. This all-important position requires that the person being guided walk one step behind and beside the guide, gripping the guide's arm just above the elbow with the thumb on the inside and the fingers on the outside of the guide's arm. This position serves two major functions. First, it allows the guide to approach obstacles first and stop or move around or over them gracefully without pushing or pulling the person with visual impairment. Second, the arm and hand position provides information to the person being guided about the path of travel (e.g., slopes, steps, lateral movement) without verbal cues. People experienced in the use of sighted guides can walk together with the guide and carry on normal conversation while all cues for travel are provided through body and arm movement. Additional sighted guide procedures provide techniques for maneuvering through narrow areas and doors, going up and down stairs, as well as accepting and refusing assistance.

As the instruction of sighted guide skills progresses, the client is taught knowledge of cardinal directions and use of sensory cues. At the end of the sighted guide instruction, clients should be able to use all procedures safely and efficiently and be aware of the path being traveled. It is recommended that the client not be passively led around the environment but be actively involved in the travel process. Rehabilitation counselors are advised to be able to perform as skilled sighted guides. Practice in the sighted guide procedures, under the supervision of an O&M instructor, is also highly recommended.

Protective Techniques

Clients are taught protective techniques during the early phases of training. These techniques (i.e., upper hand and forearm and lower hand and forearm) utilize cross-body arm and hand position to provide protection from objects extending from walls, objects at head height, or objects at waist height. Protective techniques do not afford advance contact with such terrain changes as curbs or stairs so it is required that the client be aware of the presence of these other, lower obstacles. For the most part, protective techniques are used only in familiar surroundings. Procedures for trailing a parallel surface to locate an object or to gain a line of travel are also taught.

The instruction of protective techniques provides the first opportunity for independent travel during the O&M training sequence. Orientation skills used during sighted guide instruction (i.e., cardinal directions, sensory cues, and awareness of path of travel) are emphasized and refined. Clients are taught skills for self-familiarization of indoor environments that can be applied to outdoor settings as the O&M sequence progresses.

Cane Skills

The use of a cane as a probe or extension of the arm for ascertaining objects in the path of travel is a common method for travel by people with visual impairments. The use of the long cane was instituted during World War II as a part of the group of techniques developed by Dr. Hoover. The term "long cane" is derived from the length of the cane, which is prescribed individually for each client based on height, reaction time, and length of stride. Prior to World War II, canes were usually short (about the size of a regular walking cane) and were used mostly for identification (Hill, 1986). Both long and short canes, they were usually white with a red tip. White canes are also an international symbol for pedestrians with visual impairments.

It is required that the length of the cane be matched with the needs, ability, and personal style of each individual. Although the height of the traveler, his or her length of stride, and the individual's hand position in holding the cane are generally considered in prescribing the length of a cane, individual needs vary. For example, a frail, older individual may prefer a shorter cane to preview the surface, because even stepping on an uneven sidewalk could cause injury (LaGrow, 1996). Some individuals may prefer longer canes, because they afford greater protection, allow a greater reaction time, and allow for a more comfortable arm position (Altman, 1996).

The techniques taught for the use of the long cane are based on two primary procedures, the diagonal technique and the touch technique. The diagonal technique provides a means for the cane to be used as a bumper. The cane is held diagonally in front of the body with the arm extended. The diagonal technique is designed for use in familiar environments, because the reaction time provided for changes in depth (e.g., stairs or curbs) is very short.

The touch technique is achieved by holding the cane extended from the midline of the body, with the cane moving from side to side in front of the walking pedestrian. This procedure can be used in any travel situation, because it affords maximum protection and reaction time.

Techniques for use of the long cane while maneuvering up and down stairs, trailing or shore lining a wall, and exploring objects are also taught during this part of O&M training. The client's speed of travel increases and orientation skills are honed so that a larger area is traveled more quickly and more routes are learned.

Outdoor Travel

To this point in the O&M instruction sequence, most skills have been learned and practiced indoors because indoor environments are simpler, more controllable, and provide safe opportunities for the client to concentrate on the development of basic skills. However, independent travel requires maneuvering through such outdoor environments as street crossings, business areas, and the use of public transportation (Svendsen, 1994). As might be expected, special adaptive skills are needed to travel safely through outdoor environments.

As the O&M training continues, the client progresses through increasingly more difficult outdoor environments. Starting instruction in residential neighborhoods, clients learn to travel sidewalks and cross intersections with stop and yield sign control. As skills and confidence increase, intersections with lights, wider streets, gas station crossings, and shopping areas are introduced. Finally, downtown areas with increased pedestrian traffic (including stores and malls) are traveled and public transportation is used. At the termination of O&M training, the client should be able to travel in all areas needed for everyday activity.

Adaptation of Formal O&M Skills

As has been previously noted, people who are visually impaired are not always totally blind and some may have additional impairments. The O&M skills sequence previously described was originally designed for a blind individual who had no other disability. Nevertheless, to provide the most appropriate instruction, it is sometimes necessary to adapt skills to better meet an individual's needs. Many people with visual impairments who are not blind do need O&M instruction; however, the extent and nature of the training will vary greatly. Clients with such multiple disabilities as physical and cognitive disorders, hearing impairments, and behavior disorders, also often need O&M instruction. However, as with those who are visually impaired but are not blind, skills or systems may need to be adapted to meet individual abilities and disabilities (Welsh & Blasch, 1980; Enzina, 1980). For the client with a physical disability, adapted canes or wheelchair techniques may need to be incorporated into training. Clients with cognitive limitations may need to have lessons specifically focused on functional skills in the real environment. Those with hearing or speech impairments may need augmentative communication devices (LaGrow & Mulder, 1989; Wiener, 1980) for street crossings or use of public transportation. Clients with multiple disabilities may also require more time for instruction and goals may need to be designed to meet specific vocational and daily living goals. However, for all clients who want to learn independent skills, O&M is an important part of the process.

Electronic Travel Aids

An electronic travel aid (ETA) is a "device that sends out signals to sense the environment within a certain range or distance, processes the information received, and furnishes the user with certain relevant bits of this information about the immediate environment" (Farmer, 1980, p. 372). ETAs have been and are continuing to be developed in many countries across the world, however, the three devices most commonly used in the United States are (1) the Mowat Sensor, (2) the Sonicguide, and (3) the Laser Cane. The Mowat Sensor and the Sonicguide use sound waves that are transmitted and received by the device to indicate objects within the path of travel. The Mowat Sensor is a handheld apparatus that vibrates when an object is detected. The speed for the vibration changes as the object is approached. The Sonicguide is mounted into an eyeglasses frame with earphones. This device gives information about object distance, direction, and surface characteristics. The Laser Cane uses light waves instead of sound energy and is a long cane with the mechanics mounted in the grip of the cane (Farmer, 1980; Hill & Bradfield, 1984). The Laser Cane features both auditory and tactile feedback systems. Financial support for the purchase of ETAs is generally available through private foundations (Joffee, 1987).

The extent to which ETAs are used may be inferred from a study (Stewart & Zimmerman, 1990) that included a question on six aspects of O&M. To date, no O&M instructors have reported that they offered training in ETAs. This finding supports the contention by Spungin (1985) that despite numerous laboratory attempts to develop ETAs, they have not been readily accepted by consumers. Joffee (1987) stated "electronically assisted travel has been a disappointment to both the consumer and the professional" (p. 389); however, she urged professionals not to overlook the potential of ETAs.

Some individuals who own ETAs have been satisfied, however. Based on telephone interviews with 298 ETA users, Blasch, Long, and Griffin-Shirley (1989) concluded that (1) ETA owners did use their devices for travel, (2) ETAs contributed to more rapid travel and greater obstacle avoidance (i.e., pedestrians and objects in the path of travel), and (3) travel in unfamiliar environments was enhanced.

ETAs have also been used by individuals who are unable to use a long cane, and as secondary travel tools by individuals with partial vision. Joffee (1990) described one individual who needed a support cane and was unable to effectively use both a support cane and long cane. By using a support cane with an ETA, the individual was able to travel independently much sooner.

Mobility instructors receive special training in the use of these devices before they are qualified to instruct clients. Continuing education courses have been offered at different sites around the country and vary in length from a few days to several weeks, depending on the number of devices taught. O&M specialists can apply for certification for Sonicguide and the Laser Cane through AER, Division 9, after they have completed approved courses.

Dog Guides

Dog guides were first used in the 18th century; however, formalized O&M training began in Germany toward the end of World War I, and 1929 marked the advent of dog guide training in the United States. There are now a number of dog guide schools around the country. Estimates of the number of people using dog guides range from 7,250 to 10,000, compared with 109,000 noninstitutionalized individuals who use the white or long cane (*Demographics Update,* 1994a, 1994b, 1995b).

In most cases, dog guide schools prefer that clients have had long cane training prior to entering the program. The cost of the dog guide program to the client is small, but that price varies from school to school. Clients travel to the school for a period of approximately one month (for the first dog) and receive their animal during the first week of residency. The following three weeks are spent learning commands, mobility techniques, and praise and correction procedures. As Lambert (1990) states, the 28-day residency serves two main purposes, which are as follows:

> [(a)] adequate time for initiating the important bonding between the student and the new dog, and (b) time to establish the difficult body language communication between student and dog. Communication initiated by the dog—its manner or direction of gait and body position—is conveyed through the guide harness and leash. Communication initiated by the . . . person [who is blind]—the desired pace or direction—reaches the dog through the harness and leash. (p. 155)

Dog guides were originally recommended only for individuals with very limited vision and no additional disabilities. However, several schools are now training individuals with visual impairments and multiple disabilities. The use of a dog guide, however, is not solely based on the preference of the visually impaired individual. Lambert (1990) noted that dog guide training centers scrutinize the individual's health, stamina, personal reliability, financial ability to care for the dog, and mobility skills.

Lambert (1990) identified a number of psychosocial issues associated with the use of dog guides and dog guide training centers that should be considered by rehabilitation counselors and O&M specialists. These are as follows:

1. The use of a dog guide draws attention to the impairment. Therefore, some individuals might not consider the use of a dog guide, even if they are fond of dogs. "Even a genuine dog lover might resent bitterly being an incompetent human who must entrust his or her safety to a 'mere canine'" (p. 153).
2. The use of a dog guide necessitates spending time away from home, whenever the dog needs to be replaced, to maintain mobility. This can create feelings of unfairness, when individuals with visual impairments compare themselves to sighted individuals.
3. Individuals who are visually impaired may feel anxious about or resent the "pass/fail" testing atmosphere of the dog guide training center. Moreover, failing the dog guide training program means returning home without a dog, after sacrificing both time and money to attend the program.
4. Dog guide training programs are similar to attending a summer camp, which can be demeaning for adults, who are not

used to the rules and regimentation (e.g., the inability to leave the training grounds without permission, the inability to freely invite a friend to visit). Other psychological problems related to the training programs include "risks of home sickness, fatigue-induced irritability, trouble getting along with roommates, and problems arising from the formation of social cliques. . . . anxiety over the management of their homes in their absence or about their jobs and boredom" (p. 155).

5. Individuals may hold unrealistically high expectations about the results of working with a dog guide, which can increase the level of frustration in working with a dog. Alternatively, if a new dog is replacing a dog who has died or been retired, working with a new puppy can be a bittersweet event and trigger emotional memories about the individual's previous dog.
6. The transition from training center to home can also create uncertainty and anxiety in the client. "Communication, rhythm, and confidence with which the dog-handler team left the training center is disrupted initially by the novelty of the home environment" (p. 156). Also puppies may handle new freedom at home by chewing and getting into things. The result can be "a frustrated and scared new dog owner who may risk ruining some good teamwork" and "hostility toward the new dog can possibly develop" (p. 157).

Advantages of dog guides that have been noted by Hill (1986) include the following: a dog will (1) circumnavigate obstacles, (2) disobey its master if necessary, and (3) walk at a good clip (i.e., three to four miles per hour). A dog guide also allows its user to focus on orientation issues rather than worrying about personal well-being. A dog guide may also ease social interactions. Some of the negatives associated with using a dog guide include: a dog is a large responsibility, dogs are not welcome in all environments, and a dog may travel too quickly for some elderly or physically impaired individuals. Also, the dog is occasionally the recipient of more attention than its owner. Finally, a dog is not able to communicate to its master certain environmental cues, such as intersecting sidewalks.

The recommendation for dog guides should be made only after consulting the client and providing an initial O&M evaluation. Although dog guides can be very effective for individuals with visual impairments, they will need information on the benefits and limitations associated with dog guide use. Some dog guide schools will provide an on-site evaluation, which can be useful in assisting a client in determining whether the dog guide is the best system of travel. Also, because dog guide centers generally do not have staff to assist individuals in addressing the psychological problems they may encounter (Lambert, 1990), rehabilitation counselors and O&M specialists need to be sensitive to the questions and problems that clients may experience before, during, or after acquiring a dog guide.

Roles and Functions of O&M Instructors

The roles and functions of the orientation and mobility specialist have been outlined in two studies (i.e., Beliveau-Tobey & De l'Aune, 1990; Uslan, Hill, & Peck, 1989). According to these studies, the major function of the O&M specialist is to provide instruction in specific O&M skills to individuals with visual impairments. Assessment of individuals who are visually impaired, in addition to training for follow-up with low vision devices, is also considered a priority in work activity. Case management, including working within the interdisciplinary team, writing reports, and scheduling, is the third most highly ranked job task (Beliveau-Tobey & De l'Aune, 1990).

O&M instructors function in several settings within the rehabilitation system. Rehabilitation centers will often have instructors on their staffs and clients will be scheduled for O&M as a part of their daily program. O&M instructors in centers have the advantage of the ability to access clients on a daily basis. A disadvantage of this approach is that centers are often located in sites some distance from the client's home or work area and the skills being taught and developed in areas are not necessarily those being used on a daily basis. It is important to remember that some clients have difficulty adapting skills to new environments or learning orientation to a new area on their own, which further highlights the disadvantages to learning O&M skills at a site far from the client's home or workplace.

Other mobility specialists work on an itinerant basis. They see clients in their home areas and usually work in proximity when appropriate training areas are available. This is an advantage to some clients because they can learn and practice skills in the area in which they regularly travel. A disadvantage, however, is that itinerant instructors may not be able to schedule the client more than once a week because of distances between clients and caseload demands.

When determining the type of O&M program that is appropriate for a client, the counselor must evaluate the client's needs and availability of services (i.e., center-based and itinerant). It may be appropriate to refer the client for an O&M evaluation to help determine the best model for service. When clients are referred to an O&M specialist for an initial evaluation, the instructor determines the goals, the present level of skill, and recommendations for training. The amount of hours estimated for training is also often included. It is helpful to remember that the amount of time required for O&M instruction will vary with each client, based on individual abilities and goals. For some clients, the entire mobility sequence, which has been previously described, will be appropriate. However, individual goals for independent travel will vary and clients may choose to learn only a part of the sequence.

A typical O&M evaluation for an adult client will encompass a number of aspects of travel abilities. Before beginning the assessment, the O&M specialist will establish with the client goals for O&M training. These goals will provide guidance for the extent of the assessment. Sensory abilities, including vision, audition, and proprioception will be evaluated. The client will be assessed for the present level of skill in the mobility techniques of sighted guide, protective techniques, and cane skills. When appropriate for the client's goals, these techniques will be evaluated in various environments including indoor, residential, semibusiness, and business areas. Orientation skills will also be assessed. If needed, knowledge of body image and basic concepts (i.e., environmental, directional, and positional) will also be addressed. The O&M instructor will test the client's ability to understand the relation of objects and landmarks to each other in the environment, to update that relational knowledge while walking, and to use generalizing systems (e.g., numbering systems) to predict patterns for travel (Rieser, Guth & Hill, 1982). The amount of time needed for the assessment will vary with clients and their goals; however, six to twelve hours can be considered a reasonable range. After travel skills have been evaluated, the O&M instructor will estimate how many hours of instruction will be needed for clients to meet their goals.

Clients with multiple disabilities may require more time to master skills and may need instruction oriented toward specific routes or areas. Functionally based programs that incorporate O&M skills into daily activities are often necessary, and it is reasonable to expect the O&M instructor to confer with physical and occupational therapists for assistance with individuals with physical, cognitive, or dual sensory impairments.

ASSISTIVE TECHNOLOGY AND ASSISTIVE TECHNOLOGY SPECIALISTS

When an individual has a significant visual impairment, one of the dominant effects is the elimination, reduction, or distortion of reliable sensory input from the visual sense. To compensate for the visual impairment or distortion, people use either input through another sense or an enhancement of the visual sense. A number of devices help individuals compensate for the loss of vision or a visual impairment. In the past, these devices tended to be called aids and appliances or sensory aids, but they are now referred to as assistive technology devices. The Technology-Related Assistance for Individuals with Disabilities Act of 1988 (Tech Act) defines an assistive technology device as any item, piece of equipment, or product system (whether acquired commercially off the shelf, modified, or customized) that is used to increase, maintain, or improve the functional capabilities of individuals who are disabled. For individuals who are visually impaired, such devices provide alternative sensory input or enhance existing visual input. Devices can be fairly simple or may include speech, braille, and large-print devices that enable a person who is visually impaired to use a personal computer and software programs. Members of the rehabilitation team have traditionally recommended some assistive technology devices, such as bold-lined paper, tactile markers, braille watches, low vision devices, and white canes. However, developments in computer assistive technology require the expertise and services of a professional who not only understands computer systems and programs, but also is knowledgeable about the array of devices developed specifically for computer users who are blind or visually impaired. Changes in technology, such as those involving the use of visual or graphical computer interfaces, can present new challenges to people who are visually impaired. Until 1988, the rehabilitation counselor or teacher was responsible for keeping up with new assistive technology, but the 1988 landmark legislation provided funding for centers that would develop and implement programs to assist in selecting the appropriate assistive device for each person with a disability.

The Technology-Related Assistance for Individuals with Disabilities Act

The Technology-Related Assistance for Individuals with Disabilities Act (P.L. 100–407), commonly known as the Tech Act, was signed into law by President Ronald Reagan on August 19, 1988. The law provides funding for consumer-responsive information and training programs and services designed to meet the needs of individuals who require assistive technology (AT) services. AT services are defined as any services that directly assist an individual who is disabled in the selection, acquisition, or use of an assistive device.

In March 1994, President William J. Clinton signed amendments to the Tech Act (P.L. 103–218), which not only authorized funding to Tech Act Project Centers through 1999, but also strengthened and expanded the original act by emphasizing advocacy and a change to existing delivery systems. The six mandated activities included in the legislation are as follows:

1. To develop and monitor policies and procedures that will improve access to and funding for AT devices and services.
2. To develop and implement strategies to overcome funding barriers, with particular emphasis on overcoming barriers for underrepresented and rural populations.
3. To coordinate activities among state agencies to increase access to, provision of, and funding for assistive technology devices and services.
4. To empower individuals who have disabilities to successfully advocate for increased access to and funding for assistive technology, as well as to increase their participation in, choice of, and control in the selection and procurement of assistive technology devices and services.
5. To provide outreach to underrepresented and rural populations by identifying and assessing their needs, and increasing the accessibility of services and training.
6. To develop and implement strategies to ensure timely acquisition and delivery of

assistive technology devices and services, with a special emphasis on the needs of children.

Assistive Technology Specialists

As states have been awarded grants to implement the Tech Act, the profession of assistive technology has developed. Because this profession includes individuals from a variety of specialties, as well as agency-trained and self-trained individuals with an interest in the area, establishing training procedures and job standards has been a challenge. The Rehabilitation Engineering and Assistive Technology Society of North America (RESNA) is an interdisciplinary association of people with a common interest in technology and disability that has undertaken the certification and professional development of assistive technology specialists (RESNA homepage, http://www.ari.net/resna/Certify/cib_2nd.htm).

RESNA offers certification in three areas to individuals who pass a testing and evaluation procedure. As defined by RESNA, the Assistive Technology Certification is for service providers involved in the analysis of consumer needs and training in the use of particular devices. The Assistive Technology Supplier certification is reserved for providers involved in the sale and service of commercially available devices. The Rehabilitation Engineer certification requires completion of the Assistive Technology Practitioner exam, as well as educational credentials and engineering expertise (RESNA homepage http://www.resna.org). Rehabilitation engineers are trained to solve complex problems systematically through their knowledge of physics, mechanics, physiology, electronics, materials, design, fabrication, and disabilities. However, the area of visual impairment places less emphasis on the services of rehabilitation engineers and more on those of computer access technology specialists. For the most part, specialists in assistive technology for persons who are blind or visually impaired have not participated thus far in the RESNA certification program, but the desire to ensure that quality services and consumer satisfaction are moving the field in the direction of a separate certification program or more involvement with RESNA.

People with Visual Impairments and Computers

Throughout the world, computer technology is used in an increasing number of occupational categories. From automated teller machines to the Internet, computerized services are part of daily life, but the gap between those who have access to computers and those who do not is widening. For people who are blind or visually impaired to keep pace with the changing labor market and to be fully included in society, they need access to computer technology. In 1995, an Ohio study, based on statistics collected several years before, reported that approximately 900,000 visually impaired individuals between the ages of 21 and 64 who were employed used personal computers at their jobs (*Demographics Update*, 1995a). If the individuals who use computers in nonemployment settings (such as educational settings) are added, the number of visually impaired people using personal computers will likely reach more than 1.2 million (Maxson, 1996).

Computer systems, whose function is the manipulation of data, are used to input, process, store, and output information in a variety of ways. The person who is visually impaired needs to access that information, usually viewed on the monitor or in a printed format, in an alternative format, such as large print, speech, or braille. This requires the use of special hardware and software programs that convert printed or graphic files into a format that is accessible for the computer user who is visually impaired.

This technology has been available for a number of years. The advent of optical character recognition (OCR) made it possible to convert printed text into a computer file. OCR uses a scanner, which is a hardware device that reads printed material as an ASCII file, which recognition software converts to a readable text file. For the user who is visually impaired, an assistive technology device then converts the information into large print, speech, or braille. Large-print systems translate text or graphic images into variably sized displays that can be manipulated by the user to meet specific visual demands. Synthetic speech systems use a hardware device known as a speech synthesizer and a software program called a screen reader. Translation software is also used to convert text files into braille code. Another device then takes the code and makes it readable either as a hard braille copy or as a refreshable braille display. A hard braille copy appears on paper; refreshable braille appears on a special device that displays a series of electronic braille cells with small pins that raise to form different braille characters. It is called refreshable because, as with a calculator display, the characters can change as directed by the user.

Because the basic OCR process is very popular and has many applications, prices have come down and improvements in quality and accuracy have been made. This technology is used to read bar codes in grocery stores and translate the data into pricing and sales information. With a computer-based OCR system, scanned information can be stored for later retrieval and manipulation. The development of OCR technology has been a great benefit to persons who are visually impaired because previously unavailable text materials are now accessible to them.

However, the assistive technology necessary to convert graphic materials into alternative, accessible formats has not developed as rapidly as the forms just described. Although OCR systems can convert graphic images into computer-accessible files, the technology to make them readily available to individuals using braille or speech output is still being developed. In most cases, large-print graphic images are accessible to the visually impaired user, although particularly detailed images, when enlarged, many only appear on the monitor in small sections.

The scope and range of sophistication of computer access devices are immense, and finding the most appropriate device can have a significant impact on the vocational success of the individual. For individuals with additional disabilities, a number of assistive technology devices may improve computer access. There are, for example, a variety of keyboard alternatives for people with manual dexterity difficulties. These alternatives include touch-sensitive keyboards, mouse entry systems, systems that respond to gaze- or breath-operated input, those designed for use with one hand only, and those designed specifically for individuals with limited upper mobility (e.g., quadriplegia) and cognitive impairments. If alternative keyboards cannot be used, voice recognition technology is a viable and reliable input alternative for those individuals with consistent speech patterns.

Voice recognition input systems are often composed of two components that are installed in a PC. The first component is a microphone that is connected to a sound card in the computer for data entry, and the second component is the voice recognition software. This software is loaded into the computer memory, and from that point, data received from the microphone is evaluated, translated, and displayed on the computer monitor. Depending upon the client's visual diagnosis and acuities, speech, braille, or large-print output can then be used to access the information.

Computer Access Technology

The development of popular graphic user interface (GUI) systems, such as Windows, appear to present difficulties for screen reader programs. The Windows operating system, for example, uses complex graphic images which do not convert easily to files that can be read with a screen reader. Progress is being made, but a gap is widening between the speed of access for blind versus sighted computer users. Screen reader developers are challenged to keep up with the changing software demands.

The creators of Windows continue to introduce updates and revisions, and they are exploring ways to make the programs more accessible to individuals with disabilities. The popularity of Windows is based on the quick, easy-to-understand menus and information boxes that execute commands by the click of the mouse on a small image or icon. This procedure requires that the user place the mouse in a precise location, which can be difficult for someone who is visually impaired. Assistive technology has been developed to allow the speech system user to access and process the information without a mouse by using keyboard commands.

Similarly, the Internet, which has become a tremendously convenient source of information, presents accessibility problems to people who are visually impaired. Many websites contain graphically based programming codes and may include a number of inaccessible components, such as image maps, frames, tables, and an animated programming language called JAVA, which is not easily accessible to individuals using programs designed for people who are visually impaired. Designers of websites can make the information accessible to visually impaired users by including descriptors, called alternative tags (alt tags), that provide a short description of an image for individuals using text-based systems. Some websites have text-based alternatives that allow access to individuals using speech or other text-based systems. However, the development of easy-to-use Web page publishing software has made it possible for almost anyone to design a website or homepage. Without universally accepted standards for access to web pages, accessibility for persons with disabilities has become a controversial issue. Website developers and assistive technology specialists are both addressing the issue, so that individuals with visual impairments can take advantage of the information and services that the Internet provides.

Speech Systems

All speech systems have two parts—the first is the speech software, often called a screen reader, and the second is a speech synthesizer. Screen readers are used in conjunction with popular commercial software. In essence, the computer runs two programs at the same time. The speech software allows the person to use commercial software. With extra keystrokes (commands) the person can read a character, word, sentence, or paragraph. If a commercial software program, for example, a spelling checker, highlights a misspelled word, the speech software must be able to inform the user automatically or allow the user to identify the misspelled word with a simple command. The speech program, which includes all of the phonemes and grammatical rules of a language, intercepts the information going to the monitor and translates it into speech (Galvin & Scherer, 1996).

Speech synthesizers are hardware devices that convert text into speech output, as instructed by the screen reader. The speech synthesizer is either a card installed inside the computer or an external box attached to one of the computer's parts. Some internal synthesizers have built-in speakers, whereas others use an external speaker for output. The increasingly compact size of external synthesizers can be an asset for individuals who wish to use a variety of different computer stations, because it can be easily unplugged and moved. For example, one company manufactures an external speech synthesizer that weighs only one pound, requires no special cables, and has rechargeable batteries (*Demographics Update,* 1995a). These battery-operated external speech synthesizers are primarily designed for use with portable computers.

A number of issues should be considered in selecting an appropriate speech synthesizer. The more expensive synthesizers that have human quality speech are especially useful for some clients who have both visual and hearing impairments. Some of the inexpensive units have a quality of speech that sounds more robotic than human, and the robotic sound may be more easily understood by the user at higher reading speeds. Some synthesizers are made to work with certain computer systems, while others may have large buffers that make it difficult to stop the output at a precise instant. In addition, multimedia systems, which include CD-ROM readers and sound systems, may interfere with the function of the speech synthesizer. Efforts are currently in

Computers with speech programs and synthesizers can be essential resources for individuals with visual impairments.

development to allow speech to work through some of these built-in sound systems. Given the various options, it is therefore very important to identify the type of basic computer system the person will be using, and the specific computer needs of the individual when selecting the most appropriate speech system.

Large-Print Systems

Individuals with residual vision can access printed materials and monitors in a number of ways. Depending upon the person's visual acuity, the solution can be very simple. A larger monitor may be purchased to make the work station accessible. External magnifiers that attach to the outside of the monitor, low vision devices belonging to the client (i.e., eyeglasses or hand-held systems), and electronic print magnification may provide sufficient magnification. Some programs, especially word processors and some Internet browsers, allow changes in font sizes within the program itself. There are also large-print systems, both software and hardware, which allow variation in the size of text and graphics on the monitor or from the printer. For example, Uslan and Shragai (1995) described various types of screen magnification software available for PCs, which can be used with a variety of commercial software packages. When deciding on an enlargement print system, the considerations to be made include (1) what tasks need to be performed, (2) the environment in which it will be used (e.g., lighting and glare), (3) how much the client will be using the system and how much of a factor eye strain is, (4) whether color access is important, (5) whether speed is a consideration, (6) the amount of space available in the work area, (7) whether the client is accessing a single or multiple computers, (8) whether others are using the same system, (9) whether a mouse will be used or whether it is better for the client to control the large print functions from the keyboard, (10) how large the print must be to be useful, (11) the stability of the client's vision, and (12) if the client needs access to both computer information and print at the same time.

Tactile or Braille Systems

For some situations, clients will need computer information printed in braille either on paper (hard copy) or in a refreshable braille display. For those needing hard copy braille, there are a number of braille printers and embossers on the market that vary in speed, price, and function. Some of the functions that should be considered are the ability to print graphic displays, print material sideways, print on both sides of the paper (interpoint braille), print six- and eight-dot braille (e.g., the number of dots in the braille cell), and the capacity to print jumbo braille. The choice of these functions depends on the needs of the individual client and cost considerations because braille embossers are rather expensive as is the ongoing cost of braille paper.

The reliability of the design and availability of service can also be a consideration. Braille embossers are generally divided into high-speed production embossers for printing large quan-

Refreshable braille displays, used in conjunction with computers, contain a series of pins that are arranged in six-holed cells (corresponding to the dots of the braille cell) and can be read tactilely when they are raised.

tities of braille, and moderately priced non-production systems. Both types require a special braille translation software system to translate the computer text file into a contracted braille form. Depending on the system and the function, the translation process can be fairly simple or may require an extensive knowledge of braille.

When considering a purchase of this type, the counselor is advised that braille embossers can be extremely noisy and may not be appropriate without some modifications or sound covers in certain settings. Braille embossers also require heavy weight paper. The individual using the braille embosser can reduce maintenance and repair costs by regularly cleaning and lubricating the unit. For these reasons, as well as storage considerations, some individuals prefer the refreshable or soft braille computer output. These systems do not use braille paper but display the computer information electronically. The displays come in a variety of lengths. Each cell may have the six- or eight-dot design, and each cell has movable pins that change to indicate the character that is being sent to the display. Although the displays are usually static, an advance key changes the display output at the user's chosen reading speed. This can allow for reading speeds which can exceed 100 words per minute. There are several manufacturers and distributors of refreshable braille devices with different features. The counselor needs to weigh the expense of such devices against the utility and speed the user can hope to achieve.

Portable Notebook Systems

Portable notebook systems are computers specifically designed for users with visual impairments. Most of these units are lightweight and small enough to fit into a briefcase or purse. The keyboard most frequently used is a braille design with one key for each of the braille dots. Most systems are designed for 6-dot braille entry. There are also other keys for performing such various functions as space, backspace, and carriage return. A knowledge of braille is essential for operating these devices. For individuals with excellent braille skills, the standard computer keyboard may be a hindrance, but with appropriate software and cables, most of these devices can also be used as a braille keyboard for entering data into a personal computer. For non-braille users, portable notebook systems that utilize the standard keyboard configuration for input are available. All units can be battery operated, and the time between charges varies. These systems also vary in data storage and system reliability. The main purpose of these units is to perform word processing functions such as creating, editing, and deleting text files. Other optional features include a clock and calendar, a calculator, small data management programs, such as an address book, and a stopwatch. Portable electronic notebooks have two output modes, which are speech and refreshable braille. There is also a port to transfer information to and from a personal computer. The auditory output devices also have an earphone jack for private listening. These devices have a number of advantages over standard desktop systems with portability and low cost being the two major assets.

Other Computer or Electronic Systems

A number of other systems are available to assist people with visual impairments. Some, although still in use, are being phased out. These include a portable system that converts printed text to tactile representations of letters on the finger and stand-alone braille computer terminals. New systems under development include electronic dictionaries with speech capabilities; compact disks (CDs) with encyclopedias, Bibles, and dictionaries on them; electronic travel aids (ETAs); and small, hand-held, portable CCTV systems that magnify print.

Counselor Considerations

Technology is an important consideration in the development of a rehabilitation plan with a client. Attending to the individual needs of the client in the area of technology involves melding the client's skills and preferences, the specific demands of a job or task, the availability of equipment at the job site and the selection of appropriate assistive technology from the plethora of both specialized and popular commercial technology and computer access technology.

In many instances, assistive technology specialists help the rehabilitation counselors develop the technology needs for rehabilitation plans. However, the counselor and the client are responsible for determining if the plan is feasible in terms of needs, abilities, and financial considerations. An assistive technology specialist may work on a Tech Act Project, be employed within a rehabilitation agency, or provide assistive technology evaluation and training on a consultant or contractual basis. The specialist provides a written report to the counselor that contains assessment results and recommendations. The usefulness of the reports depends on the completeness of the information the counselor provided to the assistive technology specialist at the time of referral and the specialist's familiarity with the area of blindness and visual impairment. A number of considerations need to be included in developing the rehabilitation plan, including assessment of client skills, evaluation of the work environment, and the availability of financial resources and training opportunities.

Client Skills

If a computer access system is being considered for a client, the following general criteria should be included for most career areas:

1. Keyboard skills. Although typing speed and accuracy can be an excellent indicator of potential keyboard proficiency, not all computer users have had typing experience. Typing on a keyboard is generally easier and faster than on a typewriter, but the counselor also needs to evaluate a client's manual dexterity and reach, motivation and interest, any

additional physical disabilities (particularly with the back or wrist), memory, cognitive skills, and other job requirements. For example, if a client is considering medical transcription as a career area, an employer or training program may require a minimum typing speed.

2. Language skills. Many careers require good language skills, including spelling, vocabulary, and the ability to express oneself clearly in written and spoken language. A client's skills need to be evaluated in terms of vocational objectives and assistive technology. It may be appropriate to ask the client to write a short essay on a given topic, such as why a particular career area is of interest, to evaluate his or her skills.

3. Organizational skills. One key to success for many people with visual impairments is the ability to organize and manage their personal and professional lives. This includes the ability to keep appointments, organize and maintain written documents (bills and medical records), and keep an orderly work area. When working with specialized technology, clients will need to be well-organized and able to follow and maintain sequences of directions and operations.

4. Memory. When using the various computer access technology devices, a user must keep track of a series of commands and instructions and remember the location and order of a variety of menu items in two or more programs at the same time. When using a transparent screen reader program to do word processing, a user is required to remember the commands of the screen reader and the word processor.

5. Frustration tolerance. Learning complex computer concepts may be extremely frustrating at first. If a client becomes easily frustrated and often gives up on learning new techniques or devices, learning computer access technology may need to be preceded by other activities to build confidence and patience.

6. Disability-related skills. As part of the adjustment process, individuals may learn skills that can be transferred to a variety of other areas. The ability to transfer and generalize knowledge and abilities is a valuable skill in the workplace and at home. The use of compressed speech tape players, for example, can help to develop listening skills that may assist an individual to more easily understand synthesized speech from various access devices. Large-print users who have developed the ability to glean information from taped books frequently discover that they can move more easily into the use of speech access devices than individuals who have relied heavily on residual vision to read large print. In fact, large print may be too slow for productive application in some job settings.

There are other challenges that rehabilitation counselors must face as they assist individuals who are visually impaired in using advanced technology. As Mather (1994) pointed out,

> there is no question that with the development of adaptive technologies—word processing; computerization of data bases; optical character recognition; and computers equipped with synthesized speech, large-print displays, or soft-copy braille—people who are blind or visually impaired can process and gain access to large amounts of information quickly. (pp. 545–546)

These abilities still do not mean equal access to the job market and career progression, however. Technological advances can also eliminate jobs that individuals with visual impairments once held and can also contribute to people being defined by the technology they use, rather than by their skills. Advances in automation have also contributed to the need for additional skills (i.e., higher levels of abstractness, greater independence among task levels, and new responsibilities for tasks) by individuals, including individuals who are visually impaired (Adler, 1986). These are important considerations for rehabilitation counselors who are identifying sensory aids for clients in the workplace.

Assistive Technology Planning

Individuals vary in their needs for specific types of assistive technology. For example, a desktop personal computer with a speech synthesizer will not be appropriate for all clients. One client may have a hearing impairment, which makes the use of speech impractical, whereas another client may be more accurate with the use of a particular large-print system that is not compatible with the desktop computer. A third client may not need that level of sophistication to perform a series of job tasks. At times there may be a very simple, non-computer-related solution to a client's need. A comprehensive individualized assistive technology plan is therefore recommended as part of the rehabilitation plan.

The sequence to developing an assistive technology plan is as follows:

- identify the essential job functions or job tasks the client has difficulty accomplishing because of the presence of a visual impairment, such as sorting the mail;
- use a low vision evaluation in those instances when the client has usable vision, with actual materials from the job site whenever possible, to identify such low technology alternatives as a lighted stand magnifier to read the mail;
- refer the client for an assistive technology evaluation enclosing relevant information from the job site evaluation and the low vision evaluation. If an assistive technology specialist with expertise in blindness is not available then,
- match the remaining problem areas to the use of assistive technology that will enable the client to efficiently accomplish those job tasks, for example, the use of an optical character recognition scanner to read the mail; and
- consider the practical aspects of the match, such as the cost and time efficiency of the proposed sensory aids. If the task is 10 percent of the job requirement or less and can be handled by another person in exchange for another task, it may be more practical to restructure the job, rather than spend a large amount of money on assistive technology that will allow the client to perform the task.

The assistive technology plan should have several components:

- an analysis of the job requirements and essential job functions;
- an assessment of the client's abilities and needs;
- a statement of the objective;
- a statement of the perceived problem that necessitates the purchase of specialized equipment;
- an itemized list of recommended equipment, warranties, and service contracts, shipping costs, and vendor information;
- justification for all the suggested purchases, including price justification;
- installation and training information; and
- a statement of client and employer involvement.

All the above components can be stated briefly, but, in cases that involve large expenditures of funds, thorough documentation is important. Because the assistive technology plan is usually part of an overall rehabilitation plan, it should be signed by both the counselor and the client.

Occasionally, conflicting agency policies may make it difficult to appropriately individualize a client plan. Some agencies may discourage the use of large print because they believe that speech is faster. Other agencies may have sophisticated low vision clinics that encourage clients to be assisted by their own low vision rather than by other technology services. Some state agencies are also restricted in their freedom to purchase individualized equipment for clients by state purchasing contracts. In cases such as these, the state has a sole purchase agreement with a particular computer company to buy in bulk at specially reduced rates all computer equipment used by the state. This can cause problems for accessibility because not all computer systems are equally compatible with access technology. It is recommended that the counselor remember that good casework, full documentation of a client's needs, and justification for exceptions will enable flexible operation within state policies in order to meet the client's specific needs.

Because rehabilitation counselors are frequently employed in positions in which they recommend or authorize the purchase of assistive technology devices, counselors may find themselves in a difficult position of holding the "purse strings," when a client prefers a more expensive item that cannot be justified by the stated need. Good counseling skills and conflict-resolution skills may be necessary when counselors find themselves in this position. Creative alternatives can be sought that allow counselors to function within the rules of their employing agency or organization but that also respect the wishes and desires of the client. Alternative funding sources or shared purchasing by the client and agency are some possibilities that may be explored.

Finally, there are some settings in which rehabilitation counselors may not have access to assistive technology specialists with expertise in blindness, or where each counselor is expected to develop an appropriate level of expertise to develop an assistive technology plan. In these situations, the counselor may rely on a team approach, which can include agency computer purchasing boards, or the counselor may seek advice from various vendors. Rehabilitation counselors can also benefit from the services of a number of computer resource databases, many of which are available on the Internet—these databases present facts and information on a variety of equipment and products. Professionals and consumer groups also maintain information that may be helpful in selecting appropriate assistive technology.

The Role and Function of Assistive Technology Specialists

Because assistive technology is a young and developing profession, the role and function of assistive technology specialists is still being defined. The basic role of the assistive technology specialist is to provide client evaluation, assistive technology recommendations and training, and to submit recommendations to the rehabilitation counselor and client for appropriate assistive technology solutions to stated client needs. In addition, the assistive technology specialist maintains information on the various assistive devices and refers individuals needing assistive technology solutions to appropriate resources. The assistive technology specialist provides expertise in the area of assistive technology to the rehabilitation team.

Assistive technology specialists function in several different settings. They may be part of the state Tech Act Project which has been mandated by Congress; they may be employed in rehabilitation centers specifically for individuals who are blind or visually impaired; they may be employed by companies specializing in the development and sale of specialized assistive technology devices, or as field-based agency personnel. They often function in a consulting role, but also can be involved in direct client assessment and instruction. At the Tech Act Projects, assistive technology specialists are often given responsibilities for information and referral services, assistive technology development, and direct client assessment and training services. They may install equipment, instruct clients in the use of equipment, and function as on-going consultants, providing follow-up and equipment upgrade services. As part of the federal mandate for the Tech

Act Projects, they may also function as agents of system change to make recommendations to state agency administrators. These changes require assistive technology specialists to develop strategies to overcome funding barriers, coordinate activities among state agencies, and empower individuals with disabilities by providing information about assistive technology. They have specific mandates to reach underrepresented and rural populations, and to provide delivery of AT services to children and youths.

As the profession continues to develop, the role and function of assistive technology specialists will become more clearly defined, and credentialing, professional training, and research into the implementation of federal mandates will assist in further defining the specific roles of the assistive technology specialist as part of the rehabilitation team.

SUMMARY

Individuals who provide rehabilitation teaching, O&M instruction, and assistive technology evaluation and instruction are critical members of the rehabilitation team. The services of these individuals enhance the independence and self-esteem of individuals with visual impairments by facilitating their access to activities of daily living, and vocational and avocational pursuits.

Rehabilitation teachers, as specialists in adaptive communications and daily living skills for people who are visually impaired, are knowledgeable about resources and adaptive equipment. O&M specialists provide instruction in skills including the use of sighted guides, protective techniques, cane skills, and orientation procedures. Assistive technology specialists have knowledge of the various types of assistive technology that can enhance a person's quality of life and facilitate employment opportunities. The rehabilitation counselor's role includes understanding the various services that are available and referring individuals with visual impairments for services, in addition to communicating with the client and other team members about the types of services that are needed and available. An effective team helps ensure successful rehabilitation efforts by assisting clients in making informed choices about their lives and the opportunities to implement those choices.

LEARNING ACTIVITIES

1. The narrative case example of Joe Stephens cited in the appendix to this chapter is written from the rehabilitation teacher's viewpoint. Discuss the roles and responsibilities of the counselor. What additional information is needed for writing the IWRP? Identify sources for securing the additional information for the IWRP. State clear goals for Joe and identify objectives to meet the goals.
2. Investigate how vocational and nonvocational rehabilitation services for people with visual impairments are delivered in your area. What agencies deliver the services and how are they funded? What are the roles of the counselors and rehabilitation teachers in planning and providing the services for transition-aged youth and for older adults? What are the state and local resources for information about assistive technology?
3. There are currently six university training programs for rehabilitation teaching in the United States. Graves and Maxson (1989) project from prevalence data published by the National Society to Prevent Blindness (1980) (now called Prevent Blindness America), that there are over 600,000 working-age people in the United States who are legally blind. Discuss the implications of the relatively small number of training programs and the relatively large number of people who may benefit from rehabilitation teaching services.
4. While under the instruction and supervision of an O&M specialist, learn and practice the sighted guide procedures. Use a blindfold

and low vision simulators to ascertain the different techniques required.

5. Schedule observations with an O&M instructor or rehabilitation teacher in a rehabilitation center setting and an itinerant setting. Based on your interview, what do you see as the strengths and limitations of both types of settings?
6. Discuss with a rehabilitation counselor (1) the roles of O&M specialists and rehabilitation teachers, and (2) those who provide sensory aid information. Determine referral and reporting procedures and other methods used to maintain communication among rehabilitation team members.
7. Develop a resource file of information on assistive technology and computer access devices, including sections on noncomputerized aids, large-print, braille, and speech computerized access technology and nonspecialized equipment. Include at least 50 entries with vendor names, addresses, telephone numbers; device descriptions, including price and hardware requirements; and the date the information was entered.

APPENDIX: REHABILITATION CASE STUDY

Joe Stephens, legally blind from proliferative diabetic retinopathy, was referred for rehabilitation services by his ophthalmologist after his second laser surgery (Rosenthal, 1993). Joe was concerned that he would lose his untenured faculty position. The college administrators were questioning his ability to manage his classes and to publish. The counselor interviewed Joe, opened his case, and referred him for rehabilitation teaching.

The rehabilitation teacher met Joe at his office to assess his vocational instructional needs. The teacher questioned him about the nature of his work, how he performed his job, and what tasks were difficult for him to do. The rehabilitation teacher determined that Joe was having trouble using tape recorded materials. He also needed training in listening skills and note-taking to handle the material he would be using for his classes, and to prepare him for using speech output devices. The rehabilitation teacher asked him to demonstrate his skills in keyboarding, handwriting, telephoning and using his tape recorder. The rehabilitation teacher noted that his handwriting was adequate and showed Joe how to use signature and check guides to keep his writing on straight lines. Although tape recorders were essential for him, Joe's assessment showed that he was not facile in using them. The rehabilitation teacher expected that his skills could be significantly improved with instruction. Joe had good keyboarding skills, but at times misplaced his fingers on the keys, which caused errors that he could not see on the screen. The rehabilitation teacher tactilely marked reference keys and taught him fingering techniques.

The rehabilitation teacher asked him about managing his home life and diabetes. He indicated that "maybe some hints" would be helpful. Following the initial assessment and after consultation with the counselor, the teacher developed a rehabilitation teaching plan for (1) communication and organizational skills and (2) instruction in personal management skills including diabetes care.

Joe was evaluated at the assistive technology center for people with disabilities. The counselor purchased the adaptive equipment that was recommended for him by the assistive technology specialist. Training was provided by the assistive technology specialist on a contractual basis. Working with the rehabilitation teacher, Joe learned labeling and organizational skills, and hired a reliable reader to assist him at work. With Joe's permission, the counselor and teacher met with the college administrators to describe Joe's rehabilitation plan and expected outcomes. The college agreed to retain Joe and evaluate him after his rehabilitation training.

With his work, medical, and rehabilitation appointments, Joe had to adjust to a new daily schedule including preparation of his own diabetic diet meals. He had basic cooking skills and learned adaptive techniques that were sufficient for him to safely prepare his meals. He was referred to a diabetes clinic for dietary and insulin-management instruction by diabetes educators (Williams, 1993). The recommended blood glucose monitoring system with speech output was purchased for him (Petzinger, 1993). Joe was also referred to a podiatrist for footcare and prescriptive shoes. The O&M instructor taught him how to travel safely with a long cane and to use public transportation.

The rehabilitation teacher taught Joe problem-solving skills and skills for teaching himself as a visually impaired learner. Initially, he resisted using tactile techniques but his unstable vision reinforced their value. As he learned skills for tactilely confirming what he was doing, Joe became more proficient and his tactile resistance decreased. Roberts (1977, p. 350) stated this phenomenon well, "Things don't always feel like they look."

Within a year, Joe completed his goals and the college reappointed him for one year. He continued meeting with a peer group at the diabetes clinic, because he was having difficulty adjusting to his decreasing vision. The counselor closed his case and told Joe that it would be reopened if additional vocational rehabilitation services were necessary.

CHAPTER 10

Service Systems and Resources

J. Elton Moore, Kathleen Mary Huebner, and John H. Maxson

Throughout the United States, a wide variety of services are available from public and private organizations and agencies for people with visual impairments. Although the availability of specific services may vary significantly from state to state and agency to agency, it is important for rehabilitation professionals to have knowledge of the various types of services that can assist individuals with visual impairments. The objectives of this chapter are (1) to provide a historical overview of activities related to blindness, because understanding events in the development of the profession of rehabilitation, and the resultant approaches to service form the basis for understanding the service delivery system as it exists today; (2) to describe the major public and private programs that provide services or programs for individuals with visual impairments; (3) to acquaint rehabilitation professionals with other individuals, professional associations, and consumer organizations that are involved with visually impaired individuals; and (4) to describe the legislation and related educational services and programs that can enhance opportunities for individuals with visual impairments.

Special thanks are extended to Barry McEwen for his contributions to the development of this material, and to Dr. Samuel B. Johnson for his contributions to the section on professionals within the field of blindness.

HISTORICAL OVERVIEW

Services to people with visual impairments in the United States have their historical roots in many nations. Louis Braille of France, a man who was blind, developed a raised dot communication system in 1826, which is still used today. The development of a communication system using raised dots, subsequently known as braille, brought extraordinary change in the direction of delivery of services and formed a base for educational and rehabilitative services that emphasized abilities and potentials of those with visual impairments.

Samuel Gridley Howe established Perkins School for the Blind in Massachusetts in 1829, which addressed the need to enhance learning opportunities for children and young adults who were blind. His establishment of a separate school for individuals who were blind was, in many ways, a great experiment, but it was successful and was soon replicated in many states across the country. The leadership of Howe and others convinced people of the necessity of educational preparation for young individuals who were blind in order to improve the quality of their lives.

Ultimately, the Congress of the United States agreed with this unique idea and in 1879 passed a law entitled "An Act to Promote the Education of the Blind," which recognized the need for specialized materials for children who were blind and committed the government to assist in providing such materials. A state and federal partnership was therefore established, a forerunner of today's system.

In 1895, a group of individuals (i.e., individuals who were blind, lay persons, and educators) met in St. Louis, Missouri, to form a group known as the American Blind Peoples' Higher Education and General Improvement Association. Because educational services were available in several locations in the country, the St. Louis group was formed to contend with the very real problems of adults with visual impairments who had attained an education but for whom there was neither a vocational recourse nor a recourse to advanced education. The name of the group was later changed to the American Association of Workers for the Blind (AAWB) and the group became a catalyst for improving opportunities for and strengthening services for people who were blind. The leaders of AAWB, along with the American Association of Instructors for the Blind (AAIB), incorporated the American Foundation for the Blind (AFB) in 1921 (Koestler, 1976). Because there was no central clearinghouse or coordinating body for workshops serving people who were blind, the leaders of AAWB, many of whom included workshop personnel, forged ahead to establish a National Industries for the Blind (NIB).

The mid-1930s included landmark legislation that brought about changes in the operation of services to people who were blind. Major legislation included (1) the Social Security Act (1935), which made the State-Federal Vocational Rehabilitation Program a permanent program; (2) the Randolph–Sheppard Act (1936), which allowed individuals who were blind to operate vending stands in federal buildings, and (3) the Wagner–O'Day Act (1938), which required the federal government to purchase designated products produced by people who were blind and working in rehabilitation workshops.

The roots of comprehensive services for people with visual impairments can be traced back to the decades following World War II. It was during those years that the state-federal rehabilitation program expanded to include individuals who were blind or severely visually impaired among those considered eligible for rehabilitation services. During this same period, consumer organizations began to influence service delivery, both directly or indirectly. This influence had the most impact on federal and state legislation. (For an overview of the blindness rehabilitation service-delivery system prior to 1973, the reader is referred to *Blindness and Services to the Blind in the United States—A Report to the Subcommittee on Rehabilitation/National Institute of Neurological Diseases and Blindness,* published by the Organization for Social and Technical Innovation, Inc. [1971]. For a more recent and broader review of services provided or contracted by agencies and schools in both the public and private sector, the reader should consult Kirchner and Aiello [1988]) and Moore and Fireisson [1995].)

The variety of agencies, groups, governmental entities, and private-for-profit companies and providers serving the population of individuals who are blind or visually impaired is staggering. In 1997, throughout the United States, there were more than 300 private rehabilitation facilities, 200 low vision services, 250 library and information centers, 14 dog guide schools, and 100 computer training centers providing services to people with visual impairments (AFB, 1997).

In 1969, the radio reading concept was introduced. Presently there are over 88 reading services operating in the United States. Some broadcast as little as 10 hours per week, while others broadcast 24 hours per day. With the rapid increase in the incidence of blindness, particularly among older individuals, segments of the corporate sector are analyzing the financial resources of that market as well. A variety of new companies have begun providing large-print books, devices, and appliances, and other items for people who are blind or visually impaired. In addition, a variety of consumer-oriented organizations have developed in regard to specific visual conditions.

An important resource for counselors, as well as clients and family members, includes specialty organizations such as Retinitis Pigmentosa International. Retinitis Pigmentosa International was founded in 1973 and is a national eye research foundation dedicated to finding a cure for retinal degenerative diseases [e.g., retinitis pigmentosa (RP), Usher's Syndrome, and macular degeneration]. The foundation supports basic and clinical research at many prominent institutions in the United States and serves as a worldwide source of information for RP specialists, professionals, and affected families. Examples of other visual impairment-specific organizations are: Association for Macular Diseases, Foundation for Glaucoma Research, and International Society on Metabolic Eye Disease. Programs supporting research and education, such as Prevent Blindness America, are also important resources for rehabilitation counselors. Prevent Blindness America, founded in 1908, funds research and conducts public and professional education programs. (See the Resources section at the back of this book for more information on this organization and many others discussed in this chapter.)

Because of the variety of public and private programs with missions related to blindness, directories provide valuable assistance to rehabilitation professionals. Probably the most comprehensive of these resources is the *Directory of Services for Blind and Visually Impaired Persons in the United States* (25th Edition), which is published by the American Foundation for the Blind (1997). The Directory provides comprehensive information on the kinds of services available and categorizes them according to such areas as education, rehabilitation, low vision, and taping and brailling services. Another valuable resource guide is the *Rehabilitation Resource Manual: VISION* (3rd Edition), published by Resources for Rehabilitation (1990), which contains numerous resources, addresses, and telephone numbers that will assist rehabilitation professionals to make effective referrals or to acquire additional needed information. Finally, the Internet provides a wide range of listings of employment resources (see Sidebar 10.1). Given the varied nature of programs and services undertaken in this field, the discussion that follows and the resources section of this book describe only a representative sampling of organizations and efforts that rehabilitation counselors may encounter.

PUBLIC PROGRAMS

There are a number of public programs that provide services for individuals with visual impairments. The primary programs include those relating to the state-federal vocational rehabilitation program, the Randolph–Sheppard Program, the Javits–Wagner–O'Day Act, and the U.S. Department of Veterans Affairs. (For a list of relevant legislation, see Sidebar 10.2.) A number of other programs provide services relating to people who are blind or visually impaired. The Pratt–Smoot Act, for example, provides for books for children and adults who are blind or visually impaired. Services are provided through the Library of Congress National Library Service for the Blind and Physically Handicapped. PL 89–522 extended the availability of these services to individuals with disabilities who, because of their disabilities, are unable to handle standard printed material. (See also the Resources section of this book.)

State-Federal Vocational Rehabilitation Program

The state-federal vocational rehabilitation program was established in 1920 to serve individuals with physical disabilities. During the period from 1920 to 1943, state vocational rehabilitation programs meant little to people who were blind, because few if any individuals with visual impairments were accepted for services. At this time, individuals who were blind were regarded as "too severely disabled" and "too difficult to place on jobs." Therefore, applicants who were blind were generally referred to state commissions for blind people (which at that time received no federal financial assistance) or they were rejected as poor risks for rehabilitation. Before 1943, individuals who received vocational rehabilitation services

SIDEBAR 10.1

Employment Resources on the Internet

Because of the constantly changing nature of on-line resources, this listing cannot be completely up to date. The employment resources included here are those that rehabilitation counselors might commonly encounter in assisting clients in their job searches.

The World Wide Web

America's Employers
http://www.americasemployers.com
or
http://www.americasemployers.com/Positions/

America's Job Bank (Department of Labor site with more than 500,000 help wanted ads from both public and private employment agencies)
http://www.ajb.dni.us

Best Jobs U.S.A.
http://www.bestjobsusa.com

CareerMosaic USENET Job List
http://www.careermosaic.com/cm/usenet.html

Careers On-Line
http://disserv3.stu.umn.edu/COL

Chicago Tribune Employment Listings
http://www.chicago.tribune.com/career

Cornucopia of Disability Information at Buffalo
http://codi.buffalo.edu

Employment Listings from Newspapers (*Boston Globe, Chicago Tribune, Los Angeles Times, New York Times, Washington Post, & San Jose Mercury News*)
http://www.careerpath.com

Employment Opportunities
http://www.surf.com/~cfpub/employ1.htm

Employment Research Group
http://www.ergnet.com/

Employment Resources
http://www.nova.edu/Inter-Links/employment.html

ESPAN Job Library
http://www.espan.com/

Federal Jobs Listing
http://204.216.6.21/Emplrbth/fedlist.htm

Interactive Employment Network
http://espan2.espan.com/cgi-bin/gate2?espan~simple/index.html

Job Accommodation Network (JAN)
http://janweb.icdi.wvu.edu/

Job Links
http://www.webfeet.com/jobs/links.html

JOBPLACE
http://news.jobweb.org/cgi-bin/lwgate/JOBPLACE

Job Search and Employment Opportunities: Best Bets from the Net
http://asa.ugl.lib.umich.edu/chdocs/employment

NCS Career Magazine (jobs posted to major newsgroups)
http://www.careermag.com/

MN Dept. of Economic Security, MN Employment and Blind Services
http://www.des.state.mn.us/

Employment Resources on the Internet (continued)

Project Do-IT
http://weber.u.washington.edu/~doit

Project PURSUIT (Jobs in Science, Electronics, and Math)
http://pursuit.rehab.uiuc.edu/

Raleigh News and Observer Job Listings
http://www.nando.net/classads/employment

San Francisco Chronicle and Examiner Job Listings (search string "770")
http://www.sfgate.com/classifieds
then click on "job opportunities"

Virginia-Pilot Employment Listings
http://www.pilotonline.com/jobs/index.html

Yahoo Employment Resources
http://www.yahoo.com/business/employment

Miscellaneous
http://www.spedex.com/
http://www.noicc.gov
http:/www.careerware.com

typically had vocational backgrounds and their physical disabilities had resulted from accidents (Wright, 1980). In 1943, however, there was a pronounced change. The successful rehabilitation program for veterans of World War II who were blind also provided impetus and guidance for rehabilitation programs for civilians who were blind, and the Barden–LaFollette Act was signed by President Franklin D. Roosevelt on July 6, 1943. One key provision of the Barden–LaFollette Act (PL 78–113) made it possible for that part of the state plan handling vocational rehabilitation services to people with visual impairments to be administered by state commissions or other agencies serving people who were blind. This meant that state commissions and other agencies could receive funds from the federal government to assist in their programs of vocational rehabilitation. Separate state plans were established in several states to administer a program of services to people who were blind. These state agencies expanded their staff and their scope of service, and programs to place people who were blind in industry. The structure of vocational rehabilitation services for people who are blind, as these services are known today, was created.

In the Vocational Rehabilitation Act Amendments of 1954, the ability for designated state units serving people who were blind to receive direct funds was strengthened. These amendments also improved financing for training, research, and demonstration programs, which led to improvements in professional practice and the steady improvement and establishment of rehabilitation facilities.

In 1965, additional amendments to the Rehabilitation Act were passed. These amendments authorized a higher expenditure ceiling and for the first time allocated federal funds toward initial construction, remodeling, and renovation of facilities. This mechanism provided the impetus for expansion of rehabilitation center-based services and several agencies were able to establish such services. The Rehabilitation Act was amended again in 1968, and in 1973 a new rehabilitation act was passed that has been amended several times into the 1990s.

The primary piece of federal legislation that provides for services to persons who are blind or visually impaired throughout the United States is the 1992 Amendments (PL 102–569) to the Rehabilitation Act of 1973 (PL 93–112). The following is a summary of the current provisions of the Rehabilitation Act of 1973, as amended. However, amendments to the Rehabilitation Act are under consideration by the U.S. Congress as this text is

SIDEBAR 10.2

Summary of Rehabilitation Legislation

1920 PL 66–236 *Smith–Fess Act:* Established the first civilian rehabilitation act; authorized vocational guidance, occupation adjustment, and placement services for civilians with physical disabilities.

1935 PL 74–271 *Social Security Act:* Made the state-federal vocational rehabilitation program a permanent program that could be discontinued only by an act of Congress.

1936 PL 74–732 *Randolph–Sheppard Act:* Individuals classified as legally blind could operate vending stands on federal property.

1938 PL 75–739 *Wagner–O'Day Act:* Mandated that the federal government purchase designated products from facilities for persons who are blind.

1943 PL 78–113 *Bardon–LaFollette Act:* Included rehabilitation services to persons with mental retardation and mental illness and provided the first federal-state rehabilitation support for persons who are blind.

1954 PL 83–565 *Vocational Rehabilitation Act Amendments:* Included funding to colleges and universities for preparation of rehabilitation professionals, expanded services to persons with mental retardation and mental illness, provided rehabilitation facility expansion funds and funding for extension and improvement of state agencies, and authorized research and demonstration programs.

1965 PL 89–333 *Vocational Rehabilitation Act Amendments:* Established a National Commission on Architectural Barriers, deleted economic need as a requirement for services, increased the federal share of federal-state programs (i.e., the matching requirement) to 75 percent and added an extended evaluation, which enabled counselors to provide services for periods of 6 to 18 months to determine eligibility for vocational rehabilitation services.

1967 PL 90–99 *Vocational Rehabilitation Act Amendments:* Established a National Center for Deaf-Blind Youths and Adults and authorized grants to state vocational rehabilitation agencies for pilot projects for the provision of vocational rehabilitation services to individuals with vocational disabilities who were migratory agricultural workers and members of their families.

1968 PL 90–391 *Vocational Rehabilitation Amendments:* Increased the federal share of federal-state programs to 80 percent and continued the expansion of the program.

1971 PL 92–28 *Javits–Wagner–O'Day Act:* Extended the law to cover industries that employ persons with severe disabilities other than blindness and provided paid staff for the President's Committee For Purchase From People Who Are Blind or Severely Disabled.

1973 PL 93–112 *Rehabilitation Act of 1973:* Included the Individualized Written Rehabilitation Program (IWRP) and post-employment services, established a priority of services to persons meeting the federal definition of severe disability, provided special consideration for public safety officers injured in the line of duty, authorized demonstration projects for Independent Living Rehabilitation, established client assistance pilot projects, eliminated any residency requirements for services, mandated consumer involvement in state agency policy development, stressed

Summary of Rehabilitation Legislation (continued)

program evaluation, and initiated legislation to prohibit discrimination against and provide access to persons with disabilities in federally funded programs (Sections 501–504).

1974 PL 93–651 *Rehabilitation Act Amendments of 1974:* Extended the authorizations of appropriations in the Rehabilitation Act of 1973 for one year, strengthened the Randolph–Sheppard Act (referred to as the Randolph–Sheppard Act Amendments of 1974), and provided for the convening of a White House Conference on "Handicapped Individuals."

1978 PL 95–602 *Rehabilitation, Comprehensive Services, and Developmental Disabilities Amendments of 1978:* Expanded the quality and scope of reader services for individuals who are blind and interpreter services for people who are deaf; established independent living services as part of federal-state rehabilitation program, including independent living services for "older blind individuals;" provided vocational rehabilitation services grants to Native Americans located on federal and state reservations; established the National Institute of Handicapped Research (renamed as the National Institute on Disability and Rehabilitation Research), Rehabilitation Research and Training Centers, and Comprehensive Rehabilitation Centers, and the Helen Keller Center for Deaf-Blind Youths and Adults; established the National Council on the Handicapped (later renamed the National Council on Disability).

1984 PL 98–221 *Rehabilitation Act Amendments of 1984:* Established Client Assistance Programs in each state, inserted the word "qualified" before personnel for training programs in the Act.

1986 PL 99–506 *Rehabilitation Act Amendments of 1986:* Added the definition of supported employment to the Act, established supported employment as an acceptable goal for rehabilitation services and provided funding for state supported employment programs; added rehabilitation engineering services as a vocational rehabilitation service.

1988 PL 100–407 *Technology-Related Assistance for Individuals with Disabilities Act of 1988:* Provided financial assistance to states in developing and implementing a consumer-responsive statewide program of technology-related assistance for individuals of all ages with disabilities.

1990 PL 101–476 *Individuals with Disabilities Education Act:* Required schools to provide transition services to all students with disabilities.

1990 PL 101–336 *The Americans with Disabilities Act:* Prohibited any covered entity from discriminating against a qualified individual with a disability with regard to job application procedures; the hiring, advancement, or discharge of employees, employee compensation, job training, and other terms, conditions, and privileges of employment.

1991 PL 102–52 *Rehabilitation Act Amendments of 1991:* Made technical amendments in the Rehabilitation Act of 1973, as amended, and extended the Act for one year.

1992 PL 102–569 *Rehabilitation Act Amendments of 1992:* Emphasized client choice of employment objectives, providers,

Summary of Rehabilitation Legislation (continued)

and services with a statement by the consumer on the IWRP; established consumer-controlled State Rehabilitation Advisory Councils; established a presumption of eligibility that individuals could benefit from vocational rehabilitation services, unless the agency could demonstrate otherwise; expanded services to include transition services, on-the-job services, other personal assistance services, and supported employment as a basic service; enhanced access to traditionally underserved minority populations; increased accountability measures; limited the time period for determining eligibility to 60 days from application; and directed Client Assistance Programs to include individual and systemic advocacy.

1993 PL 103–73 *Rehabilitation Act Amendments of 1993* made technical corrections or "amendments" to the 1992 Rehabilitation Act Amendments and clarified the role of the State Rehabilitation Advisory Council.

Source: Adapted from R. M. Parker and E. M. Syzmanski (Eds.). *Rehabilitation Counseling—Basics and Beyond* (Second Edition) (Austin, TX: PRO-ED, Inc., 1992).

being written, and the act itself is reauthorized periodically. It is therefore important for the rehabilitation counselor to contact his or her congressional delegation or the separate agency serving persons who are blind or visually impaired to obtain accurate information about the statutory requirements for completing a rehabilitation plan. Title I of the Rehabilitation Act of 1973, as amended, provides the primary framework for the provision of vocational rehabilitation services to people who are blind or visually impaired. Section 101 (a)(1)(A) of the Act requires each state to submit a State Plan for Vocational Rehabilitation Services. It mandates that each plan shall designate a state agency as the sole state agency to administer the plan or to supervise its administration by a local agency except that

> where under the state's law, the state agency for individuals who are blind or other agency which provides assistance or services to adults who are blind, is authorized to provide vocational rehabilitation services to such individuals, such agency may be designated as the sole state agency to administer the part of the plan under which vocational rehabilitation services are provided for individuals who are blind and a separate state agency may be designated as the sole state agency with respect to the rest of the state plan (29 USC § 720 *et seq.*).

This federal legislation has led to the formation of three different categories of state vocational rehabilitation agencies: separate agencies for people who are blind, general agencies, and combined agencies. There are presently 82 state vocational rehabilitation agencies in the United States and its territorial possessions. These are composed of 25 separate state agencies for people who are blind, and 57 general or combined agencies, which are designated to administer vocational rehabilitation programs within each state or territory. These numbers change from time to time as states make changes in their Title I State Plans. Federal regulations (34 CFR 361.10)(b) also stipulate that the state plan must meet all requirements applicable to a separate state plan, if a separate state agency for individuals who are blind administers or supervises that part of the state plan relating to the rehabilitation of individuals who are blind.

The 1992 amendments updated and added several new definitions and changed the federal share to 78.7 percent under Title I. Several key principles were added, such as the provision that individuals must be active participants in their own rehabilitation programs, including making meaningful and informed choices about the selection of their vocational goals, objectives, and services. State vocational rehabilitation agencies were also required to make eligibility determinations within 60 days unless exceptional and unforseen circumstances exist that are beyond the control of the state agency and the affected individuals concur with the extension. The eligibility process is now based on the principle that individuals with disabilities are generally presumed to be capable of engaging in gainful employment in integrated settings, if appropriate services and supports are provided. The Act provides for a wide range of services to be made available.

Scope of Services

Section 103 (a) of the Rehabilitation Act describes the extensive scope of vocational rehabilitation services that are available to individuals to help them prepare for and engage in gainful employment. Vocational rehabilitation services provided under the Rehabilitation Act of 1973, as amended, include such services as (1) assessment, (2) counseling, (3) physical and mental restoration, including eyeglasses and visual services as prescribed by an ophthalmologist or an optometrist, (4) reader services for those individuals determined to be blind, (5) vocational training and tools, (6) rehabilitation teaching services and orientation and mobility services for blind individuals, (7) sensory devices and other technological devices, and (8) rehabilitation technology services.

Individualized Written Rehabilitation Program

The 1973 Rehabilitation Act mandated an Individualized Written Rehabilitation Program (IWRP). The IWRP includes the client's vocational goal, the services needed to meet that goal, the cost of services, and the time frame for providing the services. The IWRP is developed jointly by the vocational rehabilitation counselor and the individual client or, as appropriate, that individual and a parent, guardian, or other representative (34 CFR 361.45). Each state vocational rehabilitation unit must provide a copy of the IWRP and any amendments respectively to the rehabilitation client or, as appropriate, to a parent, guardian, or other representative. Furthermore, each state must ensure that the IWRP will be reviewed as often as necessary, but at least on an annual basis. Each client must be given an opportunity to review the program and, if necessary, jointly redevelop and agree to its terms. The Rehabilitation Act Amendments of 1992 require that the IWRP be signed by both the agency and the client. If the client is dissatisfied with any determination made by the vocational rehabilitation counselor concerning the furnishing or denial of services, that client may request an administrative review or hearing before an impartial hearing officer. (A sample of a completed IWRP appears in Appendix A of this book.)

Title VII

Title VII of the Rehabilitation Act of 1973, as amended, provides for independent living services and Centers for Independent Living (CIL). The term "independent living services" includes information and referral services, independent living skills training, and peer counseling. For those states that receive federal funding under Chapter 2 of Title VII (Independent Living Services for Older Individuals Who Are Blind), a variety of services may be provided. These include (1) services to help correct blindness, such as outreach services, visual screening, surgical or therapeutic treatment to prevent, correct, or modify disabling eye conditions, and hospitalization related to such services, (2) the provision of eyeglasses and other visual devices, (3) the provision of services and equipment to assist an older individual who is blind to become more mobile and more self-sufficient, (4) orientation and mobility training, braille instruction, and other services and equipment to help an older individual who is blind adjust to blindness, (5) guide services, reader services, and transportation, (6) any other appropriate service designed to assist older individuals who are blind in coping with daily living activities, including supportive services and rehabilitation teaching services, and (7) independent living skills training, information and referral services, peer counseling, and individual advocacy training.

Client Assistance Program

Initially developed as projects in the 1973 Rehabilitation Act, Client Assistance Programs (CAPs) now exist in every state to assist people with disabilities in accessing the various services provided under the Rehabilitation Act (Patterson & Woodrich, 1986). Grants are made to the states to establish and implement client assistance programs to provide assistance in informing and advising every client or client applicant of all available benefits under the Rehabilitation Act. CAPs may also assist clients or applicants in their relationships with projects, programs, and facilities providing services to them under the Act, including assistance in pursuing legal, administrative, or other appropriate remedies to ensure the protection of the rights of such individuals under the Rehabilitation Act of 1973, as amended. CAPs services can be categorized into three areas: (1) information and referral services, (2) individual advocacy services that are available only to persons with disabilities who are receiving or seeking services under the Act and who are encountering problems concerning their benefits or rights under the Act, and (3) systems advocacy services whereby CAPs are charged with the responsibility of improving the delivery systems themselves, that is, identifying and seeking solutions to problems within each of the delivery systems (Moore, Armstrong, Lamb, & Giesen, 1992).

Randolph–Sheppard Program

The Randolph–Sheppard Vending Stand Act (PL 74–732), as amended, was passed in 1936 with the purpose of providing individuals who are blind "with remunerative employment, enlarging the economic opportunities of . . . [people who are blind], and stimulating . . . [people who are blind] to greater efforts in striving to make themselves self-supporting," (20 USCA§ 107–107f). Facility managers with visual impairments have a priority, not just a preference, in operating vending facilities and in being awarded contracts for cafeterias on federal property (Avery, 1987). The state vocational rehabilitation agency that provides services to persons who are blind is designated in the Randolph–Sheppard Act as the State Licensing Agency (SLA). Each SLA that offers services to vendors or facility managers who are blind under the Randolph–Sheppard Program [more commonly known as the Business Enterprise Program (BEP)], works cooperatively with the elected State Committee of Blind Vendors. This group actively participates with the SLA in major administrative, policy, and program development decisions.

BEP is unusual in that it is a combination of business enterprise, usually food service oriented, and vocational rehabilitation. BEP facilities operate in a partly competitive, partly subsidized market environment (Partos & Kirchner, 1986). For more detailed discussions on specific aspects of the program, see Moore, Cavenaugh, Giesen, & Maxson (1995), Moore & Tucker (1994), and Tucker & Moore (1997).

Javits–Wagner–O'Day Act

The Wagner–O'Day Act (PL 75–739) was passed by Congress in 1938 and required the federal government to purchase designated products produced by people who were blind and working in rehabilitation workshops. In 1971, the passage of the Javits–Wagner–O'Day (JWOD) Act retained the priority for purchasing products from facilities serving individuals who were blind, but also added other people with severe disabilities as eligible for participation in this program.

U.S. Department of Veterans Affairs

The Blind Rehabilitation Service in the U.S. Department of Veterans Affairs (VA) was established to provide a wide variety of services to blinded veterans. In 1948, the first Blind Rehabilitation Center was opened at the VA Hospital in Hines, Illinois. Additional centers were later added at medical centers in Palo Alto, California; West Haven, Connecticut; Birmingham, Alabama; and San Juan, Puerto Rico. The VA also established Blind Rehabilitation Clinics at VA medical centers in West Haven, Connecticut; Waco, Texas; and American Lake/Tacoma, Washington.

These centers were established as in-patient facilities to provide comprehensive adjustment programs to assist veterans who were blind to overcome the difficulties associated with daily independent functioning and to develop positive attitudes and self-concepts concerning blindness. The clinics are also in-patient programs, smaller in bed capacity, with slower-paced programs, and are designed to help veterans with long-term training and adjustment needs. Both centers and clinics offer highly specialized rehabilitation programs in a residential setting. Each facility, which serves a multiregional area, is affiliated with leading universities that provide opportunities for students in the specialized disciplines of blind rehabilitation through teaching and internship opportunities. VA Blind Rehabilitation Center programs offer services similar to those offered by many private rehabilitation agencies (e.g., orientation and mobility, communications skills, living skills, manual and visual skills, adapted physical education, social and recreation skills, and individual and group adjustment counseling).

Visual Impairment Services Teams (VIST), which have been established at many VA medical centers and out-patient clinics around the nation, provide coordinated out-patient services to veterans who are blind. VIST, which is the VA's frontline diagnostic and treatment agent, is comprised of a coordinator and representatives from all disciplines available at the facility that offer a service to blind veterans. At those VA facilities without a designated VIST, a staff social worker is assigned to serve both as coordinator of services to veterans with visual impairments and as a liaison to the Blind Rehabilitation centers, clinics, and other facilities providing services to veterans who are blind. When veterans are not eligible for assistance under VA education and rehabilitation programs, the vocational rehabilitation staff makes referrals to other programs, such as the state-federal vocational rehabilitation program.

PRIVATE REHABILITATION AGENCIES

In addition to the various public programs, there are a wide range of private not-for-profit agencies serving individuals with visual impairments. Not all communities, however, have an agency that exclusively serves individuals with visual impairments. In those communities, generally a local Goodwill Industries or other rehabilitation program may have a special unit that handles the unique needs of individuals with visual impairments. In at least two states (i.e., Wisconsin and Florida), local community technical colleges house rehabilitation and vocational training programs geared specifically to people who are blind or visually impaired. In more rural areas, the state school for blind people may also provide limited training for adults.

Private agencies are quite diverse and autonomous. With few geographic exceptions, there is no connection between the various "lighthouses for the blind," "societies for the blind," "sight or vision centers," or other organizations with similar names. In recent years, there has also been significant movement to modify names of agencies away from "blind" or "sightless" to "visually impaired" to identify with and market to the rapidly increasing population of individuals with low vision.

Programs and services offered by the private agencies are as diverse as the number of agencies that provide them. Some agencies exist to serve only (1) children, (2) adults in need of vocational training, (3) people in need of personal adjustment services, (4) older individuals, (5) individuals who are blind who also have multiple disabilities, or (6) individuals who are blind or visually impaired. Specific services provided by the private agencies may include social services, vocational counseling, work adjustment, vocational evaluation, rehabilitation teaching, occupational therapy, communication instructions

Recreational and support groups for persons with visual impairments are a component of services offered by many private rehabilitation agencies.

(e.g., braille, typing, abacus), and orientation and mobility. Other programs and services include instruction in adaptive devices and appliances, access to talking book machines, technology utilization evaluations, vocational training, dog guide training, and volunteer activities. Many include recreational programs, radio reading broadcasts, braille transcription, large-print typing, recording, camping programs, sporting events and physical activities (e.g., bowling, golf, skiing, dancing, music, mountain climbing, and tandem bicycling). Many agencies include public education as part of their program components. Still others offer programs that focus on the prevention of blindness. The agencies may be community-based programs, residential living centers, or independent living centers.

Private agencies are funded by a variety of sources, including private donations, local United Way campaigns or other fund-raising groups, Lions Clubs, state rehabilitation contracts, grants, fees for services, individual client fees, corporate or foundation grants, funding from other government agencies such as the area office on aging, human services departments, insurance companies, and school systems. Private agencies vary in their primary service areas from focusing on such limited geographic areas as a portion of a city or county, to providing services for individuals from anywhere in the United States, Canada, or foreign countries. Two examples of agencies with programs of broad scope are The Lighthouse Inc. and Lions World Services for the Blind.

The Lighthouse Inc. was incorporated in 1906 in New York City and has developed a full range of national and international education, research, and training programs. In addition to operating one of the nation's larger clinical low vision centers, the Lighthouse Inc. maintains the National Center for Vision and Aging and the National Center for Vision and Child Development. Lions World Services for the Blind (LWSB), formerly known as Arkansas Enterprises for the Blind (AEB), was incorporated in 1939 and serves as a comprehensive rehabilitation center for people who are blind or visually impaired. It has served individuals from all over the nation and countries abroad as well. LWSB provides personal adjustment training, psychological testing and counseling, prevocational evaluation, and vocational evaluation and training. (See the Resources section of this book for more information on private rehabilitation organizations.)

NATIONAL ORGANIZATIONS

There are a large number of national organizations that serve or advocate for persons with visual impairments. The following sections examine some of the representative organizations in the United States whose missions relate specifically to the area of blindness or rehabilitation of people with visual impairments.

The American Foundation for the Blind (AFB) is a national, private not-for-profit organization that advocates for programs and services to help people who are blind or visually impaired to achieve independence with dignity in all sectors of society. AFB was founded in 1921 and is recognized as Helen Keller's cause in the United States. AFB serves as a national research, information, publishing, and consultative agency that also acts as a clearinghouse for local and regional agencies serving persons who are blind. AFB sponsors institutes and workshops for professionals working with persons who are blind or visually impaired, records and manufactures talking books, evaluates special technology for people who are blind, conducts public communication programs through the media, and participates in legislative action and advocacy activities for programs and services for people with visual impairments.

The American Academy of Ophthalmology was incorporated as an independent organization in 1979 when the American Academy of Ophthalmology and Otolaryngology (AAOO) was divided into separate academies for each specialty. The American Academy of Ophthalmology is the largest association of ophthalmologists in the United States, and is dedicated to helping the public maintain healthy eyes and good vision. Its major activities include education, public and professional information, representation, member services, ethics, and relations with ophthalmologic societies. The American Academy of Optometry also promotes excellence in standards of optometric practice and fosters research and knowledge dissemination.

Since 1858, students and adults who are blind in the United States have been served by the American Printing House for the Blind (APH). APH is the largest company in the world devoted solely to producing products for people who are blind. It is the oldest organization of its kind in the United States. APH is a not-for-profit manufacturing company that grew out of the overwhelming need for special education materials that could not be made by commercial firms. For over a century, the mission of APH has been to promote independence of people with visual impairments by providing special media, tools, and materials needed for education and life.

One of the main goals of APH is providing school materials to U.S. students who are blind or visually impaired. This is accomplished through the Federal Act to Promote the Education of the Blind, passed in 1879, which provides funds that are used by the states to purchase needed educational materials for their blind students. Each year, APH conducts a census of all students with visual impairments in the United States and its possessions so that funds available under the Act can be distributed to states, based on the number of students served by each educational program.

APH provides adapted and specially designed educational materials critical in the education of blind or visually impaired students. These materials include (1) textbooks in braille, large type, recorded, and electronic formats, (2) tangible teaching devices, (3) computer hardware and software, (4) educational tests, and (5) special instructional devices, tools, and other materials. Availability of these materials promotes equal opportunity and increases the quality of education for students who are blind or visually impaired.

The Hadley School for the Blind, located in Winnetka, Illinois, was founded in 1920 as a free distance education (home study) school for people of any age who are blind. The mission of the Hadley School is to enable persons who are blind at every stage of life to acquire specialized skills in order to participate successfully in the mainstream of society. The School provides an academic and rehabilitation curriculum through a variety of communication media in a personalized home study format especially adapted for people with visual impairments. The Hadley School courses serve as an adjunctive support to rehabilitation agencies nationwide and provides materials in alternate formats (such as braille, large print, and tape) in various curriculum areas.

The Helen Keller National Center for Deaf-Blind Youths and Adults (HKNC) was established by an act of Congress in 1967 and became operational in 1969 to provide specialized services needed to rehabilitate persons who are deaf and blind. The Center provides specialized intensive services, and many other services, at the center or elsewhere in the United States, which are necessary to encourage the maximum personal development of any deaf and blind individual. HKNC also trains professionals, allied personnel, and family members at the center or elsewhere in the United States to provide services to individuals who are deaf and blind and conducts applied research in the areas of communication techniques, teaching methods, aids and devices, and delivery of services. HKNC is authorized under the Rehabilitation Act, as amended, and is funded by an annual Congressional appropriation; the Center operates under the general supervision of the Rehabilitation Services Administration (RSA).

The National Accreditation Council for Agencies Serving the Blind and Visually Handicapped (NAC) was established in 1966 as a private not-for-profit organization to set standards for and to accredit organizations that specialize in serving persons who are blind or visually impaired. NAC accreditation identifies for public purposes those organizations and programs that meet nationally accepted accreditation standards for quality services, responsible management, and public accountability.

The National Council of Private Agencies for the Blind and Visually Impaired (NCPABVI) is an association of private not-for-profit organizations that provides rehabilitation and educational services to persons who are blind or visually impaired to promote opportunities for employment and personal independence. Membership is composed of the chief executive officers of private not-for-profit organizations that render specialized services of a rehabilitative or educational nature to people with visual impairments. Established in 1978, NCPABVI is comprised of over 60 organizations.

The National Council of State Agencies for the Blind, Inc. (NCSAB) is a national organization composed of the various state unit administrators who administer and direct programs and services for persons who are blind or visually impaired. NCSAB was founded in 1975 and has a membership of approximately 50 state and territorial agencies. The primary purposes and objectives of NCSAB are to provide a specialized forum for administrators of member agencies to study, deliberate, and act upon matters affecting rehabilitation and other services for people who are blind or visually impaired; to provide a resource for the formulation and expression of the collective points of view of member agencies on all issues affecting the provision of rehabilitation and other services to blind or visually impaired persons; and to serve as an advisory body and maintain a liaison with the Division for Blind and Visually Impaired of the RSA.

National Industries for the Blind (NIB) is a national, private not-for-profit organization designed to promote the economic independence of people with visual impairments through creating, maintaining, and expanding employment opportunities. The Committee for Purchase from People Who Are Blind or Other Severely Disabled has designated NIB as the Central Non-Profit Agency under the JWOD Act representing qualified private not-for-profit or state operated industries. As such, NIB assists the committee in administering and implementing the provisions of the JWOD Act by (1) coordinating the day-to-day activities of the JWOD Act program, (2) providing for an equitable distribution of government purchase orders, and (3) ensuring adherence to the Committee's regulations by industries for blind people. NIB works cooperatively with the General Council of Industries for the Blind (GCIB) in promoting employment opportunities for people who are blind or visually impaired. Organizations serving persons who are blind associated with NIB must employ legally blind individuals for not less than 75 percent of the work hours of direct labor for either the production of commodities or provision of services during any fiscal year. They must also comply with applicable JWOD regulations, as well as the Fair Labor Standards Act. NIB was formed in 1938 and at present is associated with approximately 105 industries for blind people located throughout the United States. NIB also provides technical assistance and training in business, management, and rehabilitation areas to the associated industries. [For an excellent historical overview of NIB and the JWOD program, the reader is urged to consult *Creating Jobs/Changing Lives* by Irving R. Dickman (1988)].

Recording for the Blind and Dyslexic (RFB&D) is a private not-for-profit organization that provides educational and professional books in accessible media to people with print disabilities. RFB&D has an 80,000-volume library of books on audio cassette and a recording service for new titles. Librarians also provide reference services assisting students with research needs.

RFB&D's library, perhaps the largest resource of its kind in the world, has books on all subjects and at all academic levels, includes textbooks, research materials, and a variety of computer manuals, as well as fiction, drama, and poetry in a number of languages.

Founded in 1948 to serve World War II veterans who were blind, RFB&D now serves anyone with a "print disability." This term includes not only blindness and visual impairments, but also learning disabilities and other physical disabilities that affect reading. RFB&D's resources are available to students at all academic levels, as well as people who use educational and professional materials to pursue careers or personal interests.

PROFESSIONAL ORGANIZATIONS

The professional associations of individuals working in the area of blindness and visual impairment are important for a number of reasons: (1) they provide a forum for communication among members, (2) through their journals, they assist in disseminating the results of research that can benefit individuals with visual impairments, (3) they provide advocacy on behalf of individuals who have visual impairments, and (4) they provide a means of continuing education, which is important in a field that changes rapidly, due to advances in medicine and technology (Joiner & Saxon, 1989; Joiner, Saxon, & Bair, 1987). The organizations discussed in the following paragraphs are representative examples of the major professional organizations that are related solely to the field of visual impairments.

The American Optometric Association is a joint U.S.–Canadian membership organization, whose mission is to improve the quality of vision care through promoting high standards, information dissemination, and professional involvement.

The Association for Education and Rehabilitation of the Blind and Visually Impaired

(AER) was formed in 1984 as a result of a consolidation between two of the nation's oldest organizations in the field of blindness. The Association for Education of the Visually Handicapped, founded in 1853, and the American Association of Workers for the Blind, founded in 1895, were combined to form AER. The union of these two associations created the only international membership organization composed primarily of professionals who work with people who are blind or visually impaired. AER, as a professional organization, is dedicated to promoting and enhancing careers in the field of blindness, including, for example, vision teacher, rehabilitation counselor, orientation and mobility specialist, and rehabilitation teacher. These goals are accomplished through a certification program, professional publications, conferences, and a continuing education program. AER has a number of divisions for its members, including divisions on rehabilitation teaching, counseling, and administration.

In addition to professional organizations that are specific to the area of visual impairments, there are other organizations to which various members of the rehabilitation team may belong, including the National Rehabilitation Association (Sales, 1995), which includes such divisions as the National Association of Independent Living; the National Association of Rehabilitation Instructors; the National Rehabilitation Counseling Association (Kirk & La Forge, 1995); the National Association of Multicultural Rehabilitation Concerns; the Vocational Evaluation and Work Adjustment Association; and the National Rehabilitation Association of Job Placement and Development. Other organizations include the American Rehabilitation Counseling Association (ARCA), which is a division of the American Counseling Association and the Council for Exceptional Children (CEC), which includes as one of its 17 divisions the Division for the Visually Handicapped (DVH).

CONSUMER ORGANIZATIONS

The field of blindness is noted for active and well-organized groups of consumers. Consumer organizations have been instrumental in lobbying for many of the programs and services previously described (e.g., independent living programs, Randolph–Sheppard Program, HKNC). The following consumer organizations are representative of active, national organizations and are not intended as an exhaustive list of all those that exist in the United States.

The American Council of the Blind (ACB) is a national membership organization composed primarily of people with visual impairments. It has state and regional affiliates, and is committed to improving the lives of individuals with visual impairments. The ACB offers a broad spectrum of programs and services to promote independence and participation in employment, education, legislation, and community affairs covering such areas as information and referral on all aspects of blindness, assistance with legal problems, development and evaluation of technological aids and devices, and monitoring of existing service delivery systems.

Founded in 1940, the National Federation of the Blind (NFB) functions as a mechanism through which people who are blinded or visually impaired can come together in local, state, and national meetings to plan and implement programs to improve the quality of life for people who are blind. The NFB also promotes vocational, cultural, and social advancement in achieving the integration of blind people into society on the basis of equality with sighted persons and strives to take any other action that will improve the overall condition and standard of living of people who are blind.

The National Association for Parents of the Visually Impaired (NAPVI) was founded in 1980 and is composed of parents and families of children with visual impairments, community groups and agencies, and other interested individuals. NAPVI provides support for members and promotes public understanding of the needs and rights of children with visual impairments. The organization also seeks to address parental needs in a wide variety of areas.

The Blinded Veterans Association (BVA) is a veterans service organization serving those who are legally or totally blind. BVA encourages and assists all blinded veterans to take advantage of rehabilitation and vocational training programs and other resources through a field service program.

PROFESSIONALS WITHIN THE FIELD OF BLINDNESS

Included in the variety of professionals who are employed in the field of blindness are the following: the ophthalmologist, optometrist, orthoptist, optician, ocularist, low vision practitioner, rehabilitation counselor, social worker, rehabilitation teacher, orientation and mobility instructor, and special education teacher. No single professional can meet all of the needs of individuals who are blind or visually impaired. It is therefore important for professionals to understand each other's roles and functions and the complementary nature of the rehabilitation team. In some agencies, a team member may perform multiple functions. For example, the positions of rehabilitation teacher and rehabilitation counselor may be combined. Finally, it should be kept in mind that each of the professionals represented on a team may belong to different professional organizations, have various certification or licensure requirements, and subscribe to different codes of ethics. The following is a concise description and discussion of each of these professions.

Ophthalmologists

The ophthalmologist is a medical doctor (M.D.) who specializes in the total care of the eyes, including but not limited to (1) an evaluation of the health of the eyes and the visual system, (2) diagnosis, (3) medical interventions with drugs, noninvasive treatments, surgery, and (4) the prescription of optical corrections. Although a large number of ophthalmologists are generalists within the field of ophthalmology, there are many who specialize in specific types of visual pathology by age or by neurological condition (e.g., pediatric ophthalmology or neuro-ophthalmology). Similarly, rehabilitation clients may require the services of one or more ophthalmologists. For example, an individual with macular degeneration may see a retinal specialist, as well as a low vision specialist, both of whom may be ophthalmologists. The American Academy of Ophthalmology publishes the *Biographical Membership Directory with Resource Mart,* which lists member ophthalmologists by specialities and hospital affiliations.

Optometrists

Optometrists are doctors of optometry (O.D.) who have attended a college of optometry. Optometrists provide a wide variety of services, including diagnosis of visual conditions, prescription of optical corrections, and other noninvasive procedures, for example, patching an amblyopic (lazy) eye. The optometrist's roles and responsibilities differ according to individual state licensing requirements and regulating legislation. Most states allow optometrists to use drugs for both diagnostic and therapeutic purposes; however, rehabilitation counselors should consult their local optometric associations for specific regulations in their states. Similar to ophthalmologists, optometrists also have several specialities, including developmental optometry and pediatric optometry. Numerous optometrists specialize in low vision care, and several colleges of optometry have established their own low vision clinics.

Opticians

Opticians fill the optical prescriptions of ophthalmologists and optometrists. They grind lenses and produce different types of lens corrections for eyeglasses, bifocals, and contact lenses. When people with low vision require unique, individualized lenses (e.g., lenses with very low levels of light transmission), the optician will work closely with the eyecare specialist to accommodate the prescription. Some states have opticianary laws that regulate the strength of a prescription.

Ocularists

When someone needs a prosthesis for a missing eye, the ocularist will construct and fit a cosmetically pleasing device. The ocularist becomes a member of the rehabilitation team when a client has had an eye removed (enucleation) due to trauma or disease or when there has been a congenital condition for which an absent (anopthalmia) eye or a small (microphthalmic) eye needs to be corrected.

Low Vision or Sensory Device Specialists

Rehabilitation professionals who work in low vision clinics or in private, free-standing practices providing low vision care are referred to as low vision specialists. They assist ophthalmologists or optometrists in the instruction of people who receive optical devices and they may also deliver services for which they are otherwise qualified, such as rehabilitation teaching or orientation and mobility training. Presently, there are no state or national certifications or licensure for the specialist in low vision rehabilitation; however, the Pennsylvania College of Optometry has a master's degree program in vision rehabilitation. Professional organizations, such as AER, are exploring issues related to both certification and licensure of low vision specialists.

Ophthalmic Nurses

Some ophthalmic nurses who work under the direction of an ophthalmologist have undergone additional training to provide instruction in the use of optical devices. They will also perform a variety of duties including, but not limited to, taking clinical measurements for acuity and visual fields, and administering medications.

Rehabilitation Teachers

Rehabilitation teachers provide instruction and guidance to adults with visual impairments in six broad skills areas (i.e., adaptive techniques, home management, personal management, communication and education, leisure activity, and home orientation skills) and provide a number of services to help people who are blind or visually impaired to learn adaptive daily living skills. (See also Chapter 9, The Rehabilitation Team.)

Orientation and Mobility Specialists

The orientation and mobility (O&M) specialist provides instruction in travel skills to people with visual impairments, for example, training in the use of the sighted or human guide, the long cane, and electronic travel aids. (O&M specialists do not provide training with dog guides; dog guide training is provided by dog guide schools. See also Chapter 9, The Rehabilitation Team.)

A fairly recent development in O&M is the position of O&M assistant, a paraprofessional with basic use of O&M skills. Providing support and practice to clients, they can instruct clients in the use of the sighted guide technique, in addition to monitoring and supporting skills development in the areas of protective techniques, indoor diagonal case technique, and basic concepts and sensory skills (Wiener & Hill, 1991).

Rehabilitation Counselors

Rehabilitation counselors who work in the field of blindness rehabilitation (1) provide counseling related to adjustment to a visual impairment, (2) assist the client in identifying needs and provide information on services and resources, (3) develop rehabilitation plans, and (4) assist the client in identifying vocational or independent living goals. In most instances, both the education and training of rehabilitation counselors are not specific to the field of blindness and low vision. However, a few universities are providing graduate education for rehabilitation counselors that includes specialized course work in the area of blindness (for example, Mississippi State University and Western Michigan University).

Other members of the rehabilitation team may include a vocational evaluator, who provides vocational assessments, and a placement or job development specialist, who provides education to employers and assists individuals with visual disabilities in securing employment.

EDUCATIONAL PROGRAMS

The experiences people have in educational programs may influence their participation in rehabilitation programs and the types of services that may be needed. Knowledge of educational programs is important because rehabilitation counselors serve as team members in the transition planning that occurs when individuals prepare to leave educational programs to enter the world of work or to participate in rehabilitation programs.

There is strong evidence, through analyses of the register of children who are legally blind maintained by APH that there has been a consistent increase in the number of children with visual impairments who qualify for books and materials provided through federal quota funds available from APH under the auspices of PL 45–186, the Act to Promote the Education of the Blind. Through this legislation, Congress allocates monies annually for the production of specialized books, instructional aids, and equipment for students who are legally blind. The federal quota program, administered by APH in Louisville, Kentucky (Hazekamp & Huebner, 1989; Todd, 1986), can be a valuable resource for rehabilitation counselors. Since 1980, the number of children who are legally blind in the APH registry has increased by more than 20,000, reaching over 56,000 in the 1996 school year (American Printing House for the Blind, 1996; Kirchner, 1983; Kirchner, l988; Kirchner & Stephen, 1987).

Education Legislation

In 1975, the Education for all Handicapped Children Act (EHA) PL 94–142, the most significant legislation affecting children with disabilities, was passed (Huebner & Ferrell, 1986). This federal law was meant to guarantee a free and appropriate public education in the least restrictive environment (LRE) with special education, related services, and an individualized education program (IEP) for each child with a disability. Other provisions guaranteed under this act include protection of due process, nondiscriminatory assessment, confidentiality and record-keeping, provisions for parent surrogates, and categorical priorities.

Protection of due process provides guaranteed procedural safeguards in all matters related to identification, educational placement, and evaluation. For example, the law and its regulations outline specific procedures for parental notification (i.e., families, guardians, or surrogates), when children are to be tested. According to the law, parents must give permission for each test to be administered and be actively involved in educational placement and program decisions. The right to due process was further strengthened in the 1986 Amendments to EHA, PL 99–372, which included the authorization to award reasonable attorneys' fees to certain prevailing parties, and clarified the effect of EHA on rights, procedures, and remedies under other laws relating to the prohibition of discrimination (Office of Special Education Programs, 1987).

The issue of LRE relates to the quality of education provided within a particular placement, as measured by the degree to which the specific, unique needs of students with visual impairments as appropriately assessed and identified in their IEPs, can be met (Huebner & Marshall, 1989). The members of the CEC/DVI (Division on Visual Impairments) stated in one of its position papers that the least restrictive environment should be "the environment in which specialized services are provided by qualified staff with the intensity and frequency needed by each student commensurate with all of his or her specific needs, as appropriately identified in the IEP" (Huebner & Koenig, 1990. p.12).

The IEP is a written statement developed by those individuals who are involved and knowledgeable about the student's educational needs (Heward & Orlansky, 1988). Typically the student's teachers, parents (guardian or surrogate parents), a representative of the local education agency or administrator from the school, other personnel involved in the student's assessment or instructional programs, and in some instances the student, are involved in the development and approval process of the IEP, which must include the following:

- a statement of the student's present levels of educational performance;
- a statement of annual goals, including short-term instructional objectives;
- a statement of the specific special education and related services to be provided to the student, and the extent to which the student will be able to participate in the regular education program of the school;
- the projected date for initiation and anticipated duration of services;
- appropriate objective criteria, and evaluation procedures and schedules for determining on at least an annual basis whether the short-term instructional objectives are being met;
- justification for the type of educational placement;
- a list of individuals who are responsible for implementation of the IEP (Heward & Orlansky, 1992).

Various formats for IEPs have been developed by Local Education Agencies (LEAs) and residential schools for students who are blind or visually impaired (Ward, 1986); however, the IEP used in any educational setting can be very helpful in developing the Individualized Written Rehabilitation Program (IWRP) for rehabilitation services (Simpson, 1986). The IWRP may extend the continuum of services or objectives identified in the IEP. In some circumstances, all of the objectives of the IEP may not be met, in which case it may be appropriate for them to become objectives of the IWRP. Table 10.1 contains sample transition objectives that also demonstrate the relationship between IEPs and IWRPs. (See also Chapter 12, Placement Readiness and Supported Employment.)

In 1986, PL 99–457, an amendment to the EHA, was signed to authorize an early intervention program for infants and toddlers with disabilities and their families. The six major provisions of PL 99–457 were to: (1) extend the authorization of EHA for five years, (2) extend the rights and protection under EHA to children with disabilities ages three through five years in the school year 1990–91 (or 1991–92 if federal appropriations were not sufficient), (3) revise the prior Preschool Incentive Grant program to reflect the increased authorization for serving children three to five years, (4) establish a new state grant program for children with disabilities ages birth through two years to provide early intervention services, (5) strengthen the early education discretionary program to maximize support for achieving the objectives of the early intervention and preschool initiatives, and (6) strengthen provisions governing qualifications of persons providing services under EHA (Office of Special Education Programs, 1987).

In 1990, PL 94–142, parts C through G of the EHA, were reauthorized and PL 101–476, the Individuals with Disabilities Education Act (IDEA) was enacted. Among the changes included in the legislation were: the replacement of the word "handicap" wherever it appeared with the word "disability," and the inclusion of "counseling" and "social work services" to the definition of related services. IDEA further required that a student's IEP include a statement of needed transition services, beginning no later than age 16 and annually thereafter (and, when determined appropriate for the individual, beginning at age 14 or younger), also containing, when appropriate, a statement of the interagency responsibilities or linkages (or both) before the student leaves the school setting. This section (1401-D) of the law has significant implications for the rehabilitation counselor who is often part of the team that assists in developing transition objectives. From age 16 many individuals become part of the rehabilitation counselor's caseload. Therefore section 1401-D highlights the importance of collaborative efforts between rehabilitation and education services. This law also includes such significant

Table 10.1. Student Transition Objectives

Transition-age students with visual impairments will:

1. Recognize the impact of school experience and community experience on future vocational plans/achievement.
2. Understand job clusters/job families.
3. Understand that careers have a specific pattern of preparation, both formal (academic) and informal (experiential).
4. Recognize that adult role models (parents, teachers, siblings) have an effect on one's career choices.
5. Develop the ability after gaining information to identify various tasks that are a part of a job (job analysis).
6. Understand the concept of job accommodation and identify some personal accommodation needs (e.g., applicable technological devices, correct lighting).
7. Match personal interests and abilities with possible career choices.
8. Increase knowledge base of occupations and careers through reading, observations, and gathering information.
9. Identify job-seeking skills.
10. Internalize personal information for use in job seeking (e.g., basic job application and interview information).
11. Recognize interdependence of people in the work environment.
12. Develop a personal strategy for involving relevant resource persons in one's career planning process (e.g., school counselor, parents, career development team).
13. Seek opportunities for work responsibility in the home, school, and neighborhood.
14. Develop an understanding of the value of work to self and to society (not just monetary but personal and societal).
15. Identify occupational opportunities that are available in the local communities (including resources for the information).
16. Identify and exhibit positive work habits that generalize to all work settings (e.g., behavioral aspects, performance aspects, safety aspects, interdependent aspects).
17. Determine training needs (academic/vocational/on-the-job) and experiences to achieve chosen career goals.
18. Increase understanding and knowledge of occupations and varied work settings through involvement in actual after-school/summer work experiences.
19. Refine knowledge of job clusters/job families.
20. Develop independent living and personal management skills that are generalized to a variety of occupations and settings.
21. Refine ability to task-analyze a variety of jobs.
22. Identify personal job accommodation needs and actively seek funds, and so forth, to secure any assistive/adaptive technology that facilitates employment.
23. Refine job-seeking skills in résumé development, employment resources identification, and interviewing skills development.
24. Develop acceptable work habits with special emphasis on responding to supervision and adapting to change.
25. Identify "promotability" skills.
26. Acquire and utilize labor market information from varied resources on a continuing basis.
27. Develop the concept of work being a valuable personal experience and social contribution (Simpson, 1986, pp. 412–415).

improvements as programs to promote research, technology, and transition programs, as well as incentives to address the needs of individuals with disabilities from minority backgrounds. IDEA was re-authorized and modified in 1997.

At the local level, boards of education are responsible for direct services, which must comply with federal and state laws. Specific information on state education laws and regulations is available from each State Department of Education or Public Instruction (Hazekamp & Huebner, 1989). Because legislation is an ongoing process, it is the duty of each professional to remain up-to-date in regard to state and federal legislative activities.

Specialized Schools

Specialized schools, referred to as "schools for the blind" or residential schools, have had an important role in the education of children with visual impairments. They were originally begun to address the gaps that existed in the public educational system, because of the lack of special education programs. Although some children with visual impairments attended public school as early as 1900, a majority of students (88.4 percent) were attending specialized schools in 1950, compared with 88.4 percent attending public schools by 1988 (Erin, 1993b; Lowenfeld, 1989). In contrast to the percentages, the actual numbers of students attending specialized schools has changed from 7,892 in 1960 (American Printing House for the Blind, 1963) to 4,195 in 1991 (Poppe, 1991). The population of students in specialized schools, however, has shifted from almost exclusively students with visual impairments to students with multiple disabilities, including visual impairments, although this varies by school (Erin, 1993b).

PL 94–142 and IDEA have substantially affected the role of specialized schools. The role of the specialized school has been debated heatedly (Hatlen, 1993) and placement of students in residential schools is now considered on a case-by-case basis. In litigation involving issues related to "appropriate education" and LRE, however, "court decisions favoring specialized school placement have based their decisions on the need for instruction beyond the traditional school day, the presence of communication difficulties that preclude beneficial interaction with nondisabled peers, and the social-emotional adjustment of a student" (Erin, 1993b, p. 221).

With legislative mandates, limited resources, and changing needs of students, the roles of specialized schools have also evolved (Koehler & Loftin, 1993). Including both direct and indirect services, some of the present roles are as follows:

- Complementary service provider to children with visual impairments. The services, which would be utilized when a school district is unable to provide services or address the challenges of a particular individual, include short-term placement to address disability-specific issues (Baker, 1993; Erin, 1993b; MacCuspie, Harmer, McConnell, Fricker, & Johnson, 1993); summer programs (DeMott, 1993), including career development programs, recreational programs (McCartney, 1993), teen institutes addressing drug and alcohol issues (Finnegan, Rice, & Harris, 1993); short-term remedial programs (Curry, 1993; Scholl, 1993); life skills centers for students with multiple disabilities (Erin, 1993b); and transition and placement services (Koehler & Loftin, 1993).
- Resource centers for parents, teachers, and students. Schools serve as a central source of educational materials and serve as information and referral resources (DeMott, 1993; Erin, 1993b; Scholl, 1993).
- Diagnostic centers. Specialized schools provide educational evaluations and low vision clinics (Curry, 1993; Scholl, 1993).
- Consultation or outreach technical assistance (Baker, 1993; Miller, 1993; Stenehjem, 1993). In this capacity,

specialized schools may offer on-site consultation; workshop presentations, including presentations by students (Hinson, 1993); professional training institutes, including summer programs for teachers (DeMott, 1993); and home training to parents with infants (Smith, 1993). Recipients of these services would include small day-school programs (Scholl, 1993), rural areas (Brasher, 1993), and local educational associations.

- Research and demonstration. Specialized schools may also serve as research centers (Scholl, 1993) and as demonstration schools with best-practices instruction (DeMott, 1993).

Not all specialized schools have adopted all of these roles, but the preceding list is representative of the variety of roles and services that specialized schools continue to provide.

Bina (1993) described a number of myths identified with specialized schools that may be associated with the placement decisions of individual students. One myth is the notion that specialized schools segregate and overprotect students from the real world. Bina contends, however, that specialized schools provide for increased participation in extracurricular activities, which enhance the self-image, confidence, and skills of students. Also McMahon (1992) found that 50 percent of students in specialized schools were involved in cooperative programming with nearby public schools, and that as many as 90 percent of students with visual impairments have attended both public and specialized schools.

A second myth is the idea that specialized schools are now solely for students with multiple disabilities. Again, McMahon's (1992) research reported that 45 percent of the students in specialized schools were in academic programs, with 39 percent attending college. Some individuals believe that specialized schools are too expensive, because the cost per student is $3,000 in the public school versus $30,000 in specialized schools (Allman, 1991). But Bina maintained that the costs are reasonable, based on 24-hour-per-day coverage and the fact that many costs that are factored into specialized school expenditures (e.g., food, recreation, utilities) are not included in the per pupil costs cited by public schools. As Bina pointed out, the third myth suggests that the placement of students is not always based on LRE, but rather on the least expensive placement. A fourth myth is that specialized schools are old-fashioned. To counter this myth, Bina pointed out that most children return home every weekend and 40 percent of children attending specialized schools return home every night. Also specialized schools have reemphasized braille instruction, changed dormitories to be more homelike, added genetic counseling and instruction in the use of high-tech communication equipment and developed courses for gifted students with visual impairment. A fifth myth is that decentralized services are better than centralized services. Bina counters again that both higher education and magnet schools are based on the concept of centralized services. The final myth addressed by Bina is that visually impaired children need to be integrated with and interact with sighted children. To this myth, Bina cited the benefits of peer counseling, shared group experiences, and increased opportunities for success in a "smaller pond."

The debate over specialized schools will undoubtedly continue; however, it is evident that the programs at special schools have improved the quality of services provided to individuals with visual impairments (Geruschat, 1993) and that the concept of choice implies that students and parents should have a range of choices in both the public and private sectors (Erin, 1993a). Moreover, in an investigation of the learning and study strategies of secondary school students with visual impairments (Erin, Corn, & Wolffe, 1993), no significant differences were found by preferred medium (that is, braille versus print), school placement (namely, public versus specialized), or plans to attend college. In a national study of legally blind adults employed by NIB-associated agencies, Fireison (1997) found that persons who attended a school for the blind were considerably more braille literate than both those who attended public schools and those who experienced a combination of school settings.

Unique Learning Needs of Students with Visual Impairments

Blindness or severe visual impairment places significant obstacles before children during the formative years. Sight, the sensory mode used most frequently, efficiently, and confidently by a majority of people is not available to children who are blind, and it also has profound limitations for children with visual impairments. This sensory impairment alters the way children view, learn about, experience, and interact with the world and society (Hazekamp & Huebner, 1989). Students who are blind or visually impaired learn through alternative modes and often require individualized learning experiences and instruction in the use of specialized skills and equipment unique to visual impairments. As a result, the curriculum needs, which are the same for children with and without visual impairments must be presented differently to maximize learning.

Reading and writing are examples of curriculum needs that are the same for all children, but require modified presentation and skills for children with visual impairments. These may be thought of as the "core curriculum" (Corn, Hatlen, Huebner, Ryan, & Siller, 1995). Although the same pedagogical approaches to teaching reading and writing can be effectively applied with all students, a child who is totally blind also requires instruction in the use of braille, rather than print. The child who is totally blind learns to tactilely identify and write the braille alphabet configurations, punctuation, format indicators and other symbols in literary braille. In addition, tactile reading skills are learned to facilitate efficiency, speed, and comprehension.

There are also curriculum needs that are unique for students with visual impairments. These are referred to as "*expanded* curricula" (Corn et al., 1995). Those that will be presented in the following sections include: concept development, low vision training, some aspects of academics, communication skills, sensorimotor skills, social skills, orientation and mobility, activities of daily living, career/vocational training, and work experience programs.

Concept Development

Sighted children learn a considerable amount through indirect methods and observation or experience observational incidental learning. They watch and imitate behaviors and often do not require direct instruction. Such visual modeling may not be possible for children who are blind and is restricted for children with low vision (Hazekamp & Huebner, 1989). Therefore, concept development generally does not occur at a comparable rate for children with and without visual impairments (Warren, 1994). Students with visual impairments must be provided with direct, consistent, and meaningful instruction with active and functional participation in which concepts and applications are demonstrated.

Whenever possible, actual physical items rather than models should be used when teaching concepts. However, for things that are too large (airplanes), too small (ants), too delicate (spider webs), too dangerous (fire), models must and should be used (Lowenfeld, 1971). Before models can be used effectively, it is necessary for students with visual impairments to be taught to interpret and analyze them. Such spatial concepts as over, under, top, bottom are critical and need to be learned. Sometimes the student receives instruction in general concepts through studies in concept development classes and, as the need arises, in classes for or during daily activities. Instruction in spatial and environmental concepts integral to orientation and mobility (O&M) are frequently provided by the mobility specialist (Welsh & Blasch, 1980).

Students who have visual impairments often have the ability to utilize conceptual terminology without really understanding the concept. This is known as verbalization (Harley, 1963). Therefore, it is imperative that a student's understanding be demonstrated through action, demonstration, and application to determine if the conceptualization is complete (Swallow & Huebner, 1987).

Low Vision

Students with low vision should be evaluated periodically to determine the extent of potential use and level of visual efficiency. This process includes clinical examinations, possible prescription of electronic and nonelectronic aids along with instruction in use and functional vision assessments (Corn, 1986; Corn, 1988; Corn & Koenig 1996; Roessing, 1982).

Most students with visual impairments benefit from instruction in how to scan the environment and interpret visual information, and how to gather, combine, and use visual and other sensory information to their best advantage. Often, students with low vision do not realize that visual information is available, or if they do, they are unable to apply it. They therefore need to learn to analyze situations and to ask questions to gain verbal explanations to supplement the visual and other sensory information they are gathering. They further need to learn how to read most efficiently; this sometimes means using optical or non-optical devices, scanning/tracking strategies, enlarged print or, for others, it may mean using reduced-size print materials. Other reading strategies may also need to be learned, such as maintaining contact with the line being read or supplementing visual reading with other reading modes. For most students with visual impairment, it means learning to use a combination of reading modes for various tasks, for example, audio tapes for novels, large print for mathematics textbooks, braille for history textbooks and note-taking, and a combination of typing with closed-circuit enlargement, computers with braille or speech output, or paperless braillers for writing assignments.

Helping students with visual impairments improve their literacy skills (through braille instruction, for example) is a key part of educational services.

Academics

The vast majority of standard "core" curriculum subjects (e.g., mathematics, English, biology, history, geography, and social studies) are provided through these subject teachers (Corn et al., 1996). Although vision teachers are frequently also certified in elementary or secondary education, they are not certified in all special subject areas, such as reading, advanced mathematics, foreign languages, or the physical sciences. Their role, which does not include being subject-area tutors, is to address the *expanded core* curricular areas unique to visual impairment (Corn et al., 1995 and 1996; Hatlen, 1996). Vision teachers work with academic subject teachers in how to best (1) adapt presentation of information, (2) use specialized equipment, and (3) use alternative strategies and learning modes. Students receive instruction in the use of specialized materials, as well as strategies and skills from the vision teacher (Huebner & Strumwasser, 1987).

The regular teacher is responsible for the adaptations of the presentation of the "*core*" academic curriculum. When students experience difficulty in understanding or learning concepts associated with academic subjects and it is suspected that the cause is related to visual impairment, then it is most appropriate for the academic subject teacher and vision teacher to communicate and develop a coordinated instructional effort. Mutual, ongoing consultation among the vision and academic teachers will facilitate the process of determining how to best provide meaningful instruction so that the concepts are learned. It is recommended that the rehabilitation counselor assigned to a school-age student communicate with subject-area teachers and the vision teacher to learn about the client's academic standing, in addition to her social and emotional status.

For the most part, the education programs for students with visual impairments follow the same *core* curriculum as that of the other students in the same school or LEA. Some core curricular and expanded core curricular areas that will require modifications unique for visually impaired children include, but are not limited to

- social studies (e.g., braille, recordings, tactile relief maps);
- mathematics (e.g., models, graphic aids, abacus, talking calculator, adapted measuring devices);
- science (e.g., descriptions of diagrams, hands-on experience with materials, modification of laboratory paraphernalia, use of buddy-system for laboratory work);
- foreign languages (e.g., availability of materials in accessible media, computer software designed for the foreign language being studied, instruction in braille for accented letters that are different from unaccented English letters);
- creative arts (e.g., use of senses to assure maximum observation skills, increased first-hand experiences, opportunities to explore and participate in art, dance, and music); and
- physical education (e.g., participation with sighted students in physical education activities that are such potential life-long leisure activities as bowling, swimming, and golf) (Corn et al., 1995 and 1996; Hatlen, 1996, and Huebner et al., 1986).

Communication

Communication involves both receptive and expressive aspects of sharing ideas, feelings, and information. The receptive communication modes of students with visual impairments may include print reading with and without magnification or electronic devices, listening, and braille. Expressive communication modes may include typing, braille, handwriting, use of personal computers, and nonverbal communication cues (Heinze, 1986).

Students with visual impairments need to learn a variety of skills to communicate with one another and other people. Thorough assessments are conducted to determine students' communication abilities and to determine the most appropriate modes to be learned. For example, if students have sufficient vision to read normal-size print, but if it is a particularly laborious and time-consuming process that is not improved through magnification or other visual reading modifications and strategies, it is recommended that nonvisual methods be explored and learned. That is not to say that visual reading cannot also be taught, but reading efficiency is a major consideration. Such students may use the visual mode for reading notes and other short-term activities; listening and braille may be used for textbooks, novels, and other reading activities of longer duration.

With respect to expressive modes, students generally receive specialized instruction in nonverbal communication skills, keyboarding, handwriting, braille, and personal computers with add-ons for accessibility. Some students with visual impairments need instruction in nonverbal communication skills, if they are unaware of the effect of appropriate and inappropriate body language on communication (Huebner, 1986).

Sensorimotor Skills

Students with visual impairments also need specific instruction in the utilization and integration of senses. For example, they must be taught to (1) identify the differences between direct, indirect, and reflected sounds; (2) determine what may be causing the sounds to be one of these three distinct types; and (3) interpret and utilize such information to function effectively within the environment. Sensory training includes developing the student's ability to utilize all of the senses. Instruction is considered to be best when it is provided in controlled environments and moves progressively to natural surroundings where the sensory stimulation would most naturally be experienced (Hazekamp & Huebner, 1989).

Sensory training is an ongoing process (Swallow & Huebner, 1987). It requires cooperative efforts of teachers, parents, and all significant adults in the students' lives. Encouragement to ask questions and seek affirmation of sensory interpretation and integration is critical to a student's sensory development. For students who are congenitally blind, emphasis is generally on explanation, recognition, identification, interpretation, application, and transference of learned sensory abilities to new situations that can help in orientation.

The initial training of students who are adventitiously blind emphasizes accurate interpretation of sensory intake, confidence in using senses other than vision, and integration of sensory intake including any vision (Kimbrough, Huebner, & Lowry, 1976). With low vision students, confidence in the use of other senses and integration with existing vision is critical.

The absence or limitation of vision interferes with students' ability to observe and replicate motor actions; therefore, without early and consistent intervention, motor delay will likely occur (Warren, 1994). This is most often observed in poor muscle tone, unusual gait and stride, and poor coordination, and balance. Motor skills are refined in environments that provide opportunities for practice of physical activities (Krogman, 1972). Parents and teachers are encouraged to permit the child to explore and participate in physical activities.

Ophthalmologists will, on occasion, restrict a student's physical activity, because some physical movements can increase the potential for further damage to the eye, such as retinal detachments. Frequently, ophthalmologists who have limited experience with visually impaired individuals are not aware of the capabilities of individuals with severe visual impairments. As a result, they may be overly cautious and recommend physical restrictions that are not necessary. Therefore, it is suggested that explanations for any physical activity restriction be obtained to ensure its justification. Accordingly, it is also recommended that the student/client, parents, teachers, and rehabilitation counselors acquire specific directives from ophthalmologists as to specific physical activities that are to be limited.

Social Skills

The area of social skills encompasses a wide spectrum. Again, direct instruction is required in many areas related to social skills because of the lack of or limited ability of the student to observe behaviors. Manners, table etiquette, nonverbal communication, polite verbal exchange using appropriate voice level, taking turns, grooming, clothing selection, and appropriate clothing for a myriad of social occasions are only some of the components of a social skills curriculum (Corn et al., 1995 and 1996; Hatlen, 1996). Some units of sex education curriculum are also included in social skills courses. It is critical for all adults involved with instructional programs for students with visual impairments to recognize the long-range effects of appropriate social skills (Sacks & Wolffe, 1992; Swallow & Huebner, 1987).

Students in specialized schools have many opportunities to socialize with other students who are blind or visually impaired, but they also need to be encouraged to socialize with sighted peers in their home communities. Often, students educated in their local schools have opportunities to socialize with sighted students, but rarely with other visually impaired students. Summer camps and summer programs at specialized schools can afford these students an opportunity to meet with other students with visual impairments. Students should always be given time to interact with sighted individuals as well as individuals with visual impairments in order to develop their self-esteem and to develop a healthy and realistic self-concept (Tuttle & Tuttle, 1996). Career days representing a variety of employment options can be advantageous for students (MacCuspie et al., 1993; Simpson, Huebner & Roberts, 1986a). It is urged that students be given continuing and differing social experiences to develop the variety of skills needed in the range of casual to the most formal situations.

Orientation and Mobility

O&M are two separate functions that are nearly always presented together when discussing this area of study for students with visual impairments. This is because the components of both are interdependent. Orientation is the "process of using the senses to establish one's position and relationship to all other significant objects in one's environment" (Hill, 1986, p. 315). Mobility is defined as the "capacity, readiness, and facility to move about in one's environment" (Hill, 1986, p. 315).

Students generally begin O&M instruction, part of the expanded core curriculum, by learning specific techniques to afford safety and comfort while traveling with others; these are included in sighted guide techniques (Corn et al., 1995 and 1996; Hatlen, 1996). As students gain independence in their travel, they not only increase the physical areas in which they may move about freely, safely, and confidently, but also they begin to assume responsibility and take charge of their lives. While traveling independently in their schools, neighborhoods, and communities, they learn life skills associated with such independent movements as doing errands, visiting friends, using public transportation, being on time and adhering to schedules, and shopping for their own clothes and necessities. All these experiences have ramifications for taking on adult responsibilities later associated with independent living and employment skills. Because of the shortage of qualified O&M personnel (Uslan, Hill, & Peck, 1989), limited instructional time within the school day and other factors, many students with visual impairments are presently graduating from high school with limited independent mobility skills.

Activities of Daily Living

Activities of daily living (ADL), part of the expanded core curriculum, include a myriad of skills, generally including "table etiquette, eating, hygiene, personal grooming, organization, clothing care, food preparation, house care, money management, shopping, sewing, telephone use, time-telling, child care, and minor household maintenance" (Corn et al., 1995 and 1996; Hatlen, 1996, Huebner, 1986, p. 343). Learning such activities is an ongoing process, which takes place in many environments (Swallow & Huebner, 1987). Direct instruction is provided by many adults involved with the child in the home, and by the vision teacher in school. In some instances, rehabilitation teachers are hired by school districts to provide essential instruction, and specialized schools often have teachers whose primary responsibility is to teach ADL. In specialized schools, childcare workers or house parents also take on the responsibility for teaching many ADL skills.

Career/Vocational Training

Learning about the multitude of potential careers and jobs available in our society is a life-long activity. Children and adolescents with visual impairments need to have adults spend time with them to expose and explain career options, and to work with the students to learn job responsibilities. Students are encouraged to have chores both in the home and at school and to carry out their jobs in a timely and responsible manner (Ferris, 1991).

There are still some public school vocational training programs that resist enrolling students with visual impairments. This resistance occurs primarily because some vocational education teachers are unfamiliar with the safety techniques and other modifications in procedures that may be needed by an individual with a visual impairment. Many specialized schools have well-developed vocational training options for their students. Some of these programs are joint efforts with the public schools in the vicinity of the specialized facility. It is necessary to assess each program separately to determine its potential for meeting individual student needs.

Work Experience Programs

There are parallels between career/vocational readiness programs and work experience programs today for students with visual impairments. Strong work experience programs or work experience programs that routinely accept and involve these students are more the exception than the rule. Students with visual impairments must be encouraged and given the needed emotional and functional support, both socially and through job coaching. Many students will need assistance to seek potential after-school and summer jobs (Jeppson & Hammer, 1992). They will also need the support of the vision teacher and the rehabilitation counselor to gain access to many excellent school job experience programs that have never included students with visual impairments.

Students with visual impairments must be provided with guidance and instruction not only in job possibilities, opportunities, roles and responsibilities, but also in job-seeking strategies, résumé production and mock-job interviewing in preparation for actual interviews. Frequently, the vision teacher, rehabilitation counselor, and vocational education teacher need to work cooperatively to gain access to work experience programs (Ferris, 1991) based in or coordinated through the school.

Precollege Training and Special Summer School Options

Precollege training and summer school programs can meet a number of needs of children and adolescents with visual impairments. Because a majority of children with visual impairments participate in standard curriculum offerings in the local schools and, have curriculum areas unique to visual impairment it is difficult for students to absorb all the content that is offered to them within a nine-month school period. Research (Bishop, 1971; Wormsley, 1979) suggests that students with visual impairments may also require up to twice the amount of time it would take a sighted student to complete the same reading, research, and writing tasks. Subject areas specific to visual impairments are frequently taken during study periods, which reduces the availability of other electives and participation in extracurricular activities and after-school employment. Because of the importance of these areas in the development of a student's social and career development, summer programs can be used to balance academics and other skill training.

Many of these programs are made available through specialized schools for the blind, special education departments at college/university training sites, local school districts, state departments of education, and rehabilitation agencies. They are, for the most part, federally or state funded through short-term grants, which makes them inconsistently available (Spungin, 1975). Nonetheless, precollege and summer school programs can provide an array of offerings to facilitate such individualized programs as remedial course work, training in ADL and O&M skills, career/vocational training, and such special programs as those designed for gifted students or those specifically oriented toward college preparation.

University Programs

Most colleges and universities now have offices that provide assistance to students with disabilities (Senge & Dote-Kwan, 1995). Individuals who are working in college offices that provide disability services frequently are members of AHEAD, the Association on Higher Education and Disability. AHEAD represents more than 500 institutions in the United States and Canada and has a blindness/visual impairment special-interest group that publishes a quarterly newsletter with information to assist in advocacy and service efforts for students with visual impairments (Koek, Martin, & Pare, 1987). *A Guide to Colleges for Visually Impaired Students* (Liscio, 1986) can also be helpful when working with students who are interested in attending college. In addition to providing general information about the college or university, this guide lists general campus data about students with disabilities and the special services that are available for students with visual impairments.

Transition

Transition is an action-oriented process that encompasses a broad array of experiences and services that lead to employment (Will, 1984). In the mid-1980s, the federal government identified transition as a priority and supported research and model programs that addressed transition efforts from school to work for young adults with disabilities. This initiative facilitated a heightened level of awareness and sensitivity to the various transitions children experience, such as movement from one education level to another, and from school to work.

All people face transitions. As Will (1985) noted, "as roles, locations or relationships change, all of us must adapt, and we do so with a certain amount of disruption or stress. The transition from school to working life calls for a range of choices about career opportunities, living arrangements, social life, and economic goals that often have life-long consequences. For individuals with disabilities, this process is often made more difficult by limitations that can be imposed by others' perceptions of disability" (p. 1). Therefore, it is critically important for the IEP team members to give careful consideration to the transition plan that is devised for each student.

Collaboration, a key element of successful transition, involves students, parents, teachers, and rehabilitation counselors in an interactive process facilitated by an impartial leader who can structure opportunities for discussion and systematic planning (Dick, Moulin, Pelligrini, & Traub, 1988; Simpson, Huebner, & Roberts, 1986b; Sisson & Babeo, 1992). Most states now have formal collaborative agreements among all agencies and organizations providing services to students in transition. Collaboration requires a continuous and considerable investment of time; however, as Bellamy (1985) noted, transition is "a time when the effectiveness of our collective investment in disability services is challenged in the acid tests of employment, self-sufficiency, and community integration" (p. 11). The three needs that have been identified as contributing to transition objectives for students, parents, and education and rehabilitation professionals are as follows: (1) students with visual impairments need to develop psychosocial and work-related skills that will enable them to participate in employment; (2) parents need to be an integral part of the collaborative process that facilitates the transition from school to work for their children; and (3) professionals need to work collaboratively to facilitate the transition of youth with visual disabilities from school to work. Table 10.1 contains examples of transition objectives for students. These transition objectives can also provide a helpful framework for rehabilitation counselors to use in their assessment of the career knowledge of any individual seeking rehabilitation services (see also Chapter 11, Counseling and Career Intervention Services).

SUMMARY

A variety of public and private agencies and organizations provide services for individuals with visual impairments and their families. Legislation has also provided a number of public programs including the state-federal vocational rehabilitation programs, the Randolph–Sheppard Program, JWOD, and the VA. Private organizations, such as the AFB, the NIB, the HKNC, the Hadley School for the Blind, and an array of other private organizations have provided leadership, services, and advocacy for persons with visual impairments. Education services are another critical factor in equalizing opportunities for individuals with visual impairments. Students who are blind or who have low vision have some unique learning needs that must be addressed as part of their educational program.

Both public and private agencies are staffed by professionals who make up the rehabilitation team. These professionals (e.g., ophthalmologists, optometrists, opticians, low vision specialists, rehabilitation teachers, orientation and mobility specialists, and rehabilitation counselors) are members of professional organizations that foster research, communication, and advocacy on behalf of individuals with disabilities, including individuals with visual impairments. Futhermore, such consumer organizations as ACB, NFB, Blinded Veterans Association, and NAPVI have been a strong and vital force both in advocating on behalf of visually impaired individuals and providing education, support, and other resources that facilitate the integration of people with visual impairments into all areas of society.

Collectively, the service systems (both public and private) the educational system, and the professional and consumer organizations offer a wide array of services that can enhance the lives of individuals with visual impairments. These programs, organizations, and agencies are also major resources for the rehabilitation professional working in the field of blindness rehabilitation. Some provide information on specific types of vision loss or new technology; others provide a forum for individuals with visual impairments to network with individuals with similar impairments and concerns. By understanding the range of resources, rehabilitation counselors can better address the unique needs of individual clients.

LEARNING ACTIVITIES

1. Investigate the history of your local ACB Chapter and NFB Chapter. What are their major philosophical differences?
2. Approximately 50 percent of the states have separate agencies or commissions for people who are blind. What evidence can you generate to show that a separate state agency for the blind is more cost-effective and provides services in a more timely manner than a combined agency?
3. Working with your professor, contact a specialized school or public school program for students with visual impairments and arrange to spend a day in observation. Following the observation, identify the unique skill areas that are addressed, the strengths and weaknesses of the students' performances, and write a report of your observations.
4. Working with your professor, contact a rehabilitation counselor who is a member of a transition team for a student with a visual impairment. Arrange to attend a transition team meeting with the counselor and other team members. Prior to the meeting, spend time with the counselor to obtain background information. Observe the meeting and write a report of your observations, including that which was done well and areas that need to be improved. Be sure to explain your decisions and give examples of how you would improve the process.

CHAPTER 11

Counseling and Career Development Interventions

Gerald Miller and William H. Graves

Counseling is the foundation of the rehabilitation process and rehabilitation counselors have a critical role in helping individuals and their families understand and adapt to visual impairments. In addition to knowledge and skills in counseling, counselors who are working in the field of vision rehabilitation need to understand the counseling issues of individuals who are visually impaired, including the impact of visual impairments on career development. The objectives of this chapter are to (1) identify those counselor characteristics and personality traits that have been identified as necessary by individuals with visual impairments, (2) describe counseling considerations that are specific to visually impaired individuals and their families, and (3) identify career development interventions that can be used in working with individuals who are visually impaired.

COUNSELING INDIVIDUALS WITH VISUAL IMPAIRMENTS

The principles of rehabilitation counseling with people who are visually impaired are the same as those that govern counseling in general. As Vash (1981) stated, "Human beings are more alike than different, regardless of variances in their physical bodies, sensory capacities, or intellectual abilities" (p. xiii). The lack of visual cues and the psychological factors that are unique to being blind, however, have a deep effect upon the counseling relationship (Rusalem, 1972). Therefore, in addition to knowledge of vision and psychological factors related to visual impairments, counselors need information regarding medical and ophthalmological conditions and treatment, including low vision services. Other required knowledge areas include evaluation and training (e.g., communication skills, mobility, vocational assessment and evaluation, aids and devices, occupational information, and placement techniques). A knowledge of community resources and legislation is also valuable.

Knowledge and the application of that knowledge to individuals who are visually impaired, however, are not the sole determinants of the success of the rehabilitation process. The characteristics of counselors themselves have a significant impact on the counselor-client relationship.

COUNSELOR CHARACTERISTICS

The counselor's personality is one of the more important factors in determining the outcome of counseling effectiveness (Hardy, 1972). Kadushin (1972) noted that "a client should expect the counselor to be both technically efficient and empathetic, respectful, and genuine" (p. 3).

Counselors are also encouraged to be creative and imaginative.

At consumer meetings in five states, individuals with visual impairments were asked to identify the qualities that a rehabilitation counselor should have. The dominant characteristics identified were (1) personal qualities, (2) communication skills, and (3) specific information about visual impairments. In terms of personal qualities, most clients stated that understanding and acceptance were their greatest needs. "Supportive," "caring," "warmth," "patience," and "encouragement" were the words most frequently used by clients in identifying the personal qualities they expected a rehabilitation counselor to possess.

The expression of personal qualities has implications for working with individuals who are experiencing a visual impairment. Research (e.g., Smith-Hansen, 1977) demonstrates the importance of verbal and nonverbal cues to the client's perception of the counselor's level of empathy, respect, and genuineness. These personal qualities are communicated not only in words, but also through the counselor's tone of voice, inflection, and sound. Nonverbal cues may include body movements, direction of gaze, and smiles. Because communication occurs through visual means, as well as through conversation, the rehabilitation counselor is advised to be alert to this fact.

Communication is vitally important. Clients stated that the quality of the interview was affected by confidentiality, privacy, and an atmosphere that facilitated freedom of communication. Specific techniques that rehabilitation counselors might employ to enhance communication with clients who are blind or visually impaired were also identified. For example, speaking clearly and at a moderate rate is important for several reasons. Sighted individuals rely on additional cues from studying a person's body language or by reading lips to augment spoken words. Speaking clearly and at a moderate rate enables individuals with visual impairments to process information that is obtained primarily through the auditory sense. Also, some visually impaired individuals have diminished hearing as a result of a secondary disability or advanced age. Therefore, counselors are advised to take care to speak clearly and repeat information if there is any chance that the client did not understand.

Attentiveness is also critically important for effective communication. The rehabilitation counselor is encouraged to maintain eye contact and be alert to the client's verbal and physical expressions. One individual who is blind remembered being "turned off" when he felt that the counselor was looking out a window, instead of giving full attention to the client during a meeting. Another remembered the counselor yawning during the interview. A client's inability to see does not mean that the client is unaware when counselors are not paying attention. If a counselor is not attentive, it will usually be noted by the client, and will be viewed by the client in the same way a sighted individual would view the behavior (i.e., as disrespectful or uncaring).

Although the qualities of personality and communication were stressed, the need for relevant information was seen by clients as equally important. Many clients expressed the need to receive information about vocational opportunities and training for people with visual impairments. Clients expected complete knowledge about services of the rehabilitation agency, as well as additional community resources. At least two individuals expressed concern that the rehabilitation counselor did not provide them with information regarding sponsorship for such services as equipment or clothing.

The rehabilitation counselor must possess the requisite knowledge and skills; however, the counselor does not have to be an expert in each of the specialized areas of blindness. As part of a team, rehabilitation counselors also work with other rehabilitation professionals, including rehabilitation teachers, orientation and mobility (O&M) specialists, and low vision specialists, who have knowledge and skills that complement those of the rehabilitation counselor.

Counseling relationships are also dependent on the ability of counselors to provide an atmosphere in which clients feel free to express themselves. Rapport needs to be established so that clients feel free to talk about personal issues and, if necessary, express any feelings they may have—for example, feelings of inadequacy or anxiety. The rehabilitation counselor is encouraged to provide productive counseling as a rehabilitation service when needed, along with the psychological insight necessary for designing and implementing a beneficial plan of services. To do this well, time and patience are required. Being blind is a unique and severe impairment that requires significant attention to individual client needs. Becoming impatient or responding with quick solutions may result from organizational/agency pressures but they should not overcome the rehabilitation counselor's sounder instincts to be guided by the needs of the individual client.

THE INITIAL INTERVIEW

The counseling relationship begins with the initial interaction between the client and the counselor. The first interview, usually referred to as the "initial interview," is particularly important in the counseling process and in determining rehabilitation outcomes (Huber & Backlund, 1992; Lukas, 1993). "Authorities in the field of counseling uniformly agree that the initial interview is the most important interview in the counseling process. Because it is at this juncture that an effective counseling relationship is or is not established" (Stone, Endo, Spear, Rivera, & Petrusa, 1977, p. 75). The initial interaction between the client and counselor, however, does not usually occur in the initial interview. The client's expectations and views of the agency and counselor begin with the initial contact, which precedes the initial interview.

Before the Interview

Communication before the first face-to-face interview often sets a tone that will affect the success or failure of the individual's rehabilitation process. The first contact between counselor and client usually takes place through written correspondence. The importance of this event is underscored by the fact that many individuals with visual impairments are unable to read print. Therefore, although clients may receive letters, they may be unable to read them. Also, not all individuals who are visually impaired have access to people who are available or interested enough to read correspondence to them. Because of issues related to need for privacy or fears of dependency, some individuals may be reluctant to ask for assistance in reading this very important correspondence. Further complications may arise if the language used in the letter is neither clear to the reader nor to the client. Some individuals may have also had negative experiences with social service organizations and, accordingly, may not respond in a positive manner. Others may perceive the offer of rehabilitation services as "charity" and the letter will be ignored for this reason.

Because all of these factors may affect the degree to which an individual with a visual impairment responds to the rehabilitation counselor's letter, counselors are urged to resist the temptation to evaluate the client's lack of response to a letter as a lack of interest or as a failure to cooperate. It is recommended instead that counselors be quite careful in the interpretation of client motivation and assess all factors that may contribute to a lack of client response. Following up on initial correspondence with a telephone call can provide an opportunity for the counselor to respond to the concerns of clients.

It is also advisable, prior to the interview, to provide potential clients with materials that may assist them in understanding the services of the rehabilitation agency, as well as their rights and responsibilities. Again, counselors are encouraged to keep in mind that many clients will be unable to read these materials and are dependent on family or friends for reading or interpretation. Therefore, providing materials in alternative formats is a consideration. Some clients know braille; others may use tape recorders. The follow-up telephone call may be used to determine the client's preferred format for any agency literature.

It is suggested that the telephone call and referral material contain the elements of directness, simplicity, and courtesy. In many ways, the counselor's approach is similar to that used in marketing. To sell a product, the customer must trust the seller. Similarly, the counselor must be sincere and honest. Clients who receive telephone calls will want to know who the counselor is and how the counselor acquired their names. The client may also wonder if the organization or agency is reputable. Counselors are advised to keep communication simple in both content and language, and most important, to listen to what the client says. This is the initial step in demonstrating to the client that the counselor cares enough to learn about the needs of the client.

In the event that the client does not have a telephone, the initial contact will be a letter or a home visit, depending on agency policy. If a letter is used, it should contain the same elements of the telephone call and answer the same questions. It should also encourage the client to contact the counselor. Counselors are advised to let clients know that time has been set aside especially for them. For example, the letter might state, "I look forward to talking with you. I can meet you on Tuesday morning between 10:00 and 11:00 A.M. Please let me know if this time is convenient for you. You can telephone me at 555-4444." It is also important to provide clear instructions on location and available transportation to an agency or organization.

It is critical for rehabilitation counselors to honor the appointments they make. If a client has been told that a time is reserved, the counselor must actually reserve that time for the client. As with most people, clients, in the initial meeting, will be able to sense if the counselor has actually arranged his or her schedule to meet with the client, learn of the client's needs, and explain how the agency might meet those needs.

Above all, the rehabilitation counselors serving this particular population are urged to be more plan-oriented and thoughtful than the counselor who is serving individuals who are sighted (Hardy, 1972). For example, counselors are advised to anticipate problems that may arise for clients with visual impairments. For instance, simply getting to and from the counselor's office may be a very troublesome task. The client may be traveling over unfamiliar locations with or without the help of relatives or friends. Appointments and arrangements for counseling sessions and other contacts should be quite specific because some individuals who are visually impaired depend on others for transportation and support.

Setting for the Initial Interview

Several options exist for the choice of location for the initial interview. Because of a client's travel difficulties, the counselor may decide to conduct the initial interview at the client's home. Home interviews have a number of advantages. Significant information can be obtained regarding the home environment and the ability of the client to function independently in that environment. On the other hand, if other family members are present, clients may feel less free in discussing feelings. Therefore, the counselor may consider an initial home visit, with subsequent meetings at the counselor's office. Another choice is to meet with the client at a community center or at another agency, for example, at the agency that referred the client. Private agencies serving individuals with visual impairments frequently refer clients to state vocational rehabilitation agencies. Counselors employed by state agencies may choose to conduct the initial meetings with clients at the private agency.

At whatever point counselors elect to meet with their clients at the counselor's offices, they need to give careful consideration to the effect of the waiting room, which also provides cues about an organization and the counselors it employs. Consider the following example:

> Mr. Neal Richards, age 54, sits in the waiting room of the State Commission for the Blind. He is visibly anxious and yet, he is not sure whether anyone is there to observe him. "What can this agency do for me?" he wonders. "They won't help me get my vision back. What is expected of me? Is this going to cost me any money? I hated

to ask a favor of my brother-in-law to drive me down here. I hate being dependent." His thoughts are interrupted as he overhears conversation between two agency employees. They discuss what seems to Mr. Richards to be some fairly confidential business. "It is like they don't even know I am here," he thinks. "It seems that I have been sitting here for some time. I wonder if there are any good magazines to read while I am waiting? At least I still have my sense of humor."

Although sitting in a waiting room for a lengthy time might be uncomfortable for any person—with or without any type of disability—waiting does have some special relevance for individuals who are visually impaired. Most waiting rooms provide some reading materials for individuals to keep busy. It is recommended, therefore, that waiting rooms in agencies that serve individuals with visual impairments have materials available in large print or on cassettes. Moreover, agency staff and counselors should remember that the inability to see does not mean that a person cannot hear. It is suggested that individuals be greeted appropriately in the waiting room, and the agency personnel are advised to not allow clients and other individuals in public areas such as waiting rooms to hear confidential information being discussed.

The atmosphere of the waiting room can enhance or detract from the client's overall feelings about the agency and counselor. Although clients may glean information about the waiting room and the counselor's office, through residual vision or other senses, the counselor and receptionist are encouraged to provide a description of the environment. The detail of the description will vary according to client needs.

Preparation for the Initial Interview

Prior to the initial interview, the rehabilitation counselor is urged to review such background materials as medical and ophthalmological reports, and other referral information from educational facilities or social workers' reports. It is recommended that the counselor be familiar with this background material, but never rely solely on such information. A review of background material contributes to knowing the client only as a "case," not as a person. Moreover, rehabilitation counselors are not immune to myths and stereotypical beliefs about people who are blind (Stone, Endo, Spear, Rivera & Petrusa, 1977). Counselors are advised to resist making any assumptions about clients based on background materials or the counselor's perceptions of the visual impairments.

It is highly recommended that the initial interview follow as quickly as possible after the referral is made to the agency (McGowan & Porter, 1967). It is quite possible that the eyecare specialist has informed the prospective client that someone from a rehabilitation agency will be making contact. The importance of early contact is particularly important when the prospective contact is a person who has just recently become blind (Klemz, 1977). Undue delay in contacting the clients can contribute to negative stereotypes of the agency or counselor and may suggest that nobody cares.

Timing is important to a person with a visual impairment. The counselor also needs to remain cognizant of the effect that the visual impairment has on readiness of the person to receive rehabilitation services. Not everyone will be interested in rehabilitation at the time services are offered. Some clients will initially believe that their sight will be restored, and because they view their vision loss as temporary, they will not see the necessity of discussing their blindness or learning new skills (Peninsula Center for the Blind, 1982). Forcing rehabilitation before a person is ready to accept help will not work. In some instances, it may be more appropriate for the individual to enter a recreation program or pursue other avocational interests, during which time the client can achieve a certain degree of confidence in his or her abilities, prior to discussing future plans related solely to vocational concerns.

When preparing for the initial interview, it is suggested that the rehabilitation counselor identify questions that will yield relevant information and assist in determining needed services.

Table 11.1. Questions to be Addressed in the Initial Interview

Vision-Related Dimensions

1. How much visual impairment does the client have? What is the visual acuity and degree of field vision? (Statement of vision in functional terms is significant, e.g., "Can you read your mail?")
2. What is the cause of the visual condition? Is it related to other physical conditions, such as diabetes?
3. What is the age at onset? How long has the individual experienced diminished vision?
4. What is the progression of the visual impairment?
5. Has the client been blind since early childhood or had the advantage of adult frames of reference to use in visualizing experiences after blindness?
6. What is the prognosis for the visual disorder?
7. Are any activities or conditions apt to speed further loss?
8. How much knowledge does the client have about the visual impairment? What appears to be the client's reaction to the prognosis?
9. Is the individual fully utilizing the amount of vision that is still available?

Medical Dimensions

1. What is the client's general health?
2. Are there any additional impairments? (i.e., secondary or tertiary disabilities)?
3. What is the significance of the additional impairments and how do they limit the functioning of the individual?
4. Are there any activities that should be avoided in the future?
5. What is the status of the client's hearing?

Dimensions of Independent Functioning

1. Is the client able to travel alone? What navigational (or O & M skills) are used in the home environment and outdoors?
2. How self-sufficient is the client at home, that is, in housekeeping skills and in self-care activities? What areas does the client deem important and in what areas does the client feel that further training is needed?
3. What are the client's communication skills? What additional training is needed?

Psychosocial Dimensions

1. What is the client's attitude toward visual impairment?
2. What are the reactions of family and friends? What type of support is the client receiving?
3. What is the extent of social contacts? What has been the effect of visual impairment on recreation, social, and vocational activities? Is the individual ready to resume any or all of these activities?

Educational/Vocational Dimensions

1. What is the client's educational background? (Include information on last grade completed.) Are there any licenses or certificates or specialized training?
2. What is the client's work history? Information should include vocational training received. (Also include job skills in addition to the job titles.)
3. When did the client last work? If the visual impairment caused job termination, what aspects of the job presented specific problems?
4. What is the client's interest in assistance to return to the previous employment site?

Table 11.1 provides a list of questions that may be considered by the counselor in preparing for the initial interview. Not all of the questions are of equal importance, and not all need to be raised or addressed during the initial interview. The individual needs of the client, the client's concerns, and the type of agency dictate the relevance of the various questions. Also, more meaningful answers will be received when the client understands the relevancy of the questions and the information is presented in functional terms. For example, asking clients whether they can read headlines of newspapers yields more useful information than relying solely on visual acuity figures provided in medical reports. Finally, the rehabilitation counselor is advised to remember that restoration of vision may be possible for a person with a visual impairment. The rehabilitation counselor is encouraged to consider vision restoration, either through surgery or low vision services, as an essential part of rehabilitation.

Counseling and Interviewing Guidelines

When conducting the initial interview, the counselor will consider a number of factors, including such elements as disability etiquette, environmental factors, the use of forms, and the purpose of the interview. These factors are examined in the following sections.

Disability Etiquette

What do you do when you meet a person who is blind? How does the counselor guide the client from the waiting room to the interviewing room? How does the counselor help the client to a seat? Rehabilitation counselors who work with individuals who are visually impaired need knowledge of disability etiquette to demonstrate their respect for their clients.

Some basic behavior for rehabilitation counselors includes the following:

- Use verbal cues extensively in giving directions. Avoid such words as "turn this way" or "over there." It is helpful to use such terms as north, south, west, right, diagonal, or o'clock positions (e.g., "The form is at the 3 o'clock position on the table.");
- Use the words "look" and "see." These words are part of everyday language and they show no disrespect to individuals with visual impairments;
- Be prepared to read things aloud;
- Identify yourself and any others who may be present;
- If a person seems to need help, identify yourself and let the person know you are there by a light touch on the arm;
- To lead a person, let the person take your arm; the person will follow the motion of your body as you walk. Walk at a reasonable pace and not too far ahead, especially if there are curbs or stairs. Individuals should be told when they are approaching steps and whether the steps are going up or down; and
- In helping the person to be seated, lead the person to the chair and place the person's hand on the side or back of the chair.

Common sense and sensitivity to others are also excellent guidelines for counselors to follow. Disability etiquette does not preclude providing the necessary feedback to clients to assist them in achieving their goals. Nonetheless, as with any feedback, timing is critical. Consider the following example:

> David M., an employment consultant, is interviewing Jonathan A. in his office. Mr. A. is explaining some of the difficulties he has had in finding a job. He has a bachelor's degree in social work, has had several job interviews, but has not been able to find a job. It has been two years since he graduated from college. As Jonathan A. describes some of his frustrations in

seeking employment, Mr. M. observes that he is beginning to rock slightly in his chair. This mannerism is both disconcerting and inappropriate. This concerns Mr. M. particularly because he feels some responsibility for the placement success of this individual. He wonders why, despite this client's involvement with a rehabilitation counselor and prior attendance at a school for blind people, Jonathan is exhibiting this mannerism. Is it possible, he wonders, that no one ever told him or tried to correct it?

The rehabilitation counselor has an obligation as part of providing rehabilitation counseling to provide feedback to clients and work with them in areas that are not always comfortable to address. So-called blind mannerisms need to be addressed (McAdam, O'Cleirigh, & Cuvo, 1993) in addition to any other areas (e.g., personal hygiene) that may affect the client's ability to acquire a job or interact with other individuals. Generally, feedback prior to the establishment of a counseling relationship is inappropriate and ineffective; however, the counselor should note behavior and other areas of potential concern during the initial interview (i.e., "red flags")—areas that will need to be addressed later in the rehabilitation process, if they persist. "Confrontational" counseling, described by Warren and Gandy (1988), can also be useful, under certain circumstances.

Environmental Factors

Many meetings with clients are held in the counselor's office. Therefore, the careful review of the office conditions by the counselor is advised—particularly the amount of light: Is the office too dark, or does it have too much glare (which can be annoying to individuals with certain eye conditions)? Is the light natural or artificial? Which type of lighting contributes to or detracts from the office atmosphere? These are all questions to consider when examining the office atmosphere.

The consideration of the decor of the office or interview room is also important. What sort of messages do the decor and furniture suggest to clients? Do clients get a warm comfortable feeling, as well as a sense of privacy, or is the feeling one of a bureaucratic environment? What is the quality of sound in the interviewing room? Is there any outside noise that competes for the client's attention? Even such circumstances as the noise emitted from overhead fluorescent lights can prove distracting and can interfere with effective communication between the counselor and client. [For more specific information on appropriate office designs and on issues related to accessibility, the reader is encouraged to contact the Corporate and Access Consulting Program at the American Foundation for the Blind (AFB).]

Privacy

When clients are unfamiliar with the physical setting of the interview, they should be provided with a verbal description (Rusalem, 1972). This is particularly important because the individual needs to know whether the interview room will provide an atmosphere of privacy (Sommers-Flanagan & Sommers-Flanagan, 1993). Rehabilitation counselors who expect frank responses to questions are advised to assure the client that the interview is indeed private and that other people are precluded from overhearing. Although the counselor may be quite certain that the interviewing room allows for absolute privacy, the counselor is urged never to assume that the client is equally assured.

Interview Structure and Purpose

The initial interview is the client's introduction to the agency's purpose, services, and objectives. Certainly, the counselor would like to achieve a certain amount of structure in order to accomplish these introductory goals. At the same time, the most desirable outcome of the first interview is to establish a relationship in which the client feels he or she has freedom of expression. Also, because overstructuring the interview can promote dependency, the counselor is cautioned to avoid overly structured interviews.

An initial interview arranged around the use of questionnaires can also lead to an overly structured interview that is merely a series of questions and answers, in which specific information is acquired by the counselor, but no relationship is established with the client. The rehabilitation counselor needs to be mindful about asking closed questions that elicit only "yes" or "no" responses. It is recommended that materials be presented in such a way that the client feels free to respond. Many agencies use highly structured interview forms that counselors feel compelled to complete as early as possible. The use of forms in such a manner often inhibits the ability of the counselor to relate to the client in an effective manner. At times, some of the initial interview questions are better placed in abeyance and raised at a more appropriate time. As a general rule, to initiate the application process, the counselor will need to secure the client's name, address, Social Security number, date of birth, and referral source, if it is not known. However, basic referral information varies by state and by type of organization or agency. Other important information to obtain from the client might include educational history (the number of years of schooling or other training completed), occupational history (all positions held, including current work, and the dates of employment, and a record of military service), disability history (functional limitations, surgeries, medications, and related factors that might have a negative or positive effect on employment), functional capacities and transferable skills, and any other observations that the counselor might consider relevant (for example, mode of dress, neatness, and punctuality).

Forms also present some specific problems for individuals with visual impairments. Because of their vision loss, clients do not always know how many forms are on the counselor's desk or the length of the forms. If forms must be completed, the counselor is advised to provide a verbal description of the number, length, and purpose of the forms.

The services provided by some agencies are based on economic need. However, inquiring about economic need early in the interview may elicit barriers in clients who are concerned about privacy. People who are visually impaired may be more sensitive to privacy than other individuals, who take much of their privacy for granted (e.g., reading mail and bank statements). When economic information is required, it is recommended that the relevance of the information be discussed.

The counselor may consider emphasizing to the client that the completion of forms and questionnaires is not the goal of the interview, but the forms merely serve as a mechanism for obtaining necessary information. If certain information is unnecessary during the early stages of the interview, the counselor can delay the presentation of these forms until an appropriate time.

Agency and Counselor Limitations

It is important for counselors to know the limitations of their employing agency or organization, as well as the limitations of their professional role. The rehabilitation counselor needs to function in accordance with the policies of the employing agency; however, there will be times when the client's needs are not consistent with the types of services provided by the agency. The counselor is urged to be extremely careful not to try to fit client needs into agency or organizational services; services must be relevant to client needs. Nonetheless, if those needs cannot be met within the agency framework, they should not be ignored. Rather, it is suggested that the counselor work with the client and attempt to identify other resources that might be more appropriate. Consider the following example:

> Irene Faircloth seemed somewhat less than enthusiastic during the initial interview. She was 36 years old and had lost a considerable amount of vision due to diabetic retinopathy. Her last employed position was that of a school aide. However, she appeared to have little interest in returning to employment and the rehabilitation counselor's discussion of possible careers failed to evoke any discussion on her part. After a

> while, Ms. Faircloth said, "You know what I would really like to do? Get married."

Eventually, the client was able to successfully reach this nonvocational goal. Although the client's case was closed as "not interested," the counselor recognized Ms. Faircloth's social interest and made a referral to a local community center that offered recreational activities. During the next year, the rehabilitation counselor learned that Ms. Faircloth had met a man and they were later married. Significantly, one year later the client reapplied for services. She and her husband, who also had a visual impairment, were interested in operating a vending facility. Subsequently, both were trained and successfully placed.

There are other occasions when the purpose of the interview may change, as a result of information obtained during the interview. The following is one example of this:

> Counselor Bloch interviewed Ms. Diamond at the Madison Center for Community Services, which had referred her to the rehabilitation agency and requested sponsorship for her for mobility instruction. Ms. Diamond, who had been working in the Center's work program industry, was experiencing decreased visual functioning, which resulted in travel difficulties. The Madison Center provided the rehabilitation counselor, Mr. Bloch, with all necessary materials, including medical, eye, and economic need reports. As the interview progressed, the counselor detected a certain amount of dissatisfaction as Ms. Diamond discussed her activities at the industry. Mr. Block asked Ms. Diamond whether she had ever considered other types of employment. "To tell you the truth," she responded, "I very often thought about going to college and being a social worker."

With the exception of the names of the client, counselor, and agency, this is a true story. In many ways, this was a very "easy" referral—a person who needed financial assistance for mobility instruction. Counselor sponsorship of this activity would have been consistent with the request of the referring agency and consistent with the services the counselor could provide. The client had not been overtly suggesting any other goals. However, because of the counselor's question regarding alternative work interests, the client was later evaluated for college attendance and for a career in social work. Eventually, Ms. Diamond entered college and completed her work toward a bachelor of arts degree. After graduation, she was employed as a caseworker for the local department of social services. This change in vocational objective required the sponsoring agency to spend considerably more rehabilitation funds, and to provide many more services. In retrospect, it appears that the atmosphere of the interview and the sensitivity of the counselor promoted the change in the interview purpose from consideration for mobility training services to a broad spectrum of services, including university training, and a vocational objective more consistent with the client's interests and aptitudes.

Promoting Independence

Becoming acquainted with the client, and sometimes the client's family, seeing that material needs are met, and sowing the idea of independence for future growth are issues central to the initial interview (Klemz, 1977). Many individuals with visual impairments experience a significant loss of independence, which affects their role in the rehabilitation process (Carroll, 1961; Scott, 1969). Independence needs to be encouraged, therefore, from the very first interview. A simple example is a client who may not be ready or motivated to learn braille, but who may be able and ready to increase skills in activities of daily living (e.g., washing, dressing, personal grooming). All these function as steps toward independence.

If the client offers the counselor a cup of coffee during a home interview, the counselor is encouraged to accept the offer. Such an activity encourages client independence in household functioning, and strengthens the relationship. It is also recommended that the counselor have two or three assistive devices (e.g., a signature guide) available for the client to inspect. A device that can be used almost immediately gives a tremendous boost to a client's morale and helps improve self-concept (Marmion, McBroom, Haucke, & Jackson, 1986). Clients may also need recognition and appreciation for the progress they have made. Some clients may have already made their own adaptations to their own environments; the rehabilitation counselor is encouraged to acknowledge and reinforce the client's progress.

It is suggested that the counselor also be attuned to negative self-attitudes that may be expressed by clients. It is not uncommon for an individual who has recently experienced a vision loss to hold a number of distorted perceptions and stereotypes about being blind (McKay et al., 1983). Because these misperceptions frequently diminish the self-esteem of the client and may narrow a client's perceptions in regard to vocational and recreational opportunities, the counselor is advised to provide information and begin addressing any misconceptions when they are noted.

Interview Format

The initial interview, as well as subsequent counseling sessions, should follow a general format of (1) greeting, (2) opening, (3) body, and (4) closing (Cull & Hutchinson, 1972; Sommers-Flanagan et al., 1993). The greeting includes the initial small talk that helps put the client at ease. The less the counselor knows the client, the more time will be spent in the greeting phase of the meeting. The opening identifies the objectives of the meeting. Typical objectives of an initial interview include (1) providing the client with information about the agency, and (2) acquiring information about the client, including expectations regarding the agency and the counselor. The body of the interview represents the fulfillment of objectives. The closing includes a summary of the meeting, determination of the next meeting in terms of date, time, and place, and assignment of any responsibilities of the counselor and the client to be completed before the next meeting.

Communication: The Importance of Visual and Nonvisual Cues

If counseling is essential to the success of the client's rehabilitation, then communication may then be considered essential to the success of counseling (Wachtel, 1993). Vision plays an important role in personal communication. With the exception of some cultures, it is customary for most people to maintain eye contact. To turn away or focus on a distant object when addressing another person can be attributed to rudeness, shyness, or lack of interest. In our culture, eye contact signifies honesty, directness, attentiveness, respect, and a variety of other virtues that are the important ingredients of successful human communication. Counselors may find, however, that some individuals who are visually impaired are better able to follow conversations by turning an ear to the speaker. Because this results in turning the head away from the speaker's face, the counselor may question whether the client is attentive.

There are also instances when the client may question the attentiveness of the counselor because of the counselor's lack of "verbal following" of responses. Silence is not always golden when counseling individuals with visual impairments. Although counseling theory often suggests the importance of silence as a technique, in the absence of vision, silence can be misinterpreted or interpreted as a lack of interest or rejection. Verbal following is critical for individuals who are visually impaired because they rely on auditory cues (e.g., "ahem," "I understand," "yes," "mmmm") to indicate that the counselor is listening and paying attention. Although the "ahems" of psychotherapists are sometimes the basis of jokes, this type of response is essential because the usual eye contact and other nonverbal communication may not provide the same cues for individuals with visual impairments.

It is highly recommended that the counselor

look directly into the face and eyes of the client just as if the individual were fully sighted. People with visual impairments are often aware when sighted persons are not looking at them, and they get the impression, which may be true, that the counselor is not listening (Hardy & Cull, 1972). However, looking directly at the client may be difficult for some counselors who find the appearance of a client's eyes disconcerting. Scott (1969) stated, "when blindness is due to an accident, the face and eyes may be disfigured. Sometimes the eyes bulge or are set at peculiar angles; in other cases, they may be opaque or gray. When a person is losing vision he [she] may also lose the ability to control the eye muscles, so that the eyes constantly flutter or roll about in their sockets. These deformities present major difficulties in communication because eye contact may be not only disturbing but also repulsive to the observer" (p. 31). Although Scott's language is strong, counselors who have little experience in working with individuals with visual impairments are urged to be prepared for this situation.

Communication may also be affected both by the age at onset and the degree of visual impairment. The counselor who is used to reading emotions in various facial responses may be at a considerable loss with some people who have been blind for a number of years, and especially with those individuals who are congenitally blind and who have not learned about traditional responses. In terms of degree of visual impairment, Erber and Osborn (1994) found that the degree to which individuals with high or low extremes of visual impairments were able to discern facial cues could be fairly well predicted. However, for individuals in the midrange (e.g., 20/80 to 20/500) of visual acuity, there was wide variability. This has important implications for rehabilitation counselors who may overestimate a client's ability to perceive facial cues, based on their responses to the counselor. For example, the examiner in Erber and Osborn's study had "high contrast" facial features (e.g., dark hair, light skin, dark lipstick), which were easier for individuals to discern than such "low contrast" features as light hair, light skin, pale eyes, and no lipstick.

After the Initial Interview

The initial interview has concluded. Some clients may be talkative and others quiet. Although some may have demonstrated a great deal of enthusiasm, others may appear to lack interest. Goals may have been expressed that have been clear and realistic or they may be unexpressed or seem unrealistic. In reflecting on the initial interview, the counselor will ponder these and other questions. For example, was there expression by the client? Did the client play a role? Did the client's nod signify understanding of what the counselor was saying? Some individuals who state that they have no problems may not be ready to share their difficulties yet. On the other hand, there really may not be a need for rehabilitation services. The initial contact may have facilitated a different view of the impairment by an individual who is newly blinded. Or, some new information may have expanded the range of choices previously considered by the client. Sometimes the individual may need some time to think, or may prefer to leave certain issues to future discussions, when he or she is more familiar with the counselor.

Loss of vision creates significant challenges, and it is neither possible nor necessarily desirable for the initial interview to identify and solve all problems. The initial interview can, however, provide promise to the client. Sometimes, it is a long-range promise of a vocational goal to be achieved during a period of several years. Sometimes, it is a specific service that will be provided within a few days or weeks, such as providing talking book equipment. Klemz (1977) stated that "a promise long delayed in its fulfillment is very depressing for the . . . person [who is newly blinded] and serves to underline the feeling that all worth living for is lost and that nobody cares" (p. 77). Therefore, it is important for counselors to be responsive and honor promises promptly. This conveys to the client a feeling of confidence about the ability of the counselor and the agency or organization.

Finally, it is important to ascertain the client's perception about the initial interview. This can be accomplished in a number of ways. Such questions as "Do you have other questions that we should address?" or "I'm concerned that our meeting lived up to your expectations; did it?" may be asked at the conclusion of the initial interview. Alternatively, if it is appropriate, the counselor may encourage the client to take and mail back a "customer satisfaction card" (Patterson & Marks, 1992).

The rehabilitation counselor must remember that the initial interview is the first of many interviews. Effective counseling skills, sensitivity, and attentiveness can help ensure that the client is not "turned off," which can result in this first meeting being the last. The main goals are to establish the relationship, to become acquainted with the client and his or her family, to see that immediate material needs are met, and to encourage the idea of independence for future growth.

WORKING WITH FAMILIES

The family is a significant factor in determining rehabilitation outcomes (Kelley & Lambert, 1992; Power, 1988). Because family members, like some individuals who are blind, frequently hold myths and misconceptions about blindness, family members may need help in understanding vision loss and what rehabilitation services can accomplish. It is very important that they also understand that their support or lack of support can influence the client's success. For example, two empirical studies of family support related to individuals who are blind revealed that (1) O&M training facilitated family understanding and adjustment (Dumas & Sadowsky, 1984) and (2) successfully employed blind individuals reported more positive family attitudes than those reported by unemployed blind individuals or those who were placed in work program industries (Moore, 1984).

Kim (1970) found a high correlation between the way people with visual impairment viewed the expectations of those about them and the type of society to which they belonged. Those with close family and friends whose expectations were for the visually impaired individual to maintain a social life were more likely to do so. The social status of the families can also affect individuals with visual impairments. Kim found that when family backgrounds were of high status in the community, the family member with a visual impairment was much more apt to be integrated into society. The ability to travel independently was also seen as important to good social integration. These findings are consistent with the findings of Lukoff and Whiteman (1970), who found that individuals who were highly motivated to achieve independence were socially integrated.

A visual impairment can create disequilibrium within the family. For example, Ponchillia (1984), who reported that people who were visually impaired experienced more marriage-related difficulties than sighted individuals, indicated that the financial difficulties resulting from loss of employment, changes in family roles, reaction to dependence, rejection by the sighted spouse, and lack of participation in family activities may all contribute to major family problems.

Spousal or family overprotection can also be a difficult issue for individuals with visual impairments. There are numerous examples in which a large amount of time, money, and effort have been expended to assist an individual with a visual impairment to achieve independence in travel and in the home environment. However, when the individual returns home, the family, unprepared for the displays of independence, undermines these achievements. Undermining or overprotection result from a variety of circumstances, including lack of knowledge about being visually impaired, embarrassment, guilt, or desire for control. Consider the following example:

> Shortly after her husband's retirement, Mrs. Minter experienced significant loss of vision because of diabetic retinopathy. Her major goals were to function independently within her home environment, where she was experiencing great difficulty in performing cooking and

cleaning activities. Furthermore, she was not able to do the family shopping. Mrs. Minter was well-motivated and accepted the counselor's recommendation to receive rehabilitation training at a comprehensive rehabilitation center. She spent a period of approximately ten weeks in residence receiving evaluation, services, and subsequent training in mobility and rehabilitation teaching skills. Reports from her instructors noted that she learned these skills quickly and incorporated them into functional activities. The comprehensive rehabilitation center had a small apartment. During the last week of training, the clients lived independently and had an opportunity to perform the skills that they learned. Mrs. Minter returned home anxious to put her training to practical use. A rehabilitation teacher later visited the client in her home. Her report noted: "Client indicates that she has not had much opportunity to utilize her skills training. Her husband has taken over much of the kitchen activity. Two possible reasons for this are (1) her husband seems to be very anxious about her functioning safely in the kitchen; in particular, he has expressed concern about her using sharp objects, (2) since he has retired, her husband also considers himself an amateur chef and very much enjoys cooking the food and shopping for the appropriate ingredients. Client seems frustrated and depressed."

This underscores the importance of emphasizing family understanding and involvement. Miller (1990) noted that one of the most frequent recommendations by individuals who have experienced rehabilitation services at a comprehensive rehabilitation center was the need to involve family members to assist in their understanding of blindness and rehabilitation. Similarly, Vash (1981) stated

> The rehabilitation enterprise can be facilitated or impaired by the attitudes and behavior of the family. . . . Sometimes a rehabilitation worker's consultation with a client's family can help this family process become less of an obstacle and/or more of a help to the rehabilitation process. (p. 56)

The family also plays a major role in the career development of the individual who is visually impaired. Moore (1984), in a summary of research literature, found that a number of individuals who are blind attributed their career success to " . . . parental support, encouragement, positive reinforcement, and a positive attitude on the part of the family during the transition from a sighted world to that of blindness" (p. 101).

Parent Support Groups

In addition to working with families, rehabilitation counselors may work in settings where they lead support groups for parents of children with visual impairments. Nixon (1988) found two major areas of difference between parents of children with visual impairments and parents of children with other disabilities. The first is a low incidence of visual impairment in children, which means that parents have a much smaller potential support network, and second, the visual impairment is generally low vision, which provides parents with an opportunity to ignore the disability or postpone addressing impairment issues. Collectively, these differences contributed to a number of challenges in establishing parent support groups. The challenges included

> a sense of uniqueness of the child's . . . [disability]; the denial of the child's disability or a desire for normalcy; the low incidence of visual impairment in children and the geographic distance between families that made meetings difficult to arrange; the changing needs of parents over time; and the related fact that relatively few parents have similar support needs at the same time. . . . the tendency for parents to fall back on previous support networks (even though the support may not be satisfactory); intellectual, socio-economic, or cultural "gaps" among parents that inhibited their communica-

> tion; and parents' insecurities about their ability to contribute to a support group. (p. 273)

Of particular concern to rehabilitation counselors was Nixon's admonition that rehabilitation professionals need to respect the values, beliefs, and attitudes of parents and recognize that the adjustments of parents "may change over time and that parents have different types and degrees of needs at various stages" (p. 277). One example of changing needs relates to support groups for parents of teenagers. Assuming that parents have adjusted to any impairment issues when the teenager was a child, professionals may overlook developmental needs. A final consideration is the use of cross-disability groups and their value to parents of children with multiple disabilities, including visual impairments.

COUNSELING TECHNIQUES

The counseling techniques used with individuals who are visually impaired do not differ significantly from the techniques that counselors use with individuals who have other disabilities. Nonetheless, there are some issues and skills that are common to all disabled individuals, including individuals with visual impairments, which counselors are urged to address. These include assertiveness skills, communication behaviors, and the use of group counseling.

Assertiveness Skills and Nonverbal Communication

Some individuals with visual impairments demonstrate "learned helplessness" (Seligman, 1975), a perceived lack of control that can result in feelings of decreased competence and lowered self-esteem. Learned helplessness (or passivity) not only diminishes feelings of self-worth, but can interfere with an individual's ability to acquire and maintain a job. In contrast to passivity, other individuals may demonstrate aggressiveness. Assertiveness training, which focuses on both anxiety reduction and skill development, can be used to address issues of passivity and aggressiveness. Assertive means "being able to verbally and nonverbally communicate one's positive and negative feelings and thoughts, without experiencing undue amounts of anxiety or guilt and without violating the dignity of others" (Harrell & Strauss, 1986, p. 794).

A common occurrence for individuals with visual impairments is the sighted person who seeks to provide assistance in crossing a street, when such assistance is unwanted. An aggressive response might be, "Take your hand off me—I didn't ask for your help," whereas a passive response might be, "It is very nice of you to help me." In contrast to both of these, an assertive response would be, "Thank you. I appreciate your offer of assistance, but I would prefer to cross the street by myself."

The components of an assertiveness program include (1) addressing a person's feelings about the impairment, and (2) teaching nonverbal communication skills and assertive statements. Because individuals who are visually impaired lack visual feedback, they are often unaware of nonverbal behavior (i.e., eye contact, posture, voice, gestures, facial expression) and dress. Demonstrations of the various messages (e.g., nodding the head to demonstrate comprehension or the difference between large and small gestures) can assist individuals in understanding the importance of nonverbal behavior. Methods include having the individual with the visual impairment "feel the instructor's face and hands while demonstrating various gestures and expressions, physically motioning the . . . body, and imitating gestures" (Harrell & Strauss, 1986, p. 796). This can be followed by having the individuals act out various emotions nonverbally. Similarly, skills related to posture, leaning slightly toward the individual who is speaking, and analyzing one's tone of voice via tape-recorder can help individuals focus on nonverbal behaviors. After individuals understand nonverbal behaviors, assertive statements can be taught with individuals role--playing various situations (e.g., initiating a con-

SIDEBAR 11.1

Assertiveness Training

Assertiveness training teaches individuals with visual impairments how to express their thoughts and feelings with respect to oneself and others. After the individual understands the importance of nonverbal behavior, role-playing can be an effective training tool. The following assertive statements can be used in different situations.

1. When you want to ask for time or distance, say "I need to think about that one for awhile" or "I need more information before I make a decision."
2. When you need to obtain a commitment from someone, say "Then I am to understand that you will . . ." or "When can you give me a firm answer?"
3. When you want to make sure the receiver is getting your message, say "This is what I need: (a) . . . , (b) . . . , (c) . . . ," or "I want to make clear the point that . . ."
4. When you want to make sure you are receiving the message, say "Let me see if I got it—what you want is . . ." or "I am confused; please tell me again."
5. When you want to share a positive feeling, say "I really like the way you . . ." or "I am glad to see that you . . ."
6. When you are feeling uncomfortable or upset, say "Before we go on, I want to tell you I am uncomfortable with . . ." or "I get embarrassed when. . . ."

Source: R. Harrell & F. Strauss, "Approaches to Increasing Assertive Behavior and Communication Skills in Blind and Visually Impaired Persons," 1986, *Journal of Visual Impairment & Blindness, 80,* p. 798.

versation, handling anger, participating in a job interview) (see Sidebar 11.1).

Group Counseling

Group counseling is often an effective means of working with individuals. McCulloh, Crawford, and Resnick (1994) described a structured support group for midlife and older adults with visual impairments. Topics that they addressed in their eight-week sessions are as follows:

- Week 1: Introduction: Stress and Visual Impairment
- Week 2: Loss of Privacy and Scripts People Write for Us
- Week 3: Family, Friends, and Feelings
- Week 4: Sources of Anxiety and Fears: Issues of Mobility, Health, and Finances
- Week 5: Sources of Satisfaction: Finding Substitute Pleasures
- Week 6: Perceptions and Prejudices: Self-esteem and Self-identity
- Week 7: Adaptations: New Ways of Doing Old Things
- Week 8: What's Your Agenda Now? (p. 154)

In conducting their group, they found that a heterogeneous group was able to work well together; "substantial diversity in the participants' racial, ethnic, education, and religious backgrounds did not prove to be divisive because the participants' shared vision loss seemed to supersede other differences" (p. 155).

When conducting a group that includes one or more individuals who are visually impaired, the counselor should have all individuals identify themselves prior to speaking, until the group has met often enough for voice recognition to occur.

Group counseling frequently relies on nonverbal cues and therapeutic silence. Without visual cues, an individual with impaired vision may not understand the silence (Patterson, McKenzie, & Jenkins, 1995). It is important for the group leader to describe nonverbal cues of other group members and interpret silence or minimize its use in the screening and orientation session for a visually impaired person. Also, group techniques that require vision (e.g., color cards, mirror image, eye contact) should be eliminated when the group involves one or more individuals who are visually impaired (Patterson et al., 1995).

COUNSELING APPLICATIONS

The uniqueness of each individual precludes a description of the multitude of counseling applications to the population of individuals who are visually impaired. For illustrative purposes, however, three conditions [i.e., acquired immunodeficiency syndrome (AIDS), diabetes, and Usher's syndrome] are described in the next section.

AIDS

Individuals with AIDS and visual impairments often require a great deal of support because of the compounding effects of loss and grief that visual impairment brings to the AIDS diagnosis (Keister, 1990). The rehabilitation counselor is advised to expect a range of emotions, including fury, anger, depression, frustration, and fear. Along with pain and suffering, grief, and profound loss, the types of fear expressed can include fear of the unknown, loneliness, abandonment by family and friends, loss of bodily functioning and bodily control, and loss of identity (Strong, 1990). Because the advance of AIDS is gradual, the information needs of individuals with AIDS will vary at different points in time (Strong, 1990). One of the information needs, however, is apt to be how AIDS will affect their life goals. Rehabilitation counselors are urged to assess their knowledge of AIDS, as well as their attitudes about practices, such as homosexual activity and drug use, which can cause the transmission of the AIDS virus.

Confidentiality is assumed in all counseling relationships. However, because of special circumstances and fears surrounding individuals with AIDS, it is essential that the rehabilitation counselor undertake extra steps to maintain confidentiality. Case records should be kept in the most secure place and be available only to those professionals who must know the individual has AIDS. A rehabilitation teacher teaching activities of daily living is an example of another rehabilitation professional who might have a reason to know; however, any rehabilitation professionals should be warned that they may not break the rule of confidentiality in the planning or delivery of services.

For the rehabilitation counselor to be effective with the person who has AIDS, the counselor must have compassion and empathy. The counselor must be able to encourage the individual to continue to participate in the rehabilitation program, although the significance of the program may be questioned because of the impending death. For example, one individual with AIDS asked his mobility instructor why she was teaching him mobility skills, because neither one of them knew if he would be there tomorrow. The mobility instructor replied, "You're here today, aren't you? As long as you are here, I am going to teach you. Let's get going!" This true incident, which happened about 24 months before the person with AIDS relayed the story, is indicative of the inability of either the rehabilitation counselor or the person who has AIDS to know when the last lesson or counseling session will be. It also underscores the importance of supporting clients in their efforts to continue to participate in the community either in independent living programs or in traditional vocational rehabilitation programs.

Diabetes

Rehabilitation counselors working in the field of blindness need knowledge and skills related to diabetes. According to Prevent Blindness America (1994), there are 10 to 14 million people in the United States who have diabetes, and almost 40 percent have diabetic retinopathy. Although 80 percent of individuals with juvenile-onset diabetes (type I) will have diabetic retinopathy after 15 years, cataracts and glaucoma can also result from diabetes.

Many rehabilitation counselors will have access to diabetes educators and rehabilitation teachers who provide instruction related to diabetes. It is important, however, for rehabilitation counselors to be able to reinforce the principles and practices of diabetes education in their counseling sessions, and appropriately refer individuals when necessary. Typical areas that rehabilitation counselors may address with clients include the following:

- Insulin measurement and administration—Is the client having any problems in this area?
- Self-monitoring of blood glucose—Is this part of the individual's routine?
- Foot care—Is the individual wearing good shoes that have been appropriately fitted?
- Safe and appropriate exercise planning—In what exercise activities does the client participate?
- Nutritional needs—Is the client using exchange lists in an accessible format?
- Record keeping—Is the client maintaining appropriate records related to times the blood sugar is monitored, the levels, and the amount of insulin administered?
- Diabetes education resources—Does the client have the necessary resources? (Berkowitz et al., 1993)

The importance of strict monitoring of blood glucose levels is critical for many individuals with diabetes, because the Diabetes Control and Complications Trial found "a 70 percent reduction in the progression of detectable diabetic retinopathy" (Editor's Note, 1993, p. 325). Some individuals may need to conduct four or more blood glucose tests per day and may need three or more insulin injections. For additional resources and strategies for serving individuals with diabetes who are blind or visually impaired, see Bryant and Cobb (1997).

Diet is also an important consideration in diabetes. In addition to restrictions in carbohydrates and sugar, some individuals with diabetes may be restricted in their protein, fat, and salt intake (Rosenthal, 1993). Therefore, both menu planning and food preparation can be quite time consuming and complicated.

Because diabetes increases the risk of amputation by at least 15 times that of the general population (Harkless & Lavery, 1992; Steinberg, 1991), foot care is critical for individuals with diabetes. Pain, blisters, and objects in a person's shoes may go undetected, however, if a person has peripheral neuropathy (loss of sensation in peripheral nerves). As Ponchillia (1993) pointed out,

> the inability to see infected wounds clearly, coupled with the reduced sensation of pain, interferes with the ability to detect problems at an early stage. This point cannot be stressed strongly enough because neuropathy is the primary cause of foot lesions, and unattended wounds that become infected can lead to amputations. (p. 355)

Rehabilitation counselors are advised to inquire about any foot problems and note the condition of shoes worn by the client. Regular visits to or an evaluation by a podiatrist may be part of the rehabilitation program.

Neuropathy of the autonomic nervous system frequently affects the gastrointestinal system, resulting in diarrhea, stomach cramps, nausea or frequent vomiting from food intolerances. Because of the unpredictability of such occurrences and the drowsiness or depression caused by treatment medication, many individuals may be reluctant to leave home. Sensitivity to these issues is important for rehabilitation counselors in considering the place and duration of counseling services, vocational planning, and the potential effect on the client's self-esteem.

Damage to the kidneys is also caused by diabetes. Hemodialysis, peritoneal dialysis, transplant, and diet and medication are possible treatments, and each has implications for rehabilitation. Individuals who have had transplants take immunosuppressants, which increase their risk of infections. Therefore, rehabilitation counselors should consider the risk to the client, if the counselor is experiencing cold or flu symptoms. The scheduling of and recovery from hemodialysis sessions is an important employment issue. Balance, gait, and the time needed to replace the cleansing fluid used in continuous ambulatory peritoneal dialysis are also issues for the rehabilitation counselor to consider.

Participation in an exercise program may also be part of the client's rehabilitation plan. Exercise is helpful for many individuals with diabetes who have high levels of cholesterol. It appears to help the body better utilize available insulin (Guthrie & Guthrie, 1992); it is a source of stress-management; and it can help decrease excess body fat, which is important because 90 percent of individuals with non-insulin-dependent diabetes are considered obese (Weitzman, 1993).

Some counseling approaches that have been used with individuals with diabetes include biofeedback (Needham, Eldridge, Harabedian, & Crawford, 1993), cognitive therapy (Needham, 1988), hypnosis, and systematic desensitization (Needham et al., 1993). In situations when the many complications associated with diabetes result in clinical depression, the rehabilitation counselor is advised to consult with or refer individuals to psychiatrists or psychologists.

Usher's Syndrome

Typically, children with Usher's syndrome are born with profound deafness and experience loss of vision later in life due to retinitis pigmentosa (RP). The blindness resulting from RP is progressive. Although some individuals with Usher's syndrome become almost totally blind at an early stage of life, others have been known to retain usable vision well into their sixties or later (Barrett, 1988). Thus, the onset and degree of ultimate vision loss varies greatly among individuals, and many individuals are unaware of their impending blindness until their late twenties or early thirties (Tedder, 1987).

Tedder (1987) identified the following four questions that challenge rehabilitation counselors who work with individuals who have Usher's syndrome:

(1) Who will tell them they are going blind?
(2) Who will tell them they cannot drive any more?
(3) How should a vocational objective be chosen?
(4) How does the family support the vocational plan?

The next sections discuss these four critical questions.

Breaking the News

Although telling a client that he or she is going blind is not necessarily the counselor's responsibility, the counselor will often be involved because of communication difficulties coupled with the lack of predictability concerning the loss of vision or the period of time covered (Ingraham, Carey, Vernon, & Berry, 1994). Several counseling sessions are recommended to assure that the client understands the implications of RP, and to also give the client time to assimilate the information and develop questions. The diagnosis of RP can be especially traumatic for individuals with Usher's syndrome, in part because of their heavy reliance on vision for receptive communication (Miner, 1995). According to Tedder (1987):

> The physician's role is to provide a diagnosis and prognosis, while the counselor's role is to assist the client toward the nebulous state called "adjustment to disability," which includes both emotional resolution and the development of compensatory behavioral strategies. Whatever the level of adjustment attained, it will be achieved by the client, with the help of friends,

> family, and some skilled professionals throughout the client's lifetime. . . . The negative emotional component of the person's adjustment can often be reduced through the provision of information about compensatory skills training (e.g., that other persons who are deaf-blind can hold jobs and live independently; can travel with a sighted guide, a cane, or a dog; and can communicate with both deaf and hearing persons). The counselor is responsible for providing the best information possible through the best medium, allowing time for understanding, and checking frequently to see whether the message has been communicated. (p. 62)

Driving

Because eye exams for driving may not be sensitive enough to eliminate an individual who is legally blind, the counselor is encouraged to investigate the client's attitude toward driving and assist the client in making a responsible decision relative to driving. An excellent approach is to assist the client in eliminating the need to drive by focusing on O&M skills and identifying other reliable modes of transportation.

Selecting a Vocational Objective

Tedder (1987) identified approaches that have been taken in the selection of a vocational objective. The first focuses on the client's present situation and the client's desires. The benefit of this approach is that a client may develop a good work history before the visual impairment becomes more severe. However, the negative side of this approach is increased frustration, possible fears of failure, and feelings of increased dependency on the state-federal vocational rehabilitation program when individuals need to make a later job or career change. Another approach is to select a vocational objective consistent with a client's anticipated future limitations. Although this approach enhances the ability of the client to remain in a job or profession, it may be viewed negatively by a client who is not ready to address the future limitations that could arise as a result of diminished vision. Tedder recommends that counselors find a middle ground, in which they are sensitive to the interests, aptitudes, and desires of clients while considering the future implications of the impending vision loss.

Family Support

Many of the family support issues are similar to those experienced by any individual who experiences a disability (e.g., role changes, disequilibrium), and marriage or family counseling are recommended when problems exist. The two major differences are that many individuals who are deaf marry other individuals who are deaf, which can mean less isolation for the deaf person who also loses vision. Because RP may occur as a recessive gene, the individual may also have other family members with the impairment who can serve as positive role models. Not all relatives, however, will serve as positive role models, because some may have discontinued working as soon as they were diagnosed with RP. Nonetheless, understanding how other members of the family have responded to the visual impairment can assist the counselor in selecting appropriate interventions (Tedder, 1987). Miner (1995), noting that Usher's syndrome "requires multiple adaptations throughout the life cycle," found that (1) some individuals delayed rehabilitation because it would have placed additional stress on their spouses, (2) children may resent being forced to assume additional responsibilities, including interpreting and serving as the primary connection to the outside world, and (3) teenagers may feel stigmatized by having a parent who is deaf and blind and may also worry that their children could have Usher's syndrome.

There are other counseling issues to consider when working with adolescents who have Usher's syndrome. Fillman, Leguire, and Sheridan (1989) provide the following example:

> I was born deaf. Also I have a problem with my eyes called retinitis pigmentosa. I am afraid to become blind. I am *not* blind now—I can see in

> the day but I can't see as well in the dark. My new friends and old friends know that I have bad eyes. . . . [M]any people help me. My friends hold my arm when we go to the movies because I can't see in the dark. In class, I can't see the board. I can see close up but I can't see far away. I can't read the overhead projector. I can't see blue print on paper; I can see black better. I can't see small letters but large letters are easier to see. . . . I don't know what I would do without the help of my friends and teachers. My friends help me when we go to the restaurant. They hold my arm. The restaurants are dim. I can't read the menu so my friends tell me what it says. . . . I have problems at school, too. The halls and stairs at school are dim. Sometimes I trip. I am afraid I will fall and hurt my ankle. . . . Some people tease and joke with me because I bump into things. Some people say, "Are you blind?" I say, "No, I have problems with my eyes." They hurt my feelings. —Statement of a 17-year-old girl with Usher's syndrome, who is about to graduate from high school. (p. 19–20)

This young woman's statement demonstrates the many problems that adolescents may have with self-esteem and the value of peer support. Fillman et al. (1989), noting that counselors are urged to be alert to such defense mechanisms as denial, suggested that some adolescents may refuse to use safe mobility techniques (e.g., white cane) because of social stigma and because it calls attention to the impairment. They also stated, "at a time when there is an inherent push for independence, teenagers with Usher's syndrome find themselves more and more dependent" (Fillman et al., 1989, p. 21).

It is highly recommended that counselors who are working with adolescents be sensitive to issues related to grief, peer pressure, self-image, and dependency, and never underestimate depression, which "is common and must be taken seriously" (Miner, 1995, p. 291). Peer support groups can be especially valuable in allowing adolescents to vent feelings, increase their sense of self-worth, and enhance their feelings of belonging (Fillman et al., 1989).

THE IMPORTANCE OF TEAMWORK

The rehabilitation counselor is a member of a team, often a very large team, consisting of a number of specialized personnel. (See Chapter 9 for a discussion of the rehabilitation team.) Frequently these other professionals provide unique perceptions, as well as specialized knowledge, which can facilitate the work of the rehabilitation counselor. For example, consider the following scenario:

> Client Mike Lewis is now receiving O&M instruction from Mr. Kane. They are in the process of working on outdoor travel. Mr. Lewis has had only a one-hour interview with his rehabilitation counselor. This is, however, his fifth session with O&M instructor Kane. He is beginning to feel quite comfortable with him and during the session they discuss a number of things besides O&M—television, family, politics. Today, as they happen to discuss Mr. Lewis's newly learned travel skills, Mr. Lewis adds, "You know what I would really like to do? I really would like to go back to work."

It is possible that Mr. Lewis's expression of interest in work is something that has happened because of his increased confidence. On the other hand, it is quite possible that he was interested in employment at the time he met his rehabilitation counselor at the initial interview. The relationships that specialized rehabilitation professionals, such as O&M instructors and rehabilitation teachers, have with their clients can be very helpful in the rehabilitation counseling process. Both the rehabilitation teacher and the O&M instructor have an opportunity to meet with clients on a more frequent basis than the rehabilitation counselor and they also have an opportunity to see clients in their own environments, which may be more conducive to facilitating client trust. The performance of such activities as crossing the street safely or using cutlery offers situations in which the client has put trust in the O&M instructor or the rehabilitation teacher. Also, their relationship with the client is a more informal one. The rehabilitation counselor role may be perceived as somewhat more authoritarian, or depending on the employment setting, the counselor may be perceived as the "holder of the purse strings," or the person who can approve or refuse services.

The O&M instructor and the rehabilitation teacher have an additional advantage over the rehabilitation counselor. Because both are in the field more often than the rehabilitation counselor, they become more aware of the client's home environment and neighborhood. They are able to bring back information about family relationships and their effect on rehabilitation outcomes. Their frequent travel through the client's neighborhood may also be helpful in identifying community resources and, possibly, employment opportunities. Rehabilitation counselors are advised to maintain a free flow of communication with rehabilitation teachers and O&M specialists to ensure that they benefit from their knowledge and experiences with clients. As with other areas of rehabilitation, the importance of teamwork cannot be overemphasized in the field of rehabilitation for people who are blind or visually impaired.

CAREER DEVELOPMENT INTERVENTIONS AND VOCATIONAL COUNSELING

The lives of people with visual impairments unfold in the education–work system of our society. This system includes more than 20,000 occupations, over 120 million workers, and thousands of educational programs that train people for occupations in our post-industrial society. Despite this diversity and opportunity, unemployment and underemployment are among the most serious problems facing both those who have visual impairments and those working with them to enhance their lives (Graves, Lyon, Marmion & Boyet, 1986a). To alleviate unemployment and underemployment problems encountered by individuals who are visually impaired, it is important that rehabilitation counselors understand how to use career development interventions in the rehabilitation process.

THE CAREER DEVELOPMENT PROCESS

To understand the use of career interventions, the rehabilitation counselor must understand the meaning of such terms as career, career development, career stages, career transitions, and career development intervention. A career is the sequence of jobs or positions held by individuals during their lifetimes (Bagley, 1985). A career includes all work-related positions, as well as other positions associated with civic and family responsibilities (Graves, 1983a; Graves 1983b). A career is simply the sum of an individual's life work (Bagley, 1985).

Career Development

Career development, a concept that proposes a career is built on what a person has done, is doing, and hopes to do (Graves & Lyon, 1985), is a continuous, dynamic process in which people move through several identifiable stages throughout their lives (Crites, 1976; Ginzberg, Ginzberg, Axelrod, & Herma, 1951; Havighurst, 1964; McBroom, Tedder & Haucke, 1989; Super, 1957). It is a process of growing and learning that is affected by individual self-concepts, developmental experiences, personal histories, as well as socioeconomic and psychological environments (Marmion, McBroom, Haucke, & Jackson, 1986). Career development theory is concerned with identifying the effects over time of psychological, sociological, cultural, and economic factors influencing self-career identity, decision-making ability, and career maturity (Marmion et al., 1986).

There are a variety of explanations for the career development process. These approaches or theoretical models include trait and factor or matching approaches (Cunningham, 1969); decision-making models that emphasize such cognitive theories of motivation as expectancy theory (Lawler, 1973) and self-efficacy theory (Bandura, 1977); situational or sociological approaches (Blau, Gustad, Jessor, Pannes, & Wilcock, 1956); psychological approaches (Holland, 1973; Hoppock, 1976: Maccoby, 1980; Roe, 1956); and developmental theories (Gribbons & Lohnes, 1982; Havighurst, 1964; Knefelkamp & Slepitza, 1976; Super et al., 1957; Tiedeman, 1961).

Career Stages

Career stages are associated with developmental theories (e.g., Super et al., 1957; Havighurst, 1964). The career stage concept is derived from the work of Buehler (1933), Havighurst (1953), and Super (1957). A career stage is composed of a set of tasks that emerge at a certain period in the life of an individual, the successful achievement of which leads to happiness and to success with later tasks, whereas failure leads to unhappiness in the individual, disapproval by society, and difficulty with later tasks (Havighurst, 1953).

Stage theorists propose that career tasks are different at different stages. An individual who is in the career exploration stage, for example, has career tasks that require information-seeking and interpretation. For the individual who is in the career maintenance stage, career tasks focus on activities related to job performance, job advancement, and relating to coworkers and supervisors. Ginzberg (1972), for example, argued that careers evolve or develop through related stages that unfold over time as a result of many choices. Ginzberg emphasized options and such situational constraints as the opportunity structure of the workplace, education, family background, or personal attributes including physical disabilities, for example, being visually impaired (McBroom et al., 1989). McBroom et al. (1989) interpreted Ginzberg's theory as advancing the proposition that the individual makes a series of "optimizing" moves, despite constraints, in search of the most satisfactory occupation. They also suggested that Ginzberg's theory supported the use of intervening services to assist individuals in taking advantage of opportunities and coping with such situational constraints as being visually impaired.

Initially, career development theorists held that career development was an irreversible process, that is, after an individual had mastered the tasks associated with a specific stage, that person would not repeat the mastery process. Most theorists (e.g., Ginzberg, 1972) now accept the concept that individuals return to earlier stages, when events occur that are external to the individual—for example, adventitious blindness. As McBroom et al. (1989) stated,

> This may be particularly relevant for people who become disabled after initial employment. Theoretically, a person may revert to an earlier developmental stage and pass through any number of stages more than one time. The role of work in the life of the individual is defined in an ongoing manner by the way problems are solved and work styles are modified in various career stages. (pp. 2–3)

Movement from one career stage to another is a career transition. At any point in time, more than one-third of all adults are experiencing a career transition (Arbeiter, Schnerbeck, Aslanian & Bricknell, 1976). Career transitions are the upheaval periods occurring between periods of stability (Levinson, 1978; 1986).

Various kinds of career problems are associated with particular career stages (Campbell & Cellini, 1981). Career development interventions are events or processes that are designed to facilitate an individual's successful mastery of tasks associated with a particular career development stage. For example, the seven-year-old child with a visual impairment in the first stage of career development probably will benefit more from career development interventions that are designed to increase the child's skills, awareness of self, careers in general, economics, and education (Kirkman, 1983). A 45-year-old adult with a

By employing career development interventions that focus on providing services, assistive devices, and work-site modifications, rehabilitation counselors can play a key role in helping visually impaired individuals obtain and retain employment.

visual impairment is more apt to benefit from career development interventions that focus on providing services, assistive devices, and job- or work-site modifications that permit the adult's career development needs to be accommodated as much as possible in the present career setting with minimal lifestyle change requirements (Graves et al., 1986a). It is highly advised that the rehabilitation counselor employing career development interventions (1) identify the career development needs of the individual with the visual impairment, (2) determine which career development needs are being met by the person who is visually impaired, the individual's family, or the work environment, and (3) identify and apply the interventions or services necessary to meet that individual's career development needs.

CAREER DEVELOPMENT AND VISUAL IMPAIRMENTS

The career development of individuals with visual impairments should not be equated with the career development of those with other types of disabilities or with individuals who have no disabilities, for whom career development theories were developed. Because these theories fail to consider that assumptions made for sighted people are not accurate for others, the use of career development theories contribute little to the understanding of the career development of people with visual impairments (Graves, 1983b; Phillips, Strohmer, Berthaume, & O'Leary, 1983).

Career development theorists have implicitly assumed that all people have a number of choices about their careers, that they will be able to actively decide among career alternatives, and that they will be able to implement the most desirable alternative. These theorists also assume that after the individual has identified a career field, training will be available, which the individual can successfully complete. It is further assumed that with training, the individual will be able to locate, enter, and maintain employment in that field (Osipow, 1975). The substantial, chronically high rate of unemployment among people with visual impairments belies these assumptions of the career development theorists and suggests that the employment opportunities for people who are visually impaired are not the same as those for sighted individuals without disabilities.

Attributes Affecting Career Development

Neither intrinsic nor extrinsic attributes associated with being blind are acknowledged in career development theories (Graves, 1983a). For the purposes of this text, intrinsic attributes are those characteristics that are inherent to a visual impairment and extrinsic attitudes are such social factors as prejudice or a lack of understanding of the ability of a person who is visually impaired. As an example of these attributes, assume that an individual with reduced visual acuity, which is a characteristic basic to some visual disorders, is interested in aeronautics. Given the present technology, being partially or totally blind inherently prevents this individual from having a career as a commercial airline pilot. It does not, however, prevent this individual from pursuing a career as an aeronautical engineer specializing in drag theory because this career does not require vision. Nonetheless, extrinsic attributes associated with visual impairments could prevent this individual from achieving a career goal of aeronautical engineering.

Intrinsic attributes of visual impairments that are most pertinent to career development theory and career development interventions are age at onset, nature and severity of the visual disorder, communication skills, and mobility skills. Age at onset of the visual disorder affects career development task mastery. For example, Graves et al. (1986b) found that elementary grade level students with visual impairments had few opportunities for vicarious learning about job behaviors or about careers of men and women with visual impairments.

Incidental Learning

Reduced opportunities for vicarious or incidental learning can have important effects on career expectations or efficacy expectations (Bandura, 1977). Efficacy expectations determine whether or not a behavior will be initiated, how much effort will be used, and how long the effort will be continued in the face of such challenges as the intrinsic attributes of visual disorders and such negative experiences as the extrinsic attributes of visual impairments (Hackett & Betz, 1981).

Incidental or vicarious learning is an important reinforcer of efficacy expectations and contributes significantly to developmental task mastery. For example, adults with recent visual impairments who observe another adult who also has a recent visual impairment and who is successfully employed in a competitive situation are more apt to believe in their own abilities to return to the competitive labor force and to attempt to develop alternative skills that will facilitate labor market participation.

Career Transition Problems

McBroom et al. (1989) examined career transition problems during four stages of career development of adults with visual impairments who were employed in professional or managerial jobs. The four stages explored were beginning, establishment, maintenance, and ending. Career problems were most frequently reported by individuals at the beginning stage of career development. These problems included (1) needing to make career decisions, (2) postponing career decisions, (3) changes in the economy and limited employment opportunities, (4) difficulties in acquiring job-related information, (5) O&M skills relative to the workplace, (6) job discrimination because of the visual impairment, and (7) underestimation of skills by vocational tests or examinations. Those in the establishment stage reported experiencing fewer problems. Their problems were reported as (1) having difficulty deciding among career options, (2) postponing career decisions, (3) declining work performance because of management problems, and (4) learning large quantities of job-related information. Individuals in the maintenance stage reported job performance decline because of off-the-job pressures and those in the ending stage identified few career problems.

Lag Effects

The career development of adults who are visually impaired appears to lag behind that of sighted adults without disabilities (Graves et al., 1986a; McBroom et al., 1989). In a study of the career development needs of adults (mean age equals 44.6) with visual impairments, Graves et al. (1986a) found career development factors (e.g., personal expectations, career options, and career testing) that were not compatible with

Herr and Cramer's description (1984) of the 44-year-old sighted adult in the maintenance career development stage. The career development needs reported by Graves et al. (1986a) are more compatible with Herr and Cramer's description of the 25- to 30-year-old person who is in the later stages of career establishment. The primary career development tasks of the 25- to 30-year-old individual are trial commitment and stabilization. The function of these tasks is consolidation and advancement of the individual's career goals. These findings of delayed development or lagging are similar to those reported by Bolton (1975) and McHugh (1975) for both adults and youth who are deaf (Lerman & Guilfoyle, 1970).

Career development of individuals who are visually impaired appears to proceed in the same manner as that of sighted persons (Graves & Lyon, 1985; McBroom et al., 1989), but progresses at a slower rate. The difference in rate of development, however, appears to be less a function of intrinsic attributes than extrinsic attributes. Some of the extrinsic factors that have a slowing effect on the career development process include differences in expectations of professionals for careers of people with visual impairments (Packer, 1983), in the opportunity structure (Fiorito, 1983a), and in societal attitudinal barriers (Dixon, 1983; Graves, 1983b). These differences in rates of career development process may be reduced through the appropriate application of career development interventions that address intrinsic and extrinsic attributes of visual impairments as they affect the individual's career development.

CAREER DEVELOPMENT INTERVENTION STRATEGIES

Career development intervention strategies (CDIS) are services to facilitate career development that may be used by the individual with the visual impairment, the rehabilitation counselor, the family of the individual with the visual impairment, the employer, or other educational or rehabilitation specialists. Graves et al. (1986b) described a career development intervention services model. This model permits an examination of the relationship among the individual's career development stages, the kinds of services provided, and the service delivery system. Since the development of the model, a number of intervention services have been created that have the potential to affect the career development of individuals who are visually impaired. Two such services are supported employment and the application of computer access technology (CAT). These services could be included in the employment support services area of the model.

Community Integration Services

Community integration services is a phrase used to describe an array of services provided to youths with severe developmental disabilities. One such service is vocational transition services, which has been defined as

> a carefully planned process, which may be initiated either by school personnel or by adult service providers, to establish and implement a plan for either employment or additional vocational training of a . . . student [with a disability] who will graduate or leave school in three to five years; such a process must involve special educators, vocational educators, parents, and/or the student, an adult service system representative, and possibly an employer. (Wehman, Moon, Everson, Wood, & Barcus, 1988, p. 3)

Community integration services are based on a three-stage model (1) input and foundation, (2) process, and (3) employment outcome (Wehman et al., 1988). Youths with visual impairments and other developmental disabilities who are in the exploration stage of career development and who are receiving community integration services are placed in special education programs. A program such as this "provides for a community-based instructional model of school services," which is characterized by functional curricula and integration with students who do not have disabilities (Wehman et al., 1988, p. 7).

Transportation and Mobility Alternatives

Planning for transportation and mobility needs is an essential career transition service for people in the beginning or establishment career development stage. Rehabilitation counselors, as McBroom et al. (1989) suggested, should assist individuals with visual impairments in these stages to develop strategies or alternatives to meet their transportation and mobility needs for their careers. Services to meet immediate transportation and O&M needs are frequently included in the Individualized Written Rehabilitation Program (IWRP) (see also Chapters 5 and 10).

Planning for transportation and mobility needs is an important career transition service offered by rehabilitation counselors for people in the beginning or establishment stage of career development.

Technology as a Career Intervention Service

The provision of technology to individuals who are visually impaired is also an important career service (Marmion et al., 1986). Technology has different effects on the career development of adults who are congenitally blind and those who have adventitious visual impairments. Assistive devices were reported by rehabilitation counselors as having a greater effect on self-concept for individuals with adventitious visual impairments than for persons with congenital visual impairments. Assistive devices with various sensory information output also have differing effects on career development tasks of these two groups. Marmion and her associates (1986), for example, found that for career development tasks associated with the "selecting and preparing for an occupation" stage, assistive devices with visual output were perceived as having a significantly greater effect than either assistive devices or technology with auditory or tactile sensory output.

Jeppsson-Grassman (1986), however, cautioned that improperly applied technology or assistive devices can create difficulties that limit their usefulness as a career development intervention service. A primary difficulty is that the device has the potential of creating a rupture in the relationship between the individual who is visually impaired and the work environment. Jeppsson-Grassman cited the following example as illustrative of the kinds of problems technology can create in the worker/work environment relationship:

> When Birgitta started working at the orthopaedics consultation office, she had to sit in a little secluded room by herself, to have enough space for all the equipment the AMI-center had prescribed for her. She was supposed to assist the doctors with a telephone service. For this, she was supposed to need a tape recorder for each doctor. These took up a lot of space and the routine was disturbing and complicated in its consequences for the environment. One of the nurse's aides found a simplified solution: Birgitta could still write on paper even if she could not see, couldn't she? She could have small notebooks, one for each doctor, and note the names of each patient who wanted to be contacted by their doctors. So Birgitta developed a system for using notebooks instead. This way she could move out into the

> consultation office and work in the midst of everybody. (p. 107)

The application of technology as a career transition service requires an analysis of the job or work environment, the individual with the visual impairment, and how the technology interfaces with the individual and the work environment (Graves & Maxson, 1989). Rehabilitation engineers or technologists who specialize in visual impairments serve as consultants in much the same way as medical consultants in this phase of the rehabilitation process. Careful analysis of the worker/work environment relationship can prevent the kinds of adaptation problems identified by Jeppsson-Grassman (1986).

Job Modification Services

Job modification services are often provided to people who have recently acquired a visual impairment. Job modifications may involve application of technological devices, reordering of job tasks, or other alterations that enable the worker to perform the work tasks. Although individuals with congenital disorders receive a greater share of computerized technological devices (Marmion et al., 1986), those with adventitious visual impairments are more apt to receive job modifications (McBroom et al., 1989), particularly during the maintenance stage of career development.

Jeppsson-Grassman (1986) examined the effect of adventitious visual impairments on the return-to-work during the maintenance stage. She identified a person/work environment adaptive process. The process has four phases, which are as follows:

1. Phase I: Decline or Preparation. This phase begins when the developing visual impairment affects overtly or covertly the relationship between the individual who is visually impaired and the work environment. During Phase I, the individual copes with a series of gradual losses and gains awareness of the effects of the impairment while trying to "keep up with the demands or needs of the workplace and to live as normally as possible."
2. Phase II: Discontinuance phase. This starts when the individual leaves the workplace because of the visual impairment. Many people exit the work force forever as this phase begins because of the disruption or discontinuation of the relationship between the individual and the workplace. Jeppsson-Grassman (1986) reported that the focus on the adaptive process during Phase II is unilaterally on the individual, not the workplace. When the individual is referred to the rehabilitation counselor during this stage, the emphasis of the process (according to Jeppsson-Grassman) is on the individual, not on interventions with the work environment. The effect of rehabilitation counseling strategies that emphasize adjustment of the individual who is newly visually impaired during this phase is increased distance from the workplace. It is critical that the rehabilitation counselor focus the counseling process on ways to help the employer accommodate the individual with the visual impairment as quickly as possible to minimize the continued break between the work environment and the client.
3. Phase III: Restoration. This phase is initiated when efforts are made to reestablish a relationship between the workplace and the individual with the visual impairment. These efforts include contacts with the workplace, for example, visits, planning, and job modifications. Technological aids and devices might be found or designed that match the job requirements and the skills and abilities of the visually impaired person. An important goal of this phase is the creation of a relationship in which the individual with the visual impairment

can be productive in the workplace, while also receiving appropriate modifications in the workplace.

4. Phase IV: Normalization. This phase begins when the relationship between the individual who is visually impaired and the workplace takes on a routine character. The person with the visual impairment has mastered work responsibilities and reestablished working relationships with coworkers. It is a phase characterized by continuing adaptive efforts—both from the individual and the work environment. The visually impaired person also experiences and maintains a sense of satisfaction and meaning over time in the workplace. Maintenance of this stage requires a certain amount of vigilance and follow-up by the rehabilitation counselor because of the possibility of additional disabling symptoms and changes in the workplace.

Peer Groups

Peer groups are an important CDIS (Winer, 1982), which can provide opportunities for individuals with visual impairments to increase their knowledge of the kinds of occupations held by other individuals who are also visually impaired. It is important that peer groups provide an opportunity for individuals to converse, observe, and work with other people with visual impairments who are working in a variety of careers. Giesen et al. (1985) documented that people who are visually impaired are employed in a variety of careers with a distribution across occupational categories that is not significantly different from those of the sighted population.

The use of peer groups as a CDIS can be applied at any career development stage. If used with adults who are in the maintenance stage, prior to their visual impairment, it is preferable to have the peer group composed of individuals in the same stage. However, for individuals who are newly blind and who are in the beginning or establishment stages of career development, the peer group should be composed of a mix of stages.

Using peer group methodology as a CDIS may also be applied to special subpopulations of people with visual impairments. Project Care (Middlesex Community College, 1984), which is an example of an application of a modified peer group model, was designed to provide sighted displaced homemakers and clients of the New Jersey Commission for the Blind and Visually Impaired with an intensive job-readiness training program. The project assumed that there are commonalities in the experiences of people—especially women—with visual impairments and displaced homemakers as they seek to enter or reenter the world of work. Project Care included a recruitment and outreach process, an intake process, an assessment process, transportation services, O&M services, and access to print services as support to the vocational exploration/job-readiness program. The vocational exploration/job-readiness program included four weeks of various activities fostering self-awareness in relation to the world of work. Integrating individuals with and without vision in the same program activities successfully assisted in stimulating the career development of both sets of participants.

Networking

Networking is a career intervention strategy that has been successfully used by women to locate jobs and to move up the career ladder (Gerberg, 1986). Networking relies on personal contacts that are usually informal (Granovetter, 1974). Kirchner and Greenstein (1984) identified seven networks that might be used by people with visual impairments, including the American Foundation for the Blind (AFB) Careers and Technology Information Bank (CTIB), which is an important resource for clients and counselors seeking advice on careers and job-site modifications (see the Resources section at the end of this book).

Work Experience Programs

Work experience programs are an important CDIS for individuals who are exploring career options or who are making the transition from the exploration to the beginning stage of career development. There is ample evidence (e.g.. Graves, 1983a; McBroom et al., 1989) documenting that youths with visual impairments have fewer work experiences prior to beginning a career than sighted youths and that these fewer experiences cause the lag effect. Such community integration programs as those fashioned from the Wehman et al. (1988) model offer an opportunity to stimulate the career development of youths with visual impairments. To reap the maximum benefit, it is advised that the work experience programs offer activities which

> (1) promote growth in autonomy, (2) increase cooperation and social responsibility (social 'connectedness'), (3) lead to learning and mastery of useful skills and information, (4) advance youngsters' occupational development, (5) provide opportunities for experimentation and integration of experience (identity clarification), and (6) bring youngsters into contact with adults who can contribute to these ends (Greenberger & Steinberg, 1986, p. 209).

Vision Teacher Services as Career Interventions

The provision of educational services to enhance the career development of individuals with visual impairments begins in early childhood and continues until the youth leaves the secondary school (Graves et al., 1986b). Vision teachers, whether itinerant teacher, resource teacher, or primary teacher, can make vital contributions to the career development of youths with visual impairments. Vision teachers can play a major role in infusing career development concepts in the K through 12 curriculum (Hamel & Krumboltz, 1982; Hoyt, 1985). However, infusion is not sufficient as a stand-alone strategy of career development (Howze, 1985; Graves et al., 1986b). Such services as visits to job sites (Howze, 1985), observing workers with visual impairments (Graves et al., 1986a), work experience programs (Corn & Bishop, 1985), and community-based vocational training programs (Storey, Sacks, & Olmstead, 1985) are necessary to reinforce career development concepts infused into the curriculum. Vision teachers who recognize the career development needs of their students may incorporate these kinds of activities into the student's IEP. Rehabilitation counselors are urged to anticipate working with the student with the visual impairment, the vision teacher, and the family in developing the individualized education program (IEP) and the interface or transition program into the rehabilitation service delivery system.

SUMMARY

The initial interview and the activities leading up to the interview are extremely critical factors in the success of the rehabilitation process. It is recommended that the rehabilitation counselor understand the significance of visual impairments and how they affect clients. A number of options were presented relating to timing, structure, questionnaires and forms, and techniques of working with people who are visually impaired.

Emphasis is also placed on the significance of counseling and the unique aspects of the counseling process that are affected by visual impairment. The role of the family and significant others is especially important. Clients who successfully complete training in activities of daily living may return home only to be discouraged from putting these activities into practice because of overprotective family members. The rehabilitation counselor is encouraged to seek support of family members and arrange for family counseling services when necessary. Although the counselor plays a major role in the rehabilitation process, the significance of team membership cannot be overemphasized.

Rehabilitation counselors have a major role in alleviating unemployment and underemployment of individuals with visual impairments. Their career development is influenced by both intrinsic and extrinsic attributes, including age at onset, nature and severity of the visual impairment, communication skills, O&M skills and the manner in which these affect incidental learning and career transition and the lag effects they produce. Career development interventions that may be used by rehabilitation counselors to counter these problems include community integration services, transportation alternatives, technology, job modification services, peer groups and networks, work experience programs, and the services of vision teachers.

LEARNING ACTIVITIES

1. Review an intake form from an agency or facility that provides services to individuals with visual impairments. What questions are the most important? Are there any questions that may present difficulties for the client to answer? Are there any questions you would find difficult to ask? What questions could be delayed to subsequent interviews?
2. Observe the office waiting room and interviewing room of an agency or facility that provides services to individuals with visual impairments. What impression do you think these environments make on the client? What suggestions would you make for changes?
3. Make a list of all services provided by an agency or facility that works with individuals who are visually impaired. Think of additional services that the client might need but are not able to be provided by that agency. Identify appropriate resources for provision of these unmet needs.
4. Attend a meeting of an organization of adults with visual impairments. Identify an individual who has a career in a field that you thought might be unavailable to an individual who is visually impaired. Discuss and report on that individual's career development in that field.
5. Identify three community resources that could be used to stimulate the career development of the following three persons: (1) a 19-year-old who has a visual impairment and mental retardation, (2) a 49-year-old woman who is blind, whose work history after high school is limited to homemaking, and (3) a train conductor who was recently blinded and wishes to maintain his association with AMTRAK.

CHAPTER 12

Placement Readiness and Supported Employment

Karen E. Wolffe, Sharon Zell Sacks, and Michael D. Orlansky

Work meets a number of individual needs, including financial needs, a sense of belonging, and self-esteem. Because opportunities to work have been greatly restricted for individuals with disabilities, particularly those with visual impairments, it is important to address factors that can enhance their employability. This chapter focuses on two primary approaches to employment, which are placement readiness and supported employment. Although the goal of each of these approaches is employment, the techniques used by rehabilitation professionals vary according to the needs of individual clients. Therefore, the objectives of this chapter include helping rehabilitation counselors working with people who are visually impaired to develop an understanding of placement readiness and supported employment, determine the appropriateness of each approach for various types of clients, and develop and utilize group and individual strategies to assist people who are visually impaired to secure employment.

PLACEMENT READINESS

When an individual with a visual impairment prepares to enter the working world, questions frequently arise about whether the person is ready for placement (Fuqua, Rathbun, & Gade, 1984; Rabby & Croft, 1989). Questions asked by prospective employers, counselors, the rehabilitation client, family, or significant others may address such practical matters as whether work tasks can be performed safely and effectively by the individual who is visually impaired. Other questions may be more personal, such as whether the job will complement the prospective employee's long-term career goals, whether the employee will need sighted assistance to perform job duties or get around in the work environment, whether the employee will require additional time to complete tasks, or whether the employee will fit in. A placement-ready client will be able to answer such questions as these with confidence.

Placement readiness implies (1) individual self-awareness and (2) the identification of a vocational objective that is both realistic and compatible with a person's career goals. A placement-ready client understands how to seek employment and has a retrievable (i.e., printed, brailled, or taped) plan of action. This action plan details the steps that the individual will follow to secure a job or acquire specific skills training. The placement-ready client also knows how to keep a job and how to advance in a chosen field (Greenwood & Johnson, 1985; Howze, 1987; Marks & Lewis, 1983; Roessler & Bolton, 1984; Vandergoot & Worrall, 1979, Wolffe, 1997a).

Although placement readiness is determined in a similar manner with all people, there are some logistical issues that affect the assessment of placement readiness for those who are visually impaired (Bradfield, 1992; Davidson, 1981; Fiorito, 1983b; Graves, Lyon, Marmion, & Boyet, 1986; Rabby & Croft, 1989; Roberts, 1992; Scadden, 1986; Wolffe, 1985, 1997b). For example, the ability to move around safely and effectively in a work environment is a critical issue for an individual who is severely visually impaired. Mobility issues vary from client to client, depending upon (1) the extent of residual vision, if any, (2) age at onset of the visual impairment, (3) present age of the client, and (4) the presence of any additional physical, sensory, cognitive, or emotional impairments (Hill, 1986).

Characteristics of a Placement-Ready Client

The five major areas of concern when considering an individual's placement readiness are (1) self-awareness, (2) vocational selection, (3) job-seeking skills, (4) job-search skills, and (5) job maintenance skills. Self-awareness is characterized by an understanding of one's interests, abilities, values, and liabilities. Vocational selection involves a person's ability to match the available jobs in the labor market to that person's career goals. Job-seeking skills include such steps as identifying job openings, producing accurate applications and résumés, and interviewing (Boerner, 1994; Wolffe, 1997a). Job-search skills are the application of job-seeking skills—keeping actual records on paper or tape of the plans of whom to see, where to go, when to meet, what to discuss, and how to follow up on job leads. Finally, the job maintenance skills are concerned with job retention and advancement in a person's chosen field.

The first four placement-readiness skills are contingent on one another; that is, a successful job match under the vocational selection area is contingent upon an adequate level of self-awareness. Without self-awareness, it is virtually impossible to compare one's characteristics to job characteristics and identify discrepancies between the two. Moreover, successful application of job-seeking skills is not probable without an appropriate job selection and a job search is predictably futile without good job-seeking skills (Bolles, 1997; Porot, 1996; Wegmann, Chapman, & Johnson, 1985).

For training purposes, job maintenance skills are interwoven throughout the other content areas. In the workplace, they are evidenced by work habits such as attendance, punctuality, and cooperation. Teaching these is essential because some individuals successfully select and secure employment, only to fail in retaining their jobs. Successful job maintenance skills are, to some degree, contingent on the aforementioned placement-readiness skills and in many ways the placement-readiness skills are contingent on job maintenance skills.

Self-Awareness

Self-awareness is indicated by a thorough knowledge of one's interests (what an individual *likes* to do), abilities (what an individual *can* do), values (what an individual *believes* to be right or wrong), and limitations (what an individual *cannot* do). People who demonstrate high levels of self-awareness understand how others see them and use feedback from others' observations of them to analyze the effect of their behavior on others and themselves. In other words, they relate well to other people. People who are self-aware typically are able to set personality goals and achievement goals. This means that people who are knowledgeable about themselves understand how to change that behavior with which they are dissatisfied through goal setting (Carkhuff, 1969, 1993; Carkhuff & Berenson, 1977).

Self-Awareness Counseling Strategies

There are a number of counseling strategies that can assist clients in self-awareness. The following techniques are particularly suitable to group settings, which are encouraged whenever possible because of the valuable exchange of information that frequently occurs among clients. However, many of the suggested activities can also be utilized in individual sessions.

Values Clarification Exercises. Values clarification exercises are designed to help clients explore and define what they consider to be important. Such exercises as those detailed by Raths and his colleagues (1966); Simon, Howe, & Kirschenbaum (1995); or DeVito (1995) can be incorporated into group meetings of job seekers. Means and Roessler's (1975) *Personal Achievement Skills* (PAS) training package, which includes values clarification exercises, is a model curriculum for group work sessions.

The Lifeline Activity, which is an example from the PAS package, has participants document five accomplishments from birth to the present, and five aspirations from the present to death. This activity encourages values clarification. Moreover, an epitaph-writing exercise in the same curriculum works well to help participants analyze personal values. These activities can be shared in a group process or used in individual counseling sessions.

Interest Checklists and Tests. Many of the commercially available interest tests, such as the Strong Interest Inventory and the Self-Directed Search (available in braille), can be administered orally to individuals who are visually impaired without affecting outcome deleteriously (Bauman, 1975; Power, 1991, see Chapter 6). The Occupational Aptitude Survey & Interest Schedule (OASIS) for secondary students and young adults can be obtained on diskette (Parker, 1991). Nonreaders with adequate residual vision to discriminate pictorial information may benefit from doing the Revised Reading Free Interest Inventory (Becker, 1981). For an interviewing model to assist clients in identifying interests, see Sidebar 12.1.

Aptitude Testing. A few aptitude tests, for example, the Pennsylvania Bi-Manual Work sample and the Comprehensive Vocational Evaluation System (McCarron–Dial Evaluation Systems), are appropriate and normed on individuals who are visually impaired. In addition to these, some tests, such as the Crawford Small Parts Dexterity Test and the Purdue Pegboard, can also be adapted for people with visual impairments. Some facilities provide work samples, which simulate jobs in the community, to evaluate client aptitude. However, such samples can be difficult to maintain in relationship to an ever-changing labor market. Four other strategies for determining aptitudes include (1) informal job tryouts, (2) client self-evaluations, (3) observations on previous job sites and in classroom settings, and (4) reviews of transcripts and work histories (Power, 1991). Many contemporary career counselors (e.g., Bolles, 1997; Wolffe, 1997a) encourage job seekers to develop listings of their personal attributes, which can also provide insight into clients' aptitudes.

Special Issues. It is essential for people who are visually impaired to receive honest, open feedback concerning their personal appearance. This feedback includes such concerns as clothing, hair, skin, and cosmetic appearance of the eyes. Feedback can be solicited from significant others, including family, counselors, teachers, and peers. Some clients may also require instruction in asking for feedback from others. Rather than relying on the standard cues (i.e., facial expression and body language), clients with severe visual impairments need verbal explanations of feelings evoked by interactions with them. Furthermore, clear verbal descriptions of visual information derived from videos, films, television, and newspapers can also provide clients with a more accurate understanding of the world in which they live and work.

Vocational Selection

Vocational selection involves individuals in the process of determining what jobs would be of interest to them. Clients learn how to use career exploration materials and how to research local and national labor market demands and trends. They also learn how to conduct job analyses and how to perform a discrepancy analysis, in which they compare themselves to jobs and career

SIDEBAR 12.1

Six-Step Interviewing Model

In addition to the use of any standardized testing, Friel and Carkhuff (1974) encouraged counselors to follow a six-step interviewing model to assist clients in determining and expanding their interest areas. Briefly, the six steps are as follows:

1. Ask clients open-ended questions to help identify their interests. For example: What do you enjoy doing in your spare time?
2. Help clients explore their values by asking focused questions. For example: What kinds of things were important to you when you were in school or working?
3. Help clients organize their values into intellectual, physical, and emotional or interpersonal areas.
4. Help clients categorize interest information into people-oriented or object-oriented occupations.
5. Help clients determine the interest category that best matches their values.
6. Identify training and job requirements essential to employment areas congruent with clients' values and interests.

Source: Based on a model from T. Friel & R. Carkhuff, *The Art of Developing a Career* (Amherst, MA: Human Resource Development Press, 1974).

choices. Expected results include (1) establishing short- and long-term career objectives, (2) understanding how a person's qualifications match a job, and (3) knowing how a selected job relates to career objectives.

In summary, vocational awareness is indicated by knowledge of employers available in a person's home community who hire for positions that match as closely as possible a person's abilities, interests, and values. Jobs identified are subsequently analyzed to determine that fiscal and physical needs can be met. Finally, alternative jobs are identified that are related to life/career goals and can be sought in the event that a person's primary choice is unavailable.

Vocational Awareness Counseling Strategies

A variety of methods can be used, in either individual or group counseling sessions, to enhance vocational awareness. Although introduction to the processes can easily be presented in group settings, specific job analyses and the discrepancy analysis process lend themselves to individual work. The degree to which clients are independently able to research and analyze job choices gives the counselor concrete evidence of work performance.

Instruction in Research Methodology. Counselors will probably need to introduce clients to such occupational research materials as the *Dictionary of Occupational Titles, Guide for Occupational Exploration, Occupational Outlook Handbook* (available in taped or printed format), *Occupational Outlook Quarterly, Detroit Occupational Library for the Blind* (available on audio cassettes and diskettes), *Monthly Labor Review,* as well as the *Career Information and Training Activities for the Blind* (*CI-TAB*), which is available on audio cassettes. Internet search engines, such as Yahoo and Hot Bot, may be used to obtain additional information about careers and job openings. Clients will need training in how to access such materials through library systems and in locating related reference materials (as in local Chambers of Commerce, Better Business Bureaus, state employment commissions, business schools, and community colleges). Finally, it may be necessary to show clients how to gather information or how to sort through information they have gathered. Clients also need to know how to use such specialized services as regional libraries networked with the National Library Service for the Blind and Physically Handicapped, Recording for the Blind and Dyslexic (RFBD); and local public facilities.

Vocational Options Discussion. Wegmann, Chapman, & Johnson (1985) identified three levels of job-seeking strategies, which they identified as levels A, B, and C. People utilizing intermediaries (e.g., counselors, employment agency personnel, classified advertising—the use of others or anything removed from the actual job seeker) were identified as using C-level job-seeking strategies. The results of such endeavors were typically C-level jobs, which were characterized as mediocre jobs with high turnover rates, minimal salary, limited opportunity for growth, and few or no benefits. "Cold calls" (sales terminology for calling on customers that a person has never encountered before) were identified as B-level strategies. The initiative required to perform cold calls was repaid in the higher quality of jobs obtained. B-level jobs were typically higher paying, offered more benefits, were considerably more stable than C-level jobs, afforded greater advancement opportunity, and were more apt to accommodate individual differences. For the most part, jobs secured in this manner were not advertised to the general public. A-level jobs, which were those in which the job seeker knew someone working for the company where he or she wished to be employed, were the most advantageous. Salaries in A-level jobs were very competitive and benefit packages were generous. Some of the many benefits were travel allowances, liberal vacation and sick leave policies, opportunities for advancement, and numerous workplace amenities.

Information Interviewing. Bolles popularized the concept of information interviewing to the general public in his classic job-seeking skills manual, *What Color Is Your Parachute?* (1970, 1997, revised annually). Bolles encouraged job hunters to seek out and set interviews with workers whose jobs matched their own career interests. With a list of prepared questions in hand, the job hunter was expected to collect information about work in a chosen area. The job hunter, however, was to seek only information and not employment through this process. Actual job interviews were to follow information interviews in the job-seeking sequence.

Job Shadowing. Job shadowing is a technique in which the job seeker follows an employee during the performance of the employee's typical work duties. Often, prospective workers will shadow an employee for a number of days. This strategy enables an individual to make an informed decision regarding a potential work role.

Volunteering. Clients still in a quandary after making an earnest attempt at researching prospective jobs may need to volunteer to work in positions they are considering. In addition to clarifying career choices, volunteer positions can provide references, supervised work experiences, and a documented track record for those clients with poor job histories or limited work experience. Student teaching experiences, counseling practica, residencies, and internships, which are part of many academic programs, provide similar benefits to volunteering and job shadowing.

Special Issues. Voluminous reference materials and limited numbers of readers make access to generic vocational selection materials both difficult and time-consuming for clients with visual impairments. For nonprint readers, accessing routinely printed information, particularly newspapers (e.g., business sections, special supplements, classified advertising) and postings of help wanted signs, can be a major source of frustration. Such visual input informs job seekers about the popularity of certain positions, how frequently jobs turn over, how well certain companies are doing fiscally, where budgeted monies will be appropriated, and other valuable, job-seeking information. Some clients will be able to use computerized reading machines to access some of this information but many clients who are visually impaired will have to either rely on the reports of others or solicit such information by phone or in person.

Furthermore, observing environments from afar to ascertain whether or not one wishes to work in such a place is severely restricted without distance vision. Once again, clients must either solicit information from others and rely on their perceptions or visit workplaces and ask questions in person. Informational interviewing techniques, that is, approaching a prospective employer with a detailed list of questions about the work environment and duties, can secure input about companies being considered. However, turning around and asking for a job from an employer one has just interviewed is not a recommended tactic. Therefore, to scrutinize a prospective working environment, a person who is visually impaired may do better to ask as many people as possible for their opinions. Ideally, some present employees of the firm in question could be asked for their insights.

Finally, inadequate social networks may contribute to deficient vocational selection behavior. If a client has been living in isolation from the community at large or in a very restricted environment, knowledge of the local job market and people involved in it will probably be limited. Moreover, a significant number of individuals will have stereotypic views of what people with impaired vision can and cannot do, in part because of the low incidence of visual impairment. (For additional information on job search practices, see Fesko & Temelini [1997, sec. 2, pp. 135–160].)

Job-Seeking Skills

The job-seeking skills component of placement readiness involves learning how (1) to develop a résumé, personal data sheet, qualifications brief, or vita, (2) to access information on how to find job openings, (3) to secure and complete applications, (4) to set up interview appointments, (5) to follow up on telephone conversations, and (6) to interview successfully. A variety of job-seeking skills programs have been developed for individuals with visual impairments, for example, those described by Ferris (1991) and Ryder and Kawalec (1995).

Job-seeking skills training typically constitutes the bulk of instructional activities undertaken in placement-readiness programs. Indeed, job-seeking skills are essential when preparing to enter the work world. To secure employment, it is often necessary to submit numerous applications, set many appointments, and interview repeatedly. With effective job-seeking skills, clients can often place themselves. Without these skills, clients often require the assistance of the counselor or placement specialist to be an advocate for them when talking with employers.

Job-Seeking Skills Counseling Strategies

Job-seeking skills can be explored initially with clients in a group process. What employers are looking for in applications, résumés, and interviews can easily be discussed in either large or small groups. Comparing a variety of fictitious applicants, as a group, can also be helpful. The facilitator can bring in a series of sample applications or show a series of individuals interviewing on videotape. Clients without functional vision would have to rely on sighted assistants to read sample applications and describe video action. Group members then discuss their feelings and thoughts about the "applicants" as they appeared on paper or film.

However, the implementation of job-seeking skills can best be monitored and facilitated on an individual basis. Helping a client prepare an application or develop a résumé demands individual attention. Refining an interview style may also require one-to-one involvement. The following sections detail activities designed to enhance job-seeking skills.

Writing Activities. Résumés, vitae, qualifications briefs, and personal data sheets are paperwork variations that contain career relevant information. They are used to substantiate relevant work histories, special talents that might be missed by standard applications, and outstanding contributions or awards. An individual with limited paid work experience may choose to develop a qualifications brief rather than a formal résumé. A qualifications brief allows such a person to focus on skills developed in school or leisure activities rather than specific on-the-job training and experience. Individuals with extensive work experience and accomplishments, who desire to communicate with a prospective employer about career goals, may choose a résumé or vita, which allows for broader coverage of educational, personal, and vocational areas.

Portfolios. For some occupations (e.g., artists or jewelers), a portfolio is required for the applicant to be considered a viable candidate. Likewise, photographers, models, or writers are required to show examples of their work. Individuals pursuing careers in the performing arts may be asked to show demonstration tapes or videos, or may be required to audition, as well as showing a portfolio chronicling their careers.

Appointment Setting. In addition to reviewing these subjects individually, telephone etiquette and appointment setting are good topics for group discussion. A counselor is advised to stress the importance of documenting information obtained by phone, in order to avoid repeated calls or misinformation. It is also vital that clients understand that they may be asked to set appointments by phone, therefore, scheduling and transportation concerns must be resolved in advance of calling. Observation of problems in a client's telephone approach is best handled individually, however, and may necessitate modeling of appropriate behavior by the counselor. In a role-playing example, a counselor may have a client call from another office phone and pretend to be making an initial job interview appointment. Another choice is the counselor asks the client to play the part of a prospective employer and calls the client from another office phone to demonstrate how to make the appointment.

Interviewing. Interview structure and the consequences of leading the conversation versus following a lead imposed by another is an excellent topic for group discussion. Learning how to take the initiative, establish a friendly rapport, answer open-ended questions, and present a functional disability statement are topics amenable to either large or small group situations. In large groups, it can be very helpful to solicit volunteers to role play either with each other or with the group facilitator(s) and then discuss what has transpired. In small groups, individuals can rotate roles (i.e., employer, applicant, observer) and do situational role playing. Interviewer and interviewee rights, including those specific to individuals with visual impairments, as well as the pros and cons of filing complaints, can also be introduced in a group setting. However, some clients may need to review specifics in a one-to-one setting.

Although actual job interviews would not normally be observed by a client's counselor or other group members, videotaped practice interviews can be. Such video viewing can be particularly helpful when a client's effort is critiqued by a group of interested people. A video critique form, such as the example in Table 12.1, is another useful tool for cataloging information from others regarding a person's performance. On occasion, job seekers can also obtain feedback from an actual recruiter or personnel manager concerning interview performance. However, many job recruiters are reluctant to state their true reasons for selecting one candidate over another for fear that their comments might be held against them or their employer. In addition, many companies have instructed their human resources personnel to refrain from revealing any information that might be construed as controversial or discriminatory, because the number of discrimination-based lawsuits has increased dramatically in recent decades.

Counselors rarely, if ever, go to job interviews with clients. However, a counselor can break this

Table 12.1. Video Interview Critique Form

	Good	Average	Poor
Appearance	_____	_____	_____
Introduction	_____	_____	_____
Establishes friendly interaction with interviewer	_____	_____	_____
Brief personal description	_____	_____	_____
Explanation of disability	_____	_____	_____
Explains work experience as it relates to job	_____	_____	_____
Makes three positive statements about self	_____	_____	_____
Pays attention	_____	_____	_____
Ability to answer questions	_____	_____	_____
Ability to ask job-related questions	_____	_____	_____
Understands job duties	_____	_____	_____
Knows about company	_____	_____	_____
Body language	_____	_____	_____
Motivation	_____	_____	_____
Interest	_____	_____	_____
Seems competent/able to sell self	_____	_____	_____
Knows next step in hiring process	_____	_____	_____
Comments:			

Source: Reprinted, by permission of the publisher, from K. E. Wolffe, *Career Counseling for People with Disabilities: A Practical Guide to Finding Employment* (Austin, TX: PRO-ED, 1997a), p. 60.

rule when a client is functioning at a level that requires intervention by the counselor. In this situation, a counselor may need to attend and possibly even participate in interviews between employers and such a client. In these situations, a counselor will clarify to a prospective employer how the client will be able to perform the job duties required. If the client is utilizing supported employment strategies, which are described in the second half of this chapter, they will have to be explained in detail to a prospective employer.

Special Issues. It is important to discuss strategies on how to obtain applications with and without sighted assistance, for example, telephoning to ask a company to mail an application, or retrieving applications on-line. Issues of personal responsibility, such as having someone else fill out job applications, need attention and can be handled well in a group discussion. It is important that nonprint readers understand that the written application is a direct reflection of the person who has signed as applicant. An application tells an employer about the applicant's neatness, ability to follow instructions, ability to complete the information provided, work history, and so on, which are topics amenable to group discussion. Counselors may wish to practice presenting difficult information—for example, negative or limited work histories, chronic or progressive illnesses, criminal records, or invisible disabilities (such as learning disabilities, diabetes, or epilepsy) may be discussed in general terms within the group structure. However, specific areas of client concern may require individualized intervention. How to present positively information regarding visual impairment questions, particularly if the individual has secondary or multiple disabilities, can also be treated individually (Ryder & Kawalec, 1995).

Job-Search Skills

In actuality, the job search is putting the job-seeking skills to practical use. Job search content includes (1) how to organize time and resources, (2) how to negotiate with significant others in career plan development, (3) how to document one's efforts, and (4) how to determine when to shift to a backup plan. Job-search skills also help identify people who might be able to find job openings, recognize appropriate jobs, know when to submit a completed application and the accompanying paperwork, understand when and how to follow up after an interview, and document job-search activities.

Job-Search Counseling Strategies

Although both group and individual counseling strategies may be used, it is recommended that counselors encourage self-placement, whenever possible, and positively reinforce individual efforts. "No news is not good news" when an individual has been steadfastly pursuing work. A counselor's kind encouragement and praise for efforts made will probably be welcome. Furthermore, monitoring a client's efforts provides a counselor with valuable feedback regarding that person's level of functioning and need for additional counselor intervention.

Group Interventions. The primary function a group serves during a job search is to monitor a group member's progress externally. The group can also be a source of supportive feedback. When active job seekers report their progress to the group, other members can reaffirm those individuals' efforts. If a person reports feelings of being discouraged or frustrated, peers can often function as a safe "sounding board." Group members can also brainstorm ideas with the job seeker for changing whatever part of the job search plan appears not to be working.

An additional advantage to meeting with other job seekers in a group is the networking potential. Often, group members will report to the group about opportunities they have uncovered in the community. Providing leads to other group members and talking about job possibilities (e.g., How realistic is this job offer? Are there hidden agendas imbedded in a particular job posting? Has anyone ever heard of this company?) are possible constructive by-products of the group process.

Individualized Interventions. Some job seekers need individual assistance, perhaps in combination with group activities. With individual clients, counselors may wish to implement written job-search contracts. In such contracts, anticipated counselor and client behaviors are defined over a mutually determined time span. For example, a client might state a willingness to make a minimum of three job contacts daily over a period of two months and report to the counselor weekly. Using this as a contract, both client and counselor have a clear understanding of their mutual responsibilities and expectations. During individual job-search activities, documentation is of the utmost importance. To avoid redundancy and decrease undue reliance on memories, job seekers and their helpers need to keep adequate records of that which has transpired, in addition to those actions that still need to be accomplished.

Special Issues. Transportation concerns can be critical to success in the job search and it is advised that this issue be addressed by counselors. Topics for discussion typically include (1) private versus public transportation possibilities and consequences, such as the pros and cons of depending on a relative or friend to drive, (2) allowing ample time for bus schedule conflicts, (3) scheduling far enough in advance to ensure a reservation on a special transit service or with a taxi company, (4) how to plan a route to visit more than one prospective employer per day, and (5) appropriate statements to make upon arrival at an appointment independently.

Pursuing job leads poses another dilemma for someone with a visual impairment, particularly finding out about written notices. Whenever possible, an individual's personal network can be tapped for assistance but friends and relatives cannot be relied upon exclusively for long-term help as readers and reporters of job leads. Such intermediaries as counselors, may also need to provide assistance. Occasionally, clients may find company staff who will be willing to read the postings available to them at human resources offices and some companies routinely send out postings to applicants they have on file. Reader services will also need to be negotiated, by the client if at all feasible, as early as possible in a job search. In the ideal situation, companies provide job opening information in recorded format that clients can access by telephone or on-line in electronic format.

Some rehabilitation facilities and agencies are able to provide phone services to their clients. With this type of assistance, clients without home telephones can make calls to prospective employers. Moreover, a prospective employer can call a designated number to contact or leave word for an applicant. Some facilities also provide clerical support to copy résumés, type letters, complete forms and applications, and receive telephone messages. If such services are unavailable, client and counselor may wish to negotiate them through other community-based resources.

Finally, clients who require extensive assistance (e.g., advocacy-level clients) may have job coaches or trainers to help them with job-search skills. In such instances, the coach could possibly produce an application for a client and accompany the job candidate to the interview. The job coach or trainer can then explain to the prospective employer how the client can do the job or can be trained on the job, supported by the job coach. With advocacy-level clients, it is important to realize counselor-placement is more feasible than client-placement.

Job Maintenance Skills

Job maintenance skills are determined by a person's knowledge of how to keep a job. This includes an understanding of employer and coworker expectations, and an awareness of how these expectations change over time. Perhaps the most critical component of job maintenance is the ability to demonstrate good work habits (e.g., attendance and punctuality, interpersonal skills, cooperation, and willingness to follow written and unwritten rules). Inherent in good work habits is self-discipline. Individuals skilled in job maintenance can evaluate personal problems that may distract them from work and resolve those issues outside of the job setting. These individuals also understand such issues as job benefits, payroll deductions, and labor unions, as applicable to the client's work environment.

Job maintenance may also require the ability to adjust to a new work environment or a different location. Furthermore, adjusting to changes in supervision, duties, and schedules, as well as adapting to unofficial work-group norms, understanding rank within a work setting, and getting along as a means of getting ahead may be necessary to retain a job. Economic trends, international and national labor climates, management takeover demands, computer literacy, robotics, and similar issues require workers to develop and apply problem-solving skills to keep their jobs (Wolffe, 1997a).

Job Maintenance Counseling Strategies

Using the group to represent a work structure enables the group facilitator to solicit feedback from members regarding each person's work performance. There are a number of activities that promote this idea. Worker evaluation forms completed anonymously on each group member by other group members and reported as a composite, or reviewed face-to-face as a part of the group process, can provide some fairly realistic and objective feedback. There is also the "stroking" activity, which involves participants turning their backs (one at a time) to the group and remaining silent while group members discuss what they like about their peer. After the group has had its say, the individual rejoins the group and dialogue between group members often ensues.

Placement-Readiness Programs

A variety of placement-readiness programs and curricula have been developed over the years. The following two placement-readiness programs are representative of programs nationwide.

Job Club

The Job Club program, designed by Azrin and his colleagues, is perhaps the best known and most widely used placement-readiness program. It has been one of the most successful and frequently replicated models produced to date (Azrin & Besalel, 1980; Azrin, Flores, & Kaplan, 1975; Azrin & Phillip, 1979; Wolffe, 1986).

Job Club activities are centered around such job-seeking skills training as how to use the telephone to find job leads, how to write a résumé, how to fill out an application, and how to interview successfully. In their preface to the *Job Club Counselor's Manual,* Azrin and Besalel (1980) compare placement-readiness skills training to an interaction between vocational counseling and behavioral psychology.

New clients are allowed to enter the Job Club weekly and overlap with clients already involved in job seeking from previous weeks. Sessions are set up to accommodate this ever-changing group activity. Typically, incoming clients are involved the first week in afternoon sessions, then shift to mornings. Provided with telephone access, participants in the Job Club are requested to make at least ten contacts per day with prospective employers, a strategy based on research indicating that out of multiple contacts come job possibilities, including jobs that are available but not advertised. Job Club clients chart their progress and discuss it with on-site counselors. It is anticipated that clients will remain in the Job Club, working from 8:00 A.M. to 5:00 P.M. on a daily basis, looking for work, until they are employed (Azrin & Besalel, 1980).

Job Readiness Clinic

The Job Readiness Clinic (JRC), which operated at the University of Texas (UT) at Austin from 1975 to 1991 provided direct services to hard-to-employ rehabilitation clients (Daniels, 1978; Hansen, 1975; Wolffe, 1986). Clinic sessions were four weeks in duration and clinic training focused on assisting clients to develop career plans and go to work in jobs related to their career goals. Groups of eight to twelve rehabilitation clients participated from 8:30 A.M. to 3:30 P.M., Monday through Friday. Clients were referred to the Clinic from both the general rehabilitation agency and the rehabilitation agency serving persons who are visually impaired in Texas. Groups were composed of a heterogeneous mix of clients (16 to 65 years old).

During the first two weeks of training, clients participated in half days of instructional activities and half days of group counseling. Instructional activities were presented through facilitated group discussions or on an individual basis. Vocational exploration, job maintenance skills, and generic job-seeking skills were covered during these instructional periods. The outcome objective of the instructional track was for clients to identify their career goals and to begin to map out objectives to reach those goals.

The counseling group counterpart focused on self-awareness activities. During the two weeks devoted to group counseling, clients were introduced to a problem-solving strategy that ultimately led them to goal-setting (Carkhuff, 1969; Carkhuff, 1993; Carkhuff & Berenson, 1977). They explored and clarified their values and recognized that others' values were not necessarily the same but were right for them too. Clients received feedback from group members concerning how they were perceived by others. They learned and practiced good communication skills. The outcome objective of the counseling sessions was for clients to set personality goals and determine what behavior patterns they would attempt to change.

The entire third week was spent on job-seeking skills, with particular emphasis on interviewing and career planning. Clients produced videotaped practice interviews, which were critiqued by the group. Individuals who were totally blind were given extensive feedback from sighted participants regarding their appearance and demeanor in videotaped interviews. The critiques of participants without vision were based on the audio component of the practice interviews. The outcome goal for the third week was for each client to produce a plan for his or her job search.

The fourth week was usually spent seeking employment. Job seekers were asked to check in on a daily basis and report back to the group at the end of the week. In the fourth week, if a client was not committed to a job search or was unprepared to embark on one, that client scheduled individual work time with an instructor to practice interviewing skills or to work on a résumé or an application. Clients who were not seeking jobs set appointments in the community for information interviews or to conduct further research in area libraries, chambers of commerce, state employment programs, or similar community agencies. In addition to these activities, clients who needed further preparation to obtain work in areas of interest investigated various postsecondary training facilities during the fourth week (Wolffe, 1986).

Placement-Readiness Techniques

The following placement-readiness scenarios and circumstances are commonly faced by rehabilitation counselors.

Example 1. Rehabilitation counselors can begin to acquire placement-readiness information during the initial interview.

> A new referral, a 16-year-old man, who is blind and reported to be of average intelligence, is meeting with the rehabilitation counselor. The referral source, his mother, says her son does not plan to attend college. The prospective client is amenable to some (no more than 2 years) of postsecondary vocational training. His strongest area of interest is music and he would like to play in a band after high school graduation. However, he realizes his aspirations to be a band member may not provide him with adequate income to survive.

When a parent serves as the referral source, it is important for the rehabilitation counselor to learn as much as possible from the client, not the parent. Some of the areas the counselor is advised to explore with similar clients include (1) what is the client thinking about in terms of life goals?, (2) how does the client see himself or herself and significant others?, (3) what does the client want to be when he/she grows up?, (4) how would the client like to make his/her dreams a reality?, (5) what does the client like and dislike about the prospect of graduating?, (6) how does the client feel about the future?, and (7) what are the client's interests, abilities, values, and liabilities?

It is recommended that counselors note specific behavior at the initial interview—including punctuality, courtesy, bearing or posture, overall appearance, ability to interact comfortably with strangers, sense of humor, orientation and mobility (O&M) skills, awareness of others in the environment, and initiative. (For a discussion of issues relating to the initial interview, see Chapter 11.)

Example 2. Counselors must also determine the most appropriate placement-readiness program for a client.

> Erin is a woman in her mid-20s with a school-age child. Now that her child is in school, she would like to find a job. Her paid work experi-

> ence consists of babysitting and housekeeping jobs, which she has done off and on since she was 16. Her husband, Pete, supports the family by working as a grocery store manager. Erin married Pete the summer after she graduated from high school. Although she graduated, she did not like school and her grades were primarily on the C and D levels. The only exception was home economics, in which Erin made Bs consistently. Erin's visual problems, because of diabetic retinopathy, have steadily worsened in recent years. Presently, she has no light perception in her left eye and complains of recurring pain in her right eye, because of glaucoma. However, she reports close medical supervision of her case.

In this situation, a program similar to the JRC would be the first choice, because it offers a broader array of services than the Job Club, which focuses specifically on job-seeking activities. Programs similar to the JRC encourage self-exploration, job matching, and job-seeking skills. The JRC program provides adequate structure for a participant who is visually impaired to develop and practice interviewing skills, in addition to receiving feedback from people with similar impairments.

If the client had more clearly defined career goals or wanted to change careers, the Job Club would be a more appropriate choice. The Job Club approach is better utilized by clients with fewer vocational and physical complications than this particular client.

Example 3. The counselor must also help the client determine a preferred level of employment.

> A counselor in a fairly rural area is working with a man in his mid-40s who lost his eyesight in a hunting accident. Self-employed as a welder before his accident five years ago, the man has been a house-husband for the better part of the past five years and his wife has been the primary wage earner in the family.

In a situation in which a client was competitively employed in the past, it is recommended that the counselor start from that perspective. The counselor is advised to help the client identify any transferable skills, determine the feasibility of any occupational ideas, help determine the availability of appropriate devices and tools to perform specific jobs, and provide job-search support as needed. With the client's permission, the counselor is encouraged to consider meeting with both the husband and wife to ascertain the wife's support of her husband's efforts to return to competitive employment. Clarifying this at the outset of the rehabilitation process will benefit both the client and counselor.

Other Placement Options

For a variety of reasons, placement-readiness programs are not recommended for all individuals. When placement-readiness programs are not the program of choice, alternative programs and activities that can enhance future placement may be considered by the rehabilitation counselor.

Sheltered Work

Sheltered work experiences, both short- and long-term, are segregated employment situations in which individuals with severe disabilities are not necessarily expected to meet competitive labor quotas and frequently are paid on a piece-rate basis. Ideally, sheltered work experiences are transitional in nature and enable noncompetitive workers an opportunity to work up to competitive standards. The types of contracts secured in sheltered work settings, however, are seldom apt to produce workers capable of competing in non-sheltered jobs. The most serious concern about sheltered employment is that workers with disabilities in such settings are often isolated from the mainstream of the labor market and may be unable to move on to more integrated employment situations.

Temporary Work Experience

Summer work experiences for youths, including those available in many communities through the Job Training Partnership Act, seasonal work, and on-the-job training experiences are among the most common temporary work experiences. Individuals faced with prospective surgeries or prolonged treatments may elect to work in temporary positions until their medical situations have stabilized. Also, postsecondary students, homemakers, or others requiring flexible schedules frequently will work temporary jobs to supplement their incomes. Such experiences allow an individual to document continued employment on a résumé and generate income without committing to a permanent position. Temporary placements sometimes develop into permanent employment as some employers prefer to hire workers who have demonstrated their abilities on a temporary basis.

Volunteer Experience

Volunteer experience, which by definition is an unpaid work experience, helps develop work skills and habits that may be transferable to paid employment and may also result in professional references for future job applications. The flexibility of volunteer work appeals to many individuals, because many volunteers are able to set their own schedules. Volunteering also allows a prospective employee an opportunity to become familiar with the company and possible positions over an extended period of time.

Chores

Responsibilities or chores at home and school are vitally important to the development of self-esteem (Clayton, 1973; Tuttle, 1996, 1996; Wolffe & Sacks, 1995) and a healthy work personality (Neff, 1971, 1985; Weishan, 1973). At home, caring for pets, gardening, babysitting siblings or other neighborhood children, washing cars, mowing lawns, and other chores all build work skills and good work habits. Chores at school may involve clean-up responsibilities, monitoring of classmates or younger students, or taking messages to other classrooms and administrative offices.

Although placement-readiness activities are not appropriate for all clients, particularly those with severe cognitive impairments, there is convincing evidence that people with severe multiple impairments can often succeed in supported employment (Griffin & Lowry, 1989; Rusch, 1990; Wehman & Moon, 1988) and the Rehabilitation Act Amendments of 1986 (PL 99-506) recognized supported employment as a legitimate vocational rehabilitation outcome.

SUPPORTED EMPLOYMENT

Some individuals with little or no work experience, particularly those with visual impairments and other severe disabilities, can benefit from supported employment programs. Indeed, many of these individuals would be unemployed without such programs, and if employed, they would not be earning above minimum wage or have fringe benefits (Hanley-Maxwell, Bordieri, & Merz, 1996; Liebman, 1990).

The 1986 Rehabilitation Act Amendments contained the following definition of supported employment:

> competitive work in integrated work settings for individuals with the most severe disabilities (I) for whom competitive employment has not traditionally occurred; or (II) for whom competitive employment has been interrupted or intermittent as a result of a severe disability; and who, because of the nature and severity of their disability, need intensive supported employment services. . . . Such term includes transitional employment for persons who are individuals with the most severe disabilities due to mental illness (Rehabilitation Act Amendments, 1986).

Although definitions and program models differ considerably, most supported employment programs for people with severe disabilities have

A job coach initially remains with a worker with a visual impairment on a full-time basis as the worker masters specific job-related skills on site.

the following elements in common (Nisbet & Hagner, 1988):

1. Support services for obtaining and maintaining employment are provided by an agency staff member. The staff member is usually known as a job coach (or job trainer, job advocate, employment coordinator, or placement and training specialist).
2. The job coach typically analyzes the job to be performed, and then implements systematic instruction and data collection procedures at the work site to teach specific job-related skills and behavior.
3. The job coach initially remains on site with the worker on a full-time basis. As the worker masters tasks, the job coach's presence is gradually reduced to a point in which only occasional visits are made. The job coach must remain accessible to the employer in the event of on-the-job problems or the need for further training.
4. In addition to teaching job skills, the job coach is responsible for facilitating the client's integration into the work setting, which may include any or all of the following functions:
    - **a.** establishing rapport with supervisors and coworkers;
    - **b.** encouraging social and helping interactions between clients and coworkers;
    - **c.** demonstrating training procedures to supervisors and coworkers, and involving them in training as appropriate;
    - **d.** explaining the client's background, disabilities, and characteristics to supervisors; and
    - **e.** implementing adaptations that may be needed at the work site, such as tactile labeling, communication devices, or special transportation arrangements.
5. The job coach maintains communication with the client's family or residence staff, as well as other agencies that may be involved in the delivery of services to the client.

There can be little doubt that the growth in supported employment services in the past several years has substantially raised opportunities and expectations for people with severe disabilities. The focus of employment efforts has now shifted away from an exclusive emphasis on sheltered industries or adult activity centers, and many individuals who formerly might have been considered "unemployable" have been successfully placed, with ongoing support, in integrated community-based work settings.

In addition to the philosophical benefits such integration offers to people with severe disabilities and their families, supported employment programs have been shown to yield considerable financial benefits as well. Though the initial costs of supported employment programs are high, largely because of the one-to-one staff/client ratio at the job site for an extended period, workers who are successfully placed usually become taxpaying wage-earners rather than dependent residents of institutions. In the long run, they impose less of a financial burden on the service-delivery system, and on their own families. An extensive cost-benefit analysis completed over an eight-year period by Hill, Wehman, Kregel, Banks, and Metzler (1987) documented that a positive financial consequence of $1,057,000 accrued to the general public as the result of the placement of people with moderate and severe disabilities into supported employment programs in Virginia. Apter (1992), who examined the supported employment program of the Pittsburgh Blind Association (PBA), found that the total cost per year for 26 clients who were placed in supported, competitive employment, ranged from $900 to $6,000 per client. He indicated that if these individuals had been placed in the PBA work activity center, the costs would have been $5,400 per person during the same time period.

The employment of individuals with severe disabilities can also be good business. As an executive of a national restaurant chain that implemented a program to employ more than 2,000 workers with severe disabilities stated,

> I can present a sound business case to any employer who can provide these excellent workers with meaningful jobs. When I talk to other companies, I let our employees' records speak for themselves. Our studies show they stay on the job four to five times longer than our average employees, miss less work, and are highly dependable. And their productivity is outstanding. (Ley, 1989, pp. 1, 5)

Several successful models of supported employment programs for persons with severe disabilities have emerged. As summarized by Griffin and Lowry (1989), and sequenced in what might generally be regarded as most restrictive to least restrictive, these models include:

> *Small business approach.* A community-based enterprise, operated either by a human services agency or a private entrepreneur, employs up to eight workers with severe disabilities, as well as workers without disabilities. Training is extensive and supervision is close. Typically, workers are paid piece-rate wages according to their productivity on manufacturing or assembly tasks.
>
> *Mobile crew approach.* A group of up to eight workers with severe disabilities holds contracts to perform regular work at various locations. With the assistance of a van, this crew and its supportive personnel work at various locations around the community, usually performing such service tasks as lawn maintenance, farm work, and custodial services. Workers without disabilities may or may not be included. The mobile crew approach is well-suited to rural areas.
>
> *Enclave in industry approach.* This model is similar to the mobile crew approach, except that the group (enclave) of employees with disabilities holds a contract to perform specific work with a particular company. The individuals with disabilities are matched to a job or set of jobs within the company's

regular industrial operation. Typically, supervision is closer than with individual work placements, but the degree of integration with coworkers without disabilities is apt to be greater than in either the small business or mobile crew approaches.

Individual placement model. Only one worker with severe disabilities is placed at an employment site and matched with a position. Through training at the job site, ongoing assessment and follow-up contact, the worker is given the support necessary to maintain the job. This model affords maximum integration, flexibility, and autonomy for the worker.

Potential Problems with Supported Employment

In spite of the generally promising picture presented by the increased numbers of supported employment programs, several serious problems remain to be faced. As Nisbet and Hagner (1988) observed, the job coach model relies on the introduction of an outside source of expertise into an already established workplace. This intrusion may result in any number of difficulties, including conflicts with company supervisors, stigmatization of the worker with the disability, resentment by able-bodied coworkers, and increased dependence on the job coach. Studies of job retention in supported work programs are only moderately encouraging, with reports showing between 44 percent and 70 percent of workers with severe and multiple disabilities continuing on the job after one year.

Other problems that rehabilitation professionals have identified with supported employment programs for individuals with visual impairments and other disabilities include increased time to match the clients with visual impairments with appropriate jobs, and to work with job coaches (Liebman, 1990). In industries and regions that are affected by economic recession, unemployment, and "downsizing," opportunities for people with severe disabilities to achieve supported placements tend to diminish accordingly.

The placement of individuals with severe disabilities in vocational settings where workers without disabilities are present also does not guarantee that true integration takes place. In a social interaction study conducted in supported employment programs in food service and printing industry settings, Chadsey-Rusch, Gonzalez, Tines, and Johnson (1989) found only small amounts of interaction between workers with and without disabilities, with only few friendships formed at lunchtime, breaks, or outside of the workplace. They suggested that the training given to workers with disabilities include appropriate social interaction skills, in addition to production and other job-related tasks.

Implications for Rehabilitation Counselors

The increased awareness of the capabilities of people with severe and multiple disabilities, and their gradual integration into workplaces and communities, have brought about new challenges and new opportunities for rehabilitation counselors. Professionals who are able to look beyond traditional disciplinary boundaries are greatly needed if this integration is to continue.

How can rehabilitation counselors best serve their clients with visual impairments and multiple disabilities? Methods by which rehabilitation counselors can provide valuable interventions to clients may include the following:

1. Assisting clients in learning new skills;
2. Helping clients to identify the need for changing some aspects of their behavior or appearance;
3. Providing information on assistive devices (e.g., tactile lettering, talking calculators), and assisting the client in obtaining and learning to use them;

4. Arranging for professional consultations or ongoing services from appropriate specialists (e.g., an occupational therapist to advise on optimal seating position at work, an O&M specialist to help the client in traveling to and around the job site) (Zimmerman, 1992);
5. Assisting supervisors and coworkers in learning the most effective ways to communicate directly with the client, including how to give instruction and feedback on job performance;
6. Clarifying goals, expectations, and responsibilities with the client and with others involved in the client's overall program, such as trainers, supervisors, family members, and group home personnel;
7. Informing clients and families of available options for training and employment, and enabling them to make choices about services;
8. Remaining abreast of new developments in training techniques, employment opportunities, and avenues of financial support;
9. Providing clients with several opportunities to problem-solve and to make independent decisions.

Counselors will face additional challenges in working with individuals with severe cognitive delays who are also deaf and blind. Although only a small number of individuals have dual sensory disabilities and mental retardation, supported employment has been effective with this group. Major challenges, however, include "(a) the development and utilization of meaningful assessment procedures, (b) the utilization of effective instructional and adaptive supports, (c) the development and utilization of effective communication and interaction support services, and (d) the development of responsive and responsible funding arrangements" (Downing, Shafer, Brahm-Levy, & Frantz, 1992, p. 35). The dual sensory impairments, coupled with mental retardation, greatly restrict the ability of these individuals to have meaningful social interactions with others at the job site. Job choice may also be compromised. Noting the difficulties associated with conveying job possibilities to this group of individuals and understanding their preferences, Downing et al. (1992) reported using the enclave as a method of convenience, rather than individual preference.

The best way of overcoming skeptical or negative attitudes toward the employment of people with severe disabilities is to point to demonstrated successes. Well-functioning, established programs can serve as sources of information for the rehabilitation counselor, and can provide encouraging evidence for potential employers. Rehabilitation counselors can be referred to successful programs in their regions through state rehabilitation agencies, university research and training centers, and such professional organizations as the Association for Education and Rehabilitation of the Blind and Visually Impaired (AER) and The Association for Persons with Severe Handicaps (TASH).

Finally, supported employment has been successful for a range of individuals. Systematic follow-up analyses of work performance, such as that of Wehman, Kregel, and Barcus (1985), have shown "no statistically significant differences between the mild/multihandicapped group and the moderate/severe group when it came to assessing successful versus unsuccessful job tenure" (p. 35). It appears that such factors as an individual's adaptive behavior, and the opportunities made available to that individual to function in integrated environments and to receive on-site training and ongoing support from trainers, supervisors, coworkers, and family members, may be more critical than measured intelligence in determining the success of a placement. Yet, as Hill and Morton (1988) observed, vocational expectations for people with severe and multiple disabilities are still low. Vocational training and placement are even considered questionable in many instances, despite repeated demonstrations of this population's ability to master complex tasks and to perform successfully in integrated work settings, with appropriate support. The raising of vocational expectations, both inside and outside of professional circles, remains a central challenge to the rehabilitation counselor.

Myths about Employment and People with Severe Disabilities

There are a number of myths about employment and people with disabilities that serve as barriers to their participation in the work force (Powell, Pancsotar, Steere, Butterworth, Hykowitz, & Rainforth, 1991). This section discusses and dispels some of the most common of these. The first of these is as follows:

Myth 1. People with severe disabilities are usually "not ready" for competitive or community-based employment. They must demonstrate their readiness by progressing through a series of developmental tasks, usually in restricted and segregated settings, before such employment can be considered.

This myth is based on the belief that the placement-readiness skills previously described are required of all individuals; therefore, competitive employment can only be considered after a person has acquired these skills. To demonstrate their competence, individuals with the most severe disabilities typically progressed through a "continuum" of sheltered settings on their way to competitive employment (Beebe & Karan, 1986). Those with the most severe disabilities were placed at the bottom of the continuum, and rarely, if ever, "flowed" through it to a level as high as competitive employment. Much time and effort was fruitlessly spent in teaching tasks that had little or no relevance to actual work settings.

Although it is important for rehabilitation professionals who work with individuals with severe disabilities to be aware of the stages of "normal" development, an overly strict reliance on a developmental approach to educational and vocational training tends to result in the well-meaning but unproductive teaching of prerequisite skills that are not truly essential to later steps (Sobsey & McDonald, 1988). Sequences of behavior appropriate to people without disabilities are not necessarily relevant to individuals with severe disabilities. As Brown (1987) pointed out, "a person . . . [with a disability] may develop in a very different sequence, and the relationship among skills may be different" (p. 43). For example, head control is considered a prerequisite skill for walking, but an adult who lacks head control may nonetheless learn to operate a motorized wheelchair, thus gaining access and independence more rapidly than if lengthy attempts were made to teach head control.

Some individuals with cognitive disabilities may never learn to use mathematical computations to count change when making a purchase. However, using adaptations such as picture cards that identify the exact currency needed, or using "the next highest dollar" strategy can allow people with severe disabilities to participate in age-appropriate activities with greater independence. Efforts to teach prerequisite skills in segregated environments usually did not lead to achievements in integrated settings, as the learning seldom generalized or transferred to other settings (Bray, 1989). Further, the frequent use of developmental ages in describing clients (e.g., "This 22-year-old client is functioning at a 6-year-old level") and the use of materials that were intended for younger people reinforced the image of individuals with severe disabilities as "eternal children." Freagon (1982) offered this critique of the developmental sequencing strategy:

> In the first place, when instructional activities are based on mental, language and social, and gross and fine motor ages, . . . students [with severe disabilities] rarely, if ever, gain more than one or two developmental years over the entire course of their educational experience. Therefore, 18-year-old students are relegated to performing infant or preschool or elementary nonhandicapped student activities. They are never seen as ready to engage in 18-year-old activities. In the second place, little, if any, empirical evidence exists to support the notion that . . . students [with severe disabilities] need

> to learn and grow along the same lines and growth patterns as . . . students [without disabilities] in order to achieve the same goal of education. (p. 10)

Today, educational and vocational programs for individuals with severe disabilities are more oriented toward the client's future goals of independence and employment. Increasingly, rehabilitation professionals are making efforts to survey potential employers in their regions, for the purpose of ascertaining specific skills and behaviors that a client with severe disabilities needs to be accommodated in the work setting. Emphasis can then be placed on helping clients acquire competencies that will truly enable them to succeed in the vocational placement.

Given the influence that functional learning and working experiences may have for the visually impaired client with other severe disabilities, it is highly recommended that the rehabilitation professional consider how "traditional," summative assessment information affects the potential for successful vocational placements. Many vocational evaluations, although named for clients with visual impairments (e.g., Valpar and McCarron–Dial), do not always provide information about a person's adaptive work behaviors or their preferences and skill levels for specific job tasks. A formative assessment allows the job developer to observe a client in a real work environment, performing a variety of tasks over a period of time. This approach allows the evaluator to assess and to make decisions about attention control, and make environmental modifications (e.g., lighting, noise quality, organization of the environment for mobility purposes). It also allows the rehabilitation professional to view a client's level of social competence and behavioral control in natural contexts.

Myth 2. Attitudes of potential employers will be most favorably influenced if the client can demonstrate the ability to perform complex, multistep tasks.

Demonstrations of the ability of people with severe and multiple disabilities to perform complex, multistage vocational tasks have been extremely important contributions to the field of rehabilitation for this population. By employing a carefully structured task-analytic approach, including attention to the physical arrangement of the work station and the verbal or physical cues provided by the job trainer, Gold (1980) and colleagues provided clear evidence that individuals classified as severely and profoundly mentally retarded could successfully perform such tasks as the assembly of 24-piece bicycle brakes and the insertion of complex circuit components into television rectifier units. Other demonstration workshops or sheltered industries revealed that such clients could be taught to complete a 52-piece cam switch assembly, requiring the use of five hand tools; to assemble a 26-piece printhead device, and many similar tasks (Halpern, 1981). These demonstrations did much to document the abilities of a group of people who were previously considered to have little potential for competitive employment. Indeed, the performance of workers with severe disabilities often approached or even surpassed that of workers without disabilities, with respect to such variables as error rate, attention to task, and attendance.

However, the demonstration of work competencies in difficult manual benchwork assembly, although undeniably a pioneering research effort, has not translated into broadly improved employment opportunities for persons with severe and multiple disabilities. The willingness of employers to accept and work with clients with severe disabilities seems to be influenced more by the level of communication and support provided by the training and placement program than by the production abilities of the client. Employers need to know what is expected of them, and where to turn in the event that problems arise.

Demonstrations of competence continue to be important in expanding the work horizons of people with severe disabilities. Recent attitudinal research suggests that perceptions can be strongly influenced by the manner in which this competence is demonstrated—which is important for rehabilitation counselors. Bates, Morrow,

Pancsofar, and Sedlak (1984) presented a slide/tape show of a young woman who was mentally retarded to two groups of adults who did not have disabilities. Both groups heard the same audiotape, but the slides differed. One group saw the young woman engaging in "nonfunctional isolated" activities, while the other group viewed her engaging in "functional integrated" activities. For example, in depicting vocational (functional) abilities, one group saw the woman sorting silverware and stacking racks of glasses at a local restaurant, while the other group watched her sorting colored blocks and stacking rings on a post, nonfunctional activities associated with young children. A follow-up questionnaire found that those who observed the functional, integrated presentation had significantly higher estimates of the woman's intelligence, employment potential, and earning ability than did those who saw the nonfunctional, isolated depiction. People with disabilities who are shown to be performing realistic, age-appropriate tasks in typical community settings, the investigators concluded, could lead to "a more enhancing and optimistic perspective" of the competencies of individuals with severe disabilities (p. 77).

Myth 3. Clients with severe disabilities can be placed in a limited range of job settings, most often in repetitive and closely supervised assembly tasks.

Repetitive benchwork usually offers little opportunity for occupational advancement or for interaction with able-bodied coworkers. Training clients to perform up to a criterion level on assembly tasks may have the unintended side effects of heightening their dependency and restricting their opportunities for choice and flexibility in the job market (Szymanski & Parker, 1989). Recently, there has been greater emphasis on providing on-the-job training and assistance to workers with severe and multiple disabilities in a greatly expanded variety of work sites (see Sidebar 12.2).

Usually, such job sites do not include large numbers of employees with disabilities. In addition to encouraging integration and independence, this tends to make it easier for employers and rehabilitation professionals to identify and attend to individual workers' problems when they arise.

Part-time or flexible work schedules have also proven effective for some workers with multiple disabilities. As Fredericks (1988) noted, part-time employment can establish a successful work history, help to meet specific or seasonal needs in the community, and be less difficult to leave if the job does not work out. Part-time or flexible schedules can enable workers to accommodate some of their own specialized needs, such as medical appointments, adapted transportation, and physical therapy (Hanley-Maxwell, Rusch, & Rappaport, 1989). In addition to these benefits, satisfactory performance in a part-time job may also lead to full-time employment. Desirable as it may be in many cases, however, part-time work rarely offers the fringe benefits and job security associated with regular full-time employment.

Myth 4. When a vocational placement is unsuccessful, it is usually because the client was unable to perform the tasks required by the job.

A substantial body of research now exists on factors related to the work performance and job termination of individuals with severe and multiple disabilities. Such studies are surprisingly consistent in identifying the personal, social, and behavioral problems, rather than the inability to do job tasks, as the primary reasons for adults with severe disabilities losing their jobs (Halpern, 1981; Hanley-Maxwell, Rusch, & Rappaport, 1989). Reasons frequently cited for termination include maladaptive behavior at work (e.g., screaming, unwanted touching of coworkers, masturbation), transportation problems, inappropriate use of free time, and lack of social awareness. Inability to perform job tasks was less frequently cited, although slow production rates, poor attendance, tardiness, and specific skill deficits were occasionally mentioned as reasons (Wehman, Hill, Wood, & Parent, 1987).

There are no easy answers to the problems that result in job termination for workers with severe and multiple disabilities. It is possible that

SIDEBAR 12.2

What Types of Jobs Can People Who Are Deaf-Blind Do?

CUSTODIAN

LIBRARIAN

FACTORY CREW PERSON

BAKER'S ASSISTANT

DRAFTPERSON

LAUNDRY WORKER

CASHIER

HOUSEKEEPER

SMALL PARTS ASSEMBLER

OFFICE WORKER

RESTAURANT ATTENDANT

BUSPERSON

PAYMENT PROCESSOR

ANY OTHER JOBS IDENTIFIED BY CREATIVE JOB DEVELOPERS!

Source: Reprinted from *Transition Services for Youths Who Are Deaf-Blind: A "Best Practice" Guide for Educators,* January 1995, p. 88, with permission from the Helen Keller National Center—Technical Assistance Center.

conscientious rehabilitation counselors will have the best outcomes if they direct their efforts to both the client and the employer. For example, many clients with behavioral excesses and visual impairments can learn self-monitoring and management techniques to control inappropriate behavior (see, for example, Gast & Wolery, 1987; Griffiths, Quinsey, & Hingsburger, 1989; Park & Gaylord-Ross, 1989; Repp & Singh, 1990). Concurrently, networks in which the employer, coworkers, family members, and supportive agencies all assume specific responsibilities can often solve problems more effectively than if the problem were viewed simply as the fault of the worker with a disability (Hanley-Maxwell, Rusch, & Rappaport, 1989).

Perhaps the most powerful influence on successful employment of people with severe disabilities and visual impairments is family and caregiver support. Often family members are reluctant to allow their children to move from a safe, sheltered environment to a competitive work site where they may be vulnerable to the sophistication and reality of the work world. The astute rehabilitation professional must be sensitive to the fears and misconceptions that family members may hold about their child's potential and ultimate independence. It is important that the rehabilitation counselor work with family members to help them view their children as adults rather than perpetual children.

Enhancing Generalization of Job Success

People with severe and multiple disabilities frequently need to pay special attention to the generalization of their learning. It cannot be assumed that clients who have demonstrated certain skills or behaviors in a training setting will necessarily be able to perform in the same manner at another place and time, in the presence of different people, or over a prolonged period of time. Misunderstandings between job trainers and employers have sometimes arisen when clients with severe disabilities failed to demonstrate appropriate skills and behavior on the job, despite having "learned" them previously.

A large amount of research has focused on methods to increase the ability of people with severe disabilities to generalize and maintain their learning. At the same time, there are concerns for the efficiency and economy of training. In other words, it is useful to know how much and what kind of training is needed for generalizations to occur, without subjecting the client and job trainer to an extreme amount of training, or the wrong kind of training. Briefly, some pertinent recent findings on generalization can be summarized as follows:

- Generalization is enhanced by the presentation of multiple examples, a variety of materials, and different instructors during training sessions;
- Both new and familiar examples of tasks, cues, and materials should be incorporated into training sessions;
- It is helpful to define the "instructional universe" at the outset of training; that is, to precisely delineate the circumstances under which the targeted skill will need to be performed. This "general case" approach appears more effective than presenting multiple tasks in an unsystematic fashion (Horner, Dunlap, & Koegel, 1988; Steere, Pancsofar, Powell, & Butterworth, 1989);
- Ideally, training can be given early and often in settings where the skills will actually be used, rather than in artificial training environments. The community is the best place to teach bus travel, street crossing, shopping, and other skills that lead to independence. Even a classroom made up to resemble a workplace cannot duplicate the environment of a real job site. Sometimes, however, training in actual community or vocational settings is impractical because of safety, staffing, or transportation factors. Carefully designed simulations can be useful in these cases, particularly when they are balanced with community-based training sessions, as suggested in the helpful guidelines provided by Horner, McDonnell, and Bellamy (1986);
- Often, people with severe disabilities are taught largely or completely using a one-to-one approach. However, many children, youth, and adults with severe disabilities have been shown to benefit from instruction in small groups (Orelove, 1982; Polloway, Cronin, & Patton, 1986). When training is given in small groups (generally not more than four learners), rather than individually, persons with severe disabilities are encouraged to communicate, take turns, and pay attention to a wider variety of instructional cues and corrections. It appears that with this technique, generalization of learning may also be facilitated. Another benefit is that job trainers can also use their time more effectively in small group situations. Sidebar 12.3 presents other common problems and the methods used to resolve them.

A CONTINUUM OF OPTIONS

When considering vocational options, it is recommended that rehabilitation counselors assist clients to look at all the options, not excluding industries for individuals who are blind. In the spirit of supported employment, sheltered industries have frequently been maligned and negative research findings on sheltered industries (e.g., low wages, limited progression from workshops to competitive employment) has been generalized to all sheltered employment settings (Miller, 1993). Miller, however, provided some statistics from the National Industries for the Blind (NIB) for fiscal year 1992 that run counter to this generalization. For example, the average wage for workers was $4.97/hour with fringe benefits at 40 percent of payroll, 1,629 blind individuals were competitively placed, 374 individuals who were blind were promoted, and 1,700 line items (products and services) were produced under the Javits–Wagner–O'Day Act. Additional benefits of sheltered industries for individuals with visual impairments include the provision of (1) summer employment for teenagers, which can enhance their self-esteem and self-confidence and give them work experience, (2) part-time work for older individuals, which enables them to meet their socialization needs, (3) work and income during the transitional periods from or between

SIDEBAR 12.3

Examples of Positive Programming

Problem: A 19-year-old woman with moderate to severe mental retardation was unable to respond to verbal or pictorial instructions, because she also had a severe hearing impairment and was totally blind. An alternative prompting system had to be devised in order for her to function effectively on a job site in the community.

Approach: (Berg & Wacker, 1989): A tactile prompting system was developed to facilitate the client's attainment of envelope-stuffing and bagging tasks. This involved the use of a wooden tray, divided into two rows of six compartments each. The required materials were placed into different compartments, and raised tactile numbers or letters were affixed to indicate the order in which items should be bagged or stuffed. Later, a tactile cuebook was used, so the client could guide her own performance after the skill had been learned. The tactile cues were shown to be effective in teaching and maintaining work skills. The client was able to obtain a paying job in a supported work program in the community, and used tactile cues to guide her in performing such tasks as collating, photocopying, using vending machines, and operating home appliances.

Problem: A 17-year-old woman who was blind and also classified as profoundly mentally retarded frequently exhibited disruptive behavior. For example, the client seldom would remain seated for more than five minutes at a time. This limited her ability to attend to tasks, or to participate in functional activities.

Approach: (Hill, Brantner, & Spreat, 1989): Increasing in-seat behavior was determined to be an appropriate goal, and, consequently, music was investigated as a reinforcement. This was seen as well-suited to the client and was preferable to giving edible "rewards." With the use of a pressure-sensitive switch, taped music was played only if the client remained in her seat. The client's ability to remain in-seat increased markedly, to the point that she was able to remain seated for up to 20 minutes at a time and she was able to begin to participate in activities. Rock and jazz music were found to be more effective than classical music for this client. The special musical chair was viewed as a temporary device only, because as the investigators noted, background music is often found in work environments.

Problem: A 28-year-old woman with moderate to severe disabilities was employed as a helper in the kitchen of a large cafeteria-style restaurant. Her responsibilities included rolling silverware sets (e.g., a fork, a knife, and a spoon) into napkins. Through previous training the client was able to complete this task accurately, but when placed on the job site, it became apparent that her rate of producing silverware rolls was far too slow for continued employment.

Approach: (White & Kennedy, 1981): A point system proved effective in increasing this client's performance rate. The job trainer observed the client's silverware rolling rate during two five-minute periods daily. For producing a specified number of rolls per minute, the client received points, which were later exchanged for special privileges. As the client met each criterion, the required number of silverware rolls was successively increased. Over a period of three months, this relatively simple strategy resulted in a 100 percent increase in her rate of silverware rolling. The client met industrial norms for production rate and on-task behavior, and the satisfactory performance level was maintained after the job trainer gradually withdrew the point system and phased out her own presence at the job site.

An employee with a visual impairment operates a fastener machine in a paper products department. Individuals who are blind or visually impaired work in a wide variety of occupations and professions.

competitive employment, and (4) higher salaries than some individuals could make in traditional competitive employment.

In a survey of direct labor workers who were legally blind and employed by NIB-affiliated industries for the blind, Moore, Crudden, and Giesen (1994) interviewed 502 employees regarding their job satisfaction levels. In response to the question, "How satisfied are you working here?," 61 percent indicated that they were either "satisfied" (40 percent) or "very satisfied" (21 percent).

Rehabilitation counselors working with individuals who are visually impaired, can assist clients in evaluating their options and by recognizing that the final choice should be the client's. As Miller (1993) noted:

> Competitive employment, homemaking, vending stands, self-employment are all appropriate vocational placements. Although employment opportunities in the competitive sector are increasing for people with disabilities, the job openings are not always available, especially to individuals with unique needs. In the meantime, we should make full use of the variety of available options. Options become limited when we judge one work setting superior to another. . . . if we fail to present the option, we deny choice. (pp. 30–31)

SUMMARY

This chapter described the five major content areas that define placement readiness: self-awareness, vocational selection, and the skills associated with job-seeking, job-searching, and job maintenance. Both group and individual counseling strategies were described for each of the content areas and two examples of placement-readiness programs (i.e., Job Club and JRC) were provided. A range of placement options, from competitive employment to volunteer positions, was also detailed.

Counselors can facilitate placement readiness for clients by encouraging self-evaluation, analyzing the labor market, and helping clients compare their personal attributes with opportunities by using a discrepancy analysis process. discrepancy analysis allows the client and rehabilitation professional to examine the client's skills in contrast with those of persons without disabilities. With most clients, counselors will want to review their job-seeking strategies and provide instruction when necessary. Counselors can best influence clients' placement readiness by role modeling appropriate work habits, sharing labor market information, and practicing job-seeking skills.

When people with severe disabilities are able to attend school, work, live, and make friends in their own communities, everyone benefits. Not all clients can benefit from placement-readiness programs. However, supported employment is an appropriate, viable option, particularly for clients with multiple, severe disabilities. To use supported employment, counselors are advised to be aware of the different types of supported employment (i.e., individual, enclave, mobile crew, and small business), as well as the myths that surround the employment of individuals with severe disabilities. Counselors need to assist clients in exploring all of the employment options that are available to them and recognize the importance of client choice. Placement-readiness programs train people in job-seeking and job-keeping skills, to enable them to place themselves. Supported employment programs train clients on the job following placement by the counselor.

LEARNING ACTIVITIES

1. Attend a placement-readiness class that is offered at a local agency or with an employment service. Report on the class in terms of the following:
    - **a.** Type of program (Job Club, JRC);
    - **b.** Focus of program (self-awareness, vocational selection, job-seeking skills, job-search skills, and job maintenance skills);
    - **c.** Placement statistics (success rate) associated with the program; and
    - **d.** Accommodations for individuals with visual impairments.
2. Interview a rehabilitation counselor who works with individuals with visual impairments. Does the counselor use group or individual approaches? What community resources does the counselor use to assist with placement readiness? What does the counselor view as the greatest challenge in placement readiness?
3. To evaluate differences in clients' social behavior and work performance, visit a sheltered industry for individuals who are visually impaired and an integrated work site. Observe and report on a client in each setting in terms of the following criteria:
    - **a.** Interaction with colleagues, both with and without disabilities, during work and during break time;
    - **b.** Enjoyment of work tasks (did the individuals appear to be enjoying their jobs?;
    - **c.** Task behavior and work performance;
    - **d.** Need for supervision; and
    - **e.** Job modifications related to the visual impairment or other disabilities.

CHAPTER 13

Employer Relations: Job Development, Job Retention, and Job Accommodation

Don Harkins and Jeffrey J. Moyer

Building and maintaining relationships with employers requires the same skills and commitments as building effective relationships with clients. Understanding the other party's views, educating the other party, and being a reliable "partner" are all paramount to establishing and sustaining effective relationships with both employers and clients. Although many rehabilitation professionals believe that employers are uniformly resistant to hiring individuals with visual impairments (Kirchner, Harkins, Esposito, Isatanbuli, & Chandu, 1991), this is not true, particularly when employers understand the potential benefits associated with making that hiring decision. Most employers do, however, need information and assistance to become comfortable with the proposition that they should hire individuals with disabilities (Harris & Associates, 1987; Kirchner et al., 1991) and need assistance in identifying job accommodations that may be required.

Specific objectives of this chapter include (1) understanding job development and the significance of employer relations and employer needs in the delivery of rehabilitation services, (2) learning techniques and skills to address employer misinformation and negative attitudes to facilitate the establishment of effective working relationships with employers, (3) identifying job retention issues related to individuals who are visually impaired, and (4) understanding the types and costs of job modifications and accommodations that can benefit both employers and employees with visual impairments.

JOB DEVELOPMENT

Job development is the process of identifying businesses and industries that have existing jobs or future job openings and then educating those employers about individuals with visual impairments, as well as services and programs (e.g., work opportunities tax credits) that may benefit employers. The key to successful job development is employer relations, because "employers are the creators of and gatekeepers for jobs" (Millington, Asner, Linkowski, & Der-Stepanian, 1996, p. 277). Consider the following actual conversation:

> The Director of Constituency Relations for a major regional telephone company was complaining to an "employment specialist" about the failure of rehabilitation professionals to use more effective methods when attempting to place individuals with disabilities with his company. The director's primary complaint was that rehabilitation professionals do not understand

> what is important to his company (D. Lauer, personal communication, 1990). He indicated that most of the time when someone within the company was approached by representatives of public or private rehabilitation agencies, the professionals talked as if their clients should be hired because they had disabilities. This phone company representative was quick to point out that his company annually provided millions of dollars to support various community needs and agencies, including rehabilitation agencies. The director emphasized that the company's interest in charity extended to supporting community needs and organizations by making contributions, not in giving jobs to people just because they had disabilities. The director also pointed out that his company was very receptive to hiring qualified individuals who happened to have disabilities, and he offered proof—the phone company representative was a person who was blind.

This narration reflects a basic problem in the delivery of effective placement services—the failure to recognize the needs and interests of one key "client" as part of the process. It is sometimes difficult to appreciate that there are really three distinct clients or audiences that have to be considered in planning and delivering effective rehabilitation services. The most obvious client is the person with a visual impairment who is seeking rehabilitation services. The other clients are the rehabilitation professional's employer and the businesses in the community with job training or placement opportunities for rehabilitation clients. Understanding the "employer-client" is paramount to being successful in placing persons into employment and it is highly advised that this be a major focus of the rehabilitation professional's work.

The employer-client may be similar to the phone company, a large regional or national corporation with a personnel department and formalized policies, or the employer-client may be Mrs. Jones at the corner pharmacy. The needs and interests of employers vary widely depending on the product(s) or service(s) provided, as well as the location, size, and structure of the business. To work effectively with employers requires an appreciation for the complexity and diversity that exists across different businesses, an ability to match the abilities of persons with visual impairments to the needs of the employer, and a recognition that the bottom line for employers is not hiring a person with a disability, but hiring a person who can do the job. Without an appreciation for these three issues and an ability to translate that understanding into a method of working with employers that focuses on meeting the employer's needs and interests, the process of placing clients into competitive employment may seem elusive and frustrating.

Working with employers is often viewed as requiring different skills and abilities from those needed to work with clients (Miller & Rossi, 1988). Working effectively with clients with visual impairments and employers, however, requires essentially the same basic set of skills, namely, of asking the right questions, listening carefully, being observant, identifying options, keeping commitments, and addressing problems as they arise (Dennis, 1986). Whether the client is a person with a visual impairment or an employer, the process of service provision is driven by the following two broad principles:

> Principle 1: Services should be focused on addressing the needs of the individual.
>
> Principle 2: Services should be focused on achieving specific, shared goals.

To the degree that both principles are followed, and the skills of rehabilitation professionals are appropriately applied, then effective relationships are built and maintained.

Information and Educational Needs of Employers and Unions

In general, employers and unions need information regarding (1) blindness and people who are blind, (2) employer responsibilities when considering individuals who are blind or visually impaired for employment, and (3) information regarding specific applicant(s) relating to the specific job(s) being sought by the applicant(s). Information and education needs are also influenced by such characteristics of businesses as belief systems and company philosophy, size of the company, prior contact, and recruitment and retention policies. These characteristics are examined in the next few sections.

Belief Systems

The following statements represent stereotypes and misinformation held by 63 percent of a representative group of employers (Godley, 1981):

- Employers feel uncomfortable firing individuals who are blind,
- Individuals who are blind have trouble traveling to work,
- People who are blind have trouble filling out forms,
- Individuals who are blind have trouble getting around,
- People who are blind cannot operate high-speed machinery,
- Coworkers have difficulty interacting with individuals who are blind,
- Company supervisors have trouble training individuals who are blind,
- Hiring people who are blind increases worker compensation rates, and
- It is troublesome to deal with government agencies in hiring individuals who are blind.

Therefore, it is important for rehabilitation professionals to determine the degree to which a potential employer subscribes to these beliefs and to also have information to refute such beliefs (see Sidebar 13.1). Communicating the experiences of other employers can help dispel stereotypes held by potential employers. For example, when individuals with or without disabilities were compared on a variety of criteria (Harris & Associates, 1987), Equal Employment Opportunity (EEO) officers and department heads consistently rated applicants with disabilities very positively with regard to formal education, job skills, ability to sell themselves, leadership potential, and communication skills. Furthermore, when employers were asked to compare the performance of workers with or without disabilities, a large majority of the managers gave good or excellent ratings on the overall job performance of workers with disabilities. The managers stated that compared to nondisabled workers, workers with disabilities (1) were as reliable and punctual, if not more so, (2) worked as hard or harder, (3) produced as well or better, and (4) demonstrated average or better-than-average leadership abilities. These findings were similar to those of DuPont, which has conducted extensive surveys of its own labor force in 1958, 1973, 1981, and 1990.

Prior Contact

The more experiences employers have had with individuals who are blind (i.e., relatives, neighbors, coworkers, supervisors, employees, or friends), the more apt they are to hold positive beliefs about employing workers with visual impairments (Godley, 1981).

Recruitment and Retention Policies

It is more probable that companies with recruitment policies will hire individuals with disabilities than companies lacking recruitment policies (Harris & Associates, 1987). Generally, companies are more apt to have retention policies concerning workers who acquire disabilities than they are to have recruitment policies or programs to hire individuals with disabilities (Kirchner et al., 1991). This suggests that intervention prior to job termination tends to result in a successful outcome more so than if services are delayed until after the person has been terminated.

Size

Large companies are more inclined to have a policy or program for hiring individuals with disabil-

SIDEBAR 13.1

Barriers Perceived by Employers

- Lack of qualified applicants
- Lack of established policies or programs for the hiring of individuals with disabilities
- Job discrimination as a persistent problem
- Belief that they are already doing enough to employ individuals with disabilities
- Cost of accommodations

ities than smaller companies (Harris & Associates, 1987; Kirchner et al., 1991). Because of the positive effect that company policies have on hiring persons with disabilities (Harris & Associates, 1987), the absence of such policies, particularly in the smaller companies, suggests that individuals who are visually impaired may not as easily capitalize on future job growth and development in the work force, most of which is projected to occur in smaller companies (Toffler, 1990).

Informational Needs of Prospective Employers

If rehabilitation professionals are to address the information needs of employers, they must first identify and communicate with the employers. However, Kirchner et al. (1991) found that only 12 percent of a randomly selected group of employers indicated that they had been contacted by individuals from the state's vocational rehabilitation agency.

After the initial contact has been made, counselors are encouraged to consider the following issues when providing job development and job placement services:

1. Most companies have the personnel department screen applicants, but the final hiring decisions are made by department supervisors;
2. Employers need specific information regarding applicants with visual impairments, including the following:
    - How the applicant works with tools and equipment typically used on the job,
    - How the applicant records and retains information,
    - How the applicant accesses printed information, and
    - How the applicant accesses computer information.
3. Employers need information regarding how to handle situations such as:
    - Providing for an applicant with a guide dog,
    - Handling insurance coverage, and
    - Terminating an individual if job performance is not satisfactory.
4. Employers need such specific assistance from the vocational rehabilitation agency as follows:
    - Providing ongoing consultation if the job requirements change, and
    - Providing instruction to the person with a visual impairment on how to travel within the workplace.
5. Other types of assistance employers need include such information as follows:
    - Providing information on federal or state tax credits for employers that hire individuals with disabilities, and

- Paying companies for "on-the-job" training of newly hired workers with disabilities. (Kirchner et al., 1991)

Costs associated with making necessary accommodations are usually a concern to employers who are considering hiring an individual with a disability. Counselors can provide information to address and counter these concerns. For example, Harris and Associates (1987) found that the average cost of employing a person with a disability was similar to that for employing an individual who did not have a disability. Some types of accommodations that have been made, as reported by EEO officers, include:

- Removal of architectural barriers (90 percent),
- Purchase of special equipment (50 percent),
- Restructuring job duties or work hours (50 percent), and
- Providing readers or interpreters (23 percent).

This same group of EEO officers (72 percent) rated the cost as either not too expensive or not expensive at all and only 1 percent of the EEO officers evaluated the cost of accommodations made as very expensive. Thus, while making accommodations is a concern for some employers, those employers who have actual experience report very positively in terms of the costs of accommodations.

When discussing accommodations, counselors can also indicate to employers that accommodations that may benefit a worker with a disability may also benefit the productivity of other workers—for example, the shift to more flexible work hours. Although more flexible work hours are an accommodation for many workers with disabilities, flexible work hours may also increase satisfaction and productivity of other workers. Also, after a job has been broken down into its various elements and the essential components have been fully analyzed, it is usually the case that other workers who do not have disabilities and who are performing that same job also benefit from the time- and labor-saving steps that have been identified through a job or task analysis (Collignon, 1986).

To accommodate employees with disabilities, this employer uses an infrared device to read employees' badges during clocking in and out. The device also uses a vibrating face of a clock to acknowledge the employees' clocking in and out times for people who are deaf.

Information and Education Regarding Blindness and Visual Impairments

General information regarding blindness and visual impairments in the labor force can be provided in several ways, depending on the situation. If the goal is to educate several employers in a seminar, an employer association meeting, or any other group setting, the use of videotapes, brochures, and a short presentation is particularly effective. Some state vocational rehabilitation agencies have developed effective brochures or videotaped materials for these purposes. Materials can also be obtained from such sources as the President's Committee on Employment of People with Disabilities, the American Foundation for the Blind (AFB), the National Federation of the Blind (NFB), and the American Council of the Blind (ACB). Presentations to employer groups are, of necessity, rather broad in focus, but are usually most effective if the following issues are addressed:

- Variations in extent of visual impairments and functional implications associated with various types of impairments (central versus field),
- Range of jobs in which individuals who are blind or visually impaired are successfully employed,
- Employers' responsibilities under the Americans with Disabilities Act (ADA),
- Experiences of some employers in making accommodations, and
- Sources of consultation and support available to employers as they recruit, evaluate, and hire individuals who are visually impaired.

Group presentations are excellent vehicles to raise awareness and to encourage employers to consider the possibility of hiring people who are blind, but such presentations cannot really address the specific concerns that any given employer may have. Therefore, using group presentations as a way to establish "contact" is a particularly effective strategy, when followed by individual meetings with specific employers.

Individual meetings provide an opportunity for the counselor to try to elicit any questions that the employer may have, respond in a factual and candid manner, and thank the employer for raising the concern(s). Even if the employer does not specifically raise the following issues, it is important to touch on them (however briefly) during discussions:

- Insurance coverage and rates,
- Termination of workers with visual impairments,
- Performance expectations,
- Travel within the workplace, including the issue of dog guides,
- Available tax credits,
- Use of on-the-job training options,
- Literacy, vis-à-vis the recording, retaining and retrieving of job-related information by people with visual impairments, and
- Coworkers' reactions.

The discussion also serves to reiterate several positive beliefs that the overwhelming majority of employers seem to hold regarding applicants with disabilities, including the beliefs that they have a better-than-average education, exhibit better-than-average dependability, have a better-than-average ability to sell themselves, and possess better than average communication skills. While emphasizing these positive beliefs, even at the level of general information, it is important to begin to humanize visual impairment by stressing the uniqueness of individual workers with visual impairments. Providing brief vignettes about employed persons who are blind can be very effective in terms of reinforcing the effectiveness of such employees within that company. Attmore's (1990) book entitled *Career Perspectives: Interviews with Blind and Visually Impaired Professionals* is an example of a resource that can be helpful in this effort. This book, which describes the actual experiences of 20 individuals who are blind or visually impaired, helps employers begin to realize the uniqueness of individuals who are blind, as well as the diversity of jobs they hold.

Information and Education Regarding Employer Responsibilities

Providing education regarding employer responsibilities that are related to the consideration of applicants who are blind or visually impaired essentially means addressing the legal obligations that extend to some employers when evaluating individuals for employment. The Rehabilitation Act of 1973, as amended, was the first federal legislation to prohibit discrimination against qualified individuals with disabilities, but the Rehabilitation Act was limited in its application to employers receiving federal funds and having 50 or more employees. The ADA of 1990 (Public Law 101–336) greatly extended the protection against employment discrimination. Under the ADA, discrimination against individuals with disabilities is prohibited by employers with 15 or more employees. Specifically, the ADA provides that "no covered entity (employer) shall discriminate against a qualified individual with a disability because of the disability of such individual in regard to job application procedures, the hiring, advancement or discharge of employees, employee compensation, job training and other terms, conditions and privileges of employment" (Section 102.a). The ADA also requires that employers must make "reasonable accommodations" for employees with disabilities, unless making such accommodations would create an "undue hardship" for the covered entity. Furthermore, the ADA prohibits medical examinations prior to offers of employment. Medical examinations after an offer of employment has been made are allowable, but only if all entering employees are subjected to such examinations and if the information is treated as confidential except as supervisors and managers may need to be informed to devise necessary accommodations regarding work duties. Thus, the ADA provides for broad protection against employment discrimination for qualified individuals with disabilities and seeks to ensure reasonable treatment for such individuals.

Although the ADA is broadly framed to prohibit employment discrimination even among small employers, there are some specific limitations built into the Act. Those limitations permit a company to overlook an otherwise qualified applicant with a disability or to apply other employment-related sanctions (1) if the individual poses "a direct threat to the health and safety of other individuals in the workplace" (Section 103.b), (2) if the employer is a religious organization and requires its employee to "conform to the religious tenets of such organization," and (3) when the employer is basing an employment decision(s) on the illegal use of drugs by the worker with a disability. The limitations do not substantially lessen the impact of the ADA, but may affect its application in certain situations.

The ADA has frequently been referred to as the "Civil Rights Act for People with Disabilities," and the ADA does provide for specific remedies in the event that an individual with a disability is discriminated against under the terms of the Act. Certainly, it is highly advised that rehabilitation professionals and consumers of rehabilitation services be fully informed regarding the ADA, including the available legal remedies (Bruyere, 1994; Stude, 1994). There may even be blatant circumstances that warrant encouraging legal action against an employer based on the ADA. As a general rule, however, if it is necessary for the rehabilitation professional or the consumer to threaten or pursue legal action based on the ADA, then the possibility of building and maintaining an effective relationship with that employer has been negated. It is probable that legal action may be required in some situations; however, it is a much better idea to use the ADA as a "carrot," rather than as a "stick" when working with employers. To the extent that consultations to assist employers in addressing the provisions of the ADA can be offered as an incentive, then the possibility of building and maintaining productive relationships is significantly enhanced.

The ADA presents several challenges for the average employer. Employers covered under the ADA have a broad responsibility for the fair and equal treatment of qualified individuals with disabilities with regard to job application procedures, hiring, advancement, discharge, compensation, job training, and "other terms, conditions and privileges of employment" (Section 102.a). Even an employer who has had many years of experience in addressing employment-related issues with people with disabilities, because the company qualified as a covered entity under the terms of the Rehabilitation Act of 1973, may have difficulty in determining how to address some of the ADA issues. Therefore, smaller employers, newly covered under the ADA, may need a significant amount of assistance. For example, these employers may need assistance in determining who is and is not qualified, what is and is not reasonable, and in appropriately administering such employment issues as hiring, advancement, discharge, and other practices that might pertain to people with disabilities (see Sidebar 13.2). When working with companies in regard to these issues, the rehabilitation professional is creating a "win-win-win situation" in that the employer appreciates the assistance in defining responsibilities and responses, it enhances the company's receptiveness to provide placement opportunities to individuals with visual impairments, and it enhances the company's sensitivity to the needs of its present and future employees.

Assuming the role of employer consultant is an extremely positive position for the rehabilitation professional. That role however, can also create problems in certain situations. Two potential problems associated with attempting to develop a consulting relationship with employers are as follows:

1. Role confusion. This can occur if the employer and counselor seek to address employer needs to the detriment of adequately attending to the client's needs. There are those situations wherein the rehabilitation professional clearly must be a client advocate, and, in those situations, the employer's view of the rehabilitation professional as "the company's consultant" can complicate resolving any problems; and
2. Legal entanglements. This can happen if an employer has based company policy and procedures on the advice of a rehabilitation professional and action is taken against the company based on ADA violations. There is a possibility that in situations such as this, rehabilitation professionals could be held legally accountable for damages accruing from their advice, if the company loses the case and is ordered to pay compensation to the affected individual.

To minimize the possibility that either problem might develop, it is important for the rehabilitation professional to clearly define his or her role and goals (Pape & Tarvydas, 1993). If both "audiences" understand that the counselor is a skilled professional striving to advocate for the appropriate employment of clients with visual impairments by matching client skills and interests to available openings, and by working with employers to create a favorable employment climate within the company and community, then it is highly improbable that either audience will misinterpret the counselor's statements or actions.

Information and Education Regarding Specific Applicants and Specific Jobs

As indicated at the outset of this chapter, a critical part of building and maintaining effective relationships with employers is helping employers address their needs. One primary requirement shared by all employers is finding productive individuals to fill available job vacancies. The escalating costs associated with training new employees is increasing the pressure on companies to find the right person and the rehabilitation system is in a unique position to help employers address this need, if the client's skills and interests have been accurately evaluated, and if the employer's job has been correctly analyzed.

The Counselor as an Adviser to Employers

SIDEBAR 13.2

As a result of the Americans with Disabilities Act requirements, many employers benefit from the advice of rehabilitation counselors. Because many employers may need assistance in resolving employment concerns, the counselor can serve as a consultant to employers, making a positive contribution in the following areas:

- Developing policies to promote the hiring and retention of individuals with disabilities,
- Examining pre-employment testing procedures to ensure fairness in administration and interpretation,
- Training personnel interviewers to ensure that "qualified" individuals are identified,
- Reviewing accessibility issues as they pertain to architectural and informational "barriers,"
- Developing policies to guide "reasonable accommodation" decisions,
- Training unit managers to ensure that appropriate supervision is provided,
- Examining policies regarding annual appraisals and promotions to ensure that "successful" employees with disabilities are being fully and fairly considered,
- Working with company staff charged with the provision of employee education and training to ensure equal access to both training and training materials, and
- Training human resources department staff and unit managers to use correct procedures when remedying problems or terminating employees with disabilities.

Source: Based on K. Flippo and H. Green, "Resources for Americans with Disabilities Act Implementation: Business Accommodation Response Teams." *Journal of Vocational Rehabilitation, 4*(3), 1994, pp. 183–191.

When the evaluation of client skills and interests and the job analysis have been correctly performed, it is frequently possible to assist the employer by matching a qualified and interested person to the job. This careful matching can significantly lessen the possibility that the employer will hire someone who will not stay on or succeed in that job.

High productivity, low absenteeism, high job safety records, and low turnover have been demonstrated by people with disabilities throughout all industries in all types of jobs (Russell, 1986). This record of success is in many ways the result of the careful matching that has occurred to place qualified individuals with disabilities in appropriate jobs. However, this record of success is also partially attributable to the provision of information and education prior to employment. The types of information typically required by an employer prior to hiring a given individual with a visual impairment for a given job include the following:

- Information regarding the functional implications of the applicant's visual impairment,
- Information about the types of equipment and other modifications necessary for the applicant to competitively perform the assigned duties,
- Information for the supervisor and

The use of color contrast to signal the presence of steps, as shown here, is among the recommendations rehabilitation counselors can make to employers to help them determine "reasonable accommodation" measures for people with low vision.

coworkers in the applicant's work area regarding what to expect and how to respond, and

- Assurances that support will be available in the event that the job should substantially change.

This education and information given prior to employment assists the employer in knowing what to expect and how to prepare, which helps to ensure a successful placement (see also Sidebar 13.3).

The method for addressing the need for education and information prior to employment varies according to the circumstances. Broadly speaking, there are two parties that can provide the needed education—the rehabilitation professional and the job seeker. Whenever possible, it is always preferable for the applicant to address the employer's concerns. It is not, however, always realistic for applicants to provide this needed education and information, either because of their inability to adequately address such issues, or because the employer's perceived need to have an expert from the vocational rehabilitation agency involved in reviewing issues and concerns. To the degree that the employer in question has some prior knowledge or experience upon which to draw, then the employer is less apt to feel the

SIDEBAR 13.3

Counselor Actions and Statements That Encourage Employment

- Assisting in training
- Pointing out particular jobs done by people who are blind
- Demonstrating knowledge of jobs in employer's plant or facility
- Prescreening applicants with visual impairments
- Sharing results of studies regarding value of workers with disabilities
- Providing follow-up
- Referring only those with appropriate skills training
- Matching a person's skills to specific jobs
- Identifying available tax credits
- Leaving materials describing the agency or program
- Avoiding jargon or unfamiliar terminology

Source: C. Kirchner, D. Harkins, R. Esposito, M. Isatanbuli, and F. Chandu, *Issues and Strategies Toward Improving Employment of Blind or Visually Impaired Persons in Illinois* (New York: American Foundation for the Blind, 1991).

need for involvement by the rehabilitation counselor. Furthermore, to the extent that applicants can adequately address job-related employer education issues, then the employer is less apt to feel the need for involvement by the counselor. Given this interaction, if an assessment of a particular client's situation yielded the conclusion that the circumstances warranted more knowledge by the employer, then a greater amount of education prior to employment by the counselor would be suggested. If, however, the client's circumstances required less knowledge by the employer, then the counselor is advised to work with the client, so that the client can provide most, if not all, of the necessary information.

The final employer education concern to be addressed in regard to information and education prior to employment is the matter of ongoing support. The provision of ongoing support is a major concern for employers in the event that the client's job should change in the future. Vocational rehabilitation agency rules vary from state to state regarding this issue, but all states have some provisions for postemployment services. It is recommended that the postemployment services that are available be explained to the employer during the information and education process prior to employment so that any concern regarding ongoing support is, at least partially, addressed early in the process of the employer's consideration of the possibility of hiring a person with a visual impairment.

Knowledge Needed by the Rehabilitation Counselor

What company in a given state employs the most people? What is the fastest growing industry in a given state? These are questions that rehabilitation professionals are advised to know how to answer. Why? It is so the information can be shared in an attempt to encourage a specific client regarding a particular career goal. There are certainly times when sharing such information can be helpful to a client who is trying to make a decision. The more significant reason for regularly accessing such information, however, is to ensure that the rehabilitation professional is aware of the "big picture," which includes the following:

- Dramatic swings in particular industries,
- Shifts in types of jobs being filled,
- Major changes in unemployment applications within certain portions of a given state, and
- The level of competition for jobs, vis-à-vis the total number of individuals who are actively seeking employment.

Such information can be acquired on a local or a state level by being placed on the mailing list(s) of the Department of Labor within any particular state. Similarly, the national perspective on these significant issues can be obtained by subscribing to the U.S. Department of Labor, Bureau of Labor Statistics' *Occupational Outlook Quarterly.* By regularly reviewing such information, the rehabilitation professional can better counsel clients in regard to specific vocational goals that might be under consideration (Patterson, 1996). Rehabilitation professionals can also use such information to respond more effectively to employers, in that they will have a better appreciation and comprehension of those issues affecting employers.

Monitoring shifts in the work force is certainly an important element of understanding the "big picture." There are several other data sources and types of information, however, that rehabilitation professionals are advised to monitor on a regular basis, if they are to be efficient in building and maintaining effective employer relations. As appropriate to a given locale, the data sources and types of information that are recommended include the following:

- Local Chamber of Commerce newsletters regarding business activities,
- Business sections from the major local newspapers,
- Weekly or monthly business periodical(s),
- Local job service office listings, and
- Issues discussed informally at local service organization meetings (e.g., Lions and Kiwanis Clubs), to which rehabilitation professionals are urged to periodically offer presentations.

These sources yield important local information regarding such issues as those employers that are hiring and those that are laying off, the condition of the local economy, and who is (are) the more liberal or forward-looking local employer(s). This information can be extremely valuable in terms of targeting subsequent job development activities.

In addition to being able to synthesize and use basic business data and information, it is highly recommended that the rehabilitation counselor also be able to match the skills and interests of clients to available employment opportunities (Bradfield, 1992; Winking, O'Reilly, & Moon, 1993). Whether the matching process is done by the counselor or whether it is a service purchased from another provider, a key element in building effective employer relations is being able to correctly match clients with jobs. Job analysis and accommodation, discussed later in this chapter, are the foundations of this match. Correct job matching leads the employer to trust that the rehabilitation professional can be a valuable human resources asset for filling future vacancies.

The final issue to be addressed in this section is the importance of knowing and using other approaches with employers. Popular approaches include informational interviews and internships. Both are tools that counselors can use to enable employers to interact with job-ready clients without imposing an expectation on the employer that a hiring decision has to be made in regard to a given individual. Informational interviews are arranged by or for a job-ready individual when the individual lacks interviewing experience. In such a case, the employer is asked to help address this weakness by providing a realistic interview experience. Clients can approach the informational interview as if they are applicants (e.g., bringing a résumé, dressing appropriately, and attempting to inform the employer about their background and skills). The employer interviews the individual as if the client is an actual applicant. At the conclusion of the interview, the employer provides the client with feedback and suggestions for improving interview performance. Although the purpose of the exercise is to provide a realistic practice experience, the informational interview can lead to job offers being made by the interviewer. Because of the potential to enhance employer interest, it is another approach that can be seriously considered and used in certain circumstances.

The use of internships by counselors can also be an effective approach. An internship is arranged by or for a job-ready individual who lacks prior work experience. In a case such as this, the employer is asked to help address this lack of experience by providing a short-term employment experience. The employer provides the initial orientation and ongoing supervision during the internship period. Again, the purpose of the internship experience is to provide limited work experience, but internships can also lead to permanent positions.

JOB DEVELOPMENT STRATEGIES

> Terry C. is a rehabilitation counselor with two job-ready clients who live close to the small town of Clinton. Terry visits Clinton for a half day on a bimonthly basis to review each client's status and to set goals for the next two months' activities. Whenever Terry goes to Clinton, he arrives an hour and a half before his first appointment. During that hour and a half, Terry visits briefly and leaves business cards and brochures with the dozen or so proprietors of small retail businesses on Main Street and he usually stops to visit and leave materials with the assistant plant manager at the local foundry. Twice Terry has talked to the local ladies' auxiliary at church during their weekly noon meeting. As Terry's clients progress through the rehabilitation process, Terry is able to refer them for informational interviews to one or another of the town's employers who has agreed to help out by providing a practice interview. Terry's success for small-town placements is highly respected across the state and several colleagues wonder openly about his secret.

Although Terry C. is a hypothetical counselor conducting job development for a theoretical caseload, the principles suggested in the description of Terry C.'s work are neither hypothetical nor theoretical. Job development is the process of encouraging the decision-makers in a place of employment to seriously consider hiring a person with a disability. Terry is effective because he has applied the following basic principles in attempting to accomplish this objective:

> *First*—he is educating employers about the possibility that qualified individuals with visual impairments may be seeking employment in their companies;
>
> *Second*—he is learning about the various places of employment in the community so that he can begin to match his clients' skills and interests to the various businesses in the area;
>
> *Third*—he is building a working relationship with those employers; and
>
> *Fourth*—he is enhancing agency and community relations and expanding his network to include those who own businesses and work in human resources offices.

These four principles are at the core of providing effective job development activities, but the strategies vary according to the size of the community, the nature of the employers, and the range of the rehabilitation professional's assigned responsibilities. As was suggested in the fictional case of Terry C., a strategy successful in many smaller communities is that of networking. Networking involves making the need for employment known in as many ways as possible. This strategy is particularly relevant in a small community, because there may not be a large number of employment opportunities available at any given time and the network helps the counselor identify those opportunities, sometimes before an opening even exists. In larger communities and cities, however, a more targeted strategy can be more appropriate. That is, after the client's skills and interests are known, employers within a defined geographic area or field of work are then targeted for contact. If no opportunities are identified within the defined area or field, then the scope of the search is broadened.

Job development strategies also vary significantly according to the size of the company. Larger companies usually have human resource units that screen applicants. The final hiring decision in large companies, however, is usually made by the departmental manager or supervisor who will be monitoring the employee's work. Given the structure of large companies and the fact that being hired requires at least two decision-makers to agree, it is important to try to influence the company at both levels. It is recommended that the initial job development efforts be targeted at the human resources offices. Visits made to those offices to discuss the company's present and future hiring needs, provide information on how individuals with visual impairments may be possible employee resources, and leaving materials can create a positive hiring atmosphere. After establishing a working relationship, it is sometimes possible to offer to provide some ADA training for the staff in human resources and for the departmental managers or supervisors regarding how to evaluate and respond appropriately to applicants who are visually impaired. If an offer for training is refused, then it is frequently the case that the departmental manager or supervisor can only be reached after an applicant has applied for a position and has been interviewed by that manager or supervisor. In that case, the rehabilitation professional can still offer some job development assistance, but only if the client wants the involvement of the counselor. The assistance that the counselor can offer clients at that point includes the following:

- Referral to a database called the Job Accommodation Network (JAN). JAN is sponsored by the President's Committee on Employment of People with Disabilities. JAN puts employers who are considering the possibility of hiring a person with a disability in touch with employers who have already been through that process. (To access JAN call 1-800-JAN-PCEH);
- Offer to provide some training for staff members in the unit if the person is hired. The training would focus on basic courtesies for interacting comfortably with the person who is visually impaired and to allay any fears or misconceptions that others might have about working with a person with a visual impairment.

The unit manager or supervisor will often welcome the suggested training, but, at the same time, will emphasize that it is only for the other workers. However, managers and supervisors usually benefit at least as much, if not more, than the other workers from such sessions. For this reason, it is a good idea to suggest that any training involves everyone—including managers or supervisors.

Gaining access to the decision-maker in smaller companies can be as difficult as in larger companies, but the problems are related more to the limited time available to see the hiring authority than to a complex organizational structure. Many smaller companies assign the duty of accepting applications and scheduling interviews to a person in the administrative offices. Often this person has little or no formal training in human resources administration. It is important that counselors introduce themselves, provide some information, and educate this person, but this individual usually plays only a clerical role in the overall hiring process. Therefore, if job development efforts are to be effective with such companies, the counselor needs to approach the shop manager, owner, vice president, or whoever serves as the actual hiring authority. Two strategies that can work in such situations are, first, having the front office person suggest to the hiring authority that the individual really needs to meet with the rehabilitation counselor, and, second, providing concise, important information through the front office person to the hiring authority—information that emphasizes why meeting with the rehabilitation counselor would benefit the company. When meeting with executives from smaller companies, it is important to be sensitive to the fact that they frequently see themselves as being less equipped than major corporations in terms of their ability to hire persons with disabilities because:

1. They have smaller profit margins, so they cannot afford complex accommodations for workers with disabilities,
2. Their staff persons are not usually as specialized, so workers cannot easily be assigned a limited number of tasks and still perform productively, and
3. They view themselves as being very close-knit, so they are concerned about the impact on other workers should they hire a person who has a visual impairment.

To defuse these concerns, it is usually best to go to meetings with small company representatives armed with information about assistance that vocational rehabilitation can provide vis-à-vis accommodations and armed with real-life examples of people working productively in small companies. Given the challenges, the rehabilitation professional might question whether small companies with relatively few jobs available are worth the effort, but according to the futurist Toffler (1990), most of the job growth over the next decade will occur in these small companies.

The AFB Careers and Technology Information Bank (CTIB) (see Resources section for more information) can be of assistance in providing actual examples of successfully employed individuals who are blind or visually impaired. The CTIB, which lists a wide range of employed individuals, is a database specific to persons with visual impairments who are categorized according to the job titles they represent and the equipment that they use on their jobs. The CTIB can be reached through the AFB in New York to identify who is doing what in that employer's vicinity. Making contact with the person from the Information Bank and arranging for the employer to make contact with that person can be an effective means of alleviating an employer's concerns.

The final variations on strategies for conducting job development activities are those variations based on differences in the rehabilitation professional's job scope and responsibilities. The foregoing strategies depict situations in which the counselor has specifically allocated a significant amount of time to develop jobs. Many rehabilitation professionals, however, have job descriptions composed of 20 to 25 items and job development is only one of those items. When the counselor has this set of circumstances to contend with, then using variations on the strategy suggested in the Terry C. case study can be very successful—that is, focusing job development efforts on those clients who have completed adjustment services, have developed realistic vocational goals, and who are ready to work. Arranging regular (not less than bimonthly) meetings and trying to maintain intervening phone conversations with these job-ready clients to map strategies and set goals is highly advised for successful placement. Making sure that all major and possible employers in the vicinity are visited on a regular basis by the job seeker or the counselor, even if the companies do not have advertised vacancies is another effective activity. The counselor is also urged to consider contacting local Chambers of Commerce or local service organizations to volunteer to speak about agency services and people with visual impairments as possible resources for employers. If this aggressive strategy is followed, at least one relevant job possibility should be identified in the first bimonthly period. The goal in this effort is to develop possibilities, because it is the possibilities that lead to interviews, and interviews lead to placements.

Although many agencies have the counselor wearing multiple hats, some state and private rehabilitation agencies have a limited number of staff persons specializing in the areas of job development and placement (Stevens, Boland, &

Ranson, 1982). The specialists working for such agencies are assigned job-ready individuals who have developed specific vocational objectives. The specialists' primary focus is then to assist the clients in identifying appropriate job opportunities. Because the specialists do not have the other responsibilities, they have the flexibility to be far more active and visible within the communities in which they work. All of the foregoing strategies suggested would be applicable for the specialists to use, in addition to a number of other possibilities, such as

- Coordinating or participating in periodic job fairs for clients in urban areas where employers with vacancies would be invited to send representatives to a central site to interview candidates;
- Organizing a "barrier awareness day" during which employers would be encouraged to allow unemployed individuals with visual impairments to visit their places of employment and the employers would be invited to visit employment sites where individuals with visual impairments are presently employed, as a way of sharing information about what each person does and how jobs are performed;
- Offering to speak on radio information stations and small commercial radio stations regarding the employment of people who are blind or are visually impaired;
- Writing occasional articles for local newspapers explaining agency services and the need for employment opportunities for qualified applicants; and
- Attending the meetings of relevant professional associations (such as the Personnel Managers Association) to establish new linkages within the business community.

This list is only a brief sample of activities, because the options for job development activities are endless. Professionals who have job development and placement as their sole focus can have a tremendous impact in terms of creating employment opportunities for individuals who are blind or visually impaired within those communities where they work. Job development is at the core of providing goal-oriented vocational rehabilitation services. To be effective in this role, the rehabilitation professional must interest employers in and educate them about the possibility of hiring qualified workers with visual impairments. The scope and nature of each rehabilitation professional's job development efforts will vary somewhat according to the communities served, the companies in those communities, and the professional's specific role in the delivery of services. Nevertheless, the task of job development is enormously important and deserves and requires some commitment and attention from all vocational rehabilitation professionals.

JOB RETENTION

It is a fairly common practice for companies to have policies or programs to encourage the retention of workers who become disabled. Such policies make excellent economic sense for employers, given the escalating costs associated with training new staff. There are cases, however, in which the interventions required to retain a worker exceed the expertise held by the average employer. These situations frequently result in either the employer or the client contacting a rehabilitation agency to seek assistance. The extent to which a given state vocational rehabilitation agency can provide assistance however, may be limited by the agency's rules governing post-employment services. Such rules typically require that individuals with visual impairments be at serious risk of losing their jobs before the agency can become involved vis-à-vis the purchasing of evaluations or equipment. Thus, if the employer is at a point in which either accommodations are made or termination of the individual is imminent, and if the employer is willing to so document, then state rehabilitation agencies can typically intervene in a significant way. Should the situation not meet those criteria, however, then the counselor can usually only advise regarding actions that the employer or the individual might consider. Such actions might include a low vision evaluation, job restructuring, equipment purchase, or a leave of absence for training. The role of the adviser in such situations is important and, often, the provision of expert advice is sufficient to lead to job retention. There are also situations in which employers cannot afford to make the reasonable accommodations that are needed and the state rehabilitation agency cannot legitimately authorize postemployment services. Under these circumstances, it is sometimes possible to prevail upon a local service organization (e.g., Lions Club) to help meet the costs of the accommodations and training. For a more detailed discussion of intervention practices in the retention of competitive employment among individuals who are blind or visually impaired, see Sikka & Stephens (1997).

The average life span of Americans is increasing and, as a result, the number of people in the work force who are experiencing visual impairments is also increasing. The ADA encourages employers to provide reasonable accommodations for all qualified persons with disabilities. Normally, one would be "qualified" if he or she had a history of success on a given job prior to the onset of a disability. How, then, should the employer proceed? Assisting in job retention is an important part of the rehabilitation professional's evolving role, but there are also agency limitations that may restrict the type of service(s) that the professional can provide. Whether the role played by the rehabilitation professional is extensive or is limited to providing advice, the delivery of services to facilitate retention of employment is increasingly important, and this trend will probably continue as the costs escalate for training new employees. Because of the importance of matching the client to the right job, the need to provide information to employers about accommodations and the role of accommodations in job retention, the next section addresses these increasingly vital job accommodation issues.

JOB ACCOMMODATION AND MODIFICATION TECHNIQUES

Job accommodation and modification techniques result in expanded employment opportunities for individuals who are unemployed or underemployed. Graves, Lyon, Marmion, and Boyet (1986a) noted that in addition to unemployment, individuals with disabilities are also chronically underemployed. Moreover, unemployment and underemployment are considered among the most serious career-related problems faced by individuals who are blind or visually impaired (Graves et al., 1986a).

To understand job accommodation, the rehabilitation professional needs to know some of the key concepts and definitions. These include such concepts as reasonable accommodation, task analysis, and job restructuring. These and other essential concepts are examined in the following sections.

Key Concepts in Accommodation

Reasonable Accommodation

According to Section 504 of the Rehabilitation Act of 1973, as amended, "reasonable accommodation may include making facilities used by employees accessible to and usable by individuals with disabilities, job restructuring, modified work schedules, acquisition or modification of existing equipment, and the provision of readers or interpreters." Individuals with disabilities must be "otherwise qualified" to perform the essential functions of the job, as written in a job description, and that the reasonable accommodation by employers should not produce "an undue hardship" to employers, based on the size and type of business involved (Resources for Rehabilitation, 1991).

Job and Task Analysis

Before specific alterations or modifications of a job or working environment can occur, however, it is recommended that the rehabilitation professional analyze the work and related tasks of the existing or planned position. A job analysis includes a description of what the worker does (i.e., the tasks), how the work is done, the results of the work, worker characteristics, and context of the work. (See Appendix B for a sample of a completed Job Analysis Worksheet.) The step-by-step delineation of the work activities of a job is called task analysis (U.S. Department of Labor, 1991). A task analysis is often conducted prior to consideration of changes that might be required in order to make the job accessible to a person with a visual impairment or other type of disability (Yuspeh, 1982). Mallik (1979) stated that objectivity is the key to effective task analysis.

Job Restructuring

Mallik (1979) defined job restructuring as "a process through which one combines, eliminates, redistributes, adds, or isolates tasks from one or more jobs within the same job family to form part-time or full-time positions" (p. 145). For example, a word processing position required that the employee frequently check an updated print reference. All other aspects of the job were readily accessible to the applicant, who had a visual impairment, through an adaptive work station (i.e., a computer adapted with a speech synthesizer and screen review program). A coworker was assigned this responsibility, and the visually impaired employee was expected to produce increased word processing output.

Job Sharing

Job sharing is the dividing of what is typically a full-time job among two or more persons. A parent with childcare responsibilities, for example, might share a normally full-time job with another individual in order to be available when childcare is required. A concern about job sharing by both employer and employee is fringe benefits. Two part-time employees, both receiving full fringe benefits, will add additional expense to the employer. The organization's human resource policies and individual requirements must be considered for job sharing to be a viable option.

Work-site Modification

Work-site modification involves environmental changes to an individual's work station or workplace to make it more functional, comfortable, or convenient. Common modifications may include (1) braille or other tactile markings of file tabs, folders, containers or drawers, (2) careful organization of needed work items, such as forms or components, (3) modified tools and precision instrumentation, (4) tactile guides for such tools as drills, saws, and soldering irons, (5) use of tactile templates for work positioning, (6) removal of sources of glare, (7) installation of appropriate lighting, (8) use of adaptive print positioning surfaces, such as reading tables and copy holders, and (9) specialized technology (Scadden, 1991).

Bradfield (1992) identified the five categories of modifications and accommodations as equipment modifications, work station modifications, task modifications, time or schedule modifications, and personal modifications. For example, when determining equipment modifications, the sensory mode that is most important should first be considered. Other considerations include the importance of contrast. As Zimmerman (1992) indicated

> Two or more objects are more easily perceived when there is clear distinction between edges of each of the objects. For example, if an individual uses a white-handled knife to cut heads of cabbage on a white cutting board, then the colors of the board and the knife should be changed to provide sufficient contrast between the white head of cabbage and the utensils. Each setting must be evaluated based on the individual's visual needs. This is not an adaptation that will generalize across settings: each setting, task, and individual will require different adaptations. (p. 71)

Illumination, magnification, tactile modifications (e.g., templates), and auditory modifications are

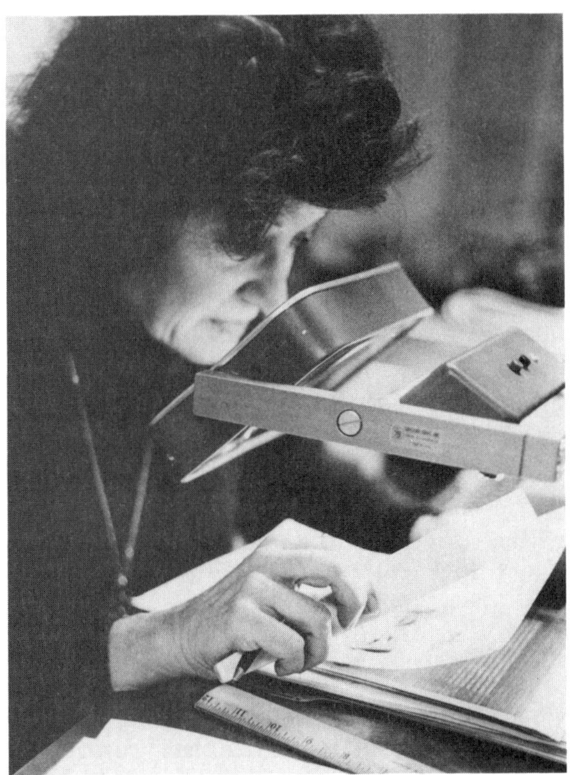

Work-site modification involves environmental and equipment changes to an individual's work station to make it more functional, comfortable, or convenient. In this instance, the worker uses a hand-held magnifier and a stand magnifier with a light to help her accomplish her tasks.

additional considerations. Work station modifications, which include both the location and organization of the work station, might be considered when the noise level precludes the use of required auditory equipment or when changes in illumination are needed. For information on technological resources, see Chapter 9.

The specifics of job modification are integrated into an overall review of multiple factors to ensure success. Crews (1976) outlined several criteria for successful job modifications, including function, adaptability, availability, cost maintainability, comparability and acceptability, which are discussed in the following sections.

Function. First and foremost, any change to an existing work site or design characteristic of a planned work station must be functional. The specific task requirements should be understood and the modification should "fit" the function required. For example, a position requiring mathematical processing may require a calculator with a paper printout, in addition to synthetic speech, to provide a running record of accuracy of accounting. The paper printout is not necessarily a modification of normal work equipment, but as a characteristic in selecting a modified calculator with speech synthesis, is necessary to fit the function required.

Adaptability. There are several factors relating to the requirement of adaptability of any aspect of job modification. On the one hand, a device may be required to be adaptable for use by sighted coworkers. For example, if an individual with a visual impairment is being employed on a job that runs multiple shifts, the same work station may be required to serve individuals without visual impairments. Hence, any modification to the equipment or work area must be adaptable for use by a sighted employee without interfering with the normal, efficient functioning of the position. For example, modified lighting may be installed for an individual requiring a reduction or an increase in illumination for maximum functioning without altering the ability to utilize standard lighting. Or, should an adapted computerized work station be installed, a standard keyboard and monitor should also be made available.

The other aspect of work station adaptability relates to the adaptability of given modifications for varying work requirements of the individual with the visual impairment. For example, a computer access system that contains a built-in calculator may serve several functional needs and therefore be adaptable to several tasks.

Availability. The availability of a piece of adaptive equipment may be a critical factor in its effectiveness in an overall job-site modification. For example, if a computer access device is needed, and the manufacturer has a 90-day backlog for delivery, a placement opportunity may be lost. Often, competing devices may have equivalent functionality, and availability may be the deciding factor in selection.

Programs providing short-term loans of assistive technology are scarce indeed, but they provide a critical link and enable the effective placement of candidates who are experiencing a delay imposed by lack of product availability. Furthermore, availability of assistive technology on loan can help in avoiding the inefficiency of "downtime" experienced by an individual when specialized equipment, such as a braille embossing printer, has to be sent back to the manufacturer for repair (Beattie, 1991).

Cost Maintainability. The cost of adaptive technology is contained in three distinct components which are the purchase price, the required services including training and engineering support, and the ongoing maintenance. Because of the extreme scarcity of specialized training in engineering support for work stations that have incorporated assistive technology, the rehabilitation professional is advised to identify appropriate human resources and incorporate realistic estimates of these costs into individual rehabilitation plans. In general, ongoing service contracts for computerized equipment cost 10 percent of the purchase price of the device annually. Such costs must be budgeted on an ongoing basis to ensure the effective maintenance of any "high tech" modification. A subtle factor regarding this point may also be that some manufacturers give preference through more rapid servicing or upgrading of equipment to those holding service contracts. Maintenance contracts are essentially insurance policies for technological devices that may become quite costly to repair without such protection.

Comparability. Any job-site modification must be comparable to the same aspect of job performance as that performed by a sighted employee. For example, if a machine shop requires measurements of work performed to the thousandth of a centimeter, tools used by an individual with a visual impairment must provide comparable accuracy. Another example is a customer service representative who is required to complete a large number of preprinted forms. A sighted employee may simply print or type the required information. A comparable modification for an individual with a visual impairment may be generating the required data on blank paper rather than on the preprinted form. If the overall organization can readily accommodate this modification, a comparable solution has been defined. However, the organization may be unable to utilize such a solution because of the use of electronic scanning equipment for form reading. Specialized applications software for use with synthetic speech output or electronic braille may enable the employee to generate data directly onto preprinted forms. Such solutions are labor intensive, require work specifically with the printer, and may be the solution of choice, although far simpler solutions may suffice. In one case, a simple cardboard template was used to enable a medical transcriber to insert a form to the specific position required for printing the medical report. In this case such a solution would not provide comparability and a computerized form-filling software program would be required.

Acceptability. Acceptability is a variable that addresses both the modification's acceptability to the individual, and to the work environment. Cosmetic factors may be important and, in spite of a modification's functionality, may interfere with an individual's willingness to accept a given system or approach. For example, telescopic eyeglasses may be of high utility in increasing visual acuity enabling the performance of given work tasks, but individuals may find their appearance unacceptable.

Concerning a modification's acceptability to the work environment, such factors as size, effect on other employees, or "fit" into overall work flow may be important. For example, a braille embossing printer may provide an office worker with needed hard copy material, but may produce too much noise to be acceptable as a desirable modification. As always, every situation must be carefully analyzed and the specifics of the work environment taken into consideration during the process of designing job modifications.

Adaptive Technology. Adaptive technology refers to specialized equipment that typically provides access to information in a modified form. For example, print may be accessed by persons with visual impairments through closed-circuit television (CCTV) magnification systems. Computers may be accessed through electronic braille, synthetic speech, or enlarged character output systems. Lights on a telephone console might be accessed through use of a "light probe" using an electronic photosensor with audible output. Although high technology tools and devices are generally thought of as examples of adaptive technology, so also are such simpler "low tech" solutions as optical devices and mechanical braillewriters. The importance of adaptive technology and its importance to one's ability to maintain employment has been well documented by Livingston and Tucker (1997). (See Chapters 4 and 9 for additional information about optical devices and adaptive technology.)

Rehabilitation Engineering. The Rehabilitation Act Amendments of 1992 mandated the provision of rehabilitation technology services by state vocational rehabilitation agencies. Among its provisions are the requirement of states to provide such services and the mandate that electronic equipment purchased by the federal government must be able to be made accessible to persons with disabilities. The term "rehabilitation technology" is defined in the Rehabilitation Act as the systematic application of technologies, engineering methodologies, or scientific principles to meet the needs of and address the barriers confronted by individuals with disabilities in areas which include education, rehabilitation, employment, transportation, independent living, and recreation. The term includes rehabilitation engineering, assistive technology devices, and assistive technology services. Rehabilitation engineering is a broadly defined class of technical specializations that address evaluating and identifying aspects of particular jobs, for example, mechanical, optical, or computer-related job requirements. When combined, they assist in the development of strategies, techniques, or recommendations of adaptive technology to "fit" the purpose and solve the problem. In the visual impairment field particularly, rehabilitation engineering services may not be provided by individuals who refer to themselves as rehabilitation engineers. Such diverse professionals as rehabilitation teachers, computer access specialists, computer scientists, mechanical engineers, industrial engineers, rehabilitation counselors, low vision specialists, and others may individually, or in combination, work as members of the rehabilitation "engineering" team.

Mechanical Engineering. Mechanical engineering involves the adaptation of the tools used by an employee or other aspects of the job setting including the addition of guards, guides, and jigs. An industrial lathe operator, for example, may be assisted in aligning work through a guide mounted on the lathe or may require scales with elevated gradations, including micrometers and insider calipers (Anand & Guha, 1986). This example suggests that job modification may involve the application of available tools and devices, rather than reliance on the fabrication of specific adaptations. Mechanical engineering-related adaptations should be developed or applied based on functionality, simplicity, and individual need, rather than assumptions about safety or any innate capabilities of people with visual impairments.

Visual Modifications. Elmfeldt, Wise, Bergsten, and Olsson (1983) suggested that the following areas require evaluation to enhance orientation and mobility (O&M) for individuals who are visually impaired within the workplace: (1) glare, which should be reduced by covering windows, (2) lighting, and (3) floors, which should also be nonglare. Eye-level high-contrast markings also should be placed on glass doors and walls to avoid collisions, and stairways should be marked for safety. Although traditional methods for marking the leading and rising edge of the stairs involve the use of a contrasting stripe approximately two inches in width, Mehr and Sakamoto (1988) suggested running stripes moving down the stairs to present a more effective means of stair demarcation.

Work Environment Visual Demands Protocol. The Work Environment Visual Demands Protocol (WEVD) was developed to be used as a tool for analyzing visual demands within work sites of individuals who are visually impaired. WEVD is a series of questions used by a low vision specialist analyzing a work environment. Personal computer software is utilized to generate a report based on these findings, which is then reviewed by the low vision team prior to clinical services. Graves, Maxson, & McCaa (1988) reported that the use of WEVD could result in fewer follow-up visits within a clinical setting, in greater use of prescribed optical devices, and in greater comfort of the individual using prescribed devices. As a tool incorporated by the professional involved with the task analysis and environmental study of the work site of the individual who is visually impaired, the WEVD offers an important and validated protocol to assist with the complex task of defining optimum prescriptive devices for maximum functionality and utility. For a sample of a completed WEVD, see Appendix E of this book.

Building on the WEVD, Bradfield and Tucker (1988) developed *The Workplace Visual Functioning Assessment for Job Modification and Accommodation.* This document examines three areas of "work evaluation," which are the job tasks, the individual's visual skills, and the match of a person to a job. The publication is a thorough instructional manual that reviews the factors to be considered as an individual who is visually impaired is integrated into a specific job environment. Unlike the WEVD, this manual does not rely on computer software, but rather on careful inventory of environmental and task analysis, individual capability, and the individual/job "fit."

Environmental and Other Considerations

Because of the wide variety of individual visual capabilities, work tasks, environmental characteristics, and the other variable factors that must be taken into consideration when developing job modifications for an individual, a thorough individual evaluation must occur prior to implementing any accommodation strategy. The professional conducting such an evaluation need not be an expert in all aspects of potential modification, but he or she needs to understand enough about possible tools, techniques, modified systems, and available expertise to organize whatever specific changes or intervention may be required. The following discussion of some specific types of modification provides an overview of the wide variety of approaches and techniques that have been used in the multifaceted art of job modification. As in other aspects of job modification, individual evaluation is required to accommodate personal needs.

Lighting. Studies have suggested that the majority of people who are visually impaired require additional light to optimize visual functioning. In addition to footcandle power, the position of the light source must allow for maximum, shadow-free illumination.

Alternatives are also available for individuals who require additional light to maximize visual efficiency. Halogen lamps, another important innovation, provide enhanced visual efficiency for many individuals who are visually impaired through the provision of high intensity, focused, and evenly distributed illumination.

The nature of the illumination may also have an effect. Incandescent light includes a broader span of the light spectrum, whereas fluorescent lighting produces more blue light that may create glare and be unusable for those individuals who experience photophobia or light sensitivity (Bandouveres, Kukish, & Giers, 1981; LaGrow, 1986). This latter group requires less-than-normal illumination for maximal visual functioning. In this situation, an employee working in a partitioned desk area required light-deflecting cardboard shields on the fluorescent lights over the work area and a draped hood over the desk to create an extremely low light environment in order to work comfortably and efficiently. Indirect lighting, windowless work areas, low-wattage lamps, or use of rheostats (devices mounted on lamps that change lighting levels) on overhead light circuits may also be considered. By using adaptive light filtering eyewear, individuals may protect themselves from painful, disruptive environmental light, although even with such eyewear, some environmental modification may be required, depending on individual needs.

Positioning. As in all matters related to low vision functionality, work positioning is as critical a consideration as is lighting and magnification. Raised work surfaces, copy holders, and slant boards can provide proper positioning of work to promote ease and speed of reading, and physical comfort. Adjustable chairs and raised computer or CCTV monitors are equally important for functional "in line" viewing of adapted visual displays. Avoiding postural strain is a secondary benefit of these types of modifications, and also has a direct bearing on productivity and worker comfort.

Another consideration pertinent to visual impairment relates to jobs that involve cathode ray tube (CRT) use. Nemeth and Childress (1987) indicated that eyestrain and visual fatigue were common complaints of video display terminal (VDT) operators in the general population. This problem may be even greater for system users with visual impairments because of the shorter viewing distance or intensity of the visual demands. Both sighted workers and those with visual impairments may benefit from appropriate ambient lighting to minimize glare, or from the use of ultraviolet filtering lenses.

Nonvisual Environmental Modifications. Although the first priority of job modification should be focused on individuals who are blind and their specific work stations, broader environmental considerations frequently must be addressed. For example, a worker who was deaf and blind was being hired as an electronics technician in a California company. A sophisticated electromechanical modification was attached to a microscope, which enabled him to solder transistor leads. The barrier to this man's employment was his inability to cross the street safely in front of the facility where he would work. As a solution, a tactile crossing signal indicator was designed and installed to enable him to accomplish this critical task after getting off the bus. In general, the assistance of O&M professionals can help avoid this type of physical adaptation; although in this case, the environmental modification was the only solution for independent travel.

Transportation. Transportation is not a job task, but can present significant challenges to workers who are blind or visually impaired (Corn & Sacks, 1994). Strategies to address transportation problems often include using public transportation or carpools, or hiring drivers, depending on the needs of the individual. The Vocational Study Center (University of Wisconsin, 1986) cited the case of a darkroom technician who was hired for a job, which included working two weekends per month. The individual was unable to commute to work on weekends because of the limitations of bus service. The employer agreed to waive the weekend work requirement and thereby made the job accessible to the employee. Similar arrangements may also need to be made regarding work shifts as they relate to bus route availability. However, rehabilitation professionals should remain cognizant of the fact that this type of accommodation may have a negative effect on other employees, if second or third shift or weekend work becomes unequally spread among sighted employees as an outcome of the accommodation. It is highly advised that the reactions of coworkers be anticipated and actions taken to minimize their effects. Clear communication with other employees can be sought and maintained, while support is given to the individual with the visual impairment (particularly in the early stages of employment on a new job).

Functional, task-specific changes may also be considered under the broad aegis of environmental modification. For example, another darkroom technician with a visual impairment was unable to determine the proper orientation of X-ray film as a result of its symmetrical packaging. The hospital agreed to have a secretary notch all film in the upper right-hand corner with a hand punch to provide a simple and expedient method for recognition by the worker. This change in the working environment facilitated this job placement.

Examples of Specific Job Modifications

The following are examples of low-cost modifications that have been successfully implemented for workers who are visually impaired.

Secretary. A secretary who was blind required the following modifications: braille tabs on hanging files, a speech synthesizer and screen review program for the existing PC work station, an optical scanner and reading system integrated into the personal computer system, and a talking calculator and dictionary.

Sewing Operator. An industrial sewing operator was hired with the following accommodations: lighting modifications, which consisted of increasing the footcandle power or illumination falling on the person's work surface, increasing the wattage of the lamp, and repositioning this incandescent light source closer to the work surface. The color of the "presser foot" or guide was altered to reduce reflective glare. Another employee in a related job required colored templates to maximize visual efficiency to be used in cutting fabric from patterns.

Radio Broadcaster. A radio broadcaster required an enlarged monitor for the station's computer system and a privately paid driver at the rate of $100 per month.

Administrator. An administrator was hired by a rehabilitation agency and required a CCTV, and screen-magnifying software for the computer work station networked within the facility. Incandescent low-wattage lamps replaced overhead fluorescent fixtures and large "foam core panels" (i.e., lightweight, sturdy, posterboard sheets) blocked daylight from striking the work surface directly from large windows.

Programmer. A computer programmer was hired to work in a networked environment. Her work station was a PC equipped with a speech synthesizer, screen-reading program, and refreshable braille display. A braille embossing printer provided her with hard-copy printouts.

The Job Modification Team

The roles assumed by the rehabilitation counselor or case manager will vary depending on the number and types of other professionals whose knowledge and skills are needed as job placement team members. As discussed earlier, a job-task analysis is generally necessary to assess all components of the targeted job. It is required that the individual client be provided with all appropriate prevocational skill development, interest and aptitude testing, counseling, and preparation for vocational placement. When a "match" is identified between the individual and the available vocational opportunity, the functional specificity of the individual modification begins.

Just as case managers must develop teams of professionals or expertise germane to the requirements of specific modifications, employers must draw on those individuals within their organizations who possess the requisite knowledge and authority to facilitate the accommodations. For example, a telephone company intended to hire a worker who was blind as a repair bureau attendant or dispatcher. A meeting was held with the head of the job placement team, which included representatives from the company's training, technical, human resources, and line supervision, all of whom had a role to play in the ultimate success of the effort. The team leader from both the company and the rehabilitation agency maintained communication and facilitated the involvement of other team members. This centralized teamwork resulted in clearer communication and coordination than would have been possible had all individuals functioned independently.

Many professionals within the field of blindness may provide significant input and expertise in the placement effort. The O&M specialist addresses independent travel to the work site, transportation-related issues, and orientation within the working environment, and may also consult on environmental modifications. The rehabilitation teacher evaluates information on handling job requirements and recommends solutions tailored to the individual. The low vision specialist may become involved with assessment of environmental factors, including lighting and positioning of work, and the functionality of prescribed optical devices in the working environment, or train the individual in the proper use of such devices. A sensory aid specialist or assistive technology specialist may specifically target the computer access needs or address electronic means for print reading. The rehabilitation engineer addresses those aspects of the job involving such technical matters as computer interface, and focuses on mechanical, optical, lighting, or positioning as they relate to the individual. And the rehabilitation counselor, as the individual who is the employer's primary contact or employee advocate, generally coordinates the activities of the various team members. It is useful to think functionally about these activities, rather than by profession, because not all counselors will have access to this full range of specialized personnel.

In short, job modifications must be considered with the overall experience in mind—with regard to not only specific task accomplishment, but with respect to the individual and the intent to establish a scheme to accomplish job duties expediently. If an optical character recognition (OCR) system or page scanner can accomplish required reading or text input tasks, it may be a cost-beneficial solution, and one that provides greater efficiency, effectiveness, and convenience for the worker, in addition to ensuring privacy and independence. All of these factors are vitally important considerations in evaluating job modifications.

Communication with Employers. Communication with the employer must be seen as an absolutely essential responsibility of the rehabilitation professional or placement specialist, particularly in terms of costs associated with job modification. A Job Accommodation Network evaluation (tabulated from October 1992 to September 1996) involving 646 employers, however, reported that 20 percent of job accommodations cost the employer nothing at all, 51 percent cost less than $500, and only 12 percent cost more than $2,000.

Another aspect of communication relates to the type of accommodation. For example, an individual with a visual impairment who uses magnifiers to read print will have no effect on the working environment. On the other hand, if a computer access modification, job restructuring, or other systemic change is required, the employer must understand the intended modifications. Depending on the size and nature of the organization, this may involve many levels and types of personnel (Moyer, 1986).

The more technical the subject matter, the greater the need for "specialist to specialist" communication. To ensure success, an electronic device specialist must communicate with a computer systems specialist on-site regarding the design of a computer access solution. Moreover, the employer must understand the requirement for ongoing communication concerning changes in the computer environment as well. For example, a human resource specialist was hired by a medium-sized business that had recently introduced a corporate intranet. Personnel-related information, such as corporate policies and descriptions of health benefits, were made available to employees through this internal computer network. However, navigation through the system depended on the selection of graphic images with the click of a mouse. During a meeting with the information systems staff who maintained the intranet, it was determined that if the graphic im-

Effective rehabilitation counseling can facilitate successful employer-employee interactions. Here a supervisor provides focused, positive feedback.

ages were labeled properly, the employee with a visual impairment could access the necessary information with his or her screen reader. As an additional advantage, employees who accessed the site from home noticed that they were able to get information more quickly over the telephone lines if they used the labels rather than the graphics, because they had to wait for the graphics to show up on the screen.

Funding Resources. Although the costs associated with job accommodation or modification may not be the responsibility of the state vocational rehabilitation agency, it is recommended that the competent rehabilitation counselor have a keen awareness of what financial resources, creative funding alternatives, and cost-sharing strategies may exist for those individuals outside the purview of the state-federal program. Mendelsohn (1987), in the preface to his landmark resource guide titled *Financing Adaptive Technology,* noted that the biggest barrier to the widespread use of computer access equipment is cost. He amassed numerous funding choices, presenting a comprehensive reference for rehabilitation counselors. Additional funding methods, including private insurance reimbursement and revolving loan funds, are outlined in two resource guides edited by Reeb (1987a, 1987b).

SUMMARY

The hiring process ultimately results in a decision-maker concluding that a particular individual has the necessary skills (e.g., technical and interpersonal) to succeed, in addition to a belief that a specific individual is the best qualified and the best "match" for that job out of all the other applicants. Depending on the type of business and type of position, the decision-maker may be the owner of the business, a unit supervisor, a personnel interviewer, or sometimes several different people. Because of the numerous ways that hiring decisions are made, the issue of educating employers is a challenge for rehabilitation professionals who need to provide general information regarding blindness and people who are blind, and information regarding specific applicants. Above all else, rehabilitation professionals are urged to understand the employer's needs and view the employer as an entity that could benefit from the rehabilitation professional's services.

To achieve the maximum effect in interacting with and informing employers about the overall goals of matching skills and interests of qualified applicants with opportunities for employment in the community, rehabilitation professionals are encouraged to be well informed about the "big picture" in that community. It is recommended that the rehabilitation professional also be able to respond to that marketplace by providing for "task analyses" of identified positions to ensure that candidate(s) being referred can succeed. Additional tools that the rehabilitation professional can employ to promote placement outcomes are informational interviews and internships. These tools may encourage employers to interact with a candidate without imposing an expectation on an employer that a hiring decision must be made. The careful use of other approaches allows the employer and the consumer to assess whether the opportunity is a good match between the person's skills and the employer's needs. The use of these tools can also significantly enhance the success of the rehabilitation professional in serving clients with visual impairments, and employers.

One of the services that rehabilitation professionals provide to employers and individuals with visual impairments is consultation on job modification. In considering possible modifications of a job or work station, the rehabilitation professional must consider such factors as function, adaptability, availability, cost maintainability, comparability, and acceptability. A wide variety of professionals are often necessary to achieve a successful job modification and accommodation. Ultimately, however, rehabilitation occurs through the motivation, effort, and will of the client. All professional service providers are advised to recognize this fact and offer such services in the spirit that holds personal dignity and individual control as the fundamental tenet upon which all else is based.

In the end, job accommodations and modifications are not cookbook methodologies. The skilled rehabilitation counselor must have a working knowledge of specific functional problems encountered by workers with visual impairments across the employment spectrum. It is recommended that the rehabilitation professional also be able to relate to the employer's perspective and organizational needs, while anticipating and overcoming unspoken concerns. Finally, it is advised that the counselor be able to anticipate the variety of costs involved with various types of modifications, and be able to navigate the diverse systems that provide payment.

Constructing and maintaining relationships with employers—assisting in job development, job retention, and job accommodation—are vital, but they are not the only services rehabilitation counselors are called on to provide to individuals with visual impairments. Rehabilitation is a goal-directed but many-faceted process. Through cooperation and mutual understanding, counselors can provide clients with appropriate services and help them make the most of their employability, independence, and participation in the community and in the workplace (Jenkins, Patterson, & Szymanski, 1992). The competitive employment and self-sufficiency of individuals who are blind or visually impaired are the primary goals of vocational rehabilitation counselors, who can play a central role in helping people pursue and resume independent, satisfying lives. Through sensitivity to the needs of the individual client, an understanding of community and other resources, and an appreciation of the importance of the activities of all members of the rehabilitation team, counselors can make a major contribution to the well-being of individuals who are blind or visually impaired.

LEARNING ACTIVITIES

1. Acquire a greater appreciation for the diversity of employers in your area by reviewing directories of businesses in the state that are available in the public or university library. Do an informal sampling of several pages of each directory to get a sense of the sizes (by

numbers of employees and sales volume), types, and distribution of businesses within the state. Compare your sampling results with U.S. Bureau of Labor statistics for the same state.

2. What employer "objections" are you most likely to encounter? Prepare a mock brochure that might be effective in addressing employers' objections and in reinforcing the positive experiences that some employers have in regard to hiring people with disabilities.
3. Contact the local Chamber of Commerce or a personnel management association group and ask them to provide you with information regarding upcoming ADA training programs. Seek permission to attend such programs to gain a better appreciation for how businesses receive and respond to such information.
4. A receptionist position for a large manufacturing firm was evaluated for its possibilities as an employment site for an individual with a visual impairment. The receptionist's desk faced a large glass wall. The receptionist was required to direct visitors, answer the multiple line telephone system, and take messages. Discuss the potential problems and possible solutions presented by this job setting.
5. An inside salesperson for an electronics company was required to utilize both print and electronic databases and converse with customers while accessing information from an electronic database. Discuss possible solutions to the problems presented by this position.
6. A large federal agency is considering hiring individuals with visual impairments to work as information specialists. The agency is converting its computer system nationwide simultaneously with this consideration. What advice would you give them concerning factors that should be evaluated to facilitate their interest in hiring workers with visual impairments? What federal laws might you cite in your discussions?
7. A state university is converting their stenographic pool through the installation of word processing equipment. A transcriptionist who is blind will be affected by this conversion. Design an optimum job placement team including personnel from both the university and the rehabilitation field.
8. A woman who is visually impaired is seeking a position in real estate that requires independent travel in a wide geographic area, the use of print documents and a computerized database, and evening and weekend travel to prospective buyer's and seller's homes. Discuss potential startup and ongoing costs that may be anticipated to accomplish this individual's vocational goal. Indicate who might be financially responsible for these costs.
9. A hospital laundry worker with a high degree of photophobia had increasing difficulty with the glare caused by the fluorescent fixtures in the hospital laundry. The hospital was not willing to alter the lighting to accommodate the individual's need. The individual's job is in jeopardy. What modifications might be undertaken to address these needs and whose responsibility would they be?

References
Appendixes
Glossary
Resources
Index

REFERENCES

Abramson, L., Metalsky, G., & Alloy, L. (1989). Hopelessness depression: A theory-based sub-type of depression. *Psychological Review, 96,* 358–372.

Abramson, L., Seligman, M., & Teasdale, J. (1978). Learned helplessness in humans: Critique and reformation. *Journal of Abnormal Psychology, 87,* 49–74.

Adler, P. (1986). New technologies, new skills. *California Management Review, 29,* 9–27.

AFB Fact Sheet (1997). Facts about aging and vision loss.

Ainlay, S. (1981). *Phenomenological study of the elderly blind.* Unpublished doctoral dissertation, Brandeis University, Waltham, MA.

Albright, L. (1980). *Strategies for assessing students' present levels of performance.* Urbana-Champaign: University of Illinois.

Alexander, M., & Bauer, R. (1988). Cerebral palsy. In V. Van Hasselt, P. Strain, & M. Hersen (Eds.), *Handbook of developmental and physical disabilities* (pp. 215–226). New York: Pergamon.

Allman, C. (1991). A study of nine state residential schools serving sensory impaired children. Florida State Legislative Study.

Altman, J. (1996). Point/counterpoint: Fitting the white cane to the real world. *Journal of Visual Impairment & Blindness, 90,* 292–293.

American Academy of Ophthalmology. (1984). *Cataract: Clouding the lens of sight.* San Francisco: Author.

American Foundation for the Blind. (1997). *AFB directory of services for blind and visually impaired persons in the United States and Canada* (25th ed.). New York: Author.

American Printing House for the Blind 1963 Registry. (1963). Louisville, KY: Author.

American Printing House for the Blind. (1988). *Reaching out since 1858: One hundred nineteenth annual report of the American Printing House for the Blind for the year ended June 30th, 1987.* Louisville, KY: Author.

American Printing House for the Blind (1996). Distribution of federal quota based on the January 2, 1996 registration of eligible students. Louisville, KY: Author.

American Psychiatric Association (1994). *Diagnostic and statistical manual of mental disorders* (4th ed.). Washington, DC: Author.

Anand, S., & Guha, S. (1986). Assessment of performance of blind center lathe operators. *Journal of Visual Impairment & Blindness, 80,* 946–949.

Anastasi, A. (1988). *Psychological testing* (6th ed.). New York: Macmillan.

Anthony, W. (1984). Societal rehabilitation: Changing society's attitudes toward the physically and mentally disabled. In R. Marinelli & Dell Orto (Eds.), *The psychological and social impact of physical disability* (pp. 193–203). New York: Springer.

Apter, D. (1992). A successful competitive/supported employment program for people with severe visual disabilities. *Journal of Vocational Rehabilitation, 2*(1), 21–27.

Arbeiter, S., Schnerbeck, F., Aslanian, C., & Bricknell, H. (1976). *Career transitions: The demands for counseling* (Vols. I, II). New York: College Entrance Examination Board and Policy Studies in Education.

Asbury, C., Walker, S., Belgrave, F., Maholmes, V., & Green, L. (1994). Psychosocial, cultural, and accessibility factors associated with participation of African Americans in rehabilitation. *Rehabilitation Psychology, 39,* 113–121.

Asch, A., & Sachs, L. (1983). Lives without, lives within: Autobiographies of blind women and men. *Journal of Visual Impairment & Blindness, 77,* 241–246.

Asenjo, J. (1975). *Rehabilitation teaching for the blind and visually impaired: The state of the art, 1975.* New York: American Foundation for the Blind.

Association for Education and Rehabilitation of the Blind and Visually Impaired. (1990). *Rehabilitation teaching university personnel preparation guidelines.* Washington, DC: Author.

Astin, H. S. (1984). The meaning of work in women's lives: A sociopsychological model of career choice and work behavior. *Counseling Pschologist, 12,* 117–126.

Atkins, B. (1982). Women as members of special populations in rehabilitation. In L. Perlman & K. Arneson (Eds.), *Women and rehabilitation of disabled persons* (pp. 38–46). Alexandria, VA: National Rehabilitation Association.

Attmore, M. (1990). *Career perspectives: Interviews with blind and visually impaired professionals.* New York: American Foundation for the Blind.

Avery, C. (1987). Challenges and choices—the changing nature of the Randolph–Sheppard Program. *American Rehabilitation, 13*(1), 6–9; 29–31.

Ayers, G. (1971). Making vocational evaluation relevant to our clients: The challenge of the disadvantaged. *Rehabilitation Literature, 32*(9) 258–262.

Azrin, N. H., & Besalel, V. A. (1980). *Job club counselor's manual: A behavioral approach to vocational counseling.* Austin, TX: PRO-ED.

Azrin, N. H., & Philip, R. (1979). The job club method for the job handicapped: A comparative outcome study. *Rehabilitation Counseling Bulletin,* 144–155.

Azrin, N. H., Flores, T., & Kaplan, S. (1975). Job-finding club: A group-assisted program for obtaining employment. *Behavior Research and Therapy, 13,* 17–27.

Babbie, E. (1975). *The practice of social research.* Belmont, CA: Wadsworth.

Bader, J. (1986). Socioeconomic aspects of aging. In A. Rosenbloom & M. Morgan (Eds.), *Vision and aging: General and clinical perspectives* (pp. 51–61). New York: Professional Press Books.

Bagley, M. (1985). Service providers assessment of the career development needs of blind and visually impaired students and rehabilitation clients and the resources available to meet those needs. *Journal of Visual Impairment & Blindness 79*(10), 434–443.

Bailey, B., & Head, D. (1993). Providing O&M services to children and youth with severe multiple disabilities. *RE:view, 25,* 57–66.

Bailey, I., & Hall, A. (1990). *Visual impairment: An overview.* New York: American Foundation for the Blind.

Baker, D. (1993). From old wisdom to future trends. *Journal of Visual Impairment & Blindness, 87,* 183–185.

Baker, P. (1987). Serving minority clientele. *Journal of Visual Impairment & Blindness, 81,* 145–146.

Baker, S. (1993). Teamwork between the healthcare community and the blind rehabilitation system. *Journal of Visual Impairment & Blindness, 87,* 349–351.

Baldwin, V. (1991). Understanding the deaf-blind census. *TRACES Newsletter, 1*(2), 1–4.

Bandouveres, E., Kukish, P., & Giers, P. (1981). Experimenting with light in a manual skills shop. *Journal of Visual Impairment & Blindness, 75,* 222–223.

Bandura, A. (1977). Self-efficacy: Toward a unifying theory of behavioral change. *Psychological Review, 84,* 191–215.

Barker, J. (1982). Women as leaders in the field of rehabilitation. In L. Perlman & K. Arneson (Eds.),. *Women and rehabilitation of disabled persons* (pp. 47–61). Alexandria, VA: National Rehabilitation Association.

Barker, S., White, P., Reardon, R., & Johnson, P. (1980). An evaluation of the effectiveness of an adaptation of the self-directed search for use by the blind. *Rehabilitation Counseling Bulletin, 23*(3), 177–182.

Barraga, N. (1964). *Increased visual behavior in low vision children.* New York: American Foundation for the Blind.

Barrett, S. (1987). Trends and issues in developing community living programs for young adults who are deaf-blind and profoundly handicapped. In A. Covert & B. Fredericks (Eds.), *Transition for persons with deaf-blindness and other profound handicaps* (pp. 39–51). Monmouth, OR: Teaching Research Publications.

Barrett, S. (1988, June). *Current issues and future trends in services to persons with deaf-blindness.* Paper presented at the 12th annual convention of the American Association of the Deaf-Blind. Baton Rouge, LA.

Barron, S. (1973). *Cause of blindness and its impact on adjustment.* Unpublished doctoral dissertation, City University of New York.

Bates, P., Morrow, S., Pancsofar, E., & Sedlak, R. (1984). The effect of functional vs. non-functional activities on attitudes/expectations of non-handicapped college students: What they see is what we get. *Journal of the Association for Persons with Severe Handicaps, 9,* 73–78.

Bauman, M. (1968). *A report and a reprint: Tests used in the psychological evaluation of blind and visually handicapped persons and a manual for norms for tests used in counseling blind persons.* Washington, DC: American Association of Workers for the Blind.

Bauman, M. (1973). Psychological and educational assessment. In B. Lowenfeld (Ed.), *The visually handicapped child in school* (pp. 93–116). New York: John Day.

Bauman, M. (1975). Guided vocational choice. *The New Outlook for the Blind, 69,* 354–360.

Bauman, M. (1976). Psychological evaluation of the blind client. In B. Bolton (Ed.), *Handbook of measurement and evaluation in rehabilitation* (pp. 249–268). Baltimore: University Park Press.

Beach, J., Robinet, J., & Hakim-Larsen, J. (1995). Self-esteem and independent living skills of adults with visual impairments. *Journal of Visual Impairment & Blindness, 89,* 531–540.

Beattie, P. (1991). Technology on the job. *Technology and Disability, 1*(1), 89–91.

Beck, R., Marr, K., & Taricone, P. (1991). Identifying and treating clients with physical disabilities who have substance abuse problems. *Rehabilitation Education, 5,* 131–138.

Becker, R. (1981). *Revised reading-free vocational interest inventory.* Columbus, OH: Elbern Publications.

Beebe, P., & Karan, O. (1986). A methodology for a community-based vocational program for adults. In R. Horner, L. Meyer, & H. Fredericks (Eds.), *Education of learners with severe handicaps: Exemplary service strategies* (pp. 3–28). Baltimore: Paul H. Brookes.

Beliveau-Tobey, M., & De l'Aune, W. (1990). *Identification of roles and functions of orientation and mobility specialists and rehabilitation teachers.* Mississippi State, MS: Rehabilitation Research and Training Center on Blindness and Low Vision.

Bellamy, G. (1985). Transition progress. *OSERS News in Print 1*(1), 11.

Benedict, R., & Ganikos, M. (1981). Coming to terms with ageism in rehabilitation. *Journal of Rehabilitation, 47*(4), 10–18.

Bennett, E., & Eklund, S. (1983a). Vision changes, intelligence, and aging: Part 1. *Educational Gerontology, 9,* 435–442.

Bennett, E., & Eklund, S. (1983b). Vision changes, intelligence, and aging: Part 2. *Educational Gerontology, 9,* 255–278.

Berg, W., & Wacker, D. (1989). Evaluation of tactile prompts with a student who is deaf, blind, and mentally retarded. *Journal of Applied Behavior Analysis, 22,* 93–99.

Berkow, R. & Fletcher, A. (Eds.) (1992). *The Merck manual of diagnosis and therapy* (16th ed.). Rahway, NJ: Merck Research Laboratories.

Berkowitz, K., Bernbaum, M., Bryant, E., Cleary, M., Davis, J., Evers, C., Kiger, D., Koenig, P., Luxton, L., Martin, R., Petzinger, R., Ponchillia, S., Schultz, J., Taft, S., Teasley, M., Thom, S., & Williams, A. (1993). Guidelines for the practice of adaptive diabetes education for visually impaired persons. *Journal of Visual Impairment & Blindness, 87,* 378–382.

Berkowitz, M. (1980). *Work disincentives.* Falls Church, VA: Institute for Informational Studies.

Bernard, H. (1972). *Psychology of learning and teaching* (3rd Ed.). New York: McGraw-Hill.

Best, A. B., & Corn, A. L. (1993). The management of low vision in children: Report of the 1992 World Health Organization Consultation. *Journal of Visual Impairment & Blindness, 87,* 307–309.

Bina, M. (1993). Do myths associated with schools for students who are blind negatively affect placement decisions? *Journal of Visual Impairment & Blindness, 87,* 213–215.

Bishop, V. (1971). *Teaching the visually limited child.* Springfield, Ill: Charles C. Thomas.

Bishop, V. (1987). Religion and blindness: From inheritance to opportunity. *Journal of Visual Impairment & Blindness, 81,* 256–259.

Blasch, B., Long, R., & Griffin-Shirley, N. (1989). Results of a national survey of electronic travel aid use. *Journal of Visual Impairment & Blindness, 83,* 449–453.

Blau, P., Gustad, J., Jessor, R., Pannes, H., & Wilcock, R. (1956). Occupational Choice: A conceptual framework. *Industrial Labor Relations* (rev.) (pp. 531–543).

Blaxall, M., & Reagan, B. (1976). *Women and the workplace.* Chicago: University of Chicago Press.

Bledsoe, C. (1980). Originators of orientation and mobility training. In R. Welsh & B. Blasch (Eds.), *Foundations of orientation and mobility* (pp. 581–624). New York: American Foundation for the Blind.

Bobash, S. R. (1988). Pre-cane mobility devices. *Journal of Visual Impairment & Blindness, 82,* 338–339.

Boerner, L. A. (1994). *Job seeking skills instructor's manual.* Menomonie, WI: University of Wisconsin—Stout.

Bolander, A., & Bolander, D. (1992). *The new Webster's medical dictionary.* Hartford, CT: Lewtan Line.

Bolles, R. (1997). *What color is your parachute?* Berkeley, CA: Ten Speed Press.

Bolton, B. (1975). Preparing deaf youth for employment. *Journal of Rehabilitation of the Deaf, 9,* 11–15.

Botterbusch, K. (1976). *The use of psychological tests with individuals who are severely disabled.* Menomonie: University of Wisconsin—Stout, Materials Development Center, Stout Vocational Rehabilitation Institute.

Botterbusch, K. (1978a). *A guide to job site evaluation.* Menomonie: University of Wisconsin—Stout, Materials Development Center, Stout Vocational Rehabilitation Institute.

Botterbusch, K. (1978b). *Psychological testing in vocational evaluation.* Menomonie: University of Wisconsin—Stout, Materials Development Center, Stout Vocational Rehabilitation Institute.

Botterbusch, K. (1983). *Short-term vocational evaluation.* Menomonie: University of Wisconsin—Stout, Materials Development Center.

Bouvier, L. & Davis, C. (1982). *The future racial composition of the United States.* Washington, DC: Demographic Information Services Center of Population Reference Bureau.

Bowe, F. (1983). *Demography and disability: A chartbook for rehabilitation.* Fayetteville: University of Arkansas Rehabilitation, Research and Training Center.

Bowe, F. (1990). Employment and people with disabilities: Challenge for the nineties. *OSERS News in Print. 3,* 2–6. Washington, DC: U.S. Department of Education.

Bradfield, A. (1992). Environmental assessment and job site modifications for people who are visually impaired. *Journal of Vocational Rehabilitation, 2*(1), 39–45.

Bradfield, A., & Tucker, L. (1988). *Workplace visual functioning assessment for job modification and accommodation.* Mississippi State, MS: Rehabilitation Research and Training Center on Blindness and Low Vision.

Branch, L., Horowitz, A., & Carr, C. (1989). The implications for everyday life of incident self-reported visual decline among people over age 65 living in the community. *The Gerontologist, 29,* 471–480.

Brasher, B. (1993). Providing services to all children with visual impairments in a rural state. *Journal of Visual Impairment & Blindness, 87,* 207–208.

Bray, A. (1989). Attitude change: Another instance of the readiness myth? *Newsletter of the Association for Persons with Severe Handicaps, 15*(9), 7.

Brown, F. (1987). Meaningful assessment of people with severe and profound handicaps. In M. Snell (Ed.), *Systematic instruction of persons with severe handicaps* (3rd ed., pp. 38–63). Columbus, OH: Merrill.

Bruyere, S. (1994). Editor's introduction and overview. *Rehabilitation Education, 8,* 3–8.

Bryant, E., & Vaughan, C. (1993). A peer support network for blind people with diabetes. *Journal of Visual Impairment & Blindness, 87,* 377.

Bryant, E., & Cobb, A. (Eds.) (1997). *Serving individuals with diabetes who are blind or visually impaired: A resource guide for vocational rehabilitation counselors.* Mississippi State, MS: Rehabilitation Research and Training Center on Blindness and Low Vision.

Buehler, C. (1933). *Der menschliche lebenslauf als psychològisches problem.* Leipzig: Hirzel.

Byers-Lang, R. (1984). Peer counselors, network builders for elderly persons. *Journal of Visual Impairment and Blindness, 78,* 193–197.

Campbell, R., & Cellini, J. (1981). A diagnostic taxonomy of adult career problems. *Journal of Vocational Behavior, 9,* 105–118.

Carkhuff, R. (1969). *Helping and human relations.* New York: Holt, Rinehart & Winston.

Carkhuff, R. (1993). *The art of helping VII.* Amherst, MA: Human Resource Development Press.

Carkhuff, R., & Berenson, B. (1977). *Beyond counseling and therapy* (2nd ed.). New York: Holt, Rinehart & Winston.

Carrick, M., & Bibb, T. (1982). Disabled women and access to benefits and services. In L. Perlman & K. Arneson (Eds.), *Women and rehabilitation of disabled persons* (pp. 28–37). Alexandria, VA: National Rehabilitation Association.

Carroll, T. (1961). *Blindness: What it is, what it does, and how to live with it.* Boston: Little, Brown.

Chadsey-Rusch, J., Gonzales, P., Tines, J., & Johnson, J. (1989). Social ecology of the workplace: Contextual variables affecting social interactions of employees with and without mental retardation. *American Journal of Mental Retardation, 94,* 141–151.

Chalkley, T. (1982). *Your eyes: A book for paramedical personnel and the lay reader.* Springfield, IL: Charles C. Thomas.

Chase, P. (1988, February). *Client assessment.* Paper presented at the midwinter meeting of the Region IV NCRE, Atlanta.

Chen, D., & Dote-Kwan, J. (1995). *Starting points: Instructional practices for young children whose multiple disabilities include visual impairments.* Los Angeles: Blind Children's Center.

Cherry, L. (1993). Institute on alcohol, drugs, and disability: From grassroots activity to systems changes. In A. Heinemann (Ed.), *Substance abuse & physical disability* (pp. 181–216). New York: Haworth.

Chess, S. (1987). Psychosocial problems and coping strategies of multihandicapped children and their families. In B. Heller, L. Flohr, & L. Zegans (Eds.), *Psychosocial interventions with sensorially disabled persons* (pp. 131–148). New York: Grune & Stratton.

Chinn, P. (1979). The exceptional minority child: Issues and some answers. *Exceptional Children, 7,* 532–536.

Cholden, L. (1958). *A psychiatrist works with blindness: Selected papers.* New York: American Foundation for the Blind.

Chute, P., & Nevins, M. (1995). Cochlear implants in people who are deaf-blind. *Journal of Visual Impairment & Blindness, 89,* 297–301.

Clayman, C. (Ed.). (1989). *The American Medical Association encyclopedia of medicine.* New York: Random House.

Clayton, I. (1973). Career opportunities for visually handicapped persons in Maryland. *The New Outlook for the Blind, 67,* 210–215.

Cleary, M. (Ed.). (1994). *Diabetes and visual impairment: An educator's resource guide.* Chicago: The American Association of Diabetes Educators Education and Research Foundation.

Cleary, M., & Hamilton, J. (1993). Nonvisual adaptive devices for measuring insulin. *Journal of Visual Impairment & Blindness, 87,* 345–347.

Coche, E. (1992). Housing modifications for persons who are blind or visually impaired. *RE:view, 24,* 23–28.

Cohen, A., & Rein, L. (1992). The effect of head trauma on the visual system: The doctor of optometry as a member of the rehabilitation team. *Journal of the American Optometric Association, 63,* 530–536.

Colbert, J., Kalish, R., & Chang, P. (1973). Two psychological portals of entry for disadvantaged groups. *Rehabilitation Literature, 34*(7), 194–202.

Colenbrander, A. (1976). *Classification of visual performance.* Unpublished manuscript. San Francisco: Pacific Medical Center.

Colenbrander, A. (1977). Dimensions of visual performance. *Transactions of the American Academy of Ophthalmology & Otolaryngology,* 83(2), 332–7.

Collignon, F. (1986). *The role of reasonable accommodation in employing disabled persons in private industry.* Disability and the Labor Market: Economic Problems, Policies and Programs. Ithaca, NY: Cornell University (ILR Press).

COMSTAC report: Standards for strengthened services. (1966). F. Koestler (Ed.). New York: National Accreditation Council for Agencies Serving the Blind and Visually Handicapped.

Connors, R. Diabetes: Some physiological considerations for the blind person. *Aids and Appliance Review, 6,* 1–6.

Corey, G. (1991). *Theory and practice of counseling and psychotherapy.* (4th ed.) Pacific Grove, CA: Brooks/Cole.

Corn, A. L. (1986). Low vision and visual efficiency. In G. Scholl (Ed.), *Foundations of education for blind and visually handicapped children and youth: Theory and practice* (pp. 99–117). New York: American Foundation for the Blind.

Corn, A. L. (1988). Socialization and the child with low vision. *Awareness* (First quarter, pp. 3–7). Austin, TX.: National Association for Parents of the Blind and Visually Impaired.

Corn, A. L., & Koenig, A. J. (Eds.). (1996). *Foundations of low vision: Clinical and functional perspectives.* New York: AFB Press.

Corn, A. L., & Sacks, S. (1994). The impact of nondriving on adults with visual impairments. *Journal of Visual Impairment & Blindness, 88,* 53–68.

Corn, A. L., & Bishop, V. (1985). Occupational interests of visually handicapped secondary students. *Journal of Visual Impairment & Blindness, 79,* 475–478.

Corn, A. L., Hatlen, P., Huebner, K. M., Ryan, F., & Siller, M. A. (1995). *The national agenda for the education of children and youths with visual impairments, including those with multiple disabilities.* New York: AFB Press.

Corn, A. L., Hatlen, P., Huebner, K. M., Ryan, F., & Siller, M. A. (1996). Developing the national agenda for the education of children and youths with visual impairments, including those with multiple disabilities. *RE: view, 28,* 5–17.

Corn A. L., Muscella D., Cannon G., & Shepler, R. (1985). Perceived barriers to employment for visually impaired women: A preliminary study. *Journal of Visual Impairment & Blindness, 79,* 458–461.

Correa, V. (1987). Working with Hispanic parents of visually impaired children: Cultural implications. *Journal of Visual Impairment & Blindness, 81*(6), 260–264.

Correa, V., & Kief, E. (1986). Ethnic minority visually impaired students and clients: Implications for education and rehabilitation. In *Yearbook of the association for education and rehabilitation of the blind and visually impaired* (Volume 4, pp. 33–39). Washington, DC: AERBVI.

Cosgrove, E. (1961). *Home teachers of the adult blind: Who they are, what they could do, and what would enable them to do it.* Washington, DC: American Association of Workers for the Blind.

Courtney, A., & Halton, I. (1993). Comment: Orientation and mobility assistants. *Journal of Visual Impairment & Blindness, 87,* 3.

Cowen, E., Underberg, R., Verrillo, R. & Benham, F. (1961). *Adjustment to visual disability in adolescence.* New York: American Foundation for the Blind.

Crews, J. (1991). Strategic planning and independent living for elders who are blind. *Journal of Visual Impairment & Blindness, 85,* 52–57.

Crews, J., & Frey, W. (1993). Family concerns and older people who are blind. *Journal of Visual Impairment & Blindness, 87,* 6–13.

Crews, J., & Luxton, L. (1992). Rehabilitation teaching for older adults. In A. L. Orr (Ed.), *Vision and aging: Crossroads for service delivery* (pp. 233–253). New York: American Foundation for the Blind.

Crews, J., Frey, W., & Peterson, P. (1987). Independent living for the handicapped elderly community: A national view. *Journal of Visual Impairment & Blindness, 81,* 305–308.

Crews, N. (1976). *Technology for independent living II.* Washington, DC: American Association for the Advancement of Science.

Crites, J. (1976). A comprehensive model of career development in early adulthood. *Journal of Vocational Behavior, 9,* 105–118.

Crofton, M. (1985). Statement before the Select Committee on Aging. U.S. House of Representatives, Washington, DC.

Crudden, A. (1997). Congenital and adventitious vision loss: A comparison based on postemployment factors. (Unpublished doctoral dissertation, Mississippi State University, Mississippi State.)

Cull, J., & Hutchinson, J. (1972). Techniques of counseling in the rehabilitation process. In J. Cull & R. Hardy (Eds.), *Vocational rehabilitation: Profession and process* (pp. 212–226). Springfield, IL: Charles C. Thomas.

Cunningham, J. (1969). *The cluster concept and its curricular implications.* (Center Monograph No. 4.) Raleigh, NC: Center for Occupational Education.

Curry, S. (1993). A model assessment program. *Journal of Visual Impairment & Blindness, 87,* 190–193.

Dale, B. (1992). Issues in traumatic blindness. *Journal of Visual Impairment & Blindness, 86,* 140–143.

Daniels, J. (1978). *Job readiness clinic final report.* Unpublished Department of Education grant #44-P-81084.

Davidson, T. (1981). Things are getting better all the time? Mainstreaming, integration and vocational development for the 1980s. *AAWB Blindness Annual 1980–81, 15,* 81–95.

Degouvea, N. (1977). Disabled women around the world suffer from multiple discrimination. *Rehabilitation World, 2*(4), 18.

DeLoach, C., & Greer, B. (1981). *Adjustment to severe physical disability: A metamorphosis.* New York: McGraw-Hill.

Demographics update. Blind persons who use dog guides. (1994a). *Journal of Visual Impairment & Blindness, JVIB News Service, 88*(1), 4.

Demographics update. Use of "white" ("long") canes. (1994b). *Journal of Visual Impairment & Blindness, JVIB News Service, 88*(1), 4–5.

Demographics update. Visual impairment, employment, and computer use. (1995a). *Journal of Visual Impairment & Blindness, JVIB News Service Part II, 89*(1), 1.

Demographics update. Alternate estimate of the number of guide dog users. (1995b). *Journal of Visual Impairment & Blindness, JVIB News Service, 89*(2), 4.

DeMott, R. (1993). New and future roles for residential schools. *Journal of Visual Impairment & Blindness,* 87, 224–226.

Dennis, W. (1986). The future of work for disabled people: Employment and the new technology. New York: American Foundation for the Blind.

DeSantis, V., & Schein, J. (1986). Blindness statistics (part 2): Blindness registers in the United States. *Journal of Visual Impairment & Blindness, 80,* 570.

DeVito, J. A. (1995). *The interpersonal communication book* (7th ed.) New York: HarperCollins.

Dial, J., Gezger, C., Massey, T., Gray, S., Hull, J. & Chan, F. (1992). *Comprehensive vocational evaluation system: A systematic approach to vocational, educational and neuropsychological assessment of visually impaired and blind.* Dallas: McCarron–Dial Systems.

Dick, M., Moulin, L., Pelligrini, S., & Traub, J. (1988). *Building bridges: Strategies for parent/professional collaboration training for transition.* Sacramento: California State Department of Education.

Dickey, T. (1975). Meeting the vocational needs of the older blind person. *New Outlook for the Blind, 69,* 218–225.

Dickinson, R. (1956). The discipline of home teaching. *New Outook for the Blind, 50,* 393–400.

Dickman, I. (1988). *Creating jobs/changing lives—the Wagner–O'Day act and the workshops for the blind 1966–1988.* Wayne, N.J.: National Industries for the Blind.

Dixon, J. M. (1983). Attitudinal barriers and strategies for overcoming them. *Journal of Visual Impairment & Blindness,* 77, 290–292.

Dodds, A., & Davis, D. (1989). Assessment and training of low vision clients for mobility. *Journal of Visual Impairment & Blindness, 83,* 449–453.

Dodds, A., Howarth, C., & Carter, D. (1982). The mental maps of the blind: The role of previous visual experience. *Journal of Visual Impairment & Blindness, 76,* 5–12.

Dodds, A., Ferguson, E., Ng, L., Flannigan, H., Hawes, G., & Yates, L. (1994). The concept of adjustment: A structured model. *Journal of Visual Impairment & Blindness, 88,* 487–497.

Dodge, L. (1979). Sexuality and the blind disabled. *Sexuality and Disability, 2,* 200–205.

Dods, J. (1993). Two exercise programs for people with diabetes and visual impairment. *Journal of Visual Impairment & Blindness, 87,* 365–367.

Downing, J., Shafer, M., Brahm-Levy, A., & Frantz, M. (1992). Supported employment for individuals with dual sensory impairments and mental retardation: Current practice and future challenges. *Journal of Vocational Rehabilitation, 2*(1), 28–38.

Dumas, A., & Sadowsky, A. (1984). A family training program for adventitiously blinded and low vision veterans. *Journal of Visual Impairment & Blindness, 78,* 473–478.

Dunn, D. (1981). Vocational rehabilitation of the older disabled person. *Journal of Rehabilitation, 47*(41), 76–81.

Du Pont, E. I. (1990). *Equal to the task II: 1990 DuPont survey of employment of people with disabilities.* Wilmington, DE: Author.

Dziekan, K., & Okocha, A. (1993). Accessibility of rehabilitation services: Comparison by racial-ethnic status. *Rehabilitation Counseling Bulletin, 36,* 183–189.

Ebener, D. (1992). The influence of negative perceptions of aging on the delivery of rehabilitation services: Implications for rehabilitation counselor education. *Rehabilitation Education, 5,* 335–340.

Edinberg, M. (1985). *Mental health practice with the elderly.* Englewood Cliffs: Prentice Hall.

Editor's Note. (1993). Diabetes breakthrough. *Journal of Visual Impairment & Blindness, 87,* 325.

Ehmer, M. & Needham, W. (1979). *The beliefs about blindness scale.* New Haven: Authors.

Ehmer, M., Needham, W., Del'Aune, W., & Carr, R. (1982, April). *Experience, expertise, and expectation: Three important factors influencing beliefs about blindness.* Paper presented at the Annual Meeting of the Eastern Psychological Association, Baltimore.

Elder, B. (1983). Rehabilitation: The double bind for blind women. *Journal of Visual Impairment & Blindness, 77,* 298–300.

Elmfeldt, G., Wise, C., Bergsten, H., & Olsson, A. (1983). *Adapting work sites for people with disabilities: Ideas from Sweden.* New York: The Swedish Institute for the Handicapped.

Elston, R. (1997). *Vocational evaluation: A screening in or screening out process for persons with disabilities.* Manuscript submitted for publication.

Elston, R., & Housley, W. (1988). Relevancy of Maslow's hierarchy of needs to the vocational evaluation process. *Rehabilitation Education, 2,* 3–4.

Emerson, D. (1981). Facing loss of vision. The response of adults to visual impairment and blindness. *Journal of Visual Impairment & Blindness, 75,* 41–45.

Enzinna, A. J. (1980). Topic 1: The visually impaired amputee. In R. Welsh & B. Blasch (Eds.), *Foundations of orientation and mobility* (pp. 413–459). New York: American Foundation for the Blind.

Erber, N., & Osborn, R. (1994). Perceptions of facial cues by adults with low vision. *Journal of Visual Impairment & Blindness, 88,* 171–175.

Erin, J. (1993a). Inclusion: What do we want it to mean to schools for students with visual disabilities? *Journal of Visual Impairment & Blindness, 87,* 165–168.

Erin, J. (1993b). The road less traveled: New directions for schools for students with visual impairments. *Journal of Visual Impairment & Blindness, 87,* 219–223.

Erin, J.N., & Corn, A. L. (1994). A survey of children's first understanding of being visually impaired. *Journal of Visual Impairment & Blindness, 88,* 132–139.

Erin, J., Corn, A. L., & Wolffe, K. (1993). Learning and study strategies of secondary school students with visual disabilities. *Journal of Visual Impairment & Blindness, 87,* 263–267.

Evans, R., Werkhoven, W., & Fox, H. (1982). Treatment of social isolation and loneliness in a sample of visually impaired elderly persons. *Psychological Reports, 51,* 103–108.

Everson, J. M. (Ed.) (1995 January). *Transition services for youths who are deaf- blind: A "best practices" guide for educators.* New York: The Helen Keller National Center—Technical Assistance Center.

Eye Research Institute of Retina Foundation (1985). Understanding macular disease. *ERI Sundial 11*(3), 2.

Eye Research Institute of Retina Foundation (1988a). An overview of retinal detachment. *ERI Sundial, 14*(3), 2.

Eye Research Institute of Retina Foundation (1988b). Treating glaucoma: Early diagnosis best defense against blindness. *ERI Sundial, 14*(2), 5–6.

Facts about aging and vision loss. (1997). (AFB fact sheet.) New York: AFB Press.

Fairweather J., & Shaver, D. (1991). Making the transition to postsecondary education and training. *Exceptional Children, 57,* 264–270.

Farish, J., & Wen, S. (1994). Effectiveness of an independent living services program for older persons who are blind. *Journal of Visual Impairment & Blindness, 88,* 525–531.

Farmer, L. (1980). Orientation aids. In R. Welsh & B. Blasch (Eds.), *Foundations of orientation and mobility* (pp. 357–412) New York: American Foundation for the Blind.

Faye, E. (1984a). *Clinical low vision.* New York: American Foundation for the Blind.

Faye, E. (1984b). The effect of the eye condition on functional vision. In: E. Faye (Ed.), *Clinical low vision* (2nd ed., pp. 171–196). Boston: Little, Brown.

Federal Register. (1977). #96, p. 42, 479.

Fergeson, R. (1979). *Disability survey 72 disabled and non-disabled: The impact of disability on employment and earnings.* U.S. Department of Health, Education, and Welfare, SSA, SSA Public #13–11717.

Ferrell, K. A. (1979). Orientation and mobility for preschool children: What we have and what we need.

Journal of Visual Impairment & Blindness, 73, 147–150.

Ferrell, K. A. (1985). *Reach out and teach: Meeting the training needs of parents of visually and multiply handicapped young children.* New York: American Foundation for the Blind.

Ferris, A. (1991). Easing a blind student's transition to employment: Suggestions to parents and teachers from a blind person's perspective. *RE:view, 22,* 85–90.

Fesko, S. L., & Temelini, D. (1997). Shared responsibility: Job search practices from consumer and staff perspectives. In F. E. Menz, P. Wehman, J. Eggers, & V. Brooke (Eds.), *Lessons for improving employment of people with disabilities from vocational rehabilitation research* (Sec. 2, pp. 135–160). Menomonie, WI: University of Wisconsin—Stout.

Fillman, R., Leguire, L., & Sheridan, M. (1989). Considerations for serving adolescents with Usher's syndrome. *RE:view, 21,* 19–25.

Fine, M., & Asch, A. (1981). Disabled Women: Sexism without the pedestal. *Journal of Sociology and Social Welfare, 8,* 233–248.

Finnegan, J., Rice, K., & Harris, G. (1993). Teen institute. *Journal of Visual Impairment & Blindness, 87,* 206.

Fiorito, E. (1983a). Choices and chances in the 80s. *Journal of Visual Impairment & Blindness, 77,* 286–288.

Fiorito, E. (1983b). The blind woman of the 80s: Her choices and chances. *American Rehabilitation, 9*(2), 30–32.

Fireison, C. K. (1997). Employment in community rehabilitation programs for persons with vision loss: A comparison of factors associated with educational setting. Mississippi State, MS: *Dissertation Abstracts International.* (In press.)

Flax, M., Golembiewski, D., & McCaulley, B. (1993). *Coping with low vision.* San Diego: Singular Publishing Group.

Flippo, K., & Green, H. (1994). Resources for Americans with Disabilities Act implementation: Business accommodation response teams. *Journal of Vocational Rehabilitation, 4*(3), 183–191.

Foulke, E., & Uhde, T. (1974). Do blind children need sex education? *The New Outlook for the Blind, 68*(5), 193–200, 209.

Fraiberg, S. (1977). *Insights from the Blind.* New York: Basic Books.

Franz, J. (1983). Cognitive development and career retraining in older adults. *Educational Gerontology, 9,* 443–458.

Fraser, K. (1992). Training the low vision patient. *Prob Optom, 4*(1), 72–87.

Freagon, S. (1982). Present and projected services to meet the needs of severely handicapped children [Keynote address]. In *Proceedings of the National Parent Conference on Children Requiring Extensive Special Education Programming.* Washington: U.S. Department of Education, Office of Special Education Programs.

Fredericks, H. (1988). *Part-time work for high school students.* Monmouth, OR: Teaching Research.

Freeman, R. (1987). Psychosocial interventions with visually impaired adolescents and adults. In B. Heller, L. Flohr, & L. Zegans (Eds.), *Psychosocial interventions with sensorially disabled persons* (pp. 153–166). New York: Grune & Stratton.

Freeman, P. & Jose R. (1991). *The art and practice of low vision.* Boston: Butterworth-Heineman.

Friel, T., & Carkhuff, R. (1974). *The art of developing a career.* Amherst, MA: Human Resource Development Press.

Fuqua, D., Rathbun, M., & Gade, E. (1984). A comparison of employer attitudes toward the worker problems of eight types of disabled workers. *Journal of Applied Rehabilitation Counseling, 15*(1), 40–43.

Galvin, J. & Scherer, M. (1996). *Evaluating, selecting, and using appropriate assistive technology.* Gaithersburg, MD: Aspen.

Gandy, M. (1988). The impact of education on the earnings of rehabilitation clients. *Education of the Visually Handicapped, 20,* 13–21.

Gardner, L. (1982). Understanding and helping parents of blind children. *Journal of Visual Impairment & Blindness, 76,* 81–85.

Gast, D., & Wolery, M. (1987). Severe maladaptive behaviors. In M. Snell (Ed.), *Systematic instruction of persons with severe handicaps* (3rd ed., pp. 300–332). Columbus, OH: Merrill.

Gaylord-Ross, R., Lee, M., Johnston, S., Lynch, K., Rosenberg, B., & Goetz, L. (1990). *Supported employment for deaf-blind individuals.* Career Development for Exceptional Individuals. Unpublished monograph. San Francisco: San Francisco State University.

Genesky, S. & Zarit, S. (1986). Low vision care in a clinical setting. In A. Rosenbloom & M. Morgan (Eds.), *Vision and aging: General and clinical perspectives* (pp. 349–362). New York: Professional Press Books.

Genesky, S., Berry, S., Bikson, T., & Bikson, T. (1979). *Visual environmental adaptation problems of the partially sighted: Final report (CPS-100-HEU).* Santa Monica, CA: Santa Monica Hospital Medical Center, Center for the Partially Sighted.

Gerberg, R. (1986). *Robert Gerberg's job changing system: World's fastest way to get a better job* (14th ed.). Kansas City, MO: Andrews, McNeel & Parker.

Geruschat, D. (1993). Guest editorial. *Journal of Visual Impairment & Blindness, 87,* 163–164.

Gianutos, R., Ramsey, G., & Perlin, R. (1988). Rehabilitative optometric services for survivors of acquired brain injury. *Archives of Physical Medicine and Rehabilitation, 69,* 573–578.

Giarratana-Oehler, J. (1976). Personal and professional reactions to blindness from diabetic retinopathy. *New Outlook for the Blind, 70,* 237–239.

Giesen, J., & Ford, K. (1986a). *The elderly blind client: Factors associated with employment outcome, executive summary.* Mississippi State, MS: Rehabilitation Research and Training Center on Blindness and Low Vision.

Giesen, J., & Ford, K. (1986b). *The unsuccessfully closed blind client: Characteristics of a nonemployment outcome.* Mississippi State, MS: Rehabilitation Research and Training Center on Blindness and Low Vision.

Giesen, J., Graves, W., Schmitt, S., Lamb, A., Cook, D., Capps, C., & Boyet, K. (1985). *Predicting work status outcomes of blind/severely visually impaired clients of state rehabilitation agencies.* Mississippi State, MS: Rehabilitation Research and Training Center on Blindness and Low Vision.

Gilbertson, K. (1973). The use of norms in a rehabilitation setting. *Vocational Evaluation and Work Adjustment Bulletin, 6*(2), 16–18.

Ginzberg, E. (1972). Toward a theory of occupational choice: A restatement. *Vocational Guidance Quarterly, 20*(3), 7–17.

Ginzberg, E., Ginzberg, S., Axelrod, S., & Herma, J. (1951). *Occupational choice: An approach to a general theory.* New York: Columbia University Press.

Glow, B. A. (1989). Alcoholism, drugs, and the disabled. In G. W. Lawson & A. W. Lawson (Eds.), *Alcoholism & substance abuse in special populations* (pp. 65–93). Rockville, MD: Aspen.

Goar, A. (1988). Information has been the most valuable thing. *Education of the Visually Handicapped, 20,* 73–74.

Godley, S. (1981). *Employer beliefs regarding employment of the blind.* Unpublished manuscript.

Goffman, E. (1963). *Stigma: Notes on the management of spoiled identity.* Englewood Cliffs, NJ: Prentice Hall.

Gold, M. (1980). *Try another way: Training manual.* Champaign, IL: Research Press.

Golden (1981). Luria–Nebraska Neuropsychological Battery. Los Angeles: Western Psychological Services.

Goldfried, M. & Davidson, G. (1976). *Clinical behavior therapy.* New York: Holt, Rinehart, & Winston.

Goldman, R., Dunham, J., & Dunham, C. (Eds.). (1978). *Disability and rehabilitation handbook.* New York: McGraw-Hill.

Goodman, H. (1985). Serving the elderly blind: A generic approach. *Journal of Gerontological Social Work, 8,* 153–168.

Goodrich, G. (1984). Applications of microcomputers by visually impaired persons. *Journal of Visual Impairment and Blindness, 78,* 408–414.

Goodrich, G. & Mehr, E. (1986). Eccentric viewing training and low vision aids: Current practice and implications of peripheral retinal research. *American Journal of Optometry and Physiological Optics, 63,* 119–26.

Granovetter, M. (1974). *Getting a job: A study of contacts and careers.* Cambridge, MA: Harvard University Press.

Graves, W. (1983a). Rehabilitation research and educational services for blind and visually impaired individuals. *Education of the Visually Handicapped, 14*(4), 126–132.

Graves, W. (1983b). *Career development theory applied to the delivery of services to blind and visually impaired persons.* Proceedings of the MacFarland Seminar. Mississippi State, MS: Rehabilitation Research and Training Center on Blindness and Low Vision.

Graves, W., & Lyon, S. (1985). Career development: Linking education and careers of blind and visually impaired ninth graders. *Journal of Blindness & Visual Impairment, 70*(10), 444–449.

Graves, W., & Maxson, B. J. (1989). Computer access technology: An ecological approach to meeting the needs of people with visual disabilities. *American Rehabilitation, 15*(2), 18–22, 31.

Graves, W., Lyon, S., Marmion, S., & Boyet, K. (1986a). *Career development needs of blind and visually impaired students and youth.* Mississippi State, MS: Rehabilitation Research and Training Center on Blindness and Low Vision.

Graves, W., Lyon, S., Marmion, S., & Boyet, K. (1986b). *Perceptions of teachers, rehabilitation counselors, and rehabilitation administrators of the career development needs of blind and visually impaired students and adults.* Mississippi State, MS: Rehabilitation Research and Training Center on Blindness and Low Vision.

Graves, W., Maxson, J., & McCaa, C. (1988). Assessing the environment of low vision persons: A validation of procedure. *Journal of Visual Impairment & Blindness, 82,* 361–365.

Greenberg, J. (1988). *Of such small differences.* New York: New American Library, Penguin.

Greenberger, E., & Steinberg, L. (1986). *When teenagers work: The psychological and social costs of adolescent employment.* New York: Basic Books.

Greenblum, J. (1979). Effect of rehabilitation on employment and earnings of the disabled: Sociological factors. *Social Security Bulletin, 42,* 11–37.

Greenough, T., Keegan, D., & Ash, D. (1978). Psychological and social adjustment of blind subjects of the 16 PF. *Journal of Clinical Psychology, 34,* 84–87.

Greenwood, R., & Johnson, V. (1985). *Employer concerns regarding workers with disabilities.* Hot Springs: University of Arkansas Research and Training Center on Vocational Rehabilitation.

Gribbons, W., & Lohnes, P. (1982). *Careers in theory and experience: A twenty-year longitudinal study.* Albany: State University of New York Press.

Griffin, S., & Lowry, J. (1989). Supported employment for persons with deaf-blindness and mental retardation. *Journal of Visual Impairment & Blindness, 83,* 495–499.

Griffiths, D., Quinsey, V., & Hingsburger, D. (1989). *Changing inappropriate sexual behavior: A community-based approach for persons with developmental disabilities.* Baltimore: Paul H. Brookes.

Grigg, C., Holtmann, A., & Martin, P. (1970). *Vocational rehabilitation for the disadvantaged.* Lexington, MA: D.C. Heath.

Griggs, N. (1986). *Florida Division of Blind Services case service file report.* Unpublished.

Grossman, H. (Ed.). (1983). *Classification in mental retardation.* Washington: American Association on Mental Deficiency.

Guthrie, D., & Guthrie, R. (1992). *The diabetes sourcebook.* Los Angeles: Lowell House.

Hackett, G., & Betz, N. (1981). A self-efficacy approach to the career development of women. *Journal of Vocational Behavior, 18,* 326–339.

Hall, A., Scholl, G., Swallow, R. (1986). Psychoeducational assessment. In G. T. Scholl (Ed.), *Foundations of education for blind and visually handicapped children and youth: Theory and practice* (pp. 187–214). New York: American Foundation for the Blind.

Hall, E. (1976). *Beyond culture.* Garden City, NY: Anchor/Doubleday.

Halpern, A. (1981). Mental retardation. In W. Stolov & M. Clowers (Eds.), *Handbook of severe disability* (pp. 265–277). Washington, DC: U.S. Department of Education, Rehabilitation Services Administration.

Halpern, A., Lehman, J., Irvin, L., & Heiry, T. (1981). *Contemporary assessment of adaptive behavior for mentally retarded adolescents and adults.* Eugene: University of Oregon, Rehabilitation Research and Training Center.

Hamel, D., & Krumboltz, J. (1982). The agenda ahead: Research priorities. In J. Krumboltz & D. A. Hamel (Eds.), *Assessing career development* (pp. 238–251). Palo Alto, CA: Mayfield.

Handler, B., & Patterson, J. (1995). Driving after brain injury. *Journal of Rehabilitation, 61*(2), 433–49.

Hanley-Maxwell, C., Bordieri, J., & Merz, M. (1996). Supporting placement. In E. Szymanski & R. Parker (Eds.), *Work and disability* (pp. 341–364). Austin, TX: PRO-ED.

Hanley-Maxwell, C., Rusch, F., & Rappaport, J. (1989). A multi-level perspective on community employment problems for adults with mental retardation. *Rehabilitation Counseling Bulletin, 32* 266–277.

Hansen, C. (1975). *Job readiness clinic.* Unpublished Department of Education grant #44-P-81084.

Hanson, T. (1980). The professionalism of rehabilitation teaching. *Journal of Visual Impairment & Blindness, 74,* 161–163.

Hardy, R. (1966). A study of manifest anxiety among blind residential school students using an experimental instrument constructed for the blind. *Dissertations Abstracts, 27,* 3693.

Hardy, R. (1972). Vocational placement. In J. Cull & R. Hardy (Eds.), *Vocational rehabilitation: Profession and process* (pp. 236–255). Springfield, IL: Charles E. Thomas.

Hardy, R., & Cull, J. (1972). *Social and rehabilitation services for the blind.* Springfield, IL: Charles C. Thomas.

Hare, B., Hammill, D., & Crandell, J. (1970). Auditory discrimination ability of visually limited children. *New Outlook for the Blind, 64,* 287–292.

Harkless, L., & Lavery, L. (1992). Diabetic food care: A team approach. *Diabetes Spectrum, 5,* 136–137.

Harley, R. (1963). *Verbalizations among blind children.* Research Series #10. New York: American Foundation for the Blind.

Harley, R., Garcia, M., & Williams, M. (1989). The educational placement of visually impaired children. *Journal of Visual Impairment & Blindness, 83,* 512–517.

Harrell, R., & Strauss, F. (1986). Approaches to increasing assertive behavior and communication skills in blind and visually impaired people. *Journal of Visual Impairment & Blindness, 80,* 794–800.

Harris, L. & Associates. (1986a). *Disabled Americans: Self perceptions.* Washington, DC: International Center for the Disabled.

Harris, L. & Associates. (1986b). *Survey of attitudes toward blindness and blind prevention.* New York: National Society for the Prevention of Blindness.

Harris, L., & Associates. (1987). *The ICD survey II: Employing disabled Americans.* New York: Author.

Harris, L. & Associates. (1994). *N.O.D./Harris survey of Americans with disabilities.* New York: Author.

Hart, V. (1988). Multiply disabled children. In V. Van Hasselt, P. Strain, & M. Hersen (Eds.), *Handbook of developmental and physical disabilities* (pp. 370–383). New York: Pergamon.

Hathaway, S., & McKinley, C. (1970). Minnesota Multiphasic Personality Inventory. Minneapolis, MN: National Computer Systems.

Hatlen, P. (1993). A personal odyssey on schools for blind children. *Journal of Visual Impairment & Blindness, 87,* 171–174.

Hatlen, P. (1996). The core curriculum for blind and visually impaired students, including those with additional disabilities. *RE: view, 28,* 25–32.

Hatlen, P., & Curry, S. (1987). In support of specialized programs for blind and visually impaired children: The impact of vision loss on learning. *Journal of Visual Impairment & Blindness, 81,* 7–13.

Havighurst, R. (1964). Youth in exploration and man emergent. In H. Borrow (Ed.), *Man in a world at work* (pp. 215–236). Boston: Houghton-Mifflin.

Havighurst. R. (1953). *Human development and education.* New York: Longmans.

Havlick, R. (1986). Aging in the eighties, impaired senses for sound and light in persons age 65 years and over, preliminary data from the supplement on aging to the National Health Interview Survey, U.S., January–June, 1984. *Advance Data from Vital Health Statistics (DHHS Publication N. PHS86–1250).* Hyattsville, MD: National Center on Health Statistics.

Havlick, R. (1986). Aging in the eighties, impaired senses for sound and light in persons age 65 years and over. Advance data from vital and health statistics. (No. 125). *Maryland: Public Health Service, 86,* 1250.

Hazekamp, J. & Huebner, K. M. (1989). *Program planning and evaluation for blind and visually impaired students: National guidelines for educational excellence.* New York: American Foundation for the Blind.

Head, D., Maddock, J., Healey, W., & Griffing, B. (1993). A comparative study of residential schools for children with visual impairments: 1985–1990. *Journal of Visual Impairment & Blindness, 87,* 216–218.

Healy, C. C. (1982). Career development: Counseling through the life stages. Boston: Allyn & Bacon.

Heinemann, A. (1993). *Substance abuse & physical disability.* New York: Haworth.

Heinze, T. (1986). Communication skills. In G. T. Scholl (Ed.), *Foundations of education for blind and visually handicapped children and youth: Theory and practice* (pp. 301–314). New York: American Foundation for the Blind.

Helen Keller National Center for Deaf-Blind Youths and Adults (1991). *Annual Report to Congress.*

Hendel, T. (1987). Providing a bilingual rehabilitation program. *Journal of Visual Impairment & Blindness, 81,* 239–43.

Henderly, D., Freeman, W., Causey, D., & Rao, N. (1987). Cytomegalovirus retinitis and response to therapy with ganciclovir. *Ophthalmology, 94,* 425–434.

Herndon, G. (1991). *Analysis of Title VII, Part C Independent Living for the Elderly Blind Grants Fiscal Year 1989–90.* Mississippi State, MS: Rehabilitation Research and Training Center on Blindness and Low Vision.

Herr, E., & Cramer, S. (1984). *Career guidance and counseling through the life span: Systematic approaches* (2nd ed.). Boston: Little, Brown.

Heward, W. (1996). *Exceptional children* (5th ed.). Englewood Cliffs, NJ: Prentice Hall.

Heward, W., & Orlansky, M. (1992). *Exceptional children: An introductory survey of special education* (4th ed.). Columbus, OH: Merrill.

Hiatt, L. (1981). Aging and disability. In N. McClusky & E. Borgatta (Eds.), *Aging and retirement* (pp. 133–152). Beverly Hills: Sage.

Hiatt, L. (1986). The need for innovation: Services and programs for vision-impaired older people. In A. Rosenbloom & M. Morgan (Eds.), *Vision and aging: General and clinical perspectives* (pp. 363–371). New York: Professional Press Books.

Hill, E. (1986). Orientation and mobility. In G. T. Scholl (Ed.), *Foundations of education for blind and visually handicapped children and youth* (pp. 315–340). New York: American Foundation for the Blind.

Hill E., & Bradfield, A. (1984). Electronic travel aids for the blind. *Exceptional Education Quarterly, 4,* 74–89.

Hill, M. & Harley, R. (1984). Orientation and mobility for aged visually impaired persons. *Journal of Visual Impairment & Blindness, 78,* 49–54.

Hill, J., & Morton, M. (1988). Transition programming: Improving vocational outcomes. In L. Sternberg (Ed.), *Educating students with severe or profound handicaps* (2nd ed.), (pp. 439–471). Rockville, MD: Aspen.

Hill, E., & Ponder, P. (1976). Orientation and mobility techniques. New York: American Foundation for the Blind.

Hill, J., Brantner, J., & Spreat, S. (1989). The effect of contingent music on the in-seat behavior of a blind young woman with profound mental retardation. *Education and Treatment of Children, 12,* 165–173.

Hill, M. (1989). Work status outcomes of vocational rehabilitation clients who are blind or visually impaired. *Rehabilitation Counseling Bulletin, 32,* 219–230.

Hill, M., Hill, E., & LeBous, C. (1994). Toward the establishment of state licensure for orientation and mobility specialists. *Journal of Visual Impairment & Blindness, 88,* 201–205.

Hill, M., Wehman, P., Kregel, J., Banks, P., & Metzler, H. (1987). Employment outcomes for people with moderate and severe disabilities: An eight-year longitudinal analysis of supported competitive employment. *Journal of the Association for Persons with Severe Handicaps, 12,* 182–189.

Hinson, N. (1993). We're not that much different. *Journal of Visual Impairment & Blindness, 87,* 207.

Hirschkatz, K. (1989). An orientation and mobility approach to problems of a neurologically impaired adult. *Journal of Visual Impairment & Blindness, 83,* 449–453.

Holcomb, L. (1983). *Challenged women: Misunderstood minority.* Unpublished manuscript.

Holland, J. (1973). *Making vocational choices: A theory of careers.* Englewood Cliffs, NJ: Prentice Hall.

Hollingsworth, D., & Pease, L. (1980). The impact of public assistance on the rehabilitation process of handicapped women. *Journal of Applied Rehabilitation Counseling, 2,* 192–195.

Holmes, G., & Karst, R. (1990). The institutionalization of disability myths: Impact on vocational rehabilitation services. *Journal of Rehabilitation, 56*(1), 20–27.

Hoover, R., & Bledsoe, C. (1981). Blindness and visual impairments. In W. C. Stolov & M. R. Clowers (Eds.), *Handbook of severe disability* (pp. 377–391). Washington, DC: U. S. Government Printing Office.

Hopkins-Best, M., Murphy, S., & Yurcisin, A. (1988). *Reaching the hidden majority: A leader's guide to career preparations for disabled women and girls.* Cranston, RI: The Carroll Press.

Hoppock, R. (1976). *Occupational information: Where to get it and how to use it in career education, career counseling and career development* (4th ed.). New York: McGraw-Hill.

Horner, R., Dunlap, G., & Koegel, R. (Eds.). (1988). *Generalization and maintenance: Life-style changes in applied settings.* Baltimore: Paul H. Brookes.

Horner, R., McDonnell, J., & Bellamy, G. (1986). Teaching generalized skills: General case instruction in simulation and community settings. In R. Horner, L. Meyer, & H. Fredericks (Eds.), *Education of learners with severe handicaps: Exemplary service strategies* (pp. 289–314). Baltimore: Paul H. Brookes.

Houser, L., Moses, E., & Kay, J. (1987). A family orientation to transition. *Education of the Visually Handicapped, 19*(3), 109–119.

Howze, Y. (1985). Increasing visually handicapped students' awareness about jobs. *Journal of Visual Impairment & Blindness, 79,* 473–474.

Howze, Y. (1987). The use of social skills training to improve interview skills of visually impaired young adults: A pilot study. *Journal of Visual Impairment & Blindness, 81,* 251–255.

Hoyt, K. B. (1985). The concept of career education: Implications for blind/visually impaired persons. *Journal of Visual Impairment & Blindness, 79,* 487–489.

Huber, C., & Backlund, B. (1992). *The twenty minute counselor: Transforming brief conversations into effective helping experiences.* New York: The Continuum Publishing Co.

Hudson, D. (1994). Causes of emotional and psychological reactions to adventitious blindness. *Journal of Visual Impairment & Blindness, 88,* 498–511.

Huebner, K. M. (1986). Social skills. In G. T. Scholl (Ed.), *Foundations of education for blind and visually handicapped children and youth: Theory and practice,* (pp. 341–362). New York: American Foundation for the Blind.

Huebner, K. M. & Ferrell, K. (1986). Ethical practice in providing services to blind and visually impaired infants, children, and youth. In *Proceedings of the 1985 Helen Keller seminar: Ethical issues in the field of blindness* (pp. 6–19). New York: American Foundation for the Blind.

Huebner, K. M. & Koenig, A. (1990). Student centered educational placement decisions: The meaning, interpretation, and application of Least Restrictive Environment. *D.V.H. Quarterly. 26,*(2), 9–12.

Huebner, K. M. & Marshall, S. (1989, June). Statement for the record of the American Foundation for the Blind to the National Council on Disability relative to its hearing on a report entitled "The education of students with disabilities: Where do we stand?". Unpublished manuscript, American Foundation for the Blind, New York.

Huebner, K. M., & Strumwasser, K. P. (1987). State certification of teachers of blind and visually impaired students: Report of a national study. *Journal of Visual Impairment & Blindness, 81,* 244–250.

Huebner, K. M., Morris, J., Rossi, P., De Lucchi, L. Malone, L., Olson, M., Shaw, R., & Craft, D. (1986). Curricular adaptations. In G. T. Scholl, (Ed.) *Foundations of education for blind and visually handicapped children and youth: Theory and practice* (pp. 363–404). New York: American Foundation for the Blind.

Hunt, C. (1993). The role of the diabetes educator. *Journal of Visual Impairment & Blindness, 87,* 329–330.

Hursh, N. (n.d.). *Diagnostic vocational evaluation with psychiatrically disabled individuals: Preliminary results of a national survey.* Boston: Boston University, Center for Rehabilitation Research and Training in Mental Health.

Hylbert, K., & Hylbert, K. (1979). *Information for human service workers* (2nd ed.). State College, PA: Counselor Education Press.

Ingraham, C., Carey, A., Vernon, M., & Berry, P. (1994). Deaf-blind clients and vocational rehabilitation: Practical guidelines for counselors. *Journal of Visual Impairment & Blindness, 88,* 117–127.

Jabs, D., Enger, C., & Bartlett, J. (1989). Cytomegalovirus retinitis and acquired immunodeficiency syndrome. *Archives of Ophthalmology, 107,* 75–80.

Jacobson, W. H. (1993). *The art and science of teaching orientation and mobility to persons with visual impairments.* New York: AFB Press.

Jenkins, W., Patterson, J., & Szymanski, E. (1992). Philosophical, historical, and legislative aspects of the rehabilitation counseling profession. In R. Parker & E. Szymanski (Eds.), *Rehabilitation Counseling Basics and Beyond* (2nd ed.) pp. 1–41). Austin, TX: PRO-ED.

Jeppson, D., & Hammer, F. (1992). Summer employment for youth. *RE:view, 24,* 29–32.

Jeppsson-Grassman. E. (1986). Work and new visual impairment: A study of the adaptive process. *Stockholm Studies in Social Work 2.* Stockholm, Sweden: University of Stockholm, Liber Forlag, School of Social Work.

Jernigan, J. (1981). Loss of physical functioning and disability. *Journal of Rehabilitation, 47*(4), 34–37.

Jernigan, K. (1974). *Definition of blindness.* Baltimore: National Federation of the Blind.

Jernigan, K. (1992, June). Equality, disability, and empowerment. *The Braille Monitor,* 295.

Joffee, E. (1987). Role of electronic travel aids: Field applications of the Russell Pathsounder. *Journal of Visual Impairment & Blindness, 81,* 389–390.

Johnson, C., & Keltner, J. (1983). Incidence of visual field in 20,000 eyes and its relationship to driving performance. *Archives of Ophthalmology, 101,* 371–375.

Johnson, G. (1997). Foreword. In Tuttle, D., & Tuttle, N., *Self-esteem and adjusting with blindness: The process of responding to life's demands.* Springfield, IL: Charles C. Thomas.

Johnson, S. (1983). *Employment discrimination and the disabled woman.* Unpublished doctoral dissertation, Southern Illinois University.

Johnson, S., & Hafer, M. (1985). Employment status of severely visually impaired men and women. *Journal of Visual Impairment & Blindness, 79,* 241–244.

Johnson, V. (1970). Counselor preparation for serving culturally deprived persons. *Journal of Rehabilitation, 36*(6), 19–20.

Johnston, W., & Packer, A. (1987). *Workforce 2000.* Indianapolis, IN: Hudson Institute.

Joiner, J. G., & Saxon, J. P. (1989). Rehabilitation practitioner contributions to professional journal literature. *Journal of Applied Rehabilitation Counseling, 20*(4), 33–35.

Joiner, J. G., Saxon, J. P., & Bair, W. (1987). Types of research and occupational roles of authors in rehabilitation journals. *Rehabilitation Counseling Bulletin, 30,* 237–242.

Jolicoeur, R. (1970). *Caring for the visually impaired older person.* Minneapolis: The Minneapolis Society for the Blind.

Jones, G. (1993). Follow-up of graduates of an orientation and mobility preparation program. *RE:view, 25,* 131–136.

Jordan, J., & Felty, J. (1968). *Factors associated with intellectual variation among visually impaired children.* New York: American Foundation for the Blind.

Jose, R. T. (Ed.). (1983). *Understanding low vision.* New York: American Foundation for the Blind.

Jose, R. T. (1992). Low vision services. In A. L. Orr (Ed.), Vision and aging: Crossroads for service delivery (pp. 209–232). New York: American Foundation for the Blind.

Jose, R. T. & Atcherson R. (1977). Type-size variability for near-point acuity tests. *American Journal of Optometry and Physiological Optics, 54,* 634–638.

Kaarlela, R. (1966). Home teaching: A description. *New Outlook for the Blind, 60,* 80–83.

Kadushin, A. (1972). *The social work interview.* New York: Columbia University Press.

Kahn, H., & Moorhead, H. (1973). *Statistics on blindness in the model reporting area 1969–1970.* DHEW Pub. No. (NIH) 73–427. Washington DC: Superintendent of Documents, U.S. Government Printing Office.

Kalafat, J., & Dehmer, J. (1993). A survey of statewide self-help groups for older persons who are visually impaired. *Journal of Visual Impairment & Blindness, 87,* 112–114.

Kelley, S., & Lambert, S. (1992). Family support in rehabilitation: A review of research, 1980–1990. *Rehabilitation Counseling Bulletin, 36,* 98–119.

Kemp, B., & Vash, C. (1971). Productivity after injury in a sample of spinal cord injured persons: A pilot study. *Journal of Chronic Disease, 24,* 259–275.

Kent, D. (1983). Finding a way through the rough years: How blind girls survive adolescence. *Journal of Visual Impairment & Blindness, 77,* 247–250.

Kiester, E. (1990). *AIDS and vision loss.* New York: American Foundation for the Blind.

Kim, Yoon Hough (1970). *The community of the blind.* New York: American Foundation for the Blind.

Kimbrough, J., Huebner, K. M., & Lowry, L. (1976). *Sensory training: A curriculum guide.* Bridgeville, PA.: Greater Pittsburgh Guild for the Blind.

Kirchner, C. (1983). Special education for visually handicapped children: A critique of data on numbers served and costs. *Journal of Visual Impairment & Blindness. 77*(5), 219–223.

Kirchner, C. (1988). *Data on blindness and visual impairment in the U.S.* New York: American Foundation for the Blind.

Kirchner, C. & Aiello, R. (1988). Services available to blind and visually handicapped persons in the U.S.: A survey of agencies. In C. Kirchner (Ed.), *Data on blindness and visual impairment in the U.S.: A resource manual on characteristics, education, employment and service delivery* (2nd ed., pp. 253–261). New York: American Foundation for the Blind.

Kirchner, C., & Greenstein, Z. (1984). Statistical brief #28: Networks for employment of blind/visually impaired persons: A review with findings from AFB's "Job Index." *Journal of Visual Impairment & Blindness, 78*(6), 270–276.

Kirchner, C., & Peterson, R. (1979). Statistical brief #5, Employment: Selected characteristics. *Journal of Visual Impairment & Blindness, 73*, 239–242.

Kirchner, C., & Peterson, R. (1981). Statistical brief #15, Men, women, and blindness: A demographic view. *Journal of Visual Impairment & Blindness, 75*, 267–270.

Kirchner, C., & Peterson, R. (1982). Statistical brief #21, Vocational and rehabilitation placements of blind and visually impaired clients: U.S. 1980. *Journal of Visual Impairment & Blindness, 76*, 426–429.

Kirchner, C., & Peterson, R. (1988a). Employment: Selected characteristics. In C. Kirchner (Ed.), *Data on blindness and visual impairment in the U.S.: A resource manual on characteristics, education, employment and service delivery* (2nd ed., pp. 169–177). New York: American Foundation for the Blind.

Kirchner, C., & Peterson, R. (1988b). Estimates of race-ethnic groups in the U.S. visually impaired and blind population: Data on blindness and visual impairment in the U.S. In C. Kirchner (Ed.), *A resource manual on characteristics, education, employment and service delivery* (2nd ed., pp. 81–89). New York: American Foundation for the Blind.

Kirchner, C., & Peterson, R. (1988c). Ethnicity and rehabilitation: An analysis of blind and visually impaired clients in the federal/state vr system. In C. Kirchner, (Ed.), *Data on blindness and visual impairment in the U.S.: A resource manual on characteristics, education, employment and service delivery*, (2nd ed., pp. 91–99). New York: American Foundation for the Blind.

Kirchner, C., & Stephen, G. (1987). Statistics on users of services related to blindness and visual impairment. *Yearbook of the Association for Education and Rehabilitation of the Blind and Visually Impaired 1986 Edition.* Alexandria, VA: AERBVI.

Kirchner, C., Harkins, D., Esposito, R., Isatanbuli, M., & Chandu, F. (1991). *Issues and strategies toward improving employment of blind or visually impaired persons in Illinois.* New York: American Foundation for the Blind.

Kirk, F., & La Forge, J. (1995). The national rehabilitation counseling association. *Journal of Rehabilitation, 61*(3), 47–50.

Kirkman, R. (1983). Career awareness and the visually impaired student. *Education of the Visually Handicapped, 14*(4), 105–114.

Klemz, A. (1977). *Blindness and partial sight.* Cambridge: Woodward–Faulkner.

Knappett, K., & Wagner, N. (1976). Sex education and the blind. *Education of the Visually Handicapped, 8*(1), 1–5.

Knefelkamp, L., & Slepitza, R. (1976). A cognitive developmental model of career development: An adaptation of the Perry scheme. *The Counseling Psychologist, 6*(3), 53–58.

Knight, R. G., & Longmore, B. E. (1994). *Clinical neuropsychology of alcoholism.* East Sussex, UK: Lawrence Erlbaum.

Koehler, W., & Loftin, M. (1993). Full-service utilization through an exit orientation: A new model for residential schools. *Journal of Visual Impairment & Blindness, 87*, 199–201.

Koek, K., Martin, S., & Pare, M. (Eds.). (1987). *Encyclopedia of associations 1988* (23rd ed.). Detroit, MI.: Gale Research Company.

Koestler, F. (1983). Visually impaired women and the world of work: Theme and variations. *Journal of Visual Impairment & Blindness, 75*, 276–278.

Koestler, F. (1976). *The unseen minority: A social history of blindness in the United States.* New York: David McKay.

Konar, V., & Rice, D. (1984). *Strategies for serving deaf-blind clients.* Eleventh Institute on Rehabilitation Issues. Hot Springs: University of Arkansas.

Krogman, W. (1972). *Child growth.* Ann Arbor: University of Michigan Press.

Kutza, E. (1981). Benefits for the disabled: How beneficial for women? *Journal of Sociology and Social Welfare, 8*, 298–318.

Kweskin, S. (1985). Understanding glaucoma: A guide to saving your sight. Daly City, CA: Krames Communications.

LaGrow, S. (1986). Assessing optimal illumination for visual response accuracy in visually impaired adults. *Journal of Visual Impairment & Blindness, 80*, 888–895.

LaGrow, S. (1996). Point/counterpoint: The case for the individual prescription of cane length. *Journal of Visual Impairment & Blindness, 90*, 293–294.

LaGrow S., & Mulder, L. (1989). Structured solicitation: A standardized method for gaining travel information. *Journal of Visual Impairment & Blindness, 83*, 469–470.

Lambert, R., (1990). Some thoughts about acquiring and learning to use a dog guide. *RE:view, 22*, 151–158.

Laus, M. (1977). *Travel instructions for the handicapped.* Springfield, IL: Charles C. Thomas.

Lawler, E. (1973). *Motivation in work organizations.* Monterey, CA: Brooks/Cole.

Lehon, L. (1980). Development of lighting standards for the visually impaired. *Journal of Visual Impairment & Blindness, 75*, 249–253.

Leja, J. (1989). The job roles of rehabilitation teachers of the blind. Doctoral dissertation, Southern Illinois University. *Dissertation Abstracts International, 50,* 3919.

Lerman, A., & Guilfoyle, G. (1970). *The development of prevocational behavior in deaf adolescents.* New York: Teachers College Press.

Leventhal, J. (1996). Assistive devices for people who are blind or have visual impairments. In J. Galvin & M. Scherer (Eds.), *Evaluating, selecting, and using appropriate assistive technology* (pp. 125–143). Gaithersburg, MD: Aspen.

Levinson, D. (1986). A conception of adult development. *American Psychologist, 41*(4), 3–13.

Levinson, D. (1978). *The seasons of a man's life.* New York: Alfred A. Knopf.

Ley, F. (1989). Quoted in article, "Pizza Hut delivers: Will hire 2,000 workers with disabilities." *Newsletter of the Association for Persons with Severe Handicaps, 15*(9), 1,5.

Lezak, M. (1983). *Neuropsychological assessment* (2nd ed.). New York: Oxford University Press.

Liebman, J. (1990). Supported employment: Does it really work? *RE:view, 22,* 84–89.

Liscio, M. (Ed.). (1986). *A guide to colleges for visually impaired students.* New York: Academic Press.

Livingston, R. & Tucker, L. (1997). Literacy, employment, and mode of access to printed information. In Increasing literacy levels: Final report. Mississippi State, MS: Rehabilitation Research and Training Center on Blindness and Low Vision.

Lockman, J., Rieser, J., & Pick, H. (1981). Assessing blind travelers' knowledge of spacial layout. *Journal of Visual Impairment & Blindness, 75,* 321–326.

Locust, C. (1995). The impact of differing belief systems between Native Americans and their rehabilitation service providers. *Rehabilitation Education, 9,* 205–215.

Long, R. G., Boyette, L. & Griffin-Shirley, D. (1996). Older persons and community travel: The effect of visual impairment. *Journal of Visual Impairment & Blindness, 90*(4), 302–313.

Lowenfeld, B. (1950). Psychological foundation of special methods in teaching blind children. In P. A. Zahl (Ed.), *Blindness* (pp. 89–108). Princeton: Princeton University Press.

Lowenfeld, B. (1971). *Our blind children: Growing and learning with them* (3rd ed.). Springfield, IL: Charles C. Thomas.

Lowenfeld, B. (1980). Psychological problems of children with impaired vision. In W. Cruickshank (Ed.), *Psychology of exceptional children and youth* (4th ed., pp. 255–341). Englewood Cliffs, NJ: Prentice Hall.

Lowenfeld, B. (1981a). *Berthold Lowenfeld on blindness and blind people: Selected papers.* New York: American Foundation for the Blind.

Lowenfeld, B. (1981b). Effects of blindness on the cognitive function of children. In B. Lowenfeld (Ed.), *Berthold Lowenfeld on blindness and blind people:* Selected papers (pp. 67–78). New York: American Foundation for the Blind.

Lowenfeld, B. (1989). Professional self-esteem or the evolution of a profession. *Journal of Visual Impairment & Blindness, 83,* 336–339.

Luck, R., & Cull, J. (1980). Attitudinal and counseling considerations in the rehabilitation of the blind. In C. Hoehne, J. Cull, & R. Hardy (Eds.), *Ophthalmological considerations in the rehabilitation of the blind* (pp. 189–298). Springfield, IL: Charles C. Thomas.

Ludwig, I., Luxton, L., & Attmore, M. (1988). *Creative recreation for blind and visually impaired adults.* New York: American Foundation for the Blind.

Lukas, D. (1993). *Where to start and what to ask: An assessment handbook.* New York: Norton.

Lukoff, I., & Whiteman, M. (1970). *The social sources of adjustment to blindness.* New York: American Foundation for the Blind.

Luxton, H. (1993). Factors affecting rehabilitation teachers' braille instruction of adults who are blind and visually impaired. Columbia University (Doctoral dissertation). *Dissertation Abstracts International, 54*(03A), (University Microfilms No. 9320991).

Maccoby, M. (1980). Work and human development. *Professional Psychology, 11,* 509–519.

MacCuspie, P., Harmer, D., McConnell, J., Fricker, J., & Johnson, J. (1993). Short-term placements: A crucial role for residential schools. *Journal of Visual Impairment & Blindness, 87,* 193–198.

Mallik, K. (1979). Job accommodation through job restructuring and environmental modification. In D. Vandergoot & J. Worall (Eds.), *Placement in rehabilitation: A career development perspective* (pp.144–165). Baltimore: University Park Press.

Mangold, S., & Mangold, P. (1983). The adolescent visually impaired female. *Journal of Visual Impairment & Blindness, 77,* 250–255.

Mann, W., Hurren, D., Karuza, J., & Bentley, D. (1993). Needs of home-based older visually impaired persons for assistive devices. *Journal of Visual Impairment & Blindness, 87,* 106–110.

Marks, E., & Lewis, A. (1983). *Job hunting for the disabled.* Woodbury, NY: Barron's.

Marmion, S., McBroom, L., Haucke, M., & Jackson, R. (1986). *Sensory aid technology: A career development intervention strategy for blind and visually impaired persons.* Mississippi State, MS: Rehabilitation Research and Training Center on Blindness and Low Vision.

Marmor, G. (1977). Age at onset of blindness in visual imagery development. *Perceptual and Motor Skills, 45,* 1031–1034.

Maslow, A. (1969). *The psychology of science: A reconnaissance.* Chicago: Henry Regnery.

Mather, J. (1994). Computers, automation, and the employment of persons who are blind or visually impaired. *Journal of Visual Impairment & Blindness, 88,* 544–549.

Maxson, B. J. (1996, December 20). *Blind computer users.* E-mail to (bsc2@ra.msstate.edu).

Maxson, J. H., McBroom, L. W., Crudden, A., Johnson, G., & Wolffe, K. (1997). A strategy to improve employment outcomes for persons who are blind or visually impaired. In F. E. Menz, J. Eggers, P. Wehman, & V. Brooke (Eds.), *Lessons for improving employment for people with disabilities from vocational rehabilitation research* (pp. 363–373). Menomonie, WI: Stout Vocational Rehabilitation Institute (National Association of Rehabilitation Research and Training Centers).

Maxson, B. J., Tedder, N., Marmion, S., & Lamb, A. (1993). The education of youths who are deaf-blind: Learning tasks and teaching methods. *Journal of Visual Impairment & Blindness, 87,* 259–262.

McAdam, D., O'Cleirigh, C., & Cuvo, A. (1993). Self-monitoring and verbal feedback to reduce stereotypic body rocking in a congenitally blind adult. *RE:view, 24,* 163–172.

McBride, D., Butler, E., & Nickolson, D. (1979). *Rehabilitation teaching counseling: A guide for practitioners working with the adult blind.* Illinois Department of Children and Family Services: Community Services for the Visually Handicapped.

McBroom, L. W., & Seaman, J. (1987). *Computerized job-matching systems: A resource guide.* Mississippi State, MS: Mississippi State University, Rehabilitation Research and Training Center on Blindness and Low Vision.

McBroom, L. W., Seaman, J., & Graves, W. (1987). *Work assessment instruments for the vocational evaluation of people with visual disabilities.* Mississippi State, MS: Mississippi State University, Rehabilitation Research and Training Center on Blindness and Low Vision.

McBroom, L., Tedder, N., & Haucke, M. (1989). *Professionally employed persons with visual disabilities: Characteristics and career transition issues.* Technical Report. Mississippi State, MS: Rehabilitation Research and Training Center on Blindness and Low Vision.

McBroom, L. W., Seaman, J., & Freeman, D. (1987). *Work assessment database* [Computer program]. Mississippi State, MS: Mississippi State University, Rehabilitation Research and Training Center on Blindness and Low Vision.

McCarron, L., & Dial, J. (1976). McCarron–Dial Work Evaluation System: Evaluation of the mentally disabled—A systematic approach. Dallas: McCarron–Dial Systems.

McCartney, B. (1993). Challenges facing residential schools: A case study. *Journal of Visual Impairment & Blindness, 87,* 204.

McCray, P. (1979). *An interpretation of VEWA/CARF: Work sample standards.* Menomonie: University of Wisconsin—Stout, Materials Development Center.

McCulloh, K., Crawford, I., & Resnick, J. (1994). A structured support group for midlife and older adults with vision loss. *Journal of Visual Impairment & Blindness, 88,* 152–156.

McDaniel, R., & Couch, R. (1980). Job analysis in vocational evaluation and adjustment. *Vocational Evaluation and Work Adjustment Bulletin, 13*(1), 17–22, 25.

McGowan, J., & Porter, T. (1967). *An introduction to the vocational rehabilitation process.* Washington, DC: Vocational Rehabilitation Administration, U.S. Department of Health, Education, and Welfare.

McHugh, D. (1975). A view of deaf people in terms of Super's theory of vocational development. *Journal of Rehabilitation of the Deaf, 9*(1), 10.

McKay, J. C., Courington, S., Lambert, R., Becker, S., Ludlow, L., & Wright, B. (1983). The measurement of attitudes toward blindness and its importance for rehabilitation. *International Journal for Rehabilitation Research, 6,* 67–72.

McKeown, J. (1992, January–February). Letter to a rehabilitation counselor. *The Braille Forum, 30*(4), 20–22.

McMahon, E. (1992). *The role of residential schools for the blind in 1990.* Bronx, NY: New York Institute of Special Education.

Means, B., & Roessler, R. (1976). *PAS: Personal achievement skills training.* Little Rock, AR: Arkansas Rehabilitation Research and Training Center.

Mehr, E., & Mehr, H. (1969). Psychological factors in working with partially sighted persons. *Journal of the American Optometric Association, 40,* 842–846.

Mehr, E., & Sakamoto, L. (1988). A new method of stair markings for visually impaired people. *Journal of Visual Impairment & Blindness, 82,* 24–27.

Mendelsohn, S. (1987). *Financing adaptive technology: A guide to sources and strategies for blind and visually impaired users.* New York: Smiling Interface.

Merrill, J. (1993). Support groups for persons with diabetes and visual impairment. *Journal of Visual Impairment & Blindness, 87,* 376–377.

Middlesex Community College. (1984). *PROJECT CARE Career alternatives through replication and education: A replication manual.* Edison, NJ: Division of Community Education.

Miller, C. (1993). A model for outreach technical assistance. *Journal of Visual Impairment & Blindness, 87,* 201–203.

Miller, G. (1990). The comprehensive rehabilitation center: Perspectives of clients and implications for professionals. *Journal of Visual Impairment & Blindness 84,* 177–182.

Miller, G. (1993). Expanding vocational options. *RE:view, 25*(1), pp. 27–31.

Miller, G., & Rossi, P. (1988). Placement of visually impaired persons: A survey of current practices. *Journal of Visual Impairment & Blindness, 82,* 318–324.

Millington, M., Asner, K., Linkowski, D., & Der-Stepanian, J. (1996). Employers and job development. In R. Parker & E. Szymanski (Eds.), *Work and disability* (pp. 277–308). Austin, TX: PRO-ED.

Miner, I. (1995). Psychosocial implications of Usher's syndrome, Type I, throughout the life cycle. *Journal of Visual Impairment & Blindness, 89,* 287–296.

Moore, J. E. (1984). Impact of family attitudes toward blindness/visual impairment on the rehabilitation process. *Journal of Visual Impairment & Blindness, 78,* 100–106.

Moore, J. E. & Fireison, C. (1995). Rehabilitating persons who are blind: 75 years of progress. *American Rehabilitation, 21*(3), 22–27.

Moore, J. E. & Stephens, B. C. (1994). Independent living services for older individuals who are blind: Issues and practices. *American Rehabilitation, 20*(1), 30–34.

Moore, J.E., & Tucker, A. (1994). *Model program operation manual for business enterprise program supervisors.* Mississippi State, MS: Rehabilitation Research and Training Center on Blindness and Low Vision.

Moore, J. E., Armstrong, G. K., Lamb, A. M., & Giesen, J. M. (1992). Information and referral needs of persons with partial sight. *Journal of Rehabilitation Administration, 16,* 94–98.

Moore, J. E., Cavenaugh, B., Giesen, J. M., & Maxson, J. H. (1995). *An assessment of the feasibility of contracting with a nominee agency for the Pennsylvania business enterprise program.* Mississippi State, MS: Rehabilitation Research and Training Center on Blindness and Low Vision.

Moore, J., Crudden, A., & Giesen, J. (1994). *The 1994 survey of direct labor workers who are blind and employed by NIB-affiliated industries for the blind.* Mississippi State, MS: Rehabilitation Research and Training Center on Blindness and Low Vision.

Moos, R. & Tsu, V. (1977). The crisis of physical illness. In R. H. Moos, (Ed.), *Coping with physical illness* (pp. 1–21). New York: Plenum.

Morris, D. (1985). *Bodywatching.* New York: Crown.

Morrison, M. (1991). Employment of older workers with disability: Attitudes and legal issues. In L. Perlman & C. Hansen (Eds.), *Aging, disability and the nation's productivity* (pp. 27–32). 15th Mary E. Switzer Memorial Seminar. Reston, VA: National Rehabilitation Association.

Morse, A., Silberman, R., & Trief, E. (1987). Aging and visual impairment. *Journal of Visual Impairment & Blindness, 81*(7), 308–12.

Moyer, J. (1986). The multiple factors of successfully integrating computer access technology into the workplace. *Yearbook of the Association for Education and Rehabilitation of the Blind and Visually Impaired, 4,* 1–7.

Murphy, S. & Hagner, D. (1988). Evaluating assessment settings: Ecological influence on vocational evaluation. *Journal of Rehabilitation, 54*(1), 53–59

Myers, T. (1980). Counseling the older disabled person for the world of work. *Journal of Employment Counseling, 17*(1), 37–48.

Nadolsky, J. (1977). The need for simulated tasks in vocational evaluation. *Vocational Evaluation and Work Adjustment Bulletin, 10*(1), 2–7.

Nadolsky, J. (1985). Vocational evaluation: An experimental trend in vocational assessment. In C. Smith & R. Fry (Eds.), *Issues papers: National forum on issues in vocational assessment* (pp. 1–9). Menomonie: University of Wisconsin—Stout, Materials Development Center.

Nagi, S. (1969). Diability and rehabilitation. Columbus: Ohio State University Press.

National Center for Health Statistics. (1975). Prevalence of selected impairments: United States—1971. *Vital and Health Statistics Series 10, No. 111, DHEW Pub. No. 7501526.* Washington, DC: Government Printing Office.

National Society to Prevent Blindness. (1978). *Vision Problems in the United States.* New York: Author.

National Society to Prevent Blindness. (1980). *Vision problems in the U.S.* New York: Author.

Needham, W. (1988). Cognitive distortions in acquired visual loss. *Journal of Visual Rehabilitation, 2*(3), 45–52.

Needham, W., & Ehmer, M. (1980). Irrational thinking and adjustment to loss of vision. *Journal of Visual Impairment & Blindness, 74,* 57–61.

Needham, W., Eldridge, L., Harabedian, B., & Crawford, D. (1993). Blindness, diabetes, and amputation: Alleviation of depression and pain through thermal biofeedback therapy. *Journal of Visual Impairment & Blindness, 87,* 368–371.

Neff, W. (1971). Rehabilitation and work. In W. Neff (Ed.), *Rehabilitation psychology* (pp. 109–142). Washington, DC: American Psychological Association.

Neff, W. (1985). Work and human behavior (3rd ed.). New York: Aldine.

Nelipovich, M., & Buss, E. (1991). Investigating alcohol abuse among persons who are blind. *Journal of Visual Impairment & Blindness, 85,* 343–345.

Nelipovich, M., & Naegele, L. (1985). The rehabilitation process for persons who are deaf-blind. *Journal of Visual Impairment & Blindness 79,* 104–110.

Nelson, K., & Dimitrova, G. (1993). Statistical brief #36: Severe visual impairment in the United States and in each state, 1990. *Journal of Visual Impairment & Blindness, 87,* 80–85.

Nemeth, S., & Childress, C. (1987). Video display terminals. *Journal of Ophthalmic Nursing and Technology, 6*(3), 108.

Neu, C. (1975). Coping with newly diagnosed blindness. *American Journal of Nursing, 75*(12), 2161–2163.

Newell, F. W. (1992). *Ophthalmology: Principles and concepts* (7th ed.). St. Louis: Mosby Year Book.

Newell, F. W. (1996). *Ophthalmology: Principles and practices* (8th ed.). St. Louis: Mosby.

Nisbet, J., & Hagner, D. (1988). Natural supports in the workplace: A reexamination of supported employment. *Journal of the Association for Persons with Severe Handicaps, 13,* 260–267.

Nixon, H. (1988). Reassessing support groups for parents of visually impaired children. *Journal of Visual Impairment & Blindness, 82,* 271–278.

O'Dea, A., & Mayhall, C. (1988). Delayed manifestations of congenital rubella. *Journal of Visual Impairment & Blindness, 82,* 379–381.

O'Toole, J., & Weeks, C. (1978). *What happens after school? A study of disabled women and education.* San Francisco: Women's Education Equity Communications Network (WEECN), Far West Laboratories.

Oehler-Giarratana, J., & Fitzgerald, R. (1980). Group therapy with blind diabetics. *Archives of General Psychiatry, 37,* 463–467.

Office of Special Education Programs. (1987). Summary of selected legislation relating to handicapped individuals: 1985–86. *OSERS News in Print, 1*(3), 8–10.

Orelove, F. (1982). Acquisition of incidental learning in moderately and severely handicapped adults. *Education and Training of the Mentally Retarded, 7*(1), 22–30.

Organization for Social and Technical Innovation, Inc. (1971). *Blindness and services to the blind in the United States—a report to the Subcommittee on Rehabilitation/National Institute of Neurological Diseases and Blindness.* Cambridge, Mass.: OSTI Press.

Orlansky, M., & Trap, J. (1987). Working with Native American Persons: Issues in facilitating communication and providing culturally relevant services. *Journal of Visual Impairment & Blindness, 81,* 151–155.

Orr, A. (1993). Training outreach workers to serve American Indian elders with visual impairment and blindness. *Journal of Visual Impairment & Blindness, 87,* 336–340.

Osipow, S. (1975). The relevance of theories of career development to special groups: Problems, needed data and implications. In J. Picou & R. Campbell (Eds.), *Career behavior of special groups* (pp. 9–22). Columbus, OH: Merrill.

Packer, J. (1983). Sex stereotyping in vocational counseling of blind/visually impaired persons: A national study of counselor choices. *Journal of Visual Impairment & Blindness, 77,* 261–268.

Padial, A. (1986). *The cataract book.* Daly City, CA: Krames Communications.

Palmer, E., & Phelps, D. (1986). Multicenter trial of cryotherapy for retinopathy or prematurity. *Pediatrics, 77*(3), 428–29.

Pape, D., & Tarvydas, V. (1993). Responsible and responsive rehabilitation consultation on the ADA: The importance of training for psychologists. *Rehabilitation Psychology, 38,* 117–132.

Park, H., & Gaylord-Ross, R. (1989). Process social skills training in employment settings for mentally retarded youth. *Journal of Applied Behavior Analysis, 22,* 373–380.

Parker, R. (1991). *Occupational aptitude survey and interest schedule—2: Interest schedule.* Austin, TX: PRO-ED.

Parker, R., & Schaller, J. (1996). Issues in vocational assessment and disability. In E. Szymanski & R. Parker (Eds.), *Work and disability* (pp. 127–164). Austin, TX: PRO-ED.

Parker, R. & Szymanski, E. (Eds.). (1996). Work and disability. Austin, TX: PRO-ED.

Partos, F., & Kirchner, C. (1986). The Randolph–Sheppard business enterprise program characteristics. *Journal of Visual Impairment & Blindness, 80,* 685–689.

Paskin, N., & Moloney-Soucy, L. (1994). *Whatever works.* New York: The Lighthouse.

Patterson, J. B. (1996). Occupational and labor market information. In R. Parker & E. Szymanski (Eds.), *Work and disability* (pp. 209–254). Austin, TX: PRO-ED.

Patterson, J. B., & Marks, C. (1992). The client as customer: Achieving service quality and customer satisfaction in rehabilitation. *Journal of Rehabilitation, 55*(4), 16–23.

Patterson, J. B. & Witten, B. (1987). Myths concerning persons with disabilities. *Journal of Applied Rehabilitation Counseling, 18*(3), 42–44.

Patterson, J. B., & Woodrich, F. (1986). The client assistance program (CAP) 1978–1984. *Journal of Rehabilitation, 52*(4), 49–52.

Patterson, J. B., McKenzie, B., & Jenkins, J. (1995). Creating accessible groups for individuals with disabilities. *The Journal for Specialists in Group Work, 20,* 76–82.

Pava, W. (1994). Visually impaired person's vulnerability to sexual and physical assault. *Journal of Visual Impairment & Blindness, 88,* 103–112.

Pavan-Livingston, D. (1985). Manual of ocular diagnosis and therapy. Boston: Little, Brown.

Peli, E. (1986). Control of eye movement with peripheral vision: Implications for training of eccentric viewing. *American Journal of Optometry and Physiological Optics, 63,* 113–8.

Peninsula Center for the Blind. (1982). *The first steps: How to help people who are losing their sight.* Palo Alto, CA: Author.

Peterson, M. (1986). *Vocational assessment of special students: A procedural manual.* Mississippi State, MS: Department of Counselor Education, VOC-AIM Project.

Peterson, M., Capps, C., & Moore, M. (1984). *Work samples and visually impaired persons: A state-of-the-art review and resource manual.* Mississippi State, MS: Rehabilitation Research and Training Center on Blindness and Low Vision.

Peterson, R., Lowman, C., & Kirchner, C. (1978). Visual handicap: Statistical data on a social process. *Journal of Visual Impairment & Blindness, 72,* 419–421.

Petzinger, R. (1993). Adaptive blood glucose monitoring and insulin measurement devices for visually impaired persons. *Journal of Visual Impairment & Blindness, 87,* 341–344.

Pfanstiehl, M. (1983). Role models for high achieving visually impaired women. *Journal of Visual Impairment & Blindness, 77*(6), 259–261.

Phillips, S., Strohmer, D., Berthaume, B., & O'Leary, J. (1983). Career development of special populations: A framework for research. *Journal of Vocational Behavior, 22*(1), 12–29.

Pogrund, R. & Rosen, S. (1989). The preschool blind child can be a cane user. *Journal of Visual Impairment & Blindness, 83,* 431–439.

Pogrund, R., Fazzi, D., & Schreier, E. (1993). Development of a preschool "kiddy cane." *Journal of Visual Impairment & Blindness, 87,* 52–54.

Polloway, E., Cronin, M., & Patton, J. (1986). The efficacy of group versus one-to-one instruction: A review. *Remedial and Special Education, 7*(1), 22–30.

Ponchillia, P. (1984). Family services: The role of the center-based teaching professional. *Journal of Visual Impairment & Blindness, 78,* 97–100.

Ponchillia, P., & Kaarlela, R. (1986). Post-rehabilitative use of adaptive skills. *Journal of Visual Impairment & Blindness, 80,* 665–669.

Ponchillia, P., & Ponchillia, S. (1996). *Foundations of rehabilitation teaching with persons who are blind or visually impaired.* New York: AFB Press.

Ponchillia, S. (1993). Complications of diabetes and their implications for service providers. *Journal of Visual Impairment & Blindness, 87,* 354–358.

Poppe, K. (1991). *Distribution of quota registrants in 1990 by grade placement, visual acuity, reading medium, school or agency type, and age: A replication of Wright's 1988 study.* Louisville, KY: American Printing House for the Blind.

Porot, D. (1996). *The PIE method for career success.* Indianapolis, IN: JIST.

Powell, T. H., Pancsofar, E. L., Steere, D. E., Butterworth, J. S., & Ranforth, B. (1991). *Supported employment: Providing integrated employment opportunities for persons with disabilities.* New York: Longman.

Power, P. (1988). An assessment approach to family intervention. In P. Power, A. Dell Orto, & M. Gibbons (Eds.), *Family interventions throughout chronic illness and disability* (pp. 5–23). New York: Springer.

Power, P. (1991). *A guide to vocational assessment* (2nd ed.). Austin, TX: PRO-ED.

Prevent Blindness America (1994). *Vision problems in the U.S.* Schaumburg, IL: Author.

Price, J. (1978). Unintentional injury among the aged. *Journal of Gerontological Nursing, 4*(3), 40.

Pruitt, W. (1977). *Vocational (work) evaluation.* Menomonie, WI: Walt Pruitt Associates.

Pruitt, W. (1983). *Work adjustment.* Menomonie, WI: Walt Pruitt Associates.

Pruitt, W. (1986). *Vocational work evaluation* (2nd ed.). Menomonie, WI: Walt Pruitt Associates.

Rabby, R., & Croft, D. (1989). *Take charge.* Boston: National Braille Press.

Randolph–Sheppard Vending Stand Act, as amended, § 20 U.S.C.A. 107 (1974).

Raths, L., Harmin, M., & Simon, S. (1966). *Values and teaching.* Columbus, OH: Merrill.

Raver, S., & Drash, P. (1988). Increasing social skills training for visually impaired children. *Education of the Visually Handicapped, 19*(4), 147–155.

Reeb, K. (1987a, July). *Private insurance reimbursement for rehabilitaion equipment.* Washington, DC: Electronics Industries Foundation.

Reeb, K. (1987b, July). *Revolving loan funds: Expanding equipment credit financing opportunities for persons with disabilities.* Washington, DC: Electronic Industries Foundation.

Regional Rehabilitation Research Institute on Attitudinal, Legal and Leisure Barriers. (1981). *Barrier awareness: Attitudes toward people with disabilities.* Washington, DC: George Washington University.

Rehab Brief. (1990). Deaf-blindness. 13(2), 1–4.

Rehab Brief. (1983). The results of helping: Empowerment or helplessness? *6*(7), 1–4.

Rehabilitation Services Administration. (1988). *Information memorandum (RSA-IM-92-25).* Washington DC: U.S. Department of Education.

Rehabilitation Act of 1973, as amended, § 29 U.S.C.A. § 721 (1974).

Rehabilitation Services Administration. (1982). *An assessment of the validity of homemaker closure.* Division of Program Administration, Basic State Grant Branch. Unpublished manuscript.

Reitan, R., & Davison, L. A. (1974). *Clinical neuropsychology: Current status and applications.* New York: Hemisphere Press.

Repp, A., & Singh, N. (Eds.) (1990). *Current perspectives on the use of non-aversive and aversive interventions with developmentally disabled persons.* Sycamore, IL: Sycamore.

RESNA (1997). Candidates information bulletin [online]. Available: http://www.ari.net/resna/certify/cib—2nd.htm/ [May 20, 1997].

Resnick, R. (1983). An exploratory study of the lifestyles of congenitally blind adults. *Journal of Visual Impairment & Blindness, 77,* 476–481.

Resources for Rehabilitation. (1990). *Rehabilitation Resource manual: Vision* (3rd ed.). Lexington, MA: Author.

Resources for Rehabilitation (1991). *Meeting the needs of employees with disabilities.* Lexington, MA: Author.

Rieser, J., Guth, D., & Hill, E. (1982). Mental processes mediating independent travel: Implications for orientation and mobility. *Journal of Visual Impairment & Blindness, 76,* 213–218.

Riffenburgh, R. (1967). Psychology of blindness. *Geriatrics,* 22, 127–133.

Roberts, A. (1977). Guidelines on rehabilitation teaching. *Journal of Visual Impairment & Blindness, 71,* 349–352.

Roberts, A. (1992). Looking at vocational placement for the blind: A personal perspective. *RE:view, 23,* 177–184.

Roe, A. (1956). *The psychology of occupations.* New York: Wiley.

Roessing, L. (1982). Functional vision: Criterion-referenced checklists. In S. Mangold, *A teacher's guide to the special educational needs of blind and visually handicapped children* (pp. 35–44). New York: American Foundation for the Blind.

Roessler, R., & Bolton, B. (1984). *Vocational rehabilitation of individuals with employability skill deficits: Problems and recommendations.* Fayetteville, AR: University of Arkansas Research and Training Center on Vocational Rehabilitation.

Roessler, R., & Rubin, S. (1991). Case management and rehabilitation counseling: Procedures and techniques. Austin, TX: PRO-ED.

Roessler, R., & Rubin, S. (1992). *Case management and rehabilitation counseling: Procedures and techniques* (2nd ed.). Austin, TX: PRO-ED.

Rogler, L., Malgady, R., Costantino, G., & Blumenthal, R. (1987). What do culturally sensitive mental health services mean? *American Psychologist, 42,* 565–70.

Rosen, G. (1978). The problem and utility of work sample reliability data. *Vocational Evaluation and Work Adjustment Bulletin, 11* (3), 45–50.

Rosenbloom, A. (1982). Care of elderly people with low vision. *Journal of Visual Impairment & Blindness, 76,* 209–212.

Rosenbloom, A. (1984). An overview of low vision care: Accomplishments and ongoing problems. *Journal of Visual Impairment & Blindness, 78,* 491–493.

Rosenthal, J. L. (1993). Special problems of people with diabetes and visual impairment. *Journal of Visual Impairment & Blindness, 87,* 331–333.

Rotter, J. (1966). Generalized expectancies for internal versus external control of reinforcement. *Psychological Monographs, 80,* 1014–1053.

RSA 911. (1995). Unpublished case service report.

Rubin, S., & Roessler, R. (1987). *Foundations of the vocational rehabilitation process* (3rd ed.). Austin, TX: PRO-ED.

Rusalem, H. (1972). *Coping with the unseen environment: An introduction to the vocational rehabilitation of blind persons.* New York: Teachers College Press.

Rusch, F. (Ed.) (1990). *Supported employment: Models, methods, and issues.* Sycamore, IL: Sycamore.

Russell, H. (1986). *Disabled Americans at work. President's Committee on Employment of the Handicapped and the Dole Foundation.* Washington, DC: U.S. Government, Public Affairs Department.

Ryder, B., & Kawalec, E. (1995). A job-seeking skills program for persons who are blind or visually impaired. *Journal of Visual Impairment & Blindness, 89,* 107–111.

Sacks, S., & Wolffe, K. (1992). The importance of social skills in the transition process for students with visual impairments. *Journal of Vocational Rehabilitation, 2*(1), 46–55.

Safilios-Rothschild, C. (1970). *The sociology and social psychology of disability and rehabilitation.* New York: Random House.

Sakata, R., & Sinick, D. (1965). Do work samples work? *Rehabilitation Counseling Bulletin, 8*(1), 121–124.

Sales, A. (1995). The national rehabilitation association. *Journal of Rehabilitation, 61*(3), 8–13.

Sampson, D. (1991). Changing attitudes toward persons with cerebral palsy through contact and information. *Rehabilitation Education, 5,* 87–92.

Sardegna, J., & Paul, T. (1991). *The encyclopedia of blindness and vision impairment.* New York: Facts on File.

Sax, G. (1974). *Principles of educational measurement and evaluation.* Belmont, CA: Wadsworth.

Saxon, S., & Etten, M. (1987). *Physical change and aging: A guide for the helping professions.* New York: Tiresias.

Scadden, L. (1984). Blindness in the information age: Equality or irony? *Journal of Visual Impairment & Blindness, 78,* 394–400.

Scadden, L. (1986). The changing work place: View from a disabled technologist. In I. Morris, *The future of work for disabled people: Employment and the new technology* (pp. 44–52). New York: American Foundation for the Blind.

Scadden, L. (1991). An overview of technology and visual impairment. *Technology and Disability, 1,* 11.

Schecter, E. (1979). *The 1974 follow-up of disabled and non-disabled adults.* U.S. Department of Health, Education, and Welfare, SSA, SSA Public #13–11725.

Schloss, P. (1987). Low-incidence handicaps. In C. Reynolds & L. Mann (Eds.), *Encyclopedia of special education* (pp. 972–973). New York: Wiley.

Schmitt, S. (1984). *The prediction of work status outcome of blind women.* Unpublished doctoral dissertation, Mississippi State, MS: Rehabilitation Research and Training Center on Blindness and Low Vision.

Scholl, G., & Schnur, R. (1976). *Measures of psychological, vocational, & educational functioning in the blind & visually handicapped.* New York: American Foundation for the Blind.

Scholl, G. (1993). Educational programs for blind children: A kaleidoscopic view. *Journal of Visual Impairment & Blindness, 87,* 177–180.

Schulz, P. (1980). *How does it feel to be blind?* Van Nuys, CA: Muse-Ed.

Scott, E., Jan, J. & Freeman, R. (1977). *Can't your child see?* Baltimore: University Park Press.

Scott, R. (1969). *The making of blind men.* New York: Russell Sage Foundation.

Seligman, M. (1975). *Helplessness on depression, development, and death.* San Francisco: W. H. Freeman.

Seligman, M. (1981). A learned point of view. In L. Rehm (Ed.), *Behavior therapy for depression: Present status and future directions* (Vol. 1, pp. 143–165). New York: Academic Press.

Selvin, H. (1979). Sexuality among the visually handicapped: A beginning. *Sexuality and Disability, 2,* 192–199.

Senge, J., & Dote-Kwan, J. (1995). Information accessibility in alternative formats in postsecondary education. *Journal of Visual Impairment & Blindness, 89,* 120–128.

Sever, J., South, M., & Shaver, K. (1985). Delayed manifestations of congenital rubella. *Reviews of Infectious Diseases, 7* (Supp.), 1.

Seybold, D. (1993). Investigating stress associated with mobility training through consumer discussion groups. *Journal of Visual Impairment & Blindness, 87,* 111–112.

Shaver, J., Curtis, C., Jesunathades, J., & Strong, C. (1987). *The modification of attitudes toward persons with handicaps: A comprehensive integrative review of research. Final report.* Logan: Utah State University.

Shaw, R., & Nye, J. (1993). An off-campus college program to prepare rehabilitation teachers of visually impaired students. *Journal of Visual Impairment & Blindness, 87,* 273–274.

Sherman, J., & Bass, S. (1984). Diagnostic procedures in low vision case management. In E. Faye (Ed.), *Clinical low vision,* 2nd ed. Boston: Little, Brown.

Sherman, S., & Robinson, N. (Eds.), (1982). *Ability testing of handicapped people: Dilemma for government, science, and the public.* Washington, DC: National Academy Press.

Shindell, S. (1988). Psychological sequelae to diabetic retinopathy. *Journal of the American Optometric Association, 59,* 870–875.

Shindell, S., Muray, L., & Needham, W. (1987, April). *Beliefs about blindness among various types of health care professionals.* Paper presented at the Annual meeting of the Eastern Psychological Association, Arlington, VA.

Sikka, A. & Stephens, B. C. (1997). Intervention practices in the retention of competitive employment among individuals who are blind or visually impaired. Mississippi State, MS: Rehabilitation Research and Training Center on Blindness and Low Vision.

Silverstone, B. (1988). *Aging & vision news.* New York: The Lighthouse National Center for Vision and Aging.

Simon, S. B., Howe, L. W., & Kirschenbaum, H. (1995). *Values clarifications.* New York: Warner Books.

Simons, K. (1983). Visual acuity norms in young children. *Survey of Ophthalmology, 28*(2), 84-92.

Simpson, F. (1986). Transition to adulthood. In G. T. Scholl (Ed.), *Foundations of education for blind and visually handicapped children and youth: Theory and practice* (pp. 405–422). New York: American Foundation for the Blind.

Simpson, F., Huebner, K. M., & Roberts, F. (1986a). Collaborative planning: Transition from school to work developing your state team—why and how. (Unpublished monograph.) New York: American Foundation for the Blind.

Simpson, F., Huebner, K. M., & Roberts, F. (1986b). Collaborative planning: Transition from school to work—programs in practice. Unpublished monograph. New York, N.Y.: American Foundation for the Blind.

Sisson, L., & Babeo, T. (1992). School-to-work transition of students with blindness or visual impairment. *Journal of Vocational Rehabilitation, 2*(19), 56–65.

Smith, A. (1987, August). *Training perceptual strategies in patients with visual loss.* Paper presented at the Annual Meeting of the American Psychological Association, New York.

Smith, D. (1993). Parent infant program. *Journal of Visual Impairment & Blindness, 87,* 208–209.

Smith, P. (1992). Providing rehabilitation teaching service to blind people: "All plus more." *American Rehabilitation, 18,*(2), 16–22.

Smith-Hansen, S. (1977). Effects of non-verbal behaviors on judged levels of counselor warmth and empathy. *Journal of Counseling Psychology, 24*(2), 87–91.

Smithdas, R. (1975). *Psychological aspects of deaf-blindness.* Sands Point, NY: Helen Keller National Center for Deaf–Blind Youth and Adults. Reprinted from presentation of 1975 Convention of the World Federation of the Deaf.

Sobsey, R., & McDonald, L. (1988). Special education: Coming of age. In B. Ludlow, A. Turnbull, & R. Luckasson (Eds.), *Transitions to adult life for people with mental retardation: Principles and practices* (pp. 21–44). Baltimore: Paul H. Brookes.

Sommers, V. (1944). *The influence of parental attitudes and social environments on the personality development of the adolescent blind.* New York: American Foundation for the Blind.

Sommers-Flanagan, J., & Sommers-Flanagan, R. (1993). *Foundations of therapeutic interviewing.* Boston: Allyn & Bacon.

Special Education Programs. (1991). *Annual deaf-blind child count data.* Washington, DC: U.S. Department of Education.

Spungin, S. (1975). *Precollege programs for blind and visually handicapped students.* New York: American Foundation for the Blind.

Spungin, S. (1985). Corridors of insensitivity: Technology and blind persons. *Journal of Visual Impairment & Blindness, 79,* 113–116.

Sreenivasan, S. (1996, December 2). New software improves Web access for the blind. *New York Times.*

Steere, D., Pancsofar, E., Powell, T., & Butterworth, J. (1989). Enhancing instruction through general case programming. *Teaching Exceptional Children, 22*(1), 22–24.

Stein, L., Palmer, P., & Weinberg, B. (1980). Characteristics of a young deaf-blind population. *The Siegel Report.* Chicago: David T. Siegel Institute for Communicative Disorders.

Steinberg, F. (1991). Rehabilitation after amputation. *Diabetes Spectrum, 4,* 5–9.

Stenehjem, D. (1993). Residential schools: An underutilized resource. *Journal of Visual Impairment & Blindness, 87,* 211–212.

Stephens, B. (1996). *Independent living services for older individuals who are blind.* Title VII, Chapter 2 of Annual Report for Fiscal Year 1995.

Stevens, P. M., Boland, J. M., & Ranson, S. (1982). Job development/placement specialists: New perspectives. *Rehabilitation Counseling Bulletin, 25,* 278–281.

Stewart, I., & Zimmerman, G. (1990). Orientation and mobility services to students with visual impairments enrolled in Iowa public schools. *RE:view, 12*(1), 23–30.

Stogner, P. (1980). The effects of typical retinitis pigmentosa, Leber's congenital amaurosis, Centro peripheral dystrophy, and Usher's Syndrome on educational and vocational success and personality development. *International Journal of Rehabilitation Research, 3,* 357–366.

Stolov, W. & Clowers, M. (1981). *Handbook of severe disability.* Washington, DC: Rehabilitation Services Administration, U.S. Department of Education.

Stone, J., Endo, G., Spear, J., Rivera, O., & Petrusa, E. (1977). Visual and auditory disability: An overview for the rehabilitation counselor. *Human Resources Institute, Monograph 4.* Salt Lake City: University of Utah.

Storey, K., Sacks, S., & Olmstead, J. (1985). Community-references instruction in a technological work setting: A vocational educational option for visually handicapped students. *Journal of Visual Impairment & Blindness, 79,* 481–486.

Strong, J. (1990). *Psychosocial components of AIDS.* A paper presented at the AIDS and Vision Loss Conference, San Francisco, January 25, 1990.

Stude, E. (1994). Implications of the ADA for master's and bachelor's level rehabiltiation counseling and rehabilitation services professionals. *Rehabilitaton Education, 8,* 17–25.

Sue, D., & Sue, D. (1990). *Counseling the culturally different: Theory and practice* (2nd ed.). New York: Wiley.

Sullivan, R. (1994). Autism: Definitions past and present. *Journal of Vocational Rehabilitation, 4*(1), 4–9.

Super, D. (1957). *The psychology of careers: An introduction to vocational development.* New York: Harper and Row.

Super, D., Crites, J., Hummel, R., Moser, H., Overstreet, P., & Warnath, C. (1957). *Vocational development: A framework for research.* New York: Teachers College, Columbia University.

Svendsen, (1994). The use of light rail or light rapid transit systems by individuals with severe visual impairments. *Journal of Visual Impairment & Blindness, 88,* 69–74.

Swallow, R. & Huebner, K. M. (1987). *Skills to thrive not just survive: A guide to developing independent life skills for visually impaired children and youths.* New York: American Foundation for the Blind.

Szymanski, E. & Parker, R. (1989). Supported employment in rehabilitation counseling: Issues and practices. *Journal of Applied Rehabilitation Counseling, 20,* 65–71.

Taheri-Araghi, M., & Hendron, G. (1994). Successful vocational rehabilitation of clients with retinitis pigmentosa. *Journal of Visual Impairment & Blindness, 88,* 128–131.

Tedder, N. (1987). Counseling issues for clients with Usher's syndrome. *Journal of Rehabilitation, 53*(2), 61–64.

Tedder, N., Warden, K., & Sikka, A. (1993). Prelanguage communication of students who are deaf-blind and have other severe impairments. *Journal of Visual Impairment & Blindness, 87,* 302–306.

Teitelbaum, L., Davidson, P., Gravetter, F., Taub, H., & Teitelbaum, C. (1994). The relation of vision loss to depression in older veterans. *Journal of Visual Impairment & Blindness, 88,* 253–257.

Temelini, D., & Fesko, S. (1997, January). Shared responsibility: Job search practices from the consumer and state vocational rehabilitation perspective. *Research Practice: Institute for Community Inclusion.*

The technology-related assistance for individuals with disabilities act [On-line]. Available: http://sapphire.ucc.nau.edu/~ihd/techact.html [May 23, 1997].

The Lighthouse, Inc. (1995) *The Lighthouse national survey on vision loss: the experience, attitudes, and knowledge of middle-aged and older Americans.* New York: Author.

The technology-related assistance for individuals with disabilities act [On-line]. Available: www.ed.gov/legislation/FedRegister/finrule/1996-1/fr0/mr6a.html [May 23, 1997].

Thomas, J. (1981). *CIL second careers exploring vocational opportunities with visually impaired older people.* New York: Infirmary Beekman Downtown Hospital/Center for Independent Living.

Thornton, G., & Byham, W. (1982). *Assessment centers and managerial performance.* New York: Academic Press.

Tiedeman, D. (1961). Decisions and vocational development: A paradigm and its implications. *Personnel and Guidance Journal, 40,* 15–20.

Tielsch, J., Sommer, A., Witt, K., Katz, J., & Royall, R. (1990). Blindness and visual impairment in an American urban population. *Archives of Ophthalmology, 108,* 287–290.

Todd, J. (1986). Resources, media, and technology. In G. T. Scholl (Ed.), *Foundations of education for blind and visually handicapped children and youth: Theory and practice* (pp. 285–296). New York: American Foundation for the Blind.

Toffler, A. (1990). *Power shift.* New York: Bantam Doubleday Dell.

Tooze, L. (1980). *Independence training for visually handicapped children.* Baltimore: University Park Press.

Townsend, O. (1970). Vocational rehabilitation and the black counselor: The conventional training situation and the battleground across town. *Journal of Rehabilitation, 36*(6) 16–18.

Trybus, R. (1984). Demographics and population character research in deaf-blindness. In J. Stahlecker, L. Glass, & S. Machalow (Eds.), *State-of-the-art: Research priorities in deaf-blindness.* San Francisco: University of California, Center on Mental Health and Deafness.

Tucker, A., & Moore, J. E. (1997). *Inclusion of women in the Randolph–Sheppard program.* Mississippi State, MS: Rehabilitation Research and Training Center on Blindness and Low Vision.

Tuttle, D. W., & Tuttle, N. R. (1996). *Self-esteem and adjusting to blindness: The process of responding to life's demands.* Springfield, IL: Charles C. Thomas.

U.S. Department of Health and Human Services. (1983). Female social security beneficiaries aged 62 or older, 1960–1982. *Social Security Bulletin, 46*(9).

U. S. Department of Health and Human Services, Public Health Service, and National Institutes of Health. (1982). *Diabetes and your eyes.* Bethesda, MD: Author.

U.S. Department of Labor. (1991). *Dictionary of occupational titles* (4th ed.). Washington, DC: U.S. Government Printing Office.

U.S. Department of Labor. (1991). *The revised handbook for analyzing jobs.* Washington, DC: U.S. Government Printing Office.

U.S. Department of Labor, Bureau of Labor Statistics. (1983). *Women at work: A chartbook.* Washington, DC: U.S. Government Printing Office.

U.S. Department of Labor, Bureau of Labor Statistics. (1997, April). *Employment and earnings, 44*(4). Washington, DC: U.S. Government Printing Office.

U.S. Department of Labor, Women's Bureau. (1980). *Facts on women workers.* Washington, DC: U.S. Government Printing Office.

United States Health Care Financing Administration. (1992). *Code of federal regulations, Title 20, Chapter III, DHHS (HCFA)* (pp. 279–282). Washington, DC: Author.

United States Health Care Financing Administration. (1995). *Evaluation of visual fields for disability determination, DHHS publication no. 367-021/20088.* Washington, DC: U.S. Government Printing Office.

University of Wisconsin. (1986). *Replicating jobs in business and industry for persons with disabilities.* Madison: University of Wisconsin, Vocational Study Center.

Uslan, M. M., & Shragai, Y. (1995). Screen-magnification software for IBM-compatible computers: An overview. *Journal of Visual Impairment & Blindness News Service, Part II, 89*(1), 19–22.

Uslan, M. M., Asenjo, J., & Peck, A. (1982). Demand for rehabilitation teachers in 1981. *Journal of Visual Impairment and Blindness, 76,* 412–416.

Uslan, M. M., Hill, E., & Peck, A. (1989). *The profession of orientation and mobility in the 1980s: The AFB competency study.* New York: American Foundation for the Blind.

Uslan, M. M., Russell, L., & Weiner, C. (1988). A 'musical pathway' for spatially disoriented blind residents of a skilled nursing facility. *Journal of Visual Impairments & Blindness, 82,* 21–24.

Van Dusen, R., & Sheldon, E. (1978). The changing status of American women: A life cycle perspective. In L. Hansen, & R. Rapoza (Eds.), *Career development and counseling of women* (pp. 78–96). Springfield, IL: Charles C. Thomas.

Van Hoose, W., & Kottler, J. (1985). *Ethical and legal issues in counseling and psychotherapy* (2nd ed.). San Francisco: Jossey-Bass.

Van Zandt, P., Van Zandt, S., & Wang, A. (1994). The role of support groups in adjusting to visual impairment in old age. *Journal of Visual Impairment & Blindness, 88,* 244–252.

Vandergoot, D., & Worrall, J. (Eds.). (1979). *Placement in rehabilitation.* Austin, TX: PRO-ED.

Vander Kolk, C. (1981). *Assessment and planning with the visually impaired.* Baltimore: University Park Press.

Vander Kolk, C. (1982). A comparison of intelligence test score patterns between visually impaired subgroups and the sighted. *Rehabilitation Psychology, 27*(2), 115–120.

Vander Kolk, C. (1987). Psychosocial assessment of visually impaired persons. In B. Heller, L Flohr, & L Zegans (Eds.), *Psychosocial interventions with sensorially disabled persons* (pp. 35–52). New York: Grune & Stratton.

Vash, C. (1981). *The psychology of disability.* Springer Series on Rehabilitation (Vol. 1). New York: Springer.

Vash, C. (1982). Women and employment in women. In L. Perlman, & K. Arneson (Eds.), *Women and rehabilitation of disabled persons* (pp. 21–27). Alexandria, VA: National Rehabilitation Association.

Vaughan, D. G., Asbury, T., & Riordan-Eva, P. (1992). General ophthalmology (13th ed.). Los Altos, CA: Lange Medical Publications.

Vaughan, D. G., Asbury, T., & Riordan-Eva, P. (1995). *General ophthalmology* (14th ed.). Norwalk, CT: Appleton & Lange.

Verplanken, B., Meijnders, A., & van de Wege, A. (1994). Emotion and cognition: Attitudes toward persons who are visually impaired. *Journal of Visual Impairment & Blindness, 88,* 504–511.

Vickers, R. (1987). A psychological approach to attitudes toward blind persons. *Journal of Visual Impairment & Blindness, 81,* 323–325.

Vinger, P., Knuttgen, H., Easterbrook, M., Pashley, T., & Schnell, D. (1988). Eye injuries and eye protection in sports. *Physician and Sports Medicine, 16*(11), 49–51.

Vocational Evaluation and Work Adjustment Association. (1975). *Vocational evaluation project: Final report.* Menomonie: University of Wisconsin—Stout, Materials Development Center.

Vroom, V. H. (1964). *Work and motivation.* New York: Wiley.

Wachtel, P. (1993). *Therapeutic communication: Principles and effective practice.* New York: Guilford.

Wagner-Lampl, A., & Oliver, G. (1994). Folklore of blindness. *Journal of Visual Impairment & Blindness, 88,* 267–276.

Wainapel, S. F. (1989). Vision loss: A patient's perspective. In S. L. Greenblatt (Ed.), *Providing services for people with vision loss—a multidisciplinary perspective* (p. 7). Lexington, MA: Resources for Rehabilitation.

Waiss, B. & Cohen J. (1991). Glare and contrast sensitivity for low vision practitioners. *Prob Optom, 3*(3), 433–48.

Walker, S., Akpati, E., Roberts, V., Palmer; R., & Newsome, M. (1986). Frequency and distribution of disabilities among blacks: Preliminary findings. In S. Walker, F. Belgrave, A. Banner, & R. Nicholls (Eds.), *Equal to the challenge: Perspectives, problems, and strategies in the rehabilitation of the nonwhite disabled* (pp. 27–38). Washington, DC:

Howard University, Bureau of Educational Research.

Wallace, J. (1972). Attitudes and blindness. In R. Hardy & J. Cull (Eds.), *Social and rehabilitation services for the blind* (pp. 139–152). Springfield, IL: Charles C. Thomas.

Walters, D. (1980). *Performance of older workers.* Paper presented at meeting of American Foundation for the Blind.

Ward, M. E. (1986). Planning the individualized education program. In G. T. Scholl (Ed.), *Foundations of education for blind and visually handicapped children and youth: Theory and practice* (pp. 215–238). New York: American Foundation for the Blind.

Warren, D. (1994). *Blindness and children: An individual differences approach.* New York: Cambridge University Press.

Warren, D., Asooshian, L., & Bollinger, J. (1973). Early vs. late blindness: The role of early vision in spacial behavior. *American Foundation for the Blind Research Bulletin, 26,* 151–170.

Warren, M. (1992). A hierarchical model for evaluation and treatment of visual perceptual dysfunction in adult acquired brain injury, parts 1 and 2. *American Journal of Occupational Therapy, 47,* 42–65.

Warren, J., & Gandy, M. (1988). Counseling to maximize potential: Case study of a disaffected blind worker. *Journal of Visual Impairment & Blindness, 82,* 10–12.

Wegmann, R., Chapman, R., & Johnson, M. (1985). *Looking for work in the new economy.* Salt Lake City: Olympus Publishing.

Wehman, P. (1981). *Competitive employment: New horizons for severely disabled individuals.* Baltimore: Paul H. Brookes.

Wehman, P., & Moon, M. (Eds.). (1988). *Vocational rehabilitation and supported employment.* Baltimore: Paul H. Brookes.

Wehman, P., Hill, J., Wood, W., & Parent, W. (1987). A report on competitive employment histories of persons labeled severely mentally retarded. *Journal of the Association for Persons with Severe Handicaps, 12,* 11–17.

Wehman, P., Kregel, J., & Barcus, J. (1985). From school to work: A vocational transitional model for handicapped students. *Exceptional Children, 52,* 25–37.

Wehman, P., Moon, M., Everson, J., Wood, W., & Barcus, J. (1988). *Transition from school to work: New challenges for youth with severe disabilities.* Baltimore: Paul H. Brookes.

Weil, M., & Karls, J. (1985). *Case management in human service practice.* San Francisco: Jossey-Bass.

Weinstock, F. (1987). Vision in the 1980s: A bright outlook for senior citizens. *Journal of Visual Impairment & Blindness, 81*(7), 313–16.

Weishan, R. (1973). Toward involving the total community in career education. *New Outlook for the Blind, 67,* 414–423.

Weitzman, D. (1993). Promoting healthful exercise for visually impaired persons with diabetes. *Journal of Visual Impairment & Blindness, 87,* 361–364.

Welsh, R. (1981). Promoting adult independence through orientation and mobility. *Journal of Visual Impairment & Blindness, 75,* 115–121.

Welsh, R., & Blasch, B. (Eds.). (1980). *Foundations of orientation and mobility.* New York: American Foundation for the Blind.

Westin, M., & Reiss, D. (1979). The family role in rehabilitation: Early warning systems. *Journal of Rehabilitation, 45*(1), 26–29.

Wetstein-Kroft, S., & Vargo, J. (1984). Changing children's attitudes towards disability: A review and analysis of the literature. *International Journal for the Advancement of Counseling, 7*(3), 181–195.

White, S., & Kennedy, K. (1981). Improving the work productivity of a mentally retarded woman in a city restaurant. In P. Wehman (Ed.), *Competitive employment: New horizons for severely disabled individuals* (pp. 68–70). Baltimore: Paul H. Brookes.

Whitstock, R. H. (1980). Dog guides. In R. Welsh & B. Blasch (Eds.), *Foundations of orientation and mobility* (pp. 556–580). New York: American Foundation for the Blind.

Who cares: A handbook on sex education and counseling services for disabled persons. (1979). Washington, DC: George Washington University Sex and Disability Project.

Wiener, W. (1980). Audition. In R. Welsh & B. Blasch (Eds.), *Foundations of orientation and mobility* (p. 115–185). New York: American Foundation for the Blind.

Wiener, W., & Bussen, P. (1988). Shortages in personnel serving children and adults who are blind: A recruitment dilemma. *The yearbook of the Association for the Education and Rehabilitation of the Blind and Visually Impaired (AER).* Alexandria, VA: AER.

Wiener W., & Hill, E. (1991). *Manual for orientation and mobility assistant trainer/supervisors.* Alexandria, VA: Association for Education and Rehabilitation of the Blind and Visually Impaired.

Wiener, W., & Joffee, E. (1993). The O&M personnel shortage and university training programs. *RE:view, 25,* 67–75.

Wiener, W., & Luxton, L. (1994). The development of guidelines for university programs in rehabilitation teaching. *RE:view, 26*(1), 7–14.

Wiener, W., & Uslan, M. (1990). Mobility assistants: A perspective on new service providers. *RE:view, 22,* 56–68.

Wiener, W., & Welsh, R. (1980). The profession of orientation and mobility. In R. Welsh & B. Blasch (Eds.), *Foundations of orientation and mobility* (pp. 625–651). New York: American Foundation for the Blind.

Wilkinson, G. S. (1993). WRAT3 Administration Manual. Wilmington, DE: Wide Range.

Will, M. (1985). Transition: Linking disabled youth to a productive future. *OSERS News in Print, 1*(1), 1.

Will, M. (1984). *Bridges from school to working life: OSERS programming for the transition of youth with disabilities.* Washington, DC: Office of Special Education and Rehabilitation Services, U.S. Department of Education.

Williams, A. (1993). Diabetes education for visually impaired people at Cleveland Sight Center, *Journal of Visual Impairment & Blindness, 87,* 352–353.

Williams, D. (1996). Functional adaptive devices. In: E. Cole, & B. Rosenthal, (Eds.), *Remediation and management of low vision.* St. Louis: Mosby-Year Book.

Winer, M. (1982). Self-help programs for people with sight loss. *Journal of Visual Impairment & Blindness, 76,* 393–397.

Winking, D., O'Reilly, B., & Moon, M. (1993). Preference: The missing link in the job match process for individuals without functional communication skills. *Journal of Vocational Rehabilitation, 3*(3), 27–42.

Winkler, D. (1975). Family role adjustment to blindness in one member. *Travailler Social, 43,* 19–23.

Witkin, H., Oltman, P., Chase, J., & Friedman, F. (1971). Cognitive patterning in the blind. In J. Helmuth (Ed.), *Cognitive Studies* (Vol. 2, pp. 16–46). New York: Brunner/Mazel.

Wolffe, K. E. (1985). Don't give those kids fish! Teach 'em how to fish! *Journal of Visual Impairment & Blindness, 79*(10), 470–471.

Wolffe, K. E. (1986). *The relationship between pre-employment skills training and successful placement of hard-to-employ rehabilitation clients* (Doctoral dissertation, University of Texas 1986). Dissertation Abstracts International, DES86-18595.

Wolffe, K. E. (1997a). *Career counseling for people with disabilities: A practical guide to finding employment.* Austin, TX: PRO-ED.

Wolffe, K. E. (1997b). *Do the rules change when you hire a person with a visual impairment?* Austin: Texas Commission for the Blind.

Wolffe, K. E. & Sacks, S. Z. (1995). *Social network pilot project: Final report.* (Department of Education grant H023A30108). Unpublished manuscript.

Work, aging, and vision. (1987). Report of a conference. Washington, DC: National Academy Press.

World Health Organization. (1973). The prevention of blindness: Report of WHO study group. *Report services 518.* New York: Author.

World Health Organization. (1980). *International classification of impairments, disabilities, and handicaps.* Geneva: Author.

Wormsley, D. (1979). *Effect of a hand movement training program on the hand movements and reading rates of young braille readers.* Unpublished Dissertation. Pittsburgh: University of Pittsburgh.

Wright, B. (1990). *Physical disability: A psychosocial approach* (2nd ed.). New York: Harper and Row.

Wright, G. N. (1980). *Total rehabilitation.* Boston: Little, Brown.

Wynne, B. (1980, June). *The power of touch: Communication and education.* Presented at Helen Keller Centennial Congress, Boston, MA.

Wynne, B. (1987). The population—who are they? In S. Barrett, T. Carr, T., & A. Covert (Eds.), *Community-based living options for young adults with deaf-blindness: Philosophy, directions, and strategies* (pp. 3–26). Sands Point, NY: Helen Keller National Center.

Yeadon, A. (1984). The informal care group: Problem or potential? *Journal of Visual Impairment & Blindness, 78,* 149–154.

Yee, A. (1983). Ethnicity and race: Psychological perspectives. *Educational Psychologist, 18*(1), 14–24.

Young, C. E. (1995). A focus group on employment. *Journal of Visual Impairment & Blindness, JVIB News Service, 89*(1), 14–17.

Yuspeh, S. (1982). *Handbook of job analysis for reasonable accommodation (PMS 720—B).* Washington, DC: U.S. Government Printing Office.

Zasler, N. (1990). The role of the psychiatrist. In P. Wehman & J. S. Kreutzer (Eds.), *Vocational rehabilitation for persons with traumatic brain injury.* Rockville, MD: Aspen.

Zavon, B. & Slater, N. (1988). A surgical counseling plan for patients undergoing cataract surgery. *Journal of Ophthalmic Nursing & Technology 7(2),* 68–71.

Zimmerman, G. (1992). Orientation and mobility training: Enhancing the employment prospects for people with blindness and visual impairments. *Journal of Vocational Rehabilitation, 2*(1), 66–72.

Zitnay, G. (1995). Head injury. In A. E. Dell Orto & R. P. Marinelli (Eds.), *Encyclopedia of disability and rehabilitation* (pp. 361–366). New York: Macmillan.

Commission for the Blind
Individualized Written Rehabilitation Program

Client's name Heraldo A. Gomez ______ **Extended evaluation**

Agency representative John D. Thomas __X__ **Initial rehabilitation program**

Case number 12345 ______ **Major program revision**

______ **Independent living program**

This Is Your Rehabilitation Program

Part 1. Vocational Goal Accountant **D.O.T. No.** ______

Part 2. Date of Program Initiation ______ **Date That Goal Is Expected to Be Reached** ______

Part 3. Major Steps Needed to Reach the Goal (Numbered intermediate objectives and dates of expected completion)

1. Heraldo will follow the instructions of his ophthalmologist to maintain maximum visual acuity and overcome functional limitations.
2. Heraldo will obtain assistive technology needed to function as an accountant.
3. Heraldo will learn to use his CCTV in an effective and efficient manner.
4. Heraldo will actively participate in a mental health treatment program for his depression.
5. Heraldo will acquire orientation and mobility (O&M) skills needed to travel safely to and from work and in his community at large.
6. Heraldo will come to work on time and will carry out his assigned accounting responsibilities in a timely and effective manner.

(continued on next page)

Appendix A. Sample Individualized Written Rehabilitation Program

Source: Reprinted from A. Corn and A. Koenig (Eds.), *Foundations of Low Vision: Clinical and Functional Perspectives* (New York: AFB Press, 1996).

Individualized Written Rehabilitation Program (*continued*)

Part 4: Services Necessary to Reach Objectives

Client's Name Heraldo A. Gomez **Case Number** 12345

Objective Number	Services Necessary to Reach Objectives	Starting Date	Ending Date	Resources/Provider	Rate (Amount per hour)	Total Cost	Progress Review[a]
1.	Clinical low vision examination and treatment as required.			Vocational Rehabilitation for the Blind			
2.	Purchase a CCTV and personal computer with magnification software for use in performing accounting duties.			Vocational Rehabilitation for the Blind Local Lions Club			
3.	Training in the use of adaptive equipment at the local rehabilitation center.			Vocational Rehabilitation for the Blind			
4.	Guidance and counseling as needed.			Vocational Rehabilitation for the Blind and regional mental health center			
5.	O&M training at the local rehabilitation center.			Vocational Rehabilitation for the Blind			
6.	Public transportation services.			Metro Handilift			

Note: (The counselor should complete this section on the basis of scheduled reviews)

[a]*Periodic Progress Review: Please record a cross reference to the case file for each periodic review.*

(*continued on next page*)

Individualized Written Rehabilitation Program (*continued*)

Client's Name Heraldo A. Gomez **Case Number** 12345

Part 5. Comparable Benefits and Services

The local Lions Club will be used to obtain partial payment for the purchase of a CCTV. The local handilift van service will be used to provide transportation to and from work. Heraldo will use his health insurance for follow-up visits to the ophthalmologist.

Part 6. Specific Responsibilities of the Client and Agency Representative

The client agrees to keep all appointments and to cooperate with the vocational rehabilitation counselor in completing his rehabilitation program. The counselor, in turn, will work closely with the local Lions Club and the handilift transportation service to coordinate the purchase of a CCTV and make arrangements for transportation to and from work.

Part 7. Progress Will Be Evaluated by (list by numbered intermediate objects. Note: Status 06 must be evaluated at least every 90 days).

1. Eye examination report from the low vision clinic.
2. Evaluation report from the assistive technology specialist with regard to which personal computer and adaptive software is recommended for purchase.
3. Monthly facility progress reports that reflect the client's progress in learning to use his adaptive hardware and software.
4. Weekly meetings of the client and the vocational rehabilitation counselor and monthly progress reports from the regional mental health center.
5. Monthly progress report from the O&M instructor.
6. Periodic contact with the employer regarding the client's work performance.

(*continued on next page*)

Individualized Written Rehabilitation Program (*continued*)

Client's Name Heraldo A. Gomez **Case Number** 12345

Part 8. Statement in client's, parent's, guardian's, or representative's own words of how he or she participated in formulating his or her program:

Client	Date	Agency Representative	Date

Part 9. Program Annual Progress Reviews: (Includes 06 cases at 12 months)

The client and agency representative have reviewed and discussed the program and agree on the program, the progress being made, and program changes, if any. See case-record entry for details.

Client	Date	Agency Representative	Date	(first review)

Client	Date	Agency Representative	Date	(second review)

Client	Date	Agency Representative	Date	(third review)

Job Analysis Worksheet: ADA Essential Functions

Job Title: Vocational Rehabilitation Counselor

D.O.T. Code: 045.107-042 **S.I.C. Code:** N/A

Consultant ______

Company State Commission For the Blind

Address ______

City, State, Zip ______

Contact Person: John Q. Supervisor

Education/Training/Experience/License Required

Circle: 8th HS: 1 2 3 4 Col: 1 2 3 4 5 (6) 7

Special Training: Graduate training in rehabilitation counseling

Certification/License: CRC preferred

Suggested resources for completing the **Job Analysis Worksheet**

ADA Manual for Rehabilitation Consultants, Field, T. & Norton, L. (1992). Elliott & Fitzpatrick, Inc. Athens, GA

The **Revised Classification of Jobs,** Field, J. & Field, T. (1992). Elliott & Fitzpatrick, Inc., Athens, GA.

The **Revised Dictionary of Occupational Titles.** (1991). U.S. Government Printing Office.

The **Revised Handbook for Analyzing Jobs.** (1991). U.S. Government Printing Office.

Evaluate each of the following job elements that are critical to the performance of the job; leave blank if not applicable.

- **Critical to the performance of the job.**
- **Enter percent of time performing task, e.g., "Standing" — 60%/Time**
- **Risk to self or others (enter "S" or "O").**
- **Relevant to Essential Function # ____ (see page 8).**

(continued on next page)

Appendix B. Sample Job Analysis Worksheet: Americans with Disabilities Act Essential Functions

Source: Reprinted with permission from Elliott & Fitzpatrick, Inc., Athens, GA, 1992.

Job Analysis Worksheet: ADA Essential Functions (*continued*)

SPECIFIC VOCATIONAL PREPARATION

Rate Level of Performance

SVP: "1" = Low; "9" = High.
GED: "6" = High level of performance; "1" = Low level.
Aptitudes: "1" = High; "5" = Low

Factor	Time	Rating	Relevant to Function #
Duration *For the purpose of rating jobs, TRAINING TIME is defined as the amount of general educational development and specific vocational preparation required of a worker to acquire the knowledge and abilities necessary for average performance in a particular job-worker situation.*	______	8	1-4

1. Short time only.
2. Anything beyond short demonstration up to and including 30 days.
3. Over 30 days up to and including 3 months.
4. Over 3 months up to and including 6 months.
5. Over 6 months up to and including 1 year.
6. Over 1 year up to and including 2 years.
7. Over 2 years up to and including 4 years.
8. Over 4 years up to and including 10 years.
9. Over 10 years.

GENERAL EDUCATIONAL DEVELOPMENT

Factor		Time	Rating	Relevant to Function #
1. Reasoning	*GED embraces those aspects of education (formal and informal) which contribute to the worker's (a) reasoning development and ability to follow instructions, and (b) acquisition of "tool" knowledge P=3 such as language and mathematical skills. This is education of a general nature which does not have a recognized, fairly specific occupational objective. Ordinarily, such education is obtained in elementary school, high school, or college. However, it derives also from experience and self-study.*	______	5	1-4
2. Mathematics		______	3	1-4
3. Language		______	5	1-4

(*continued on next page*)

Job Analysis Worksheet: ADA Essential Functions (*continued*)

APTITUDES

Rate Level of Performance

1. **The top 10 percent of the population. This segment of the population possesses an extremely high degree of the aptitude.**
2. **The highest third exclusive of the top 10 percent of the population. This segment of the population possesses an above average degree of the aptitude.**
3. **The middle third of the population. This segment of the population possesses a medium degree of the aptitude, ranging from slightly below to slightly above average.**
4. **The lowest third exclusive of the bottom 10 percent of the population. This segment of the population possesses a below average or low degree of the aptitude.**
5. **The lowest 10 percent of the population. This segment of the population possesses a negligible degree of the aptitude.**

Factor	Time	Rating	Relevant to Function #
1. **Intelligence** *General learning ability.*		2	1 - 4
2. **Verbal** *Ability to understand meanings of words and ideas associated with them, and to use them effectively.*		2	1 - 4
3. **Numerical** *Ability to perform arithmetic operations quickly and accurately.*		3	1 - 4
4. **Spatial Perception** *Ability to comprehend forms in space and understand relationships of plane and solid objects.*		4	2 - 4
5. **Form Perception** *Ability to perceive pertinent detail of objects in pictorial or graphic material.*		4	2 - 4
6. **Clerical Perception** *Ability to perceive pertinent detail in verbal or tabular matter.*		3	2 - 4
7. **Motor Coordination** *Ability to coordinate eyes and hands or fingers rapidly and accurately in making precise movements.*		4	4
8. **Finger Dexterity** *Ability to move the fingers and manipulate small objects with the fingers rapidly and accurately.*		4	4
9. **Manual Dexterity** *Ability to move the hands easily and skillfully.*		4	4
10. **Eye/Hand/Foot Coordination** *Ability to move the hand and foot coordinately with each other in accordance with visual stimuli.*		5	
11. **Color Discimination** *Ability to perceive or recognize similarities or differences in colors, or in shades or other values of the same color or to identify a particular color.*		5	

(*continued on next page*)

Job Analysis Worksheet: ADA Essential Functions (*continued*)

PHYSICAL DEMANDS

Factor	Time	Critical to Performance	Risk	Relevant to Function #
1. Strength	______	______	______	______
— Standing *Remaining on one's feet in an upright position at a work station without moving about.*				
— Walking *Moving about on foot.*	______	______	______	______
— Sitting *Remaining in the normal seated position.*	______	______	______	______
— Lifting *To exert physical strength necessary to move objects from one level to another.*	______	______	______	______

	Never	Rarely	Occas.	Freq.	Cont.
Under 10 lbs.	______	______	______	x	______
10 to 25 lbs.	______	______	______	______	______
26 to 60 lbs.	______	______	______	______	______
61 to 75 lbs.	______	______	______	______	______
76 to 100 lbs.	______	______	______	______	______
Over 100 lbs.	______	______	______	______	______

Factor	Time	Critical to Performance	Risk	Relevant to Function #
— Carrying *Transporting an object, usually holding it in the hands or arms or on shoulders.*	______	______	______	______

	Never	Rarely	Occas.	Freq.	Cont.
Under 10 lbs.	______	______	______	x	______
10 to 25 lbs.	______	______	______	______	______
26 to 60 lbs.	______	______	______	______	______
61 to 75 lbs.	______	______	______	______	______
76 to 100 lbs.	______	______	______	______	______
Over 100 lbs.	______	______	______	______	______

Factor	Time	Critical to Performance	Risk	Relevant to Function #
— Pushing *Exerting force upon an object so that the object moves away from the force (includes slapping, striking, kicking, and treadle actions).*	______	______	______	______
— Pulling *Exerting force upon an object so that the object moves toward the force (includes jerking).*	______	______	______	______

(*continued on next page*)

Job Analysis Worksheet: ADA Essential Functions (*continued*)

PHYSICAL DEMANDS (continued)

Factor	Time	Critical to Performance	Risk	Relevant to Function #
2. Climbing *To ascend or descend ladders, scaffolding, stairs, poles, inclined surfaces.*	______	______	______	______
3. Balancing *To maintain a body equilibrium to prevent falling when walking, standing, crouching, or running on narrow, slippery or erratically moving surfaces.*	______	______	______	______
4. Stooping *Bending the body downward and forward by bending the spine at the waist. This factor is important if it occurs to a considerable degree and requires full use of lower extremities and back muscles.*	______	______	______	______
5. Kneeling *Bending the legs at the knees to come to rest on the knee or knees.*	______	______	______	______
6. Crouching *Bending body downward and forward by bending legs and spine.*	______	______	______	______
7. Crawling *Moving about on hands and knees or hands and feet.*	______	______	______	______
8. Reaching *Extending the hand(s) and arm(s) in any direction.*	______	______	______	______
9. Handling *Seizing, holding, grasping, turning or otherwise working with hand or hands (fingering not involved).*	______	______	______	______
10. Fingering *Picking, pinching, or otherwise working with fingers primarily (rather than with whole hand or arm as in handling).*	______	______	______	______
11. Feeling *Perceiving attitudes of objects such as size, shape, temperature or texture by means of receptor in skin, particularly those of finger tips.*	______	______	______	______
12. Talking *Expressing or exchanging ideas by means of the spoken word.*	______	x	______	1-4
13. Hearing *Perceiving the nature of sounds by the air.*	______	x	______	1-4
14. Tasting/Smelling *Distinguishing, with a degree of accuracy, differences or similarities in intensity or quality of flavors and/or odors, using tongue and/or nose.*	______	______	______	______
15. Near Acuity *Clarity of vision at 20 inches or less. This factor is important when special and minute accuracy is demanded and when defective near acuity would adversely affect job performance and/or the safety of others.*	______	______	______	______

(*continued on next page*)

Job Analysis Worksheet: ADA Essential Functions (*continued*)

PHYSICAL DEMANDS (continued)

Factor	Time	Critical to Performance	Risk	Relevant to Function #
16. Far Acuity *Clarity of vision at 20 feet or more. This factor is important when visual efficiency in terms of far acuity is required and defective far acuity would adversely affect job performance and/or the safety of others.*	______	______	______	______
17. Depth Perception *Three-dimensional vision. Ability to judge distances and spatial relationships so as to see objects where and as they really are. This factor is important when depth perception is required for successful job performance and/or for reason of safety to oneself and others.*	______	______	______	______
18. Accommodation *Adjustment of lens of eye to bring an object into sharp focus. This factor is important when doing near point work at varying distances from eye.*	______	______	______	______
19. Color Vision *Ability to identify and distinguish colors.*	______	______	______	______
20. Field of Vision *Observing an area that can be seen up and down or right to left when eyes are fixed on a given point. This factor is important when job performance requires seeing a large area while keeping eye fixed.*	______	______	______	______

ENVIRONMENTAL CONDITIONS

Factor	Critical to Performance	Risk	Relevant to Function #
1. Exposure to Weather *Exposure to hot, cold, wet, humid, or windy conditions, caused by the weather. This factor is rated important when exposure to weather results in marked bodily discomfort.*	______	______	______
2. Extreme Cold *Exposure to nonweather-related cold temperatures. This factor is rated important when temperatures are sufficiently low to cause marked bodily discomfort.*	______	______	______

	Code	Level	Illustrative Examples
____	1	Very Quiet	isolation booth for hearing test; deep sea diving; forest trail
____	2	Quiet	library; many private offices; funeral reception; golf course; art museum
x	3	Moderate	business office where typewriters are used; department store; grocery story; light traffic; fast food restaurant at off-hours
____	4	Loud	can manufacturing department; large earth-moving equipment; heavy traffic
____	5	Very Loud	rock concert—front row; jackhammer work; rocket engine testing area during test

(*continued on next page*)

Job Analysis Worksheet: ADA Essential Functions (*continued*)

ENVIRONMENTAL CONDITIONS (continued)

Factor	Critical to Performance	Risk	Relevant to Function #
3. Extreme Heat *Exposure to nonweather-related cold temperatures. This factor is rated important when temperatures are sufficiently high to cause marked bodily discomfort.*	______	______	______
4. Wet and/or Humid *Contact with weather or other liquids; or exposure to nonweather-related humid conditions. This factor is rated important when contact with wter or other liquids or exposure to humidity causes marked bodily discomfort.*	______	______	______
5. Noise *Exposure to constant or intermittent sounds of a pitch or level sufficient to cause marked distraction or possible hearing loss.*	______	______	______
6. Vibration *Exposure to a shaking object or surface. This factor is rated important when vibration causes a strain on the body or extremities.*	______	______	______
7. Atmospheric Conditions *Exposure to conditions, such as fumes, noxious odors, dusts, mists, gases and poor ventilation, that affect the respiratory system, eyes, or the skin. This factor is rated important if these conditions are present to a degree or length of time sufficient to cause marked bodily discomfort or possible injury.*	______	______	______
8. Hazards *A hazard is a condition in the work environment that subjects or exposes the worker to the possibility of serious bodily injury or danger to the worker's life or health. A hazard is specific, related to the job, and has a greater likelihood of occurring than it would away from the job. The following conditions are evaluated as possible hazards in specific jobs.*			
a. Moving Parts	______	______	______
b. Electrical Shock	______	______	______
c. High, Exposed Places	______	______	______
d. Radiant Energy	______	______	______
e. Explosives	______	______	______
f. Toxic Chemicals	______	______	______
g. Other Hazards	______	______	______

TEMPERAMENTS

Factor	Time	Critical to Performance	Relevant to Function #
1. Working Alone *Performing work activities by oneself and away from others.*	______	______	______
2. Directing Others *Adaptability to accepting responsibility for the direction, control, or planning of an activity.*	______	______	______
3. Expressing Personal Feelings *Adaptability to situations involving the interpretation of feelings, ideas, or facts in terms of personal viewpoint.*	______	x	1

(continued on next page)

Job Analysis Worksheet: ADA Essential Functions (*continued*)

TEMPERAMENTS (continued)

Factor	Time	Critical to Performance	Relevant to Function #
4. Influencing People *Adaptability to influencing people about the opinions, attitudes, or judgments about ideas or things.*	______	x	2-3
5. Making Judgments *Adaptability to making generalizations, evaluations or decisions based on sensory or judgmental criteria.*	______	x	1-4
6. Performing Repetitive Work *Adaptability to performing work, or to continuously performing the same work, according to set procedures, sequence, or pace.*	______	______	______
7. Performing Under Stress *Adaptability to performing under stress when confronted with emergency, critical, unusual, or dangerous situations; or in situations in which working speed and sustained attention are make or break aspects of the job.*	______	______	______
8. Attaining Tolerances *Adaptability to situations requiring the precise attainment of set limits, tolerances, or standards.*	______	______	______
9. Working Under Instructions *Adaptability to dealing with people beyond giving and receiving instructions.*	______	x	1-4
10. Performing a Variety of Duties *Adaptability to performing a variety of duties, often changing from one task to another of a different nature without loss of efficiency or composure.*	______	x	1-4

ESSENTIAL FUNCTIONS

Brief Narrative Description of Essential Job Functions (tasks and activities)

1. Provides counseling and other vocational rehabilitation services to individuals with disabilities
2. Interviews and evaluates applicants for vocational rehabilitation services based on established eligibility criteria
3. Assists individuals with disabilities in selecting a vocational objective
4. Conducts job development and placement activities in collaboration with individuals with disabilities
5. ______

Comprehensive Vocational/Psychological Evaluation Report

NAME: Robert O'Brian

SOCIAL SECURITY # : 123-45-6788
DATE OF BIRTH : 10/15/79
DATE OF EVALUATION: 2/12/97
HEIGHT: 5/6 **AGE:** 17 yrs/04 mos

WEIGHT: 120 **SEX:** M
HAND PREFERENCE : L
EVALUATOR: Lynn Jones, M.Ed.
Psychologist/Diagnostician

ADDRESS : 7 Rock Trail
University City, TX 78100
TELEPHONE : (410) 000-0000

CONTACT : Dennis O'Brian, Father
Same address as consumer

VR STATUS : 18
PREPARED FOR: Susan Smith, VRC
Starkville, D. O.

PRIMARY DISABILITY: Visual Functioning Level: Legally Blind. VA = LP-OS, 10/200 w < 10 degree VD-OD.

Etiology or Diagnosis of Visual Impairment: Robert is legally blind due to bilateral aphakia and severe retinopathy of prematurity (ROP) with extensive retinal scarring and a repaired retinal detachment resulting in a less than 10 degree visual field OD, and a total retinal detachment OS.

REASON FOR REFERRAL: Robert was referred for a vocational/psychological evaluation for assistance in determining his level of vocational potential, and for help with program planning.

TESTS ADMINISTERED

INTELLECTUAL
Wechsler Adult Intelligence Scale-Revised (WAIS-R), Verbal Scale only
Cognitive Test for the Blind (CTB)

ACADEMIC ACHIEVEMENT
Wide Range Achievement Test-Revised² (WRAT-R²)

SENSORY
Haptic Sensory Discrimination Test (HSDT)

MOTOR
McCarron Assessment of Neuromuscular Development (MAND)

EMOTIONAL/BEHAVIORAL
Emotional Behavioral Checklist (EBC)

(*continued on next page*)

Appendix C. Sample Comprehensive Vocational/Psychological Evaluation Report

Source: Reprinted with the permission of the Texas Commission for the Blind, Austin, Texas, and based on the CVES protocol of the McCarron-Dial Systems, Dallas, Texas.

COPING/ADAPTIVE BEHAVIOR
Survey of Functional Adaptive Behaviors (SFAB)

VOCATIONAL INTEREST/EXPLORATION
Self-Directed Search, Form E (SDS-E)

OTHER
Diagnostic Interview

BACKGROUND INFORMATION

Robert is a 17-year-old legally blind junior at Sam Houston High School in Shiner, Texas. Robert lives with his parents and three brothers. Robert also has one older sister. Robert's father is a teacher. His mother is a registered nurse, however, she is currently unemployed. Robert is currently working for Aztec Mobile Phones and Paging as a sales representative.

PHYSICAL/MEDICAL

Robert is legally blind due to bilateral aphakia and retinopathy of prematurity (ROP) with extensive retinal scarring and a repaired retinal detachment-OD and a total retinal detachment-OS. Robert's visual acuity with best correction is 10/200-OD, Bare Light Perception Only-OS. Robert has left esotropia and nystagmus. His visual field in the right eye is less than 10°. Robert wears a +29 Silosoft extended wear aphakic contact lens in his right eye. He uses a 10x hand-held monocular for distance viewing and a 10x hand-held illuminated magnifier for close work. Robert is able to visually access large-print materials with the aid of a closed-circuit television (CCTV). He also utilizes a computer with voice access, braille access and large-print access. Robert does much of his written work with the aid of a tape recorder.

Robert reports that he is generally in good health. He does not take any medication on a regular basis. His appetite is good and he sleeps well. Robert is a member of the varsity wrestling team at his high school.

EDUCATION/VOCATIONAL TRAINING/WORK HISTORY

Robert is currently a junior at Sam Houston High School in Shiner, Texas. He reports that his best subject is English. He has had the most difficulty with Math and foreign languages. Robert attended Texas School for the Blind and Visually Impaired (TSBVI) during the 6th, 7th and 8th grades. He also attended the summer program at TSBVI from 1985 to 1989 and in 1994. Last summer, while attending TSBVI, Robert worked doing auto detailing. He held a job this school year for several months with Cameron Communications and he is currently employed with Aztec Mobile Phones and Paging. Robert reports that he

(*continued on next page*)

has a patent on a pager with braille access. Robert would like to go into the field of research and development in an effort to make telephones and paging devices more accessible for people with disabling conditions. Robert's hobbies include water skiing, wrestling, ham radio, and playing the guitar. He is an Eagle Scout and he is a member of an amateur radio rescue unit.

SUMMARY OF IMPRESSIONS

Robert presented as a legally blind Caucasian male in his late teens. Robert was well groomed and appropriately dressed at the time of evaluation.

Robert spoke in complete sentences using good grammar. He was able to relay information about himself in a clear and understandable manner and he followed test instructions without any difficulty. Robert's expressive and receptive English language skills appear to be in the high average range.

Robert travels with the aid of a mobility cane. He is able to travel independently in familiar indoor and outdoor environments. When traveling in unfamiliar locations, Robert is able to identify major landmarks and then find his way around. He has traveled by common carrier to another city without assistance.

Robert was cooperative throughout the evalution process. He appeared to put forth his best effort. Test results are felt to be an accurate and reliable reflection of Robert's current ability level.

INTELLECTUAL

The Verbal Scale of the Wechsler Adult Intelligence Scale-Revised (WAIS-R) and the Cognitive Test for the Blind (CTB) were used as measures of Robert's intellectual functioning. The Performance Scale of the WAIS-R was omitted due to his legal blindness. The following scaled scores were obtained on the WAIS-R:

Verbal Subtests	*Scaled Scores*
Information	8
Digit Span	10
Vocabulary	10
Arithmetic	7
Comprehension	14
Similarities	14

Verbal IQ = 115

(*continued on next page*)

Comprehensive Vocational/Psychological Evaluation Report (*continued*)

The following scores were obtained on the CTB:

Verbal Subtests	*Scaled Scores*	*Performance Subtests*	*Scaled Scores*
Auditory Analysis	12	Category Learning	16
Immediate Digit Recall	11	Category Memory	11
Language Comprehension	14	Memory Recognition	10
Letter Number Learning	13	Pattern Recall	15
Vocabulary	9	Spatial Analysis	13

Verbal Standard Score = 110 Performance Standard Score = 117

Total CTB Standard Score 113

Robert's Verbal IQ on the WAIS-R of 115 is within the high average to above average range. His Verbal Standard Score of 110 on the CTB is also within the high average range. Robert's Performance Standard Score of 117 on the CTB is within the high average to above average range and his Total Standard Score on the CTB is also within the high average to above average range. Robert demonstrated significant strength on measures of common sense and social judgment, verbal abstract reasoning, listening comprehension, abstract reasoning when information is presented tactilely and tactile pattern recall. Robert scored within the above average range in all of these areas. Robert scored within the high average range on measures of rote learning through memorization and tactile spatial analysis skills. He scored within the average range on measures of general fund of information, short-term auditory recall, the ability to recall word meanings and short-term tactile memory. Robert scored within the low average range on a measure of the ability to solve mathematical problems mentally. Overall, Robert's subscale scores range from low average to significantly above average.

VERBAL-SPATIAL-COGNITIVE INTERPRETATION

Robert's Verbal-Spatial-Cognitive (VSC) standard score of 114 is in the bright normal range of verbal-intellectual functioning. His sensorimotor functions are consistent with verbal-cognitive abilities; however, deficits in adaptive-coping functions that may compromise cognitive abilities were observed. His adaptive-coping deficits may interfere with learning and problem-solving activities. Robert's Verbal and Performance factor scores on the CTB do not significantly differ, thus suggesting approximately equal skills or aptitudes related to both verbal-language and non-language cognitive functions (thinking and/or learning of a non-verbal, image-oriented nature). Vocational objectives should primarily consider Robert's overall cognitive abilities and any specific strengths and/or deficits described below.

(*continued on next page*)

Comprehensive Vocational/Psychological Evaluation Report (*continued*)

Robert revealed strengths contrasted to his overall cognitive abilities in the following areas:

> Solving abstract spatial and conceptual problems—This factor is not only considered a "relative strength," but is also above average for the general population. Some consideration might be given to vocational objectives which involve further education or training.
>
> Learning concepts and symbols using feedback and practice—This factor is considered a "relative strength" and is also above average for the general population.

Robert would appear to have above average abilities to understand and communicate analogies and form concepts from his experience. He can transfer learning from one situation to another; therefore, consideration should be given to the applicability of any previously learned, vocationally relevant skills to Robert's present vocational objective.

Although Robert's reading ability (6th grade) is lower than would be expected for his intellectual level, it is, nevertheless, functionally relevant for many specific occupations in the community. He demonstrates seventh grade equivalency in writing (taping). Robert also demonstrates a math skill equivalency of grade eight. He can make precise measurements using a marked ruler, protractor, or balance scale. He can also mark and identify currency, count money, and make change.

Despite relatively higher VSC scores, Robert's overall evaluation profile would suggest the possible need for some further training/accommodation prior to community job placement.

ACADEMIC ACHIEVEMENT

Robert's level of academic achievement was measured using the Wide Range Achievement Test-Revised[2] (WRAT-R[2]). Test administration procedures were modified to accommodate for Robert's legal blindness. The following grade equivalents were obtained:

Subtests	*Grade Equivalents*
Reading Recognition	6th grade (Ending)
Oral Spelling	4th grade (Beginning)
Arithmetic	8th grade (Beginning)

The Reading Recognition subtest was presented in a Grade I braille format. Robert also uses a closed-circuit television (CCTV) for reading large print; however, he was unable to see the one-inch letters used in the large-print format of the Reading Recognition subtest. The Spelling subtest was responded to orally. The Arithmetic subtest was responded to orally first.

(*continued on next page*)

Comprehensive Vocational/Psychological Evaluation Report (*continued*)

Robert was then given an opportunity to solve additional mathematical equations using a large-print format. Robert is able to solve mathematical equations without the aid of any adaptive devices at a 4th to 5th grade level. With the aid of a talking calculator, he is able to solve mathematical problems at an 8th grade level. He demonstrated an understanding of addition, subtraction, multiplication, division, decimals, percentiles, and basic fractions.

SENSORY INTERPRETATION

Robert's Sensory factor score of 108 is in the high normal range when compared to the norms for the general population. Robert's sensory functions on the right side are significantly above average. He demonstrates very good skills in discriminating among various shapes, sizes, textures and configurations if they are presented to the right hand. Robert's sensory functions on the left side of the body are in the average range.

Robert appears to have basic orientation skills including orientation of body parts, orienting to stationary objects in space and tracking objects in space. He demonstrates unrestricted travel skills including travel by common carrier between distant points.

MOTOR INTERPRETATION

Robert's Motor factor score of 110 is in the normal range when compared to norms for the general population. He demonstrated approximately equal performance on both sides of the body as reflected by measures of speed, strength and coordination. Tasks of lower body balance, gross coordination and/or strength were performed significantly better than upper body tasks involving speed and/or coordination. Robert revealed "relative" deficits contrasted to his overall motor abilities in the following areas:

> Muscle Power—He may have less upper and/or lower body strength than his overall Motor factor score would predict. Tasks which require heavy lifting, carrying, pulling and/or pushing may be slightly more difficult for him; nevertheles, these abilities are also in the normal range when compared to the norms for the general population.

Robert's motor skills are sufficiently developed to permit safe operation of air powered and/or motor driven equipment. He is able to manipulate and place some objects that are as small as 1/8 inch. Robert is able to stand and maintain continuous performance for a full day. Robert has the ability to lift and carry items which weigh up to 50 pounds.

(*continued on next page*)

PSYCHOLOGICAL/EMOTIONAL

Robert appeared well oriented in regard to time, place, and person. His affect was generally appropriate for the evaluation session. No mentation of either a psychotic or neurotic nature was observed. Robert reports that he has never had any problems with drugs or alcohol. He has participated in psychological counseling in the past, which he found helpful. Robert appears to have a good relationship with his family and several friends. He is excited about his new job and he appears to be optimistic about the future. On the whole, Robert appears to have normal attitudes and interests for an adolescent beginning to make the transition to adulthood. It should be noted, however, that Robert has a tendency to start tasks without waiting for complete instructions and he may occasionally interrupt other people when they are talking. Robert appears to have some minor problems with impulsivity and frustration tolerance. Robert may benefit from participating in personal social awareness classes to assist him in recognizing these behaviors and learning strategies to accommodate for this tendency.

INTEGRATION/COPING INTERPRETATION

Robert's Integration-Coping factor score of 99 is in the normal range for adaptive behavior as compared to the norms for the adult general population. Considering his relatively higher verbal-cognitive functions, Robert would be expected to acquire additional adaptive skills through training and experience.

Residential Living Skills—Robert's Residential Living Skills factor score is consistent with his overall adaptive behavior level.

Daily Living Skills—Robert's Daily Living Skills factor score is consistent with his overall adaptive behavior level.

Academic Skills—Robert's Academic Skills factor score is consistent with his overall adaptive behavior level.

Vocational Skills—Robert's Vocational Skills factor score is consistent with his overall adaptive behavior level.

VOCATIONAL INTERESTS

Robert's vocational interests were assessed using the Self-Directed Search, Form E (SDS-E). Robert's summary code profile is A/E/S (Artistic, Enterprising/Social). This vocational interest code indicates an interest in occupations related to the arts, sales, management, teaching and social work. Occupations which are classified as Artistic generally involve creative work in the arts, music, writing, performance,

(*continued on next page*)

Comprehensive Vocational/Psychological Evaluation Report (*continued*)

sculpture or other relatively unstructured and intellectual endeavors. Enterprising occupations tend to involve working with people in a supervisory or persuasive way to achieve organizational goals. Social occupations generally involve working with people in a helpful or facilitative way.

Specific occupations within this vocational interest pattern include:

Account Executive	164.167-010
Sales, Service Promoter	165.167-010
Young-Adult Librarian	100.167-034
Field Representative	163.267-010
Public Relations Representative	165.167.014
Lawyer	110.107-010
Sales Manager (Any Industry)	163.167-018
Sales Representative, Telephone Services	253.257-010
Buyer	162.157-018
Teacher, Secondary School	091.227-010

All of the occupations listed above require a high school diploma and additional training. Some of the occupations listed above may be learned on-the-job. Others require additional training within a technical school or college setting. Robert appears to have the necessary general aptitude for success within a college or technical school setting.

When asked informally about the kinds of work that Robert has considered in thinking about his future, he reported that he is most interested in doing research and development for making communication systems more accessible to people with disabilities. He has also expressed interest in sales, management, teaching, and coaching.

(*continued on next page*)

Comprehensive Vocational/Psychological Evaluation Report (*continued*)

RECOMMENDATIONS

1. Robert's predicted level of vocational potential is within the Technical/Professional range of community employment. At this level career development and vocational placement activities are emphasized. Robert has expressed an interest in attending college after he graduates from high school. He appears to have the necessary general aptitude for success within a college setting. However, his academic skills are somewhat below what is generally expected for success within a college setting. Robert reports that he prefers to use auditory media for most of his studies. He prefers talking books and utilizing auditory tape for written assignments and a talking calculator for mathematical calculations. Considering Robert's above average listening comprehension skills and verbal abstract reasoning skills, it appears appropriate for Robert to use an auditory means of communication.

2. Robert started a new job at Aztec Mobile Phones and Paging approximately two weeks ago. He has expressed a need for a talking calculator. It is recommended that Robert's adaptive technology needs be reevaulated by the Employment Assistance Specialist in his area for an assessment of specific adaptive technology needs related to this employment.

3. Robert's predicted level of residential functioning is within the Independent Community Living range. At this level autonomous living within the community with only occasional normal need for assistance from others is generally possible. On the whole, Robert appears to have good adaptive skills; however, he appears to have some minor problems with impulsivity and frustration tolerance. It is recommended that Robert participate in the College Preparation program at Austin Rehabilitation Center (ARC) following his senior year of high school. While attending ARC it is recommended that he participate in a personal social awareness class to assist him in identifying strategies to compensate for problems with impulsivity and frustration control.

Lynn Jones

Lynn Jones, M.Ed.
Licensed Psychological Associate
TSBEP #43843

(*continued on next page*)

Comprehensive Vocational/Psychological Evaluation Report (*continued*)

Robert O'Brian 2/12/97 ADDENDUM

EVALUATION PROFILE FOR AN INDIVIDUAL WHO IS BLIND OR VISUALLY IMPAIRED

Age: 17Y/ 4M **Sex:** M **Program:** TECHNICAL/PROFESSIONAL
Residence: INDEPENDENT COMMUNITY LIVING

MEASUREMENT	Raw	STD	25 40 55 70 85 100 115 130
Wechsler Verbal IQ	115	115	: . . . . : . . . . : . . . . : . . . . #
CTB—Total	113	113	: . . . . : . . . . : . . . . : . . . . #
CTB—Verbal	110	110	: . . . . : . . . . : . . . . : . . . . #
CTB—Performance	117	117	: . . . . : . . . . : . . . . : . . . . : #
HSDT—Right	28	115	: . . . . : . . . . : . . . . : . . . . #
HSDT—Left	25	100	: . . . . : . . . . : . . . . : . . . . . #
HSDT—Total	53	108	: . . . . : . . . . : . . . . : . . . . #
Fine Motor	396	102	: . . . . : . . . . : . . . . : . . . . . #
Gross Motor	355	116	: . . . . : . . . . : . . . . : . . . . #
Total Motor	751	110	: . . . . : . . . . : . . . . : . . . . #
EBC	7	77	: . . . . : . . . . : . #
SFAB	243	99	: . . . . : . . . . : . . . . : . . . . . #

	STD	SP mean → ← GP mean
AVG STD SCORE, ALL FACTORS	102	: . . . . : . . . . : . . . . : . . . . . #
PREDICTED VOCATIONAL LEVEL		: . . . . : . . . . : . . . . : . . . . . . #########

Daycare ^————^ ^–^ Semi-Skill
Work Activity ^—^ ^—^ Skilled
Extended ^—^^—^ ^————————>
Transitional ^———^ Technical/Professional

SP is Special Population Mean
GP is General Population Mean

Robert's predicted level of vocational functioning is within the Technical-Professional range of employment. The standard score range for this vocational level is >= 105. This person would appear to have the necessary ability and aptitude structure to pursue technical or professional vocational objectives. In general, these objectives will involve the completion of a defined academic or technical educational program as well as specific certification or licensure considerations. However, specific motivation, interests, and possible effects of disability should be considered in vocational counseling.

Robert's predicted level of residential functioning is within the Independent Community Living range. The standard score range for this level is >= 85. Autonomous living in the community with only occasional (normal) need for assistance from others would appear possible for this individual.

(*continued on next page*)

Comprehensive Vocational/Psychological Evaluation Report (*continued*)

Robert O'Brian | 2/12/97 | ADDENDUM

SUMMARY of Robert O'Brian's COMPUTERIZED FACTOR/TRAIT ANALYSIS

Robert's AVERAGE FACTOR STANDARD SCORE for all factors measured is 102.0.

Standard Score Range for the General Population:
greater than 115 . . . . . . above average
85 to 115 . . . . average
less than 85 . . . . .below average

** ** ** ** ** ** ** ** ** ** ** ** ** **
PROGRAMMING PRIORITIES
** ** ** ** ** ** ** ** ** ** ** ** ** **

The present analysis indicates that program planning for Robert should include the following factors listed in order of remediation/accommodation priority:

Priority:	*STD Score:*	*Factor:*
1st	77	Emotional
2nd	99	Integration-Coping
3rd	114	Verbal
4th	108	Sensory
5th	110	Motor

(*continued on next page*)

Comprehensive Vocational/Psychological Evaluation Report (*continued*)

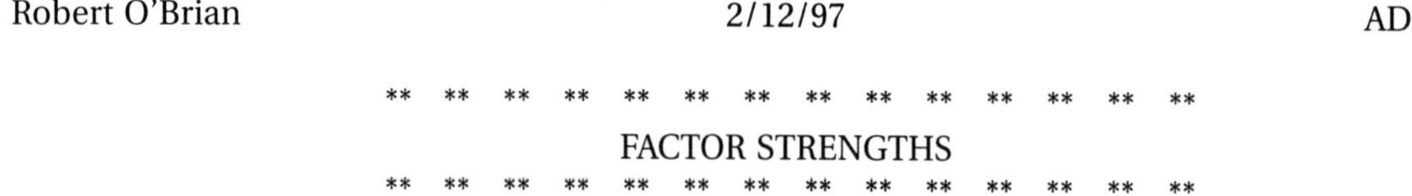

Robert O'Brian 2/12/97 ADDENDUM

** ** ** ** ** ** ** ** ** ** ** ** ** **

FACTOR STRENGTHS

** ** ** ** ** ** ** ** ** ** ** ** ** **

Strengths relative to the individual's average level of functioning which may be considered in goal setting, general programming, or placement were observed in the following areas (strengths are defined as those factors with STD Scores 10 points or more above the individual's average factor standard score):

STD	Score	Factor	Description
**	114	VERBAL	Verbal and spatial intellectual functioning; memory and information processing using auditory and touch senses.

** ** ** ** ** ** ** ** ** ** ** ** ** **

STRENGTHS WITHIN SPECIFIC FACTORS

** ** ** ** ** ** ** ** ** ** ** ** ** **

Strengths within specific factors relative to the individual's overall score on that factor which may be considered in individual programming or placement were observed in the following areas (strengths are defined as sub-factors with STD Scores 10 points or more above the overall factor score to which they relate):

VERBAL-SPATIAL-COGNITIVE (Factor Score = 114)

STD	Score	Sub-Factor	Description
***	127	CTB-LEARNING	Learning concepts and symbols using feedback and practice
***	124	CTB-CONCEPTUAL	Solving abstract spatial and conceptual performance

*** Above average when compared with the general population
** Average when compared with the general population
* Below average when compared with the general population

(*continued on next page*)

Comprehensive Vocational/Psychological Evaluation Report (*continued*)

Robert O'Brian 2/12/97 ADDENDUM

** ** ** ** ** ** ** ** ** ** ** ** ** **

FACTOR WEAKNESSES

** ** ** ** ** ** ** ** ** ** ** ** ** **

Weaknesses relative to the individual's average level of functioning which may affect goal setting, general programming, remediation, accommodation, and/or placement were observed in the following areas (weaknesses are defined as those factors with STD Scores 10 points or more below the individual's average factor standard score):

STD	Score	Factor	Description
*	77	EMOTIONAL	Reaction or response to environmental stress, disability, and/or interaction with others.

** ** ** ** ** ** ** ** ** ** ** ** ** **

WEAKNESSES WITHIN SPECIFIC FACTORS

** ** ** ** ** ** ** ** ** ** ** ** ** **

Weaknesses within specific factors relative to the individual's overall score on that factor which may be considered in individual programming or placement were observed in the following areas (weaknesses are defined as sub-factors with STD Scores 10 points or more below the overall factor score to which they relate):

MOTOR (Factor score = 110)

STD	Score	Sub-Factor	Description
**	93	MAND-RHPI	Speed, coordination and strength on the right side of the body
**	94	D-LHPI	Speed, coordination and strength on the left side of the body
**	95	MAND-MP	Muscle Power—Strength in the upper and lower body

*** Above average when compared with the general population
** Average when compared with the general population
* Below average when compared with the general population

(*continued on next page*)

Comprehensive Vocational/Psychological Evaluation Report (*continued*)

Robert O'Brian 2/12/97 ADDENDUM

PROGRAMMING WORKSHEET

(San Francisco Vocational Competency Scale + Electrical Assembly Task)/2 : 106.1
Average Factor STD score : 102.0
Predicted Vocational Program Level : TECHNICAL/PROFESSIONAL
Voc. Program Range for CVES STD scores: 105.0 to 190.0
Predicted Residential Program Level : INDEPENDENT COMMUNITY LIVING
Res. Program Range for CVES STD scores : 85.0 to 190.0

CVES STD scores are normalized scores with a mean of 100 and a standard deviation of 15.

HIERARCHY				PRESENT PERFORMANCE		
RANK	FACTOR	TESTS	RAW SCORES	STD SCORES	FACTOR STD SCORE	FACTOR PRIORITY
1	VERBAL	WAIS CTB-T CTB-V CTB-P	115 113 110 117	115 113 110 117	114	3
1	EMOTIONAL	EBC	7	77	77	1
2	COPING	SFAB	243	99	99	2
3	SENSORY	HSDTR HSDTL HSDTT	28 25 53	115 100 108	108	4
3	MOTOR	Fine Gross Total	396 355 751	102 116 110	110	5

The evaluator should review all other sources of information about this case. Factor priorities should be adjusted if other data suggests problems related to factors for which there are no factor scores.

APPENDIX D

Code of Professional Ethics for Rehabilitation Counselors

The Commission on Rehabilitation Counselor Certification has adopted the Code of Professional Ethics for Certified Rehabilitation Counselors; and the following professional organizations have adopted the Code for their memberships: American Rehabilitation Counseling Association, National Rehabilitation Counseling Association, and National Council on Rehabilitation Education.

Preamble

Rehabilitation counselors are committed to facilitating personal, social, and economic independence of individuals with disabilities. In fulfilling this commitment, rehabilitation counselors work with people, programs, institutions, and service delivery systems. Rehabilitation counselors recognize that both action and inaction can be facilitating or debilitating. Rehabilitation counselors may be called upon to provide counseling; vocational exploration; psychological and vocational assessment; evaluation of social, medical, vocational, and psychiatric information; job placement and job development services; and other rehabilitation services, and do so in a manner that is consistent with their education and experience. Moreover, rehabilitation counselors also must demonstrate adherence to ethical standards and must ensure that the standards are enforced vigorously. The Code of Professional Ethics, henceforth referred to as the Code, is designed to facilitate the accomplishment of these goals.

The primary obligation of rehabilitation counselors is to their clients, defined in this Code as people with disabilities who are receiving services from rehabilitation counselors. The basic objective of the Code is to promote the public welfare by specifying and enforcing ethical behavior expected of rehabilitation counselors. Accordingly, the Code consists of two kinds of standards, Canons and Rules of Professional Conduct.

The Canons are general standards of an aspirational and inspirational nature reflecting the fundamental spirit of caring and respect which professionals share. They are maxims which serve as models of exemplary professional conduct. The Canons also express general concepts and principles from which more specific Rules are derived. Unlike the Canons, the Rules are more exacting standards that provide guidance in specific circumstances.

Rehabilitation counselors who violate the Code are subject to disciplinary action. A Rule violation is interpreted as a violation of the applicable Canon and the general principles embodied thereof. Since the use of the Certified Rehabilitation Counselor (CRC) designation is a privilege granted by the Commission on Re-

Source: Reprinted by permission of the Commission on Rehabilitation Counselor Certification, Rolling Meadows, Illinois.

habilitation Counselor Certification (CRCC), the CRCC reserves unto itself the power to suspend or to revoke the privilege or to approve other penalties for a Rule violation. Disciplinary penalties are imposed as warranted by the severity of the offense and its attendant circumstances. All disciplinary actions are undertaken in accordance with published procedures and penalties designed to assure the proper enforcement of the Code within the framework of due process and equal protection of the laws.

When there is reason to question the ethical propriety of specific behaviors, persons are encouraged to refrain from engaging in such behaviors until the matter has been clarified. Certified Rehabilitation Counselors who need assistance in interpreting the Code should request in writing an advisory opinion from the Commission on Rehabilitation Counselor Certification. Rehabilitation counselors who are not certified and require assistance in interpreting the Code should request in writing an advisory opinion from their appropriate professional organization.

Rehabilitation Counselor Code of Ethics

Canon 1—MORAL AND LEGAL STANDARDS

Rehabilitation counselors shall behave in a legal, ethical, and moral manner in the conduct of their profession, maintaining the integrity of the Code and avoiding any behavior which would cause harm to others.

Rules of Professional Conduct

R1.1 Rehabilitation counselors will obey the laws and statutes in the legal jurisdiction in which they practice and are subject to disciplinary action for any violation, to the extent that such violation suggests the likelihood of professional misconduct.

R1.2 Rehabilitation counselors will be thoroughly familiar with, will observe, and will discuss with their clients the legal limitations of their services, or benefits offered to clients so as to facilitate honest and open communication and realistic expectations.

R1.3 Rehabilitation counselors will be alert to legal parameters relevant to their practices and to disparities between legally mandated ethical and professional standards and the Code. Where such disparities exist, rehabilitation counselors will follow the legal mandates and will formally communicate any disparities to the appropriate committee on professional ethics. In the absence of legal guidelines, the Code is ethically binding.

R1.4 Rehabilitation counselors will not engage in any act or omission of a dishonest, deceitful, or fraudulent nature in the conduct of their professional activities. They will not allow the pursuit of financial gain or other personal benefit to interfere with the exercise of sound professional judgment and skills, nor will rehabilitation counselors abuse their relationships with clients to promote personal or financial gain or the financial gain of their employing agencies.

R1.5 Rehabilitation counselors will understand and abide by the Canons and Rules of Professional Conduct which are prescribed in the Code.

R1.6 Rehabilitation counselors will not advocate, sanction, participate in, cause to be accomplished, otherwise carry out through another, or condone any act which rehabilitation counselors are prohibited from performing by the Code.

R1.7 Rehabilitation counselors' moral and ethical standards of behavior are a personal matter to the same degree as they are for any other citizen, except as these may compromise the fulfillment of their professional responsibilities or reduce the public trust in rehabilitation counselors. To protect public confidence, rehabilitation counselors will avoid public behavior that clearly is in violation of accepted moral and ethical standards.

R1.8 Rehabilitation counselors will respect the rights and reputation of any institution, organization, or firm with which they are associated when making oral or written statements. In those instances where they are critical of policies, they attempt to effect change by constructive action within organizations.

R1.9 Rehabilitation counselors will refuse to participate in employment practices which are inconsistent with the moral or legal standards regarding the treatment of employees or the public. Rehabilitation counselors will not condone practices which result in illegal or otherwise unjustifiable discrimination on any basis in hiring, promotion, or training.

Canon 2—COUNSELOR-CLIENT RELATIONSHIP

Rehabilitation counselors shall respect the integrity and protect the welfare of people and groups with whom they work. The primary obligation of rehabilitation counselors is to their clients, defined as people with disabilities who are receiving services from rehabilitation counselors. Rehabilitation counselors shall endeavor at all times to place their clients' interests above their own.

Rules of Professional Conduct

R2.1 Rehabilitation counselors will make clear to clients, the purposes, goals, and limitations that may affect the counseling relationship.

R2.2 Rehabilitation counselors will not misrepresent their role of competence to clients. Rehabilitation counselors will provide information about their credentials, if requested, and will refer clients to other specialists as the needs of clients dictate.

R2.3 Rehabilitation counselors will be continually cognizant of their own needs, values, vis-à-vis clients, students, and subordinates. They avoid exploiting the trust and dependency of such persons. Rehabilitation counselors make every effort to avoid dual relationships that could impair their professional judgments or increase their risk of exploitation. Examples of dual relationships include, but are not limited to, research with and treatment of employees, students, supervisors, close friends, or relatives. Sexual intimacies with clients are unethical.

R2.4 Rehabilitation counselors who provide services at the request of a third party will clarify the nature of their relationships to all involved parties. They will inform all parties of their ethical responsibilities and take appropriate action. Rehabilitation counselors employed by third parties as case consultants or expert witnesses, where there is no pretense or intent to provide rehabilitation counseling services directly to clients, beyond file review, initial interview and/or assessment, will clearly define, through written or oral means, the limits of their relationship, particularly in the areas of informed consent and legally privileged communications, to involved individuals. As case consultants or expert witnesses, rehabilitation counselors have an obligation to provide unbiased, objective opinions.

R2.5 Rehabilitation counselors will honor the right of clients to consent to participate in rehabilitation services. Rehabilitation counselors will inform clients or the clients' legal guardians of factors that may affect clients' decisions to participate in rehabilitation services, and they will obtain written consent after clients or their legal guardians are fully informed of such factors. Rehabilitation counselors who work with minors or other persons who are unable to give voluntary, informed consent, will take special care to protect the best interests of clients.

R2.6 Rehabilitation counselors will avoid initiating or continuing consulting or counseling relationships if it is expected that the relationships can be of no benefit to clients, in which case rehabilitation counselors will suggest to clients appropriate alternatives.

R2.7 Rehabilitation counselors will recognize that families are usually an important factor in clients' rehabilitation and will strive to enlist family understanding and involvement as a positive resource in promoting rehabilitation. The permission of clients will be secured prior to family involvement.

R2.8 Rehabilitation counselors and their clients will work jointly in devising an integrated, individualized rehabilitation plan which offers reasonable promise of success and is consistent with the abilities and circumstances of clients. Rehabilitation counselors will persistently monitor rehabilitation plans to ensure their continued viability and effectiveness, remembering that clients have the right to make choices.

R2.9 Rehabilitation counselors will work with their clients in considering employment for clients in only jobs and circumstances that are consistent with the clients' overall abilities, vocational limitations, physical restrictions, general temperament, interest and aptitude patterns, social skills, education, general qualifications and other relevant characteristics and needs. Rehabilitation counselors will neither place nor participate in placing clients in positions that will result in damaging the interest and welfare of either clients or employers.

Canon 3—CLIENT ADVOCACY

Rehabilitation counselors shall serve as advocates for people with disabilities.

Rules of Professional Conduct

R3.1 Rehabilitation counselors will be obligated at all times to promote access for people with disabilities in programs, facilities, transportation, and communication, so that clients will not be excluded from opportunities to participate fully in rehabilitation, education, and society.

R3.2 Rehabilitation counselors will assure, prior to referring clients to programs, facilities, or employment settings, that they are appropriately accessible.

R3.3 Rehabilitation counselors will strive to understand accessibility problems of people with cognitive, hearing, mobility, visual and/or other disabilities and demonstrate such understanding in the practice of their profession.

R3.4 Rehabilitation counselors will strive to eliminate attitudinal barriers, including stereotyping and discrimination, toward people with disabilities and will enhance their own sensitivity and awareness toward people with disabilities.

R3.5 Rehabilitation counselors will remain aware of the actions taken by cooperating agencies on behalf of their clients and will act as advocates of clients to ensure effective service delivery.

Canon 4—PROFESSIONAL RELATIONSHIPS

Rehabilitation counselors shall act with integrity in their relationships with colleagues, other organizations, agencies, institutions, referral sources, and other professions so as to facilitate the contribution of all specialists toward achieving optimum benefit for clients.

Rules of Professional Conduct

R4.1 Rehabilitation counselors will ensure that there is fair mutual understanding of the rehabilitation plan by all agencies cooperating in the rehabilitation of clients and that any rehabilitation plan is developed with such mutual understanding.

R4.2 Rehabilitation counselors will abide by and help to implement "team" decisions in formulating rehabilitation plans and procedures, even when not personally agreeing with such decisions, unless these decisions breach the ethical Rules.

R4.3 Rehabilitation counselors will not commit receiving counselors to any prescribed courses of action in relation to clients, when transferring clients to other colleagues or agencies.

R4.4 Rehabilitation counselors, as referring counselors, will promptly supply all information necessary for a cooperating agency or counselor to begin serving clients.

R4.5 Rehabilitation counselors will not offer on-going professional counseling/case management services to clients receiving such services from other rehabilitation counselors without first notifying the other counselor. File review and second opinion services are not included in the concept of professional counseling/case management services.

R4.6 Rehabilitation counselors will secure from other specialists appropriate reports and evaluations, when such reports are essential for rehabilitation planning and/or service delivery.

R4.7 Rehabilitation counselors will not discuss in a disparaging way with clients the competency of other counselors or agencies, or the judgments made, the methods used, or the quality of rehabilitation plans.

R4.8 Rehabilitation counselors will not exploit their professional relationships with supervisors, colleagues, students, or employees sexually or otherwise. Rehabilitation counselors will not condone or engage in sexual harassment, defined as deliberate or repeated comments, gestures, or physical contacts of a sexual nature unwanted by recipients.

R4.9 Rehabilitation counselors who know of an ethical violation by another rehabilitation counselor will informally attempt to resolve the issue with the counselor, when the misconduct is of a minor nature and/or appears to be due to lack of sensitivity, knowledge, or experience. If the violation does not seem amenable to an informal solution, or is of a more serious nature, rehabilitation counselors will bring it to the attention of the appropriate committee on professional ethics.

R4.10 Rehabilitation counselors possessing information concerning an alleged violation of this Code, will, upon request, reveal such information to the Commission on Rehabilitation Counselor Certification or other authority empowered to investigate or act upon the alleged violation, unless the information is protected by law.

R4.11 Rehabilitation counselors who employ or supervise other professionals or students will facilitate professional development of such individuals. They provide appropriate working conditions, timely evaluations, constructive consultation, and experience opportunities.

Canon 5—PUBLIC STATEMENTS/FEES

Rehabilitation counselors shall adhere to professional standards in establishing fees and promoting their services.

Rules of Professional Conduct

R5.1 Rehabilitation counselors will consider carefully the value of their services and the ability of clients to meet the financial burden in establishing reasonable fees for professional services.

R5.2 Rehabilitation counselors will not accept for professional work a fee or any other form of remuneration from clients who are entitled to their services through an institution or agency or other benefits structure, unless clients have been fully informed of the availability of services from other such sources.

R5.3 Rehabilitation counselors will neither give nor receive a commission or rebate or any other form of remuneration for referral of clients for professional services.

R5.4 Rehabilitation counselors who describe rehabilitation counseling or the services of rehabilitation counselors to the general public will fairly and accurately present the material, avoiding misrepresentation through sensationalism, exaggeration, or superficiality. Rehabilitation counselors are guided by the primary obligation to aid the public in developing informed judgments, opinions, and choices.

Canon 6—CONFIDENTIALITY

Rehabilitation counselors shall respect the confidentiality of information obtained from clients in the course of their work.

Rules of Professional Conduct

R6.1 Rehabilitation counselors will inform clients at the onset of the counseling relationship of the limits of confidentiality.

R6.2 Rehabilitation counselors will take reasonable personal action, or inform responsible authoritics, or inform those persons at risk, when the conditions or actions of clients indicate that there is clear and imminent danger to clients or others after advising clients that this must be done. Consultation with other professionals may be used where appropriate. The assumption of responsibility for clients must be taken only after careful deliberation and clients must be involved in the resumption of responsibility as quickly as possible.

R6.3 Rehabilitation counselors will not forward to another person, agency, or potential employer, any confidential information without the written permission of clients or their legal guardians.

R6.4 Rehabilitation counselors will ensure that there are defined policies and practices in other agencies cooperatively serving rehabilitation clients which effectively protect information confidentiality.

R6.5 Rehabilitation counselors will safeguard the maintenance, storage, and disposal of the records of clients so that unauthorized persons shall not have access to these records. All non-professional persons who must have access to these records will be thoroughly briefed concerning the confidential standards to be observed.

R6.6 Rehabilitation counselors, in the preparation of written and oral reports, will present only germane data and will make every effort to avoid undue invasion of privacy.

R6.7 Rehabilitation counselors will obtain written permission from clients or their legal guardians prior to taping or otherwise recording counseling sessions. Even with guardians' written consent, rehabilitation counselors will not record sessions against the expressed wishes of clients.

R6.8 Rehabilitation counselors will persist in claiming the privileged status of confidential information obtained from clients, where communications are privileged by statute for rehabilitation counselors.

R6.9 Rehabilitation counselors will provide prospective employers with only job relevant information about clients and will secure the permission of clients or their legal guardians for the release of any information which might be considered confidential.

Canon 7—ASSESSMENT

Rehabilitation counselors shall promote the welfare of clients in the selection, utilization, and interpretation of assessment measures.

Rules of Professional Conduct

R7.1 Rehabilitation counselors will recognize that different tests demand different levels of competence for administration, scoring, and interpretation, and will recognize the limits of their competence and perform only those functions for which they are trained.

R7.2 Rehabilitation counselors will consider carefully the specific validity, reliability, and appropriateness of tests, when selecting them for use in a given situation or with particular clients. Rehabilitation counselors will proceed with caution when attempting to evaluate and interpret the performance of people with disabilities, minority group members, or other persons who are not represented in the standardized norm groups. Rehabilitation counselors will recognize the effects of socioeconomic, ethnic, disability, and cultural factors on test scores.

R7.3 Rehabilitation counselors will administer tests under the same conditions that were established in their standardization. When tests are not administered under standard conditions, as may be necessary to accommodate modifications for clients with disabilities or when unusual behavior or irregularities occur during the testing session, those conditions will be noted and taken into account at the time of interpretation.

R7.4 Rehabilitation counselors will ensure that instrument limitations are not exceeded and that periodic reassessments are made to prevent stereotyping of clients.

R7.5 Rehabilitation counselors will make known the purpose of testing and the explicit use of the results to clients prior to administration. Recognizing the right of clients to have test results, rehabilitation counselors will give explanations of test results in language clients can understand.

R7.6 Rehabilitation counselors will ensure that specific interpretation accompanies any release of individual data. The welfare and explicit prior permission of clients will be the criteria for determining the recipients of the test results. The interpretation of assessment data will be related to the particular goals of evaluation.

R7.7 Rehabilitation counselors will attempt to ensure, when utilizing computerized assessment services, that such services are based on appropriate research to establish the validity of the computer programs and procedures used in arriving at interpretations. Public offering of an automated test interpretation service will be considered as a professional-to-professional consultation. In this instance, the formal responsibility of the consultant is to the consultee, but the ultimate and overriding responsibility is to clients.

R7.8 Rehabilitation counselors will recognize that assessment results may become obsolete. They make every effort to avoid and prevent the misuse of obsolete measures.

Canon 8—RESEARCH ACTIVITIES

Rehabilitation counselors shall assist in efforts to expand the knowledge needed to more effectively serve people with disabilities.

Rules of Professional Conduct

R8.1 Rehabilitation counselors will ensure that data for research meet rigid standards of validity, honesty, and protection of confidentiality.

R8.2 Rehabilitation counselors will be aware of and responsive to all pertinent guidelines on research with human subjects. When planning any research activity dealing with human subjects, rehabilitation counselors will ensure that research problems, design, and execution are in full compliance with such guidelines.

R8.3 Rehabilitation counselors presenting case studies in classes, professional meetings, or publications will confine the content to that which can be disguised to ensure full protection of the identity of clients.

R8.4 Rehabilitation counselors will assign credit to those who have contributed to publications in proportion to their contribution.

R8.5 Rehabilitation counselors recognize that honesty and openness are essential characteristics of the relationship between rehabilitation counselors and research participants. When methodological requirements of a study necessitate concealment or deception, rehabilitation counselors will ensure that participants understand the reasons for this action.

Canon 9—COMPETENCE

Rehabilitation counselors shall establish and maintain their professional competencies at such a level that their clients receive the benefit of the highest quality of services the profession is capable of offering.

Rules of Professional Conduct

R9.1 Rehabilitation counselors will function within the limits of their defined role, training, and technical competency and will accept only those positions for which they are professionally qualified.

R9.2 Rehabilitation counselors will continuously strive through reading, attending professional meetings, and taking courses of instruction to keep abreast of new developments, concepts, and practices that are essential to providing the highest quality of services to their clients.

R9.3 Rehabilitation counselors, recognizing that personal problems and conflicts may interfere with their professional effectiveness, will refrain from undertaking any activity in which their personal problems are likely to lead to inadequate performance. If they are already engaged in such activity when they become aware of their personal problems, they will seek competent professional assistance to determine whether they should suspend, terminate, or limit the scope of their professional activities.

R9.4 Rehabilitation counselors who are educators will perform their duties based on careful preparation so that their instruction is accurate, up-to-date and scholarly.

R9.5 Rehabilitation counselors who are educators will ensure that statements in catalogs and course outlines are accurate, particularly in terms of subject matter covered, bases for grading, and nature of classroom experiences.

R9.6 Rehabilitation counselors who are educators will maintain high standards of knowledge and skill by presenting rehabilitation counseling information fully and accurately, and by giving appropriate recognition to alternative viewpoints.

Canon 10—CRC CREDENTIAL

Rehabilitation counselors holding the Certified Rehabilitation Counselor (CRC) designation shall honor the integrity and respect the limitations placed upon its use.

Rules of Professional Conduct

R10.1 Certified Rehabilitation Counselors will use the Certified Rehabilitation Counselor (CRC) designation only in accordance with the relevant GUIDELINES promulgated by the Commission on Rehabilitation Counselor Certification.

R10.2 Certified Rehabilitation Counselors will not attribute to the mere possession of the designation depth or scope of knowledge, skill, and professional capabilities greater than those demonstrated by achievement of the CRC designation.

R10.3 Certified Rehabilitation Counselors will not make unfair comparisons between a person who holds the Certified Rehabilitation Counselor (CRC) designation and one who does not.

R10.4 Certified Rehabilitation Counselors will not write, speak, nor act in ways that lead others to believe Certified Rehabilitation Counselors are officially representing the Commission on Rehabilitation Counselor Certification, unless such written permission has been granted by the said Commission.

R10.5 Certified Rehabilitation Counselors will make no claim to unique skills or devices not available to others in the profession unless the special efficacy of such unique skills or device has been demonstrated by scientifically accepted evidence.

R10.6 Certified Rehabilitation Counselors will not initiate or support the candidacy of an individual for certification by the Commission on Rehabilitation Counselor Certification if the individual is known to engage in professional practices which violate this Code.

IDENTIFICATION

(Computer Section 1)

NAME	Angela Labpugian
AGE OF INDIVIDUAL	57

MEDICAL EYE REPORT INFORMATION

1st Right Eye	MACULAR DEGENERATION
1st Left Eye	MACULAR DEGENERATION
2nd Right Eye	CENTRAL SCOTOMA
2nd Left Eye	PERIPHERAL SCOTOMA
3rd Right Eye	DEFICIENT COLOR VISN
3rd Left Eye	DEFICIENT COLOR VISN

JOB TITLE	Secretary 8
DOT TITLE	SECRETARY
DOT NUMBER	201362030
REPORTER	W RUFF

Appendix E. Sample Work Environment Visual Demands Protocol

Source: Rehabilitation Research and Training Center on Blindness and Low Vision, Mississippi State University, Mississippi State, Mississippi.

Work Environment Visual Demands Protocol (*continued*)

JOB 1 - JOB DESCRIPTION

(Computer Section 2)

ACTION	TYPING LETTERS
PURPOSE	CORRESPONDENCE

Alone	1	Time Present at Activity	2
Critical to Job	1	Work Station	1
Footcandles Observed	020	Illuminance Category Observed	D
Job Setting	1	Recommended IES Illuminance Category	E

VISION REQUIREMENTS:

Near	1	Midrange	1
Far	0	Depth Perception	0
Shifts in Work Distances	1	Color Vision	0
Field Vision	0	Speed and/or Accuracy	1
Eye-Hand	1	Eye-Foot	0
Eye-Hand-Foot	0		

Appendix E. Sample Work Environment Visual Demands Protocol (*continued*)

Work Environment Visual Demands Protocol (*continued*)

JOB 2 - JOB DESCRIPTION

If a description of a second job is not needed, enter "NA" in the space for Action and proceed to next section.

(Computer Section 2)

ACTION: answer telephone

PURPOSE: schedule appointment

Alone	1	Time Present at Activity	2
Critical to Job	1	Work Station	1
Footcandles Observed	020	Illuminance Category Observed	C
Job Setting	1	Recommended IES Illuminance Category	D

VISION REQUIREMENTS:

Near	1	Midrange	0
Far	0	Depth Perception	0
Shifts in Work Distances	1	Color Vision	0
Field Vision	0	Speed and/or Accuracy	1
Eye-Hand	0	Eye-Foot	0
Eye-Hand-Foot	0		

Appendix E. Sample Work Environment Visual Demands Protocol (*continued*)

Work Environment Visual Demands Protocol (*continued*)

JOB 3 - JOB DESCRIPTION

If a description of a third job is not needed, enter "NA" in the space for Action and proceed to next section.

(Computer Section 2)

ACTION: GREET GUESTS

PURPOSE: PROMOTE POSITIVE REL

Alone	0	Time Present at Activity	2
Critical to Job	1	Work Station	1
Footcandles Observed	020	Illuminance Category Observed	C
Job Setting	1	Recommended IES Illuminance Category	C

VISION REQUIREMENTS:

Near	0	Midrange	1
Far	1	Depth Perception	1
Shifts in Work Distances	1	Color Vision	0
Field Vision	1	Speed and/or Accuracy	0
Eye-Hand	0	Eye-Foot	0
Eye-Hand-Foot	0		

Appendix E. Sample Work Environment Visual Demands Protocol (*continued*)

Work Environment Visual Demands Protocol (*continued*)

JOB 1 - LIGHTING

(Computer Section 3)

DIRECTION OF ILLUMINATION ON VISUAL TASK

1. CEILING

Left of subject	0	Right of subject	0
Behind subject	0	Front of subject	1

2. WALL MOUNTED

Left of subject	0	Right of subject	0
Behind subject	0	Front of subject	0

3. TASK LIGHTING

Left of subject	0	Right of subject	0
Behind subject	0	Front of subject	0

4. WINDOW, EXTERNAL

Left of subject	0	Right of subject	1
Behind subject	1	Front of subject	1

Appendix E. Sample Work Environment Visual Demands Protocol (*continued*)

Work Environment Visual Demands Protocol (*continued*)

JOB 1 - LIGHTING

TYPE OF LIGHTING

	Ceiling	Wall	Task	Window
1. Standard Incandescent Light Bulb	☐	☐	☐	☐
2. Fluorescent				
Cool white	☐	☐	☐	☐
Deluxe cool white	1	☐	☐	☐
Warm white	☐	☐	☐	☐
Deluxe warm white	☐	☐	☐	☐
White	☐	☐	☐	☐
Daylight	☐	☐	☐	☐
3. Mercury	☐	☐	☐	☐
4. Metal halide	☐	☐	☐	☐
5. Sodium	☐	☐	☐	☐
6. Natural daylight	☐	☐	☐	☐

SIZE OF ILLUMINATION AREA

1. Length in inches	0 7 2
2. Width in inches	0 6 0
3. Height in inches	0 3 0

Appendix E. Sample Work Environment Visual Demands Protocol (*continued*)

Work Environment Visual Demands Protocol (*continued*)

JOB 2 - LIGHTING

(Computer Section 3)

DIRECTION OF ILLUMINATION ON VISUAL TASK

1. CEILING

Left of subject	☐	Right of subject	☐
Behind subject	☐	Front of subject	1

2. WALL MOUNTED

Left of subject	☐	Right of subject	☐
Behind subject	☐	Front of subject	☐

3. TASK LIGHTING

Left of subject	☐	Right of subject	☐
Behind subject	☐	Front of subject	☐

4. WINDOW, EXTERNAL

Left of subject	☐	Right of subject	1
Behind subject	1	Front of subject	1

Appendix E. Sample Work Environment Visual Demands Protocol (*continued*)

Work Environment Visual Demands Protocol (*continued*)

JOB 2 - LIGHTING

TYPE OF LIGHTING

	Ceiling	Wall	Task	Window
1. Standard Incandescent Light Bulb	☐	☐	☐	☐
2. Fluorescent				
Cool white	☐	☐	☐	☐
Deluxe cool white	1	☐	☐	☐
Warm white	☐	☐	☐	☐
Deluxe warm white	☐	☐	☐	☐
White	☐	☐	☐	☐
Daylight	☐	☐	☐	☐
3. Mercury	☐	☐	☐	☐
4. Metal halide	☐	☐	☐	☐
5. Sodium	☐	☐	☐	☐
6. Natural daylight	☐	☐	☐	☐

SIZE OF ILLUMINATION AREA

1. Length in inches 0 7 2
2. Width in inches 0 6 0
3. Height in inches 0 3 0

Work Environment Visual Demands Protocol (*continued*)

JOB 3 - LIGHTING

(Computer Section 3)

DIRECTION OF ILLUMINATION ON VISUAL TASK

1. CEILING

Left of subject	0	Right of subject	0
Behind subject	0	Front of subject	1

2. WALL MOUNTED

Left of subject	0	Right of subject	0
Behind subject	0	Front of subject	0

3. TASK LIGHTING

Left of subject	0	Right of subject	0
Behind subject	0	Front of subject	0

4. WINDOW, EXTERNAL

Left of subject	0	Right of subject	1
Behind subject	1	Front of subject	1

Appendix E. Sample Work Environment Visual Demands Protocol (*continued*)

Work Environment Visual Demands Protocol (*continued*)

JOB 3 - LIGHTING

TYPE OF LIGHTING

	Ceiling	Wall	Task	Window
1. Standard Incandescent Light Bulb	☐	☐	☐	☐
2. Fluorescent				
Cool white	☐	☐	☐	☐
Deluxe cool white	1	☐	☐	☐
Warm white	☐	☐	☐	☐
Deluxe warm white	☐	☐	☐	☐
White	☐	☐	☐	☐
Daylight	☐	☐	☐	☐
3. Mercury	☐	☐	☐	☐
4. Metal halide	☐	☐	☐	☐
5. Sodium	☐	☐	☐	☐
6. Natural daylight	☐	☐	☐	☐

SIZE OF ILLUMINATION AREA

1. Length in inches	0	7	2
2. Width in inches	0	6	0
3. Height in inches	0	3	0

Work Environment Visual Demands Protocol (*continued*)

JOB 1 - VISUAL WORK DIMENSIONS

(Computer Section 4)

PRIMARY WORKING SIGHT LINE DISTANCE IN INCHES | 2 | 7 |

Indicate if the Display Object is ABOVE OR BELOW HORIZONTAL SIGHT LINE. See Manual for Definition of Horizontal Sight Line. 1 = Above; 2 = Below | 2 |

PRIMARY HORIZONTAL SIGHT LINE | 3 | 2 |

Note: Measure from eye or eyes to object at a right angle to the floor.

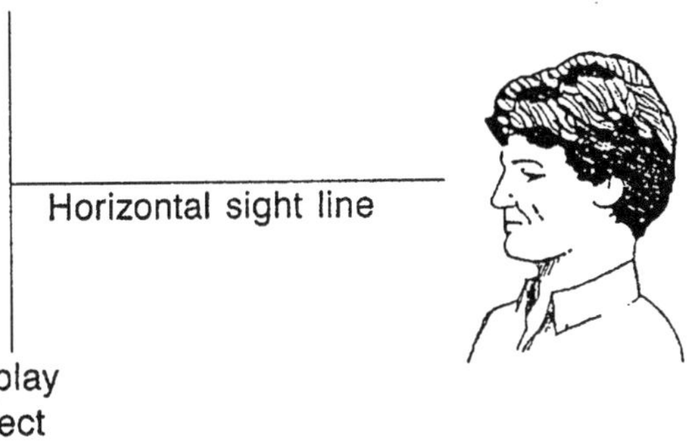

PRIMARY VERTICAL VIEWING ANGLE
COMPUTER CALCULATED - NO ENTRY REQUIRED | | | | °

SECONDARY WORKING SIGHT LINE DISTANCE | 2 | 7 |

Note: Proceed as in primary working sight line, if applicable.

SECONDARY HORIZONTAL SIGHT LINE | 3 | 2 |

Note: Proceed as in primary horizontal sight line, if applicable.

SECONDARY VERTICAL VIEWING ANGLE
COMPUTER CALCULATED - NO ENTRY REQUIRED | | | | °

Work Environment Visual Demands Protocol (*continued*)

JOB 1 - VISUAL WORK DIMENSIONS

PRIMARY WORKING LATERAL VIEWING ANGLE
COMPUTER CALCULATED - RECORD MEASUREMENTS ON DIAGRAM BELOW. THE COMPUTER PROGRAM WILL USE THESE MEASUREMENTS TO CALCULATE THE VIEWING ANGLE.

0	1	7	°

Note: Instruct worker to assume a usual working position as in measure for working sight line. Measure from eyes to center of display object; RECORD IN INCHES. Measure from eye or eyes to right edge of display; RECORD IN INCHES. Measure from eye or eyes to left edge of display. RECORD IN INCHES.

Working sight line

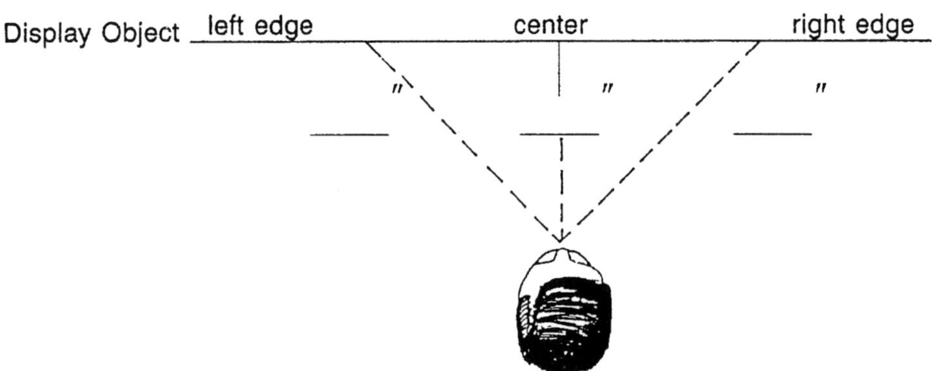

SECONDARY WORKING LATERAL VIEWING ANGLE
COMPUTER CALCULATED - PROCEED AS DESCRIBED ABOVE.

0	1	0	°

Working sight line

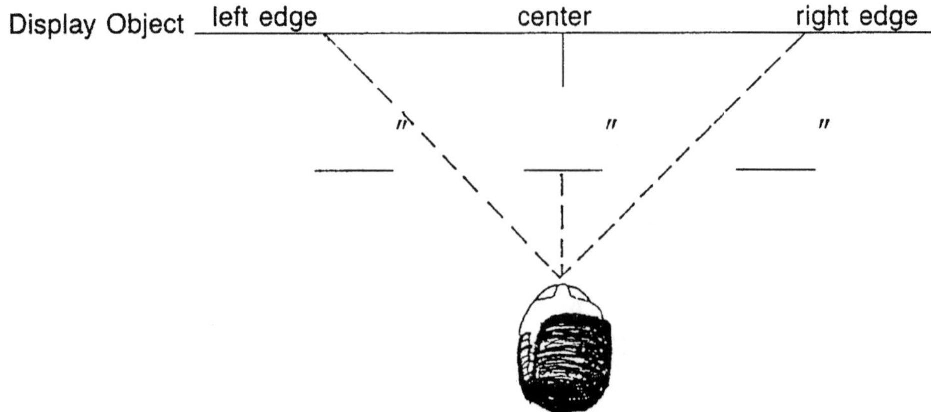

Work Environment Visual Demands Protocol (*continued*)

JOB 1 - VISUAL WORK DIMENSIONS

MEASUREMENTS OF SITTING WORKPLACE

1. Work surface height in inches | 3 | 2 |
2. Primary display height in inches | 3 | 7 |
3. Secondary display height in inches | 3 | 2 |
4. Seated eye height of worker in inches | 4 | 8 |

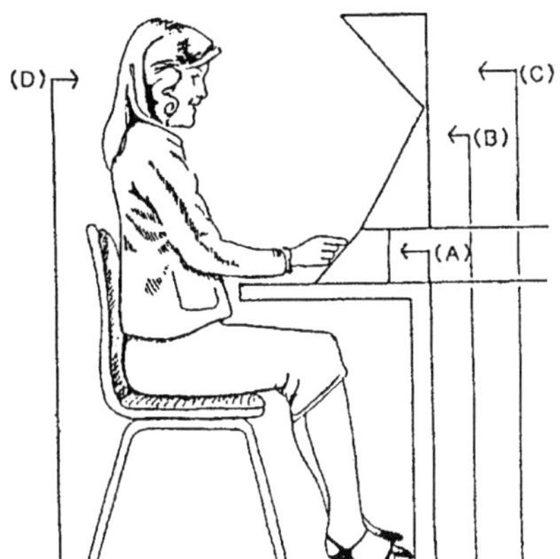

MEASUREMENTS OF STANDING WORKPLACE

1. Work surface height in inches
2. Primary display height in inches
3. Secondary display height in inches
4. Standing eye height of worker in inches

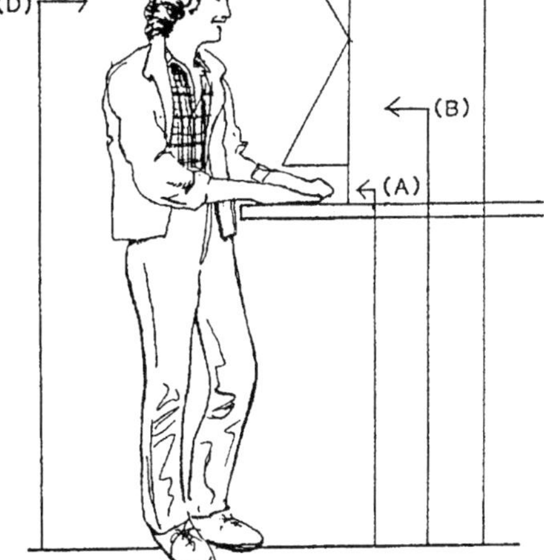

Appendix E. Sample Work Environment Visual Demands Protocol (*continued*)

Work Environment Visual Demands Protocol (*continued*)

VISUAL DISPLAY

(Computer Section 5)

Different work tasks often have different types of visual tasks. Analyze each work task which has different visual demand requirements than covered above. This is necessary, as different aids may be needed or portable aids may be necessary to accommodate the partially sighted individual.

TYPES OF DISPLAY

PRINTED FORMS AND TASKS	JOB 1	JOB 2	JOB 3
1. 20 - 24 point print (5M) NEWSPAPER HEADLINES	☐	☐	☐
2. 14 - 18 point (2 - 3M) LARGE TYPE TEXTS	☐	☐	☐
3. 8 - 10 point (1 - 1.5M) CLEAR PRINT WITH GOOD CONTRASTS	☐	☐	☐
4. 8 - 9 point (1M) REGULAR BOOK PRINT	☐	☐	☐
5. 7 - 8 point NEWSPAPER PRINT	☐	☐	☐
6. 4 - 5 point (.08M) TELEPHONE DIRECTORIES	☐	☐	☐
7. GLOSSY MAGAZINES	☐	☐	☐
8. MAPS	☐	☐	☐
9. TYPED ORIGINALS	☐	☐	☐
10. TYPED 2nd CARBON	☐	☐	☐
11. COLORED FORMS	☐	☐	☐

Appendix E. Sample Work Environment Visual Demands Protocol (*continued*)

Work Environment Visual Demands Protocol (*continued*)

VISUAL DISPLAY

HANDWRITTEN TASKS	JOB 1	JOB 2	JOB 3
1. #3 PENCIL AND HARDER LEADS	✓		
2. #2 PENCIL AND SOFTER LEADS	✓	✓	
3. BALL - POINT PEN	✓	✓	
4. FELT - TIP PEN, FINE	✓	✓	
5. FELT - TIP PEN, MEDIUM	✓	✓	
6. FELT - TIP PEN, BOLD	✓	✓	
7. HANDWRITTEN CARBONS			
8. CHALKBOARDS			
9. UNRULED PAPER	✓		
10. NARROW RULED PAPER	✓		
11. LEGAL RULED PAPER	✓		

COPIED TASKS	JOB 1	JOB 2	JOB 3
1. DITTO COPY			
2. MICRO - FICHE READER			
3. MIMEOGRAPH			
4. PHOTOGRAPHS			
5. XEROGRAPH	✓	✓	

Appendix E. Sample Work Environment Visual Demands Protocol (*continued*)

Work Environment Visual Demands Protocol (*continued*)

VISUAL DISPLAY

TYPES OF DISPLAY	JOB 1	JOB 2	JOB 3
CRT MONITOR	1	1	
DOT MATRIX Segmented number readout			
ANNUNCIATOR LIGHTS			
GAUGE WITH MOVING POINTER			
KEYBOARD READING	1		
MACHINERY OPERATION			
BUILDING MATERIALS			
TOOLS			
OTHER			

WORK DEVICES ASSOCIATED WITH VISUAL DISPLAYS

Identify Work Device	Frequency of Use	JOB Number
CRT MONITOR	2	1
COMPUTER KEYBRD	2	1
TELEPHONE	2	2

Appendix E. Sample Work Environment Visual Demands Protocol (*continued*)

Work Environment Visual Demands Protocol (*continued*)

JOB 1 - VISUAL DISPLAY CHARACTERISTICS

(Computer Section 6)

DISPLAY NUMBER 1

1.	COLOR OF VISUAL DISPLAY	DARK GRAY
2.	MUNSELL NOTATION	N4.75/
3.	COLOR OF VISUAL DISPLAY BACKGROUND	LIGHT GRY
4.	MUNSELL NOTATION	N8.75/
5.	ILLUMINANCE MEASURED	002
6.	LUMINANCE REFLECTANCE MEASURED	010
7.	PERCENT OF REFLECTANCE	
8.	MOVEMENT OF VISUAL DISPLAY	3
9.	SPEED OF MOVEMENT OF VISUAL DISPLAY	2
10.	DIRECTION OF MOVEMENT OF VISUAL DISPLAY	3

Appendix E. Sample Work Environment Visual Demands Protocol (*continued*)

Work Environment Visual Demands Protocol (*continued*)

JOB 2 - VISUAL DISPLAY CHARACTERISTICS

(Computer Section 6)

DISPLAY NUMBER 2

1. COLOR OF VISUAL DISPLAY — BLACK
2. MUNSELL NOTATION — N2.5/
3. COLOR OF VISUAL DISPLAY BACKGROUND — WHITE
4. MUNSELL NOTATION — N9.25/
5. ILLUMINANCE MEASURED — 020
6. LUMINANCE REFLECTANCE MEASURED — 007
7. PERCENT OF REFLECTANCE —
8. MOVEMENT OF VISUAL DISPLAY — 1
9. SPEED OF MOVEMENT OF VISUAL DISPLAY — 2
10. DIRECTION OF MOVEMENT OF VISUAL DISPLAY — 5

Appendix E. Sample Work Environment Visual Demands Protocol (*continued*)

Work Environment Visual Demands Protocol (*continued*)

JOB 3 - VISUAL DISPLAY CHARACTERISTICS

(Computer Section 6)

DISPLAY NUMBER 3

1. COLOR OF VISUAL DISPLAY | N | A | | | | | | | |
2. MUNSELL NOTATION | | | | | | | | | | | |
3. COLOR OF VISUAL DISPLAY BACKGROUND | | | | | | | | | |
4. MUNSELL NOTATION | | | | | | | | | | | |
5. ILLUMINANCE MEASURED | | | |
6. LUMINANCE REFLECTANCE MEASURED | | | |
7. PERCENT OF REFLECTANCE | | | |
8. MOVEMENT OF VISUAL DISPLAY | |
9. SPEED OF MOVEMENT OF VISUAL DISPLAY | |
10. DIRECTION OF MOVEMENT OF VISUAL DISPLAY | |

Appendix E. Sample Work Environment Visual Demands Protocol (*continued*)

Work Environment Visual Demands Protocol (*continued*)

ENVIRONMENTAL FACTORS

(Computer Section 7)

ENVIRONMENTAL FACTORS SURROUNDING VISUAL DISPLAY

	JOB 1	JOB 2	JOB 3
Shadows created by other objects are present which darken areas of the visual display	0	0	0
Shadows created by worker's head or body position are present which darken areas of the visual display	0	1	0
Direct or indirect glare interferes with observation of the visual display	1	1	1
Visual indicators are uniformly aligned	0	0	0
Visual indicators are in the same position for standard functioning	0	0	0
Visual displays are distorted optically	0	0	0
Other unused displays surrounding primary visual display are covered or removed	0	0	0

Appendix E. Sample Work Environment Visual Demands Protocol (*continued*)

Work Environment Visual Demands Protocol (*continued*)

MOBILITY

(Computer Section 8)

MOBILITY REQUIREMENTS OF THE WORKPLACE

Is the worker required to move from one workplace to another to perform the work tasks?	1
Does the move require light and/or dark adaptation?	1
To travel to and from the workplace(s) is it necessary that the worker use	
1. STAIRS	1
2. RAMPS	1
3. WALKWAYS, INTERNAL	1
4. WALKWAYS, EXTERNAL	1
5. AISLES	1
6. CORRIDORS	1
7. ELEVATORS	1
8. ESCALATORS	0
9. CONVEYORS	0

Appendix E. Sample Work Environment Visual Demands Protocol (*continued*)

Work Environment Visual Demands Protocol (*continued*)

MOBILITY

(Computer Section 8)

MOBILITY REQUIREMENTS OF THE WORKPLACE

Are there likely to be fixed (non-moving) obstacles in the work path? [1]

If yes, are they

1. ABOVE HORIZONTAL SIGHT LINE [0]
2. BELOW HORIZONTAL SIGHT LINE [1]
3. AT HORIZONTAL SIGHT LINE [1]
4. DO THE OBSTACLES HAVE POOR CONTRAST? [1]

Are there likely to be moving (non-fixed) obstacles in the work path? [ ]

If yes, are they

1. ABOVE HORIZONTAL SIGHT LINE [0]
2. BELOW HORIZONTAL SIGHT LINE [1]
3. AT HORIZONTAL SIGHT LINE [1]
4. DO THE OBSTACLES HAVE POOR CONTRAST? [1]

Appendix E. Sample Work Environment Visual Demands Protocol (*continued*)

Work Environment Visual Demands Protocol (*continued*)

FLEXIBILITY

(Computer Section 9)

FLEXIBILITY OF WORKPLACE

Is the workplace adaptable for

1. CEILING SUPPLEMENTAL LIGHTING [0]
2. WALL SUPPLEMENTAL LIGHTING [1]
3. TASK SUPPLEMENTAL LIGHTING [1]

Is the workplace adaptable for

1. STAND TYPE MAGNIFIER [1]
2. CLAMP-ON TYPE MAGNIFIER [1]

What is the range within which a task can be performed?

1. MINIMUM DISTANCE IN INCHES [ ][4]
2. MAXIMUM DISTANCE IN INCHES [3][6]

Is the distance from the worker's eyes to the visual display adaptable? [1]

The data entered into the computerized program shown here in the sample Work Environment Visual Demands Protocol generates the following report.

(*continued*)

Work Environment Visual Demands Report

SUMMARY

Social Security No.: 000-00-6044 **Name:** Angela Labpugian **Age:** 57

Medical Eye Report

Primary condition	**Right eye:**	macular degeneration
	Left eye:	macular degeneration
Secondary condition	**Right eye:**	central scotoma
	Left eye:	peripheral scotoma
Tertiary condition	**Right eye:**	deficient color vision
	Left eye:	deficient color vision

Job Title: Secretary-8

Job Activities

- Job 1: Typing letters
- Job 2: Answer the telephone
- Job 3: Greet guests

Reporter: W. Ruff

Date: August 21, 1997

Appendix E. Sample Work Environment Visual Demands Report

Work Environment Visual Demands Report (*continued*)

Social Security No.: 000-00-6044 **Name:** Angela Labpugian **Age:** 57

Medical Eye Report

Primary condition	Right eye:	macular degeneration
	Left eye:	macular degeneration
Secondary condition	Right eye:	central scotoma
	Left eye:	peripheral scotoma
Tertiary condition	Right eye:	deficient color vision
	Left eye:	deficient color vision

Job Title: Secretary-8

JOB ACTIVITY NO. 1: TYPING LETTERS

- Time present: often (20 percent to 50 percent of time).
- Activity is critical to the job.
- 20 footcandles are observed.
- Illuminance category observed: D (20 to 50 footcandles); general lighting is an observed option.
- Job setting: Commercial, institutional, residential, and public assemblies
- Illuminance category recommended: E (50 to 100 footcandles); Illuminance on task is a recommended option.
- Vision requirements: Near, midrange, shifts in work distances, speed and accuracy, and eye-hand coordination.

Lighting

- Ceiling light—Direction: Front of subject
- Ceiling light—Type: Deluxe cool white fluorescent light
- Window (external) light—Direction: Right of subject, behind subject, front of subject
- Size of illumination area: Length = 72 inches, width = 60 inches, height = 30 inches

Primary Display: Vertical Measurements

- Primary working sight line = 27 inches
- Display object is below horizontal sight line
- Primary horizontal sight line = 32 inches

Secondary Display: Vertical Measurements

- Secondary working sight line = 27 inches
- Secondary horizontal sight line = 32 inches

Measurements of Sitting Workplace

- Work surface height: 32 inches
- Primary display height: 37 inches
- Secondary display height: 32 inches
- Eye height of worker: 48 inches

Types of Displays

- Printed and forms tasks
  Typed originals
- Handwritten tasks
  No. 3 pencil and harder leads
  No. 2 pencil and softer leads
  Ball-point pen
  Felt-tip pen, fine
  Felt-tip pen, medium
  Felt-tip pen, bold
  Unruled paper
  Narrow ruled paper
  Legal ruled paper
- Copied tasks
  Xerograph
- Other displays
  CRT monitor
  Keyboard reading

Work Devices

- CRT monitor often used (20 percent to 50 percent of the time)
- Computer Keyboard often used (20 percent to 50 percent of the time)

Visual Display Characteristics

- Color of visual display: dark gray

Appendix E. Sample Work Environment Visual Demands Report (*continued*)

Work Environment Visual Demands Report (*continued*)

Visual Display Characteristics (*continued*)

- Color of visual display background: light gray
- Percentage of reflectances: 50 percent

Environmental Factors Surrounding the Visual Display

- Direct or indirect glare interferes with the observation of the visual display.

Mobility Requirements

- Client must move from one workplace to another to perform work tasks.
- Moving requires light and dark adaptation.
- It is necessary for the client to use stairs, ramps, internal walkways, external walkways, aisles, corridors, and elevators.
- There are likely to be fixed (nonmoving) obstacles in the work path.
- Fixed obstacles in the work path are below the horizontal sight-line or at the horizontal sight line.
- Obstacles have poor contrast.

Flexibility of the Workplace

- The Workplace is adaptable for:
  Wall supplemental lighting
  Task supplemental lighting
  Stand-type magnifier
  Clamp-on type magnifier.
- Range within which a task can be performed:
  Minimum Distance = 4 inches; Maximum Distance = 36 inches.
- Distance from the worker's eyes to the display is adaptable.

Appendix E. Sample Work Environment Visual Demands Report (*continued*)

Work Environment Visual Demands Report (*continued*)

Social Security No.: 000-00-6044 **Name:** Angela Labpugian **Age:** 57

Medical Eye Report

Primary condition	Right eye:	macular degeneration
	Left eye:	macular degeneration
Secondary condition	Right eye:	central scotoma
	Left eye:	peripheral scotoma
Tertiary condition	Right eye:	deficient color vision
	Left eye:	deficient color vision

Job Title: Secretary-8

JOB ACTIVITY NO. 2: ANSWER THE TELEPHONE

- Time present: often (20 percent to 50 percent of the time).
- Activity is critical to the job.
- 20 Footcandles are observed.
- Illuminance category observed: C (10 to 20 footcandles); General lighting is an observed option.
- Job setting: commercial, institutional, residential, and public assemblies.
- Illuminance category recommended: D (20 to 50 footcandles) General lighting is a recommended option.
- Vision requirements: Near, shifts in work distances, speed and accuracy.

Lighting

- Ceiling light—Direction: Front of subject
- Ceiling light—Type: Deluxe cool white fluorescent light
- Window (external) light—Direction: Right of subject, behind subject, front of subject
- Size of illumination area: Length = 72 inches, width = 60 inches, height = 30 inches

Types of Displays

- Printed and forms tasks
  Typed originals
- Handwritten tasks
  No. 2 pencil and softer leads
  Ball-point pen
  Felt-tip pen, fine
  Felt-tip pen, medium
  Felt-tip pen, bold
- Copied tasks
  Xerograph
- Other displays
  CRT monitor

Work Devices

- Telephone often used (20 percent to 50 percent of time)

Visual Display Characteristics

- Color of visual display: Black
- Color of visual display background: White
- Percent of reflectance: 35 percent

Environmental Factors Surrounding the Visual Display

- Shadows created by the worker's head or body position are present, which darken areas of the visual display.
- Direct or indirect glare interferes with the observation of the visual display.

Mobility Requirements

- Client must move from one workplace to another to perform work tasks.
- Moving requires light and dark adaptation.
- It is necessary for the client to use: Stairs, ramps, internal walkways, external walkways, aisles, corridors, and elevators.
- There are likely to be fixed (nonmoving) obstacles in the work path.
- Fixed obstacles in the work path are below the horizontal sight line or at the horizontal sight line.
- Obstacles have poor contrast.

Appendix E. Sample Work Environment Visual Demands Report (*continued*)

Work Environment Visual Demands Report (*continued*)

Flexibility of the Workplace

- The workplace is adaptable for:
  Wall supplemental lighting
  Task supplemental lighting
  Stand-type magnifier
  Clamp-on type magnifier.
- Range within which a task can be performed
  Minimum distance = 4 inches
  Maximum distance = 36 inches.
- Distance from the worker's eyes to the display is adaptable.

Appendix E. Sample Work Environment Visual Demands Report (*continued*)

Work Environment Visual Demands Report (*continued*)

Social Security No.: 000-00-6044 **Name:** Angela Labpugian **Age:** 57

Medical Eye Report

Primary condition	Right eye:	macular degeneration
	Left eye:	macular degeneration
Secondary condition	Right eye:	central scotoma
	Left eye:	peripheral scotoma
Tertiary condition	Right eye:	deficient color vision
	Left eye:	deficient color vision

Job Title: Secretary-8

JOB ACTIVITY NO. 3: GREET GUESTS

- Time present: often (20 percent to 50 percent of time).
- Activity is critical to the job.
- 20 Footcandles are observed.
- Illuminance category observed: C (10 to 20 footcandles) general lighting is an observed option.
- Job setting: Commercial, institutional, residential, and public assembles.
- Illuminance category recommended: C (10 to 20 footcandles) general lighting is a recommended option.
- Vision requirements: Midrange, far, depth perception, shifts in work distances, and field vision.

Lighting

- Ceiling—Direction: Front of subject
- Ceiling Light—Type: Deluxe cool white fluorescence light
- Window (external) light—Direction: Right of subject, behind subject, front of subject
- Size of illumination area: length = 72 inches, width = 60 inches, height = 30 inches

Types of Displays

(no information for job 3)

Visual Display Characteristics

- Color of visual display
  Not applicable

Environmental Factors Surrounding the Visual Display

- Direct or indirect glare interferes with the observation of the visual display.

Mobility Requirements

- Client must move from one workplace to another to perform work tasks.
- Moving requires light and dark adaptation.
- It is necessary for the client to use: Stairs, ramps, internal walkways, external walkways, aisles, corridors, and elevators.
- There are likely to be fixed (nonmoving) obstacles in the work path.
- Fixed obstacles in work path are below horizontal sight line or at the horizontal sight line.
- Obstacles have poor contrast.

Flexibility of the Workplace

- The Workplace is adaptable for:
  Wall supplemental lighting
  Task supplemental lighting
  Stand-type magnifier
  Clamp-on type magnifier.
- Range within which a task can be performed:
  Minimum Distance = 4 inches
  Maximum Distance = 36 inches.
- Distance from the worker's eyes to the display is adaptable.

Appendix E. Sample Work Environment Visual Demands Report (*continued*)

GLOSSARY

The following listing includes terms that are used in this text. The terms are defined as they are used in the field of rehabilitation counseling and in working with persons who are blind or visually impaired. The terms relate to such areas as the anatomy of the eye, eye conditions, and treatment that rehabilitation professionals are likely to encounter when providing services to blind and visually impaired individuals.

Accommodation The ability of the eye to adjust its focus for seeing at different distances by changing the shape of the lens through action of the ciliary muscle.

Acquired immunodeficiency syndrome (AIDS) A disease of the immune system that is caused by infection with the human immunodeficiency virus. Cytomegalovirus retinitis is the most frequent opportunistic intraocular infection among individuals with AIDS, and its prevalence rate is from 15 to 40 percent.

Activities of daily living (ADL) Work and daily living activities, such as food preparation and home management, whose performance often determines the need for nonmedical rehabilitation services.

Adaptive device *See* Assistive technology device.

Added correction *See* Bifocal add.

Adventitious Occurring after birth; in the context of blindness or visual impairment, postnatal loss of sight, that is, a vision loss that develops after one's birth, as compared with a congenital visual impairment.

Age-related macular degeneration (AMD) A condition associated with vascular diseases such as arteriosclerosis and stroke, in which central vision is gradually lost and acuity may decrease to 20/200 or less, but peripheral vision is usually retained. AMD is also called age-related maculopathy.

AIDS *See* Acquired immunodeficiency syndrome.

Albinism *See* Ocular albinism.

Amblyopia Diminished vision that is not totally attributable to organic causes and is often associated with strabismus or a high, uncorrected refractive error.

Amblyopia exanopsia Uncorrectable blurred vision because of long disuse.

Americans with Disabilities Act (ADA) of 1990 An act granting civil rights to individuals with disabilities. The ADA prohibits discrimination against individuals with disabilities in the areas of public accommodations, employment, transportation, state and local government services, and telecommunications.

Amsler grid A graphlike card used to determine central field losses, as in macular degeneration.

Aniridia A congenital or traumatically induced absence of the iris.

Anoxia A deficiency of oxygen to the body tissues that is of such severity as to cause permanent damage.

Anterior chamber The aqueous-filled space bounded in the front by the cornea and in the back by the iris and the middle part of the lens.

Aphakia The absence of the crystalline lens, usually resulting from the removal of a cataract.

Aptitude test A standardized examination that evaluates the abilities of an individual to learn or develop proficiency in a particular area if appropriate education or training is provided.

Aqueous humor The clear, watery fluid that fills the anterior and posterior chambers of the eye.

Arteriosclerosis A chronic disease characterized by thickening and loss of elasticity of arterial walls.

Assessment In ophthalmology, an appraisal of the integrity, health, and function of the eye and the optic pathways that lead to the occipital lobe of the brain; in rehabilitation counseling, the process through which the counselor determines the present needs and skill levels of the client.

Assistive technology device A device used to help individuals compensate for the loss of vision or a visual impairment. Devices can be simple, such as tactile markers, braille watches, or bold-lined paper, or they may include speech, braille, and large-print devices that enable a person who is visually impaired to use a personal computer and software programs.

Assistive technology plan A plan for provision of assistive devices that includes an assessment of the client's abilities and needs; an analysis of the job requirements; a statement of the objective; a statement of the perceived problem that necessitates the purchase of specialized equipment; an itemized list of recommended equipment, warranties, and service contracts, shipping costs, and vendor information; justification for all the suggested purchases, including price justification; installation and training information; and a statement of client and employer involvement.

Assistive technology specialist A rehabilitation professional who assists a client in identifying which assistive device(s) most effectively meet a specified need. Assistive technology specialists are classified differently by organization, agency, and state, and come from a variety of professional groups, including rehabilitation counselors, rehabilitation teachers, and computer access technology specialists.

Astigmatism A refractive error that is caused by an irregular curvature of the cornea and that prevents light rays from coming to a point or focus on the retina.

Asymptomatic Without functional evidence of a condition or disease.

Autosome Any nonsex-determining chromosome, of which there are 22 pairs in a human.

Best correction Optimal visual function with the use of prescription eyeglasses, contact lenses, or low vision lenses.

Bifocal add In a bifocal lens, the smaller, near vision lens that is placed below the center of the larger, distance vision lens. The additional power is reported as an add.

Bifocal lens A compound spectacle with a smaller, near vision lens placed below the center of the larger, distance vision lens.

Binocular vision Vision that uses both eyes to form a fused image in the brain and results in three-dimensional vision.

Biomicroscopy The examination of the eyelids and anterior portion of the eyeballs with a slit lamp (a biomicroscope) for magnification.

Blepharoplasty Reconstructive surgery performed on the eyelids for functional or cosmetic enhancement.

Blindness The inability to see; the absence or severe reduction of vision.

Blind spot A scotoma or "blank" area (point of loss of vision) in the central or peripheral visual field.

Braille A system of raised dots that enables functionally blind persons to read and write.

Brain injury A physical impairment resulting from anoxia, trauma, tumors, or stroke. The effects range from little to no visual impairment to a combination of poor visual acuity, visual field loss, diplopia (double vision), distortion, glare sensitivity, and such visual perceptual difficulties as visual agnosia (objects are seen but not recognized).

Buckle *See* Scleral buckle.

Canal of Schlemm A circular channel at the limbus that drains the aqueous humor from the anterior chamber to the veins and into the blood stream.

Career development theory A body of principles that identify the effects over time of psychological, sociological, cultural, and economic factors on self-career identity, decision-making ability, and career maturity.

Case management The process of overseeing an individual's progress, as in rehabilitation counseling, from the initial interview through closure. It includes case finding and referral, evaluation and assessment, planning, service delivery and coordination, job placement and follow-up.

Cataract An opacity of either the crystalline lens of the eye or the capsule that contains it.

CCTV *See* Closed-circuit television.

CF *See* Count fingers.

Choroid The vascular, middle layer between the retina and the sclera that provides the blood supply for the retina; part of the uveal tract.

Choroidoretinitis An inflammation of the choroid and retina.

Ciliary body The tissue inside the eye that is composed of the ciliary muscle and the ciliary processes.

Ciliary muscle The part of the ciliary body that helps adjust the thickness of the transparent lens by regulating the tension of the suspensory ligaments.

Ciliary process The portion of the ciliary body that produces aqueous humor.

Client assistance program (CAP) A federally mandated program developed as a part of the Rehabilitation Act of 1973 to provide (1) information and referral services, (2) individual advocacy services that are only available to persons with disabilities who are receiving or seeking services under the Act and who are encountering problems concerning their benefits or rights under the Act, and (3) systems advocacy services in which CAPs are charged with the responsibility of improving the delivery systems themselves, namely, identifying and seeking solutions to problems within each of the delivery systems.

Closed-angle glaucoma A form of primary glaucoma characterized by an increase in intraocular pressure as a result of a blockage of the anterior chamber at the base of the iris. Closed-angle glaucoma can cause sudden vision loss and immediate pain. Also called narrow-angle glaucoma.

Closed-circuit television (CCTV) An electro-optical video magnification device that is used primarily as a reading aid for persons with low vision and that is available with a black-and-white or color video monitor. It can be a stationary camera (under which the material is moved), a hand-held camera, or a head-mounted camera system. A CCTV not only affords maximum magnification for individuals with very poor visual acuity, but also allows for the manipulation of contrast, which can be an important concern for some types of visual impairments, such as glaucoma.

Cochlear implant The surgical insertion of an amplifying device into the spirally wound tube that forms part of the inner ear. An implant may be appropriate for some individuals who have profound bilateral sensorineural hearing loss and cannot be helped by conventional amplification devices.

Cognitive abilities Functions involving those operations of the mind by which persons become aware of objects or thought or perception, including understanding and reasoning.

Coloboma A congenital fissure in any part of the eye, including the choroid, iris, lens, optic nerve, and retina.

Comparability The concept that any job-site modification that is made for an individual with a visual impairment must be comparable to the same aspect of job performance as that performed by a sighted employee.

Competitive employment According to the Rehabilitation Act of 1973, as amended, work in a fully integrated setting at the prevailing minimum wage. The Rehabilitation Services Administration has determined that the phrase "fully integrated" means that the setting is as integrated as that for other, able-bodied workers performing the same functions.

Computer access technology (CAT) The use of personal computers to perform four major functions for persons with visual impairments: (1) input, (2) processing, (3) output, and (4) storage.

Comprehensive Vocational Evaluation System (CVES) A system developed specifically for individuals with visual impairments, it is a norm-referenced test battery that assesses intelligence, academic achievement, motor skills, tactile processing skills, adaptive behavior, work behavior, and emotionality.

Concave lens A spherical (divergent or minus) lens that bends light rays outward and is used to compensate for myopia.

Cone cells Photoreceptor cells that are located in the retina, primarily in the fovea and macula, that are sensitive to bright lights and give the clearest, sharpest sense of color and resolution.

Congenital Existing at birth; in the context of visual impairment, a condition of blindness or visual impairment that exists at birth, as compared with an adventitious vision loss, which occurs after birth.

Conjunctiva The mucous membrane that lines the eyelids and part of the outer surface of the eyeball.

Contrast sensitivity (CS) Subjective measure of an individual's ability to detect and discriminate objects and fine detail under conditions of reduced or low contrast. CS curves indicate how a person can see large targets (low-spatial frequency) of poor contrast, in addition to such small targets (high-spatial frequency) as printed letters or road signs of poor contrast.

Converging lens *See* Convex lens.

Convex lens A spherical (convergent or plus) lens that bends light rays inward and is used to compensate for hyperopia.

Cornea The transparent tissue at the front of the eye that is curved and provides approximately 66 percent of the eye's refracting power.

Cortical blindness Blindness that is the result of damage to any part of the visual pathways in the brain. Sometimes the optic chiasma (the point at which images are transmitted to the right or left brain) may be injured and unable to transmit the visual impulses. Individuals who are cortically blind may exhibit a reduced visual field or a hemianopia (blindness in half of the visual field).

Count fingers (CF) A standard test of vision that records the ability of the patient to identify the number of fingers held up by an examiner.

CRT screen A cathode ray tube screen, or the viewing screen of a video display.

Cryopexy The use of extreme cold (as with liquid hydrogen) to seal the retina to the choroid in retinal detachment or for repair of a retinal tear or hole.

Crystalline lens *See* Lens.

Cylindrical lens A lens that can be shaped with different refractive powers along specific meridians to compensate for the convergent or divergent power a specific eye lacks to bring light rays to focus on the retina; used to correct astigmatism.

Cytomegalovirus (CMV) A virus, such as CMV retinitis, that is frequently bilateral and, if left untreated, is almost always progressive and often leads to blindness. The drugs ganciclovir and foscarnet generally retard the progression of the disease, but do not cure it. The speed with which vision loss occurs varies from months to years. Ninety percent of the population that is infected with the human immunodeficiency virus (HIV) carries the CMV virus.

Deafness A lack or loss, incomplete or total, of the sense of hearing.

Diabetes, type I *See* Insulin-dependent diabetes mellitus.

Diabetes, type II *See* Noninsulin-dependent diabetes.

Diabetes mellitus A metabolic disorder related to faulty pancreatic activity and an inability to oxidize carbohydrates, resulting in the inadequate production or utilization of insulin; it results in an elevated blood sugar level and presence of sugar in the urine.

Diabetic retinopathy A noninflammatory disease of the retinal blood vessels caused by both type I and type II diabetes; a leading cause of blindness in the United States.

Diopter A unit of measurement of the refractive power of a lens equal to the reciprocal of the focal distance in meters.

Diplopia A vision disorder in which two images of a single object are seen because of unequal action of the muscles in the eyes. Also called double vision.

Disability A condition that exists when, in a particular setting, an individual cannot independently perform a specific set of functional activities.

Disincentives Social or governmental systemic criteria that make progress through the rehabilitation process toward employment less desirable than a nonproductive, supported activity.

Distal Anatomically located far from a point of reference.

Distance vision acuity The ability to perceive objects at a distance; distance visual acuity is measured using distance vision test charts, such as the Snellen chart, in which distance is measured at a length of 20 feet.

Diverging lens *See* Concave lens.

Dog guide A specially trained dog that assists a person who is blind or visually impaired in orientation and mobility; dog guides can learn to respond to commands and to judge when doing so would endanger the owner.

Drusen The yellow spots of waste material that appear on the retina; drusen are a symptom of "dry" acute macular degeneration.

E chart *See* Snellen chart.

Electronic travel aid (ETA) A mobility device that emits ultrasound vibrations or laser beams that probe the immediate environment and provide tactile or auditory signals, or both, to the traveler who is visually impaired.

Electro-oculography A test to determine the functionality of retinal pigment epithelium, one of the nine layers of the retina, in which the patient changes fixation from one visual target to another. As the gaze shifts, the skin electrodes record shifts in corneal-retinal electrical potential, which are considered indicative of problems in the retinal pigment epithelium.

Electroretinopathy A test utilizing the electroretinogram (ERG), which measures electrical responses from the retina when a checkerboard pattern or flashing lights are presented to both the light- and dark-adapted eye. The pattern, amplitude, and latency of the wave form that results from the stimulation of the retina by the flashing lights or the reversing pattern is displayed.

Entropion The inversion, or turning inward, of the edge of the eyelid.

Enucleation The surgical removal of the entire eye.

Epithelium The tissue that covers the internal and external surfaces of the eye.

Esotropia A form of strabismus in which one or both eyes deviate inward.

Evisceration The surgical removal of the contents of the eye with the exception of the sclera, which is left intact.

Eximer laser sculpturing Use of a laser to change the shape of the cornea to improve its refractive functioning.

Exotropia A form of strabismus in which one or both eyes deviate outward.

Extended employment Work in a nonintegrated or sheltered setting for a public or private nonprofit agency or organization that provides compensation in accordance with the Fair Labor Standards Act.

Extraocular muscles The muscles located outside the eyeball but within the orbit that are responsible for turning the eyeball in different directions; also called extrinsic muscles.

Field loss A measure of deficiency of vision based on what a fixed eye can or cannot see; it may be either peripheral or central vision loss.

Field of vision *See* Visual field.

Fine motor function Dexterity in performing acute tasks, such as closing a button, opening a safety pin, or removing a match from its box.

Floaters Deposits or particles in the vitreous humor that appear as thin, transparent strings or specks that flutter and float through the visual field; a sudden appearance of floaters or flashes of light may indicate a serious eye disorder, such as a retinal tear. Also called muscae vilantes.

Focal distance In optics, the distance between a lens and the point at which parallel light rays are brought to a focus.

Fovea centralis An indentation in the center of the macula that is about the size of the head of a pin; it is packed with cone cells, has no blood vessels, and is where the clearest, sharpest vision takes place.

Fundus The posterior pole of the eye, that is, the part opposite the pupil.

Fundus fluorescein angiography (FFA) A procedure that shows the capillaries, arteries, and veins of the choroid and retina. It is especially helpful in diagnosing and treating diabetic retinopathy, retinal vein occlusion, and macular degeneration. Vascular leaks, edema, neovascularization, and hemorrhages can be detected by observation with an ophthalmoscope during the procedure and by examination of the fundus photographs later.

Fusion *See* Binocular vision.

Genetic counseling The provision of specific facilitative assistance to individuals with hereditary conditions who may be considering having children. This area of counseling, which should be provided by qualified practitioners, requires an in-depth knowledge of possible outcomes of pregnancies because of various genetic disorders.

German measles *See* Maternal rubella.

Glaucoma A disease in which increased intraocular pressure results in the degeneration of the optic disk and eventual defects in the visual field. If not treated, the outcome is total blindness.

Globe The eyeball.

Goldmann perimetry A standard test of the field of vision losses that uses a moving target in a bowl-like apparatus to measure the entire visual field. It is called kinetic perimetry because the target moves.

Gross motor function The dexterity in performing such tasks as walking, jumping, and swimming.

Hand movement (HM) A method of measuring visual acuity; the examiner moves a hand in front of the individual being tested and records the distance at which the hand can be perceived.

Head injury *See* Brain injury.

Hemianopia Blindness in one half of the field of vision in one or both eyes.

HIV *See* Human immunodeficiency virus.

Home signs In manual communication methods for persons who are deaf, use of informal gestures.

Homologous Having the same relative structure, position, or origin.

HOTV test A visual acuity chart using irreversible letters that is effective in testing the distance vision of preschool children who are able to match letters.

Human immunodeficiency virus (HIV) The submicroscopic agent of acquired immunodeficiency syndrome (AIDS) that infects and destroys cells of the immune system. Ninety percent of HIV-infected individuals also carry the cytomegalovirus (CMV), which can attack the retina.

Hydrostatic pressure Tension produced by the fluid in the eye. In glaucoma, this may damage optic nerve cells on the retina.

Hyperopia (farsightedness) A refractive error in which light rays converge at a hypothetical point behind the retina, resulting in vision that is better for distant than for near objects; corrected with a plus (convex) lens.

Hypertension High blood pressure. With hypertension, changes in the retinal arterioles may suggest either recent, reversible pathology or fixed, longstanding alterations.

Hyperthyroidism A condition caused by excessive production of thyroid hormones. If left untreated, vision loss may occur because of optic nerve involvement. Graves's disease, a common form of hyperthyroidism, is characterized by a slight protrusion of the eyeballs.

Hypertropia Eyes that are turned upward because of a disorder of the extraocular muscles.

Hypotropia Eyes that are turned downward because of a disorder of the extraocular muscles.

Independent living skills Skills for performing daily tasks and managing personal needs, such as those for self-care, planning and cooking meals, maintaining a sanitary living environment, traveling independently, budgeting one's expenses, and functioning as independently as possible in the home and in the community.

Individualized Education Program (IEP) Originally developed as part of the Education for all

Handicapped Children Act, which provided for a free and appropriate public education in the least restrictive environment with special education and related services for each child with a disability. A written plan of instruction by a transdisciplinary educational team, the IEP includes the student's present levels of educational performance, annual goals, short-term objectives, specific services needed, duration of services, evaluation, and related information. Under the Individuals with Disabilities Education Act (IDEA), each student receiving special services must have such a plan.

Individualized Written Rehabilitation Program (IWRP) Mandated by the Rehabilitation Act of 1973, the IWRP is a contract between the client and a rehabilitation agency that describes the services needed to achieve the client's employment objective.

Individual placement model The concept that, in supported employment, only one worker with severe disabilities is placed at an employment site and matched with a position. Through training at the job site, ongoing assessment, and ongoing support, the worker is given the support necessary to maintain the job. This model affords maximum integration, flexibility, and autonomy for the worker.

Initial interview The first time an applicant and rehabilitation counselor interact in a formal way.

Insulin-dependent diabetes mellitus A form of diabetes mellitus that develops during childhood and is characterized by a severe deficiency in insulin secretion; it can usually be controlled by insulin injections. Also known as type I diabetes and juvenile diabetes.

Intraocular lens (IOL) implant An artificial (plastic) lens that is inserted surgically when a cataract is removed to replace the function of the crystalline, or natural, lens.

Intraocular pressure (IOP) The force of the aqueous and vitreous humors on the inner surfaces of the eyeball that gives it its firm, round shape.

Iridectomy The surgical removal of part of the iris.

Iridocyclitis An inflammation of the iris and the ciliary body. Also called anterior uveitis.

Iridotomy A surgical incision of the iris.

Iris The colored, circular membrane of the eye that is suspended between the cornea and the lens and that expands or contracts to control the amount of light entering the eye.

Islet of Langerhans The area within the pancreas that produces insulin, an internal secretion connected with the metabolism of carbohydrates.

Isopter A visual field map, which is a line connecting points where a target was seen or not seen.

Itinerant program In the context of rehabilitation, a program in which orientation and mobility instructors, educators, and other service providers see clients in their home areas and usually work in proximity when appropriate training areas are available.

Jaeger scale A test of near vision using graded sizes of letters or numbers.

Job accommodation In the workplace, the methods of providing expanded employment opportunities for individuals with disabilities; these accommodations may include making facilities accessible and usable, modifying work schedules, restructuring jobs, and acquiring adaptive equipment to help qualified individuals perform the essential functions of a job.

Job analysis The rehabilitation professional's description of what the worker does on the job, how it is done, the worker's characteristics, and the context of the work; a job analysis and a task analysis must be performed before recommending specific modifications of a job or work environment.

Job coach A professional who works with one or more individuals with a visual impairment, in a new job to help the person(s) learn the responsibilities of the position.

Job modification The application of assistive devices, the reordering of job tasks, or other alterations made to a job site that enable an employee with a disability to perform work tasks.

Job restructuring A process involving the redistribution of tasks and responsibilities in a particular job to another employee to accommodate an individual with a visual impairment, who, in turn, would be expected to increase output in other aspects of the position.

Job retention In the context of rehabilitation counseling, the ability of a worker to retain his or her job.

Job sample Job samples utilize the same tools, materials, procedures, and work standards as specific jobs, as compared with occupational cluster work samples, which emphasize select tasks common to several different jobs.

Job search skills A component of job placement readiness that involves learning the following skills: (1) how to organize time and resources, (2) how to negotiate with significant others in career plan development, (3) how to document one's efforts, and (4) how to determine when to shift to a backup plan; the ability to identify potential employers or job openings, apply and interview for jobs.

Job shadowing A technique in which the job seeker follows an employee, often for a number of days, to better understand the employee's responsibilities. This strategy enables an individual to make an informed decision regarding a potential work role.

Job sharing The division of what is typically a full-time job among two or more part-time persons.

Job tryout A situation in which an individual performs actual work tasks on a real job either in the community or in a community rehabilitation program. During this time, his or her performance, work, and learning skills are assessed.

Keratitis Any of a variety of corneal infections, irritations, and inflammations.

Keratoconus A cone-shaped deformity of the cornea that is a hereditary degenerative disease and is manifest in adolescence or later.

Keratoplasty Reconstructive surgery on the cornea, particularly corneal grafting and transplantation.

Lacrimal gland A gland that is located in the upper outer quadrant of the orbit; it secretes tears that flow down over the front surface of the globe.

Large print or type The size of type that is 14 points (3/16 inch) or larger in height.

Laser surgery The use of a concentrated, very powerful beam of light to perform various procedures in the eye, including coagulation of retinal vessels (argon laser) and destruction of secondary cataracts (YAG laser).

Lateral Lying away from the median axis of the body; lying at or extending toward the right or left side.

Legal blindness Visual acuity for distance vision of 20/200 or less in the better eye after best correction with conventional lenses, or a visual field of no greater than 20 degrees in the better eye.

Lens The transparent biconvex structure within the eye that allows it to refract light rays, enabling the rays to focus on the retina; also called the crystalline lens. Also, any transparent material that can refract light in a predictable manner.

Lens implant See Intraocular lens implant.

Lens opacity A clouded area on part or all of the lens through which light rays do not pass; a cataract.

Light perception (LP) The ability to discern the presence or absence of light, but not its source or direction.

Light projection The ability to discern the direction or source of light, but not enough vision to identify objects, people, shapes, or movements.

Limbus The junction of the cornea and sclera.

Low vision A visual impairment after best correction, but with the potential for use of available vision, with or without optical or nonoptical compensatory visual strategies, devices, and environmental modifications, to plan and perform daily tasks.

Low vision devices A wide variety of optical and nonoptical devices used to enhance the visual capability of persons with visual impairments.

Macula The small, avascular central area of the retina that surrounds the fovea; a depression on the retina that has a high concentration of cones and that is the point of clearest vision.

Macular degeneration A degenerative disease of the macula that causes a loss of central vision resulting in a central scotoma, or a blind or partially blind area in the central visual field; a leading cause of visual diminution in persons who are elderly. *See also* Age-related macular degeneration.

Magnification power The number of times of enlargement of an image by a lens; for example, a 10X magnifier enlarges an image 10 times.

Magnifier A device used to increase the size of an image through the use of lenses or lens systems; a magnifier may be used at any distance from the eye (e.g., stand type, hand held, or spectacle mounted).

Marfan's syndrome An inherited congenital disorder of the connective tissue characterized by abnormal elongation of the extremities, partial dislocation of the lens, cardiovascular abnormalities, and other disorders.

Maternal rubella An acute contagious viral disease (German measles) that is contracted by a pregnant woman and that may cause complications in the fetus, such as cataracts, uveal colobomas, searching nystagmus, microphthalmus, strabismus, retinopathy, and infantile glaucoma, when occurring during the first trimester.

Medical assessment A comprehensive medical evaluation consisting of a complete, general medical examination, a visual examination by either an ophthalmologist or an optometrist, examinations by specialists in medical or related fields, a hearing examination, and clinical laboratory tests and procedures.

Metabolic disorder A deficit in one of the chemical or physical processes in which living organized substance is produced or maintained.

Microscope A high-power convex lens that magnifies near-point objects and is usually mounted into eyeglasses and prescribed for one eye only.

Minification The reduction in size of the image of an object; it is the opposite of magnification.

Minus lens *See* Concave lens.

Mobile crew approach A model of supported employment in which a group of up to eight workers with severe disabilities holds contracts to perform regular work at various locations. With the assistance of a van, the crew and its supportive personnel work at various locales, usually performing such service tasks as lawn maintenance, farm work, and maintenance services. Workers without disabilities may or may not be included in this approach.

Mobility The ability to move from one's present position to one's desired position in another part of the environment. *See also* Orientation.

Monocular Relating to one eye or having one eyepiece, as opposed to binocular, which pertains to both eyes.

Multiple disabilities Two or more concomitant disabilities (physical, mental, or emotional) that have a direct effect on the ability to learn.

Muscae vilantes *See* Floaters.

Myasthenia gravis A syndrome of fatigue and exhaustion of the muscular system marked by progressive paralysis of muscles without sensory disturbance or atrophy. Loss of function is the result of an autoimmune attack on acetylcholine receptors, which are key agents in neuromuscular transmission.

Myopia (nearsightedness) A refractive error in which the light rays from an object beyond a specific distance are focused in front of the retina; the condition can be the result of too great refractive power or of an eyeball that is too long; it is corrected with a minus (concave) lens.

Nasopharynx The part of the pharanyx that is behind and above the soft palate, directly continuous with the nasal passages.

Near vision acuity The ability to perceive objects up close (at a reading distance).

Neovascularization New blood vessel growth, as on the retina; it is one sign of diabetic retinopathy.

Nephropathy An abnormal state of the kidney that commonly accompanies later stages of diabetes mellitus.

Neurological disability A deficit of the nervous system, the causes of which vary and may be the result of maternal infection, injury during the birth process (e.g., anoxia), injury or trauma after birth (e.g., brain tumor, blows to the head), or strokes.

Neuropathy An abnormal and usually degenerative state of the nervous system or nerves, as in the reduced tactile sensitivity in diabetic neuropathy.

Neuropsychological test A psychological assessment that studies the relationship between the functioning of the brain and the cognitive processes or behaviors to evaluate central nervous system function and diagnose specific behavioral or cognitive deficits or disorders.

No light perception (NLP) A description of visual functioning in which an individual reports the inability to detect light or shadow of any kind or degree.

Noninsulin-dependent diabetes mellitus A form of diabetes mellitus that develops in adults and is characterized by hyperglycemia that results from the inability to utilize insulin together with the inability to compensate with increased insulin production; this type of metabolic disorder can typically be controlled by weight loss and diet. Also known as type II diabetes and adult onset diabetes.

Nonoptical devices Low vision devices that do not involve optics, such as lamps, filters, large print, typoscopes, bold-lined paper, and writing guides.

Norms Set standards or patterns derived from a representative sampling of median achievement of a large group; norms offer a range of values against which individual comparisons may be made.

"Null point" In nystagmus, the direction in which there is the least amount of rapid eye movement and the best possible vision.

Nystagmus An involuntary rapid movement of the eyeball that may be horizontal, vertical, rotary, or mixed.

Obliterative lesions The pathological discontinuity of tissue, as with lesions of the small, tufted blood vessels of the kidney (glomerular capillaries).

Occipital lobe The posterior part of the brain that is responsible for vision and visual perception; it includes the visual cortex, which is the cerebral end of the visual pathway.

Occupational cluster work sample A work sample that is derived from the more common work tasks associated with a group of related jobs; occupational cluster work samples emphasize select tasks common to several different jobs, whereas job samples mimic specific jobs in their entirety.

Ocular albinism A hereditary condition that results in pigmentation loss in the retinal pigment epithelium, iris, and choroid.

Ocularist A person who makes and fits an artifical eye (prosthesis).

OD Oculus dexter (right eye).

Open-angle glaucoma The most common type of primary glaucoma, in which the aqueous humor does not filter through the trabecular meshwork and out of the Canal of Schlemm; it is bilateral, asymptomatic in onset until visual impairment occurs, and then is slowly progressive. See also glaucoma.

Ophthalmic nurse A nurse who works under the direction of an ophthalmologist and who has undergone specific training to provide instruction in the use of optical devices; duties may include taking clinical measurements for acuity and visual fields, and administering medications.

Ophthalmologist A physician who specializes in the diagnosis and treatment of defects and diseases of the eye; performs surgery, when necessary, and prescribes other types of treatment, including eyeglasses or other optical devices.

Ophthalmoscope An instrument for viewing the interior of the eye that consists of a concave mirror with a hole in the center through which the examiner views the eye; a source of light is reflected into the eye by the mirror and can be rotated into the opening in the mirror.

Optical character recognition (OCR) A system used to convert printed material into computer files so it can be produced in a form (such as braille, voice output, or closed-circuit television) that is useful for people with sensory losses, using a scanner interfaced with a computer.

Optical devices Low vision devices that incorporate optics, such as magnifiers, microscopes, and telescopes.

Optic atrophy The damage to the optic nerve that can result from occlusion of the central retinal artery, degeneration of the retina, direct injury to the optic nerve, or pressure against the nerve from a tumor or aneurysm. In the latter case, if the pressure can be relieved, vision may improve; in other cases, often little can be done. Loss of vision may occur slowly and may be the only symptom of the problem.

Optic chiasm The junction where the fibers coming from the nasal portion of the retina of each eye split off from their optic nerves and cross over to the opposite side to join fibers coming from the temporal portion of each retina from the opposite side.

Optic disk The point at which the nerve fibers from the inner layer of the retina become the optic nerve and exit the eye (that is, the point at which the optic nerve intersects with the retina); the "blind spot" of the eye.

Optician A professional who fills the optical prescriptions of ophthalmologists and optometrists and who grinds lenses and produces different types of lens corrections for eyeglasses, bifocals, and contact lenses.

Optic nerve The sensory nerve that carries visual impulses from the retina to the brain.

Optic neuropathy A functional disturbance or pathological change in the optic nerve.

Optics The science that deals with light and phenomena associated with it, applied in the prescription of low vision devices.

Optometrist A licensed nonmedical doctor of optometry who is trained to work with the functioning but not the pathology of the eyes and who measures refraction and prescribes and fits eyeglasses or contact lenses. In most states, optometrists are also able to prescribe and dispense medications.

Orbits The two pyramidal cavities in the front of the skull that contain the eyeballs, eye muscles, and fatty cushioning layers, as well as nerves and blood vessels.

Orientation The process of becoming familiar with and establishing one's position and relationship to significant objects in the environment. *See also* Mobility.

Orientation and mobility (O&M) The field dealing with systematic techniques by which blind or visually impaired persons orient themselves to their environment and move about independently. The O&M specialist provides instruction in travel skills (e.g., working with the sighted or human guide, the long cane, and electronic travel aids).

Orthoptist A nonmedical technician who directs and supervises ocular control training or visual training involving the exercise of the eye muscles to develop coordination and correct vision.

OS Oculus sinister (left eye).

Osteoporosis A condition in which bones become increasingly porous, brittle, and subject to fracture because of the loss of calcium and other minerals.

OU Oculi unitas (both eyes).

Pathological nystagmus Rapid eye movement as a result of a sensory or motor defect or upon occlusion of either eye (latent nystagmus).

Peripheral vision The ability to perceive the presence, motion, or color of objects outside the direct line of vision or by other than the central retina.

Personal adjustment The process of how one lives with an impairment in terms of individual functioning and emotional acceptance.

Personality test A test that determines the basic characteristics of individuals that can be used to predict their reactions to various situations; a test designed to give an indication of a person's psychological strengths and weaknesses, coping styles, and ability to handle various forms of stress.

Placement The end goal of vocational rehabilitation, namely, the attainment and retention of employment by an individual with a disability.

Placement readiness program A program of assistance for job seekers, the activities of which may include training in such areas as how to use the telephone to find job leads, how to write a résumé, how to fill out an application, and how to interview successfully.

Plus lens *See* Convex lens.

Posterior chamber The space between the front of the vitreous and the back of the iris that is filled with aqueous fluid.

Power of a lens In lens magnification, power is measured in diopters; the principle that the stronger the lens is, the shorter is the focal distance or the distance necessary to bring light rays to a point of focus.

Prescription eyeglasses Corrective lenses prescribed by an eyecare specialist after examination to determine which lens configuration would best refract light to the individual's retina.

Prism lens A special triangle-shaped lens that is incorporated into regular eyeglasses, to redirect the rays of light entering the eye, resulting in a realignment of the eyes or, in some cases, a shifting of images to permit binocular vision.

Projection The ability to determine from which direction light comes.

Prosthesis An artificial device to replace a missing part of the body, as in an artifical eye.

Protective techniques The utilization of cross-body arm and hand positions to provide protection from objects extending from walls, objects at head height, or objects at waist height.

Psychological assessment A professional determination of whether an individual possesses the emotional stability to handle stresses associated with performing a particular job, learning a particular skill, or participating in a vocational training program.

Psychosocial abilities Patterns of behavior, personality, or emotional functioning in terms of oneself and one's relation to others.

Pterygium A triangular fold of tissue that extends from the conjunctiva over the cornea and that can impair vision by warping the cornea.

Ptosis A drooping of the upper eyelid that may be congenital and requires surgical correction if the droop interferes with vision.

Pupil The hole in the center of the iris through which light rays enter the back of the eye.

Radio reading An auditory information resource, usually operating on noncommercial bands of radio frequencies and requiring a special receiver, that provides persons with visual, physical, and reading impairments, newspaper articles, commentary, advertisements, best sellers not available in adapted forms, consumer information, and information on issues such as jobs, access, and transportation.

Reasonable accommodation Any change in the work environment or in the way things are customarily done that enables an individual with a disability to enjoy equal employment opportunities. It may include such changes as making facilities used by employees accessible to and usable by individuals with impairments by job restructuring, modified work schedules, acquisition or modification of existing equipment, and the provision of readers or interpreters. Individuals with impairments must be otherwise qualified to perform the essential functions of the job, as written in a job description.

Recessive genetic transmission The incapability of expression unless carried by both sets of homologous chromosomes.

Refraction The bending of light rays as they pass through a substance; also, the determination of the refractive errors of the eye and their correction with eyeglasses or contact lenses.

Rehabilitation counselor A professional who works with individuals with physical or mental disabilities to become or remain self-sufficient, productive citizens. Rehabilitation counselors help individuals with disabilities deal with societal and personal problems, plan careers, and find and keep satisfying jobs. They also may work with individuals, professional organizations, and advocacy groups to address the environmental and social barriers that create obstacles for people with disabilities. Job tasks frequently include: (1) evaluating an individual's potential for independent living and employment, (2) arranging for medical and psychological services and vocational assessment, training, job placement, and (3) working with employers to identify and modify job responsibilities to accommodate individuals with disabilities.

Rehabilitation engineering The systematic application of engineering sciences to design, develop, adapt, test, evaluate, apply, and distribute technological solutions to problems confronted by individuals with impairments in functional areas, such as mobility, communications, hearing, vision, and cognition, and in activities associated with employment, independent living, education, and integration into the community.

Rehabilitation teacher A professional who provides instruction and guidance to adults with visual impairments in five broad skill areas—home management, personal management, communication and education, leisure activity, and home orientation skills—to enable the individual to live and function independently.

Rehabilitation technology The systematic application of technologies, engineering methodologies, or scientific principles to meet the needs of, and address the challenges confronted by, individuals with disabilities.

Reliability The extent to which data demonstrate consistency on repeated trials across time or from one part of a test to another. An assessment device is reliable if clients consistently score near the same level regardless of the number of times they take the test.

Residential school A place of instruction at which dormitory or other maintenance facilities provide room and board for students. State schools for the blind often serve individuals whose homes are located too far away for them to commute. By providing for their maintenance, the most efficient use of specialized teachers and resources may be applied.

Retina The innermost layer of the eye, containing light-sensitive nerve cells and fibers connecting with the brain through the optic nerve that receives the image formed by the lens.

Retinal degeneration A classification of a number of conditions in which retinal cells break down; one condition commonly seen by rehabilitation counselors is retinitis pigmentosa.

Retinal detachment The separation of the retina from the underlying choroid, nearly always caused by a retinal tear, which allows fluid to accumulate between the retina and the retinal pigment epithelium. It usually requires surgical intervention to prevent loss of vision.

Retinal edema The swelling of the retina because of leaking blood vessels.

Retinal hemorrhage A copious discharge of blood caused by any condition that compromises the endothelial cells, and results from diapedeses (outward passage of corpuscular elements of blood through intact vessel walls) from veins or capillaries.

Retinitis An inflammation of the retina marked by impairment of sight, perversion of vision, edema, and exudation or occasional hemorrhages into the retina.

Retinitis pigmentosa (RP) A group of progressive, often hereditary, retinal degenerative diseases that are characterized by decreasing peripheral vision. Symptoms include night blindness and progressive contraction of the visual field. Some progress to tunnel vision, whereas others result in total blindness if the macula also becomes involved.

Retinopathies Diseases of the retina as a result of various causes, including diabetes mellitus and hypertension.

Retinopathy of prematurity (ROP) A common cause of blindness in premature infants, ROP results from exposure to a high concentration of oxygen at birth and leads to retinal detachment and various degrees of vision loss. Extremely premature infants weighing less than 1 kilogram at birth have an increased risk of ROP.

Retrolental fibroplasia (RLF) Oxygen, necessary in many instances to preserve infant life, triggers changes in retinal blood vessels and, in some cases, proliferation of vessels into the vitreous with predisposition to retinal detachment. For many babies, the net result was blindness, for others, visual impairment. When the relationship between low birthweight, prematurity, and the administration of high concentrations of oxygen over extended periods of time was discovered in the early 1950s, monitoring procedures were introduced, and the incidence of RLF decreased dramatically.

Rod cells Specialized retinal photoreceptor cells that are located primarily in the peripheral retina. They are responsible for seeing form, shape, and movement and function best in low levels of illumination.

Safety lens A shatterproof lens that prevents the cutting of eyelids or penetrating wounds into the cornea or deeper into the globe that may occur if standard lenses are fragmented.

Scanning The surveying of the environment in an organized manner; repetitive fixations that are required to look from one object to another.

Scleral buckle A surgical procedure used for retinal detachment, in which a strap of preserved sclera or a silicone band is placed around the eyeball, and tightened to indent the sclera, which pushes the retina against the choroid and encourages reattachment of the retina.

Scotoma A blind or partially blind area in the visual field that may be caused by damage to the retina or visual pathways; also called a "blind spot."

Screen reader Speech software designed to "read" material on a computer screen.

Secondary disability In this context, a physical or mental disability in addition to vision loss; in cases where an individual has two or more disabilities, the secondary disability is the one having the most impact on functioning that is not affected by the visual impairment.

Severe disability A physical or mental disability that acutely affects one or more major life activities.

Severe visual impairment As defined by the National Center for Health Statistics, a person with severe visual impairment is unable to read ordinary newspaper print even with the aid of corrective lenses, or, if under six years of age, a person who is blind in both eyes or has no useful vision in either eye.

Sex-linked genetic transmission A characteristic transmitted by a gene located on a sex chromosome.

Sighted guide technique A specific orientation and mobility technique in which a person who is blind takes the elbow of a sighted person and, walking a half-step behind, learns to utilize nonverbal and brief verbal clues to negotiate travel on flat surfaces, up and down stairways, through doors opening towards and away from the pair, and through narrow openings.

Situational assessment The systematic observation of a person's behavior in work situations; the four types of situational assessment are simulated job situation, community rehabilitation program setting, job tryout or job-site evaluation, and vocational classroom tryout.

Small business approach A model of a supported employment program that is a community-based enterprise operated either by a human services agency or a private entrepreneur, and that employs up to eight workers with severe impairments, as well as workers without impairments. Training is extensive and supervision is close. Typically, workers are paid piece-rate wages according to their productivity on manufacturing or assembly tasks.

Snellen chart A chart used for testing central visual acuity, usually at a distance of 20 feet, containing letters, (*the top line consists of the letter E*), numbers, or symbols in graduated sizes, labeled with the distance at which each size can be read by the "normal" eye.

Social Security Disability Insurance (SSDI) Disability benefits awarded unter Title II of the Social Secutiry Act.

Specific learning disability In contrast to mental retardation, in which all areas of mental functioning are impaired, specific learning disabilities affect discrete areas of functioning, such as reading or use of numbers.

Specific norms The standards that provide the average performance of a specified group; the term specific refers to the relationship of the standards to the actual characteristics of a client or client group, as opposed to general norms, namely, standards for the general population.

Spectacle-mounted lens Eyeglasses, as opposed to contact lenses or intraocular lenses.

Speech system A generic classification for adaptive systems that have two components: a speech software (often called a screen reader) and a speech synthesizer. A synthetic speech system is a computer-based system that converts the electronic signals that appear on the screen as text into spoken units; it is generally composed of an internal or external synthesizer, which does the speaking, and screen-access software, which tells the synthesizer what to say.

Spherical lens A lens whose shape is a segment of a sphere, as compared with a cylindrical lens, whose shape is columnar. In eyeglasses and prescriptive lenses, concave spherical (divergent or minus) lenses are used to compensate for myopia and convex spherical (convergent or plus) lenses are used to compensate for hyperopia. Cylindrical lenses are used to correct astigmatism.

Standardized tests Measures that compare an individual's performance with the performance of a representative sample group, including tests of achievement, personality, intelligence, aptitude, interests, and motor skills.

Stand magnifier An image-enlarging lens that is mounted on a device so that the hands are not required to hold it during use.

Stargardt's dystrophy A condition transmitted in an autosomal recessive manner, in which the macular pigment epithelium slowly degenerates, leading to loss of central vision.

State-federal vocational rehabilitation program In operation since 1920, it is a partnership of federal funding and oversight, along with state administration and service delivery, that has helped millions of Americans with disabilities to find employment. The federal partner is the Rehabilitation Services Administration, operated under the Office of Special Education and Rehabilitative Services in the U.S. Department of Education. The state partners, referred to in the law as designated state units (DSUs), are vocational rehabilitation agencies or commissions. The program operates under authority of the Rehabilitation Act of 1973, as amended.

Stereotype An often oversimplified or biased mental picture held to characterize the typical individual of a group. These prevailing misconceptions and stereotypes, rather than the physical loss of sight, often have a significant negative effect on self-esteem, availability of services, and employment opportunities for individuals who are blind or visually impaired.

Strabismus An extraocular muscle imbalance that causes misalignment of the eyes.

Substantial gainful activity A term used by the Social Security Administration to determine eligibility for benefits.

Supplemental Security Income (SSI) Disability income awarded under Title XVI of the Social Security Act.

Supported employment Competitive work in integrated job settings with ongoing support services for individuals with the most severe disabilities.

Suspensory ligaments The circle of fine fibers that are attached to the ciliary body and hold the lens in place; they allow the lens to change shape in accommodation.

Systemic lupus erythematosus A chronic, remitting, relapsing, inflammatory, and often fever-associated multisystemic disorder of the connective tissue. Acute or insidious in onset, it is characterized by involvement of the skin, joints, kidneys, and mucous membranes; retinal damage may be associated with lupus.

Talking books Books in an audible format (on tape or vinyl recordings) supplied through the federal-state system of library services for persons with visual or physical impairments. The borrowers in the program need special devices on which to play the recordings.

Task analysis The step-by-step delineation of the work activities of a job.

Task-oriented work samples The measures of the ability of an individual to perform a specific job task; for example, an individual's ability to measure yards of material or to type 50 words per minute. There are two kinds of task-oriented work samples: job samples and occupational cluster work samples.

Team A number of rehabilitation professionals, which may include individuals who provide rehabilitation teaching, O&M instruction, and assistive technology evaluation and instruction, who work together to ensure efficient, nonduplicative, and effective rehabilitation services to persons with disabilities.

Telemicroscope A low vision device that combines a telescope and a microscope. Telemicroscopes are adapted to focus at a near or intermediate distance by the use of a cap or a variable focusing mechanism, and they allow hands-free magnification at a greater focal distance than equivalent-powered microscope reading glasses, but at the expense of the field of view.

Telescope A low vision lens system that uses magnification for viewing objects at distance of about 2 feet or greater; telescopes optically increase the apparent size of the far objects and thus enlarge the retinal image.

Tertiary disability A disorder in addition to the visual impairment and major secondary condition.

Tonometer An instrument used for measuring intraocular pressure.

Tonometry The measurement of intraocular pressure.

Touch technique A specific cane technique used by travelers with visual impairments in outdoor and unfamiliar indoor areas. The cane is swung from side to side, low to the ground and touching down at each end of the arc. The cane serves as a bumper, informing the user about characteristics of the terrain, including texture, gradient changes, and drop-offs such as stairs and curbs.

Toxoplasmosis An infection with, or a condition produced by, a protozoal parasite found worldwide in epithelial cells of most mammals, including humans. In congenital toxoplasmosis, uveitis and retinal inflammation and scarring may occur.

Trabeculum The area where fluid flows from the eye.

Transition In rehabilitation, a stage that occurs when an individual prepares to leave an educational program to enter the world of work or to participate in rehabilitation programs.

Traumatic brain injury *See* Brain injury.

Trifocal lens A spectacle lens that contains three refractive surfaces: one that corrects for near vision, one for intermediate vision, and one for distance vision.

20/20 A measure of "normal" visual acuity for distance; that which should be seen at 20 feet is seen at 20 feet.

20/200 A commonly used term to describe "legal blindness" if the remaining vision in the better eye after best correction is 20/200 or less.

Type I diabetes *See* Insulin-dependent diabetes mellitus.

Type II diabetes *See* Noninsulin-dependent diabetes mellitus.

Ultrasonography A test that provides a measure of the structural integrity of the eye by using the reflection of extremely high-frequency waves to determine shape, size, thickness, position, and density of soft tissue in the orbit and the eyeball; also called echography, this test is helpful in locating tumors and foreign bodies and in detecting detached retinas.

Undue hardship An action requiring significant difficulty or expense in providing a reasonable accommodation.

Usher's syndrome An autosomal recessive syndrome in which congenital deafness is accompanied by retinitis pigmentosa, often ending in blindness; sometimes mental retardation and disturbances of gait may occur.

Uveal tract The middle, vascular layer of the eyeball that includes the choroid, the ciliary body, and the iris.

Uveitis An inflammation of one or all portions of the uveal tract.

Validity The degree to which an assessment device accurately reflects the concept or task it was designed to measure.

Values clarification exercises Activities designed to help persons explore and define what they consider to be important.

Verbal cues The use of spoken phrases in place of nonverbal expressions of communication to assure that persons unable to perceive nonverbal cues obtain the full import of dialogue.

Visual acuity The sharpness of vision with respect to the ability to distinguish detail, often measured by the eye's ability to distinguish the details and shapes of objects at a designated distance; it involves central (macular) vision.

Visual acuity test An assessment of detailed central vision; infants are tested by ascertaining pupillary responses to light and, later, light fixation reflexes; subsequent assessments include the illiterate "E" chart and standard Snellen chart.

Visual cognition The recognition and assimilation of specific environmental objects through vision.

Visual disability A term that refers to a visual impairment of sufficient magnitude to cause a real or perceived disadvantage in performing specific tasks by an individual and to require the specialized services of a counselor or agency serving individuals with visual impairments.

Visual field Peripheral vision, that is, sight transmitted to the brain from areas of the retina other than the macula; the area that can be seen when looking straight ahead, measured in degrees from the fixation point; also called field of vision.

Visual impairment Any degree of vision loss that affects an individual's ability to perform the tasks of daily life, caused by a visual system that is not working properly or not formed correctly.

Visual memory The retention of mental imagery of environments or objects in one's environment gained through original visual input.

Visual modifications Areas that require evaluation to enhance orientation and mobility within the workplace for individuals who are visually impaired. These include glare, which should be reduced through covering of windows; lighting; floors, which should also be nonglare; eye-level high-contrast markings on glass doors and walls to avoid collisions; and stairways marked for safety.

Visual processing The entire process by which one receives visual information, integrates it, performs an action, and adjusts one's behavior accordingly.

Vitrectomy The surgical removal of part of the vitreous, and its replacement with a saline solution.

Vitreous The transparent physiological gel that fills the vitreous cavity, the back portion of the eye between the lens and the retina; it is 99 percent water and its surrounding cavity accounts for 75 percent of the weight and about 66 percent of the volume of the globe; it maintains the shape of the eyeball and any injury or insult that allows the vitreous gel to escape can result in the collapse of the eyeball.

Vitreous cavity The third chamber of the eye, located behind the lens and filled with vitreous gel.

Vocational assessment A determination of the vocational strengths, interests, and functional limitations of individuals with visual impairments to enhance their opportunities for education, training, and employment.

Vocational evaluation A process that consists of using real or simulated work to assess an individual's work skills, capabilities, and interests. Also called work evaluation.

Vocational evaluator A professional trained in vocational evaluation techniques, measurements, and systematic reporting of results.

Vocational rehabilitation A system of services that evaluates personal, work, and work-related traits, resulting in optimal placement in employment.

Vocational stereotypes Misconceptions of the capabilities of persons with vision loss in terms of employment.

Work Environment Visual Demands (WEVD) Protocol An instrument developed to analyze the visual demands within work sites of individuals who are visually impaired; a series of questions answered by a low vision specialist who visits the work environment of a visually impaired individual.

Work evaluation *See* Vocational evaluation.

Work incentives Strategies used by the Social Security Administration to encourage people to work, such as a trial work period, extended period of eligibility, or continuation of medicare coverage.

Work samples Simulated tasks or work activities that are based on actual industrial/business operations. It provides an assessment of an individual's skills, capabilities, and interests in a particular job by having the individual perform the actual work.

Work-site modification Environmental changes to an individual's work station or workplace to make it more functional, comfortable, or convenient.

For definitions of opthalmological and technical terms, the following books are examples of those that can be consulted: D. M. Anderson, J. Keith, P. D. Novak, and M. A. Elliott, *Dorland's Illustrated Medical Dictionary* (28th ed; Philadelphia, PA: W.B. Saunders Company, 1994); R. Berkow and A. J. Fletcher (Eds.), *The Merck Manual* (16th ed.; Rahway, NJ: Merck Research Laboratories, 1992); Mayo Foundation for Education and Research, *Mayo Clinic Family Pharmacist* (CD-ROM; Minneapolis, MN: IVI Publishing, 1994); U.S. Equal Employment Opportunity Commission and U.S. Department of Justice Civil Rights Division, *The Americans with Disabilities Act—Questions and Answers.* (Washington, DC: Author, 1992); and D. G. Vaughan, T. Asbury, and P. Riordan-Eva, *General Ophthalmology* (13th ed.; Norwalk, CT: Appleton & Lange, 1992).

RESOURCES

This resource guide is a representative sampling of information for rehabilitation professionals to begin to find material about pertinent government agencies and national organizations that provide information, consumer education materials, services, and referrals to services for blind and visually impaired individuals. Professional organizations of interest to rehabilitation counselors are also included here. The American Foundation for the Blind (AFB) acts as a national clearinghouse for information about blindness and visual impairment and operates a toll-free national hotline. The National Technology Center at AFB ([212] 502-7642) is a repository of information about assistive technology. AFB's Careers and Technology Information Bank ([212] 502-7639) contains data from more than 1,900 blind and visually impaired people who use adaptive equipment in a variety of jobs and who mentor others seeking career advice.

An essential part of working with blind or visually impaired individuals is providing information about a wide variety of products and services they may require. Many of the specialty items used daily by clients—such as magnifiers, writing guides, braille paper, and adaptive devices (including computer software)—are not easily found in local stores. An extensive listing of sources of products and services may be found in the *Directory of Services for Blind and Visually Impaired Persons in the United States and Canada,* 25th edition, published by AFB Press. The *Directory* also lists university programs in various states offering training in the area of rehabilitation counseling. Additional information about continuing education in the area of rehabilitation counseling can be obtained by contacting the National Council on Rehabilitation Education (NCRE), the Commission on Rehabilitation Counselor Certification (CRCC), or rehabilitation counseling professional organizations. Information on continuing education related to the fields of blindness and visual impairment can be obtained by contacting AFB and the Association for Education and Rehabilitation of the Blind and Visually Impaired (AER).

SOURCES OF INFORMATION AND SERVICES

U.S. Federal Agencies

U.S. Department of Education

Office of Special Education Programs
330 C Street, S.W., Switzer Building
Washington, DC 20202
(202) 205-5507
URL: http://www.ed.gov/

Administers the Individuals with Disabilities Education Act and related programs for the education of disabled children, including grants to institutions of higher learning and fellowships to train educational personnel; grants to states for the education of disabled children; and research and demonstration projects, such as centers and services for children who are deaf-blind.

Rehabilitation Services Administration (RSA)
330 C Street, S.W., Switzer Building
Washington, DC 20202
(202) 205-5482
URL: http://www.ed.gov/offices/OSERS/RSA.rsa.html

Oversees programs that help individuals with physical or mental disabilities to obtain employment through the provision of such supports as counseling, medical and psychological services, job training, and other individualized services. RSA's major formula grant program provides funds to state vocational rehabilitation agencies to provide employment-related services for individuals with disabilities, giving priority to individuals who are severely disabled.

U.S. Department of Health and Human Services

National Institutes of Health
National Eye Institute Information Center
9000 Rockville Pike
Building 31, Room 6A03
Bethesda, MD 20892
(301) 496-5248; (301) 496-2234
FAX: (301) 402-1065
URL: http://www.nei.nih.gov

Finances and conducts research on the eye and vision disorders; supports training of eye researchers; and publishes materials on visual impairment.

U.S. Department of Veterans Affairs

Blind Rehabilitation Service
810 Vermont Avenue, N.W., Room 1071
Washington, DC 20420
(202) 535-7637
URL: http://www.bva.org

Oversees programs for blinded veterans within the Veterans Health Administration. Services offered include Visual Impairment Services Teams (VIST) assistance and Blind Rehabilitation Center and Clinic Programs. Visual Impairment Services Teams are diagnostic and treatment agents who provide periodic evaluations of physical, visual, hearing, and adjustment status and ongoing individualized treatment according to needs, goals, and eligibility. There is at least one VIST designated for each state. Blind Rehabilitation Center and Clinic Programs offer comprehensive rehabilitation services.

Veterans Benefits Administration
810 Vermont Avenue, N.W., Room 520
Washington, DC 20420
(202) 273-6763
URL: http://www.va.gov/benefits.htm

Furnishes compensation and pensions for disability and death to veterans and their dependents. Provides vocational rehabilitation services, including counseling, training, and assistance in securing employment, to blinded veterans disabled as a result of service in the armed forces during World War II, the Korean conflict, and the Vietnam era; also provides rehabilitation services to certain peace-time veterans. Offers and guarantees loans for the purchase or construction of homes, farms, and businesses.

Veterans Health Administration
810 Vermont Avenue, N.W.
Washington, DC 20420
(202) 273-5781
URL: http://www.va.gov/facilities.htm

Provides hospital and outpatient treatment, as well as nursing home care, for eligible veterans in Veterans Administration facilities. Services elsewhere are provided on a contract basis in the United States and its territories. Provides nonvocational inpatient residential rehabilitation services to eligible legally blinded veterans of the armed forces of the United States.

Other U.S. Federal Agencies

Library of Congress National Library Service for the Blind and Physically Handicapped
1291 Taylor Street, N.W.
Washington, DC 20542
(202) 707-5100 or (800) 424-8567
URL: http://lcweb.loc.gov/nls/nls.html

Conducts a national program to distribute free reading materials of a general nature to individuals who are blind or who have physical disabilities. Provides reference information on all aspects of blindness and other physical disabilities that affect reading. Conducts national correspondence courses to train sighted persons as braille transcribers and blind persons as braille proofreaders.

The President's Committee on Employment of People with Disabilities
1331 F Street, N.W.
Washington, DC 20004-1107
(202) 376-6200 or TDD (202) 376-6205
FAX: (202) 376-6200
URL: http://www.pcepd.gov/contents.htm

Promotes development of maximum employment opportunities for disabled persons. Consists of volunteer members throughout the country.

Consumer Organizations

American Council of the Blind
1155 15th Street, N.W., Suite 720
Washington, DC 20005
(202) 467-5081; (800) 424-8666
FAX: (202) 467-5085
URL: http://www.acb.org

Promotes effective participation of blind people in all aspects of society. Provides information and referral; legal assistance and representation; scholarships; leadership and legislative training; consumer advocate support; assistance in technological research; speaker referral service; consultative and advisory services to individuals, organizations, and agencies; and program development assistance. Publishes *The Braille Forum.*

Canadian Council of the Blind
396 Cooper Street, Suite 405
Ottawa, ON K2P 2H7, Canada
(613) 567-0311
FAX: (613) 567-2728
URL: http://www.cnib.org

Provides social, recreational, and blindness prevention programs and advocacy on behalf of blind and visually impaired persons.

Council of Citizens with Low Vision International
c/o American Council of the Blind
1155 15th Street N.W., Suite 720
Washington, DC 20005
(800) 733-2258
FAX: (317) 251-6588
URL: http://www.acb.org/Affiiliates/Nva/index.html

Promotes rights of partially sighted individuals to maximize use of their residual vision. Educates the public about the needs of visually impaired people. Informs people with low vision of available services. Supports groups and chapters throughout the United States.

National Association for Parents of the Visually Impaired
P.O. Box 317
Watertown, MA 02272-0317
(800) 562-6265
FAX: (617) 972-7444
URL: http://www.spedex.com.NAPVI/

Provides support to parents and families of children and youths who have visual impairments. Operates a national clearinghouse for information, education, and referral. Publishes the newsletter *Awareness.*

National Federation of the Blind
1800 Johnson Street
Baltimore, MD 21230
(410) 659-9314
FAX: (410) 685-5683
URL: http://www.nfb.org

Strives to improve social and economic conditions of blind persons; evaluates and assists in establishing programs; and provides public education and scholarships. Interest groups include the Committee on the Concerns of the Deaf-Blind. Publishes *The Braille Monitor* and *Future Reflections.*

National Organizations

American Academy of Ophthalmology
655 Beach Street
P.O. Box 7424
San Francisco, CA 94120-7424
(415) 561-8500
URL: http://www.eyenet.org

Promotes continuing education for ophthalmologists and quality care in ophthalmology. Publishes informational material for professionals and the public. Sponsors the National Eye Care Project to give free eyecare to the elderly.

American Diabetes Association
National Center
1660 Duke Street
P.O. Box 25757
Alexandria, VA 22314
(800) 342-2383
FAX: (703) 836-7439
URL: http://www.diabetes.org

Promotes knowledge of diabetes through public and professional education. Seeks to prevent and cure diabetes and to improve the lives of all people affected by diabetes. All services provided at the local level by more than 800 chapters throughout the United States and 54 affiliates in all 50 states.

American Foundation for the Blind
11 Penn Plaza, Suite 300
New York, NY 10001
(212) 502-7600 or (800) 232-5463
TTY/TDD: (212) 502-7662
FAX: (212) 502-7777
URL: http://www.afb.org

Provides services to and acts as an information clearinghouse for people who are blind or visually impaired and their families, professionals, organizations, schools, and corporations. Stimulates research and mounts program initiatives to improve services to visually impaired persons; advocates for services and legislation, maintains the M. C. Migel Library and Information Center and the Helen Keller Archives; provides information and referral services; operates the National Technology Center and the Careers and Technology Information Bank; produces videos and publishes books, pamphlets, the *Directory of Services for Blind and Visually Impaired Persons in the United States and Canada,* and the *Journal of Visual Impairment & Blindness.* Maintains the following offices throughout the country in addition to the headquarters in New York:

AFB Midwest
401 N. Michigan Avenue, Suite 308
Chicago, IL 60611
(312) 245-9961
FAX: (312) 245-9965

AFB Southeast
National Initiative on Literacy
100 Peachtree Street, Suite 620
Atlanta, GA 30303
(404) 525-2303
FAX: (404) 659-6957

AFB Southwest
260 Treadway Plaza
Exchange Park
Dallas, TX 75235
(214) 352-7222
FAX: (214) 352-3214

AFB West
111 Pine Street, Suite 725
San Francisco, CA 94111
(415) 392-4845
FAX: (415) 392-0383

Governmental Relations
820 First Street, N.E., Suite 400
Washington, DC 20000
(202) 408-0200
FAX: (202) 289-7880

American Optometric Association
243 North Lindbergh Boulevard
St. Louis, MO 63141
(314) 991-4100
FAX: (314) 991-4101
URL: http://www.aoanet.org

Improves the quality of vision care through promoting high standards, continuing education, information dissemination, and professional involvement. Conducts conferences; operates a placement service; maintains an optometric museum and library; also maintains a Virginia office [1505 Prince Street, Suite 300, Alexandria, VA 22314, (703) 739-9200]. Publishes *AOA News* and *Journal of the American Optometric Association.*

American Printing House for the Blind
1839 Frankfort Avenue
P.O. Box 6085
Louisville, KY 40206-0085
(502) 895-2405 or (800) 223-1839
URL: http://www.aph.org

Produces materials in braille and large print, and on audio cassette; manufactures computer-access equipment, software, and special educational devices for visually impaired persons; maintains an educational research and development program and a reference-catalog service providing information about volunteer-produced textbooks in accessible media.

American Rehabilitation Counseling Association
c/o American Counseling Association
5999 Stevenson Avenue
Alexandria, VA 22304
(800) 545-ARCA

Serves as a professional membership association representing rehabilitation counselors. Promotes professional development and effective rehabilitation counseling services.

Association for Education and Rehabilitation of the Blind and Visually Impaired
4600 Duke Street, Suite 430
Alexandria, VA 22304
(703) 823-9690
FAX: (703) 823-9695
E-mail: aernet@laser.net

Promotes all phases of education and work for blind and visually impaired persons of all ages, strives to expand their opportunities to take a contributory place in society, and disseminates information. Certifies rehabilitation teachers, orientation and mobility specialists, and classroom teachers. Interest groups include the Multihandicapped and Deaf-Blind Division. Publishes *RE:view, AER Report* and *Job Exchange Monthly.*

Association for Macular Diseases
210 East 64th Street
New York, NY 10021
(212) 605-3719
URL: http://www.macula.org/asso.htm

Provides information and education. Maintains a support group for persons with macular degeneration, and funds an eye bank devoted to research on macular degeneration. Counsels individuals by phone and mail. Publishes *Eyes Only.*

Blinded Veterans Association
477 H Street, N.W.
Washington, DC 20001-2694
(202) 371-8880 or (800) 669-7079

FAX: (202) 371-8258
URL: http://www.bva.org

Encourages and assists all blind veterans to take advantage of rehabilitation and vocational training benefits, job placement assistance, and other aid from federal, state, and local resources by means of a field service program. Promotes extension of sound legislation and rehabilitation through liaison with other agencies. Through 48 regional groups and field service offices, operates a volunteer service program for blinded veterans in their communities and provides information and referral services.

Canadian National Institute for the Blind
1929 Bayview Avenue
Toronto, ON M4G 3E8, Canada
(416) 480-7580
FAX: (416) 480-7677
URL: http://www.cnib.org

Provides services to people who are blind or visually impaired through a network of divisional offices throughout Canada.

Commission on Accreditation of Rehabilitation Facilities
4891 East Grand Road
Tucson, AZ 85712
(520) 325-1044
URL: http://www.carf.org/bascaccr.html

Sets standards and accredits organizations providing services to people with disabilities. Encourages the development and improvement of uniformly high standards of performance of all organizations serving individuals with developmental, physical, or emotional disabilities. Surveys and accredits rehabilitation organizations, and conducts research and educational activities related to standards. Publishes *CARF Report* and *Standards Manuals for Organizations Serving People with Disabilities.*

Commission on Rehabilitation Counselor Certification
1835 Rohlwing Road, Suite E
Rolling Meadows, IL 60008
(847) 394-2104

Serves as the national certification body for rehabilitation counselors.

Council on Rehabilitation Education
1835 Rohlwing Road
Rolling Meadows, IL 60008
(847) 394-1785
URL: http://www.core-rehab.org

Promotes effective delivery of rehabilitation services to people with disabilities. Accredits university-based graduate programs in rehabilitation counseling. Publishes *CORE News* and lists of recognized rehabilitation counselor education programs.

Foundation Fighting Blindness
Executive Plaza 1, Suite 800
11350 McCormick Road
Hunt Valley, MD 21031-1014
(410) 785-1414 or TDD (410) 785-9687 or
(888) 394-3937 or TDD (800) 683-5551
FAX: (410) 771-7470
URL: http://www.blindness.org/

Provides public education, information and referrals, workshops and research through its main office and 60 affiliates. Raises funds for research into the cause, prevention, and treatment of retinitis pigmentosa. Publishes *Fighting Blindness News* and *Macular Update.*

The Glaucoma Foundation
33 Maiden Lane, 7th Floor
New York, NY 10038
(212) 504-1901 or (800) 452-8266
FAX: (212) 504-1933
URL: http://www.glaucomafoundation.org

Provides free literature and referrals to the public, available through a toll-free worldwide hotline:

1-800-GLAUCOMA. Promotes and funds research into the causes of glaucoma and potential cures for the disease, and funds public education projects to provide information about glaucoma and the importance of early detection and treatment. The Foundation also hosts an annual scientific think tank that brings together leading scientists to pool their insights regarding the protection and regeneration of the optic nerve.

Glaucoma Research Foundation
490 Post Street
Suite 830
San Francisco, CA 94102
(415) 986-3162 or (800) 826-6693
FAX: (415) 986-3763
URL: http://www.glaucoma.org

Protects the sight of individuals with glaucoma through research and education. Publishes *Gleams Newsletter;* the patient guide *Understanding & Living with Glaucoma;* and fact sheets on a variety of glaucoma-related issues.

Hadley School for the Blind
700 Elm Street
Winnetka, IL 60093-0299
(847) 446-8111 or (800) 323-4238
FAX: (847) 446-9916

Provides tuition-free home studies in academic subjects as well as vocational and technical areas, personal enrichment, parent and child issues, compensatory and rehabilitation education. Rehabilitation courses include topics such as braille, abacus, and, for deaf-blind adults, independent living without sight and hearing.

Helen Keller National Center for Deaf-Blind Youths and Adults
111 Middle Neck Road
Sands Point, NY 11050-1299
(516) 944-8900 (voice/TDD)
FAX: (516) 944-7302
URL: http://www.ed.gov/OSERS/RSA/PGMS/hkncp.html

The national center and its 10 regional offices provide diagnostic evaluations, comprehensive vocational and personal adjustment training, and job preparation and placement for people who are deaf-blind from every state and territory. Provides technical assistance and training to those who work with deaf-blind people. Publishes *The Nat-Cent News, National Parent Newsletter,* and *TAC Newsletter.*

The Lighthouse Inc.
111 East 59th Street
New York, NY 10022
(212) 821-9200 or (800) 334-5497
TDD: (212) 821-9713
FAX: (212) 821-9705
URL: http://www.lighthouse.org/

Aims to overcome visual impairment for people of all ages through rehabilitation services, education, research, and advocacy. Undertakes regional, national, and international programs to enable people who are blind or have partial sight to lead independent lives. Publishes *Lighthouse News; Aging and Vision News; Envision;* and *Sharing Solutions* newsletters.

National Accreditation Council for Agencies Serving the Blind and Visually Handicapped
260 Northland Boulevard, Suite 236
Cincinnati, OH 45246
(212) 683-5068 (Will change after 10/1/97)
FAX: (212) 683-4475

Administers a program of standards development and accreditation for programs, agencies, and schools serving children and adults who are blind or visually impaired. Publishes standards that are available in print, braille, cassette, tape, and disk.

National Association for Visually Handicapped
22 West 21st Street
New York, NY 10010
(212) 889-3141
FAX: (212) 727-2951

Acts as an information clearinghouse and referral center regulating resources available to persons who are visually impaired.

National Clearinghouse of Rehabilitation Training Materials
Oklahoma State University
5202 North Richmond Hill Drive
Stillwater, OK 74078-4080
(405) 624-7650 or (800) 223-5219
FAX: (405) 624-0695
URL: http://www.nchrtm.okstate.edu

Provides information on recent publications, videotapes, and other rehabilitation training materials. Publishes a quarterly newsletter, *NCHRTM Memo.*

National Council of Private Agencies for the Blind and Visually Impaired
c/o Vital Rehab Inc.
348 Elmington Avenue
Nashville, TN 37205
(615) 321-2643
FAX: (615) 321-4092

Serves as an advocate concerning issues that relate to programs, operations, and funding affecting voluntary agencies serving blind and visually impaired persons. Acts as a unified voice in negotiating with federal and state agencies about fees and other matters concerning private agencies.

National Council of State Agencies for the Blind
1213 29th Street, N.W.
Washington, DC 20007
(202) 298-8468
FAX: (202) 333-5881

Promotes communication and advocacy among state VR agencies offering services to severely visually impaired individuals.

National Council on Rehabilitation Education
Department of Special Education
Utah State University
Logan, Utah 84322-2870
(801) 797-3241
URL: http://www.nchrtm.okstate.edu/ncre/ncre.html

As a membership organization for professionals involved in the education of rehabilitation personnel. NCRE promotes the improvement of rehabilitation services available to persons with disabilities through quality education and rehabilitation research. Publishes *NCRE Newsletter* and *Rehabilitation Education.*

National Industries for the Blind
1901 North Beauregard Street, Suite 200
Alexandria, VA 22311-1727
(703) 998-0770
FAX: (703) 820-7816
URL: http://www.nib.org

Enhances opportunities for economic and personal independence for persons who are blind by creating, sustaining, and improving employment. Allocates, among qualified industries for blind persons, purchase orders of the federal government for approved goods and services as designed by the President's Committee for Purchase from Persons Who Are Blind and Other Severely Disabled. Coordinates the production of 106 industries in 36 states. Researches and recommends new products, prices, and price revisions to the President's Committee. Devises quality control systems and provides management and engineering services to increase plant efficiency and broaden production opportunities for people who are blind. Publishes *Opportunity* and *Annual Report.*

National Rehabilitation Association
633 Washington Street
Alexandra, VA 22314
(703) 836-0850
TTY/TDD: (703) 836-0849
FAX: (703) 836-0848
URL: http://www.nationalrehab.org

Serves as a membership organization for professionals in the field of rehabilitation and as an advocate for the rights of persons with disabilities. Publishes the *Journal of Rehabilitation* and *Contemporary Rehab.*

National Rehabilitation Counseling Association
8807 Sudley Road, Suite 102
Manassas, VA 22210-4719
(703) 361-2077
TTY/TDD: (703) 361-1596
URL: http://www.ed.wriht.edu/cehs/nrca/NRCAHome.html

Serves as a professional membership organization representing rehabilitation counselors. Serves as a primary source of rehabilitation and disability information.

National Rehabilitation Information Center
8455 Colesville Road, Suite 935
Silver Springs, MD 20910-3319
(301) 588-9284 (Voice/TDD)
(800) 346-2742
FAX: (301) 587-1967
URL: http://www.naric.com/naric

Serves as a library and information center on disability and rehabilitation. Funded by the National Institute on Disability and Rehabilitation Research. NARIC collects and disseminates the results of federally funded research projects. Services include quick reference and referral, database searches of all documents at NARIC on a particular topic or combination of topics, and document delivery.

Prevent Blindness America
500 East Remington Road
Schaumburg, IL 60173
(847) 843-2020 or (800) 221-3004
(800) 331-2020 PBA Center for Sight
FAX: (847) 843-8458
URL: http://prevent-blindness.org

Conducts, through a network of state affiliates, a program of public and professional education, research, and industrial and community services to prevent blindness. Services include screening, vision testing, and dissemination of information on low vision devices and clinics.

Recording for the Blind and Dyslexic
20 Roszel Road
Princeton, NJ 08540
(609) 452-0606 or (800) 221-4792
FAX: (609) 987-8116
URL: http://www.rfbd.org

Provides recorded and computerized textbooks, library services, and other educational resources to people who cannot read standard print because of visual, physical, and perceptual disabilities. Maintains a lending library of recorded books and acts as a recording service for additional titles.

Rehabilitation Engineering and Assistive Technology Society of North America
1700 North Moore Street, Suite 1540
Arlington, VA 22209-1903
(703) 524-6686 or TDD (703) 524-6639
FAX: (703) 524-6630
URL: http://www.resna.org/resna/reshome.htm

Serves as an information center to address research and the development, dissemination, integration, and utilization of knowledge in rehabilitation and assistive technology.

Rehabilitation Research and Training Center on Blindness and Low Vision
Mississippi State University
P.O. Drawer 6189
Mississippi State, MS 39762
(601) 325-2001 or (800) 675-7782
FAX: (601) 325-8989
URL: http://www.msstate.edu/dept/rrtc/blind.html

Conducts a variety of applied research projects concerning blindness, visual impairment, and deaf-blindness. Conducts in-service training programs for state agencies, national training conferences, and research forums. Publishes monographs on related subjects in alternate media and a newsletter, *Worksight.*

Resources for Rehabilitation
33 Bedford Street, Suite 19A
Lexington, MA 02173
(617) 862-6455
FAX: (617) 861-7517

Provides training and information to professionals and the public about the needs of individuals with disabilities and the resources available to meet those needs. Publications include the *Living with Low Vision* series and large-print publications.

SOURCES OF ADDITIONAL INFORMATION

Books

Attmore, M. (1990). *Career perspectives: Interviews with blind and visually impaired professionals.* New York: American Foundation for the Blind.

Blasch, B. B., Wiener, W. R., & Welsh, R. L. (Eds.). (1997). *Foundations of orientation and mobility* (2nd ed.). New York: AFB Press.

Brodwin, M. G., Tellez, F., & Brodwin, S. K. (1993). *Medical, psychosocial, and vocational aspects of disability.* Athens, GA: Elliott & Fitzpatrick.

Corn, A. L., and Koenig, A. J. (Eds.). (1996). *Foundations of low vision: Clinical and functional perspectives.* New York: AFB Press.

Dickman, I. (1983). *Making life more livable.* New York: American Foundation for the Blind.

Eisenberg, M. G., Glueckauf, R. L., & Zaretsky, H. H. (Eds.). (1993). *Medical aspects of disability.* New York: Springer.

Falvo, D. R. (1991). *Medical and psychosocial aspects of chronic illness and disability.* Gaithersburg, MD: Aspen.

Griffin-Shirley, N., & Groff, G. (1993). *Prescriptions for independence.* New York: AFB Press.

Jacobson, W. H. (1993). *The art and science of teaching orientation and mobility to persons with visual impairments.* New York: AFB Press.

Kendrick, D. (1993). *Jobs to be proud of: Profiles of workers who are blind or visually impaired.* New York: American Foundation for the Blind.

Marinelli, R. P., & Dell Orto, A. L. (Eds.). (1991). *The psychological and social impact of disability.* New York: Springer.

Marshak, L. E., & Seligman, M. (1993). *Counseling persons with physical disabilities.* Austin, TX: PRO-ED.

Parker, R. M., & Szymanski, E. M. (1997). *Rehabilitation Counseling* (3rd ed.). Austin, TX: PRO-ED.

Pogrund, R. L., Fazzi, D. L., & Lampert, J. S. (Eds.). (1992). *Early focus: Working with young blind and visually impaired children and their families.* New York: American Foundation for the Blind.

Ponchillia, P. E., & Ponchillia, S. V. (1996). *Foundations of rehabilitation teaching for persons who are blind or visually impaired.* New York: AFB Press.

Power, P. W. (1991). *A guide to vocational assessment.* Austin, TX: PRO-ED.

Roessler, R. T., & Rubin, S. E. (1992). *Case management and rehabilitation counseling* (2nd ed.). Austin, TX: PRO-ED.

Rubin, S. E., & Roessler, R. T. (1995). *Foundations of the vocational rehabilitation process* (4th ed.). Austin, TX: PRO-ED.

Szymanski, E. M., & Parker, R. M. (Eds.). (1996). *Work and disability.* Austin, TX: PRO-ED.

Zunker, V. G. (1994). *Career counseling.* Pacific Grove, CA: Brooks/Cole.

Journals

American Rehabilitation
Rehabilitation Services Administration
330 C Street, S.W.
Washington, DC 20202-0001
(202) 205-8296
FAX: (202) 205-9874

Information Technology and Disabilities
URL: http://www.rit.edu:80/~easi/itd.html

International Journal of Rehabilitation Research
URL: http://www.chapmanhall.com/rr/default.html

Journal of Applied Rehabilitation Counseling
National Rehabilitation Counseling Association
8807 Sudley Road, Suite 102
Manassas, VA 20110
(703) 261-2077; (703) 361-1596 (TTY/TDD)

Journal of Rehabilitation
National Rehabilitation Association
633 South Washington Street
Alexandria, VA 22314
(703) 836-0850; (703) 836-0848 (TTY/TDD)
FAX: (703) 836-0848

Journal of Rehabilitation Administration
Journal of Rehabilitation Administration, Inc.
San Diego State University
P.O. Box 19891
San Diego, CA 92159
(619) 594-6406
URL: http://interwork.sdsu.edu/jra/

Journal of Vision Rehabilitation
Media Publishing, Division of Trozzolo Resources
1102 Grand Blvd., Suite 2300
Kansas City, MO 64106-2305
(916) 842-8111
TTY: (816) 756-1490
FAX: (816) 842-8188

Journal of Visual Impairment & Blindness
American Foundation for the Blind
11 Penn Plaza, Suite 300
New York, NY 10001
(212) 502-7648 or (800) 232-5463
TDD: (212) 502-7662
FAX: (212) 502-7774
URL: http://www.afb.org

Journal of Vocational Rehabilitation
Andover Medical Publishers, Inc.
80 Montvale Ave.
Stoneham, MA 02180-3602
(617) 438-8464
FAX: (617) 279-4851
URL: http://www.elsevier.com:80/locate/inca/525014

Rehabilitation Counseling Bulletin
American Rehabilitation Counseling Association
c/o American Counseling Association
5999 Stevenson Avenue
Alexandria, VA 22304
(703) 823-9800; (800) 347-6647
URL: http://www.counseling.org

Rehabilitation Education
Elliott & Fitzpatrick, Inc.
1135 Cedar Shoals Dr.
Athens, GA 30605
(706) 353-2632
FAX: (706) 546-8417

Rehabilitation Psychology
Springer Publishing Company, Inc.
536 Broadway, 11th Floor
New York, NY 10012-3915
(212) 431-4370
FAX: (212) 941-7842

RE:view
Association for Education and Rehabilitation of the Blind and Visually Impaired (AER)

4600 Duke Street, Suite 430
Alexandria, VA 22304
(703) 823-9690
FAX: (703) 823-9695

On-line Resources

These listings include Internet addresses for sources of electronic information. E-mail addresses and web-site addresses for organizations listed elsewhere in this section are included in the main organizational listing.

Adaptive/Assistive Technology Information
http://www.lib.uwaterloo.ca/discipline/Disability_Issues/

Americans with Disabilities Act—U.S. Department of Justice
http://www.usdoj.gov/crt/ada

Americans with Disabilities Act—NARIC Guide
http://www.cais.com/naric/pubs.html

Apple Computers Disability Connection
http://www2.apple.com/disability/welcome.html
Content: Disability information.

Center for Assistive Technology
University of Buffalo
http://cosmos.ot.buffalo.edu/aztech.html

Descriptive Video Service
http://www.wgbh.org/dvs

IBM Special Needs Solutions
http://www.austin.ibm.com/sns
Content: Information about IBM products for people with disabilities.

Job Accommodation Network
http://janweb.icdi.wvu.edu

MedWeb
http://www.cc.emory.edu/WHSCL/medweb.html
Content: List of file servers concerning disability, and some articles and databases.

NIDRR
National Institute on Disability and Rehabilitation Research
http://www.ed.gov

National Rehabilitation Information Center
http://www.naric.com/naric

Project ENABLE
http://www.icdi.wvu.edu/enable.html

Rehabilitation Information System
West Virginia RRTC
http://www.icdi.wvu.edu

Smith-Kettlewell Eye Research Institute Rehabilitation Engineering Center
http://www.ski.org/rerc

Trace Research and Development Center
http://trace.wisc.edu

W3C Web Accessibility Initiative (WAI)
http://www.w3.org/wai

INDEX

Photo Credits

American Foundation for the Blind, 322, 331; Howard Becker, Signature Works, 317; Oraien Catledge, 280; Janet Charles, 155; Don Denney, The Clovernook Center—Opportunities for the Blind, 139, 301, 311, 338; Kathleen E. Fraser, 90, 97, 98; Adrienne Helitzer, 65; Bradford Herzog, 63, 184; Jewish Guild for the Blind, 15, 67, 99, 234, 277; Lighthouse for the Blind of the Palm Beaches, 138, 153; Lighthouse Low Vision Products, 88; National Eye Institute, National Institutes of Health, 35; Montana Department of Public Health and Human Services, 77; Oregon Commission for the Blind, 66; Pinellas Center for the Visually Impaired, 103, 109, 157, 192, 214, 247; Dona Sauerburger, 188; Mark Sauerburger, 202; VA Puget Sound Health Care Systems Photography Service, 11; Ruth Solomon, 115; TeleSensory Corporation, 195, 215.